D1617228

Realm of the Black Mountain

For Ivor and for my parents

ELIZABETH ROBERTS

Realm of the Black Mountain

A History of Montenegro

Cornell University Press
Ithaca, New York

Originally published in the United Kingdom by
C. Hurst & Co. (Publishers) Ltd, London

First published 2007 by Cornell University Press

ISBN 978–0–8014–4601–6

Printed in India

Librarians: Library of Congress Cataloging-In-Publication
Data are available.

Cloth printing: 10 9 8 7 6 5 4 3 2 1

Contents

Illustrations

Maps

Preface and Acknowledgements

On May 21 2006 Montenegrins took the momentous step of voting to restore the independence they had lost more than eighty years before under the Versailles Peace Treaty when the kingdom was subsumed into what became Yugoslavia. The vote paves the way for Montenegro to be the first independent state of the new century and millennium. Already in 2003, the name of Yugoslavia had disappeared from maps to be replaced by the Union of Serbia and Montenegro. To the disappointment of the few remaining Yugonostalgics, the change passed largely unnoticed. The reasons for this were not difficult to find: while international public attention had largely moved on, those still directly involved were aware that the renaming was really a piece of window-dressing, and that despite its founders' best intentions, the resulting Union of Serbia and Montenegro was an unbalanced and unpromising hybrid, which was unlikely to offer a lasting solution to the problem of political relations between Serbia and Montenegro. And so it proved.

The Belgrade Agreement, which laid the foundation for the new Union, accepted the parties' right to revisit the arrangement by referendum. The May 2006 referendum in Montenegro produced a 55–45 per cent majority in favour of independence, which just cleared the barrier set by the European Union to determine whether the result was conclusive enough to settle the statehood question and ensure that the country would regain the international recognition it had lost at Versailles. The political debate in the run-up to the referendum was predictably acrimonious, reflecting the fundamental disagreement within the majority Orthodox population of Montenegro over what it means to be Montenegrin and whether indeed it is a meaningful classification. Orthodox Montenegrins, who make up roughly 74 per cent of the Republic's total population, are to many Serbs in Serbia simply ethnic Serbs. Within Montenegro the question has long been deeply divisive with the Orthodox population split roughly down the middle in a way that has greatly complicated the political debate.

The finely balanced and divisive nature of the debate over independence has been both a plus and a minus for anyone writing about Montenegro at this time. On the one hand, it might be counted upon to stimulate interest in a book on Montenegro's history among those who hope to find in it arguments to grind their particular axes. On the other, it is likely to raise expectations that can only be fulfilled at the price of being seriously partial. I have outlined below the arguments on both sides of the debate in a way which I hope both sides will judge to be fair. My own preference for independence is not relevant since the decision has now been taken by the people who matter, the Montenegrins, not by the Great Powers or their successors.

However tempting it is to remain on the fence over independence, it is all but impossible to avoid taking a stance on the issue of Montenegrin identity, since merely writing a book on Montenegro in which its history is not presented as an adjunct of Serbia is itself implicitly making the distinction. This is above all a narrative history, and I have preferred not to interrupt the flow by revisiting the identity issue repeatedly. Instead I consider the subject of Montenegrin identity in an introductory chapter which at the same time provides some further geographical and historical orientation in order to make sense of what follows.

Very little has been written exclusively on Montenegro by non-Montenegrins. This book attempts to fill a gap by offering a consecutive general history without neglecting the underlying themes. It aims to be informative rather than polemical. Readers will judge for themselves whether this approach is well-founded.

The attempt to write such a history presented a number of difficulties. First, particularly in the earlier chapters, covering such a long period inevitably required reliance on secondary sources where these exist and recognition of the lack of detailed knowledge at other times. At times the story had to be pieced together from contradictory accounts, and there are gaps which have to be accepted. Primary sources were more readily available from the nineteenth century and, where possible, I have consulted them, while for the later part of the twentieth century and the early years of the twenty-first I have drawn to some extent on personal experience. Second, there was a need to guard against the danger that a history of Montenegro with its evident thematic concern with Montenegrin identity might result in a definition of Montenegriness which was nothing more than anti-Serbianism. A further risk stemmed from the fact that in a country so small the history of major individuals at times threatens to overshadow more ordinary everyday realities. Lastly and most difficult of all was the challenge of writing a history at a time when the outcome of the vote on independence, which might otherwise have been thought to provide a natural conclusion, remained uncertain. Such uncertainty might be held sufficient to dissuade a prudent person from attempting a history until more clarity emerges. But I have perhaps rashly gone ahead in the belief that a knowledge of the past is important at a time when Montenegro is certain at least of entering a new phase in its history.

My father's barber-shop rendition of a Lehar tune 'I come by cruel fate from a little Balkan state' was my unwitting first exposure to Montenegro. When many years later I went to live in what became Serbia and Montenegro, I was quickly given a warning by a professor of English there against becoming interested in Montenegro's past. As an Australian, he said, echoing George Eliot, I was indeed fortunate in coming from a country with 'so much geography and so little history'. Why, he wondered, would I want to involve myself in a country which was placed at the extreme opposite end of the spectrum? Why indeed? But needled by the challenge I have gone ahead, surprised that while so much attention has been focused on Kosovo, Bosnia and Serbia, so little has been devoted to a constituent part of the former Yugoslavia whose defining characteristics—good and bad—have been instantly recognisable to all other Yugoslavs.

Acknowledgements

Over the long period I have taken to complete this book I have received help and advice from friends and colleagues of many different backgrounds—British, Irish, American, Canadian, Australian, Italian, as well as Serbian, Albanian and Montenegrin. I owe a particular debt to Professor Richard Crampton, who read the manuscript and provided many invaluable suggestions. My thanks are also due to Aleksa Djilas, Miodrag Lekić and particularly Maureen

MacGlashan for her painstaking work on the index and her perceptive comments on the text as a whole. Professors Stevan Pavlowitch, Tim Garton Ash, James Gow, Šerbo Rastoder and Antun Sbutega all provided generous assistance, as did Anne Willitts, Branko Lukovac, Shaun Byrnes, Nebojša Čagorović, Cathy Carmichael, Andje Kapičić, Aleksandar Berkuljan, Robert Fowler, Fardus Sultan, Kenneth Morrison, Ivan Vukčević, Irena Radović and Colonel Calogero Scolaro of the Biblioteca Militare Centrale in Rome. I am also grateful to Jane Adamson and Meg Miller who read parts of the manuscript and to my daughter Hannah who prepared the family trees. I am greatly indebted to the publishers in London—Michael Dwyer for his energy and patience, and Christopher Hurst for his meticulous attention to the text and the book as a whole. Sebastian Ballard, the map-maker, had to cope with an exceptionally difficult task. Mistakes that remain are of course my responsibility. My main debt has been to my family for their remarkable forbearance, above all to my husband Ivor for his unswerving support and to my father for his encouragement in a project which he did not live to see completed.

Rome, June 2006   ELIZABETH ROBERTS

Nomenclature and Transliteration

All writers on the Balkans encounter problems of nomenclature and transliteration. The problem is compounded in a full-length history of this kind when places change their names, sometimes more than once, as a result of conquest or colonisation. Consistency is not always possible: it would be incongruous to describe the *strategos* of Dyrrachium located in present-day Albania as exercising his office in Durazzo (as the city was subsequently known to the Venetians), or even in Durrës, its modern name, although the region was at that time already inhabited by ancestors of today's Albanians. Likewise, the crisis that brought the European powers to the brink of war in 1912 was internationally known as the Scutari crisis, although when writing earlier of this city as the capital of the fourteenth-century Balšići dynasty I have referred to it by the local Slav name used at the time, Skadar. To complicate matters further, Skadar/Scutari, known to its present-day Albanian population as Shkodra, was earlier commonly referred to as Shkodër, and stands on the shores of the largest lake in the Balkans which may be similarly referred to by all four names depending on the speaker's language of origin. Here in order to avoid further confusion I have consistently opted for the term used in Montenegro—Lake Skadar. Elsewhere too I have generally used local Slav names rather than their Italian (or Albanian) equivalents: thus Zadar in preference to Zara, Dubrovnik to Ragusa, Bar to Antivari, Ulcinj to Dulcigno, with the most frequently used alternatives being given in brackets when the name is first used. This does not, however, apply to cities such as Belgrade, Constantinople or Vienna where to use to use Beograd, Carigrad or Beč would simply be pedantic. In the case of personal names the question of whether to anglicise them is a further cause of inconsistency. With regard to the former, I have preferred to use the local variants, that is King Nikola not Nicholas, and King Petar, not Peter, Karadjordjević, although an exception has been made in the case of the Karadjordjević Regent, Prince Paul, who was internationally known by this name rather than by the Serbo-Croatian Pavle.

The problem of transliteration—that of converting Cyrillic words into their Latin forms has been made soluble by the use of diacritics. But if agreeing to write Milošević rather than Miloshevich has simplified matters at one level, since the early 1990s a new area of difficulty has been created by a nationalistically-inspired bout of linguistic fracturing with what used to be called Serbo-Croatian giving way to Serbian, Croatian, Bosnian, Montenegrin and so on. Intended or no, the effect has been to create a minefield for the outsider who can inadvertently cause offence by preferring one variant to another where no slight was ever intended. With little hope of avoiding this trap I have endeavoured to choose the Montenegrin variant over its Serbian equivalent in names pertaining strictly to Montenegro but not in the case of people or places beyond the county's present borders.

A few individual preferences may be worth mentioning. In writing of the Second World War, I have preferred the internationally recognised terms Chetnik and Ustasha to Četniks and Ustaša. By contrast, I have preferred Hercegovina to Herzegovina, the former being the variant used locally when the name is written in Latin script.

In abbreviating institutions I have generally used the initials of the Serbo-Croatian original: KPJ, not CPY for the Communist Party of Yugoslavia, except in a very few cases such as that of the FRY (Federal Republic of Yugoslavia) where the acronym has become too well-known to make the Slav version variant, the FRJ, a sensible alternative. The Ottoman Empire is sometimes referred to as Turkey and its inhabitants as Turks since this was common usage during the period, although it is not of course to imply that the people so referred to are exclusively ethnic Turks.

Dates throughout use the Gregorian rather than the Julian calendar, which was twelve days behind the Gregorian calendar during the nineteenth century and thirteen days behind it during the twentieth. Both dates were generally given in official documents and newspapers until 1919, when Montenegro became part of the Kingdom of the Serbs, Croats and Slovenes (SHS), after which time the Julian calendar was retained only by the Serbian Orthodox Church.

Montenegro in the Balkans

Montenegrin Identity in Time and Space

'Few nations have been less known than the Montenigrians [*sic*]; and the name of the country is seldom found on maps.' (The English traveller Charles Lamb after visiting Montenegro in 1844[1])

'There is no Montenegrin nation in the sense that there is an Italian or French nation. The Montenegrins are to the Jugoslavs what Cornishmen are to England or the men of Argyle and Morven are to Scotland. They are a small section of the Serbian nation, who favoured by their wild and inaccessible mountains, and thanks to their own headlong valour and endurance, contrived to maintain their independence during the period of Turkish domination in Serbia, and attracted to their eagle's nest many of those Serbs who found existence under the Ottomans intolerable.' (R. W. Seton-Watson[2])

'I am not a Montenegrin because I am a Serb, but a Serb because I am a Montenegrin. We Montenegrins are the salt of the Serbs. All the strength of the Serbs is not here [in Montenegro] but their soul is.' (Milovan Djilas[3])

'The Montenegrins are, despite provincial and historical differences, quintessential Serbs, and Montenegro the cradle of Serbian myths and of aspirations for the unification of Serbs.' (Milovan Djilas[4])

---

[1] Charles Lamb, 'A Ramble in Montenegro,' *Blackwood's Edinburgh Magazine*, no. 57, January 1845, p. 33.

[2] R. W. Seton-Watson, 'The Question of Montenegro', *New Europe*, no. 14, London, 1 April 1920, p. 265.

[3] A character from the novel *Montenegro* by Milovan Djilas, transl. by Kenneth Johnstone, London: Methuen, 1964, p. 55. Set in the years 1916–19, Djilas's novel explores the conflict between supporters of the Union with Serbia and those whose loyalty to the Montenegrin ruling dynasty caused them to rebel in the name of Montenegrin independence.

[4] *Wartime* (transl. by Michael B. Petrovich), New York and London: Harcourt Brace Jovanovich, 1977, p. 149.

'Serbia and Montenegro are like two eyes in the same head.' (Slobodan Milošević[5])

Who are the Montenegrins?

There is no fixed line at which Montenegrin history can be said to begin. The name Montenegro—the Black Mountain (*Crna Gora* in the language that used to be called Serbo-Croatian)—has a timeless ring to it, but this is deceptive. According to the Montenegrin historian Šerbo Rastoder, the name was first mentioned in a papal epistle of 1053 in which the Latin *Monte nigro* referred to an area within the medieval Slav state of Duklja, while Cyrillic sources mention it for the first time in 1276.[6] Yet the name was only brought into common use by Venetian sailors in the late fourteenth century when it was applied to Mount Lovćen and the surrounding mountainous hinterland of the Gulf of Kotor (Ital. Cattaro, Serb. Boka Kotorska), a spectacular drowned river canyon (invariably referred to as a fjord) set deep into the Adriatic coast and for centuries the principal gateway into Montenegro.[7] At the time Montenegro was not a country but simply a wild region, yet its identity had been recognised, as had its enduring if quasi-mythical link with another South Slav state, former Raška, later medieval Serbia. This symbiotic relationship is a *leitmotiv* of this book, and before examining the history we should pause to look at its impact on the complex and divisive question of Montenegrin identity.

Slobodan Milošević is unlikely to be one of the sons most Montenegrins will want to claim as their own although his parents were both from Montenegro and only moved to Serbia in the year he was born. Nevertheless, his view (above) of Montenegro as for ever coupled with Serbia is one that has deep roots within both the Serbian and Montenegrin traditions, and there is no need to share

---

[5] Quoted in Duško Doder and Louise Branson, *Milošević: Portrait of a Tyrant*, New York: The Free Press, 1999, p. 13.

[6] See Šerbo Rastoder, 'A Short Review of the History of Montenegro' in Florian Bieber (ed.) *Montenegro in Transition: Problems of identity and statehood*, Baden-Baden: Nomos, 2003, p. 107. Other Montenegrin sources date the first reference to Montenegro to a charter issued by the Serbian King Milutin in 1282.

[7] John V. A. Fine, *The Late Medieval Balkans: A Critical Survey from the Late Twelfth Century to the Ottoman Conquest*, Ann Arbor: University of Michigan Press, 1991, p. 532.

Milošević's Greater Serbian views[8] or Serbian-Montenegrin origins in order to subscribe to it. Both Milovan Djilas, a Montenegrin by birth and Communist Yugoslavia's most prominent dissident, and the great British pre-war authority on Eastern Europe R.W. Seton Watson were in very different ways deeply opposed to Greater Serbian ideology, yet both saw Orthodox Montenegrins as 'quintessential' Serbs, whose historic role was to keep alive the flame of Serbdom during the long years when Serbia was under Ottoman occupation.

Montenegrins themselves are aware of another tradition that rejects the idea that Orthodox Montenegrins are Serbs and instead claims that they constitute a separate ethnic group of mixed Slav-Albanian-Vlach origins, emphasising the importance of Montenegro's divergent history.[9] Hardline supporters of this tradition go further, insisting that Montenegrins are not Slavs at all but descendants of ancient Illyrians and seeking to trace the origins of the 'nation' back to earliest times in a way that suggests a seamless fit between past and present.[10] Montenegro is thus portrayed as possessing a form of proto-nationhood predating the establishment of a Roman province in the region in the second century AD and encompassing the various early and late medieval fiefdoms and principalities that flourished in the same Adriatic coastal region of the peninsula following the arrival of the Slavs in the sixth century AD.[11]

The reality is more multi-faceted than either of these traditional approaches suggests. Montenegrins are not simply a collection of mountain Serbs, nor are they 'pure' Montenegrins. Identities are neither primordial nor set in stone, as nationalists would have us believe. Instead they are, within limits, fluid and opportunistic; they evolve over time. Moreover, identity is not necessarily based

[8] Most first-hand accounts of Milošević express scepticism about the genuineness of his 'Greater Serbian' views, suggesting that he was prepared to adopt any ideology he saw as offering a short-cut to power.
[9] See Ivo Banac: *The National Question in Yugoslavia: Origins, History, Politics,* Cornell University Press, Ithaca, 1984, pp. 274–5 and Mark Thomson, *A Paper House: The Ending of Yugoslavia,* London: Hutchinson Radius, 1992, pp. 151–2.
[10] See, for example, Radosav Rotković, *Odakle su došli preci Crnogoraca,* Podgorica: Matica Crnogorska, 1992.
[11] Srdja Pavlović; 'Who are the Montenegrins? Statehood, identity and civic society', in Bieber (ed.), *Montenegro in Transition,* pp. 83–106.

solely on ethnic criteria: clearly relationships with the state and with civil society are also important, but when the state is weak and civil society poorly developed, ethnicity as the source of group solidarity is bound to play the larger part. Nor are all Montenegrins directly caught up in the ethnic dimension of the identity problem. Apart from its Orthodox majority, Montenegro also contains a number of minorities—among them Slav Muslims (or Bosniaks), Albanians (both Catholic and Orthodox), Croats and Roma[12]— all of whom are 'Montenegrins' in the political sense of being citizens of that territory. Taken together these minorities make up approximately 26 per cent of Montenegro's total population of 672,000 people, and a majority within each of these minorities— overwhelming in the case of the Albanians—favoured Montenegrin independence.[13] Given that the Orthodox population has in recent years tended to be split roughly equally over the question of independence, the minorities have the power to determine the outcome of the vote. But however sensitive the issue, the existence of substantial minorities is not specific to Montenegro: with the exception of Slovenia, minorities are present to a greater or lesser extent in all the new states that emerged from the former Yugoslavia. Instead it is the ambivalent and often contested identity of the Orthodox majority that remains the essential and defining 'Montenegrin question'.

How then are we to describe and account for the problem? One prominent Montenegrin sociologist, Srdjan Darmanović, describes the Montenegrin condition as that of a 'national *homo duplex,*

---

[12] According to the figures provided by the Montenegrin statistics bureau, MONSTAT, the results for the 2003 census are: Montenegrins – 43.16%, Serbs – 31.99%, Bosniaks (also spelt Bosniacs) – 7.77%, Muslims – 3.79%, Albanians – 5.03%, Croats – 1.10% and Roma – 0.42%. For a general overview of the situation of the minorities in Montenegro see František Šístek and Bohdana Dimitrovová, 'National minorities in Montenegro after the break-up of Yugoslavia', in Bieber (ed.), *Montenegro in Transition*, pp. 159–79. Their impact on the independence issue in Montenegro is considered in Chapter 12.

[13] While the Albanians were almost all in favour of an outcome which placed a greater distance between them and Serbia, Slav Muslims (or Bosniaks), who live mostly in the area adjoining Serbia known as the Sandžak, were thought to be divided on the issue of independence but surprised observers by voting overwhelmingly in favour.

a victim of his 'double or divided consciousness'.[14] Why is this so? Why, if Croats define themselves clearly as Croats and Serbs as Serbs are Montenegrins different?[15] The most common explanation is that the sense of shared Serbian-Montenegrin identity conferred by religion and language—both powerful totems of ethnicity in the Balkans[16]—is offset in Montenegro's case by recent political history. As Darmanović explains, 'Many of those who nationally declare themselves Montenegrins have besides their "Montenegrin-ness" a strong Serbian ethnic feeling, based on sharing the same language and religion. Consequently Montenegrins as a nation have been caught—especially in the twentieth century—between their "Montenegrin-ness" and their "Serbian-ness", between the particular interests of the Montenegrin state and those of Serbs in general.'[17]

This analysis is valuable especially in so far as it helps to account for changes in the number of citizens declaring themselves one thing or another in response to a variety of domestic or external events in the course of the twentieth and into the twenty-first century, but it does not fully explain the fact that the ambivalence over identity is not experienced uniformly in all parts of the country. Opinion polls show that most people living in the vicinity of the old royal capital of Cetinje have no hesitation in declaring themselves 'Montenegrin' while those to the north and east in the regions closest to Serbia frequently define themselves simply as 'Serbs'. In the capital Podgorica and along the coast the response is more mixed. To shed light on this aspect of the identity problem we need to go further back than twentieth-century political history to see how the question of identity in Montenegro relates to that of lands.

---

[14] Srdjan Darmanović, 'Montenegro: Destiny of a Satellite State', *Eastern European Reporter*, no. 27, March–April 1992, pp. 27–9.

[15] Bosnian Muslims in the Tito period exhibited a sense of uncertainty over whether they were Yugoslavs first and Muslims second, or vice versa.

[16] Of course it is not only in the Balkans that religion and language are seen as principal markers in determining ethnicity and nationhood. See John Hutchinson and Anthony D. Smith (eds), *Nationalism*, Oxford University Press, 1994, and Adrian Hastings, *The Construction of Nationhood: Ethnicity, Religion and Nationalism*, Cambridge University Press, 1997.

[17] Darmanović, *ibid.*

Lands and identities

The relationship between 'lands and identities'[18] has often been the
starting-point for histories of the Balkans. But if it offers insights, it
also carries risks. All too often, and especially during the break-up of
the former Yugoslavia, the past movements of peoples from one
place have been hijacked by nationalist historians seeking to
establish irredentist claims to 'ancestral lands' or to reinforce the
privileges of one ethnic group at the expense of others on the basis
of the 'who was there first' school of history. Such claims cannot be
entertained, not only because they risk causing chaos but also because the underlying assumption that ethnic groups have remained
somehow pure and unsullied does not stand up to examination, least
of all in a region which for millennia has been at the crossroads of
trade routes and on the borders of great multinational empires.

   The lands that today comprise Montenegro were acquired—
whether as a result of migration, conquest or political agreement—
in discrete portions at different times over many centuries. This
pattern of historical acquisition helps to account for the presence of
the various minorities referred to earlier. Also, as we shall see, it
partly explains the differences that exist within the Orthodox majority over the issue of national identity.

   In pre-classical times these lands were part of Illyria—a proto-
state covering much of the central and western Balkans and inhabited by an indigenous Indo-European people.[19] Subsequently
the coastal region experienced Greek maritime colonisation, before
being incorporated together with much of the hinterland into the
Roman Empire in the course of the first century AD. With the fragmentation of the Roman Empire into its eastern and western halves
in the fourth century AD, the area which was to become Montenegro was left at the border between two worlds. For centuries
afterwards the coastal region oscillated between the cultural influence of Greek and Roman civilisations, and subsequently, after the

[18] The terms are linked by Ivo Banac in his seminal history, *The National Question
in Yugoslavia.* See pp. 31–59.
[19] John V. A. Fine, *The Early Medieval Balkans: A Critical Survey from the Sixth to the
Late Twelfth Century,* Ann Arbor: University of Michigan Press, 1991, pp. 9–10.
For more on the Illyrians and on the other early inhabitants of the lands relevant
to the development of Montenegro see Chapter 1.

great ecclesiastical schism of 1054, between Orthodoxy and Catholicism. In the late Middle Ages the littoral was again the focus of competing civilisations, Ottoman and Venetian.

Rich and varied though they were, these cultures were to have only a limited impact on the peoples of the hinterland, primarily for geographical reasons. Although from Roman times roads ran from the Adriatic coast through the interior to connect with the major north-south Belgrade-Constantinople axis, these arteries of communication ran to the north and south of the lands that were eventually to be incorporated in Montenegro. The physical features of the littoral—the narrow coastal strip, the high and barren mountains—created a formidable barrier comparable to the mountains of northern Albania but elsewhere unequalled along the whole length of the Dinaric Alps that extend for some 700 kilometres along the western edge of the Balkan peninsula. With the coast of Italy so near it was simply easier for the coastal populations to look outwards across the Adriatic and seek their living through maritime trade, fishing and even piracy rather than to attempt to forge links with the peoples beyond the mountains.

From the third to the fifth centuries AD the Balkan peninsula was subjected to repeated attack by waves of invaders: first the Germanic Goths, then the Asiatic Huns and, more feared than either of these, the Turkic Avars. Within their walled cities the inhabitants of the Adriatic coastal towns held out against the invaders, while the inland settlements were attacked and mostly destroyed. When they had laid the countryside waste and pillaged all they could, the invaders departed.

The sixth century saw a short interval of peace during which Byzantine civilisation, with its Christianising influences, penetrated the southern Balkans, but it was not to last. Lured by rumours of fabulous Byzantine wealth, a new group of invaders from the north made their way into the peninsula and into its western regions at some time in the seventh century AD. The newcomers were the Slavs who, unlike all their predecessors, had come to stay. Their arrival prompted further waves of ethnic migration as the indigenous and often Romanised inhabitants fled from the river valleys and plains into the more remote and mountainous areas including those of modern Montenegro.

Byzantine culture was forced to retreat in the face of a way of life based on the extended family commune or *zadruga*, which was

further organised around loose tribal areas known as *županije*. It was
not till the ninth century that the Slav inhabitants of the regions in
the western part of the peninsula—by now known as Serbs—began
to come together in larger and more organised political units. The
first to emerge was in an area known as Raška, to the north of
modern Kosovo, near the Sandžak town of Novi Pazar.

A century later a second nascent Slav state, Duklja, expanding out
from its nucleus on the shores of Lake Skadar (Ital. Scutari, Alb.
Shkodra) on the border between modern Montenegro and Albania,
extended its control along the Adriatic coast from the Pelješac peninsula in the north to the city then known as Skadar (later Scutari,
then Shkodra) in the south although it did not control the city state
of Ragusa (modern Dubrovnik). Duklja's inland territories extended
into the mountains of modern Montenegro and northern Albania,[20]
and in due course expanded to include the adjacent Serb-inhabited
entities of Raška and Zahumlje (modern Hercegovina). Over the
next eighty years Duklja—or Zeta, as it came to be called—shook
off its allegiance to Byzantium, which had re-emerged as the dominant power in the east. But by the beginning of the twelfth
century Zeta's brief moment of glory was over: its position as the
foremost Serb state was soon taken by Raška.

Over the next two centuries the achievements of the rulers of
Raška were to overshadow those of all other Balkan rulers as they
forged the medieval Serbian empire of the Nemanjić dynasty,
stretching from the Adriatic to the Aegean and from the Gulf of
Corinth to the Danube. No doubt its size was a contributing factor
when Raška too fell victim to the pattern of dynastic rivalry that had
been the downfall of previous Slav princedoms. As the empire
declined and weakened, a new and formidable power from beyond
the Balkans was poised to make rapid inroads into the peninsula. In
the fourteenth century the Ottoman Turks, emerging out of
Anatolia, thrust rapidly up through the Balkans, and defeated the
Serbs in famous battles on the Maritsa river (in modern Bulgaria)
and at Kosovo Polje.

In the wake of the Ottoman advance many Serbs sought refuge in
the mountains of Zeta. As the Ottomans strove to consolidate their
hold in the central Balkans a new noble family, the Balšić dynasty of

---

[20] Dimitri Obolensky, *The Byzantine Commonwealth: Eastern Europe 500–1453*,
London: Phoenix Press, 1971, p. 220.

mixed Serbo-Albanian origins, was able to take control of Zeta—
both the hinterland and the coast—and re-establish for some fifty
years a measure of that entity's former independence. But it was only
a matter of time before the rulers of Zeta would experience the
menace that had overtaken the Serbs of Raška. In an atmosphere of
mounting instability, the Balšići were ousted by a rival family, the
Crnojevići. Feudal lords from the area of Zeta, which was by this
time known as Montenegro, the Crnojevići briefly extended their
control over a large part of Zeta, presumably causing the name
Montenegro to spread with them.[21]

In turn the Crnojevići were to find themselves driven out as the
Ottomans pushed relentlessly on. Driven out first from the old
Zetan capital of Skadar on the lake of the same name, and then from
the hilltop stronghold of Žabljak near the site of modern Rijeka
Crnojevića, the Crnojevići finally abandoned the fertile river valley
of the Zeta and led a retreat of some of the peasantry into the mountainous hinterland above the Gulf of Kotor. Here, on a high plateau
encircled by hills of bare stone, they built a monastery and established a court at Cetinje, the future royal capital. From Cetinje the
Crnojevići planned ill-fated campaigns and uprisings against the
Ottomans, finally provoking threats of retaliation which forced them
to flee to Venice for protection. With their departure the region
around Cetinje, the last Orthodox redoubt in the Balkan peninsula,
finally fell to the Ottomans.

Viewed in retrospect, the principal events of the Crnojević era—
the doomed struggle against the Ottoman advance, the migration
from fertile lowlands into a mountain wilderness, the founding
of a new 'capital' with its own Orthodox metropolitan—provided
highly suggestive material for the construction of a national story.
It mattered little that at the time the Crnojevići themselves were
local rulers whose sense of identity was likely to be primarily Orthodox[22] and whose peasant followers were no doubt driven to follow
them for reasons which included the avoidance of vassal status
and religious affiliation in an age that knew nothing of notions of
national identity; the narrative contained enough ambiguous elements to allow it to be interpreted as both a celebration of Serb con-

[21] Fine, *The Late Medieval Balkans*, p. 532.
[22] See Fine, *ibid.*, p. 603, on their attempts to promote Orthodoxy.

BORDER CHANGES

1. Zeta and Serbia, mid–13th century

2. Old Montenegro and the Brda

3. Expansion, 1859–80

4. After the Balkan Wars, 1912–13

tinuity and the beginning of a new Montenegrin epoch.[23] The abandonment also meant relinquishing several important towns of the Adriatic coast and the fertile plains and valleys of the Zeta and Morača rivers. It was therefore not surprising that Zeta itself later provided a source of inspiration for future rulers of Montenegro intent on wresting back some of the coastline as a way of breaking out of their mountain isolation.[24]

Old Montenegro

The area into which the Zetans now retreated was of necessity inaccessible. It was also supremely inhospitable, mountainous, rocky and largely barren—a land dominated by the eponymous Black Mountain. That it should be so was fitting, because over the ensuing four centuries the physical characteristics of the landscape were to have a defining effect on the inhabitants' way of life and future political history. A much-quoted Montenegrin myth makes the point. 'When God finished making the world,' the tale goes, 'He found He had a great number of rocks left in His bag so He tumbled the whole lot out on a wild and desolate bit of country— that is how Montenegro was formed.' In the way of myths the story links an ineluctable fact of life with God's purpose. This purpose, retold by bards and bishops over the centuries, was to preserve in Old Montenegro a corner of the Serbian Orthodox world free from Islam.

Like many myths this one is based rather more on wishful thinking than on historical accuracy. With the departure of the Crnojevići at the end of the fifteenth century these lands too—comprising no more than four Turkish sub-districts or *nahije*—became part of the Ottoman Empire, but whenever the opportunity presented itself, the Montenegrins rebelled against Ottoman authority, acting at different times in co-operation with different neighbours—Venetians, Hercegovinians, Albanians and Serbs. Their unruliness coupled with the difficulty of the terrain soon led the Ottomans to renounce the

[23] On the latter see Rastoder, 'A Short Review of the History of Montenegro', p. 111.
[24] See Chapter 9 on Montenegro's attempt to take Skadar (Scutari) during the Balkan Wars of 1912–13.

struggle to collect anything but the basic poll tax, and to tolerate, grudgingly and within limits, an increasing degree of self-rule.

This semi-autonomous system differed significantly from the stratified social structure with its divisions into peasants and nobility that had characterised the preceding periods of Balšići and Crnojevići rule in coastal and lowland Zeta.[25] As they retreated into the mountains the Zetans had come into contact with mobile tribes of Vlach pastoralists, who were taking advantage of the chaos unleashed by the Ottoman invasion to advance further into Zeta.[26] Who exactly these Vlachs were and where they had come from has generated controversy among historians, but most authoritative scholarship accepts that they were the descendants of pre-Slavic peoples—native Illyrians blended with later Romanised and Latin-speaking populations—who had dispersed into the interior as a result of the various invasions of the Balkan peninsula from the third to the sixth centuries.[27] The Vlachs grazed their flocks over large communally-owned and locally-defined areas known as *katuns*, a practice allowing for the movement of livestock between summer and winter pastures. At the same time their contact with neighbouring Slav populations—to whom they supplied horses and other livestock—led many of them to become increasingly Slavicised to the point where they accepted Orthodoxy and spoke the same language.

It was thus hardly surprising that within a relatively short time the Zetans had intermarried and blended with the Vlachs, adopting their tribally-based and patriarchal way of life in which authority was vested in clan chiefs and above them in the headmen of the most powerful tribes.[28] As the sixteenth century advanced, this pattern of

---

[25] Traditionally the mountainous regions of Zeta had been inhabited by tribes of herdsmen who were never fully under the control of the area's successive rulers. See Fine, *The Late Medieval Balkans*, p. 415.

[26] Rastoder points out that some degree of social change had already begun to take place during the brief period in which the Crnojevići still had control of coastal and lowland Zeta. (Rastoder, 'A Short History of Montenegro', p. 110.)

[27] See Noel Malcolm, *Bosnia: A Short History*, London: Macmillan 1994, pp. 72–81.

[28] See Banac, *The National Question*, p. 44. For more on the tribal pattern of Montenegrin social organisation see Christopher Boehm, *Blood Revenge: The Anthropology of Feuding in Montenegro and other Tribal Societies*, Lawrence: University of Kansas Press, 1984, and Chapter 3.

tribal organisation expanded to cover most of former Zeta with the exception of the coastal towns of Kotor and Budva, which remained under the control of Venice. In this respect life in Old Montenegro had much in common with that of the neighbouring Albanian tribesmen to the south and Hercegovinians to the north, while diverging significantly from the pattern of settled farming and larger towns which predominated in the lush valleys and fertile farmlands of Serbia.

But if differences in geography and social mores set the inhabitants of Old Montenegro and Serbia apart, the distinction was not perceived as significant in an era when modern notions of 'nation' and 'state' had yet to be invented and the individual Montenegrin was tied more closely to his tribe and its jealously guarded autonomy than to any idea of Montenegro as a whole. Identity, as is often pointed out, is relational, most obviously in its need to be defined in opposition to something else. For almost the whole of the Ottoman period, concepts of Serbian and Montenegrin identity tended to coalesce in opposition to the 'Turk', a category that included both Ottoman functionaries and Slav converts to Islam. Predictably this shared hostility found its strongest expression in support for a common Serbian Orthodox Church, the one traditional institution permitted to exist under the Ottoman *millet* system which sought to rule subject peoples indirectly through their own religious hierarchies.[29] In defence of Orthodoxy both Serbs and Montenegrins embraced a tradition that honoured medieval Orthodox saints who were at the same time Serbian rulers, while maintaining a quasi-messianic belief in the eventual restoration of a powerful Serbian state. Nor was it only a matter of belief—the Cross against the Crescent. Patriarchal Montenegrin society was warlike: barren lands and poverty gave rise to the practice of raiding, which in turn provoked the Ottomans to renew their campaigns of 'pacification'. Dedicated to preserving their autonomy, the tribesmen fought back; their attempts to find allies led to repeated involvement in the prolonged wars between Venice and the Ottoman Empire during the seventeenth century. Hostilities between the Ottomans and Montenegrins con-

[29] On the Ottoman *millet* system, see Barbara Jelavich, *History of the Balkans,* 2 vols: *Eighteenth and Nineteenth Centuries,* vol. 1, Cambridge University Press, 1983, pp. 48–53.

tinued into the next century with the Montenegrins frequently managing to hold their own against the immeasurably greater forces of the Ottoman commanders. Perhaps almost as bad from the Ottoman viewpoint was the fact that the need to defend themselves against the invader constantly prodded the Montenegrin tribes towards greater integration, thereby boosting their capacity to resist while at the same time deepening and strengthening the horizontal links on which a sense of common identity ultimately depends.

Indeed the first manifestation of this growing tendency was the development of a further level of self-government above that of the primitive clan and tribal assemblies, which had traditionally controlled life within their respective territories. This was the formation of an all-tribal general assembly (*opštecrnogorski zbor*), which by the early seventeenth century had begun to offer advice and formulate policies for the conduct of the tribes' relations with neighbours, although it lacked executive and judicial powers and therefore its conclusions depended for their enactment largely on the weight of moral force.[30] Clearly the existence of such an institution, drawing in representatives of all the tribes of Old Montenegro, fostered a sense of common identity among those whose interests it represented and underscored the Montenegrins' experience of self-governance and increasing autonomy at a time when the rest of the Balkans was under Ottoman rule.

Running roughly parallel with the increasing unity of the tribes was the gradual transformation of the office of metropolitan or Vladika, which having at first been an ecclesiastical position, subordinate to and elected by the tribes, had begun by the early seventeenth century to serve as both a focus for and agent of central authority, with the Vladika often mediating between the various fractious chiefs. Progressively in the course of its evolution the office took on the political and hereditary characteristics which were increasingly to distinguish it as a uniquely Montenegrin institution, eventually referred to in English as Prince-Bishop. The year 1697 marked a highly significant step in its development when Metropolitan Danilo became the first in a line of hereditary bishops to descend from the powerful Petrović clan. Not content solely with strengthening his own position, Danilo also sought to extend the

---

[30] Rastoder, 'A Short Review of the History of Montenegro', pp. 113–14.

tribesmen's horizons beyond the very narrow borders of Old Montenegro. The clearest indication of his ambitions emerges from the title he chose for himself: 'Danilo, Vladika of Cetinje and Warlord of the Serbian land'. The designation is indeed revealing: not only does it stress Danilo's 'Serbness' (in counterpoint to the Ottomans), but it also lays claim, in a preposterously grandiloquent way, to the leadership of the Serb peoples, an interesting early example of Montenegrin 'self-centredness'[31] with its characteristic intimations of superiority.

Having transformed the role of the Vladika, Danilo's next innovation was of equal and lasting importance in deciding the future course of Montenegro. This was to establish a close connection with Russia, the country which over the next three centuries was to provide material and spiritual succour to Montenegrins, engendering a loyalty unparalleled among the other South Slavs.[32] Clear evidence of Montenegrins' developing pro-Russian sympathies was already apparent at the very beginning of the eighteenth century when Montenegrins, supported by some highland and Hercegovinan tribes but not by other South Slavs, rallied to Peter the Great's call to rise against the Ottomans in support of his Balkan campaign. Later links with Russia were fostered by succeeding Vladikas, who made numerous visits to Russia designed to secure subventions for the paltry Montenegrin budget and to solicit moral and material support for their struggle against the Ottomans. In 1754 the first *History of Montenegro* was published in Russia as part of a campaign by Vladika Vasilije to persuade St Petersburg to agree to the establishment of a Russian protectorate over Montenegro.[33] Just how pervasive the cult of Mother Russia in Montenegro had come to be was made fully apparent when in 1767, during a hiatus in the authority of the ruling Vladika, the Montenegrins accepted a bizarre impostor, Šćepan Mali (Stephen the Small) as their ruler after he had claimed to be Tsar Peter III, the murdered husband of the Empress Catherine.

Critically for relations with Serbia, the closer relationship with Russia coincided with a period of uncertainty for the Serbian Patri-

[31] The term is used by Banac in *The National Question*, p. 274.
[32] See Rastoder, 'A Short Review of the History of Montenegro', p. 115.
[33] Jelavich, *History of the Balkans*, vol. 2, p. 85.

archate in Peć whither the Montenegrin Vladikas went for consecration. Following its abolition by the Ottomans in 1766 in retaliation
for drawing too close to Russia, it was forced to remove to Habsburg-
ruled territory at Sremski Karlovci in Vojvodina. The Ottomans
then appointed a new patriarch who was under the authority of the
Ecumenical Patriarch of Constantinople (i.e. a trusted Greek, not
pro-Russian), but the Serbian Church was effectively split and could
no longer provide a single focus for the Serbian world. The Orthodox Church in Montenegro, while maintaining a nominal association with the displaced Patriarchate, reacted by being equally
inclined, if not more so, to associate their Orthodoxy with Russia.

Both internally and in terms of a fledgling foreign policy the
Montenegrins over this period took decisions, pursued policies and
formed attitudes designed to further their own interests, a course of
action largely forced upon them by their military vulnerability, precarious economic situation and physical isolation. In short, they
were caught up in an appreciably different and distinctively Montenegrin way of life. But is leading such an existence tantamount to
possessing a sense of separate and specifically Montenegrin identity?

All the evidence we can produce—the little we know from the
folk tradition, from ballads and oral history—suggests that the
Montenegrins of this time drew support from their sense of com-
monality with Serbs in Ottoman-ruled territories elsewhere in the
peninsula. Indeed they went further, tracing their origins back to
remnants of the Serbian nobility who had fled into the mountains of
Montenegro following the heroic defeat in 1389 at Kosovo Polje,[34]
and burnishing, in repeated clashes with the enemy, a reputation as
'the best of Serbs'. But ostensibly harmonious as it appeared, this
sense of accommodation contained within it seeds of conflict from
which later divisions were to grow: for Montenegrins to be seen and
to see themselves as 'the best of Serbs' was to invite feelings of superiority, which once instilled and assimilated could not be easily relin-
quished.[35] None of this was apparent at the time, but when in the
future the two cultures were weighed on their merits and the smaller

[34] See Milovan Djilas, *Njegoš: Poet, Prince, Bishop,* transl. Michael B. Petrovich, New
York: Harcourt, Brace & World, 1966, p. 11.
[35] Banac, *The National Question,* p. 273.

and weaker Montenegrin culture was found wanting, there could be no mistaking the fact that divergent experiences and centuries of separation had engendered a sense of being different. For some these were challenges that could be overcome, but for others they would make the prospect of co-existence, especially co-existence on unequal terms, not just difficult but completely impossible.

Montenegro expands to the highlands (Brda)

The first expansion beyond the heartlands of Old Montenegro did not take place till 1796 when, following crucial battles against the Ottomans at Martinići and Kruši, Montenegro acquired a substantial piece of territory to the north-east of Cetinje, known as the Brda or highlands. In 1820 the Montenegrins again defeated the Ottomans at a battle on the river Morača and as a result were able to incorporate lands belonging to two further highland tribes, the Rovci and the Moračani. Still later, in 1858, after the defeat inflicted on the Ottomans at the battle of Grahovo, Montenegro gained additional territory in Hercegovina, together with adjacent areas to the north-east. As a result of these successive victories, the Montenegrins more than doubled the total area of territory under their control. But while they had been able to expand into the uplands they did not succeed in regaining the fertile Zeta valley, which almost bisected Montenegrin lands from the south. Old Montenegro and the Brda were effectively separated from one another along almost the full length of the river valley by a strip of Ottoman-controlled territory, and they were joined only at the head of the valley by a stretch of land no more than 12 km. in length, north of modern Danilovgrad. Montenegro therefore remained highly vulnerable: Ottoman forces could attack from either end of this narrow funnel.

The risks posed by this physical vulnerability were heightened in the years immediately following Montenegro's annexation of the Brda by the notorious unreliability of the region's inhabitants. In the past these Orthodox tribesmen, fiercely committed to defending local interests, had on occasion fought for Montenegro against their Ottoman overlords. Similarly their transfer to Montenegro did not prevent them from rebelling against control from the centre, particularly in times of famine. Aware of the need to respect the highlanders' sense of independence and consequently limited identification with Montenegro, the Montenegrin authorities refrained from amalgamating the Brda into Montenegro, and instead continued to treat it as a separate entity, for example by ensuring that the first general law code and the first court, which were established in 1798, contained separate references to Montenegro and to the Brda.

At about the same time as Montenegro was first expanding into the Brda, it was also acquiring new neighbours to the north-west as a result of the great changes brought about in Europe and the Mediterranean by the Napoleonic wars. In 1797 Napoleon Bonaparte, having destroyed the enfeebled Venetian Republic, then proceeded to force Austria to sign the Treaty of Campo Formio under which the Habsburg Empire was obliged to take over Venetian lands in Istria and Dalmatia in exchange for ceding its lands in Belgium to France. Austria thus gained control not only of the territory north of Cetinje but also of the Gulf and town of Kotor. But not for long: after the Austrian defeat at Austerlitz in 1805 Napoleon seized back Austria's Venetian possessions in order to incorporate them into his Kingdom of Italy. With all the Great Powers competing for supremacy in the Mediterranean, Montenegro saw its chance to involve Russia in an attempt to gain some of the disputed coastline for itself, and began a campaign against Napoleon's forces for possession of Kotor. In 1807, with Russian-Montenegrin cooperation at its height, Vladika Petar I tried to interest Tsar Alexander I in a proposal to create an enlarged South Slav state in which Montenegro would play the central role and Petar himself would be the ruler. Improbable as the scheme was, it underlined two recurring and related themes in Montenegrin political history—an active policy of expansion, which included the belief that special merit had earned Montenegrins a place at the heart of an expanded South Slav state, and an over-inflated trust in a beneficent Russia. Turned down by the Tsar, Montenegro continued the fight with Napoleon's forces, and in 1813, with British naval backing, was able to capture Kotor from the French. Almost immediately a joint body of Montenegrins and representatives of the coastal tribes voted to form a union, giving

Montenegro a sizeable stretch of coastal territory. The vote was significant since it underlined the shared aims of the coastal communities and their Montenegrin neighbours, but its significance was short-lived. Five months later, under pressure from Russia, the Congress of Vienna returned Kotor to Austria which thus regained possession of the whole of Dalmatia. Montenegro was once again completely landlocked.

A direct border with Austria-Hungary was to have unimagined consequences for Montenegro.[36] Throughout the nineteenth century Austria's rulers consistently opposed all efforts by Montenegro to gain a direct outlet to the sea, convinced that this would amount to giving Russia a base on the Adriatic. In 1838, under Petar I's successor Petar Petrović II Njegoš, Montenegro's most famous ruler and greatest poet, this goal seemed on the verge of being achieved when the Montenegrins managed to purchase a strip of coastline below the Gulf of Kotor from a local tribe, the Paštrovići. Not surprisingly the Austrians refused to accept this *fait accompli* and instead demanded that the Montenegrins hand the territory over to them in return for £40,000.[37] But while Petar I had nurtured dreams of Montenegrin hegemony, Njegoš's political agenda was appreciably different. On the one hand, he continued and developed his predecessor's policy of Montenegrin state-building—creating new executive organs of government, introducing the first taxes and arranging for Petar I's canonisation, a gesture designed to aggrandise Montenegro and its rulers by evoking comparison with saintly rulers of Serbia's medieval empire. On the other hand, Njegoš was in touch with Ilija Garašanin, the dominant political figure in mid-nineteenth century Serbia and originator of the Greater Serbian project. In essence Garašanin's programme envisaged the construction of a large South Slav state, taking as its core the great medieval Serbian empire, whose glories it aimed to recreate. Yet although Garašanin and Njegoš seemingly saw eye-to-eye, the success of Garašanin's expansionist project would ultimately imply Serbian

---

[36] In the twentieth century Austria's land border with Montenegro made its fateful invasion of Montenegrin territory in 1914 incomparably easier. See below and Chapter 9.

[37] *Foreign Office Handbook on Montenegro*, no. 20, HMSO, November 1918, p. 15.

dominance at the expense of Montenegro. At the time this scarcely mattered as both Montenegro and Serbia were still individual entities, separated from one another by the swathe of territory that made up the Ottoman-ruled—and later the Austro-Hungarian-ruled—Sandžak. Serbs and Montenegrins could therefore continue to see themselves as the closest of brothers, a state of affairs that persisted well into the nineteenth century and even beyond.

The Congress of Berlin

In 1875 a rebellion against the Ottomans broke out in neighbouring Hercegovina. Serbia and Montenegro quickly entered the conflict, which spread throughout the region. Montenegrin forces distinguished themselves, capturing a vast expanse of territory from the Ottomans. When the Great Powers intervened in Montenegro's favour, the country was able to achieve international recognition for many of its territorial gains. At the Congress of Berlin of 1878, which resolved the so-called Eastern Question, Serbia and Montenegro achieved independence from the Ottoman Empire. In recognition of Prussian and Austro-Hungarian anxieties about Russian influence, the terms agreed were less favourable to Montenegro than those of the immediately preceding Treaty of San Stefano. However, in the north Montenegro was granted possession of the important town of Nikšić, which had fallen to its army after a long siege, together with the adjacent districts of Piva and Banjani. To the east the country was permitted to make some limited inroads into Hercegovina, gaining some but not all of the area claimed by the ruling dynasty as part of its ancestral lands. To the south Montenegro's gains were still more significant. They included not only the Ottoman trading centre of Podgorica (the present capital) and the former Crnojević capital of Žabljak, but also the Zeta river valley and the broad plain stretching south to Lake Skadar.

The Congress of Berlin marked a watershed in Montenegro's fortunes, the culmination of a centuries-long struggle against the Ottomans. Not only had the country gained its longed-for independence, but its remarkable contribution to the war had propelled it to prominence on the international stage. In Britain Gladstone regaled the House of Commons with exploits of a race of heroes, while Tennyson composed his sonnet 'Montenegro' in celebration of the 'rough rock-throne of freedom'. Both to outsiders and in their own eyes Montenegrins were now confirmed in their role as 'the best of Serbs', an accolade which while gratifying was also storing up trouble for the future. With Montenegro's reputation so high and its international standing as an independent state now equal to that of Serbia, how would Montenegrins in the future reconcile themselves to being something less?

Predictably Montenegro's enhanced status did not improve the country's standing in the eyes of Serbia and Austria. The Obrenović dynasty, which had returned to power in Serbia in 1858, had previously entertained cordial relations with Montenegro's ruler Nikola Petrović, culminating in an agreement in 1866 between the two reigning princes to work together for the unification of Serbian historic lands, although each prince was in reality working to his own agenda. In the wake of the changes brought about by the Congress of Berlin, Serbian rulers—first Miloš Obrenović and then his successor Aleksandar—grew suspicious of the ambition of the autocratic Montenegrin monarch.

Meanwhile Austria-Hungary's occupation of Bosnia-Hercegovina, which had been conceded at the Congress, acted as a block to Montenegrin territorial ambitions in Hercegovina, whose Orthodox Slav inhabitants were culturally close to the Montenegrins. Instead Montenegro was able to expand only to the south and east into lands populated largely by Albanians—both Muslims and Catholics—and Slav Muslims. Along the coast in the vicinity of Ulcinj the almost exclusively Albanian population was largely Muslim. The areas to the south and east of Podgorica were inhabited by Albanians from the predominantly Catholic tribes, while further to the east there were also concentrations of Slav Muslims. Podgorica itself had long been an Ottoman trading centre with a partly Turkish but largely Slav Muslim and Albanian population. To incorporate such a population was to dilute the number of Montenegrins, whose first loyalties lay with the Montenegrin state and Petrović dynasty, not that this was seen as sufficient reason for the Montenegrins to desist from seeking to obtain further territory.

One reason for this was that the Montenegrins' most important acquisition through the Congress of Berlin—the longed-for outlet to the sea at Bar—did not prove to be quite the godsend they had expected. In part this was because it represented a reduction of the long strip of coastal territory Montenegro had seized from Turkey during fighting the previous year. In part too it was because Austria-Hungary, determined to restrict Montenegro's gains, had secured permission to patrol these Montenegrin waters. As if this were not enough, Austria-Hungary was also extending its influence to the south among the Catholic Albanians of Skadar (more widely known at his time as Scutari) and to the east, where it now occupied certain points in the Sandžak of Novi Pazar. Montenegro, though significantly expanded, found itself hemmed in less by Turkey than by Austria. It was only in 1880 after further fighting with local Albanians that the Montenegrins gained an additional 45 km. stretch of seaboard extending from just north of Bar down to Ulcinj. But even after the Congress of Berlin and these later adjustments, certain parts of the Montenegrin frontier continued to be disputed by Albanian tribes which were strongly opposed to rule by Montenegro. Raiding and feuding took place along the whole length of the porous Montenegrin-Albanian border. For Edith Durham, the nineteenth-century Balkan traveller, the borders drawn by the Congress of Berlin were 'impossible: the frontier floated on blood.'[38]

A second and more fundamental reason for Montenegro's continued quest for territory was the country's unrelieved poverty, reflected in the continuing exodus of Montenegrins bound for neighbouring countries or, increasingly, for North America. One possibility still somewhat unrealistically entertained by Prince Nikola—incorporating Hercegovina into a Greater Montenegrin state—was conclusively thwarted in 1908 when, to counter the threat posed to its interests by the Young Turks' revolution in Istanbul, Austria-Hungary suddenly annexed Bosnia-Hercegovina. The disappointment could not have come at a less propitious moment for the Montenegrin regime, by this time experiencing serious unrest as a result of the growing strength of the political opposition whose goals were nothing less than the overthrow of the Petrović

[38] Edith Durham, *The Struggle for Scutari*, London: Edward Arnold, 1914, p. 159.

regime and Montenegro's unification with Serbia. Worse still, the
rebels' goals if achieved would place Montenegro under the rule of
the dynasty which in 1903 had returned to rule Serbia and whose
present incumbent was none other than Nikola's own son-in-
law, Petar Karadjordjević. By 1909 any temporary improvement in
Serbian-Montenegrin relations as a result of shared outrage and disappointment at Austria-Hungary's actions in Bosnia and Hercegovina the previous year had evaporated and, following the discovery
of what was believed to be a Serbian-backed conspiracy[39] to overthrow Nikola and his government, Serbian-Montenegrin relations
reached a new nadir. How this affected the identity issue can easily
be imagined. As Ivo Banac comments, 'It could no longer be
assumed that a good Montenegrin was the best Serb, or even an
acceptable Serb.'[40] Nikola's second son put it more bluntly: 'Montenegrins are not Serbians, neither cowards nor traitors, nor regicides... We do not want to have anything to do with Serbia.'[41] As
relations between the two states deteriorated, Nikola decided to use
the pretext of his fiftieth anniversary on the throne to place Montenegro on an equal footing with Serbia by raising the country's
status to that of a kingdom.

Far from slaking the new king's ambitions, this act of self-
aggrandisement merely stimulated his determination to acquire
further territory, which he believed to be essential to the country's
economic survival. In 1910 the Catholic Albanian Malissori tribes
along Montenegro's southern border rose in rebellion against their
Ottoman overlords. With Scutari and even Tsar Dušan's medieval
capital of Prizren as possible prizes, Nikola attempted to fan the flames
of rebellion by offering the insurgents a refuge in Montenegro.

[39] While the Montenegrin authorities believed that the Serbian government was
behind the conspiracy, many Serbs believed that Austria-Hungary and the
Montenegrin government had together hatched the plot with the intention of
discrediting Serbian nationalists' attempts to gain support for an enlarged South
Slav state. See Treadway, *The Falcon and the Eagle*, pp. 53–4.

[40] Banac, *The National Question*, p. 277.

[41] Treadway, *The Falcon and the Eagle*, p. 57. The regicide referred to is that of
Petar Karadjordjević's predecessor Aleksandar Obrenović, who was murdered,
together with his hated wife Queen Draga, by a group of army officers in 1903.
See Chapter 8.

But the revolt of 1910 and a second one the following year both failed, and it was not till 1912 that the small Balkan states—Bulgaria, Serbia, Greece and Montenegro—formed an alliance designed to force the dismemberment of Turkey-in-Europe.

The Balkan Wars

Ostensibly the inclusion of both Serbia and Montenegro in this alliance suggested that relations between them were now on an even keel, but below the surface rivalries persisted. Indeed so anxious was Nikola to demonstrate Montenegro's primacy on national issues that he arranged for his son to fire the first shot of the war. Although the Balkan Wars of 1912 and 1913 resulted in yet another substantial increase in Montenegrin territory (the settlement reached with the mediation of the Great Powers allowed Montenegro to keep its gains to the north of Lake Skadar as well as Bijelo Polje, Berane, Plav and Gusinje in the Sandžak, important towns along the old caravan route across Kosovo and Macedonia and on to Istanbul), these territorial additions were intended to compensate the Montenegrins for the most disastrous loss during the entire campaign—the surrender of Scutari, which they had taken in April 1912 after a prolonged siege. Under the strongest pressure from Austria-Hungary, the self-appointed protector of the Albanians, the Great Powers had insisted that Montenegrin troops hand the city over to an international administration. Effectively the territory awarded to Montenegro amounted to almost half of the Sandžak and extended into Kosovo to encompass the fourteenth-century monastery at Dečani and the Serbian holy town of Peć, although it did not include Prizren. Montenegro's territory had increased by some 8,200 sq. km. and its population, swollen by the more densely populated lands in Kosovo, had almost doubled to some 450,000. It was far more crucial, however, that for the first time in five centuries Serbia and Montenegro now had a common frontier, running through the middle of the Sandžak. As the climate of rivalry intensified over the last years of the nineteenth century and the early years of the twentieth, an increasing number of young Montenegrins began to compare the liberalism of Serbian rulers with their own reactionary Petrović dynasty, and with

a common frontier now a reality saw no reason to delay the realisation of their earlier goal of Serbian–Montenegrin unification.

The First World War and Montenegro's loss of independence

When the elections in January 1914 brought to power a party
wedded to union, Nikola was realist enough not to reject these
demands out of hand. Instead he expressed support for them provided that both royal houses would be maintained and the rights of
each guaranteed.[42] Negotiations, ostensibly aimed at bringing about
a Serbian–Montenegrin commonwealth along Prussian-Bavarian
lines but ultimately intended to bring about unification, were begun
but then interrupted by the assassination of the Archduke Franz
Ferdinand in Sarajevo and never completed.[43] Serbia, served with an
ultimatum by Austria, quickly found itself under immense pressure.
Meanwhile in Montenegro Nikola, at first attracted by the idea of
staying out of the war, found the pressures from an increasingly pro-
Serb population ever harder to contain. Accordingly, when Austria-
Hungary finally declared war on Serbia on 28 July 1914 Nikola
responded by issuing his own declaration of war on the Dual Monarchy a week later. With Russia increasingly frustrated and by now
taking an openly pro-Serbian line, the Montenegrin monarch had
little choice but to accept a Serbian general, Boža Janković, as commander of the Montenegrin army. In June 1915 the Montenegrins
briefly re-occupied Scutari in defiance of the wishes of both the
Great Powers and General Janković, who promptly submitted his
resignation only to be replaced by another Serbian.

Meanwhile the situation on the wider checkerboard of war
was moving rapidly against both Serbs and Montenegrins. In October the same year Austria-Hungary launched a massive offensive,
pushing the Serbs to the south and entering Montenegro before
taking the capital Cetinje in January 1916 and forcing Montenegrin
capitulation. King Nikola had ingloriously fled into exile a few days,
earlier earning unfavourable comparison with his Serbian counterpart King Petar who accompanied his army on an epic retreat all
the way to Corfu. Although some guerrilla (*komiti*) fighters took to

---

[42] See Treadway, *The Falcon and the Eagle*, pp. 174–5, and Chapter 8.
[43] Treadway, *ibid.*

the hills to mount a resistance campaign against the occupiers, the surrender was a national trauma for the Montenegrins. They had been let down as much by Serbian generals as by their own dynasty. For some Montenegrins neither would be forgiven, but others saw the debacle as strengthening their belief in unification, while a remnant still clung to the ideal of restoration of the Petrović dynasty. But while the divisions were clearly apparent, it was only when the victorious Serbian army entered Montenegro, following the defeat of Austro-Hungarian forces in the Balkans in 1918, and supervised its union with Serbia that civil war became inevitable.

The sudden collapse of the Central Powers in 1918 took both sides by surprise. In Montenegro the retreat of the Austro-Hungarian forces was followed by the successful re-entry of the Serbian army into Montenegro. Accompanied by British, French and Italian troops, the Serbians were formally under the command of a French general who, in line with the French policy of backing Serbia's plans for unification with Montenegro, ordered the allies to take up positions along the coast while leaving the interior of the country to the Serbians. Meanwhile Nikola, detained in France, was prevented from leaving for Montenegro. In November 1918 a 'Grand National Assembly', convened in the former Ottoman town of Podgorica rather than in the royal capital of Cetinje, voted under the watchful eye of the Serbian army to dethrone the Petrović dynasty and unite Montenegro with Serbia. The result was to be expected. Before entering Montenegro the Serbian army had received its instructions from the Regent Aleksandar, who told their commander: 'In your work in Montenegro do not be tenderhearted. King Nikola must be prevented from returning to Montenegro at all costs, even if we have to use extreme measures.'[44] The following year, only forty-one years after the Congress of Berlin had granted international recognition to the principality of Montenegro, the Paris Peace Conference confirmed the country's incorporation within the new Kingdom of the Serbs, Croats and Slovenes. Clever diplomacy on the part of the Serbian government, together with the Allies' desire to achieve a unified South Slav state, meant that Montenegro was not represented at the Conference.

---

[44] Banac, *The National Question*, p. 284.

Although officially closed by the Paris Peace Conference, the issue of Montenegrin independence was kept alive through the early 1920s by armed insurgents who took the name Greens (*zelenaši*) after the colour of their candidates' list for the Grand National Assembly of 1918. Opposing them were the Whites (*bjelaši*)—pro-Serbian units, many from those parts of Montenegro adjoining Serbia, although the divisions cut across tribes and even families. For a time the Greens received support from Victor Emmanuel III of Italy, who was married to Nikola's daughter Jelena. Ultimately, however, the Italian king proved a fickle ally, who was bought off after Italy settled its border dispute with Yugoslavia over Trieste at the Treaty of Rapallo in November 1920. Deprived of outside support, the Greens took refuge in caves in the mountains, swooping down to harry their opponents. Atrocities committed on both sides were compounded by famine as the rebels and their pursuers plundered and burnt their way through the countryside leaving ruin and desolation behind them. But when the White tendency finally triumphed in the mid 1920s, the divisions created by the fighting did not disappear. Instead they remained, in the words of Ivo Banac, 'as permanent fixtures of the Montenegrin landscape'.[45]

The turmoil of the period threw the vexed question of Montenegrin loyalties into sharp relief. Once a benevolent and inspiring motherland, Serbia had eclipsed Montenegro's existence as an independent state. How were Montenegrins, accustomed to see themselves as the most valiant of Serbs, to reconcile themselves to Serbia's role in the disappearance of their country? In truth the response was divided, although the divisions were not as clear-cut as is sometimes made out. In the years immediately following Nikola's departure, his supporters—the Greens—attempted to mount a fruitless rearguard action to revive the dynasty and reclaim Montenegro's independent existence. The monarchy's younger and better educated Serbophile opponents sought to convey the conflict as 'an explicit collision between Serbdom and Montenegritude, between love of freedom

---

[45] Banac, *The National Question*, p. 289. While the divisions remained, by the mid-1920s most Greens had of necessity accepted the move from military to political means. They formed the Montenegrin Party, committed to the creation of a federal Yugoslavia in which Montenegro would have a status equal to that of the other constituent nations, the Croats and the Slovenes. See Chapter 9.

and reaction.'[46] However, many ordinary Montenegrins, while not necessarily supporters of the dynasty or opposed to a union on equal terms, were deeply affronted by the way in which unification had been imposed by the Serbs and without respect for Montenegro's separate traditions and longstanding historical identity. Thus while 1918 marked a critical turning-point in the debate over Montenegrin identity, what resulted was not simply a clear polarization between those who viewed themselves exclusively as either Serbs or Montenegrins, but rather a wide spectrum of opinion which included both these views while at the same time leaving many Montenegrins stranded somewhere in the middle. Moreover, the picture was complicated by the fact that while the original division between supporters and opponents of union with Serbia had tended to set young, educated town-dwellers against the older and less sophisticated rural population, there was also clear evidence of a geographical divide: the population around Cetinje and in the region that had made up Old Montenegro proved to be the strongest supporters of the Green insurgency while those in the areas which had been more recently joined to Montenegro—the Brda and the northern part of the country bordering Serbia—were predominately Whites.[47]

Montenegro in the first Yugoslavia

Montenegro's incorporation in the Kingdom of the Serbs, Croats and Slovenes—renamed the Kingdom of Yugoslavia in 1929—did nothing to assuage the wounded sentiments of those Montenegrins who deeply resented the country's loss of sovereignty and separate identity. On the contrary, the treatment meted out to Montenegro during the inter-war years, which ranged from economic neglect and abolition of the autocephalous Montenegrin Church to the elimination of the country's historic name, was designed to blur all distinctions between Serbia and Montenegro: in reality it produced an increasing sense of alienation. In particular the Serbian regent's decree of 1920 unilaterally proclaiming the unity of all the autoce-

[46] Banac, *The National Question*, p. 277.
[47] See, *ibid.*, pp. 286–7 and Chapter 9.

phalous churches and episcopates within Yugoslav lands under the jurisdiction of a single Serbian patriarch with his see in Belgrade was a real blow to Montenegrin self-esteem, not because Montenegrins were especially religious—they were, and are, not—but because of the traditional links between church and state in the Ortho-dox world and specifically because of the Montenegrin Church's centuries-long association with the country's path to self-rule and independent statehood. In 1929, following the institution of a dicta-torship, the Kingdom of Yugoslavia was reorganised into nine provinces, the boundaries of which were drawn with the aim of diluting historic loyalties and identities. Montenegro was now the *Zetska banovina*, a province based on the river Zeta that, disregarding old borders, included parts of southern Dalmatia and Hercegovina as well as most of the Sandžak of Novi Pazar.

The Second World War and the second Yugoslavia

In marked contrast to the inter-war period, characterised by a loss of identity and concomitant neglect, the traumatic events of the Second World War refocused attention on Montenegro. Occupied by the Italians in 1941 after the Kingdom of Yugoslavia's capitu-lation, the country was quickly involved not only in a war of resistance against the occupiers but also in a bitter civil war between Tito's communist Partisans and royalist Chetniks, who looked forward to the restoration of a Serb-dominated Kingdom of Yugo-slavia after the war. Here again identity issues were involved in both the war of resistance and in the civil war, at times reinforcing, at times cutting across previously existing divisions over Montenegrin iden-tity. First Montenegrin separatists, offshoots of the old Greens, sup-ported the Italian invaders in the establishment of a puppet state which the occupiers claimed would bring about the restoration of the former Petrović dynasty. But the charade soon collapsed as a result of a popular uprising organised jointly by the Communists and pro-Serbian Chetniks, who at an early stage cooperated to fight the occupiers. Subsequently, however, both Communists and Chet-niks devoted a large proportion of their time and energy to fighting one another, but while the Communists continued at the same time to attack the Axis forces, the Chetniks were prepared to collaborate with them in order to defeat the Partisans, whom they believed to pose a more immediate threat to their goal of a future Serbian-dominated Yugoslavia. Significantly the bulk of Chetnik support came from the Brda tribes and from the north of Montenegro, strongholds of the former Whites. Meanwhile the Partisans, despite the fact that their foot-soldiers included Montenegrins of all backgrounds and beliefs, took up a position closer to the former Greens in arguing that the Montenegrins were indeed a separate people, a position they assumed partly in response to the politics of Serbian hegemony espoused by their Chetnik opponents. Throughout the war the fighting in Montenegro was exceptionally savage. In particular, the country's traditional history of resistance to the invader and the population's experience of what was essentially guerrilla warfare proved invaluable to the Partisans' need to find fighters prepared to go the bitter end in the quest for victory.

After the war Tito recognised the Montenegrins' contribution to the Partisan cause by making Montenegro a full Republic within the new Federal People's Republic of Yugoslavia (FNRJ). In an attempt to prevent a resurgence of the intractable inter-war national conflicts, the new Yugoslavia was divided into six Republics and (within Serbia) two autonomous provinces. Montenegro's borders were extended to take in the coastal strip north of Bar and up to and including the Gulf of Kotor—an invaluable acquisition. At the same time, however, Montenegro was obliged to cede some of the territory it had gained as a result of the settlement of the Balkan Wars, lands that were then incorporated in Serbia's province of Kosovo. The resulting borders are those that continue to delimit the territory of the newly independent state of Montenegro, an area of some 13,812 square km. on the map, about the size of Northern Ireland.[48]

---

[48] Montenegro is one of the least densely settled parts of Europe. It has approximately 290 km. of coastline; Italy lies less than 100 km. away across the Adriatic. It has land borders with Croatia and Bosnia-Hercegovina to the north and Serbia to the east, while to the south its border with Albania is delimited by the aptly named Prokletije or Accursed Mountains. To the north-west Montenegro borders Bosnia-Hercegovina along a jagged frontier beyond the massif of the 2,500-metre Mount Durmitor in a region of empty uplands, precipitous ravines and extensive cave systems. To the east the border with Serbia runs through

Of course, bolstering the notion of a separate Montenegrin identity also suited Tito's policy of cutting the two largest 'nations'—the Serbs and Croats—down to size by strengthening the smaller 'nations' within the federation. Irrespective of the motive, for many Montenegrins the creation of a separate Republic of Montenegro managed to resolve the conundrum of Montenegrin identity. On the one hand this quasi-statehood helped to assuage the patriotic feelings of those who wished to see themselves as independent actors on the Slav stage. On the other it provided membership of a common state for those Montenegrins who wished to remain in a continuing close relationship with Serbia.

At least superficially Tito's Yugoslavia seemed to have reached a balanced solution, with which many Montenegrins declared themselves satisfied. However, problems arose when in 1948 Tito split with Stalin. Given their strongly Russophile sentiments and rigid traditional values, it was not surprising that many Montenegrins had enthusiastically followed the hard-line Stalinist approach and were not prepared to compromise. Rebellions, which some 'deviationists' thought might spread across Yugoslavia, broke out in 1948 and continued into the following year before the movement was finally crushed. A considerable number of rebels paid the price. Some were tracked down and executed, while many more were imprisoned. Of all the Yugoslav republics, the repression was harshest in Montenegro.

In the ensuing decade, as Montenegro began to benefit from its position within Tito's Yugoslavia, the memory of repression faded, but, as elsewhere in the former Yugoslavia, the bitterness did not entirely disappear. Not everyone was content with Yugoslavia. There were persistent pockets of support for Montenegrin independence, especially around the old royal capital of Cetinje, and although many Montenegrins were willing to think of themselves as Yugoslavs, this

---

almost equally remote terrain, sparsely inhabited by tough shepherds and pastoralists, many of whom consider themselves to be ethnic Serbs. Modern Montenegro cannot be said to constitute a natural geographical unit. On the contrary its physical features—narrow coastal plain, barren limestone ranges and interior plateau with high mountains—mark it out as part of the larger geographic area running parallel to the Adriatic all the way from the Gulf of Trieste to the mouth of the Drin river in northern Albania.

tended to overlay rather than replace their existing sense of identity. In a society as small as that of Montenegro it was not possible to erase the memory of old allegiances, still less of past misdeeds. Divisions—those between Greens and Whites, now compounded by those between Partisans and Chetniks (though they did not always co-incide)—continued to exist under the surface of a regime ostensibly committed to the Titoist goal of 'brotherhood and unity'.

Overall, however, the relatively high level of satisfaction with life in Tito's Yugoslavia was reflected in the fact that Montenegro had more members of the Communist Party per head of population than any of the other Republics in Federal Socialist Yugoslavia. Montenegrins were significantly over-represented in the Yugoslav army, especially in the officer corps, where their traditional affinity for warfare stood them in good stead. This caused no problem for the Serbs, who were themselves strongly represented in the armed forces, but like other Yugoslavs they were less happy with what they saw as the Montenegrins' natural propensity for elbowing their way into comfortable positions at all levels in the sprawling Communist bureaucracy. Montenegrins, so conventional wisdom had it, were ready for anything that smacked of status and involved a minimum of real work, And, as always where differences are small, the need to exaggerate them is greater. So Serbs were also among the first to single out what they saw as specifically Montenegrin defects—laziness, vanity and misogyny, overlaid with a primitive belligerence.

These were petty grievances; jokes made at each other's expense co-existed with a more favourable view of Montenegrins—as brave, intelligent, educated and proud.[49] If nothing else, such stereotyping is a testimony to widespread recognition of a distinct Montenegrin identity, accepted at the time not only by Serbs and Montenegrins but also by other Yugoslavs. In the early years Titoist policies intended to improve the position of Yugoslavia's less developed regions ensured that Montenegro received a somewhat disproportionate share of investment, and this understandably added to resentment. In Montenegro, as elsewhere in Yugoslavia, the relatively high level of satisfaction endured as long as the state was able to deliver not only 'brotherhood and unity', but a measure of prosperity.

[49] See Srdja Pavlović, 'Who are the Montenegrins?', p. 92.

The end of Communism

However, Montenegro was no exception when at the end of the 1980s the collapse of Communism and a myriad of economic ills brought Tito's Yugoslavia to its knees. In these dire conditions the ambitious Serbian Communist Party apparatchik Slobodan Milošević played the national card in Kosovo. In a climate of mounting social and economic insecurity he launched his bid for power, manipulating people's atavistic fears and ousting potential opponents. In Montenegro, as in Vojvodina, Serbia and Kosovo, so-called 'antibureaucratic revolutions', instigated by Milošević's henchmen, swept the old Communist authorities from power. In mass demonstrations Montenegrins stood shoulder to shoulder with Serbs in support of their brothers in Kosovo. When, in 1991, war broke out with Croatia, Montenegrins did not demur as Montenegrin paramilitaries embarked on a campaign of destruction, ravaging the ancient city of Dubrovnik and the beautiful Dalmatian littoral. In 1992 Montenegro went further, with over 90 per cent of the population voting in a plebiscite to remain in a rump federation with Serbia, the new Federal Republic of Yugoslavia (FRY).

Yet despite the overwhelming vote, the identity issue was again emerging as some in Montenegro recoiled from Milošević's nationalistic and Greater Serbian policies. One manifestation of this was the revival in 1993 of the dispute over the abolition of the Montenegrin Orthodox Church, which though ostensibly a religious matter, was in reality a political issue intended to reinstate the submerged concerns over Montenegro's separate identity and independence from Belgrade to their former place on the political agenda.[50] In 1997 the political debate took a further turn following a split within the ruling party in Montenegro, when the winner in the ensuing conflict, the thirty-eight-year-old Milo Djukanović, broke formally with Milošević. Naturally this was warmly welcomed by

---

[50] For information on both the history of the Montenegrin Orthodox Church and the state of relations between the rival churches in Montenegro the author is indebted to a paper by Nebojša Čagorović entitled 'The War of the Churches: Montenegrin and Serbian Orthodox Churches, 1992–2003', delivered at a conference on 'After Yugoslavia: antagonism and identity revisited', held at the University of Kent, Canterbury, England, on 29–31 March 2003.

the West as he rapidly made the transition from authoritarian apparatchik to pro–Western democrat. Backed by Western governments, Djukanović became increasingly assertive in his readiness to take on Milošević. Not content with refusing to recognise Milošević's writ in Montenegro, he also attacked his policies of repression in Kosovo and refused to allow Montenegrins to fight alongside Serbs in the ensuing Kosovo war.

A tense period followed. Djukanović played a cautious waiting game, manoeuvring where necessary with sufficient skill to avoid provoking full-scale retaliation from Milošević's federal forces stationed inside Montenegro. At the same time, he took more power into his own hands, gradually claiming for Montenegro competences which had previously been exercised at the level of the Yugoslav federation. And as the international community redoubled its efforts to isolate or, better still, topple Milošević, Djukanović was received by Western leaders in Washington, London and Paris. Visiting journalists noticed that a portrait of King Nikola now looked down from the wall in the room in which he received his guests,[51] and at about this time he began to listen to the advice of those who advocated not just enhanced autonomy for Montenegro but Montenegrin independence.

Yet it was not only opportunism that prompted the move towards the restoration of Montenegro's independence. As Serbs were increasingly seen as international pariahs, many ordinary Montenegrins were anxious to draw a line between Serbs and Montenegrins and to distance themselves from uncomfortable memories of Montenegrin support for the Serbs' war against Croatia. A considerable number of intellectuals and other prominent individuals were keen to denounce Milošević's attempts at domination as a continuation of the Greater Serbianism of the Karadjordjević period, thus erasing lingering memories of Montenegrin involvement in the Greater Serbian dream.

The fall of Milošević in October 2000 after losing the elections of the previous month took the Montenegrin government by surprise: it had never expected the fractious leaders of the Serbian opposition parties to overcome their divisions, and—anticipating Milošević's

[51] Tim Judah, 'Goodbye to Yugoslavia', *New York Review of Books*, 8 February 2001.

victory, had refused to participate in the September elections in which he was convincingly defeated. Djukanović was in an uncomfortable position. Not only had he failed to play a direct role in the overthrow of Milošević; Serbia's new President Vojislav Koštunica, rapturously welcomed by the international community, had well-known Greater Serbian sympathies and was expected to favour restoring the by now largely defunct federal link with Montenegro. Worse still, the international community had begun to urge Djukanović to engage with Koštunica and the other Serbian leaders in order to find a solution to the problem of Montenegro's status which would retain the link with Serbia, primarily to prevent the situation between the two having any spill-over effect on the still fragile situation in Kosovo.

Djukanović and his supporters took the logical way out by embracing the cause of Montenegrin independence, a course from which he was deflected by the European Union's initiative: the Belgrade Agreement and through it the end of the Third Yugoslavia and the creation in February 2003 of the Union of Serbia and Montenegro.[52] Enshrining a theoretical equality, the new union soon proved unworkable, bitterly disappointing the hopes of those who sought to portray it as a stabilising solution in a region still at obvious risk from instability. Should that have been surprising? The answer is no—first, because a number of the parties—principally the Montenegrin government, but also some on the Serbian side[53]—did not wish to see the union succeed and were determined to undermine it. This constituted an immediate obstacle but there was also a more fundamental reason for doubting the union's ability to provide a lasting solution to the relationship between Serbia and Montenegro. Realistically the enormous imbalance between the two parties in population, size and wealth meant that the equality enshrined in the Belgrade Agreement could be no more than notional. Instead Montenegrins would have had to come to terms with their mark-

[52] See Chapter 12 and also the author's paper, 'Serbia and Montenegro: A new federation?', *Conflict Studies Research Centre*, G108, March 2002.

[53] For example, some leading Serbian economists, members of the influential G-17 Plus political group, believed that Montenegro would be an impediment to Serbia's economic reform programme and as a result supported the line taken by the Montenegrin authorities. See Chapter 12.

edly inferior status, a requirement which they have never been conditioned to accept.

Serbs and Montenegrins have much in common: in many respects their religious and cultural tradition is overlapping; they are the closest of all the peoples of the former Yugoslavia. And yet, as we have seen, other important aspects of the Montenegrin experience—history, geography and the persistence at least till very recently of a clan-based society with its own value system—have made Montenegrins different. The result, as many observers have pointed out, is a multi-layered identity which may be construed differently, not merely as a result of individual experience or inclination but also depending on clan affinity, which is in turn linked to geographical location. In general, Montenegrins who live in areas or trace their identity back to clans that have had the longest association with what we might call core or Old Montenegro are likely to feel their 'Montenegrin-ness' most strongly, and *vice versa*. People who live in the coastal region, where the sense of clan affinity is often attenuated or non-existent, may also feel less 'Serb' as a result of greater exposure to what might be described as Mediterranean influence, although here too there are evident local as well individual variations.[54]

In voting in favour of independence in the referendum of May 2006, Montenegro duly made the key decision on its future for at least the next generation. The referendum led to mobilisation of the political and social elites. All relevant arguments were mustered; even language was enlisted as part of the identity issue.[55] Meanwhile the

---

[54] For example, it is noteworthy that Herceg Novi, which was only joined to Montenegro after the Second World War and contains a high proportion of people who originate from outside Montenegro—whether from Hercegovina or from Serbia proper—registers a high proportion of people calling themselves 'Serbs'.

[55] Following the line taken by Croatians and Bosnians after the break-up of the former Yugoslavia in 1992, Montenegrin nationalists are now demanding the right to have 'Montenegrin' recognised as a separate language. In fact while most Montenegrins speak *ijekavian*, the western variant of the *štokavian* dialect of what used to be called Serbo-Croatian, and most Serbs speak the eastern variant known as *ekavian*, this has never proved a problem in the past. (The principal difference is in the pronunciation of the long vowel *e*: the speakers of *ijekavian* pronounce it as *ije*, while those of *ekavian* pronounce it as *e*. The word for river, for instance, is *rijeka* or *reka* according to which variant is used. A further variation is

struggle between the rival churches escalated, while the various minorities were dragged into arguments for and against independence. The trick now will be for the winners and losers to handle the result in a way which acknowledges the sensitivity and complexity of the identity question and allows Montenegrin and Serbian identities to flourish in apposition not in opposition to each other.

---

that 'Montenegrin', to emphase its difference from 'Serbian', is generally written using the Latin rather than Cyrillic alphabet.)

1. Early History: Between East and West

Prehistory

Early history is for the most part elusive. In the western Balkans, and specifically in the lands that were to comprise Montenegro, it is not only prehistory that is unspecific and inchoate; the early historical period too fails to provide a smooth narrative. Instead what we have appears in fragmentary form as occasional individuals and events emerge to illuminate periods of darkness.

In the late Iron Age future Montenegrin lands were occupied by Illyrian tribes, who by that time had settled throughout the Balkan peninsula west of the Morava river. The origin of the Illyrians remains a controversial subject. Most Albanian archaeologists regard modern Albanians as the direct descendants of the Illyrians, who they maintain are an autochthonous people. This claim can be seen as giving Albanians historic rights to lands once inhabited by Illyrians.[1] Other scholars argue, often for equally partisan reasons, that the Illyrians were themselves invaders, but neither school of thought has been able to provide conclusive proof. By the first millennium BC the Illyrians, whatever their origins, had developed a common language and culture which spread throughout a wide region of the central and western Balkans, covering areas that are today south-eastern Bosnia, south-western Serbia, the northern half of Albania, and Montenegro. Numerous hill-forts scattered throughout the region show that these early communities often banded together for protection, and that warfare and violence were commonplace.

[1] On the origins of the Albanians and their claimed links with the Illyrians see Noel Malcolm, *Kosovo: A Short History*, London: Macmillan, 1998, pp. 28–40. Malcolm himself specifically rejects linking 'historic rights' to questions of chronological priority in ancient history.

39

However, graves excavated at sites in modern Montenegro have been found to contain objects of considerable beauty and craftsmanship, with amber and bronze jewellery, as well as a variety of weapons.[2] By the late fifth or early fourth century BC a number of these communities had come together to form an Illyrian tribal confederation. Although this at first had its capital in Macedonia, its centre of power subsequently moved to the northern Albanian region.

Contact with the classical world

From the fourth century BC onwards the Greeks established trading centres along the Adriatic coast, often on the sites of former Illyrian settlements. Budva, on the central coast of Montenegro, which had existed as an Illyrian town in the fifth century BC, became a Greek emporium in the early fourth century. Although the period of Greek colonisation was relatively short (from the late fourth till almost the end of the third century), the Greeks had a dramatic impact on the cultural and social development of the coastal area, introducing urban forms of life where town-dwellers practised a variety of trades and crafts within settlements defended by impressive stone walls. By contrast, the cultural changes introduced by these new arrivals penetrated only very gradually and indirectly into the remote interior, where the traditional semi-nomadic pattern of life remained largely unchanged.

Unlike the Greeks, the Romans were to establish a far-reaching presence in the peninsula. Their first incursions were to suppress piracy in response to the Greek colonists' appeals for protection, but they were soon drawn inland by the Balkans' ready supply of raw materials and of manpower for their armies. Major hostilities between the invaders and the native Illyrians broke out in 229 BC when Queen Teuta, widow of the Illyrian King Agron, attempted to recapture a number of the Greek coastal cities. Of the many stories about Queen Teuta, some at least more properly belong to mythology. T.G. Jackson wrote in 1887 that the Romans were provoked to fight the queen when she ordered that two of their envoys sent to

[2] Čedomir Marković and Rajko Vujičić, *The Cultural Monuments of Montenegro*, Novi Sad: Presmedij, 1996, pp. 26–7.

urge her not to attack the Republic's allies be put to death and a third imprisoned. According to Jackson, the Romans responded by sending two consuls with 20,000 infantry and 2,000 cavalry into Illyria. Their mission to subdue the unruly queen was assisted by treachery: Demetrius, a Greek who held Corfu for her together with nearby Pharos (Lesina), surrendered the islands to the Roman consul Fulvius, after which Teuta, driven from one stronghold to another, was finally forced to seek asylum in Rhison (Risan) in the Gulf of Kotor and sue for peace. She was compelled to surrender to Rome a quarter of her territory, which was all that remained to her. Whatever the truth of these accounts, mythology seems to have portrayed Teuta as a queen who kept up the fight against the invaders until, when finally defeated by the Romans, she committed suicide by leaping into the sea. After her death, resistance by the native Illyrians to the Roman invaders continued well into the second century BC. The last Illyrian king, Gentius, an ally of Rome's opponent Perseus, King of Macedonia, was defeated in Skadar in 168 BC, which marked the effective end of Illyrian power.

By the first century AD both the Adriatic coastal region and the interior of the Balkan peninsula south of the Danube were under Roman control. The Romans had established the province of Dalmatia, which incorporated the whole of the present-day territory of Montenegro as well as much of modern Croatia. Early in the fourth century Dalmatia was divided into eleven provinces. The southern province of Praevalitana encompassed much of the territory that was to become Montenegro but also included future Albanian lands.

As elsewhere throughout their vast empire, the Romans swiftly established forts and towns in the plains and valleys along roads they built to connect the coast with the interior. Such trading centres included the first-century town of Birziminium on the site of present-day Podgorica, as well as an important settlement near modern Pljevlja, referred to in ancient texts only as Municipium S.[3] Outside the towns, however, the Illyrians and other indigenous peoples continued to follow their traditional way of life, retaining their language together with many of their customs and religious practices.

---

[3] See Draško Šćekić, *Travelling through Montenegro*, Podgorica, 1966, p. 150, and Marković and Vujičić, *Cultural Monuments*, pp. 37–8.

The most important and best preserved of the Roman settlements in what was to become Montenegro was Roman Dioclea (later Duklja) at the confluence of the Morača and the Zeta rivers near modern Podgorica. Once thought to have been the birthplace of the Emperor Diocletian, it is now believed to have acquired its name from an Illyrian tribe, the Docleati, who had settled the area before the Roman conquest. In the first century AD Dioclea was established as the seat of the local Roman rulers (*imperatores*) and awarded the highest status for a Roman town—that of a *municipium*, which conferred citizenship upon its inhabitants while permitting them some degree of self-rule.[4] The town was surrounded by strong defensive walls with towers, and was rich in public buildings, temples, palaces and baths. Artefacts unearthed in the excavation of one of its two necropolises include fine jewellery, glassware and ceramics, some from distant parts of the empire, giving an idea of the town's wealth and extensive trading contacts.[5] However, in the late sixth or early seventh century AD it was struck by a disastrous earthquake and later suffered further devastation at the hands of the invading Slavs and Avars.[6]

From the beginning of the third century AD the Roman Empire entered a period of chaos with civil wars leading to stagnation and decline. Like the rest of the empire, the Roman territories of the Balkan peninsula experienced misery, made more acute by the onset of a period of intensive raiding by 'barbarian' Germanic tribes lasting from the third till the fifth century. Diocletian sought a way out of the chaos by dividing the empire between two senior and two junior emperors to each of whom he allocated specific territories.[7] As the senior emperor he chose to establish himself in the east, a decision that was ultimately to prove fatal to the Western Empire. In 395 a still more historically momentous division shook the empire when the Emperor Theodosius on his deathbed divided it between his two sons, assigning the east to the elder, Arcadius, and the west to the younger, Honorius. The unintended result was the permanent division of the empire, which was thereafter to evolve along two dif-

[4] Marković and Vujičić, *Cultural Monuments*, p. 34.
[5] *Ibid.*, pp. 34–5.
[6] Šćekić, *Travelling Through Montenegro*, p. 150.
[7] Fine, *The Early Medieval Balkans*, p. 14.

ferent paths, Latin and Greek. (The same broad fault-line would be maintained when, in 1054, the church finally split into its Eastern Orthodox and Western Catholic branches.) While populations to the north of the Theodosian line looked to Rome and spoke Latin, those to the south spoke Greek and focused their attention on Constantinople (Byzantium).[8] The region that would one day become Montenegro was astride the cultural line: Kotor was incorporated within the Western Empire, while the Eastern Empire controlled future Montenegrin lands to the south and east.

Momentous as its consequences were in other respects, Theodosius's division failed to stem growing anarchy within the empire. No longer the seat of imperial power, the Roman Empire in the west continued on its long path to disintegration. Meanwhile successive waves of barbarians invaded the Balkan provinces, plundering and destroying many of the towns along the main trading routes and carrying off some of the population as slaves. In the fourth century Praevalitana suffered successive incursions by two related Germanic tribes, the Visigoths and the Ostrogoths. At the end of the fifth century the Ostrogoth leader, Theodoric, led his people out of the Balkans into Italy where, after defeating the barbarian general Odoacer, then ruling the land, he established an Ostrogothic kingdom in Italy. Theodoric's kingdom, formally a vassal state of the Eastern Roman Empire, soon expanded to take in some of the territory previously ruled by Rome in the western Balkans including parts of Praevalitana around Nikšić and the Gulf of Kotor.[9] But Gothic ascendancy in the region was short-lived. In about 537 the energetic Byzantine Emperor Justinian I, who had made it his life-mission to

[8] The city of Constantinople took its name from the Roman Emperor Constantine (307–37). Born in what today would be Serbia, Constantine spent most of his youth in the eastern part of the empire before going to rule Britain and Gaul. In 312 he invaded Italy and conquered Rome, but subsequently moved his court to the former Greek city of Byzantium on the shores of the Bosphorus. There in 330 he founded the new Christian city of Constantinople that was to become the capital of the Byzantine Empire and maintain the traditions of Rome for a further 1,100 years.

[9] Marković and Vujičić, *Cultural Monuments*, p. 42. As the authors point out, in medieval times the town on the site of present-day Nikšić was known as Onogošt, a name derived from the earlier Gothic name 'Anagast'.

recover the empire's territories in both east and west, succeeded in driving the Goths from the Balkans.[10] The departing Goths left behind few traces of their culture, but the area had been weakened by centuries of raiding and social chaos. Over the years many of the inhabitants had fled to the hills and mountains leaving the towns and valleys depopulated. With the exodus of the Goths the Balkan region remained more vulnerable than ever.[11]

In the centuries preceding Justinian's reign the Byzantine emperors had suffered a series of setbacks and defeats in attempting to maintain their sway over the fragmented and unstable Balkan region. Some steps towards reasserting control were taken by the Emperor Zeno at the end of the fifth century but real progress towards the restoration of Byzantine rule over the wider region would have to await Justinian. In fact Justinian's plans for the reconquest went well beyond waging war to include the recovery of many devastated areas and activity ranging from the rebuilding of fortresses and city walls to the repair and construction of churches and palaces. Significantly for the future of the southern Balkans, the increased contact built up over this period greatly assisted the spread of Christianity.

Arrival of the Slavs

The invaders of the third, fourth and fifth centuries had come to raid, not to settle. This pattern was to change in the sixth century when Justinian's ambitious prosecution of war on both eastern and western fronts of the empire left the Byzantine presence spread too thinly throughout the Balkan peninsula. The new arrivals—the Slavs—had occupied the northern banks of the Danube in the fifth century, after moving southwards from lands now generally thought to be in present-day Ukraine.[12] There had been some Slav incursions southwards into the Balkans from the fifth century onwards, but the mass movement of Slavs south across the Danube from the middle of the sixth century appears to have been triggered by the

---

[10] Fine, *The Early Medieval Balkans,* p. 22.

[11] *Ibid.*

[12] Fine, *The Early Medieval Balkans,* p. 25, and Obolensky, *The Byzantine Commonwealth,* p. 42.

activities of a still more warlike Turkic people, the Avars, who had themselves been driven across the Asian steppes by the Central Asian Turks. Initially the Avars were the dominating invaders in the western part of the peninsula, while the Slavs were present in greater numbers in the east. Archaeologists have found what appear to be sixth- and seventh-century Turkic/Avar sites in what is now Montenegro at a time when there is no comparable evidence for a Slav presence. Such recent scholarship tends to confirm the accounts of the tenth-century emperor turned historian, Constantine VII Porphyrogenitus, who described the Avars as conquering Dioclea, together with Zahumlje and lands around the mouth of the Neretva river to the north.[13] In what was to become Montenegro only Butua (Budva) and Acruvium (Kotor) withstood their attacks to remain, like other Dalmatian cities further up the coast, outposts of romanised Byzantine culture.[14]

In 626 the Avars, who were masters in the art of siege warfare, suffered a massive defeat at the hands of the Byzantines after they had rashly set their sights on taking Constantinople. Although the Slavs played a subservient role in the battle, their victory essentially turned the tables, allowing them to gain the upper hand in many areas previously dominated by the Avars. This reversal of fortune appears to have been assisted by the arrival of a second wave of Slavs, who had entered the peninsula in the course of the seventh century, possibly in response to a request for help against the Avars by the Byzantine emperor at the time.[15] Byzantine sources now referred to the incoming Slavs as divided into two different groups—Croats and Serbs—although it seems likely that these names derived originally from minority Iranian peoples who had at some stage managed to impose their authority upon larger groups of Slavs before becoming assimilated by them in their turn.[16] Nevertheless, given their fearsome reputation the true reason for the eclipse of the Avars remains something of a mystery. Although 'they died away like Avars' is a traditional Balkan saying, it can reasonably be assumed that their

[13] Fine, *The Early Medieval Balkans*, pp. 34–5.
[14] Obolensky, *The Byzantine Commonwealth*, p. 53.
[15] Noel Malcolm, *Kosovo*, pp. 24–5.
[16] Fine, *The Early Medieval Balkans*, pp. 56–7.

genetic and cultural impact—still not fully explored—left its traces among the populations of the western Balkans.

Despite the Slavs' later arrival in the western parts of the peninsula, some of them had reached the Adriatic by the early seventh century and were moving from the coastal lands in what is now Montenegro down into modern Albania. While the Croats established themselves to the north and west, the Serbs settled further south in the vicinity of a region now in southern Serbia that is commonly known by its Turkish name, the Sandžak (literally 'district') of Novi Pazar. From these areas the Serbs are presumed to have spread out into lands that roughly correspond to modern Montenegro and Hercegovina (in territories then known as Duklja, and Zahumlje and Travunia). However, they often failed to penetrate the major towns where Roman walls helped to protect them from the invaders. Here both Christianity and a Byzantine-inspired literary and artistic culture were to survive and ultimately re-emerge to influence the peoples of the interior.

Not surprisingly, given the upheaval created by the arrival of the Slavs, there are few sources for the history of the western Balkans in the seventh century, which was thus a dark period. The Slavs themselves had no written script at this stage and what little is known of their way of life in this early period is largely derived from the descriptions given by Byzantine historians, most of whom were writing more than two centuries later.[17] However, one earlier account by John of Ephesus, a Syrian historian at the Byzantine court, records the Slavs' devastating incursion into the peninsula:

That same year [AD 574] ... was famous also for the invasion of the accursed people, called Slavonians. ... And four years have now elapsed and still, because the king is engaged in war with the Persians, and has sent all his forces to the East, they live at their ease in the land, and dwell in it, and spread themselves far and wide as God permits them, and ravage and burn, and take captives. And to such an extent do they carry their ravages, that they have even ridden up to the outer walls of the city [the Long Wall of Constantinople], and driven away the king's herds of horses, many thou-

---

[17] The major source for this period is Constantine Porphyrogenitus whose *De Administrando Imperio* was written in the late 940s or early 950s. See Fine, *The Early Medieval Balkans*, p. 49.

sands in number, and whatever else they could find. And even to this day they still encamp and dwell there...free from anxiety or fear, and lead captive, slay and burn: and they have now grown rich in gold and silver, and herds of horses, and arms, and have learned to fight better than the Romans, though at first they were but rude savages, who did not venture to show themselves outside the woods and the covets of the trees; and, as for arms, they did not even know what they were, with the exception of two or three javelins or darts.[18]

Little wonder then that outside the towns some of the original inhabitants fled into the more inaccessible regions of the peninsula where the invaders would not trouble to pursue them. There they continued to live as pastoralists speaking a variant of Latin. Among these people were those thought by some to be the ancestors of the modern Albanians (the Illyrians), while others only reappear in historical accounts in the fourteenth century where they are referred to as Vlach, meaning 'shepherd' in Greek. The remote mountains and uplands of Montenegro, as well as parts of Bosnia and Hercegovina, sheltered many of them. Later Slavs themselves sought refuge in these barren regions, and followed similar patterns, leading a way of life that continued unchanged in these areas almost into modern times.

At first the Serbs who had settled in the south-western parts of the Balkan peninsula lived in small tribal territories called *županije*, ruled over by local chiefs or *župani*, who at times co-operated. With the principal east-west and north-south routes no longer safeguarded, trade declined and the few remaining Roman cities in Dalmatia became isolated from Constantinople and instead built closer links with Italy. Further south along the Adriatic coast, the important port of Dyrrachium (later Durazzo, then Durrës, in modern Albania) remained under the control of Byzantium. Communications between Byzantium and Rome became more difficult, deepening the division between the two worlds. In border regions such as the lands that were to become Montenegro local rulers would in the future exploit the possibilities which this rivalry offered to manoeuvre to their own advantage.

---

[18] Quoted by Obolensky, *The Byzantine Commonwealth*, p. 51.

The first Slav states

The first partially Slav state was formed only at the end of the seventh century, by the Bulgarians at Pliska to the south-east of the Danube near the Black Sea.[19] From the seventh century to the beginning of the tenth the first Bulgarian medieval empire expanded, challenging when it could Byzantium's position as the pre-eminent power in the southern Balkans. The alternating balance of power between the Byzantine and Bulgarian empires left Serb-inhabited lands caught in the middle, struggling to maintain a territorial foothold in a highly insecure environment. Local Serbian *župani* had to work in the interstices between the great empires, entering into and out of relationships of vassalage with more powerful rulers and trading allegiances and territory to their maximum advantage.

The early Bulgarian efforts at state building were a powerful catalyst for the future independence of the South Slavs. Most important of all in this respect was the decision of the ninth century Bulgarian ruler Prince Boris to promote the development of a Slavonic written language for the Orthodox liturgy, inviting the followers of Cyril and Methodius to continue their work translating Byzantine religious texts into the Slavonic language, using the eponymous Cyrillic script. The creation of a liturgical language based on written Slavonic not only enabled the Bulgarian Orthodox Church to avoid Byzantine domination;[20] it also paved the way for future Slav kingdoms to develop as political entities independent of Byzantium and led ultimately to the creation of spiritual, as well as linguistic bonds, between Slav peoples within the Balkan peninsula and beyond.

In the mid-ninth century the leaders of various Serb tribes in an area called Raška near modern Novi Pazar banded together under a single ruler to resist the Bulgarian threat. For a short time this first Serbian entity was successful, but internal rivalries soon erupted and were exploited by the Bulgarians who by the end of the ninth century had become overlords of these Serb-ruled lands. However,

[19] R.J. Crampton, *A Concise History of Bulgaria*, Cambridge University Press, 1997. In fact, as Crampton points out, the first Bulgarian state comprised two groups: the proto-Bulgarian conquerors and the more numerous conquered Slavs. (See pp. 9–10)

[20] *Ibid.*, p. 16.

Bulgarian expansionism did not stop there. Under Simeon, the only Bulgarian ruler ever to be celebrated as 'the Great', the Bulgarian empire expanded to the Aegean in the south and the Adriatic in the west, taking in most of the lands today included in Montenegro.[21] Clearly Simeon could not directly control all this territory. Raška he simply annexed in the conviction that its feuding princes could not be counted on to remain loyal in the face of the bribes offered by Byzantium. His campaign against the Serbs was remarkable for its ferocity if we are to believe the Byzantine historian Porphyro-genitus, who described Serbian lands as deserted wastes where people were forced to hunt in order to survive.

Elsewhere, Simeon followed the prevailing feudal practice of ruling through vassal princes. His lands in inland Duklja, the successor to Roman Dioclea—which were under the control of a neighbouring vassal prince, Mihajlo of Zahumlje—seemingly escaped the devastation meted out to Raška. After Simeon's death around 927, Raška was able to free itself from Bulgarian control under a dynamic prince, Časlav, who had himself been held captive by the Bulgarians. In place of Simeon, Časlav recognised the Byzantine Emperor as overlord, establishing close ties with the empire that were to remain in force throughout his reign. While we know little about life in these Serb-inhabited lands at this period, it was clearly a time of growing Byzantine preponderance throughout the peninsula, which in turn led to increasing Christianisation. Orthodox influence had already spread from Bulgaria under Simeon and, with Byzantium replacing Bulgaria as the predominant influence in Raška, continued to do so under Časlav. Although the formal split between the Eastern and Western Churches had not yet taken place, differences between them had already reached a level where they could properly be described as falling into two distinct ecclesiastical camps, each bent on increasing the amount of territory and number of adherents under its jurisdiction. Raška's strengthening of ties with Byzantium at this time would be an important factor in determining the eventual religious affiliation of its inhabitants.

But while in the interior of the peninsula Orthodoxy was making progress, along the Adriatic seaboard the religious status of the

[21] Crampton, *A Concise History of Bulgaria*, p. 17.

coastal cities and their hinterland was less certain. Mihajlo of Zahumlje, at the time when he was overlord of Duklja, had been under
papal jurisdiction. However, after the death of his ally Simeon he
seems to have followed the prevailing trend in moving closer to
Byzantium, even accepting the Byzantine rank of proconsul, but he
continued to maintain close relations with Rome in a way that aptly
reflected the ambivalent religious climate of the coastal region.

The rise of early medieval Duklja

In about 960 Čarslav died and Raška began to disintegrate. As
always, a strong ruler's death spelt hope for his ambitious vassals, and
this time the man to seize the opportunity was a noble of Duklja,
Vladimir, who quickly reversed Zahumlje's earlier dominance over
Duklja and then captured Travunia, the mountainous region between modern Dubrovnik and Kotor, before going on to bring
Raška too under his control. In keeping with the practice of the time
Vladimir swiftly allied himself with Byzantium, thereby incurring
the hostility of Tsar Samuil (997–1014), ruler of a resurgent Bulgarian state, whose centre had shifted from near the Danube to
Ohrid and Prespa in modern Macedonia. Under Samuil, Ohrid was
raised to the status of a patriarchate, which subsequently spread its
cultural and religious influence throughout much of the Balkan
peninsula.

   In a historical landscape replete with petty rulers and local magnates, the story of Prince Vladimir has been preserved as a result of
the treacherous circumstances of his death and his subsequent elevation to sainthood. Much of the detail is based on the lively but
often unreliable *Chronicle of the Priest of Dioclea*, an account written
by an anonymous priest from Bar (ancient Antebareos, later Antivari) some two centuries later. Whatever its shortcomings, the Chronicle affords a glimpse into the highly unstable world of tenth-
century princelings and upstarts.[22] Tsar Samuil soon defeated and
imprisoned Vladimir, gaining control of all his lands, and the *Priest of
Dioclea* records that Samuil's daughter Kosara fell in love with the

---

[22] On the *Chronicle of the Priest of Dioclea* and its account of the marriage of Vladimir and Kosara, see Fine, *The Early Medieval Balkans*, pp. 193–4.

pious Vladimir while washing his hands and feet as an act of Christian charity. When she begged her father's permission to marry him he not only agreed but allowed the couple to return to rule Vladimir's former lands in Duklja, even going so far as to throw in part of the valuable Duchy of Dyrrachium as a dowry.

Hostilities, in which Vladimir appears to have played no part, continued between Samuil of Bulgaria and Basil II of Byzantium, with the latter slowly gaining the upper hand. The end came for Samuil with the defeat of his army in 1014 at Kledion near the river Struma in what is today Macedonia. Basil, the story goes, ordered the blinding of some 15,000 of Samuil's soldiers, leaving only one man in every hundred with one eye to help guide the returning army home. This act of barbarity helped to earn Basil the sobriquet of Bulgar-Slayer.[23] Samuil is said to have died of grief.

Samuil's death plunged Bulgaria into a period of dynastic rivalries and murder. Not content with wreaking havoc at home, his nephew Vladislav, the eventual victor in the struggle for the throne, conspired to murder Vladimir of Duklja, possibly as part of a blood feud, or perhaps simply out of ambition to annex Duklja. Vladimir had received an invitation from his kinsman to visit him at his residence on an island in the middle of Lake Prespa (now in Macedonia), but fearing treachery requested reassurance. In response Vladislav sent him a gold cross as a pledge of safe conduct. The saintly Vladimir then reportedly replied that Christ was crucified not on gold or indeed silver, but on a cross of wood. An emissary was then sent with a cross of wood and Vladimir, reassured, journeyed to Prespa and entered a church to pray. It was while he stood with the wooden cross in his hands that soldiers sent by the treacherous Vladislav entered the church and cut Vladimir to pieces. Like the English King Henry II following the equally sacrilegious murder of Thomas à Becket two centuries later, Vladislav reverted to a state of fearful repentance while the site where Vladimir was hacked to death became associated with numerous miracles. Vladimir's bones, were

---

[23] Paul Stephenson's *The Legend of Basil the Bulgar-Slayer* (Cambridge University Press, 2003) argues convincingly that Basil's reputation as the 'Bulgar-Slayer' is a myth which has its origins in the political aspirations of later Byzantine rulers and in the nineteenth-century Greek national movement.

collected by his widow Kosara, who took them to a monastery on the shores of Lake Skadar; they were later transferred to a church near Elbasan in present-day Albania. However, the wooden cross that the saint was supposedly clutching when he died was preserved in a church near Mount Rumija in Montenegro. Subsequently, in a development that typifies the religious syncretism of this coastal region, Vladimir became the patron saint of the city of Durazzo (Durrës), and was subsequently venerated by Serbs, Greeks and Albanians along the Adriatic coast from that city to Lake Skadar.[24] However, in the interior of Serbia the cult of Vladimir did not survive the Middle Ages. One possible explanation is that Vladimir's sainthood did not suit the future rulers of Raška—the great Nemanjić dynasty—who were shortly to bring all lands inhabited by Serbs under their sway.[25] Saint Vladimir of Duklja could well have appeared as a rival to their own tradition of canonised rulers who, in the eyes of Serbs everywhere, were to represent a single holy Serbian state.

    After Vladimir's murder the historical sources are silent concerning the fate of Duklja; it may have been annexed by Basil of Byzantium or ruled by a vassal prince whose name has not come down to us. For a time Duklja's rulers may even have been vassals of Croatia, but whatever its exact status, it appears to have suffered sufficiently under Byzantine domination to prompt the next ruler of whom we have a record, Vojislav, to rebel in 1034 at the very moment when Constantinople was once again between emperors.[26] In response the Byzantines launched an attack from Dyrrachium in which Vojislav was captured and taken to Constantinople. At some time in 1038–9 Vojislav managed to escape back to Duklja and was able to expand

---

[24] The tradition has continued to the present: on All Souls Day local Orthodox, Muslims and Catholics follow in procession behind St Vladimir's cross to the summit of Rumija to await sunrise. Hence the outcry in August 2005 when the Serbian Orthodox Church in Montenegro, without reference to the Montenegrin government, arranged for members of the armed forces to helicopter in a prefabricated Orthodox church and install it on the summit.

[25] See Obolensky, *The Byzantine Commonwealth*, pp. 311–12, for an account of the martyrdom of Vladimir of Duklja and its significance.

[26] Sima M. Ćirković, *The Serbs* (transl. from the Serbian by Vuk Tošić), Oxford: Blackwell, 2004, p. 22.

his control further up the Dalmatian coast. When an imperial ship laden with gold was wrecked off the coast, Vojislav was reckless enough to seize it in defiance of the emperor. A punitive expedition was duly launched but Vojislav managed to defeat it, inflicting heavy losses. In 1040 the imperial governor (*strategos*) of Dyrrachium[27] assembled in response to what the sources describe as the largest invasion force ever mustered against Duklja, reinforced by troops from Raška, Bosnia and Zahumlje. Bent on plunder and revenge, he entered the narrow valley of the Zeta,[28] but as the imperial army was proceeding along the valley, weighed down with booty it had seized on its advance, it was set upon from above by Vojislav's forces who, despite their small numbers, were able to inflict heavy losses on the enemy with enormous stones and arrows.

Vojislav's triumph in this unequal struggle marked the beginning of Duklja's short-lived period of ascendancy. Such was Vojislav's success that he not only succeeded in shaking off Byzantine suzerainty but went on to annex neighbouring Zahumlje and territories around Dyrrachium, establishing a new capital at Skadar. Although Vojislav did not long survive the epic battle with Byzantium, already by the time of his death his independent principality extended up the coast as far as Ston, north of Dubrovnik, and included the important coastal towns of Kotor and Bar.[29]

Vojislav died in 1043 and bitter wrangling followed between his sons over the succession. At first the brothers agreed to form an alliance to protect themselves against the Byzantines, who were poised to take advantage of any instability. The agreement they signed has survived in a version recorded in the twelfth-century *Chronicle of the Priest of Dioclea* and has some claim to be the oldest treaty in Serb history.[30]

However, the brothers soon clashed again, with Mihajlo (c.1052–81) at length prevailing. He quickly sought peace with Byzantium,

---

[27] Both Dyrrachium and Ragusa were at this time outposts of the Byzantine Empire. Neither city controlled extensive hinterlands although the Byzantines attempted to use these 'bridgeheads' as bases from which to extend their control over local rulers. (See Ćirković, *The Serbs*, p. 22.)

[28] Fine, *The Early Medieval Balkans*, p. 206.

[29] *Ibid.*

[30] *Ibid.*, p. 212.

even accepting the title of a Byzantine official (*protospatharius*) in the hope of being thus protected from further dynastic challenges, but in reality like his father, he was intent on shaking off imperial control. By this time the towns of the Adriatic coast, though still nominally under the suzerainty of Byzantium, were coming increasingly under Latin influence as much because of the growing naval and mercantile power of Venice as through the religious authority of Rome. The situation was further confused by the overlapping of Roman and Byzantine ecclesiastical organisations and practices, mostly along the coast but also in the hinterlands. In 1072, following the momentous defeat of Byzantium by the Seljuk Turks in Asia Minor, Mihajlo lent his support to a revolt against the empire that had broken out among the Bulgarians in Macedonia. Recognising an opportunity to extend his own power to the interior,[31] he sent an army under his son Constantine Bodin. The extent of Duklja's prestige at this time can be gauged from the fact that when Bodin and his army reached Prizren on his way into Macedonia he was crowned by some of the Bulgarian chiefs as their tsar. But the fanfare was premature. After some early successes, which included briefly holding Skopje, the insurgents recklessly divided their forces, the revolt was suppressed, and Bodin was captured and taken to Constantinople where he remained a prisoner for some six years. Mihajlo was correspondingly weakened to the extent that the *strategos* of Dyrrachium was able to attack and capture all the towns in the interior which had previous been under the control of Duklja. Pushed further towards the coast, Mihajlo established courts in both Kotor and Prapatna near modern Bar.[32] Duklja now possessed two courts but lacked its own archdiocese since its churches—or those of them under the jurisdiction of Rome—were variously subjected to the archdioceses of Ohrid, Split, and Durazzo, none of which was within Duklja's own territory. Accordingly Mihajlo began petitioning the Pope for an archdiocese at Bar.

In 1077 Mihajlo went a step further in his campaign to escape control by an encroaching Byzantium when he requested a royal crown from Pope Gregory VII. The Eastern and Western Churches

---

[31] Ćirković, *The Serbs*, p. 25.
[32] *Ibid.*, p. 26.

had split definitively in 1054, making this a significant move. More-over, by becoming in effect a papal vassal Mihajlo widened his political options: he was now formally on the same side as the newly-emerging power in the Adriatic, the Normans, who were soon to capture the city of Bari as well as Calabria and Apulia from Byzantium. This made Mihajlo's new allegiance particularly expedient: not only was he entitled to hope that the Pope would now be obliged to caution the Normans against invading Duklja, but he might also, should the need arise, call on the Normans for help against the Byzantines. Alliances at this time were fluid with individuals prone to switch sides when they judged it advantageous. Typical of this trend was the fact that in 1081, shortly before Mihajlo's death, both he and Bodin joined with Venetians and Albanians in supporting the new Byzantine Emperor, Alexius I Comnenus, after the Normans attacked Dyrrachium, a city known to them, and increasingly referred to at this time, as Durazzo.[33] However, in October that year the Dukljans stood aside in the decisive battle for Durazzo—a move which, since it helped to ensure an eventual Norman victory, would not be forgotten by the Byzantines.

Some time in the 1080s Mihajlo was succeeded by Bodin, who had earlier managed to escape from Constantinople with the help of Venetian merchants.[34] As ruler Bodin attempted to move closer to Rome, thus continuing his father's policy. The centre of Byzantine influence on the southern Adriatic seaboard and in the spread of Orthodoxy into Duklja had long been the Greek metropolitanate of Durazzo. In 1081, shortly before the Dukljans' failure to support Alexius I against the Normans at Durazzo, Bodin had married a Catholic, the daughter of the prominent Norman from Bari, just across the straits from Bar. Then, in 1089, Bodin apparently secured the agreement of the anti-pope Clement III to the creation of the archdiocese of Bar.[35] In the years that followed a number of bishops

---

[33] On this incident see Ćirković, *The Serbs*, p. 27, and Fine, *The Early Medieval Balkans*, pp. 221–2.

[34] Fine, *ibid*.

[35] Some scholars claim that Bodin's father Mihajlo had persuaded Pope Alexander II to agree to the creation of an archbishopric in Bar as early as 1066/7. See Fine, *The Early Medieval Balkans*, pp. 215–16, and Obolensky, *The Balkan Commonwealth*, p. 220.

in towns now in Serbia, Bosnia and Albania were placed under Bar, making inroads into territory previously under the ecclesiastical jurisdiction of Constantinople and the Greek Church. Bodin's success in obtaining the archbishopric at Bar provoked hostile reaction from their former ecclesiastical superiors in Dubrovnik, who had hitherto exercised jurisdiction on behalf of Rome over part of the coastal area to the south as well as over Travunia, Zahumlje and Serbia. For the rest of the eleventh century the church in Duklja was, at least in theory, subject to Rome, although away from the coast, and certainly in Serbia, most of the population remained unaffected.[36]

Duklja becomes Zeta before declining into civil war

Bodin's reign was to mark a high point in the history of Duklja (or Zeta as it was beginning to be called).[37] Under Vojislav and then Mihajlo it had become the principal centre of resistance to Byzantine rule. For a time Mihajlo had exercised control over neighbouring Raška, where he installed a member of the Dukljan royal family to rule the principality on his behalf. Soon after assuming power Bodin succeeded in reasserting his authority over a rebellious Raška and extended his control over the local rulers of Bosnia. However, Bodin did not seek to eliminate the local nobility in either Raška or Bosnia, but instead allowed both entities to exist as vassal states under their own nobles, contenting himself with imposing a member of the Dukljan royal family at their head.[38]

About 1083–4 Raška attempted to break away from Zeta. Bodin crushed the revolt and installed two *župani*, probably members of his own family, to ensure his continuing control,[39] but this was not to last. Some time in the 1080s the Byzantines, in reprisal for Bodin's refusal to aid them in their ongoing struggle against the Normans,

---

[36] Fine, *ibid.*, p. 224.

[37] Zeta was originally one *župa* within Duklja but from the end of the eleventh century this name was increasingly being used to refer to what had previously been Dukljan lands. See Fine, *The Early Medieval Balkans*, p. 212.

[38] *Ibid.*, 1991, p. 223.

[39] *Ibid.*, pp. 222–3. As Fine points out, the available sources on this period are often contradictory with the result that dates can only be approximate.

attacked and defeated Zeta, and according to certain accounts Bodin was again taken prisoner. However, if this was indeed so, he appears to have returned to Zeta since he is mentioned elsewhere as having graciously received the leader of the First Crusade when it passed through Dukljan territory in the winter of 1096–7.[40] In any case Zeta was clearly weakened. Vukan of Raška, Bodin's kinsman and appointee, seized his chance to break free of its control, and Bosnia and Zahumlje quickly followed.

Shorn of its outlying territories, Zeta was further undermined by ongoing civil war as members of Bodin's family began to feud among themselves.[41] Typically at this time, dynastic feuding was accompanied by myriad cruelties—beheading, poisoning, blinding, castration and imprisonment—as one side or another sought to incapacitate its opponents to eliminate them from the contest for succession. The Zetan royal family proved characteristically adept, with Bodin's widow, the Italian-born Jakvinta, allegedly resorting to poisoning and beheading in the attempt to secure the succession of her own minor son in place of one of her husband's older half-brothers or nephews. And, as always, the intriguing and the accompanying desire for revenge created opportunities for outside powers as one faction or another sought protection or enlisted intervention. Before long both Byzantium and Raška were involved in Zeta's civil war, each backing its own candidate for the throne.

At first Vukan succeeded in installing his candidate Kočopar (1102–3), but then withdrew his support, allowing the Zetan nobles to install their own favourite, Vladimir, a descendant of the former king, Mihajlo. Vladimir's accession was followed by an interval of peace between Raška and Byzantium, which Vladimir secured by prudently marrying Vukan's daughter and accepting Byzantine suzerainty. But Vladimir's death—possibly the result of poisoning by Jakvinta—brought more chaos as a Byzantine army arrived to drive out Jakvinta's heir and install an imperial appointee.

From this time onwards for about eight years (1118–25) Zeta was again at peace. But in 1125 the prince of Raška again attacked Zeta,

---

[40] Ćirković, *The Serbs*, pp. 28–9.
[41] This account outlined by Fine (*The Early Medieval Balkans*, pp. 228–33) is based on the *Chronicle of the Priest of Dioclea*.

installing his candidate, none other than Jakvinta's son Juraj, and unleashing further internal conflict within the now severely weakened
state. Predictably Byzantium intervened, occupying much of Zeta
and unleashing perhaps the most destructive phase in the long civil
war. Ultimately the Byzantines prevailed, and from being the
foremost Serb state in the peninsula Zeta was now reduced to vassal
status, its final quasi-independent ruler, Radoslav, no longer a king
but simply a prince (*knez*).

For much of the eleventh century Duklja/Zeta had been the foremost Serbian state in the Balkans, galvanising resistance to Byzantium, but its success had depended on strong rulers and their
capacity to neutralise or attract support from outside powers. The
end was never really in doubt once the years of bitter civil war and
anarchy in Zeta had taken their toll. By the beginning of the twelfth
century the focus of Serb power had shifted conclusively from Zeta
to the rival state of Raška, which with intermittent success was
struggling to free itself from Byzantine suzerainty. Whenever the
opportunity presented itself, Raška's rulers' sought strength in their
revolt through alliance with Hungary, which the ambitious Byzantine emperor Manuel Comnenus had long been attempting to
incorporate within the empire. But while Byzantium's wars with
Hungary and Hungary's willingness to come to Raška's assistance
whenever possible delayed its pacification, they were never enough,
and eventually the rebellions of the Raškan rulers were forcibly
put down.

The Nemanjić dynasty

The event that changed all this took place in the late 1160s when a
new dynasty, which took its name from its founder Nemanja, came
to power in Raška. Given the immense importance of the dynasty in
Serbian history it is hardly surprising that Nemanja's origins have
been linked to Raška's, and thus indirectly Duklja's, previous rulers
as a means of strengthening the dynasty's historical legitimacy. In
reality, however, it is not so clear-cut—Nemanja may have been a
grandson of Uroš I, himself a descendant of the rulers of Raška, but
neither of the biographies written by his sons provides incontrovertible evidence of this.[42]

---

[42] John V. A. Fine, *The Late Medieval Balkans*, p. 2. A recent history of Montenegro

What we are told in the biography written by his second son Stefan is that Nemanja was born in Zeta, in a village called Ribnica near the modern city of Podgorica.[43] From what can be pieced together from this account Nemanja's father had fled to Zeta to escape an internal power struggle. Since the area around Podgorica was then under Catholic jurisdiction, Nemanja was baptised a Catholic, although he was later re-baptised into the Orthodox faith. At first Nemanja was not sole ruler of Raška but obliged to share power with his brothers under the overall control of the eldest, Tihomir, but by 1168 he had defeated both Tihomir and a Byzantine force which rallied to his defence, and was established as grand *župan* of Raška. Like his predecessors Nemanja attempted to resist Byzantium's demands for the auxiliary troops required from a vassal state, but in 1172 he was famously defeated in battle by the Emperor Manuel Comnenus and forced to appear before him with a rope around his neck as part of the emperor's victory parade through Constantinople. For all the humiliation, Nemanja's period in captivity was to mark him in a number of ways: it not only ultimately inclined him to become re-baptised into the Orthodox faith, but before leaving Constantinople he swore an oath of allegiance to Manuel to whom he remained loyal until the emperor's death in 1180.[44]

Manuel's death was the first of a number of events that led to the weakening of Byzantium and created the opportunity for Raška to prosper and expand. Not only was Stefan Nemanja freed from his oath, but Manuel's son, still a child, was soon murdered by a member of his family, plunging Byzantium into a period of instability. In 1183 Stefan formed an alliance with Bela III of Hungary and together they invaded the empire, sacking Belgrade, Niš and Sofia—cities which were still partly in ruins when the Crusaders passed through them six years later.

denies any link between Nemanja and Duklja/Zeta, describing him simply as the 'prefect' of Raška. (See Živko Andrijašević and Šerbo Rastoder, *The History of Montenegro from Ancient Times to 2003*, Podgorica: Montenegrin Diaspora Centre, 2006, p. 16.)

[43] Ribnica arose on the site of the ancient Roman city of Birziminium. See above.
[44] Obolensky, *The Byzantine Commonwealth*, pp. 221–2.

In Bulgaria too Byzantium's weakness had created new opportunities: an uprising in 1185 led ultimately to the emergence of a new Bulgarian empire. Against this background, Stefan Nemanja was able first to obtain the independence of Raška and then to set about acquiring new territories in modern Kosovo and Macedonia. By 1190 he had annexed Zeta, including the important towns of Kotor and Bar. All members of the former Dukljan dynasty were ousted and in their place Nemanja named his eldest son, another Vukan, as prince of Zeta. Zahumlje, formerly controlled by the rulers of Zeta, was now assigned to another of Nemanja's sons, Miroslav.[45] Although these western principalities and their dependent cities were formally part of Nemanja's expanding empire, they were never merged within a single unified state. Thus a degree of separate Zetan identity was maintained under which both local rulers and archbishops retained their independent titles.[46]

In 1196 or 1197 Stefan Nemanja abdicated and, following the example of his youngest son Sava who had run away to become an Orthodox monk, entered the monastery Sava had founded on Mount Athos. Here they jointly founded the monastery of Hilandar, still today a focus for Serbian religious feeling and a meeting point of Serbian and Byzantine culture. Nemanja was succeeded by his second son, another Stefan whose marriage to the daughter of the Byzantine emperor had earned him the honorific title of *sebastokrator* and a place in the imperial line of succession.[47] In choosing Stefan, Nemanja passed over his eldest son Vukan who, stung by the slight to his birthright and not content with controlling only Zeta, attempted to assert control over both Zeta and Raška. In 1202 he enlisted the support of the Catholic King Imre of Hungary. At first he was successful; not only was Byzantium, beset by both internal and external enemies, unable to offer help to the imperial son-in-law, but Imre's attack on Serbia succeeded in defeating Stefan,

---

[45] It may also subsequently have been ruled for a time by Nemanja's youngest son, Rastko, who was later ordained as the Orthodox monk, Sava. (See Fine, *The Late Medieval Balkans*, pp. 19–20.)

[46] Ćirković, *The Serbs*, p. 32.

[47] Stefan Nemanjić's wife was the niece of the Byzantine Emperor Isaac II Angelus but her father managed to overthrow his brother making himself Alexius III Angelus and Stefan the imperial son-in-law. See Ćirković, *The Serbs*, pp. 32–3.

allowing Vukan to replace him and assume the title of grand *župan*. In return for the favour Imre, with Vukan's co-operation, planned to convert the Orthodox Serbs to Catholicism, choosing a Hungarian Catholic bishop for the task of rooting out his Orthodox brethren in Serbia, but he died before he could implement the scheme and Stefan was able to regain his throne, this time with help from Bulgaria rather than from Byzantium.[48]

Meanwhile in 1199 Nemanja had died at the monastery on Mount Athos. In 1204 his son Sava brought his body back to Serbia and, using the occasion to effect a reconciliation between his brothers, oversaw Nemanja's canonisation. Sava then set about consolidating the Nemanjić domination, taking advantage of the calamity that had overtaken the Byzantine state. In the year of Nemanja's death the Crusaders had launched the Fourth Crusade and in a devastating campaign captured Constantinople, massacring many of its inhabitants. Urged on by the formidable Doge Enrico Dandolo of Venice, the Catholic Crusaders carved up the empire into a number of feudal Latin states. The Venetians, for some time already a rising power in the Adriatic, now seized the Greek seaports on the islands and along the coast, which gave them effective command of the sea route from their mother city all the way to Constantinople, so setting the scene for their commercial domination of south-eastern Europe over the next six centuries.

Following the sack of Constantinople exiles from Byzantium set up a rival Orthodox empire at Nicea in Asia Minor, from where its ruler, Theodore Laskaris (1204–22), could only look on when, in 1217, Sava requested a papal crown for Stefan. Pope Honorius III agreed and Stefan was crowned king by a papal emissary, earning him the sobriquet Stefan the First-Crowned (*Prvovenčani*). In making their request to the Pope, the brothers referred to their father's birthplace Zeta, the ancient Dioclea, having been recognised as 'a great kingdom from the beginning'.[49] A further link with the West was secured when Stefan contracted a second marriage with Anna Dandolo, granddaughter of the Venetian Doge. For a time Catholic

[48] Tim Judah, *The Serbs: History, Myth and the Destruction of Yugoslavia*, New Haven: Yale University Press, 1997, p. 19.
[49] Judah, *The Serbs*, p. 39.

influence within Raška increased, although it did little to alter the underlying loyalty to Orthodoxy. Nevertheless this religious dualism, motivated by politics rather than religion, remained for much of the thirteenth century a characteristic feature of Serb life.[50]

If these close links with Venice and the Roman Catholic West had continued, the subsequent history of the Serbs might have been very different. They might for instance have had much closer contacts with Croats, as well as with Hungarians and with Venice and Rome. But Stefan the First-Crowned was in reality attracted to the state-building potential of ecclesiastical independence. Raška at that time had no archdioceses, and the link with Rome was therefore established in place of an autocephalous Orthodox Church within its own territory. However, in 1219 Sava was able to secure a vital agreement with the Byzantine patriarch whose authority, closely linked to that of the state, had been weakened by the existence of the Byzantine Empire-in-exile in Nicea. The agreement granted the Serbian Church autocephalous status and Sava became its first archbishop. Thereupon King Stefan supported his brother and set about distancing himself from the Catholic Church. Dioceses were set up throughout Raška and in Zeta, where the bishop established his seat on the Prevlaka peninsula in the Gulf of Kotor. The inclusion of Zeta within the jurisdiction of the Serbian Orthodox Church was of great significance for the future of these lands. It not only helped to undermine the influence of the Roman Catholic Church, hitherto particularly strong in this part of the western Balkans, but also encouraged the inhabitants of Zeta to establish closer links with the Serbs of Raška and develop a sense of shared identity.

However, certain coastal cities still retained a large proportion of Catholics who continued to practise their faith alongside their Orthodox brothers. In Kotor, for example, the largely Catholic population was guaranteed many privileges, which were at times fiercely contested by another Catholic coastal city, Bar.[51] And channels to the Catholic West were by no means entirely cut off. In the later Middle Ages an important land route ran from the Adriatic coast along the shores of Lake Skadar, across the mountains of Montenegro to Peć

[50] Obolensky, *The Byzantine Commonwealth*, p. 247.
[51] Fine, *The Late Medieval Balkans*, p. 141.

and then through Kosovo to Niš. Called the Via di Zenta (a variation
on the name Zeta), it was used by the Venetians and the Ragusans
(inhabitants of present-day Dubrovnik) in their trading operations
with Serbia and Bulgaria. The existence of this route (one of many)
was instrumental in bringing the interior of Serbia into contact with
the Romanised cities on the Adriatic coast and through them with
Venice.

As Catholicism weakened throughout the Serb-inhabited lands,
the association between church and state grew stronger. It was nurtured especially by members of the Nemanjić dynasty, who became
the first native saints of the Serbs. The close association between
church and state implied by the ruler's canonisation owed much of
its inspiration to Byzantium.[52] The wealth and foremost cultural
position of Byzantium inclined all local Balkan rulers to imitate its
rituals and practices, and even to attempt to make themselves into
Slav versions of Byzantine emperors.

The reign of Stefan the First-Crowned in Raška was to see the
eclipse of Zeta as an independent kingdom, an eclipse which lasted
for almost 150 years. Stefan successfully put down attempts to reassert Zetan independence by both his brother Vukan and Vukan's
son Djordje, who sought to ally himself with Venice against his
uncle. Djordje continued to rule as some sort of governor in Zeta
under Stefan's first son Radoslav, when records from Dubrovnik
refer to Djordje as 'Prince of Duklja'. Djordje's tenure over Zeta was
maintained when Serbian nobles overthrew Radoslav in favour of
Stefan's second son Vladislav. But when Vladislav was in turn ousted
by a third brother, the forceful Uroš I, Djordje risked his position by
backing Dubrovnik's right to be the sole archdiocese for the coastal
region while Uroš backed the rival town, Bar. Fighting broke out
with Uroš launching a number of attacks on Dubrovnik in spite of
which the ecclesiastical situation remained essentially unchanged.
Bar continued as an archdiocese but failed to gain jurisdiction over

---

[52] The close link between the state and official religion set a pattern that characterised Serbian society for centuries to come. It continued under the Ottomans,
while in Montenegro it was reflected in the highly unusual institution of the
Prince-Bishop or Vladika. There are echoes of this concern in the recent
conflict within Montenegro over whether the Montenegrin Church should be
allowed to exist as an officially sanctioned institution alongside the Serbian one.

the Catholics of the hinterland, who remained under the diocese of Kotor which was in turn subordinated to the archdiocese of Bari in southern Italy. Exactly what happened to Djordje is unclear since we hear no more about him.[53] More lasting fame was achieved by Djordje's brother Stefan, who in about 1252 built the famous Morača monastery near Podgorica with its beautiful frescoes illustrating the life of the prophet Elijah. Another monastery, Davidovica on the Lim River, is attributed to a third son of Vukan, Dimitrije, a local *župan* who subsequently became a monk.[54] Thereafter Vukan's descendants and indeed all reference to a separate Zetan nobility disappear from the records, the one noteworthy exception being the Princess Milica, wife of the famous Serbian Prince Lazar who was defeated in the battle of Kosovo Polje by the Ottoman Turks and as a result passed into legend. Milica claimed descent from Nemanja's son Vukan of Zeta, a connection which posthumously helped to promote Lazar's candidature for canonisation.

Under Uroš I Serbia, as Raška was now beginning to be called, became a leading Balkan power, eclipsing its former rivals Bulgaria and Greek Epirus. Uroš undoubtedly understood the dangers involved in installing royal relations as rulers in the more far-flung parts of his realm. His title pointedly contained no reference to subordinate rulers or principalities; instead he styled himself 'King of all Serbian land and the coast',[55] an all-encompassing title that did however imply some recognition of the separate identity of the coastal region. Yet for all Uros's pretensions his court was far from sophisticated. A contemporary account written in about 1268 by a Byzantine envoy notes with disdain: 'The Great King, as he is called, lives a simple life in a way that would be a disgrace for a middling official in Constantinople; the king's Hungarian daughter-in-law works … at her spinning wheel in a cheap dress; the members of the household eat like a pack of hunters or sheep-stealers.'[56]

Precautions further afield did not spare Uroš trouble at home. In 1276 he was overthrown by his elder son Dragutin and, following the trend set by his predecessors, spent the years until his death as a

---

[53] Ćirković, *The Serbs*, p. 48.
[54] *Ibid.*, p. 48.
[55] Fine, *The Late Medieval Balkans*, p. 203.
[56] Quoted by Fine, *ibid.*, p. 204.

monk in the monastery he had built at Sopćani near modern Novi Pazar. The new king, however lacking in filial duty towards his father, provided generously for his widowed mother Jelena, who was granted control of Zeta along with a large section of the coast including Cavtat (in modern Croatia) right down to Skadar. There Helen set up her court and as a pious Catholic established a number of Franciscan missions in Bar, Kotor and Ulcinj, some of which later became monasteries.

After Uroš's death the centralisation he achieved began to give way to the more common pattern of different centres developing some degree of autonomy under their own rulers, a situation more to the liking of the local nobility. Towards the end of the thirteenth century, Dragutin suffered an injury after falling from his horse, and perhaps for this reason but more probably because the nobles believed they could more easily control his younger brother, he was replaced at this time by Uroš's second son Milutin, who was declared king for life while Dragutin withdrew to lands he was granted in western and northern Serbia. It was during Milutin's reign that Serbia expanded southwards into Byzantine lands in Macedonia and eastwards into lands hitherto occupied by Bulgarians. Although the Byzantine Empire in Constantinople had been restored in 1261, the state remained weak and the Emperor Michael Palaeologus died before his forces could recapture lands seized by Milutin. His successor Andronicus II fared no better: during his reign Milutin was able to go on the offensive and capture yet more territory to consolidate his hold over central Macedonia, effectively doubling the size of the Nemanjić state.[57]

Around the beginning of the fourteenth century Milutin appears to have awarded Zeta to his son Stefan Dečanski, a decision that could well have provoked the hostilities which now broke out between the king and his brother Dragutin, who had grounds for fearing that his own son would be passed over in the succession. To shore up possession, Milutin set about improving relations with Byzantium. New borders were agreed through Macedonian lands, and Milutin sealed the arrangement by taking as his fourth wife a five-year-old Byzantine princess, Simonida. The relationship between the child and a man some forty years her senior was pre-

---

[57] Ćirković, *The Serbs*, p. 50.

dictably unhappy and unfruitful, yet Simonida's presence in Serbia was marked by a significant increase in Byzantine influence on all aspects of Serbian courtly, religious and artistic life. Byzantine titles, customs, taxes and systems of land tenure were introduced, and churches and monasteries were built, earning Milutin the strong backing of the Orthodox Church.

From Zeta in 1314 Stefan Dečanski, backed by local nobles, launched a revolt against his father, perhaps intending to force Milutin to recognise him as his heir. Instead Milutin defeated Stefan and, following the gruesome practice of the times, had his son blinded and banished, together with his wife and children, to the imperial court in Constantinople. Milutin then awarded Zeta to Dečanski's younger brother or half-brother Constantine.

When Milutin died in 1321 without naming an heir, civil war broke out between Constantine, the blind Stefan Dečanski who had finally been allowed home and granted control of the Budimilje *župa* (near modern Berane) shortly before his father's death, and Dragutin's son Vladislav. Constantine immediately declared himself king of Zeta. Dečanski, perhaps because he had never been effectively blinded, proclaimed himself miraculously cured, which was enough for the church whose archbishop crowned him king of Serbia, together with his son Dušan, proclaimed the 'Young King'. War with Zeta followed, and in the battle Constantine was defeated. Sources—admittedly unfavourable to Dečanski—record that he had his brother nailed to a cross and sawn in two. For all the Nemanjić dynasty's patronage of the church, the pattern of violence was to occur repeatedly in the relationships between its members. Perhaps, as Rebecca West writes,[58] this reflected the spirit of the age as the acts of vengeance and cruelty of the Tudor dynasty in England did more than two centuries later. But it also doubtless reflected the weakness of the state and the frequent remarriages of rulers.

Stefan Dečanski held all Zeta and most of northern Albania, but in the confusion caused by the uncertainty and warfare that had followed the death of Milutin, he lost control of the province of Zahumlje which offered vital access to the sea. Under Milutin it had seemed for a time that Serbia might have expanded westwards to the

---

[58] Rebecca West, *Black Lamb and Grey Falcon: The Record of a Journey through Yugoslavia in 1937*, vol. 2, London: Macmillan, 1941, pp. 258–9.

Adriatic, but the opportunity was now lost and in future Serbia would concentrate on expanding its territories and influence over Bulgarian lands to the east and Byzantine territories to the south. This expansion helped to consolidate Serbia's links with the Greek-speaking world and in that sense to distance it from those parts of Zeta that remained open to influence from the West and Latin Christendom.

In 1331 Dečanski's son Dušan, who had taken up residence in Zeta, was attacked by his father. This time the cause was probably only partly due to uncertainty over the succession. Dušan had distinguished himself fighting the Bulgarians and had thus built up support among the nobles who favoured his candidature over that of his half-brother, the son of Dečanski's new Byzantine wife. At the same time nobles critical of Dečanski's failure to pursue a more aggressive policy towards Byzantium and its territories to the south had come to favour Dušan over his father, and in the fighting that followed Dušan proved victorious. When, shortly after his son's coronation, Dečanski was found strangled in prison, suspicion inevitably fell on Dušan. The following year Zeta, under the leadership of a noble called Bogoje, attempted to secede from Serbia, and discontented chieftains from Albania rose in support, but Dušan suppressed the revolt. How far this movement in Zeta was due to a desire for greater autonomy and how far it simply reflected the discontent of nobles who had expected to receive favours from their former lord is difficult to determine, but the eruption of a new revolt in Zeta immediately after Dušan's death suggests that pressure for separation from Serbia may indeed have existed.

Dušan was not only the greatest of the Nemanjić rulers; in his time he was also the foremost figure in the Balkans, a man whose military skill was accompanied by an astute diplomatic mind. On his accession in 1331 he found himself surrounded on all sides by potentially hostile powers—Bulgaria to the east, Hungary to the north, Catholic Bosnia to the west and Byzantium to the south, but in his reign Serbian lands reached their farthest expansion. Taking advantage of Bulgaria's weakness after a period of military defeat and civil war, he overran much of Bulgaria's territory in Macedonia. Within about fifteen years Serbia almost doubled in size while Bulgaria lost almost half its territory. However, Dušan had spent much of his childhood in Constantinople while his father Stefan Dečanski was in exile, and his familiarity with the Byzantine court allowed him at one time to make an alliance against the empire with John Canta-cuzenus, a former co-ruler of the empire turned rebel, and subse-quently to forge a close relationship with the dowager empress, who helped him to arrange a marriage with a Byzantine princess for his five-year-old son.[59] Not surprisingly his preference was always to expand into the richer Byzantine-ruled Greek-inhabited lands of southern Macedonia rather than to the west, where the inhabitants were fellow-Slavs.

In 1346 Dušan raised the Serbian archbishop to the rank of patriarch, establishing the seat of the Patriarchate at Peć in modern Kosovo. Here on Orthodox Easter Day he had himself crowned by the newly-appointed Serb patriarch as Emperor of the Serbs, Romans, Bulgarians and Albanians. Having taken for himself the imperial title and proclaimed his rule over the 'Romans', as the Greeks of Byzantium still called themselves, Dušan set about the 'Byzantification' of both his court and his country's administration.

In recognition of its great size and different languages, Dušan's empire was divided into two halves, Greek and Serb, with the em-peror ruling the Greek lands while his son Uroš, the 'Young King', ruled those inhabited by Serbs. But the division was more theoretical than actual since Dušan's son was still a child and unable to rule alone. In reality Dušan's empire was neither national nor monoglot but effectively multi-national and multi-lingual. Greek, Serbian and Albanian were widely spoken in different parts of the empire, and Serbs were placed over Greeks and Albanians in the areas that the Greeks formerly controlled. However, at the lower levels of the administration local officials remained in place, making for much cultural interpenetration. But the greatest force for unity remained, as it had been since Milutin's time, the Orthodox Church.

Like the Byzantine emperors, members of the Nemanjić dynasty were famous as the builders of monasteries from whose walls their own halo-crowned images gazed down on an illiterate population. As in the Christian West, the monasteries themselves were to be-come centres of learning, their high-ranking clergy, often members

[59] Ćirković, *The Serbs*, p. 64.

of the royal family, playing an important role in affairs of state. The expansion of Dušan's empire southwards into Macedonia and the Greek-speaking areas contributed further to this process, ensuring that the cultural and religious influence of Byzantium would not only permeate medieval Serbian culture but also leave its imprint for centuries to come. The links established at that time between the Serbian royal dynasty and the Orthodox Church were to make Orthodoxy the natural religion of the vast majority of the Nemanjić empire's inhabitants.

For much of this period Zetan lands had not altogether conformed to the general pattern as Catholic and Italian influence had expanded from the important archdiocese at Bar into the interior. But from the foundation of the Orthodox archdiocese in Peć in 1346, the Catholic Church began to lose ground more generally throughout Zeta until it was confined to the cities of the coast and their immediate hinterland.

A second source of unity within the Serbian lands of Dušan's empire was the promulgation of his famous law code or *Zakonik*, again much influenced by Byzantine practice but also reflecting the influence of Serbian customary law. In a period when historical sources were very much chronicles of the kings and nobles, the *Zakonik*, promulgated in 1349, is a particularly valuable resource for what it reveals of contemporary society.[60] But if, in its widespread application, the *Zakonik* was a unifying force, its detailed inventory also reveals the varying conditions prevailing within the different Serb territories. For instance, its many penalties for brigandage reflect the continuing insecurity afflicting the more remote areas, which would naturally have included the mountainous regions of Zeta. Its provisions also reveal something of the conditions of dependent peasants, who made up a large proportion of the population, and suggest some variation throughout Dušan's lands. One difference to emerge was that while most peasants paid their dues to their lord in labour, those in Zeta, especially on the Adriatic coast, where trading contact with the West was frequent, were more likely to meet their obligations with payments in cash or in kind. Land-

[60] For more on Dušan's *Zakonik* and its social implications see Fine, *The Late Medieval Balkans*, pp. 314–21, and Ćirković, *The Serbs*, pp. 68-74.

holdings in these areas tended to be smaller than those in the more fertile eastern regions of Serbia.

Differences such as these can only be indicative: we have all too little information about the lands that were to become Montenegro as they were at this time. But the variation apparent within the Serbian lands prompts the question whether one can justifiably speak of any sense of separate identity which set medieval Zetans apart from Serbs elsewhere.

The question of Zetan identity

There is at least some evidence favouring a sense of Zetan identity. The revolts that broke out intermittently in Zeta during the long period of Nemanjić rule may be seen as suggesting that the Zetans considered themselves as a distinct people who did not want to live under the Raškan yoke. In 1332 Dušan had to suppress a serious revolt that broke out when some nobles in Zeta tried to secede and form their own principality. Scholars have argued that this suggests that there was, at least within the nobility, a reluctance to submit to rulers from Raška, who were perceived to be foreigners. The fact that the Raškan ruler's son was often given direct charge of Zeta is equally suggestive of some sense of difference attaching to it. Possibly such a volatile entity was thought to require close attention if it were to be incorporated effectively into the larger Serb state. Finally, at least where the coastal towns are concerned, there is evidence of a marked degree of difference in terms of the penetration of Catholicism and of Latin culture, and even in the promulgation of their own laws,[61] a distinction observed even by the centralising Uroš when he chose to describe himself 'King of all Serbian land and the coast'.

But there are also good arguments against this view of Zetans as possessing a separate sense of identity. Indeed, as the medievalist John Fine points out, events initially suggestive of separateness may on closer examination be susceptible to the opposite explanation.[62] Nemanja's elder son Vukan who in 1204 launched a rebellion

[61] Ćirković, *The Serbs*, p. 71.
[62] On the question of separate Zetan identity see Fine (*The Late Medieval Balkans*, pp. 42–3) to whom I am indebted for several of the following points.

against Serbian rule from his base in Zeta and briefly took over control of Serbia, converted to Catholicism and even accepted Hungarian suzerainty. But we know that he also took in and sheltered his brother's spurned wife, the Byzantine princess Eudocia, when she was accused of adultery. Thus it may be that Vukan's ostensibly political acts, far from reflecting any specifically Zetan consciousness, were directed principally against his brother Stefan, whose control of Serbia he bitterly resented. While Zeta was the base for his rebellion, he is likely have seen himself as a Serb prince and to have had the ambition of ruling over all Serb lands.

Whether the ordinary people felt any sense of Zetan identity is still more doubtful. Borders were porous and constantly changed. In the feudal society of Dušan's time it is likely that the inhabitants of Zeta would have felt themselves to belong to a particular locality and to have owed allegiance to a local lord or bishop. In a hierarchically ordered world rulers, nobles and ordinary people, whether free or in a state of serfdom, were bound together by military and personal obligations rather than by effective state administration and abstract concepts of patriotism and statehood.[63] Indeed the precedence of the personal over abstract conceptions of the state is well illustrated by the case of Stefan Nemanja himself, who remained loyal to the oath of fealty he swore to Manuel Comnenus for as long as Manuel was alive, but thereafter attempted to rebel against the state of Byzantium.

Zeta at this stage was thus one of a number of inherently unstable and loose-knit Balkan kingdoms, whose *raison d'être* was the concept of loyalty to a particular potentate or ruling dynasty. Lacking clearly defined territorial boundaries and offering little to their populations beyond a life of toil and military service, these entities were vulnerable both to conquest and to internal revolt and fragmentation whenever a powerful ruler died. Such a fate was soon to befall even the greatest of these, Dušan's empire, which would make way for the emergence of new magnates and powerful families in the Zetan lands.

---

[63] On the fundamental characteristics of the 'dynastic realm' see Benedict Anderson, *Imagined Communities: Reflections on the Origins and Spread of Nationalism*, New York: Verso, 1991, pp. 19–22.

2. Zeta between Venice and the Ottomans

Dušan's empire did not fall apart immediately after his death; its demise was gradual. Dušan had never succeeded in unifying his vast lands or welding its peoples into one; it was largely the strength of his personality that kept the empire together. Over the next twenty years his successors battled against a host of exogenous forces: not only the Serbs' traditional foes and rivals—Byzantium, Venice, Hungary and Bulgaria—but, increasingly, the enemy that was ultimately to prove the nemesis of all the Christian kingdoms—the Ottoman Turks.

Dušan's son, the nineteen-year-old Uroš V, clearly lacked his father's abilities and charisma, to the extent that he was known as Uroš the Weak. Challengers abounded, both internal and along the periphery in the non-Serb parts of the empire. First, certain Greek magnates were able to wrest some of the Aegean coastal lands away and soon Albanian nobles followed, aided by Venice, taking over control of lands in what is today southern Albania.[1] To the north Hungary was able to exploit inter-Serbian rivalries to install its own appointee and ultimately bring about the secession of these lands from Serbia.

The rise of the Balšići

To the west the Hungarian king had also ejected Venice from a number of the Adriatic cities and by 1359 had secured overall control of Dubrovnik.[2] Meanwhile just to the south in Zeta, another family—the Balšići—had risen to prominence and were beginning

---

[1] Fine, *The Late Medieval Balkans*, p. 357.
[2] Ćirković, *The Serbs*, p. 76.

to challenge Serbian control of these lands. Who exactly the Balšići were and where they had come from is far from clear. The story that they were descended from a son of Bertrand de Baux who was said to have settled in Albania after fighting on the side of Charles of Anjou when he seized the kingdom of Naples, is disputed. Most writers follow Francis Seymour Stevenson's dismissal of the claim while a more recent work by two Montenegrin historians seeks to reassert it.[3] But whether the Balšići were of Serb or Albanian origin, or perhaps something in between such as Serbo-Albanian or even Vlach has never been conclusively established. Among the aristocracy of the various Balkan principalities, the importance of constructing wide-ranging dynastic alliances meant that mixed marriages were common during much of the medieval period. Although they were doubtless less so among the common people and the petty nobility from which the Balšići seem to have emerged, similar ways of life, fluctuating religious affiliation and highly porous borders all helped to blur the distinction between Serb and Albanian in these western lands. Whatever his origins, Balša and his sons were 'culturally Serbianized';[4] the family's founder, Balša, is first mentioned in a charter issued by the Serbian King, Uroš V, to Dubrovnik, which allowed its merchants trading privileges in lands specified as being under Balša's control. The Balšići soon established their base in Skadar, in territory that is now part of Albania. From Skadar they moved rapidly northwards, first to take over the surrounding lands of lower Zeta, before expanding their control into upper Zeta and up the coast as far as, but not including, Kotor.[5] Although Balša and his sons did not hesitate to use violence where necessary, they also resorted to trickery and exploited the advantages offered by marriage alliances to neutralise rivals and cement their territorial gains.

The relationship with Venice and with Serbia

On Balša's death around 1360, he was succeeded jointly by his three sons Stracimir, Djuradj (George) and Balša II. By this time, Venice

---

[3] Francis Seymour Stevenson, *A History of Montenegro*, London: Jarrold, 1912, pp. 30–1 and Andrijašević and Rastoder, *History of Montenegro*, p. 18.
[4] See Dragoje Živković, *Istorija Crnogorskog Naroda*, Cetinje, 1989, vol. 1, p. 255–6.
[5] On the above see Fine, *The Late Medieval Balkans*, pp. 358–9.

had become a major power in the Adriatic region, and the Balšici, with their territories along the coast, were naturally brought into close contact with the Venetian colonists. As far back as the tenth century Venice had gained Byzantine approval for its presence in the Adriatic in return for suppressing piracy along the coast. A century later Byzantium granted Venice free access to its Adriatic ports in return for help in countering the increasing inroads made by other outside powers, in particular the Normans. Yet Venice proved an untrustworthy ally whose real interests lay in expanding its own commercial empire, which was backed by formidable naval power.

To the north Venice continued its struggle with Hungary over control of Dalmatia. Here geography gave Venice the advantage because the Adriatic shore, cut off as it is from the hinterland, was particularly susceptible to occupation by a naval power.[6] Failing this, any would-be occupier required supply routes through Bosnia and Hum (former Zahumlje). This was something Hungary grew progressively less able to achieve as Bosnia came under the sway of its most powerful medieval ruler, King Tvrtko. In the fourteenth century Venetian influence continued to extend down the Adriatic coast. It was thus quite natural for the Balšici, by now the native rulers of the central coastal region from just south of Skadar to Kotor, to bow to local custom by becoming enrolled as patricians of Venice.[7]

Critical though it was to be to the future of Montenegro, the relationship with Venice did not go smoothly. Conflict over the cities of Kotor and Dubrovnik soon drew in Venice and the Balšici on opposite sides. Dubrovnik had retained its independence during Dušan's rule, but Kotor had come under the formal control of the Nemanjić dynasty, while nonetheless retaining its own political institutions and other elements of local independence. Following Dušan's death, Kotor had been included in the domains of Uroš V. Uroš's weakness, however, and the ambitions of other local rulers, now left both Kotor and Dubrovnik vulnerable to predatory actions of local magnates aided, where interest so dictated, by outside powers.

The conflict was precipitated by the attempt of Vojislav Vojinović, a noble whose lands adjoined Zeta's to the north, to force Dubrovnik (already by this time under Hungarian suzerainty) to pay its

[6] Stevenson, *History of Montenegro*, pp. 33–4.
[7] *Ibid.*, p. 37.

annual tribute to him. While Dubrovnik struggled to resist, the citizens of Kotor came out on the side of Vojislav and against Dubrovnik, possibly out of fear of the Balšići's designs on their city. When a truce was signed in 1362 it was only through the mediation of an outside power, Venice; greatly inconvenienced by the disruption to its commercial traffic, it successfully put pressure on both sides into suspending hostilities. The episode introduced a certain tension into relations between the Balšići and Venice; Kotor in particular remained a source of friction, with Venice insisting on the right to protect its friends and allies along the coast. For their part, the Balšići alternated between plunder and attempts to gain outright control.

Meanwhile, in Serbia itself, Uroš had been forced to bolster his own position by enlisting the support of two of his father's courtiers, the brothers Vukašin and Uglješa, descendants of the Mrnjavčevići, a poor family of emigrants, originally from neighbouring Hercegovina who had risen in Dušan's time to become great landholders in Macedonia. That the two leading western noble families—that of Vojislav and the Balšići, theoretically both vassals of Uroš—could go to war against one another illustrates the Serbian king's loss of control over the Serb-inhabited parts of the empire.[8] Uroš's need for support was further demonstrated when he made Vukašin his co-ruler, even agreeing, since he himself was childless, to designate Vukašin's son Marko as the 'Young King'. Intent on strengthening his position, Djuradj Balšić of Zeta married Vukašin's daughter, thereby allying himself with the real master of Serbia.

Having secured the relationship with Serbia, the Balšići turned their attention to consolidating their acquisitions on the coast, even converting to Catholicism in the belief that this would make them more acceptable to the local population. The coastal towns of Bar and Budva had both fallen to them, but they had to wait till 1368 to take a third town, Ulcinj, where Dušan's widow Jelena held out on her own until her death some thirteen years after her husband. Further south the Balšići were simultaneously involved in warfare with the most powerful of the northern Albanian nobles, Karlo Thopia, a local ruler dignified by Venice as 'Prince of Albania'. In 1364, in the course of the fighting, Karlo Thopia managed to

[8] Fine, *The Late Medieval Balkans*, p. 359.

capture Djuradj Balšić and hold him captive until 1366 when his release was secured through the good offices of Dubrovnik.[9]

Soon Djuradj was at war again, this time in an attempt to take Kotor, where the prosperous and sophisticated citizens were facing hard times as a result of the prevailing instability and its impact on inland and maritime trade. Kotor resisted and, failing to receive support from either Serbia or Venice, offered to submit to Hungary in return for protection from the Balšići. Far from bringing an improvement in Kotor's fortunes, the move unleashed a succession of claims against it by predatory local magnates, threatening to bring in both Dubrovnik and Serbia. But the danger posed to Kotor on this occasion never materialised as the forces of Uroš and Vukašin suddenly found their presence urgently required far closer to home.

The arrival of the Ottomans

While the local barons were disputing the spoils of Dušan's Serbian empire, the real threat to all the Balkan Christian populations had been growing largely unchecked, if not entirely unrecognised, in the lands formerly ruled by Byzantium to the south. The Ottoman Turks were originally one among a number of Turkic tribes which, under their leader, Osman, were able to form a small independent state in northern Anatolia following the decline of the Seljuk Turkic empire in the thirteenth century. As the Osmanli or Ottoman state expanded rapidly through Anatolia it drew in many other Turkic and Muslim peoples, attracted by its military success. In a prime example of historical irony, the Ottomans' fateful appearance on European shores had been instigated by Europeans themselves, when in the Byzantine civil war of the 1340s the Emperor John Cantacuzenus turned to the Ottomans for support against his rivals. Once in Europe, however, the Ottomans refused to return to the Asian side of the Dardanelles.[10] In 1354 from their foothold at Gallipoli Ottoman forces under the direction of Osman's younger son and successor Sultan Murat made rapid progress through the peninsula. West European countries, devastated at the time by the

---

[9] Fine, *The Late Medieval Balkans*, p. 372.

[10] In fact, as Noel Malcolm points out, Christian rulers had previously made use of Turkish auxiliaries, but on these occasions the soldiers had returned home when the fighting was over. (Malcolm, *Kosovo*, pp. 59–60.)

ravages of the Black Death, were unable to muster forces for effective resistance. Moving up through Thrace, Bulgaria and Macedonia, Murat's men began to plunder lands belonging to Vukašin's brother, Uglješa.

Keenly aware of the danger the Ottomans represented, Uglješa tried to rally support from Byzantium as well as from the rulers of the small Slav fiefdoms and territories, but his endeavours met with little success. Only Serbia, under the effective control of his brother, was prepared to assist. With the Serbian ruler no longer in a position to compel support, the remaining Balkan magnates—the Balšići included—either failed to recognise the extent of the threat or felt too vulnerable to the menace of local adventures to undertake a campaign so far from home.

Superficially, at least, the decision seemed a wise one. The ensuing battle of Maritsa,[11] intended to stop the Ottomans in their tracks, resulted in a massive defeat in 1371 for the Serbs in which both Vukašin and Uglješa were killed. So overwhelming was the defeat and so large the numbers killed, that most historians believe the battle of Maritsa to have played a far more significant role in the Ottoman conquest of the Balkan peninsula than the much better known battle of Kosovo Polje.[12] Fatally weakened and with its lands in Macedonia and southern Serbia gone, Serbia was vulnerable, not only to the Turks, but to land-hungry upstarts closer to home. When, barely three months after the battle, Uroš died childless and the Nemanjić line came to an end, Vukašin's son Marko, the 'Young King', was not in a position to defend his claim to the throne. Beset by predatory barons, he soon found himself pushed into a corner of his kingdom and forced to seek Ottoman suzerainty.

Djuradj Balšić wasted no time. Divorcing his wife, Vukašin's daughter, as soon as news of the defeat reached him, he moved swiftly to seize the rich trading centre of Prizren in Kosovo. At about the same time the family acquired more territory in Albanian-inhabited lands when Balša II married the daughter of John Comnenus Asen, brother of the Bulgarian tsar. These territorial gains soon brought the Balšići into conflict with a powerful local Albanian

---

[11] For a detailed account of this period and the ensuing battle of Maritsa see Fine, *The Late Medieval Balkans*, pp. 377–84.

[12] Malcolm, *Kosovo*, p. 58.

family, the Thopia, who found their territory wedged between Zeta and the new lands acquired through Balša's marriage.[13] These new territories in Albanian lands were the principal focus of Balšići activity in the 1370s with the rich city of Durrës (formerly Dyrrachium but by now known to the Venetians as Durazzo) their overriding goal. Although they were not to achieve this aim till 1385, when Balša II briefly succeeded in wresting the city from Karlo Thopia, they were able to extend their sway over a number of prominent Albanian families whose lands they then controlled indirectly.

In 1373 the eldest of the Balšići, Stracimir, died. His death had little impact on the family fortunes since his younger brother Djuradj had long been the dominant personality in the family. Stracimir's place was nonetheless filled by his son, Djuradj II.[14] By the mid-1370s the Balšići controlled an extensive and territorially consolidated swathe of land extending from Peć and Prizren in Kosovo as far as the Adriatic and from the Gulf of Kotor to the Mati river, making their importance in a pan-Slav context at this time unquestionable. When, in 1375, the Patriarch of Constantinople agreed to recognise the autocephalous status of the Serbian Church (in return for Serbian renunciation of the right to hold the title of tsar), the ceremony to install the new Serbian Patriarch took place in the Balšići's city of Prizren. Bearing in mind that the Balšići had by this stage converted to Catholicism, and that the agreement had been negotiated by the leading Serbian noble Lazar Hrebeljanović, the decision suggests the temporary ascendancy of the Balšići over Lazar.

But the Balšići did not achieve this prominence without incurring antagonism, nor would they long retain it. Elsewhere other ambitious magnates were poised to seize what lands they could. The Serbian heartlands and the rich mining centre of Novo Brdo were under the control of Lazar Hrebeljanović, the future prince whose name was to become the most emblematic in Serbian history following his defeat in 1389 on the field of Kosovo Polje at the hands of the Ottoman sultan. Lazar was the son of Dušan's chancellor and as such had inherited lands along the Morava and Ibar rivers north of Novi Pazar.[15] Although he had no Nemanjić blood, he was married to Milica, a princess who claimed descent from Vukan, one-time

---

[13] Fine, *The Late Medieval Balkans*, pp. 383–4.
[14] *Ibid.*, p. 386.
[15] *Ibid.*, p. 374.

governor of Zeta and Stefan Nemanja's eldest son. Moreover Lazar had obtained the particular favour of the Orthodox Church by ending the schism with Constantinople and securing recognition for an autocephalous Serbian Church. In 1373, seeking to gain more territory and further consolidate his position, Lazar also formed an alliance with the most powerful of all the local potentates at this time, King Tvrtko, ruler of Bosnia. Together they seized the lands of a neighbouring noble Nikola Altmanović, had him blinded and forced him to enter a monastery. The Balšići, too, were able to benefit from Nikola Altmanović's overthrow to the extent of gaining some of his lands which abutted their own territory. But their good fortune did not last. Soon Tvrtko was challenging the Balšići's interests along the Adriatic coast, seizing from them a section of it between Dubrovnik and the Gulf of Kotor.

The dynasty under threat

Worse was to follow. In 1379 the family strongman Djuradj I died, an event that led to a weakening of the family's position within the fractured and unstable hierarchy of Balkan principalities. Without his commanding personality, Tvrtko was able to annex the territory around Dubrovnik and the Gulf of Kotor, which hitherto he had merely occupied. In 1382, when the Hungarian King Louis I died, Tvrtko who somewhat vaingloriously had already arranged to have himself crowned 'King of Bosnia and Serbia', attempted to seize the valuable port of Kotor. But the aristocrats of Kotor managed to thwart his attempt by obtaining outside help, first from the Venetians, and then again from Hungary. When the contest over Kotor deepened the enmity between Tvrtko and the Balšići, it was ultimately Tvrtko who emerged the stronger. Not only did he secure further lands at the Balšići's expense but he also acquired additional coastal territory where in 1382 he built the port of Sveti Stefan, later Novi (literally 'New'), and finally renamed Herceg Novi after the Bosnian Duke (*Herceg*) Stefan Vukčić Kosača who ruled the city in the mid-fifteenth century shortly before it fell to the Turks.

While Tvrtko was successfully opposing the Balšići's interests in their northern lands, another long-standing rival, Vuk Branković[16]

---

[16] Vuk Branković and Djuradj II were in fact brothers-in-law since both had married daughters of the Serbian Prince Lazar. See below.

from Kosovo, moved to oust the family from the territories they had acquired there, including the town of Prizren. In the space of only a few years the Balšići's extensive landholdings had been eaten into on both sides. And, as so often in the past, the detrimental impact of these external attacks on a local ruling family was soon to be aggravated by self-inflicted wounds.

Djuradj's death in 1379 had left Zeta's remaining lands under the control of the third remaining brother Balša II and his nephew Djuradj II, while Djuradj I's own son Constantine by his second marriage was effectively excluded. At the time Constantine was still a minor and could do little to avenge his treatment at the hands of his uncle and cousin. Nor was Constantine yet in a position to act when, in September 1385, Balša II himself was killed in battle with the Ottomans. Balša had died attempting to defend his conquest of the city of Durrës, which he had seized from the Albanian Thopia clan in April that same year. It was in an attempt to regain the prized possession of Durrës that the Thopia had first called on the Ottomans for help. According to the sixteenth-century historian Orbini—not always a reliable source for the period—Balša's head was cut off and sent to Hajredin, the sultan's representative in his newly-conquered territories in Macedonia.[17] Irrespective of how Balša met his end, however, the importance of this first successful Ottoman incursion into the Adriatic[18] lay in the introduction of the Ottoman presence as a factor in local power struggles. Just as in the past they had called upon Christian rulers, local nobles now invoked the help of the new Muslim power to strengthen their position against neighbouring potentates or even rivals within their own family. The inevitable demand note was not long in coming. First Djuradj II, despite his desire to build closer links with Venice, was obliged to become an Ottoman vassal.[19] The same step would be taken in 1390 or 1391,

---

[17] Živković, *Istorija Crnogorskog Naroda*, vol. 1, p. 265.

[18] *Ibid.*, pp. 265–6, and Fine, *The Late Medieval Balkans*, pp. 390–1.

[19] The date of Djuradj II's acceptance of Ottoman suzerainty is uncertain. Fine notes that, while it may have been on his succession in 1385 or during the Ottoman raids on Zeta the following year, the first reference we have to Djuradj as an Ottoman vassal is found in documents from 1388. (*Ibid.*, p. 392.) Djuradj's formal subordination to the Ottoman sultan did not, however, prevent him from becoming at around the same time a vassal of the Serbian Prince Lazar, a step he appears to have taken at the time of his marriage to Lazar's daughter in 1386. See below.

after the battle of Kosovo Polje, by the young Constantine who called upon the Ottoman Sultan Bayezid I to back his attempt to gain control of Zeta from his cousin Djuradj II.[20] In essence this acceptance of vassal status was no more than a continuation of past practice, but the consequences were to prove as inimical to the Balšići's interests as they were to Slav rulers in general.

Already by the 1380s the Balšići, faced with threats from Tvrtko to the north and Albanian nobles seeking emancipation to the south, had taken steps to shore up their position—seeking alliances with more powerful families through marriage and vassalage. The situation was highly unstable, but there was no doubt that the Balšići's fortunes were in decline. In 1386 or 1387 Djuradj married Jelena, one of Lazar's four daughters, and Lazar's other daughters made equally advantageous marriages—one to Vuk Branković of Kosovo, and the remaining two to influential families in Bulgaria and Hungary, alliances which both reflected and consolidated Lazar's pre-eminent position. Coming under increasing pressure from rivals at home, Djuradj II accepted Lazar's suzerainty at the time of his marriage, hoping in this way to reduce his own vulnerability.

Lazar's ascendancy among his Slav peers was not, however, enough to safeguard the peace within his own lands. From at least as early as the battle of Maritsa, Turkish *ghazis* (warriors for the faith) had been raiding Slav territories in the peninsula with increasing frequency while the mercenaries recruited by the local magnates to oppose them were an almost equal menace. In 1386, the Ottomans took Lazar's southern city of Niš, an important cross-roads since ancient times for merchants and travellers throughout the region. With this strategic stronghold in his possession, Sultan Murad set his sights on Serbia and Bosnia and their rich silver mines.

The Balšići themselves may also have played a part in prompting the Ottoman onslaught which was to culminate on the field of Kosovo. Djuradj II's acceptance of Ottoman suzerainty obliged him to allow the sultan free passage through his lands. Whether or not he actually encouraged Murat's invasion of Bosnia in 1388 in order to strike a blow at his enemy, Tvrtko, has not been conclusively established, but there is little doubt that when the Ottoman forces were unexpectedly crushed by Tvrtko's general Vlatko Vuković, Sultan

[20] Fine, *ibid.*, p. 417.

Murad was spurred on to the attack at Kosovo by the necessity of expunging the disgrace of this defeat.

The battle of Kosovo Polje

While the Balšići may have wittingly or unwittingly helped to instigate the fateful encounter on the field of Kosovo it is unlikely that Djuradj's forces were present on the day.[21] The battle has been depicted by Serb historians as the most tragic and sacred event in Serbian history—a heroic defeat that ushered in five centuries of Turkish Muslim rule while reserving for the Serbs the moral high ground. For nineteenth century Serbian national leaders the need to avenge Kosovo became the most potent source of inspiration in the uprisings against the Turks. On 28 June 1989, the six hundredth anniversary of the battle, Slobodan Milošević told a crowd of over a million people gathered to protest at alleged mistreatment of Serbs and Montenegrins by largely Muslim Albanian Kosovars: 'We are again in battle. It is not an armed battle, but even that cannot be excluded.'[22]

But for all its potent symbolism we have very little historical information about the battle itself beyond the fact that both Lazar and Murad perished in it. Considerable uncertainty surrounds the composition of the opposing forces, although the issue is understandably an emotional one with national historians lauding the part played by their co-nationals and correspondingly denigrating that played by others. Not surprisingly therefore, Montenegrin and Albanian historians have mostly taken the view that Djuradj's forces participated on the Serbian side, possibly as part of the contingent sent by Tvrtko of Bosnia.[23] Historians of other nationalities have challenged this view, pointing out that the known enmity between Tvrtko and Djuradj would have made their co-operation unlikely and citing documents purporting to show that the Zetan ruler was

[21] For a detailed discussion of the issues surrounding the battle of Kosovo see Noel Malcolm, *Kosovo*, pp. 60–80.

[22] Slavoljub Djukić, *Milošević and Marković: A Lust for Power*, Montreal: McGill-Queen's University Press, 2001, p. 29.

[23] See Živković, *Istorija Crnogorskog Naroda*, vol. 1, p. 267, and John Allcock, *Explaining Yugoslavia*, London: Hurst, 2000, p. 431.

occupied in putting down a rebellion at Ulcinj on the Adriatic coast on the day of the battle.[24]

There is regrettably no conclusive evidence one way or the other. In one sense at least this is immaterial: popular culture has been less concerned with the contributors of forces than with the battle's mythic importance.[25] At the centre of the myth is the heroic but self-sacrificial decision which Lazar is said to have made on the night before the battle when in a vision God offered him the choice between a heavenly and an earthly kingdom. Predictably Lazar chose the heavenly kingdom and thus accepted defeat in the coming battle in exchange for eternal triumph in the hereafter. His choice, known as the 'Kosovo covenant',[26] provides the foundation both for the often-quoted Serbian penchant for victimhood, as well as for the quasi-biblical belief that Serbia is finally destined to regain its promised land.[27]

For Montenegrins, however, the import of the story is slightly different. In popular culture Montenegrins trace their origins back to the flight of the Serb nobility who sought shelter in their mountains after the fall of the empire at Kosovo.[28] Yet here the emphasis is less on victimhood than on heroism born of the desire to avenge the defeat.[29] Certainly it is likely that at least some of the vanquished

---

[24] Stevenson, *History of Montenegro*, p. 54, and Malcolm, *Kosovo*, p. 62.

[25] The myth-engendering potential of the Kosovo story not surprisingly reached its high point in the nineteenth century when Serbs were struggling to free themselves from foreign domination. The depiction of the event in hundreds of epic poems and folk songs owes much to the general Romantic climate of the time. For more on the impact of the battle of Kosovo within a Montenegrin context see especially Chapters 4 and 6 below.

[26] Malcolm, *Kosovo*, p. 80.

[27] For more on the import of the myth for Serbia see Judah, *The Serbs*, pp. 29–47 and, for a particularly negative view, Branimir Anzulović, *Heavenly Serbia: From Myth to Genocide*, New York University Press, 1999, pp. 38–44.

[28] Milovan Djilas, *Njegoš, Poet, Prince, Bishop*, New York: Harcourt, Brace & World, 1966, p. 11. The claim is also made for Milošević's family. See Slavoljub Djukić, *Milošević and Marković*, p. 3.

[29] In part this can be explained by the deep influence of Njegoš's *Mountain Wreath* which castigates cowardice and, in recounting the massacre of Muslim Slavs by Montenegrins ('The Montenegrin Vespers') on Orthodox Christmas Eve 1702, stresses the need to avenge the defeat at the battle of Kosovo. See Chapter 6 below.

remnants of Lazar's forces did seek refuge from the Ottomans in the more remote regions including Montenegro's Dinaric mountains. Yet many more were killed, while others stayed on to accept Ottoman overlordship and even serve in the Ottoman armies. Moreover, inaccessible as they were, the mountainous areas of the western Balkans already sheltered groups of people—many of them Vlachs—who had fled from earlier invaders. In the years that followed the battle of Kosovo, these groups were to be joined by others as Christian populations from the more accessible regions withdrew from the advancing Ottomans. The notion that the people who were eventually to become Montenegrins are direct descendants of the warriors of Kosovo Polje thus contains more myth than reality; nonetheless it continues to provide an important strand in the tangle of Montenegrin identity.

Despite the large numbers killed on both sides, the Serbian defeat at Kosovo was not the pivotal event that later historians and poets have made it. On the contrary, with both Lazar and Murad dead, it was not even clear at first which side could claim genuine victory. Viewed in the longer term, however, the Ottomans were the undoubted victors since they alone had sufficient manpower to continue the struggle after their huge losses on the battlefield. A year after the battle Lazar's widow Milica, who ruled on behalf of her minor son Stefan Lazarević, had accepted Ottoman suzerainty as a means of protecting her lands from Hungarians and from Vuk Branković, who were threatening Serbian lands respectively from north and south.

The weakening control of the Balšići

Djuradj II of Zeta was in no position to benefit from Serbia's weakness immediately following the battle of Kosovo. Even before the battle the Balšići dynasty had lost control of some of its territory in the hinterland of Kotor to an upstart family, the Crnojevići, who from obscure origins had expanded to hold lands in the vicinity of Lake Skadar as well as in the mountains behind Kotor.[30] In itself the nature of the pastoral life, characteristic of much of Zeta, contributed to the weakening of central control as mobile herdsmen

---

[30] Fine, *The Late Medieval Balkans*, p. 392.

drove flocks over large areas, across ill-defined borders and into inaccessible mountainous regions. In the aftermath of the battle and in conditions of increasing instability, local leaders began to reassert themselves as people banded together in smaller groups for protection. Often the extended family or tribe was a more effective source of security than the more distant authority of the nominal ruler.

In 1391 and again the next year the Ottomans launched major raids that reached as far as Zeta and the coast. Meanwhile Djuradj was facing opposition not only from the Crnojevići and various Albanian nobles but also from his cousin Constantine, the son of Djuradj I whom Djuradj II, together with his uncle, had excluded from power in Zeta. Constantine, already well connected through his mother Theodora,[31] was by this time, as we have seen, an Ottoman vassal. It was possibly he who encouraged the Ottomans to imprison Djuradj when he visited Skopje in 1392 to discuss his conflict with the Crnojevići.

Zeta oscillates between Venetian and Ottoman suzerainty

Djuradj's detention gave the Crnojevići, with support from the Venetians, the opportunity they needed to seize further territory. Determined to defend his lands against the Crnojevići, Djuradj took the only course open to him by agreeing to pay the Ottomans tribute and surrendering to them a number of coastal cities, including Skadar, in exchange for his freedom. In return he was allowed to retain the town of Ulcinj where he proceeded to establish his 'capital'.

From their base in Skadar the Ottomans began to consolidate their position in Albanian lands putting pressure on local lords who usually had no choice but to submit or seek terms with the other major power in the region, Venice. In their weakened state the leading noble families oscillated between Venetian and Ottoman suzerainty, often fighting wars with one another on behalf of their patrons. In 1395, taking advantage of the Ottomans' need to defend them-

---

[31] Theodora was both a niece of the great Dušan and the former wife of Žarko of Zeta who had been a leading noble in the region before the rise of the Balšići. (Fine, *The Late Medieval Balkans*, pp. 310, 358 and 390.)

selves against Christian Crusaders gathered round the Hungarian King Sigismund, Djuradj was able to throw off Ottoman suzerainty and regain Skadar and a number of other coastal towns. For a short time too he was granted administrative control of the Adriatic islands of Korčula and Hvar when King Sigismund, seeking a safe passage home in a Venetian galley after suffering a massive defeat at the hands of the Ottomans at Nikopolis in 1396, nominated him as honorary ruler.[32] But with the victorious Ottomans poised to stage a major comeback, Djuradj could not expect to hold on to his newly acquired lands on his own. Within a year he was forced to yield most of the conquered territory as well as Lake Skadar and its islands to Venice and to accept Venetian overlordship in exchange for a yearly pension for himself and his descendants. The transaction was to have lasting consequences, since Venice, once established there and at Durazzo, which was purchased by the Republic in 1392, would in time become a significant actor in Zeta itself.[33] Djuradj retained for himself only Bar and Ulcinj on the coast, together with part of the mountainous region of Zeta.

While Djuradj had been preoccupied with preserving his lands to the south, the powerful Crnojevići had been attempting to make further inroads into the Balšići's territory around Kotor. Unlike Djuradj the Crnojevići were Orthodox, which may have assisted them in attracting the support of some of the leading local families in the territory they were now able to bring under their control. That both the Balšići and the Crnojevići were vassals of Venice was not enough to prevent hostilities breaking out between them. In May 1396 the most powerful of the Crnojevići, Radić, was killed in combat with Djuradj's army and Djuradj, following established practice, moved to seize what lands he could. But as constant fighting had left the Balšići impoverished and lacking manpower, he was ill placed to gain much from his victory over the Crnojevići. Years of raiding by both the Crnojevići and the Ottomans had left towns and the country despoiled. The Venetian commissioner who took over Skadar had declared the city to be 'in wretched order, and without any decent dwelling place',[34] while Djuradj's coastal towns of Bar

---

[32] Živković, *Istorija Crnogorskog Naroda*. p. 272.
[33] Ćirković, *The Serbs*, p. 92.
[34] Stevenson, *History of Montenegro*, pp. 60–1.

and Ulcinj had been badly damaged in an earthquake in 1396.[35] In this weakened state Djuradj had also to suffer attacks from a leading Bosnian noble Sandalj Hranić, the son of Tvrtko's commander, Vlatko Vuković, who had revived the old struggle over Kotor and captured Budva with help from a prominent local tribe, the Paštro-vići (a name derived originally from *pastor*, shepherd[36]).

Venice in fact found less to be gained from its Adriatic coastal pos-sessions than it had expected, and in reaction taxed them heavily.[37] When, at the very end of the fourteenth century, revolts broke out in Skadar and nearby Drivast (Alb.: Drisht), both Djuradj and the Ottomans sought to take advantage of them, and Venice's role in the Adriatic suffered a temporary setback as the hinterland fell gradually to local rulers under the sway of the Ottomans or to the Ottomans themselves. But the Venetian eclipse was short-lived, and subsequent attempts at rebellion were to be less than successful. In 1402 the still aggrieved Constantine Balšic attempted to take Durazzo from the Venetians. The timing seemed propitious with the Ottomans and most of their Albanian vassals in deep disarray after the massive de-feat inflicted on Sultan Bayezid, and his allies at Ankara by Tambur-laine, the last great warlord and conqueror to emerge from Central Asia. Unlucky to the last, Constantine met with defeat and the Venetians promptly executed him. Any rejoicing Djuradj may have felt at the death of his cousin and rival was to be brief, for he himself died in 1403, leaving his lands in the possession of his widow Jelena, sister of Stefan Lazarević of Serbia and their seventeen-year-old son Balša III.

For the next eight years until her marriage to Sandalj Hranić of Bosnia Jelena greatly influenced the policies of her son, seeking to bring him closer to her brother, Stefan Lazarević, who by this time was already both a Hungarian and Ottoman vassal. With the Otto-mans no longer threatening the Balšići's possessions in Zeta, Jelena felt free to distance herself from Catholic Venice, bringing her

---

[35] Fine, *The Late Medieval Balkans*, p. 421.

[36] Ćirković, *The Serbs*, p. 130.

[37] While trade was relatively unimportant, the Republic valued the Adriatic coast for its splendid natural harbours, not to be found on the Italian side of the Adriatic, for the stone and timber provided by the hinterland and finally for the mariners who were so often to crew Venetian ships. (See John Julius Norwich, *A History of Venice*, Penguin Books, 2003, p. 260.)

policies more in line with her sympathies—with Serbia and the Orthodox world. In this she had the support of many ordinary people who had suffered considerably as a result of the determination of Venice to make the empire pay its way. The scale of the Ottoman defeat and subsequent strife between Bayezid's successors had given Venetian policy in the Adriatic a new lease of life. One after another Albanian and Zetan nobles had exchanged their vassalage with the Ottomans for a similar relationship with Venice. But under Jelena's influence things were about to change. Balša III converted to Orthodoxy and went so far as to support an uprising against the Venetians in Skadar. In 1405, as hostilities between Balša and Venice deepened, Balša sought help from Bayezid's son Suleiman, agreeing to become an Ottoman vassal in exchange for protection from Venice.

Over the next four years Suleiman's forces waged intermittent war with Venice.[38] As a prime protagonist Balša III lost no opportunity to tighten his grip on power. The cost to the local population was high as towns changed hands between the rival powers amid periods of bitter fighting and bloodshed. In 1407, however, Balša married Mara, the daughter of Nikola Thopia, a prominent Albanian noble who was a Venetian vassal. With his father-in-law and wife in the role of mediators, Balša now embarked on a drawn-out process of negotiation with the Venetians, which saw his mother Jelena briefly in Venice in an unsuccessful attempt to secure a peace treaty. Only in 1412, after her marriage to Sandalj of Bosnia, was agreement finally secured and a peace treaty signed. Under pressure from Sandalj, Venice agreed that both parties should revert to their pre-1403 borders, giving the Zetan ruler once again control of Skadar, Bar and Ulcinj.

Taking up residence in Bar, Balša III now set about reasserting his authority in Zeta, rewarding those who had supported him during his long struggle with Venice and dealing out retribution to former enemies. As part of the reckoning the Crnojevići, already greatly weakened by the death of their leading member Radić, were further reduced in status. However, one branch of the family, the Djuraševići, having consistently supported Balša through his difficulties, was now raised to the highest position at court and granted lands and

---

[38] For a fuller account of this period see Fine, *The Late Medieval Balkans*, pp. 512–17.

other privileges. In 1412 or 1413 Balša took his favours to the family still further when he divorced Mara Thopia and took as his second wife a kinswoman of the Djuraševići.

Balša III, reportedly 'of a turbulent disposition',[39] was not temperamentally inclined to bury the hatchet with Venice permanently. Nor did Venice prove much more accommodating despite the peace treaty. The fortunes of the Balšići dynasty, pressed as they were between two major outside powers, Venice and Ottoman Turkey, were on the decline. But Balša was not ready to give up the struggle. After Suleiman's death in 1411[40] Balša renewed his oath of fealty to the new Sultan, Suleiman's brother, Mehmet, earning himself a period of respite from the Ottoman forces, which were continuing their steady inroads into surrounding lands. Meanwhile, taking advantage of the general instability, other noble families were beginning to emerge in the interstices of power while keeping a wary eye on local Ottoman commanders. But Balša, though prepared to reach an accommodation with the Ottomans, continued to act as a thorn in Venice's side: terms of trade, war reparations, the repossession of Skadar, the position of the Orthodox Church, the struggle for ownership of the valuable salt works on the Luština peninsula (on the southern side of the Gulf of Kotor), even grazing rights, were all elements of this provocation. In 1417 Balša went further, ordering the imprisonment of all Venetian subjects within his territories. Exasperated and over-stretched by a simultaneous campaign against Hungary in northern Dalmatia, the Venetians placed a reward of 2,000 ducats, a vast sum at this time, upon Balša's head. They need not have worried; time was already on their side as Balša was seriously ill. Sensing his death approaching and determined above all to protect his possessions from his enemy, Venice, Balša turned to his uncle Stefan Lazarević for help. Balša's position was complicated by the fact that he had no male heir and his two surviving daughters were both under fourteen years old. Despite his illness he made the journey to Lazarević's court where he died on the 28 April 1417, nine days after his arrival.[41]

---

[39] Stevenson, *History of Montenegro*, p. 65.

[40] Suleiman was strangled in 1410 by his brother Musa, who was in turn overthrown by another brother, Mehmet. (See Malcolm, *Kosovo*, p. 84.)

[41] Živković, *Istorija Crnogorskog Naroda*, p. 288.

Venice, which had secured its northern frontiers against Hungary, now moved to take advantage of the vacuum created by Balša's death by seizing some towns along the coast. Kotor had already placed itself under Venetian suzerainty as a means of protecting itself from the ongoing demands for tribute made by the Zetan and Bosnian rulers. Simultaneously the Djuraševići saw the opportunity to expand their control over the interior regions of Zeta.

However, Stefan Lazarević was not prepared to forfeit his claim to Zeta without a struggle. In 1421 and 1422 he went on the attack, achieving some success along the southern stretch of the coast, but he could not afford to remain away from his lands in Serbia for long. In his absence Venice's willingness to allow the coastal towns a high degree of autonomy, together with the application of handsome bribes, had brought many of the towns and their leading families, including even the highly independent-minded Paštrovići, over to the Republic's side.

The (re)emergence of the Djuraševići/Crnojevići

Meanwhile Stefan Lazarević, having secured the backing of Sultan Murad, sent his ally Djuradj Branković of Kosovo back into Zeta. If, as is alleged, he was accompanied by 8,000 horsemen,[42] it is not surprising that the Venetians were moved to seek terms. Under a treaty known as the Peace of Sveti Srdj of 1423, Serbia was awarded a number of the coastal towns, regaining its former access to the sea. Over the next few years, Serbia and Venice avoided open warfare, although they continued to squabble over territorial borders and over the payment of tribute each claimed from different towns along the coast. However, Kotor was permanently under Venetian suzerainty, together with Lake Skadar, its islands and the immediately surrounding area. This still left Serbia, at least formally, in control of most lands in the inland area of Zeta, but in reality the distances involved meant that local families, in particular the Djuraševići, were increasingly able to live their lives free of Serbian interference.

While Venice and Serbia had been establishing some sort of *modus vivendi*, the Ottoman presence was increasing in strength. To the south of Zeta two of the most important Albanian families had

---

[42] Fine, *The Late Medieval Balkans*, p. 519.

been obliged to send their sons to Adrianople (Edirne) west of the Bosphorus where the Ottomans held them as hostages. Of these one, Gjergj son of Gjon Castriot, was to convert to the Muslim faith and become, under his Islamic name Iskander or Skanderbeg, a famous general in the Ottoman army.

In 1427 Stefan Lazarević died childless, leaving his kingdom to his nephew, Djuradj Branković, ruler of Kosovo and already at the time an Ottoman vassal. Formally, at least, Djuradj Branković still retained Stefan Lazarević's territories in Zeta but growing opposition from both the Ottomans and the Hungarians left him unable to enforce his rule in these western lands. Here a new generation of the Djuraševići emerged as the leading local family. Perhaps to signal a departure with their immediate forebears or perhaps to confer fresh distinction, the Djuraševići now began increasingly to revive the old name of Crnojevići, last used by Radić Crnojević's branch of the family. Concentrating on building up local ties in opposition to Serbia, the leading Djuraševići-Crnojević, Stefan, married Mara Castriot, the daughter of the prominent Albanian noble family and sister of Skanderbeg who by this time was already both a Muslim convert and Ottoman general. Clearly neither Albanian blood nor the Muslim/Ottoman connection was deemed disadvantageous at the time; on the contrary, the marriage strengthened the position of the Crnojevići by linking them with powerful neighbours beyond Zeta's borders.

The Crnojevići were soon to need all the help they could muster. Not only were the Ottomans edging ever closer, but a noble from Bosnia, Stefan Vukčić Kosača, was also hatching plans to dismember Zeta. Surrounded though they were by the Ottomans and Venetians and hard-pressed by Kosača, the Crnojevići were at least better off than Djuradj Branković. From the time he took over Stefan Lazarević's lands, Djuradj had been forced to accept the Ottomans' creeping annexation of Serbia. Gradually he was forced back on the once rich mining centre of Novo Brdo, though legally he still remained suzerain of Zetan lands. In 1441 he could hold out no longer: the Ottomans stormed his territory, took Novo Brdo and blinded his sons, leaving Djuradj to flee to Hungary.[43]

---

[43] Malcolm, *Kosovo*, p. 87.

The eclipse of Djuradj Branković meant that the Zetan lords of the interior were free of his largely nominal suzerainty, making them an attractive target for the Crnojevići's ambitions. But even as they attempted to strengthen their position in the hinterland, the Crnojevići were forced to concede the upper hand to Stefan Vukčić Kosača of Bosnia by handing over Ivan—one of the younger members of the family—as a hostage and accepting the status of vassal. In support of their new suzerain, the Crnojevići were drawn into competition with Venice over the possession of the towns along the coast that had reverted to a state of quasi-independence since Serbia's collapse. Sailing its fleet along the coast, Venice was able to divide the Crnojevići brothers among themselves, bringing the three younger ones over to the Republic's side while the two elder ones strengthened their alliance with Vukčić and seized their siblings' land in Upper Zeta.

Venice, from its position of strength, now proceeded to occupy Budva in an act of annexation that was to last till 1797 and the collapse of the Venetian Republic.[44] The independent Metropolitan of Zeta, the senior dignitary of the Orthodox Church in the region, was displaced from his seat at Budva and sought refuge in a monastery on an island in Lake Skadar. The struggle between Kosača and Venice continued, with the Venetians gradually gaining the upper hand. In 1443 they captured Bar, and with its surrender the whole of the Zetan portion of the Adriatic coast lay in their hands.[45] The departure of the Metropolitan of Zeta and the consolidation of the Venetian presence had the expected effect of weakening the Orthodox presence along the coast. Although the Venetians themselves counselled patience, Kotor in particular set about expelling Orthodox clergy and appropriating church lands with ruthless determination. By 1455 not a single Orthodox monk remained in the Gulf.[46]

The year 1443 saw great upheaval in eastern Europe as the Polish King Vladislav mustered a vast multi-national army of Crusaders

[44] See Fine, *The Late Medieval Balkans*, pp. 533–4, for a more detailed account of the struggle with Venice.
[45] *Ibid.*
[46] *Ibid.*, p. 534.

under his Hungarian general, Janos Hunyadi, to drive the Turk from
Europe.[47] At first the Christian armies were successful. Marching
south through Serbia they defeated the Ottoman Sultan Murad at
Niš, continuing through Bulgaria to take the capital, Sofia. The
sultan, needing to buy time to organise his defence, offered to reinstate the Serbian Djuradj Branković provided the despot was prepared to block the Hungarian army's passage south through Serbia.
Branković agreed, obtaining a reprieve for his Serbian kingdom and
indirectly contributing to the massive defeat of the Christian army at
Varna on the Black Sea coast in the autumn of 1444.

Such tumultuous events had profound effects elsewhere. In Serbia
the Ottomans' re-instatement of Djuradj Branković meant the restoration of the despot's feudal rights, including those over inland
Zeta. Djuradj Branković continued to observe the terms of his vassalage by backing the Ottoman side against his fellow-Christians.[48]
Further afield, in the Albanian-inhabited lands to Zeta's south, the
Crusade of Varna and its aftermath pushed the Ottoman general,
Skanderbeg, to launch the daring and, for a time at least, successful
uprising against his former Ottoman masters that made him Albania's greatest national hero. Uniting the tribesmen behind him, the
newly re-Christianised Skanderbeg defeated first the Ottomans and
then the Venetians, skilfully playing the two powers off against each
other and retreating to the wild mountains of Albania when threatened with a large standing army. Next he declared himself heir to the
Balšići lands[49] and launched raids along the coast from Ulcinj to Bar
in a bid to claim his 'inheritance'. The Venetian possessions along
the coast were naturally a target, and the Republic strove to defend
them first from Skanderbeg and subsequently from Djuradj Branković who, backed by Stefan Crnojević, had attempted to join in
the carve-up. Djuradj must have been confident as he marched
7,000 men from Serbia to do battle with Venice, but his presump-
tion was misplaced: not only did Venice defeat the Serbian forces,
but it also succeeded in inveigling Stefan Crnojević into abandoning
Djuradj and allying himself with the Republic.

---

[47] At the time Vladislav also ruled Hungary. See Malcolm, *Kosovo*, p. 87.
[48] *Ibid.*
[49] Živković, *Istorija Crnogorskog Naroda*, p. 307.

In 1451 the Republic concluded an agreement with Stefan as the brother possessing effective rights to Zeta. The territory he held with Venice's agreement was small—no more than a smattering of settlements on Lake Skadar and the Bojana river, together with some villages in Upper Zeta, his fortress at Žabljak and the territory above Kotor that included Mount Lovćen.[50] But Stefan defended it tenaciously against further attempts by Djuradj to seize it in 1452 and 1453, inflicting a number of defeats on his ageing adversary. As both men struggled over a constantly changing border, they gradually lost ground to the Turks.

For Djuradj nemesis was not long in coming. In 1454 the Ottomans again attacked his fortress of Novo Brdo, scattering its inhabitants and taking the women and boys into slavery. In Zeta, however, Stefan Crnojević, helped by his continuing relationship with Venice, was still clinging on as the Ottomans advanced on all sides. Although legally Venice was by this stage suzerain of both Upper and Lower Zeta, Stefan Crnojević remained the first among his peers in the conduct of daily affairs. As one Montenegrin historian points out, the treaty with Venice, which attests to Stefan's pre-eminent position, required the acquiescence of fifty-one military brotherhoods or clans based on territorial divisions, in itself an early example of the importance attached to gaining the assent of the tribe to acts by the leader.[51] The pact itself, signed with Venice on the island of Vranina on Lake Skadar, guaranteed the rights of Stefan's Orthodox inhabitants and protected their bishops from falling under the domination of the Roman Catholic Church. In return it stipulated that local nobles would agree to serve away from home in the Venetian armies in Albanian-inhabited lands.[52] Venice was by now benefiting not only from the ties with client rulers but from the connections between them, an outcome the Republic sought to replicate by instituting a similar arrangement with an Albanian *vojvoda* (military leader), Gjergj Arainite, over lands to the south. As a further act of

[50] Fine, *The Late Medieval Balkans*, p. 560. The fortress at Žabljak on the foreshores of Lake Skadar should not be confused with the town of the same name at the foot of Mount Durmitor in what is today northern Montenegro.

[51] Živković, *Istorija Crnogorskog Naroda*, p. 314.

[52] Fine, *The Late Medieval Balkans*, p. 561.

favour Venice was able to secure the release of Stefan Crnojević's son, Ivan, who had been held hostage for ten years in Bosnia.[53] When this son married the daughter of Gjergj Arianite, all the principal actors appeared to have cause for satisfaction. However, the protective mantle of Venetian overlordship was already fraying around the edges. Ottoman troops made regular incursions across the lines of contact, heightening the insecurity of local populations already exposed to the depredations of frequent cross-border raiding.

In 1464 Stefan Crnojević died and was buried in the monastery of Kom on one of the islands of Lake Skadar.[54] His son, Ivan was already hardened from his years in captivity in Bosnia and by long campaigns undertaken against the Ottomans. Ivan's reputation among his descendants benefited greatly from his warlike exploits although it is more difficult to say how much they reflect events of fifteenth century Zeta and how much the impact of the intensely romantic and nationalist nineteenth century when the Montenegrin Prince-Bishop, Petar Petrović Njegoš, wrote the following lines:

> *Beg Ivan-beg of ancestry heroic,*
> *Like tawny lion fought against the Turks,*
> *On every side, and deep in gory woods:*
> *Half of his lands the Turks did take from him.*[55]

The Crnojevići retreat

Certainly Ivan Crnojević's circumstances were anything but propitious. Along with the defeats at Varna and Kosovo, Constantinople had fallen in 1453, and Bosnia ten years later. Yet even after he had formally accepted Ottoman suzerainty in 1470 Ivan continued to fight against the Ottomans, often in support of the Venetians. In 1474 he battled alongside the Venetians in their defence of Skadar, where together they inflicted a partial defeat on the enemy. Again, in 1476, he joined the Hercegovinian noble Vlatko Kosača (son of his father's old rival, Stefan Vukčić Kosača) to continue the struggle, and

[53] *Ibid.*, p. 560.
[54] Stevenson, *History of Montenegro*, p. 88.
[55] *The Mountain Wreath of P. P. Nyegosh, Prince Bishop of Montenegro, 1830–1851* (transl. by James. W. Wilkes), London: George Allen and Unwin, 1930, p. 102.

then battled on alone when the Bosnian agreed to seek terms. In 1477 or 1478 the Ottomans launched a mighty wave of attacks against Zeta, attacking Ivan's fortress at Žabljak on Lake Skadar. To judge by what remains of the fortress, a vast stone structure some 44 by 25 metres in extent, with walls two metres thick and 14 metres high[56]—Ivan's citadel was well-protected. But it was not strong enough to withstand Murad's forces and Ivan was forced to flee.

About 1479 the Ottomans ousted the Venetians from Skadar. The ensuing peace settlement allowed Venice to retain a strip of coastal territory, which included Ulcinj, Bar, Budva and Kotor, but when Venice attempted to include Ivan Crnojević in the treaty by declaring him a Venetian subject, the Ottomans, who viewed him as a rebellious vassal, insisted that his lands be forfeit and he himself pursued and punished.[57] Wisely he fled to the coast. Medieval Zeta—apart from the coastal strip now in the possession of Venice—was at an end.

Ivan Crnojević made one final attempt to regain his Zetan heartland. In 1481 he used the unrest that had accompanied the installation of a new sultan, Bayezid II, to return to the coast and try to recruit local tribesmen to his cause. Sending envoys to Bayezid, he pleaded to be allowed to return under the terms of Ottoman suzerainty that had prevailed in 1470. Faced at that moment with an Albanian revolt, Bayezid II agreed to allow Ivan to occupy a small area between the coast and the Zeta River extending as far as Lake Skadar.[58] In return Ivan was to pay tribute, relinquish any control over foreign relations and surrender his youngest son Staniša as a hostage. Although, under the agreement, Ivan was spared the presence of Ottoman officials in his tiny principality, he was to suffer further indignity when his son, following the prevailing practice, converted to Islam, taking the name of his father's former companion-in-arms against the Turk, Skanderbeg.[59]

The centre of Ivan's greatly reduced patrimony was now the small settlement of Obod above a river draining into Lake Skadar, not far

---

[56] Šćekić, *Travelling through Montenegro*, pp. 160–1.
[57] Fine, *The Late Medieval Balkans*, p. 600.
[58] *Ibid.*, p. 603.
[59] *Ibid.*, p. 603.

from the Crnojević's earlier citadel of Žabljak. As Ottoman raids became ever more frequent Ivan resolved on a further move to the still more remote site of the future royal city of Cetinje at the foot of Mount Lovćen. Here in 1482 he brought his monks and began work on the court and monastery that were to form the austere 'capital' of his remaining lands. Although his territory was small, Ivan's vision must have been expansive since he commissioned masons from Dubrovnik to build the church in what, sources reveal, was the early Renaissance style.[60] In 1485, with the church completed, the Metropolitan of Zeta was brought to Cetinje to establish the bishopric. Neither the monastery nor the church was to survive after suffering Turkish attacks on many occasions, but the bishopric itself was to prove the single most durable institution—indeed the central core—of the future Montenegro.

Ivan was by this stage already old, and his eldest son Djuradj began to play a part in ruling his lands even before his father's death. When Ivan died in 1490 Djuradj Crnojević was recognised by the sultan as the official ruler of Montenegro, as his mountainous domain was now increasingly called. Djuradj—'brave, tall, a fine horseman and a lover of books',[61] and a man who knew the classics, mathematics and astronomy, was seemingly well suited to rule. In fact Djuradj's most noteworthy achievement was his commissioning of the first book printed in Cyrillic by the South Slavs—the *Oktoih prvoglasnik* (a book of hymns to be sung in eight parts), which was probably printed in Cetinje in 1493 or 1494 although the printing press was originally located at Obod. Based on Italian designs but actually made in Montenegro, the press produced between 1493 and 1496 a few extraordinarily beautiful liturgical books after the manner of illuminated manuscripts as well as a copy of Tsar Dušan's famous law code.[62] As historians have never failed to remark, both the time and setting of this event seem remarkable, but there are indeed reasons for its introduction in Montenegro. At the practical level the Crnojevići had a history of close contact with Venice, and Djuradj himself, as we have seen, was a deeply cultured man. But at a time when Orthodox culture and the accompanying way of life were under the

[60] Šćekić, *Travelling through Montenegro*, p. 113.
[61] Fine, *The Late Medieval Balkans*, p. 603.
[62] *Ibid.*

most acute threat, the natural reaction was perhaps to turn to something that would help preserve it. The fact that the few books printed at the Cetinje press were almost all devotional and that the master-printer Makarije was a monk would have helped to ensure that they were viewed as holy items in themselves, together with the church and monastery. There is a poignancy about this brief flourish of artistic activity in Cetinje, since it was so soon to vanish, not to reappear for over three centuries.

Djuradj himself tempted providence. Through his kinship links with the Albanian family of his uncle by marriage Constantine Arianite he was drawn into a fateful last adventure, which was plotting the formation of a new coalition against Ottoman power. The scheme was launched by King Charles VIII of France who, having seized Naples in 1495, sought to draw in Albanian rulers from southern Italy and others with promises of aid. When the uprising was launched, the plan was swiftly uncovered and Djuradj held to be a prime suspect. Bayezid decided to deal with the problem once and for all by ridding the region of Djuradj and suppressing any vestige of Montenegrin independence. Djuradj, given the option of surrendering in person to the sultan or leaving Montenegro, prudently chose the latter course. In 1496 he embarked from Budva for Venice and took the treasures from the Cetinje monastery with him. In his place the Ottomans attempted to make use of Djuradj's younger brother Stefan who had sided with the sultan against him. But the Ottomans soon lost faith in Stefan and in 1499 he too was expelled from Montenegro. He remained for some time in Venice where he was kept under close supervision by the authorities, but his final years, and those of his brother Stefan, remain something of a mystery. Some historians claim that Djuradj then sought the sultan's permission to return to Montenegro. Although, according to this version of events, Djuradj's request was turned down, he was given a province to rule in Anatolia, an act which, if true, sounds remarkably generous.[63] For the Ottomans his departure and the change of ruler offered a chance to tighten their grip: Montenegro lost its autonomy and was simply absorbed into the Ottoman administrative structure, first as part of a *kadiluk* (an administrative district normally under a magistrate or *kadi*) and incorporated within the Sandžak of Skadar.

[63] See Andrijašević and Rastoder, *History of Montenegro*, pp. 51–2.

The war between Venice and Turkey continued till 1503, with Venice in a steadily weakening position and unable to render effective assistance to potential allies among the Montenegrin tribes. Under pressure many tribesmen transferred their allegiance to the Ottomans, who in this way gained possession of Grbalj (between Kotor and the sea) with its valuable salt mines. In 1513 or 1514 Ottoman predominance over Venice in the battle for influence in Montenegro was signalled by Sultan Bayezid II's appointment of Ivan's youngest son, the Islamicised Skanderbeg, as provincial governor of what was now declared to be the separate Sandžak of Montenegro. Like Serbia and Bosnia before it, Montenegro was now under Ottoman sway.

The fourteenth and fifteenth centuries as a whole

If the above account of events in the western Balkans in the fourteenth and fifteenth centuries has thrown up a confusing succession of rulers and battles, of alliances and betrayals, of towns and hostages taken and surrendered, the primary reason is that the period from the end of the fourteenth to the beginning of the sixteenth century was one of great and traumatic change in the whole of the Balkan region as the Ottomans were gradually defeating their opponents in Bulgaria, Serbia, Bosnia and Albania. Meanwhile, over roughly the same period, Venice was extending its control of the eastern shore of the Adriatic, an expansion that impacted directly on Zetan lands. As the fifteenth century progressed, little Zeta and its rulers were increasingly squeezed between two giants.

The second reason for the admitted preponderance of those traditional mainstays of historical narrative—battles and kings—is the dearth of information about everyday life in that period. Although we know quite a lot about the principal families and something of the clergy, we can be sure of very little about the life of the common people. Books and written records were few, and excepting some of the monks and the leading families, like Jelena Balšić[64] and Djuradj Crnojević, illiteracy was the norm. The lives of ordinary people were hard, less because they tilled the soil—most were pastoralists

---

[64] The author of a famous collection of letters known as the 'Gorica Anthology'. See below.

who moved frequently with their flocks—than because the harsh terrain and uncertain weather meant that reliable food supplies were short and they often lacked enough to eat. To the precarious nature of daily life could be added the danger of raiding by bands of marauders, often soldiers from the Ottoman armies, whose activities gradually pushed the population into the less fertile and more mountainous areas. As central authority weakened, the tribe or clan increasingly stepped in to organise defence, administer justice and fulfil any number of other essential roles.[65]

To an extent even more pronounced than in earlier periods, borders were porous with tribes wandering back and forth across each other's lands. When an early twentieth-century historian of Montenegro writes 'At no period probably in their history have the Serbs [the inhabitants of Zeta] and the Shkipetars [the Albanians] been brought into closer contact with one another than during the rule of the Balšas' we understand what he means, as we do when he regards 'that period of transition and expansion .... as furnishing in large measure, an explanation of the reason why certain common elements have permeated the manner and customs of both races'.[66] Of course, much too can be made of the broad topographical similarities which influence the way of life across the region and of continuing cultural interchange and even intermarriage at intervals over a much longer period. Nevertheless, the Zetans' exposure to Albanian influences at this stage in their history is an experience that finds no ready parallel among the Serbs.

At first the Balšići dynasty was able to exploit the growing instability around it in order to prosper. At its zenith its power extended over more land than was held by medieval Duklja. But already by the time of Djuradj II in the 1380s the Balšići's fortunes had begun to decline in consequence both of the growing insecurity of the times and of internal divisions and rivalries. But for all the turmoil the cultural achievements of the Balšići's seventy years of ascendancy were considerable. Djuradj I built a number of churches with accompanying monasteries on the islands in Lake Skadar. Here communities of monks produced liturgies, gospels, psalters and other devotional works notable for the quality of their illuminations. One

---

[65] Fine, *The Late Medieval Balkans*, pp. 415–16.
[66] Stevenson, *History of Montenegro*, p. 71.

of the most famous of these is *The Prologue of Gorica* (*gorice*, islands) produced 'on the island of the holy old man Makarije in the time of the generous lord Djuradj Bašilic'.[67] A work of special interest is the *Gorički Zbornik* (Gorica Anthology), a collection of the correspondence between Jelena Balšić, wife of Djuradj II and daughter of Prince Lazar, addressed to her spiritual mentor, the monk Nikon of Jerusalem in 1441–2, written after she had returned from Bosnia as a widow and become a nun. Although the collection was not illustrated, it has literary merit and is of particular significance in being the correspondence of a woman in an age when women's voices were seldom heard.

The monasteries and churches themselves were generally decorated with frescoes but because of their destruction we do not know whether they were in the Byzantine tradition of the preceding Nemanjić era or were influenced by the separate tradition of the 'Greek'[68] painters of the coast. As the Ottomans advanced, *scriptoria* were established further inland in monasteries around Bijelo Polje, Pljevlja and Morača. There copying and illumination were undertaken by some of the best painters of the day, continuing in some places even under Ottoman administration.

Meanwhile on the coast and at Kotor in particular a rich cultural and artistic life continued. Goldsmiths from Kotor enjoyed considerable prestige, even in Italy. Painting flourished there with the famous school of 'Greek' painters whose blend of Byzantine iconography with later techniques was a feature of their style. At times saints venerated in both the Catholic and the Orthodox traditions were portrayed on the same church walls with parallel inscriptions in Old Slavonic and Latin, an indication of the degree of religious interpenetration at the time. The most famous of these fifteenth century painters of the domestic school was the master Lovro Dobričević of Kotor, whose work reflects the transitional stage between the Gothic and the Early Renaissance. One of the best known of Dobričević's works, still extant, is the icon of Our Lady of the Rocks

[67] Now in the State Library in Berlin. Marković and Vujičić, *Cultural Monuments of Montenegro*, p. 64.

[68] Many of these painters were indeed Greek, but others were local painters whose work revealed the influence of earlier Byzantine artists. See Marković and Vujičić, *Cultural Monuments of Montenegro* (pp. 67–9) and below.

(*Gospoda od Škrpjela*), which adorns the altar of a little church sited on a small island in the Gulf of Kotor. Painters in Kotor worked with artists abroad—from Venice, of course, but also from Dubrovnik—, and their work was sent as far afield as Prague.[69]

Unlike the Balšići, the Crnojevići had little time or resources for the construction of churches, hard-pressed as they were by both the Venetians and the Ottomans. For the coastal towns too the menace of the ever-closer Turkish threat required the building and upkeep of fortifications, allowing less time and resources to be devoted to artistic undertakings and religious monuments. Further inland, the Crnojevići began to build fortresses, like the one at Djurdjevac, guarding the mountain pass above Budva, and the impressive redoubt at Žabljak.[70]

The world of the Crnojevići owed much to the relationship with Venice, fluctuating though that association proved to be. Paradoxically, however, their enduring legacy owes its existence to the Ottomans, whose unrelenting advance forced their acceptance of a way of life dedicated to pastoralism, tribalism and dogged resistance. In subsequent centuries, this way of life, which can be said to have been pioneered by the Crnojevići, became emblematic of Montenegro, and indeed is so closely associated with its people that all that had gone before seemed in comparison to carry little weight.

Unlike the Balšići (at least until Balša III), the Crnojevići were Orthodox. The definitive shift to Orthodoxy meant a turning away from what had at times been a shared Serb-Albanian culture in which both sides were often Catholic. Under the Crnojevići something of the Byzantine heritage lived on in an austere and simplified form, and this provided a frail connecting thread linking the past with the future. For many years the local nobility had tried to save what they had and preserve an ever-shrinking degree of autonomy, but in the end it was beyond their powers. When the last of their secular rulers set sail for Venice, the efforts of Montenegro's inhabitants were bent on survival.

[69] Marković and Vujičić, *Cultural Monuments of Montenegro*, p. 69.
[70] *Ibid.*, p. 56.

3. Clansmen and Empires

Montenegro of the sixteenth and seventeenth centuries is for historians the proverbial backwater. Given the absence of contemporary indigenous sources, this neglect is understandable,[1] but wherever possible an attempt should be made to fill the gap. These centuries, unsettled and violent as they mostly were, form an important link between the last years of Crnojević rule and the emergence of the small theocratic state that Montenegro became in the course of the eighteenth century.

The Ottoman expansion of the late fourteenth and fifteenth centuries had driven inhabitants of the valleys and plains of lower Zeta into the barren upland regions of the Dinaric mountains of modern Montenegro and eastern Hercegovina. Many of these areas were sufficiently remote and infertile to have escaped the feudal society characteristic of earlier Slav polities and supported only small populations living an austere patriarchal and pastoral way of life. Now they offered not only sanctuary for refugees but places where popu-

---

[1] This period is swiftly passed over in most foreign-language accounts of the Balkans. Historians from the region who do pay it some attention have been obliged to draw largely on the available sources in foreign archives, mostly Turkish or Venetian, and thus, unsurprisingly, devote the bulk of their attention to the Turco-Venetian wars of the period. The Dubrovnik historian Mavro Orbini left a detailed, if not always reliable, account in his *Il Regno degli Slavi* but this was printed in 1601 and therefore offers no information on the seventeenth century. Further information comes from Turkish documents, often from Ottoman censuses (*defteri*), or from Venetian chronicles and records, many of them compiled in Kotor, which was under Venetian rule for almost four centuries (1420–1797). For more detailed information on the Ottoman period, see Branislav Djurdjev, *Turska vlasta u Crnoj Gori u XVI i XVII veku* (Turkish power in Montenegro in the 16th and 17th Centuries), Sarajevo, 1953. For a recent perspective on the period I have drawn in this chapter on works by two Montenegrin historians—Dragoje Živković, *Istorija Crnogorskog Naroda* (2 vols), Cetinje, 1992, and Milinko Djurović, *Istorija Crne Gore* (3 vols), Titograd (Podgorica), 1967–75.

lations intermingled, introducing new blood and exchanging historical memories in a way that managed to keep some part of the past alive.[2] Deprived of their traditional leaders, newcomers to these unpromising regions fell back upon a simplified pattern of social and political life centred on small, semi-autonomous units—the tribe and its sub-unit, the clan.[3] The rugged terrain and a fluctuating population ensured the tribesmen's dependence on a way of life based on stock-breeding when they were not engaged as warriors or bandits. Materially the population lived at the edge of survival, but spiritually they sought comfort and cohesion in the preservation of their Orthodox religion. And wherever they could they sought outside help to protect their lands from domination by the Muslim conquerors. Taken together, these developments were of fundamental importance in shaping the future. Within the emerging tribal society of the sixteenth and seventeenth centuries, the distinctive ethos of Montenegro—warfare and resistance linked to support from an outside power—was beginning to develop.

Ottoman rule

As we saw in the previous chapter, the Crna Gora of the Crnojevići, in itself only a small part of the former state of Zeta, had become an Ottoman vassal state in 1481. But it was only at the end of the fifteenth century with the departure of the last Orthodox Crnojevići, the brothers Djuradj and Stefan, that this long-enduring enclave of Orthodox resistance came under direct Ottoman rule. Regions to the south, east and west of this last remnant of Crnojević territory— areas now part of modern Montenegro—had fallen to the Ottomans some fifty years earlier. Here half a century of occupation had allowed the conquerors to establish complete control over fertile

[2] Stevan K. Pavlowitch, *Serbia: the History behind the Name*, London: Hurst, 2002, p. 14.

[3] In using these terms I have chosen to translate the word *pleme* as 'tribe' and *bratstvo* as 'clan', following Christopher Boëhm, *Montenegrin Social Organisation and Values: A Political Ethnography of a Refuge Area Tribal Adaptation*, New York: AMS Press, 1983, pp. 42 and 52. Other writers prefer to translate *pleme* as clan and *bratstvo* as brotherhood but the latter, though a more literal translation of the Serbian, seems misleading for a group which can comprise some 250 members.

lands that included the foreshores of Lake Skadar and the Zeta and Bjelopavlićka valleys. The Ottomans had also overrun, though not in all cases secured, areas to the north and east of the small Crnojević enclave—the Brda or highlands immediately to the north, the lands around Nikšić, and those in the vicinity of the settlements of Pljevlja and Bijelo Polje. Here, following the customary pattern of imperial administration, they established *timars* (feudal estates) on which they settled *sipahis*[4] (Ottoman feudal knights), who in return incurred certain military and fiscal obligations and owed allegiance to the sultan. Although the Ottomans had not secured control of Venetian possessions along the coast, by 1497 they had established a foothold on the central coast at Grbalj near Kotor—a region valued both for its strategic importance to the town and for its productive salt mines. Protected by massive walls, Kotor itself continued to hold out against repeated attempts at capture and occupation, although at times it had to pay tariffs to the sultan.

In 1503, after several years of warfare, the Venetians signed a peace treaty with Sultan Bayezid II under which they formally recognised Ottoman authority over all former Crnojević lands. At first the Ottomans were content to annex this territory, which they called by its Turkish name Kara Darg, to the *sanjak*[5] of Skadar (or Shkodra).[6] For administrative convenience it was originally placed under the direct control of the Skadar *sanjak-bey's*[7] deputy or *subashi*, based in the former Zetan centre of Žabljak, but by 1513 Montenegro had become a *sanjak* in its own right under the control of Skanderbeg, Ivan Crnojević's Islamicised youngest son. The total area under Skanderbeg's administration consisted of six or seven sub-districts, known in Turkish as *nahiye* (Serb. *nahija*). From the beginning there

---

[4] Initially some of the *sipahis* were Christians, former landowners, such as the family who, at the end of the sixteenth century, sponsored the building of the Pljevlja monastery (then in the *sanjak* of Novi Pazar but now in modern Montenegro). Gradually, however, these Christian *sipahis* either died out or converted to Islam. See Malcolm, *Kosovo*, pp. 97–8, and Ćirković, *The Serbs*, pp. 112–13.

[5] A subdivision of an *eyalet* or province of the Ottoman Empire, originally corresponding to a military district.

[6] The Skadar *sanjak* extended over a large area, from the coast as far inland beyond Peć and western Kosovo (Metohija).

[7] The administrator of a *sanjak*.

were differences in the 'subject' people's attitude to the conquerors: while those in the more accessible areas could hardly avoid compliance, the population of the most recently conquered region— an area just inland from the Adriatic and in the shadow of the mighty Mount Lovćen—proved far less yielding. This barren area of karstic limestone, roughly no more than 30 by 60 km. in extent,[8] derived a paradoxical benefit from its unpromising geography. To begin with, its proximity to the Venetian-controlled coast provided an important yet easily defensible gateway to the non-Ottoman world. Moreover, an area so mountainous and infertile was scarcely worth the trouble of subduing and holding it, a fact its inhabitants were quick to exploit. Therein lies the historical importance of the 'Under Lovćen' region.[9] Although in the sixteenth century it was not the 'eagle's nest of freedom' romantic historians and mythmakers later proclaimed it to be, this rocky heartland already provided a kernel of separateness from which the future independent principality of Montenegro would grow. It is this area that, for the next two centuries until its union with the Brda, can accurately be referred to as Old Montenegro.

The Ottomans may at first have believed that their appointment of Skanderbeg as ruler of the former Crnojević lands would significantly assist their occupation of the region. Not only might his Crnojević background help to conciliate the fractious Montenegrin tribesmen, but to the Venetians it could even, and for the same reason, represent him as continuing the rule of their former allies. Skanderbeg did indeed play a skilful hand in dealings with his neighbours, but his treatment of the native Montenegrins was harsh. In the lands they had previously overrun the Ottomans had built garrison towns and fortresses such as those at Podgorica and Medun, outposts from which they now attempted to control their new and less easily secured territories.[10] But success was not always guar-

---

[8] This area comprised four *nahije*: Katuni, Rijeka, Crmnica and Lješnjani. Each *nahija* was further sub-divided into tribes, Katuni having nine tribes, Rijeka five, Crmnica seven and Lješnjani, being incomplete, only three.

[9] Some Montenegrin sources refer to this core area as 'Under Lovćen' Montenegro but for anglophone readers the commonly-used designation 'Old Montenegro' seems preferable.

[10] Živković, *Istorija Crnogorskog Naroda*, vol. 2, pp. 14–15.

anteed or, when it came, necessarily lasting. When, almost a century and a half later, the Turkish traveller and writer Evlija Çelebi broke his journey at 'the merciless fortress of Podgorica, which is at the extreme frontier', he admired the size and structure of the fortress but noted that its seven hundred 'doughty *ghazis*' were occupied in 'battling day and night' against their enemies, among whom he numbered not only the population of Kotor but also 'the Albanian [*sic*] infidels of…Kelmendi and Montenegro'.[11]

The Ottoman response to resistance included reform as well as punishment. In 1523 the Ottoman administration promulgated a legal code, the *kanun-nama*, which regulated taxes, fixed conditions of labour—for instance, the population had to provide fifteen days labour in the salt mines at Grbalj—and laid down penalties for particular crimes. As time went on the Ottoman administration resigned itself to taking a more pragmatic approach to the issue of taxation. Recognising that the infertility of such an 'impassable mountainous country'[12] made payment of their dues in taxes or in tithes difficult for the tribesmen, the Ottomans resorted to designating them 'free Vlachs' who were obliged to pay only an annual tax of a gold coin (*filurya*) for each household (hence the term *filurdjis*) instead of the customary poll tax (*haraç*) and duties on livestock and produce.[13] Far from eliciting loyalty, any concessions by the conquerors were viewed by Montenegrins as evidence of their special status, and subsequent attempts to curtail some of the 'privileges' were met with a rejection that would in time mature into open revolt.[14] Although taxes were periodically collected and conditions of labour fulfilled, some of the population preferred to decamp to the neighbouring Venetian territories.[15] Still the sit-

---

[11] Robert Dankoff and Robert Elsie (eds), *Evliya Çelebi in Albania and Adjacent Regions (Kosovo, Montenegro, Ohrid)*, Leiden: E. J. Brill, 2000, pp. 47–9.

[12] Quoted from Turkish document of 1523. See 'Serb land of Montenegro', www.njegos.org/mnhistory/hist1.htm, accessed on 08/04/2005.

[13] Ćirković, *The Serbs*, p. 113.

[14] Banac, *The National Question*, p. 271. See also B. Djurdjev, 'Karadagh' in *Encyclopaedia of Islam*, 2nd edn, ed. H. A. R. Gibb, J. H. Kramers, E. Levi-Provençal and J. Schacht, vol. IV, pp. 574–5. See also Djurović, *Istorija Crne Gore*, vol. 2, p. 36.

[15] Oppression by the Ottoman authorities was not, however, the only cause of population displacement. Djurović (*Istorija Crne Gore*, vol. 2, pp. 41–3) notes that the population increased in the central Katuni *nahija* from 665 households in

uation remained unsatisfactory. Skanderbeg's death in 1528 or 1530 led to further tinkering with the system as the Ottoman administration annulled Montenegro's separate status, attaching it first to the *sanjak* of Skadar, then to the *sanjaks* of Dukadjin and Hercegovina, and finally, when presumably these experiments too proved a failure, back to Skadar. Revolt, when it occurred, was punished harshly. When in 1565 the tribes of the outlying regions—the Piperi, Bratonožići and Kuči—refused to pay their taxes and took up arms, the Ottoman state ordered the execution of the men involved and the enslavement of their wives and children.[16]

The Ottomans' lack of success in the mountains of Montenegro was certainly an irritant, yet it counted for far less than their interest in gaining territory along the Adriatic coast. And here as the sixteenth century progressed they began to see signs of progress. While the peace agreement of 1503 may have secured a respite for Venice, it in fact marked a turning-point in relations between Venice and the Ottoman Empire as the Ottoman fleets began to challenge Christian dominance on the seas, just as their armies had done over a century earlier on land.[17] For all his advances north of the Danube and forays into the Adriatic, Sultan Bayezid II had devoted much of his reign to consolidating Ottoman conquests. His successors, Selim I and Suleiman I (the Magnificent), pursued more aggressive policies, defeating their enemies in Asia before turning their attention once again to Europe. After conquering Belgrade in 1521, Suleiman was led by his ambitions to challenge the Christian powers throughout the Mediterranean, including the Albanian and Dalmatian coasts.

In 1538 an Ottoman victory at Preveza,[18] a Turkish stronghold on the coast of western Greece, further turned the tide in the empire's favour. Kotor came under siege and only managed to survive thanks in part to provisioning supplied by Montenegrins. The following year, building on the Ottoman victory, the notorious pirate chief and captain Barbarossa (Khayreddin), by this time in the service of

---

1523 to 861 households in 1570, suggesting that this population increase put pressure on land and hence drove the population to leave.

[16] Djurović, *Istorija Crne Gore*, vol. 2, p. 40.

[17] *Encyclopaedia Britannica*, vol. 28, 'Turkey and Ancient Anatolia', p. 923.

[18] It was here at the Battle of Actium 1,569 years earlier that the young Octavian won a great naval victory over Antony and Cleopatra.

the sultan, recaptured the town of Novi, decimating the defending Spanish garrison. However, Kotor was more fortunate, resisting the huge invading force with which Barbarossa attempted to take the town.

War broke out again in 1570 when the sultan sent a letter to Venice demanding the surrender of the island of Cyprus, in reality a prelude to a renewed campaign of conquest. Although other European powers joined in alliance against the Ottomans, Venice was forced to yield Cyprus in order to concentrate on defending its possessions along the Adriatic coast, which now came under Ottoman attack. Ulcinj, Bar, Spič and Budva sent emissaries to Venice with pleas for military assistance and for food since the population was in the grip of famine. Kotor too was suffering after an outbreak of the bubonic plague struck the town, killing at least 3,500 people. Perhaps afraid of the plague, the Ottoman commander Ferhat Pasha, instead of attacking Kotor, sailed the fleet south to Ulcinj, defeating a mercenary force of Italians and French Huguenots and capturing the town. On hearing this both Bar and Spič, further up the coast, surrendered without a fight. Only the Paštrovići tribe of Budva resisted and saw its town destroyed in consequence.

The balance appeared to shift with the Christian victory at the battle of Lepanto in October 1571 when the fleet of the Holy League, commanded by Don Juan of Austria, half-brother of Philip II of Spain, defeated the Ottoman fleet at the mouth of the Gulf of Patras. The success of the Christian alliance at this famous battle owed a debt to the seamen of the Gulf of Kotor: men from the small town of Perast on the northern side of the Gulf piloted the Venetian galleys. The pilot of Don Juan's own ship was a sea captain from Perast, Petar Marković.[19]

Lepanto was hailed as a great Christian victory, yet it conferred no obvious strategic advantage and one of its consequences was to prove a lasting thorn in the side of Venice. Fighting on the side of the sultan, the Barbary pirate chief turned Ottoman admiral, Uluz Ali Pasha, succeeded in avoiding the fate of the rest of the Ottoman fleet[20] by sailing into the Adriatic as far as Ulcinj with thirty surviving galleys. For the next 200 years Uluz Ali's followers and their

[19] Djurović, *Istorija Crne Gore*, vol. 2, pp. 52–3.
[20] Lovett F. Edwards, *The Yugoslav Coast*, London: Batsford, 1974, pp. 71–2.

descendants, often using ships manned by slaves, made Ulcinj a by-word for piracy. Focused as they were on attacking Christian ships and towns on both sides of the Adriatic, the pirates' activities were tolerated and even encouraged by the Ottoman state.

The following year, 1572, the Ottomans were again on the offensive, this time against Kotor. Aware of the gravity of the threat, Venice sought to enlist the support of both Montenegrins and Albanians. The Albanians failed to respond, but the Montenegrins offered limited support with tribesmen helping to bring supplies into the town. Though weakened by plague, the citizens of Kotor managed to hold out till 1573 when a renewed force of Venetian troops, assisted by a fleet of twenty-two galleons, succeeded in raising the siege.

For a brief moment these victories raised hopes that the Ottomans might be ejected from the Adriatic, but it was soon apparent that Venice was emerging from the wars as the net loser. The Ottomans had captured Cyprus. Less important perhaps but still critical for the future of Montenegro and the coast, they had secured possession of all the coastal region south of Budva, although it was not till March 1573 that Venetian emissaries signed a peace treaty with the sultan, giving formal recognition to the changed situation. Cut off from Venice and under the shadow of the nearby pirates of Ulcinj, the once important town of Bar fell into decay.

Situated on the fringes of two great empires, the tribesmen of Montenegro and the surrounding areas could not escape the effects of the Christian powers' struggles against the Ottomans. Even in times of relative peace the Montenegrins' relations with their Ottoman overlords were characterised by a high degree of insecurity, which could be the result of ambitious Ottoman feudatories seeking to extend or pacify the areas under their control, sometimes in direct retaliation for raids they had in fact carried out themselves. In such cases retribution might range from the destruction of livestock or property to killing and the kidnapping of women and children. Just how precarious existence could be for such people is well illustrated in an account by an anonymous agent of the Venetian government whose diary for the years between 1571 and 1574 is quoted extensively by the nineteenth-century writer and traveller Sir John Gardner Wilkinson. At one point the diarist records the fate of members of the Paštrovići tribe who, continuing to resist Ottoman demands, had appealed to the Venetian *provveditore* in nearby Cattaro (Kotor) to afford them the protection they had received in the past. Having sought and received assurances from the *provveditore*, the emissaries for the Paštrovići departed, only to return to Kotor several days later to give the following account:

Eighty of the enemy's cavalry have invaded the valleys which skirt our district, and have begun to levy tax, as from their captive subjects, with threats of burning houses, corn, and everything else, if it be not paid; and… they were advancing further up the country when our people raised the alarm, and rang the bells from one village to the other. All is fighting and confusion. We belong to the Serene Republic, and we trusted that the peace would surely include us poor Pastrovichi also; but it seems not; and none can tell where the storm will end.[21]

Even beyond the evident threat to life and property, the Ottoman advance and the loss of easy access to much of the coast increased the Montenegrins' dependence on Venetian-controlled Kotor. Lacking an artisan class, the mountaineers relied principally on the coastal population for the supply of essential goods such as textiles, ceramic wares and especially weapons.[22] Indeed the trade was vital to both sides since Kotor was heavily dependent, particularly during times of siege, on primary produce—dried meat, skins, cheese, honey, wax and timber—brought in from Montenegro. The resulting connections were close, the more so since many Montenegrins found employment as domestics or guards in the noble houses of Kotor. A number of the women, having come to trade or act as servants, remained to marry and became Catholics.

While Montenegro's position, astride yet another fault-line, imposed both constraints and dangers, it was clearly not always detrimental to Montenegrin interests. For example, Montenegrins often acted as couriers, maintaining a link between the Ottomans and Venice despite long periods of warfare. Venetian merchants needed to be in constant communication with their agents in Constan-

[21] Quoted by John Gardner Wilkinson, *Dalmatia and Montenegro*, 3 vols (facsimile of edition published by John Murray, London, 1848), Elibron Classics replica edition, vol. 2, pp. 330–1.

[22] Montenegrins also made use, although to a lesser extent, of the Ottoman markets in towns such as Podgorica, Bijelo Polje and Pljevlja, but such relations were frequently disturbed by banditry or periods of outright warfare.

tinople, and entrusted their despatches from Venice to Montenegrin messengers who secured their safe passage through Ottoman territories by means of guarantees and protection paid for by Venetian gold. The route, from Kotor to Priština, crossed the mountains of Hercegovina but with the passage of time this route was felt to be too slow and in 1612 a Venetian from Kotor, Marino Bolizza, was charged with developing a new route. Messengers would then travel from Kotor to the former Constantinople now Istanbul, crossing the territory of the warlike Kuči and Klimenti tribes along the mountainous borders of Kosovo, and on through Peć to Priština, Philippopolis and Adrianople, taking only eighteen days to complete the journey. Ultimately this route was found to be too insecure with the result that the couriers returned to the older, slower route.[23] But this change was only made after many costly incidents; mostly the service continued in spite of war. A sixteenth-century traveller, Fynes Moryson, writing from Dubrovnik (Ragusa) in 1595, recalled: 'When we inquired of the way from Raguza [*sic*] to Constantinople by land, all the Postes and Messengers passing that way told us that the warre of Hungarie made all those parts full of tragedies and miserie.'[24]

But if Montenegro's borderland position made a degree of contact with both empires inevitable, it might also have been expected—given the climate of the times—to lead to their direct involvement in the fighting. From the Venetian point of view, both the tribesmen's evident hostility to Ottoman rule and their close links with Kotor meant that Montenegro's involvement as an ally was likely to be welcome. But while such prospects stirred hope, the results were generally nugatory—and not only where they involved Montenegro's relations with the Venetians. At different times during the Austro-Ottoman war of 1593–1606 agents of the Pope[25] and

[23] Stevenson, *History of Montenegro*, pp. 109–10. While the Kuči were Orthodox and later joined Montenegro, and the Klimenti (also known as Kelmendi) were Catholic, both tribes frequently fought together against first the Ottomans and later the Austrians in an attempt to preserve their quasi-independent status and a way of life based on raiding and stock-herding.

[24] *Ibid*, p. 111. The Habsburg-Ottoman war of 1593–1606 saw much of central Hungary taken by the Austrians only to be restored to Ottoman rule after the signing of the treaty of Zsitvatorok in 1606.

[25] Clement VIII (1593–1605) despatched emissaries to carry letters addressed by the Hungarian King Rudolf II to the then Montenegrin Metropolitan, Ruvim

other Christian statesmen urged both the Albanian and Montenegrin clans to revolt in the hope that this would precipitate a wider uprising leading to the eventual overthrow of Ottoman rule. Plans were hatched and emissaries, sometimes including priests, travelled to and fro between Naples, where the Spanish viceroy was to lend support, and the chiefs of the mountainous regions straddling Hercegovina and Montenegro.[26] But while local tribal leaders were prepared to exploit any opportunity that might secure the restoration of their own privileges and the restoration of the powers and property of the monasteries, they were destined to be disappointed when their foreign allies failed to provide the sustained backing needed for such rebellions to succeed. One such revolt in 1597, led by Grdan, *vojvoda* of Nikšić, spread quickly over a large area from Nikšić to Lake Skadar, but ended in failure when outside support originally promised by the Holy League disappeared following Austria's conclusion of a peace treaty with the Ottoman Empire.[27]

Clans and chiefs

The course of the Habsburg-Ottoman war, though ultimately indecisive, exposed to the European powers the weakness of the Ottoman state. For the first time since beginning its march into Europe Ottoman expansion stalled, forcing the authorities to undertake a review of practices and policies within the empire. This in turn led to renewed attempts to secure the empire's borderlands, among which was the karst region of Old Montenegro. Thus prompted, local Ottoman officials attempted to strip away the population's privileges, bringing their position closer to that of subject peoples elsewhere. In part too they were determined to control the tribesmen's constant raiding of their lands, a practice which stemmed from many years of warfare and endemic poverty. Ironically the long-term consequence of this more punitive approach was to propel the

---

II, in which he requested the participation of the Montenegrins in an uprising against the Ottomans, which failed to materialise. (See Živković, *Istorija Crnogorskog Naroda*, vol. 2, pp. 38–9).

[26] Ćirković, *The Serbs*, p. 142.

[27] Živković, *Istorija Crnogorskog Naroda*, vol. 2, pp. 38–40. See also Ćirković, *ibid*.

tribesmen towards greater social and political unity as a means of self-defence.[28]

From the fifteenth century onwards the Ottoman policy of indirect rule had left day-to-day control in the hands of the tribal leaders, with the rank of *knez* (prince or duke) *or vojvoda* (clan chief, often a military leader). Beneath the tribes (*pleme*) were smaller units or clans (*bratstvo*) consisting of families who traced their descent from a putative common ancestor in the male line with defined links to a specific piece of territory[29]; ancestors through the female line did not count and marriage took place outside the clan. While small family plots could be held individually, water and grazing lands were held communally. The *bratstvo* was the most important unit, not only socially and politically but also militarily; in a society practising the blood feud, it was also the basis of the feuding group. Almost anything, it seemed, could be the cause of bloodshed—raiding, a broken engagement, a woman running away from her husband, an abduction, a killing. Often the motive appeared unimportant; it was enough that honour had been slighted. Obviously the blood feud was costly and worked against a broader sense of social unity. Yet in other ways the clan system was a useful adaptation, and it extended well beyond the borders of modern Montenegro into the mountainous regions of northern Albania and Hercegovina. It not only suited the semi-nomadic way of life made necessary by the lack of suitable land for cultivation or permanent grazing, but also engendered strong bonds of social solidarity that were of great value in times of war. This was partly because it embodied a rudimentary democracy: local assemblies of adult males elected the leaders of clan and tribe on the basis of qualities—physical strength, skill in warfare, courage—which in the climate of those times best served the interests of the group. Tribal solidarity, as the Balkan historian Ivo Banac points out, gave rise to 'a hierarchy of valour' which in turn enabled the Montenegrins 'to hold their own against the Turks in centuries of mutual ravage'.[30]

Above the level of the clan and tribe, at least within Old Montenegro, a measure of co-ordination had begun to be achieved through

---

[28] Banac, *The National Question*, p. 271.

[29] On the structure of clan society in Montenegro see Boehm, *Montenegrin Social Organisation*, especially pp. 40–8.

[30] *Ibid.*, p. 272.

a council of chiefs known as the *glavarski zbor*. There was also a general assembly (*opšti zbor*), which consisted of all adult males and usually convened only once a year, initially on the day of the nativity of the Virgin and later on a national saint's day. But for all this Montenegro at this stage lacked a strong form of central leadership, just as it lacked almost all the characteristic institutions of a state.

The Orthodox Church under the Ottomans

The one institution that had flourished from the early days of the country's existence was the Orthodox Church. When and how the story originated is hard to tell, but it was soon accepted lore that Ivan or his son Djuradj had entrusted the people's fate not to any representative of the sultan but to the Vladika or metropolitan of Cetinje. Soon this tale was being further embellished by myths linking the Cetinje monastery and the clans belonging to the Katuni *nahija* around Cetinje in particular to a more remote and glorious past. The idea was to prove a powerful one. Milovan Djilas, writing more as a romantic Montenegrin than a hard-headed Communist, explained:

The great myths—a doomed Serbia, the flight of its nobility into the Montenegrin mountains after the fall of the empire at Kosovo, the duty to avenge Kosovo, Miloš Obilić's sacrifice, the irreconcilable struggle between Cross and Crescent, the Turks as an absolute evil pervading the entire Serbian nation—all these myths took on their sharpest and most implacable aspects here, among the men of Katuni. Here these sentiments went beyond and above all others. Obilić and Kosovo were not something that happened some time ago and far away, but they were here—in daily thoughts and feelings and life and struggle with the Turks. It was a struggle against extermination—for the survival of the clan—in which faith and nationality, the Cross and freedom, were more perfectly merged than in any other province and anywhere else in the Balkans.[31]

For early generations perhaps such foundation myths helped to erase the bitter memory of Skanderbeg and the Turks and restore a sense of 'national' dignity. But such a move was also politically astute since the Ottoman system allowed only religious figures and not civil ones to serve as leaders of subject peoples.[32] Naturally the link with the

[31] Milovan Djilas, *Njegoš: Poet, Prince, Bishop*, p. 11.
[32] This was the Ottoman *millet* system according to which a community was distinguished exclusively by its religious affiliation: e.g. Muslim, Orthodox, Jewish.

Crnojevići helped to ensure that the immediate focus of religious life remained the monastery at Cetinje. Moreover, the choice of Cetinje—too wild and barren to support an outside force, yet within a hard day's march of the outside world—made excellent strategic sense, as Ivan Crnojević knew. Thus Cetinje was the centre of the Montenegrin nation, and its inhabitants—members of the Njeguši tribe of the Katuni *nahija*—in the future were to provide the leadership, first elective and later hereditary, of the state. At this stage the Vladika was not appointed by the Patriarchate of Peć, which had been abolished, but elected from different families by the chieftains meeting as representatives of their tribes in the *glavarski zbor* and approved by the general assembly.[33] This not only helped to ensure his independence, but it further ensured that he himself would possess qualities which were valued by the tribesmen, qualities which were likely to be political and military as much as spiritual.

Gradually the church grew stronger. In 1557 Bayezid's grandson Suleiman II, under the influence of his Bosnian-born son-in-law, the Grand Vizier Mehmet Pasha Sokolović, permitted the restoration of the Orthodox patriarchate to its traditional see at Peć. Under the leadership of the new Patriarch Makarije, a kinsman of Sokolović, its jurisdiction included large parts of the South Slav Orthodox world extending from Bulgaria and Macedonia in the south and east, through Serbia, to Bosnia-Hercegovina and Montenegro in the north and west.

The year 1557 was also marked by the issuing of an Ottoman *firman* (decree), which allowed the restoration of Orthodox churches while prohibiting the building of new ones. Not only in Montenegro proper but also in the Brda and beyond in the regions bordering on Hercegovina churches began to be restored, and new monasteries erected secretly on the foundations of the old. In a

---

The heads of the religious community were allowed a considerable degree of control over the flock's daily life provided this did not interfere with the basic Ottoman requirements in terms of taxation and military service.

[33] After the restoration of the Patriarchate at Peć in 1557 the choice was normally validated by the patriarch. Still later, Montenegrin metropolitans travelled to Moscow where their ordination was confirmed by the Russian patriarch. See below.

primitive world such churches and monasteries were centres of learning and cultural influence and, like the Morača monastery on the edge of the canyon of that name near Kolašin, kept a sense of separate identity and ethnic consciousness alive.

Rebels and retribution

The response of the Ottomans to the progressive strengthening of the ecclesiastical institutions and leadership was an attempt to alter the pattern of settlement in the hope of diluting Orthodox and clan identity. Indeed for a time they trusted in re-population rather than military means as a way of pacifying the local inhabitants. This worked well enough in the plains around Podgorica and along the river valleys where, alongside fortresses and barracks, the Ottomans or their Muslim subjects took over fisheries and fertile lands and built mosques and *medrese* (theological schools), but was not appropriate in the region's more barren areas. Here the tribesmen's persistent raiding and insubordination proved too much to bear and from the late sixteenth century onwards the local Ottoman lords turned increasingly to punitive expeditions to crush resistance and enforce payment of taxes. Banditry—attacks on caravans and settlements as well as stock-raiding—had been endemic in the pastoral life of poor and mountainous regions of the Balkans since the earliest times. The bandits known as *hajduks* (outlaws) ranged widely, sometimes travelling as far as the Sandžak, Kosovo and Macedonia and even into Bulgaria. Banditry was not confined to native Montenegrins attacking wealthy Muslims: the tribesmen often stole each other's cattle and women, a practice that, as we have seen, gave rise to the blood feud. But the Ottoman conquest was to impart another dimension. As in early Norman England, the relationship between the outlaws and those they robbed was generally that of subjects to rulers and this, at least in popular culture, facilitated the transition from bandit to freedom fighter. Like the English outlaws in the time of Robin Hood and the Scottish cateran, the Balkan *hajduk* emerges as a romanticised figure, celebrated in song and poetry from the fifteenth century onwards. Here too Montenegrin society appears to provide the template for the Balkans. The *hajduk* was equally part of Serbian society, but the Montenegrin version was, in John Allcock's words, somehow 'nobler'.[34]

However, *hajduks* were not the only outlaws to plague the conquerors in the sixteenth and seventeenth centuries. Concurrently with these outlaws, who operated in lands fully or partly under the control of the the Ottoman state, the empire's expansion had caused a further class of dispossessed people to emerge, known as *uskoks*[35] (defectors or refugees), who, having fled in large numbers from Ottoman rule in the early sixteenth century, established their principal settlement at Senj on the Croatian coast. Here and in a number of smaller coastal settlements in Venetian-ruled territory they were joined after each subsequent bout of fighting by other refugees from Montenegro and Hercegovina fleeing hunger and the consequences of war. With no means of support and cut off from the native mountains many of these refugees became pirates, preying on ships that plied up and down the Adriatic coast;—originally these were largely Turkish, but later also included those of their former Venetian allies. Within a short time the *uskoks* had become excellent seamen, even developing their own light and shallow-drafted galleys—*braceras*—which easily outstripped the slower Venetian vessels.[36] Soon the inhabitants of nearby Dubrovnik and other coastal towns on both sides of the Adriatic were suffering from their depredations, although in their own eyes the *uskoks* were continuing the glorious tradition of outlawry in the spirit of the *hajduk*. The havoc wreaked by the *uskoks* reached a high point in the first quarter of the seventeenth century when they raided as far away as Istria and, on one occasion, Venice itself.[37] Their continued raiding unleashed the

---

[34] The role of the *hajduk* is discussed by John Allcock in *Explaining Yugoslavia*, pp. 531–7. Many of the most famous Serbian *hajduks* came from mountain regions either within or bordering Montenegro. The progenitor of the first Serbian national uprising, Karadjordje Petrović, or Black George, was originally from the Vasojevići tribe of the Lim valley region, while his rival, Miloš Obrenović, leader of the second Serbian uprising of 1813, came from stock originating in the Bratonožići tribe of the Brda. See Banac, *The National Question*, p. 45.

[35] As the Balkan scholar, Lovett F. Edwards, explains, the term *uskok* derives from a verb meaning 'to leap over' and originally referred to people who had fled across the borders into what was still Christian-controlled territory to escape Ottoman domination (*The Yugoslav Coast*, London: Batsford, 1974, p. 61).

[36] *Ibid.*, p. 63.

[37] *Ibid.*, p. 69.

Uskok war of 1615–17 when, not without considerable difficulty, a combined force of Venetian and Austrian troops succeeded in defeating them, burning their ships and securing their forcible movement inland to the districts of Otočac and Žumberak where they were resettled by the Austrians to form part of the force guarding the southern frontier against the Ottomans.[38]

Both *hajduks* and *uskoks* had largely emerged not from the Montenegrin heartland around Cetinje but from tribes of the Brda and the regions adjoining eastern Hercegovina. Throughout the period of renewed confrontation with Ottoman overlords, which had begun towards the end of the sixteenth century, clans from these areas were to prove more warlike and rebellious than their counterparts from Old Montenegro. Possibly this was because the Brda region, though equally mountainous, was, as we have seen, somewhat more productive than the area of 'Under Lovćen' Montenegro and thus of greater value to neighbouring Ottoman potentates. Whatever the reason, the exploits of the Brda tribesmen were often impressive: they inflicted defeats and at times even instigated revolts which spread as far as areas that are today in Serbia. In an attempt to reduce banditry and force the highlanders to pay taxes, local Ottoman feudatories launched punitive expeditions, but any success was usually short-lived. For all this the highland tribesmen's efforts suffered from a lack of unity that prevented them from consolidating any temporary gains, while in contrast the population of Old Montenegro were further advanced in this respect and inching their way towards a more unified form of resistance. A significant step was taken when, in 1603, the Montenegrins inflicted a major defeat on Ali Beg Memibegović, *sanjak-bey* of Skadar at Lješkopolje, wounding him and killing his deputy.[39] The event might have been just one of many such encounters between Montenegrins and Ottoman forces occurring at this time had the Montenegrins on this occasion not been led into battle for the first time by the Vladika, Ruvim II. This combination of military and ecclesiastical roles in the person of the Vladika was to become one of the distinguishing features of Montenegrin society, persisting till 1852 when the then ruler of Montenegro, Danilo, opted to become a secular prince in order to marry.[40]

---

[38] *Ibid.*, p. 70.
[39] Živković, *Istorija Crnogorskog Naroda*, vol. 2, p. 42.
[40] See Chapter 7 below.

Shortly after his defeat at the hands of the Montenegrins, Ali Beg was replaced as *sanjak-bey* of Skadar by Mustafa-beg, who at first took a less belligerent approach to Montenegro. Nevertheless the pattern of sporadic conflict between Montenegrins and the Ottomans continued as other Muslim lords such as Ibrahim, Pasha of Bosnia, went on the offensive against the tribes of the Brda and the border area with Hercegovina in an attempt to enforce the payment of taxes. Figures of 40–60,000 soldiers given by Venetian sources for an expedition of 1611 are scarcely credible,[41] but irrespective of numbers the pasha achieved meagre results in revenue and pacification for the effort expended. As time went on, the almost constant skirmishing with its toll in lives and burnt settlements led the Christian tribes to hope once again for a larger war between the Ottomans and the Christian powers. Yet when war came, it was far from proving the panacea that the Montenegrins anticipated.

The Candian war (1645–69)

In 1645 the Ottoman Empire was again at war with Venice, provoked on this occasion by Turkish designs on the island of Crete. In Montenegro the renewed warfare was seen as an opportunity. Naively over-estimating the political and military power of Venice at a time when it had declined considerably, the Montenegrins prepared to engage on its side. Early successes appeared to justify their hopes as in February 1649 first Risan on the Gulf of Kotor and then Nikšić and the surrounding areas were wrested from the Ottomans. But an attempted attack on Podgorica in which the Montenegrins, possibly short of food and armaments, did not take part, ended in failure. The consequent cooling of relations with Venice suggested that the Republic and Montenegro would drift apart, but in the event the Venetians' decision in April 1649 to pay a number of prominent Montenegrins a small monthly retainer was enough to keep the chiefs on side.

None of this sufficed to keep the Ottomans at bay for long. Not only did they soon recapture the areas previously taken by the Venetians and Montenegrins, but spurred on by a vigorous leader, Ali Pasha Čengić, they built a fortress at Kolašin and opened a new front

---

[41] Živković, *Istorija Crnogorskog Naroda*, vol. 2, p. 44.

to the north-west. The response of the Venetians was characteristically devious. They set about implicating Ali Pasha and another
Ottoman *bey* in a web of corruption and intrigue sufficient to
convince Istanbul that their feudatories had gone over to the other
side. Under pressure and facing replacement, Ali Pasha unleashed a
series of brutal attacks on the local population, and as the wave of
reprisals widened to include territory near Kotor the town itself
came under threat of renewed siege.

For some time Kotor, penetrated by enemy agents, had been alive
with rumours of impending attack. Other accounts suggest that the
tribesmen of Old Montenegro and the Brda were now fully under
Ottoman control and prepared to join the siege on the enemy side.[42]
In the summer of 1657 Sultan Mehmed IV ordered Ali Pasha Čengić and his counterpart from Skadar, Mehmed Pasha Varlac, to sur-
round the town with 10,000 troops, but as on earlier occasions
Kotor's walls and the bravery of its defenders, as much as the enemy's
lack of adequate siege equipment, succeeded in thwarting the
attackers. When after twenty-two days the siege was abandoned on 1
October 1657, all the church bells of Kotor rang in celebration of
the town's deliverance.[43] Within the decade many of these churches
were no longer standing. On the afternoon of 6 April 1667 Kotor
was struck by a devastating earthquake—the worst in its history.
Along with the churches and many fine civic buildings, three-quar-
ters of the town's dwellings were reduced to rubble. There were many
deaths not only in Kotor but in the nearby towns of Budva, Novi
and Perast as well as in villages around the Gulf of Kotor.

With Kotor freed from danger, the way was opened for a strengthening of the relationship between Venice and the different Montenegrin and Brda tribes. In November 1657 chiefs from Nikšić and
from the tribes of the regions of the Morača and Tara rivers sent representatives to Venice to offer their services against the Ottomans
in exchange for money and arms. Three years later in 1660 the Vladika of Cetinje, Visarion Kolinović, sent his own emissaries to the
provveditore of Kotor, offering his people's help in fighting the
Ottomans on similar terms. In December that year Montenegro and
Venice signed a treaty of military co-operation under which the

[42] *Ibid.*, p. 54. See also Andrijašević and Rastoder, *History of Montenegro*, p. 66.
[43] *Ibid.*

Montenegrins promised to defend the borders of La Serenissima against Ottoman attack.

But if the situation was improving for the tribesmen of Old Montenegro and Brda regions, the same could not be said for neighbouring Hercegovina and the surrounding areas. In this wild part of Dalmatia the Ottoman offensive continued unabated and in 1651 the monastery of Tvrdos in the Zahumska area of Hercegovina came under attack. In fear for his life the Metropolitan Vasilije Jovanović fled first to nearby Nikšić before finding refuge in a cave in the face of Mount Ostrog at some distance beyond the town. Here, at a site that commanded an immense view over the plain below, Vasilije and his followers cut a small chapel deep into the face of the cliff. Vasilije was to spend the remaining fifteen years of his life in the monastery he founded at Ostrog, where he began to acquire a reputation as a miracle worker. On his death stories of further miracles began to circulate. A vine was said to have sprouted from the stony ground around his burial place, and the wife of his enemy the Pasha of Sarajevo was apparently cured of painful and debilitating illness thanks to his intercession. Seven years after his death monks opened his grave and discovered his body wholly uncorrupted, and he was declared a saint. Today he remains the saint most revered by Montenegrins.[44]

As the war continued Hercegovina suffered major outbreaks of fighting which spread into tribal areas in what is today northern Montenegro. In 1662 the *sanjak-bey* of Hercegovina, fearing that he was losing control of the situation, summoned fifty-seven local *knezovi* from the districts of Nikšić, Piva, Drobnjak and Morača to swear an oath of loyalty, promising to safeguard their lives. Instead he had them all summarily put to death, and taking advantage of the

[44] Not surprisingly given its location, Ostrog monastery has continued to serve as a place of refuge up till very recent times. Rebecca West in the epilogue to her massive work, *Black Lamb, Grey Falcon*, recalls that the monastery, 'a bleak pigeon hole in a Montenegrin cliff', sheltered King Petar of Yugoslavia when he was spirited out of Belgrade to escape the Nazi air-raids which blitzed the city in 1941 (see West, *Black Lamb, Grey Falcon*, vol. 2, p. 547 and Chapter 18 below). More recently, the former Bosnian Serb leader and indicted war criminal Radovan Karadžić was rumoured to be hiding in the cave complex behind the monastery, disguised as an Orthodox monk. (See BBC 2 Television programme, 'Looking for Karadžić' by Maggie O'Kane, 19 May 2002.)

disarray launched a major offensive against the local Christian population.[45] Many fled in terror to Venetian-controlled territory.

In 1669 the Candian war was brought to an end by the Ottomans' conquest of Crete. Although the eastern Adriatic and its hinterland had seen little major warfare since 1657, the unsettled and poverty-stricken conditions of everyday life, the constant raiding and the activities of the *hajduks* and *uskoks* had taken a heavy toll on the population. Outsiders saw the region as wholly beyond the pale. In 1662, the year of the massacre of headmen by the *sanjak-bey* of Hercegovina, the Turkish traveller Evliya Çelebi journeyed as far as the Ottoman fortress at Podgorica. Prevented by the conflict from visiting Kotor, he was loftily dismissive of Montenegro—'a large headland ... of thickets and barren mountains'. The inhabitants, he observed dryly 'had gone over to the Venetian side'.[46]

However, such changes were relatively unimportant; after twenty-five years of warfare the frontiers of the Ottoman and Venetian Empires in the Adriatic remained largely as they had been before the war, with Ottoman feudatories ever more firmly entrenched in the valleys. But in a political sense the changes brought about by the Candian war were significant. Years of conflict during which the tribes of Old Montenegro, the Brda and those in the northern and western regions bordering on Hercegovina had all thrown their lot in with Venice against the Ottomans provided the first foundations for the future unification of these tribes within a significantly enlarged Montenegro. Such a union was still far from a reality, but a further period of prolonged warfare lasting till the end of the century would confirm these early bonds of solidarity on which eventual union would be based.

Fifteen years were to elapse before the Montenegrin tribes were again to find themselves involved in a major war between the Christian powers and the Ottomans. Naturally the local Ottoman *beys* did not abandon their efforts at pacifying the Montenegrin tribes over this time. Yet already the Ottoman Empire's power was in decline from its apogee at the time of Mehmed II and Suleiman the Magnificent. In 1683 the sultan's forces experienced a catastrophic defeat before Vienna at the hands of a combined force of the Polish-

[45] Živković, *Istorija Crnogorskog Naroda*, vol. 2, pp. 55–6.
[46] Robert Dankoff and Robert Elsie (eds), *Evliya Çelebi*, p. 53.

Habsburg alliance, an event that proved to be one of the major turning-points of European history. Soon the Ottomans were suffering further reverses: in 1686 Budva was recaptured and in 1688 Belgrade was taken by the Austrians, who continued southwards to capture Niš and onwards into Kosovo and Macedonia.

In their determination to halt the Ottoman tide the Orthodox and Catholic Churches had for some time been seeking rapprochement, and the Montenegrins, placed as they were on the fringes of both empires, were natural intermediaries. Thus Pope Clement X, in making contact with the Orthodox Patriarch of Peć, Arsenije III Čarnojević, employed the offices of both the Montenegrin Vladika Ruvim III Boljević and the Catholic Archbishop of Bar, Andrija Zmajević. Arsenije, whose name would later pass into history as the patriarch who led the great exodus of Serbs out of Kosovo in 1690,[47] was not slow in urging his flock to rebel, but the Ottoman forces rallied and put down the rising. Arsenije was forced to flee from Kosovo into Montenegro where he sought the protection of Venice.[48]

The Morean war (1684–99)

Still smarting from defeat in the Candian wars, the Venetians chose this moment to join the Polish-Habsburg alliance and declare war on the sultan, and immediately urged the Montenegrin tribesmen to join them. Even before 1684 when war was formally declared, *hajduks* from the Gulf of Kotor and further up the coast had been carrying out raids against Ottoman settlements. During one such attack in 1684 a *hajduk* chieftain, Bajo Pivljanin, succeeded in capturing the ancient town of Risan: this town, which had fallen to the Ottomans in 1539, had once been the principal residence of the Illyrian Queen Teuta.

Still the tribesmen hesitated. In the past the Venetians had proved unreliable allies and the chiefs were reluctant to engage before measuring the strength of Venice's commitment to this war; only after a year of prevarication did events themselves propel them into war.[49]

[47] On the Serbian exodus from Kosovo and northern Macedonia see Ćirković, *The Serbs*, pp. 143–4, and Tim Judah, *The Serbs*, p. 1.
[48] Pavlowitch, *Serbia: The History behind the Name*, p. 19.
[49] Živković, *Istorija Crnogorskog Naroda*, vol. 2, pp. 62–3.

In 1685 the newly-appointed Pasha of Skadar, Suleiman Pasha Bušatlija (Bushati), launched an attack on Cetinje, choosing the moment when the Vladika Visarion II (1685–92)—also newly-established in his position following the death of his predecessor the previous year—had travelled to Peć for consecration by Patriarch Arsenije. Taken unawares, the Montenegrins sought help from Kotor, and in response the Venetian governor sent a contingent under Bajo Pivljanin, who joined battle with the enemy at Vrtijeljka just outside Cetinje. Despite heroic attempts at resistance during which Bajo Pivljanin lost his life the Montenegrins were forced to yield, and Bušatlija advanced at the head of his men into Cetinje. But his troops remained in occupation for only four days before attacks from neighbouring tribes forced the pasha to withdraw to Skadar after first setting fire to Cetinje.[50] If the experience did little to strengthen the tribesmen's faith in Kotor as an ally, it gave them a new bandit-hero: Bajo Pivljanin, who received a hero's burial and passed into legend.[51]

The shortcomings of Venice as an ally were at least partly remedied in the eyes of the Montenegrins in 1687 when they succeeded with the tribesmen's support in capturing the important coastal town of Novi. The town with its great fortress, many fine buildings and mosques had been held by the Ottomans for two centuries and its loss dealt a severe blow to their hopes of retaining a significant presence in the Adriatic. For Venice the capture of the town which the Republic was to hold until its conquest by Austria in 1797, was one of the more important victories of the Morean war. Undeniably it strengthened La Serenissima's alliance with the Montenegrins while helping to reinforce a sense of solidarity between the chiefs.

Meanwhile the skirmishes with the Ottomans and their feudatories continued. As time went on, the Pasha of Skadar proved a fearsome enemy whose determination to crush his Christian opponents extended to the Brda tribes and in particular the most rebellious among them, the Kuči. So successful were they that on one occasion, when they had successfully stormed the important Ottoman fortress at Medun and wounded the pasha himself, the

---

[50] *Ibid.*, pp. 64–5.
[51] Some sources claim that he was buried together with a succession of *Vladikas* in the church in Cetinje. (Djurović, *Istorja Crne Gore*, vol. 2, p. 175).

Venetian senate voted to award the Kuči 1,000 ducats in recognition of their fighting spirit.

In 1691 Vladika Visarion prevailed on the Venetians to join forces in an attempt to seize the fortress at Rijeka Crnojevića on the marshy foreshores of Lake Skadar. Although they succeeded only in destroying the fortress rather than holding it, the attack unleashed a campaign of retribution which was to end in the total destruction of Cetinje. Only at the beginning of 1692, after the death of Visarion himself, did Bušatlija feel ready to begin his assault on Cetinje. Crossing the Lješnjani and Crmnica districts, his troops encountered the Montenegrins who had secured Venetian reinforcements under the leadership of the *provveditore* of Kotor, Nikola Erizzo. Bušatlija's forces were bolstered by 4,000 fresh troops brought up from Skadar under the command of the pasha's son. The Venetians then took up a position within the monastery while the Montenegrins, having sent their dependants into the hills, stationed themselves around its perimeter. There are two accounts of what happened next. According to one the Venetians, confronted by a re-invigorated enemy, offered to surrender the monastery on condition that the monks were spared and permitted to withdraw. Bušatlija accepted the terms, but the Venetians before withdrawing secretly mined the monastery and church, and when the pasha's forces entered the monastery they were blown to bits. The monastery's destruction was thus accompanied by the deaths of perhaps 100 Ottoman soldiers, victims of Venetian treachery.[52] This is a fine story and it may be true, but it has to be admitted that the temptation to lay the blame on the Venetians would have had its attractions for local historians either at the time or afterwards.

The alternative account which claims that the Montenegrins, realising that they could not defend the monastery, stacked it with gunpowder and thus took their own lives together with those of the enemy, arguably shows the defenders in a less appealing light.[53] Regardless of who was responsible for the destruction of Ivan Crnojević's monastery, the attack on Cetinje and the punishment meted out by Bušatlija must have been both psychologically and physically

[52] See Živković, *Istorija Crnogorskog Naroda*, vol. 2, p. 75, and Djurović, *Istorija Crne Gore*, vol. 2, p. 205.
[53] Drasko Šćekić, *Travelling through Montenegro*, pp. 114–15.

devastating. But far from abandoning their territory, the Montene-grins remained to carry out a series of guerrilla attacks on the occu-pying forces, which were sufficient to force Bušatlija's withdrawal to Skadar. Clearly too, trust between the Venetians and Montenegrins was dealt a severe blow by the events at Cetinje. Not only did the Venetians pull out hastily, never again to return to Cetinje, but the defeat marked the final attempt at close military co-operation between Venetian and Montenegrin forces in the Morean war.

The war was in any case losing its intensity and by 1696 fighting had effectively ceased along a front stretching from the Neretva river to Ulcinj, bringing some relief to the hard-pressed population of the hinterland. However, elsewhere in Dalmatia and in the Morea (Peloponnese) the conflict continued for a further three years. The fifteen-year war was finally brought to an end in January 1699 when Austria, Poland, Russia and Venice jointly signed a peace agreement with the Ottomans at Sremski Karlovci on the Danube. Under the treaty of Karlowitz (Karlovac) the Ottoman Empire gave up a signi-ficant portion of its territory permanently to the European powers. Venice acquired increased territory in Dalmatia as well as the Morea, and the Habsburg Empire gained Croatia, Slavonia and other lands. Although the treaty stipulated that borders were established on the basis of *uti possidetis*, it took two years for Venice and the Ottoman Empire to agree on borders within Hercegovina.[54]

Viewed from the Montenegrin standpoint, both the war and the alliance with Venice had some positive consequences although the costs in human suffering were undoubtedly high. Risan and Novi had been liberated, removing the Ottoman presence from the fore-shores of the Gulf of Kotor. As a result Venice had a compact region under its control, a situation which, regardless of the Montenegrins' doubts as to the good faith of the Republic, was undoubtedly pref-erable to what had gone before.[55]

Indeed there were to be concrete gains for Montenegro. In time this more peaceful environment would permit towns and set-tlements to flourish within the region under Venetian rule, a devel-opment that brought some economic benefit to the tribesmen. But rather than any immediate territorial or economic gain, the real

---

[54] Živković, *Istorija Crnogorskog Naroda*, vol. 2, p. 77.
[55] *Ibid.*

advantage for Montenegro was political and longer-term. In the first place the degree of co-operation manifested by the different Montenegrin tribes during the war gave a powerful impetus to moves towards closer integration, a trend that was to become more apparent in the early years of the next century.[56] However, it was more significant that as a result of the war both Austria and Russia had been brought to focus on the peoples of the Balkans, including on the margins, those of tiny Montenegro. And, as at least a few Montenegrins were beginning to realise, capturing the interest of these major powers in the region would be of the utmost importance for the future.

The sixteenth and seventeenth centuries in perspective

Throughout the sixteenth and seventeenth centuries, Montenegro's relations with the outside powers followed a discernible pattern. First the Montenegrin, the Brda and the more far-flung tribes were incited to rebel by foreign European powers. This in turn provoked Ottoman retaliation: pillaging, the burning of villages and the seizure of potential hostages and slaves. Punishment inflicted, the Ottoman forces would then pull back since the cost of staying put and holding down the population was simply too great. Not only was the land too poor to support an occupying army but the Montenegrins' aptitude for the guerrilla campaign made settlement seem doubly undesirable. As a local saying put it, 'In Montenegro a small army is defeated, a large one dies of hunger.'

Naturally such a pattern of existence took a heavy toll on the population, leaving little time for other pursuits or achievements. Sixteenth- and seventeenth-century Montenegro remained a poor and exceptionally backward place. Even when not caught up in war, ordinary people's lives were plagued by insecurity because of the activities of *hajduks* and the constant feuding of the clans. Hardship and emigration kept the population at fairly static levels. Records of 1570 show the five central *nahije* as having just under 3,000 households with twenty-six estates paying taxes and thirty-five Muslim households on which taxes were not levied.[57] Population

---

[56] Djilas, *Njegoš*, p. 22, and Živković, *Istorija Crnogorskog Naroda*, vol. 2, pp. 77–8.
[57] The *nahije* concerned were Katuni, Rijeka, Lješnjani, Crmnica and Pješivci. The latter is only occasionally considered to be one of the four *nahije* making up

levels were broadly the same a century later.[58] Society was organised simply, and after the serfs had been freed from working monastery lands towards the end of the sixteenth century, it did not suffer from the rigidities imposed by social hierarchy or occupational class. The mountainous terrain supported no community bigger than the village. Only beyond the borders of Old Montenegro were there larger settlements, areas populated mostly by Muslims where the Ottoman rule prevailed.

Culturally the period was in many ways one of stagnation. Even in the previously rich towns along the coast, astride the 'fracture zone'[59] so frequently contested between Venetians and Ottomans, the population was largely cut off from the European mainstream. Yet the region was not a complete cultural desert. From time to time patrons emerged to attract and encourage important artists. One such figure was the Catholic Archbishop of Bar, Andrija Zmajević, whose patronage encouraged literature and painting. Significantly Zmajević worked towards building close links between the Orthodox and Catholic world, composing his own church chronicle in both Slavic and Latin and through contact with Venice and France ensuring a channel of communication with the outside world.[60]

The situation in the interior was far worse. But here too manuscripts continued to be copied by the monks in centres of religious learning like Nikoljac near Bijelo Polje, the Holy Trinity at Pljevlja, and Morača. Later, after the restoration of the Patriarchate at Peć, there was something of a resurgence of fresco and icon painting, with some of the work executed by the monks themselves under the direction of artists and craftsmen from the coast. Perhaps the most

---

Old Montenegro. See http://www.njegos.org/mnhistory/hist1.htm, accessed 05/06/02.

[58] In an account of 1612, Marino Bolizza, a Venetian noble of Kotor, charged with re-organising the postal service, gives a figure of 3524 households, but the area he defines as Montenegro may well be somewhat larger. (Stevenson, *History of Montenegro*, p. 111.) Stevenson himself believes the statistics given by Bolizza to be 'so precise as to invite scepticism'.

[59] *The Fracture Zone: A Return to the Balkans* is the title of a book by the travel writer and correspondent Simon Winchester (London: Viking, 1999).

[60] Sreten Perović (ed.) *Montenegro: Culture and the Arts*, Podgorica: Official publication, 1980, p. 138.

talented painter of the period, Georgije Mitrofanović, had trained at
a workshop on Mount Athos before coming to Montenegro where
he worked on frescoes in the Morača monastery. Other famous
painters included the mysterious Kozma, responsible for beautiful
frescoes in both the Morača and Piva monasteries; Piva has the
unique distinction of having been built with the permission of the
Ottoman rulers over a period of more than ten years from 1573 to
1585. Its founder was the Metropolitan of Hercegovina, later the
Serbian Patriarch, Savatije, kinsman of the Grand Vizir, Mehmed
Pasha Sokolović, who was taken from his home as a boy and rose to
become one of the empire's most famous statesmen.[61] As a result the
church contains a fresco depicting both Savatije and Sokolović and is
thus a rarity for an Orthodox church in being adorned with the
portrait of a 'Turk'.[62]

Rare as it is, such a work of art reflects the fact that Montenegro,
like the rest of the Balkans, was at that period influenced by a sym-
biosis of cultures—Byzantine/Orthodox and Ottoman /Muslim.
Indeed many of the tribes contained members who were Muslim
converts. Montenegrins also shared many aspects of their culture
with the tribes in regions which are today in northern Albania. In
the sixteenth and seventeenth centuries, identities which were later
to crystallise along sharply delineated and religiously inspired lines
were only beginning to take shape. But as the seventeenth century
closed, such 'ambiguities of identity'[63] were about to experience significant and irreversible change. Under a new Vladika, Danilo, the
boundary between who was and who was not a Montenegrin was to
be harshly and inflexibly defined. And, together with its population,
Montenegro as a polity was to gain a clearer identity that would bind
it still more closely to Orthodox Christianity. Admittedly the process was gradual, being influenced partly by the country's relationship with a new sponsor, Orthodox Russia. Furthermore, early
in his period of office Danilo was to succeed in making the position

---

[61] Savatije was one of Sokolović's relatives, who in turn succeeded Markarije as
patriarch of the restored see at Peć. See Banac, *The National Question*, p. 64.
[62] In the patriarch's palace in Istanbul is a modern mosaic in traditional style
showing Mehmet II with the then patriarch (in 1453).
[63] Allcock, *Explaining Yugoslavia*, p. 439.

of Vlakida hereditary rather than elective, significantly strengthening the centralising power of the embryonic state. Difficult as it is to draw sharp lines in a people's history, these developments taken together perhaps mark the true beginnings of Montenegro as a theocracy and thus of a new era in its history.[64]

[64] Harold W. V. Temperley, *History of Serbia*, London, 1919, p. 146.

4. Montenegrin Theocracy

The Christmas Eve massacre: myth or history

According to tradition, on Christmas Eve in 1702 the Vladika, Danilo, summoned the chiefs of the Montenegrin tribes and ordered them to go out and murder their fellow clansmen who had converted to Islam and refused to recant in favour of Christianity.[1] Of all the chiefs only the five Martinović brothers were prepared to carry out the Vladika's command, and together set to slaughtering men, women and children. This is a terrible story if indeed it is true, but no contemporary record of such a massacre survives and historians differ over what happened and even whether it actually took place. In the past some of those seeking to substantiate the historicity of the event based their case on a note purportedly written by Vladika Danilo himself. When doubts arose over the authenticity of the document most historians chose either to ignore them or explain them away. The first verifiable reference to the massacre dates from 1833 when a poem entitled 'Serbian Christmas Eve around 1702' by another Vladika, Petar I (1747–1830) and based on a popular folk ballad, was published in Cetinje. The following year the theme of the massacre was taken up again in the drama *Dika Crnogorska* (The Pride of Montenegro) by Sima Milutinović Sarajlija, tutor to Petar I's successor, another Petar Petrović, known as Njegoš. In 1846 Njegoš himself dramatised the massacre in a long epic poem, *The Mountain Wreath* (Gorski Vijenac), later to become the most famous work in the history of South Slav literature.[2]

---

[1] Uncertainty over the historical nature of the event is increased by the different dates on which it is alleged to have taken place. In addition to 1702, some accounts give 1707 while Ivo Banac opts for 1709.

[2] *The Mountain Wreath* was composed in Cetinje in 1846 and published the following year in Vienna. The original edition has the subtitle *Historical event from the end of the Seventeenth Century* although an earlier work by Njegoš, entitled

But however great its literary impact in the Slav world, Njegoš's *magnum opus*, written almost a century and a half after the events it purports to describe, can scarcely be said to constitute decisive proof of the massacre's historicity. Nor indeed do the various ballads and songs on which *The Mountain Wreath* was based. Yet the story's place in popular tradition requires explanation, a fact acknowledged even by those who believe that no such massacre ever took place.[3]

Of the two schools, the believers and the sceptics, the true believers were mostly to be found among nineteenth- and early twentieth-century writers who, coming from an age more given to admiring martial values, were not only convinced that the massacre did take place, but expressed understanding for its goal of protecting national identity despite the loss of innocent human life.[4] Writing in 1876, the French correspondent of the widely-read travel journal *Le Tour du Monde* interpreted the event as part of an 'unceasing struggle', adding: 'It is sufficient to read the history of this country to understand the traditional hatred which is passed on through generations.' Later a British Foreign Office report expressed similar understanding, referring to Danilo's 'memorable Montenegrin Vespers'[5] as 'rid[ding] the country of the .... dangerous internal foe—the renegades'.[6]

Ogledalo Srpsko (The Serbian Mirror), which also refers to the massacre, ascribes to it the date 1702. *The Mountain Wreath* has twice been translated into English—first by the English scholar James W. Wiles, *The Mountain Wreath of P. P. Nyegosh, Prince-Bishop of Montenegro, 1830–1851*, London: Geo. Allen and Unwin, 1930, and second by Vasa D. Mihailovich, *The Mountain Wreath of P. P. Njegoš*, Chapel Hill: University of North Carolina Press, 1986. For a fuller discussion of the poem and on Njegoš as Vladika of Montenegro see Chapter 6.

[3] On the relationship between popular tradition (legend and myth) and historical context see George Schöpflin, *Nations, Identity, Power: The New Politics of Europe*, London: Hurst, 2000, pp. 87–9.

[4] One dissenting voice at this time was that of the nineteenth-century historian Ilarion Ruvarac in his *Montenegrina* published in 1899. See Milovan Djilas, *Njegoš: Poet, Prince, Bishop*, pp. 310–11.

[5] The analogy is with the notorious 'Sicilian Vespers' of 1282 when the subject population of Palermo massacred possibly as many as four thousand of their French/Norman rulers.

[6] *Montenegro: Handbook prepared under the direction of the historical section of the Foreign Office*, no. 20, November 1918, p. 12.

After the Second World War Yugoslavia's Communist ideologues, committed as they were to 'brotherhood and unity', were more circumspect, denying the event's historicity while extolling the literary qualities of Njegoš's work. It was from this time onwards that the sub-title 'A historical event from the end of the seventeenth century' was removed from all editions of the Njegoš poem.

In the late 1950s Milovan Djilas, serving a long prison sentence after his break with Tito, wrote a lengthy biography of Njegoš, which was smuggled out of prison and published in the West.[7] Dissident though he was, Djilas shared the now accepted view of the massacre as purely fictional, and argued that the extirpation of Muslims in Montenegro was the result of a process rather than a single incident. In support of his argument Djilas pointed out that a *History of Montenegro* written by one of Danilo's successors, Vladika Vasilije, and published in Moscow in 1754, did not mention the massacre although it gave prominence to many less significant clashes.[8] The point is a valid one, although—given the nature of Vasilije's book, a panegyric more than a factual history—it can hardly be seen as conclusive. For Djilas the ties of clan would have overridden those of religion and he accordingly interpreted the story of the massacre as 'a social and spiritual event, [which] signified the first step in putting an end to the pro-Turkish leanings of the clan chieftains in their resistance to the central government'.[9]

Not surprisingly, the Yugoslav wars of the 1990s, in which the Muslim population suffered so greatly at the hands of Serbs, encouraged a number of critics of Serbian nationalism to see the events described in *The Mountain Wreath* as based on an incontrovertible historical reality.[10] More recently a Canadian scholar, Srdja Pavlović, has contested the reality of the massacre and suggests instead that the story might have arisen from the conflation of two documented historical events—the first being the conversion to Islam in 1485 of a number of Montenegrins, including Djuradj Crnojević's youngest son Staniša, and the second the expulsion from Montenegro around 1704 of the Medojević family, who were blacksmiths employed by

[7] Djilas, *Njegoš: Poet, Prince, Bishop,* cited in fn 8 above.
[8] *Ibid.*, p. 310.
[9] *Ibid*, p. 313.
[10] See, for example, Branimir Anzulović, *Heavenly Serbia*, pp. 51 and 189.

the Cetinje monastery, as a result of a dispute over property.[11] Pavlović's main concern is to ensure that *The Mountain Wreath* is read primarily as a work of literature, situated within the context of its time. Accordingly he seeks to show that the account of the 'Montenegrin Vespers' given in the poem tells us more about the political aspirations of Petar Petrović Njegoš and the romantic nationalistic ideology of his age than it does of early eighteenth-century Montenegro, a view which is surely correct. But however right Pavlović may be in cautioning against a direct read-across from *The Mountain Wreath* to early eighteenth-century Montenegro (or indeed, as others would have it, to our own times), his explanation of the origins of the massacre story remains an interesting possibility rather than an established certainty.

In the light of so much that is hypothetical what then can be said of relations between Christians and Muslims in the early years of Danilo's reign? Undoubtedly Danilo took office at a time when changes brought about by the long wars between the Ottoman Empire and the Christian powers were threatening what little stability and economic security the tribesmen may have had. Essentially the Ottoman Empire, forced by the Treaty of Karlowitz to cede territory to the Christian powers, was being further weakened by anarchy at home. Increasingly the Sublime Porte[12] lacked the capacity to impose order in its more far-flung borderlands. Nevertheless the Ottoman authorities were unwilling to give up the Porte's claim to Montenegro which the terms of the treaty still held to be a part of the empire. The resulting vacuum provided opportunities for local Ottoman feudatories to strengthen their control by demanding recognition of their feudal claims and their entitlement to levy new taxes.

The effect was to provoke further rebellion. To bolster their attempts to break the resistance of the Montenegrin tribes, the local *beys* set about constructing a system of forts stretching from Nikšić and Gusinje in the north and east to Žabljak and Ulcinj in the south and west, so creating an effective military belt encircling the whole

[11] Srdja Pavlović, '*The Mountain Wreath*: Poetry or a Blueprint for the Final Solution?' available at http://www.univie.ac.at/spacesofidentity/vol_4/_html/pavlovic.html
[12] From the time of the Grand Vizier Mehmed Pasha Köprülü (served 1656–61) onwards the foreign affairs of the Ottoman Empire were centred in the Grand Vizier's headquarters whose gateway was known as the Sublime Porte. The latter term thus came to stand for the Ottoman state itself.

of Old Montenegro and the Brda. Increasingly these fortress towns attracted the local Muslim population. This had further consequences: first, Muslims began to be seen as a relatively wealthy and town-based social group, so that that religion became equated with higher social class and a range of urban occupations. Secondly, the Muslim population's move into the towns permitted the development of more effective peasant resistance movements in the villages and hamlets of Montenegro. Promising access to a privileged way of life, conversion to Islam was bound to prove attractive, as it also did among neighbouring Bosnians and Albanians. Faced with such a threat, the Montenegrins, as we have seen, responded differently. Possibly only a part of Montenegro was affected, and many people may have been simply expelled rather than murdered.[13] But in specific areas such as the lands of the Ćeklići clan near Cetinje—the fact that Muslim families were killed or at least driven out is supported by local memory with the names of the clans concerned still remembered.[14] While the details cannot be established, the change in attitude such acts implied is certainly significant. While the Montenegrins had fought many battles against the Ottomans in the past, they had done so as against outsiders; now they were violating codes of tribal solidarity by turning against their own people who had converted to Islam. Although those now under attack had never been seen as privileged or notably different, this was to change as the struggle became more narrowly ideological—the Cross against the Crescent, as Montenegro's admirers would continue to claim. Paradoxically this change of attitude owed something to the culture against which it was directed: under the Ottoman *millet* system religion was placed above clan or tribe in determining national identity, and membership of a particular *millet*—Muslim, Orthodox, Catholic, Jewish—governed almost all aspects of an individual's existence.

The origins of the Petrović dynasty

While Danilo's stance in relation to these events cannot be outlined with any certainty, he is nevertheless the first of the Vladikas whose character emerges with sufficient clarity for a clear picture of him

[13] See Judah, *The Serbs*, p. 76.
[14] See Djurović (ed.), *Istorija Crne Gore*, book 3, part 1, pp. 244–9.

as an individual to be formed. Writing around 1720 Vicentije Zmajević, an important figure in the Catholic Church from Perast, remarked of Danilo that he was 'a relentless enemy of the Turks against whom he swore undying animosity'. In any event the milestones of Danilo's political career suggest a man who was likely to leave his mark on history. To begin with, his election as Vladika in the spring of 1697 was by no means a foregone conclusion. The death of his immediate predecessor Vladika Savatije Kaludjerović after only three years in office left a gap which both the Venetians and the Ottomans were eager to fill with men of their choosing. The tribesmen thus had to move quickly to select a convincing candidate if they were to pre-empt outside interference. Danilo, then a twenty-five year old monk at the Cetinje monastery, had impressed them not only by his lineage but also by his evident patriotism and serious demeanour. In most ways his background was that of a typical Montenegrin: baptised Nikola Šćepčević, he was the son of Šćepac from Njeguši, a poor hamlet of no more than a few houses on a stony outcrop half-way between Cetinje and Kotor. But the Herak (later Petrović) clan[15] to which Danilo belonged had arrived in Montenegro from Hercegovina some time in the late fifteenth century and over the intervening years had gained a reputation for skill and courage in the long anti-Ottoman campaign. Indeed what we know of Danilo suggests that he was more warrior than monk, and that certainly was how his compatriots perceived him. A portrait of 1912 shows him at once solemn and purposeful, standing with hand on sword and dressed in the finery of a mountain chief against a background of stone ruins and soaring mountain peaks. Romanticised as the portrait is, its darkly handsome figure may well bear some likeness to the historical Danilo: physical attributes were generally regarded as prerequisites for leadership in tribal Montenegro, while the sobriquet, the 'Black Vladika,' can be taken, as with the later Serbian leader Karadjordje, as referring to Danilo's dark colouring rather than his character. That Danilo saw himself as the military as well as spiritual leader of his people is clear from the title he later

---

[15] All descendants of Danilo's father Šćepac Heraković and his uncle Ivan took the name Petrović (son of Petar), after the founder of the dynasty, who was known as the monk Petar. After Petar II, known as Njegoš, the dynasty took the name Petrović-Njegoš to distinguish itself from other Petrovići since the name was common in both Montenegro and Serbia.

assumed—'Danilo, Vladika of Cetinje and War Lord [*vojvodić*] of the Serbian land'. The choice of words is revealing of Danilo's soaring ambition. In 1697 Montenegro was still restricted to four *nahije* and, cut off from the sea, had to make do with a short stretch of coastline on Lake Skadar. Conveniently discounting these geographical limitations and the country's lack of political status, the Vladika looked to a Greater Montenegro as the hub of restored Serb power.[16]

However, during his first few years in office Danilo was engaged at home, consolidating his position within a country that had been impoverished and destabilised by the long Morean wars. Not till 1700 did circumstances allow him to travel to Secui (Sečuj) in Hungary to be formally consecrated as metropolitan by the Serbian patriarch. Danilo's decision to make the difficult journey across Bosnia to Secui for this ceremony was not undertaken lightly. Patriarch Arsenije Čarnojević III, then residing in Hungary under Habsburg protection, had abandoned the traditional see of Peć in 1690 accompanied by thousands of his flock who, having joined the Austrians and Venetians in battle against the Ottomans, feared reprisals. The Ottomans installed a placeman, whom Danilo refused to recognise, in this way taking a stand which, as Serbian historiographers have insistently pointed out, demonstrated his solidarity with fellow Serbs under the Habsburg Empire and elsewhere.[17]

At the same time such a stance underlined the Montenegrins' determination to assert their independence of the Sublime Porte, a position which clearly could only be sustained with outside support. Relations with Venice had cooled since the end of the Morean wars. Trade with the population of Venice's Dalmatian territories declined and the relationship was further strained both by the tribesmen's tendency to stray into Venetian territory when seeking winter pasture for their stock and by the much more seriously threatening activity of the *hajduks*. In 1707, however, a deterioration in the relations between Venice and the Porte led the Venetian *provveditore* of Dalmatia, Giacomo Riva, to invite a number of the Montenegrin tribal leaders to Herceg Novi (formerly known as Novi) in order to set Venetian-Montenegrin relations on a better footing. The results, though broadly beneficial to the Montenegrins, were not sufficient

[16] See Banac, *The National Question*, p. 272.
[17] François Lenormant, *Turcs et Monténégrins*, Paris: Didier, 1866, p. 140.

to offer them the economic or military security they sought. While some of the chiefs received money and other gifts, it was made clear that the Venetian senate would no longer pay the regular stipend granted in the past, partly because this could provoke the Ottomans to further action.

Relations with Russia

If Montenegro were to survive at all it needed new allies. Fortunately a combination of circumstances—the Montenegrins' record of hostility to Ottoman domination and their proximity to the Adriatic—meant that such an ally was to hand. In the late seventeenth and early eighteenth centuries Russia's interest in the Balkan region was driven primarily by Peter the Great's determination to acquire a port on the Mediterranean. Peter was aware that his countrymen, with no naval tradition, required seafaring experience if his ambitions were to be realised, and he accordingly enlisted the help of the great maritime nations: the Dutch, the Venetians and the English. In 1698 two groups of young Russian noblemen were duly despatched from Moscow to acquire the best traditions of seamanship through training under Dutch and Venetian master-mariners. The Venetian senate determined that the seventeen future Russian naval officers consigned to them should train under the great Captain Marko Martinović at the prestigious Venetian naval school at Perast on the Gulf of Kotor. Famous Russians followed in their wake, among them a certain Count Tolstoy (envoy of the tsar and later Russian ambassador in Istanbul) who was moved to write of the local Orthodox population: 'Although very far from the motherland, there live a people with our same faith …, brave and loyal, with a coast which could well serve the cause of Russian military expansion.'[18] Contacts between Russia and the seafaring population of the Gulf multiplied. The admiral of Peter's Baltic fleet was a native of Perast, Matija Zmajević, a great sailor and member of a famous Zmajević family, which had produced the forceful and charismatic Archbishop of Bar. The story of Matija Zmajević's arrival in Russia captures the flavour of life in the Gulf region at the time. Suspected of involvement in a plot to murder a fellow sea captain who had

---

[18] Quoted in Nicoló Carnimeo, *Montenegro: A Timeless Voyage*, Milan: Mondadori, 1999, pp. 56–7.

abducted the adopted daughter of Captain Martinović—a beautiful girl of Bosnian origin freed from captivity by the Captain during a raid on the North African coast—Zmajević fled to Istanbul where he sought the help of the Russian ambassador. It was the ambassador who, knowing Zmajević's reputation for seamanship, arranged his introduction to Peter the Great.[19]

Thus it was through their contact with the mariners of the Gulf of Kotor that the Russian political class were made aware of the warlike reputation of the local Slav Orthodox population and of the mountaineers' long history of resistance to Ottoman domination, which had been demonstrated most recently in 1692 by their gallant but unsuccessful defence of Cetinje. In 1696 Peter's expansionist policies had led him to join the Holy League in its attack on the Ottoman Empire. A peace signed in 1700 resulted in Russia's acquisition of the port of Azov affording an outlet to the Black Sea, and the appointment of a Russian diplomatic representative in Istanbul. In 1710 Peter resumed his war against the Ottomans, sending his armies into Balkan lands and calling on the population to rise against their Muslim overlords. One of the tsar's envoys to Montenegro was a Captain Ivan Lukačević, originally from Podgorica, while another was Colonel Mihajlo Miloradović from Hercegovina, who travelled through Montenegro promising liberation under Russia's protection once the conquerors had been driven out. The Montenegrins, and some Hercegovinians, responded enthusiastically, but elsewhere the subject peasant population remained largely unmoved. With neither the Venetians nor the people of nearby Dubrovnik offering support, the Montenegrins faced the old problem of securing supplies of armaments and ammunition. But they had taken a decisive step. Of all the Balkan countries it was Montenegro that established the closest relationship with Russia, which, despite some fallow periods, continued till the fall of the Romanov dynasty in 1917.

In 1711 the tsar's attempt to invade Ottoman-ruled Moldavia resulted in a serious reverse on the River Pruth. News of the terms of the Treaty of Pruth under which Russia was forced to return Azov to the Ottoman Empire took some time to reach Montenegro,

[19] Carnimeo, *Montenegro: A Timeless Voyage,* pp. 56–7. The museum in the town of Perast still contains the naval banner presented to Admiral Zmajević by Peter the Great.

where it was greeted with dismay and disbelief. Despite their failure to capture Ottoman fortresses—among them Nikšić, Grahovo and Spuž—and the signing of a temporary truce with the Ottomans, the Montenegrins had no intention of abandoning the struggle and continued trying to acquire arms in preparation for another uprising. But their enemies were one step ahead of them, and the following year launched a campaign to capture and destroy Cetinje and punish Danilo and Colonel Miloradović, whom they held responsible for the uprising.

In the second half of July 1712 two Ottoman forces advanced from opposite directions into Montenegro, the larger led by Ahmed Pasha, the vizier of Bosnia, the smaller advance force under the command of the *sanjak-bey* of Skadar, Tahir Pasha. In the ensuing battle of Carev Laz, near present-day Rijeka Crnojevića, the Montenegrins, led by Vladika Danilo, were able to engage and inflict losses on Tahir Pasha's forces while Ahmed Pasha's troops were still advancing towards Cetinje over a much broader front.[20] But before the Montenegrins had time to recover, Ahmed Pasha, at the head of his still fresh troops, was able to enter Cetinje, raze the monastery (which Danilo had rebuilt in 1701) and burn many of the surrounding houses. Yet this act of retribution failed to erase the damage done to the Ottomans' reputation by their earlier defeat. Fleeting though it was, news of the Montenegrins' success against a larger and better-equipped adversary spread as far as Russia. It is hardly necessary to add that in Montenegrin accounts the battle of Carev Laz is celebrated as one of the great national triumphs, a status it does not truthfully deserve.

Ahmed Pasha and his men did not remain long in Cetinje where they experienced all the old problems of coming under guerrilla attack and suffering serious food shortages. For his part Vladika Danilo, who had been preparing to travel to Russia to seek formal protection and further support, suddenly abandoned his mission when it seemed likely that a renewed Russian campaign might require his presence at home. Such optimism proved misplaced: not only did the Russian campaign fail to materialise, but a renewed attack on Montenegro by some 30,000 janissaries and irregulars[21]

---

[20] Živković, *Istorija Crnogorskog Naroda*, vol. 2, p. 135.
[21] Djurović (ed.), *Istorija Crne Gore*, book 3, part 1, p. 256. Once again the figures given in Venetian sources seem likely to be exaggerated.

commanded by the new vizier of Bosnia, the capable and feared Numan Pasha Ćuprilić, resulted once again in the Ottomans seizing Cetinje and the surrounding lands and villages. This time the scale of the defeat was devastating: the countryside was laid waste as never before. Venetian sources tell of half the women, children and old people being carried off by the Turks with the male population facing death or being taken into slavery.[22] Those who managed to escape took refuge in caves or fled to Venetian territory. Within a short time the refusal of Venice to hand over these refugees, numbering around 2,500, had been seized on by the Ottomans as a pretext for renewing hostilities. On 10 December 1714 the Ottoman Empire and Venice were again at war. Where they could, remaining bands of Montenegrin fighters continued a guerrilla campaign against occupiers from the mountains until the onset of winter forced them to retreat.

Meanwhile Vladika Danilo had managed to flee to Venetian territory, first to the coast and later to Venice itself. In late 1714, only a few days before the outbreak of war between Venice and the Ottoman Empire, he set off on his long-postponed journey to Russia in the hope of obtaining help to rebuild his devastated country.[23] Small though Montenegro was, its reputation ensured Danilo a courteous reception in St Petersburg. Yet the high hopes he had invested in his mission were not to be realised. While the Russians provided funds to help with the restoration of the Cetinje monastery, together with an assortment of Russian medals to bestow upon worthy citizens and charters promising friendship, they were unwilling to offer Danilo what he most desired—support for Montenegro's independence underwritten by promises of political and military backing.

Relations with Venice

In the absence of the expected backing from Russia, Danilo transferred his hope for outside support to Austria whose army, under the great commander Prince Eugene of Savoy, had once again joined Venice against the Ottomans. Aware of the risk to their position which this rapprochement involved, the Venetians increased their

[22] Živković, *Istorija Crnogorskog Naroda*, vol. 2, p. 139.
[23] *Ibid*, p. 141.

efforts to woo the Montenegrins, attempting to drive a wedge between Danilo and some of his chiefs. Against the wishes of the Vladika, tribal leaders from the Katuni region sent to Venice representatives, led by a local chief from the village of Čevo, Vukadin Vukotić, to negotiate the creation of a Venetian protectorate encompassing Old Montenegro, in exchange for which the Montenegrins would receive guarantees of local self-rule and religious freedom, as well as supplies and payments to the chiefs themselves. On 7 March 1717 the Venetian senate accepted the proposal, to which was added a provision for the appointment of a civil governor (*guvernadur*) for Montenegro. The first governor was to be Vukadin Vukotić himself, who according to the terms of the agreement was to reside in Kotor, on Venetian territory, and receive a subsidy from the Venetian authorities. Although the agreement stipulated that the civil governor was to be chosen jointly by the tribal headmen and Venice, the Venetians doubtless intended the new civil governor to represent their interests and thus counterbalance or diminish the influence of the Vladika. But Danilo refused to fall in with their plans and was soon working to turn the agreement with Venice to his own advantage, insisting on the signing of a further treaty between himself and the Venetian *provveditore generale*, Alvise Mocenigo. So successful was he that the civil governor soon abandoned Venetian territory for Cetinje where he came to serve as the Vladika's deputy, both presiding over the assembly of the chiefs and, in the Vladika's absence, leading the country in times of war. Over time the office itself, like the position of Vladika, would become the effective monopoly of one family the Radonjić clan, who like the Petrovići belonged to the Njeguši tribe. For the time being, it seemed, Danilo had neutralised the Venetians' attempts to weaken his hold over the tribesmen, but as would later become apparent, the threat of a potential conflict of interest between civic and ecclesiastic authority remained.

For the present, however, external events worked in the Vladika's favour as Austria's success in capturing Belgrade in August 1717 and overrunning northern Serbia heightened Venice's fears that Montenegro might again turn to the Habsburgs for protection. Exploiting the leverage this gave him, Danilo was able to persuade the authorities in Venice to commit their navy to a joint Montenegrin-

Venetian attack on the Ottoman-held town of Bar. Although the offensive was unsuccessful and had eventually to be abandoned, the Vladika nonetheless maintained his position as the dominant political figure among the Montenegrin tribes and Venice's principal interlocutor. Restlessly active and ambitious, he continued to formulate plans in other directions, for the incorporation of Lake Skadar and its surrounding lands into Montenegro, for the improvement of Montenegro's trading links, and finally for the extension of his own role as the religious leader of the Orthodox population to include the Orthodox communities under Venetian jurisdiction. But although formal agreement on the last question was apparently reached in the Vladika's favour, the real position was never decisively settled to the satisfaction of both churches, and the allegiance of the population of the Gulf of Kotor continued to be a source of conflict between the Montenegrin Orthodox Church and the Catholic Church for years to come.[24]

In 1718 the signing of the Treaty of Passarowitz (Požarevac in Serbia) brought an end to the war and with it a weakening of the relationship with Venice since it also spelt the effective end of the Venetian protectorate of Montenegro. But while Venice was awarded considerable coastal lands to the north and south of Kotor, the Montenegrins received no increase in territory. The treaty did however delineate a formal border between Venetian and Montenegrin territory henceforth known as the Mocenigo line after the Venetian *provveditore generale* of Dalmatia. The Stanjevići monastery, the secondary residence of numerous Montenegrin Vladikas from Danilo onwards, was on the Venetian side of the Mocenigo line, providing Montenegrin rulers with a perch on Venetian soil. Although Montenegro's *de jure* status under the treaty was still that of a part of the Ottoman Empire, the *de facto* position of at least the Katuni *nahija*, the core area of Old Montenegro, was by this time effectively one of independence.[25]

The remainder of Danilo's period in office was relatively peaceful. Taking advantage of this refreshingly novel state of affairs, the Vladika was able to turn his attention to strengthening the few internal institutions his countrymen possessed and improving their very

---

[24] Djurović, *Istorija Crne Gore*, book 3, part 1, p. 274.
[25] Banac, *The National Question*, p. 271.

Above, pages from the Oktoih, a hymnal with eight parts, printed at Cetinje in 1494 on the first printing press in the Balkans.

Coat of arms of the Balsici dynasty who ruled Zeta from the late 14th to the early 15th century.

The 17th-century monastery at Ostrog (recent photo).

Journey to market: a Montenegrin woman's lot as seen by the French traveller Theodore Valerio, 1877.

Montenegrin lullaby: Cradle and Gun, by Valerio, c. 1876.

Vladika Danilo (*c.* 1670–1735), reconstruction by Milo Vrbica, 1912.

Vladika Sava (1700–81).

Vladika Vasilje (1709–66).

Vladika Petar I, Saint Peter of Cetinje (1813–51), mid-19th century painting by Johann Boss.

Vladika Petar II (Njegos)

poor material circumstances. In the latter task he was helped by Venice's payment of stipends to some of the headmen, which it continued not so much out of charity as through a desire to maintain some degree of influence in the face of the growing threat to its interests from Austria and Russia.

Danilo remained in power till his death in January 1735 at around sixty years of age. The character and policies of this ambitious and forceful individual left an indelible mark on his country. It is a paradox that, while he saw himself as the future leader of a revived Serbian state, his period in office is often seen as the beginning of a specifically Montenegrin history.[26] Two of the institutional changes of his time were of lasting significance. The first, introduced as early as 1713, was the setting up of a court of twelve elected members to adjudicate in the frequent disputes between the different clans and tribes. The second concerned the nature of the office of Vladika. Such was Danilo's force of character that he was able not only to name his successor in his will but to ensure that the office, from being elective, became hereditary, in effect laying the foundations for the institution of 'prince-bishop' to which many later writers on Montenegro refer. But since Orthodox bishops were required to be celibate, the succession could not be direct but in most instances passed from uncle to nephew within the Petrović clan. Such a development at once strengthened central authority and to some extent diminished the fractious influence of the clans. Still more important, it gave the Orthodox Church in Montenegro its own distinctive character: although the Montenegrin metropolitans remained formally dependent on the Serbian Patriarchate in Peć until its abolition in 1766, their effective autonomy—already in evidence from the fact that they were chosen locally—was confirmed and strengthened. At the same time the contacts Danilo had succeeded in establishing with Orthodox Russia, and his active proselytising among the popu-

---

[26] See, for instance, Milovan Djilas who wrote: 'The Montenegro from the time of the Crnojevići and before them was not Montenegro, but vassal medieval Zeta. The very name Montenegro ... referred to a region and to a feudal holding, not a state. All that transpired from the time of the Crnojevići to Danilo was slavery and struggle. It was not until the time of Bishop Danilo that Montenegro became the independent spark of a new Serbdom, and more than that—a mentality and a frame of mind recognized as something separate, a world within a world.' *Njegoš*, p. 255.

lation beyond the immediate borders of Old Montenegro, increased the prestige of the Cetinje Metropolitanate throughout the entire region.[27]

Sava and Vasilije

Danilo was succeeded by two close kinsmen, first his cousin Sava and then his nephew Vasilije, who for more than two decades was able to push aside the unworldly Sava and become effectively the highest authority in Montenegro and its representative abroad. Throughout this period and during the bizarre interregnum that followed Vasilije's death in 1765, Sava survived in the background and re-emerged in his final years to preside over a faction-ridden society which, lacking effective leadership, was drifting increasingly into anarchy.

Danilo's choice of Sava as his successor may seem puzzling since he so manifestly lacked the strength of character and sense of purpose required by his society and the times. Family ties and clan membership were clearly important, helped by the fact that Sava's family came from the Petrovići's native Njeguši. Like Danilo, Sava became a monk, serving in the Majine monastery on the coast where he was consecrated as an archpriest (*arhijerej*) in 1719 by the Patriarch of Peć.[28] From the time of his ordination onwards, Danilo sought to introduce the young man gradually to political life, conferring on him the title of co-adjutor or assistant bishop in confirmation of his future role. But little about Sava's later career suggests that he gained much from early exposure to Danilo's experience. A contemplative who was happier herding flocks[29] than tackling conflict, he preferred to leave his countrymen as they had been in the past: dependent on Venice and where necessary paying taxes to the Ottoman *beys*.

In 1735, the year in which Sava became Vladika, a new war broke out between the Ottoman Empire and Russia, which Austria soon entered on Russia's side. Predictably this was welcomed by the Montenegrin tribesmen, who were ready as ever to boost any chance to

---

[27] According to H.W.V. Temperley the success of Danilo's activities led to complaints by the Venetian Catholic prelate of Bar, *History of Serbia*, p. 152.

[28] Živković, *Istorija Crnogorskog Naroda*, vol. 2, p. 153.

[29] Djilas, *Njegoš*, p. 50.

bolster their struggle for independence. *Hajduk* activity increased, threatening not only Ottoman-controlled Hercegovina but also the coastal territory ruled by Venice and by nearby Dubrovnik. Lacking the capacity to impose firm leadership, Sava could have little influence on events; in so far as he interested himself in political matters at all, he continued to seek good relations with Venice, a stance that suited his natural conservatism and may well have been influenced by his early life on the coast. Sava's aim was to secure more open borders for Montenegro, which was already suffering under blockades imposed by its neighbours on all sides. But his inability to break the blockades, which were to endure for a full seven years, coupled with his powerlessness to control the brigandage threatening his neighbours was enough to doom such policies to failure.

Meanwhile early Austrian successes in the campaign against the Ottomans, supported both by Montenegrin and Albanian tribesmen, were followed by serious reverses, after which Austria was forced to yield territory. By the autumn of 1739 the Austrians had been forced to sign the Peace of Belgrade which required them to return to the Ottomans most of the gains made in the wars of 1714–18 including the Serbian city of Belgrade itself. To the Montenegrin tribesmen the peace counted for little: the pattern of raids and counter-attacks continued with the Brda tribes taking the brunt of Ottoman reprisals. In 1740 a new pasha of Skadar began preparations for an offensive in the region on a scale that appeared to make successful resistance impossible. Unusually opting for negotiations in preference to warfare, the Brda tribesmen sent a number of their chiefs to parley, only to have forty of them put to death and another 400 of their compatriots taken into slavery on the orders of the pasha himself.[30]

Hard-pressed on all sides, Sava decided to follow his predecessor's example and seek help from Orthodox Russia, offering to provide Montenegrin troops to serve in Russia's armies in return for some form of Russian protectorate over Montenegro. In the autumn of 1742 he set off in person, and on reaching St Petersburg the following spring presented Montenegro's case to the newly-enthroned Empress Elizabeth. Initially sympathetic, Elizabeth promised financial help, including further funds for the Cetinje monastery, but was

---

[30] Živković, *Istorija Crnogorskog Naroda*, vol. 2, p. 158.

unwilling to broach the question of a political arrangement that would afford Montenegro any military protection.[31] Journeying back by way of Berlin, Sava was presented with a beautiful gold cross by Frederick the Great, but such tokens of consideration fell far short of meeting his exaggerated hopes, and his journey, far from proving a turning-point in Montenegro's fortunes, served rather to prompt his withdrawal from public life.

Already that same year (1744) the younger and much more energetic Vasilije had travelled to Venice in the hope of improving relations and in particular gaining access for Montenegrins to the Venetian markets of the coast. These efforts met with some success, but the negotiations sparked conflict between the cousins, fanned perhaps by the Venetian predilection for intrigue. Sava was not entirely without supporters, a number of whom were reluctant to see a potentially more effective leader gain control. Yet despite their best efforts Vasilije advanced by degrees, gaining first the honorary title of archimandrite and then in 1750 consecration as a full bishop by the Serbian Patriarch Atanasije II.[32] Now effectively Sava's equal as Co-Vladika, Vasilije was able to push his older relation more and more into the background.

Disillusioned with Venice, which, from the time of the Treaty of Passarowitz had been reluctant to back the Montenegrins' anti-Ottoman struggle, Vasilije now turned to other big-power backers who might support his goal of securing Montenegro's independence. First among these was the Empress Maria Theresa of Austria. Vasilije's letter to the empress entreating her to make Montenegro a Habsburg protectorate displayed all the literary verve and disregard for accuracy which was to characterise his later communications with the Russian Empresses Elizabeth and Catherine II. Montenegro, he argued, had never been subjugated but had 'since the time of Alexander the Great been a pure virgin, a separate Republic, [over which] rules her Metropolitan, not only in religious affairs but in all worldly things'.[33]

---

[31] Živković, *Istorija Crnogorskog Naroda*, vol. 2, p. 160.

[32] Gligor Stanojević, *Le Métropolite Vasilije Petrović et son Époque (1740–1766)*, Belgrade, 1978. (Book in Serbian with a French résumé as given on http://www.-njegos.org/French/frvasil.htm)

[33] Banac, *The National Question*, p. 274. See also Živković, *Istorija Crnogorskog Naroda*, vol. 2, p. 167.

Vienna was not seriously interested in this proposal, which Vasilije himself may even have considered only a preparatory step designed to advance his principal goal of attracting Russian support.[34] In 1752, seeking to put this plan into action, he set off on a journey to Moscow and St Petersburg which was to last a full two years. Over this time he attempted to convince his hosts of the need to accept Montenegro as a Russian protectorate, but when this approach failed to produce results—Russia was more than fully occupied with its conflict with Sweden in the Baltic and the quest for expansion in the Black Sea—Vasilije determined to put his people's case in a *History*, the first of its kind ever written about Montenegro. Published in Russian in St Petersburg in 1754, the work was somewhat vaingloriously attributed to 'the Metropolitan of Montenegro, Skadar and the Coastlands, and heir to the Serbian throne, Vasilije Petrović'.[35] Only forty-three pages long, this account was less a history than a political tract enlivened with a heavy dose of mythology and designed to depict his countrymen as a race of heroes. The Russian authorities were presumably unimpressed since Vasilije's overtures and entreaties continued to receive no response. But the book was not without effect. The Vladika's endeavours, combined with the presence in St Petersburg of a sizeable number of his compatriots, sparked a vogue for Montenegro in Russia, even persuading some Serbian refugees to pass themselves off as Montenegrins.[36] Vasilije, first and foremost a Montenegrin, would have none of this. Fearing that some of these impostors might besmirch Montenegro's reputation, he warned the Russian senate that the only real Montenegrins were those who had in their possession his personally written confirmation of their nationality.[37]

---

[34] Živković, *ibid.*

[35] www.njegos.org/mnhistory/histlit.htm.

[36] Further evidence of the vogue for Montenegro is provided by the existence of a second 'book', by Jovan Stefanov Balević, entitled *A Brief and Objective Description of the Present State of Montenegro*. Balević, an Albano-Montenegrin, had attended school in Sremski Karlovci, before fleeing to Russia, where he had become a major in the Russian army. Balević's book, written in 1757, may well have been commissioned by the Russians themselves anxious to receive a more accurate picture of the situation in Montenegro. But the work never appeared in Russia and was only finally published in Cetinje in 1884.

[37] Živković, *Istorija Crnogorskog Naroda*, vol. 2, p. 169.

Obliged eventually to settle for 5,000 roubles and a gift of books for Cetinje monastery in place of the hoped-for Russo-Montenegrin alliance, Vasilije returned home to discover that during his two-year absence events had drifted in a direction to which he was utterly opposed. The tribesmen, under the nominal control of the distinctly unwarlike Sava, had been persuaded to pay the tribute demanded with threats by the Bosnian vizier Hadži Mehmed-Pasha. Deeply dismayed by this development, Vasilije immediately set about sabotaging any understanding with the vizier, encouraging banditry and all forms of anti-Ottoman activity. The Venetians, wholly opposed to renewed war between the Montenegrins and the Ottomans, were angered by Vasilije's activities, and attempted to have him poisoned. As if this were not enough, Vasilije, having brought most of the tribesmen round to accepting his call for rebellion, now faced Ottoman reprisals.

The Ottoman campaign began in November 1756, but the Montenegrins, though heavily outnumbered, were helped by torrential autumn rains which thwarted the Ottomans' hopes of destroying Cetinje. For many Montenegrin historians and mythmakers this in itself amounted to evidence of another national victory; however, for all the bravery of their resistance the defenders were unable to prevent the devastation of much of the countryside, and the effective occupation by the vizier's forces of a swathe of territory around Nikšić.[38]

The following year a truce was signed under which at least some Montenegrin tribes agreed to pay the hated *harač* and abandon banditry. Vasilije, who had fled the country before the Ottoman attack, now attempted yet again to interest Russia in Montenegro's plight, begging Empress Elisabeth to intercede with the Sublime Porte on his countrymen's behalf. Taking up residence once again in Russia he deluged the authorities with ever more far-fetched proposals for securing Montenegro's independence, highlighting the role Montenegrins had played in the struggle to liberate South Slav Christians from Islam. At the same time he had some success in encouraging poverty-stricken Montenegrins to emigrate to Russia. But the Vladika's activities were not universally welcome. Even among his own people there were now some who out of conviction or self-interest

---

[38] Žiković, *Istorija Crnogorskog Naroda*, p. 179.

declared themselves opposed to his grandiose schemes. Foremost among his detractors in Russia were two native Montenegrins, a monk Teodosije Mrkojević and an army officer Major Stevan Sarović, who together began a campaign against the Vladika. While Montenegrins in Russia were divided, the Russians themselves, conscious of the large sums already disbursed, decided to send an envoy, Colonel Puchkov, to assess the situation in Montenegro itself. In March 1760, after spending some weeks travelling in the country, Puchkov presented his report to the Russian Collegium for Foreign Affairs. While his broad conclusions were far from favourable, Puchkov's most scathing remarks were reserved for the clergy: 'The people are wild; they live in disorder; heads roll for the least offence; the clergy are grasping; the churches are deserted; Russian assistance [is] distributed among the Bishop's cousins.'[39] For Vasilije the report could not spare a single good word: the Vladika was egotistical, avaricious and duplicitous, and Sava was little better. Not surprisingly, Puchkov's report had a highly damaging impact in Russia, and for some time its negative findings were influential, not least with the Empress Elizabeth. The prospect of a closer relationship with Russia, on which Vasilije had built all his hopes for Montenegro's future security and prosperity had been dealt a blow from which recovery would take years.

Possibly chastened by this experience and steadied by the realisation that it was impossible to continue the fight on two fronts at once, Vasilije now embarked on a more circumspect course which included on occasion accepting the payment of tribute to Ottoman feudatories.[39] However, he had not given up his hope of re-establishing a close relationship with Russia and worked tirelessly to erase the impression of wrongdoing in Russian minds. The death of Empress Elizabeth presented him with an opportunity, and in 1762 he sent a delegation, which included his son, to sound out the situation with her successor Catherine II. At last in 1765 he gained permission to travel to Russia, but it was a journey from which he never returned. Falling sick in St Peterburg, the Vladika was tended by his nephew, the future Petar II, but died on 21 March 1766. Kept

[39] Quoted in English on the website www.njegos.org.mnhistory/histl.htm
[40] *Ibid.* (website) See also Jelavich, *History of the Balkans*, vol. 1, p. 86.

at a distance for many years from the Russian court and refused an audience with the Empress, Vasilije was eventually buried with full honours and at state expense in the Church of the Annunciation in St Petersburg.

Catherine's ukase, issued on the occasion of the burial, assured the Montenegrin people of 'our unchanging imperial good will and clemency', but added a note of caution: 'We advise the principal chiefs …to live together with their neighbours in peace, tranquillity and unity and as far as possible to eliminate all cause for discord, hate or warfare.'[41] Russia was not about to underwrite any Montenegrin adventurism.

News of Vasilije's death took at least three months to reach Montenegro. If his final visit had failed in its principal aim, it at least achieved something positive for his countrymen. Catherine sent another representative to prepare a fresh report on Montenegro and, having received a more favourable verdict, agreed to continue the regular financing of the upkeep of Cetinje's monastery. Such gains were slight compared to the immense hope Vasilije had placed in the relationship with Russia. Yet it is not the full measure of Vasilije's contribution to Montenegrin history. Far more telling in the longer term was the strongly pro-Russian orientation he helped to instil in his compatriots, which in turn shaped the future direction of Montenegro's foreign relations and buttressed the strong place that Orthodoxy occupied in determining the national identity.

Restless, ambitious and with little sense of moderation, Vasilije schemed and travelled in pursuit of the glorious role to which he believed the Montenegrins' history and their present struggle entitled them. As his letters make plain, he believed that Montenegro's struggle should set an example for Serbs everywhere.[42] But his vision took little account of reality, and his actions often fell short of his high aims, investing his patriotism with a degree of pathos. Yet, like his regard for Russia, Vasilije's patriotism left a strong legacy. The primacy he attached to Montenegro's role in history was to become something of an *idée fixe* for future Montenegrin rulers, and even

---

[41] Catherine's ukase is quoted in French in Lenormant, *Turcs et Monténégrins*, pp. 344–5.

[42] Stanojević, *Le Métropolite Vasilje Petrović et son Époque*, as quoted at *www.njegos.org/ french/frvasil.htm*.

today its traces linger on in the continuing debate over Montenegrin identity and the relationship with the Serbs.[43]

In the immediate aftermath of Vasilije's death it was scarcely likely that the chiefs would abide by Catherine's injunction to keep the peace among themselves and with their neighbours. The older Sava was no more capable than he had ever been of imposing firm leadership, and the general situation within the country became increasingly anarchic. For some time the old metropolitan had confined himself to church affairs, assisted by his sister's son Arsenije Plamenac whom he intended to name as his successor. In 1766 Arsenije had been consecrated archbishop by the Serbian Patriarch Vasilije Brkić who had fled his see at Peć under pressure from the Ottomans and was living in Montenegro. Together with his protégé Plamenac, Sava spent most of his time at a monastery in the Crmnica *nahija*. Removed from Cetinje and out of touch with influential chiefs, neither man had any impact on the growing social and political turmoil. Within Montenegro inter-tribal feuding was perpetuated by the blood feud, and beyond its borders the Ottoman Empire's increasing inability to rein in local feudatories and curb the activities of out-of-control janissaries was fuelling rebellion, which in turn intensified cross-border banditry. In the consequent political vacuum the rival clans of the Petrović and Radonjić competed to challenge Sava's authority and block Arsenije's route to power.

The false tsar, Šćepan Mali

As the various factions manoeuvred, a bizarre impostor moved in to fill the gap. Capitalising on the Montenegrins' love of Russia, this interloper claimed to be Tsar Peter III (husband of Catherine II, who had in fact been murdered years before), embellishing his fantastic claim with details of a miraculous escape from his Russian prison. The impostor's real name and origins were never discovered, and he was known in Montenegro simply as Šćepan Mali, or Stephen the Small. Physically unimpressive as this sobriquet suggests, Šćepan's success was the more astonishing among a people who traditionally attached great importance to physical strength, vigour and

[43] See Banac, *The National Question*, pp. 274–5.

good looks. Yet the description given by his contemporaries is of a nondescript man of middle height, around thirty-five years of age.[44]

Why then was this 'false tsar' so readily accepted?[45] Part of the answer may lie with the man himself: Šćepan first came to notice on the coast as a purveyor of herbal medicines, an occupation in which a degree of charlatanism would prove useful. But part of the answer surely also lies in the nature of Montenegrin society at the time. The people were illiterate and unsophisticated and, being reared on a diet of folklore and quasi-religious mythology, naturally credulous.[46] Shared Orthodoxy and the cult of Russia, so heavily promoted by Vasilije, predisposed them to accept an outsider claiming to embody the quasi-mystical qualities of a Russian tsar. In all probability Šćepan was not so very foreign and may even have come from the Dalmatian coast or from inland Hercegovina.[47] Whatever the reality he was far from being the only usurper to impose himself upon the Montenegrins. Milovan Djilas mentions no fewer than four other pretenders who at different times in Montenegro's history managed to find backing for a range of dubious claims.[48]

Like many charismatic leaders Šćepan claimed to be sent by God, and used religious language to overawe his audience.[49] Part of his appeal lay in his proclamation of himself as a peacemaker, able to heal all manner of social ills just as he had produced cures for physical ones. For the ordinary people, exhausted by constant warfare, raiding and hunger, his appeal was irresistible but Šćepan also had support among some of the few Montenegrins with experience of the outside world. Two of them, Teodosije Mrkojević and Captain Marko Tanović, Vasilije's opponents in Russia, not only solemnly swore that Šćepan was indeed the 'murdered' tsar but in 1767, in a declaration

---

[44] Djurović (ed.), *Istorija Crne Gore*, book 3, part 1, p. 376.

[45] *The False Tsar: Stefan Mali* is the title of another long poem by Petar Petrović Njegoš. In the poem Njegoš lays considerable weight on Šćepan's claim that he will restore the great Serbian Nemanjić empire, though it is far from certain that the historical Šćepan made this claim.

[46] See Djilas, *Njegoš*, pp. 374–5.

[47] *See* Djurović (ed.), *Istorija Crne Gore, ibid.*, p. 375, and Marco Houston, *Nikola and Milena: King and Queen of the Black Mountain*, London: Leppi Publications, 2003, p. 31.

[48] Djilas, *Njegoš*, pp. 374–5. Meanwhile in Russia itself at least seven people claimed to be the murdered Peter III.

[49] Djurović (ed.), *Istorija Crne Gore, ibid.*, p. 376.

made before the gates of Budva, proclaimed his arrival in Montenegro as marking the beginning of a new age.[50]

However, Sava, in spite of apparently accepting Šćepan's claims, decided to inform the Russian representative in Istanbul. When the envoy assured him that Peter III had indeed died in 1762, Sava hurried to inform the chiefs meeting in the *zbor* that they were about to saddle themselves with an impostor.[51] But he was too late. The chiefs had already voted in favour of making Šćepan the effective ruler of Montenegro, and were not about to revoke their decision. Instead it was Sava who found himself briefly imprisoned.

News of Šćepan's election as leader by the *zbor* soon reached the Brda tribes, where it was welcomed enthusiastically. Further afield, however, the reaction was less positive. The Venetians were immediately antagonistic, but for all their intriguing failed to shake the tribesmen's faith in their new leader. In turn the Sublime Porte, convinced of Šćepan's part in some heinous Venetian plot, dismissed the attempts by Venice to find common ground against him. In desperation the Venetians tried to find a way to poison him but failed to penetrate his circle of followers.

The Ottomans' next step was predictable. In the autumn of 1768 their forces under the command of the Bosnian vizier attacked near Nikšić. They were met in the narrow Ostrog pass by a Montenegrin force of some 2,000 men and accompanied by Šćepan himself. Hugely outnumbered, the Montenegrins suffered a major defeat, although Šćepan, whose capture had been the vizier's prime objective, escaped. The Ottoman forces then plundered their way through the Crmnica and Bjelopavlići tribal areas, while the Venetians seized the opportunity to attack the coastal areas of Majine, Pobor and Brajić, where support for the self-styled tsar had been especially strong. It was at this low point in Montenegrin fortunes that outside forces intervened. As the Ottoman army was about to launch a second assault, massive storms soaked their ammunition and made it unusable. Then, before the vizier's forces had the chance to prepare a new offensive, the Montenegrins were saved a second time by the outbreak of a new Turco-Russian war. Once again Montenegro's lucky escape became the stuff of myth. Over a century later W.E. Gladstone, then

[50] *Ibid.*, p. 377.
[51] Živković, *Istorija Crnogorskog Naroda*, pp. 201–2.

leader of the Opposition in the British House of Commons and self-appointed tribune of oppressed Christians in the Balkans, wrote of the battle:

[The Montenegrins] assailed before dawn the united forces of the Pashas of Roumelia from the south and Bosnia from the north. Again they effected the scarcely credible slaughter of 20,000 Turks with 3,000 horses, and won an incredible booty of colours, arms, munitions and baggage. So it was that the flood of war gathered round this fortress of faith and freedom, and so it was that flood was beaten back. *Afflavit Dominus, ac dissipantur.*[52]

A few years later[53] Francis Seymour Stevenson, like Gladstone a great admirer of Montenegro and Montenegrins, likened the outcome of the battle to that achieved by England against the Spanish Armada. Given the prominent role played by the elements in the two encounters, his comparison seems closer to the mark than Gladstone's encomium.

Even at the time the Montenegrins' reputation as indomitable fighters against the Turk travelled far beyond the territory's narrow borders, evoking admiration among fellow-Slavs. Looking for allies in the western Balkans to help her pursue the renewed Turco-Russian war, Catherine II invited the Montenegrins to join with other Balkan Christians in rising against the Turks. To drive home the message she despatched as her envoy a member of one of Russia's most illustrious noble families, Prince Vladimir Dolgorukov, but fatally for the success of his cause Dolgorukov was also instructed to call on the Montenegrins to expel Šćepan Mali whose preposterous claims were naturally denied by the Russian court. This had not been the first failure of Russian diplomacy to oust Šćepan. Earlier attempts to warn against the impostor by sending an envoy from Vienna had met with obstruction from the Venetians, who both feared a Russian-Montenegrin plot against their interests and were anxious lest the Sublime Porte should interpret any Russian presence in Montenegro as part of a Venetian-motivated plot against

[52] 'The Lord breathed upon them and they were dispersed.' W. E. Gladstone, 'Montenegro: A Sketch', *The Nineteenth Century: A Monthly Review*, no. 3, May, 1877, pp. 368–9.
[53] Stevenson, *History of Montenegro*, pp. 155–7. Stevenson's history was only published in 1912 although, apart from the final chapter, the work had been written some twenty-eight years earlier.

the empire.[54] In a nice piece of historical irony, the suspicions and intriguing of all three powers played into the interloper's hands, enabling him to survive the various attempts to unseat him which must surely have worked had they been co-ordinated rather than sabotaged by the parties involved.

Bearing an imperial ukase, Dolgorukov embarked for Montenegro accompanied by a large retinue. In Cetinje he addressed an assembly of perhaps 2,000 leading Montenegrins, urging them to support the war against the Ottomans and throw out the impostor. The Montenegrins rejected his demands; not only were they determined to have Šćepan as their leader irrespective of his origins, but they were sufficiently affronted by Russia's interference in the affair to decline—uncharacteristically,—the Russian call to arms. Although in this sense the mission was a failure, Dolgorukov left Montenegro two months later convinced of Šćepan's extraordinary sway over the tribesmen, and even supporting him with the provision of funds. One account has Dolgorukov going further and indulging the false tsar with the uniform of a Russian staff officer, although it is hard to imagine this going down well with the empress.[55]

With the neighbouring countries caught up in larger affairs, Šćepan was left a free hand to tackle the chaotic state of daily life within Montenegro. He now turned his charismatic qualities to achieving pragmatic goals, attempting to give Montenegro some form of civil government. Acting ruthlessly where necessary he suppressed the blood feud which had ravaged so many families and caused havoc among the tribes and clans. In its place he instituted a system of justice, supported by harsh punishments, which for the first time succeeded in protecting life and property. He also initiated the first register of population[56] and tried to regulate and improve markets. As part of his attempt to unify Montenegrins, Šćepan set about building roads in an area where previously there had been none. Per-

---

[54] See Živković, *Istorija Crnogorskog Naroda*, vol. 2, pp. 203–4.
[55] Stevenson, *History of Montenegro*, p. 158.
[56] At the time the population of Montenegro proper numbered at the most some 25,000. But close links now existed with the Brda region to the east whose tribes included the Kuči, Piperi, Bjelopavlići and Vasojevići and with the area adjoining Hercegovina to the north west, home to the Nikšići, Drobnjaci and Pivljani tribes. See Živković, *Istorija Crnogorskog Naroda*, p. 211.

sonally engaged in the project, he lost the sight of one eye in 1770 when laying mines to clear rocks.

But barely six years after it had begun Šćepan's programme of reforms was brought to an end. In August 1773 the false tsar was murdered while asleep in bed by a Greek servant who had been bribed by the vizier of Skadar. Yet, incongruous as it may appear, the interlude of Šćepan's rule stands as rather more than a footnote in Montenegrin history. Autocratic in style and at times cruel, this mysterious outsider succeeded in reining the tribesmen back from the anarchy that was threatening to overwhelm them. Although tribal norms persisted and the society remained exceptionally primitive compared to other parts of Europe, this brief taste of civil order laid a foundation on which Šćepan's successors—Petar I and his nephew Petar Petrović Njegoš—began to build something more closely approximating to a state.

But this did not happen immediately. After Šćepan's death a further eight years passed during which the tribesmen were again led by Sava. Now an old man and less able than ever to impose control, Sava still intended that the succession should pass to his protégé Arsenije Plamenac, but Arsenije too was old and in poor health and, besides, he was not a Petrović. Predictably the impasse triggered a struggle over the succession. On one side were the Petrovići, who were not about to let the most important office slip from their control. They had in mind the young archimandrite Petar, who had tended Vladika Vasilije in St Petersburg at the time of his death. On the other side was Montenegro's second family, the Radonjići, who under a change introduced in 1770 by Šćepan Mali claimed the position of civil governor as a hereditary right, although in earlier times it had been held intermittently by members of the powerful Vukotić clan. Originally intended by Venice to guarantee its influence within Montenegro, the role of civil governor was now becoming a wholly indigenous institution whose incumbent was effectively the second power in the land.[57] Building on the power-base conferred by this office, the Radonjići declared their contender to be Jovan, younger son of the last governor Stanislav Radonjić who had died in St Petersburg in 1758.

[57] Živković, *Istorija Crnogorskog Naroda.*

Petar, who had benefited from four years' schooling in Russia in 1762–6, was known to have been Vasilije's choice as successor and had strong support among the chiefs. However, in the troubled times both preceding and following Sava's death (on 7 March 1781) the success of his claim was by no means guaranteed since Jovan Radonjić also held certain cards in his hand: he not only already possessed a title and formal office while Petar had neither, but had good links with Venice and was intent on developing connections with Austria, which by this time was increasingly taking the place of the crumbling Venetian Republic as the foremost regional power.

Montenegro could ill afford the uncertainty because at this time Kara Mahmud (Black Mahmud), Vizier of Skadar and an Ottoman renegade, was poised to take advantage of any weakness while weighing up his chances of mounting a successful invasion. For Jovan Radonjić the threat offered a chance to display his statesmanship, and he immediately sent a letter to Catherine II seeking again to interest her in the possibility of making Montenegro a Russian protectorate. However, Catherine did not respond and a further mission despatched to Russia by Sava in 1777 was equally unsuccessful. Radonjić saw this as an opportunity to approach Austria with an offer to provide fighting men to defend the Habsburg border in exchange for the protectorate he had failed to obtain from Russia. Already irregular contacts with Austria had been launched by an adventurer, Nikola Marković,[58] who offered to form a legion of Montenegrins to fight for Austria, a scheme that failed when Venetian ships blocked his attempt to embark men from territory under their control. Unfortunately for Radonjić, the activities of this fraudster and his accomplices made his attempt to reach an agreement with them suspect in the eyes of the Habsburg authorities. The governor had aroused great hopes among his fellow Montenegrins who would not easily forgive their disappointment when he failed to deliver on his promises. Worse still, the arrival in Montenegro of an Austrian envoy, Colonel Paulić, sent to Montenegro to prepare a report, excited the suspicions of both the Venetians and the ambitious Ottoman renegade Kara Mahmud.[59] Although the Venetians received assurances

---

[58] Jelavich, *History of the Balkans*, vol. 1, p. 86.
[59] Živković, *Istorija Crnogorskog Naroda*, p. 255.

from Radonjić that this was simply a private visit of experts to advise on minor matters like printing, they did not believe him and encouraged Mahmud in his preparations to attack Montenegro.[60]

Meanwhile the Austrians withdrew to Vienna and presented their report. Although Paulić's conclusions, including his strong endorsement of Radonjić and his pro-Austrian sentiments, were supported by the Austrian Chancellor Kaunitz, the ever-cautious Emperor Joseph II, successor to Maria Theresa, was opposed to a scheme which he believed would not cover its cost.[61] Radonjić might have expected to reap some benefit but, having raised exaggerated hopes, it was not enough to save his position. In 1783 another visit to Austria to plead directly with Kaunitz proved equally fruitless. Moreover, his absence from the country played into Petar's hands when the chiefs meeting in the *zbor* voted to approach the Serbian metropolitan at Sremski Karlovci, Mojsije Putnik, asking him to agree to consecrate Petar as the next Metropolitan of Cetinje. This Mojsije agreed to. Deprived of Austrian support, and rejected by the majority of the Montenegrin chiefs, there was little Jovan Radonjić could do. When Sava's old protégé Arsenije died on 15 May 1784, the way was open for Petar's consecration as metropolitan, which took place in Sremski Karlovci on 13 October the same year.

Internal dynamics and the traditional esteem enjoyed by the Petrović clan thus had more influence than external factors in resolving the power struggle within Montenegro. This was not surprising: despite the developments that had taken place during the eighteenth century, Montenegro was still an essentially conservative society in which the tribal chiefs played a predominant part. Few ordinary Montenegrins knew much of the world beyond Kotor and most lived in isolated hamlets. There were no schools. The extent of tribesmen's insularity and backwardness had been demonstrated by their readiness to accept the false tsar and, except during Šćepan's period of draconian rule, by the continued prevalence of the blood feud and raiding.

There was, however, some opening to the outside world compared to the two preceding centuries. The many letters written to

[60] Živković, *Istorija Crnogorskog Naroda*, p. 256.
[61] *Ibid.*, pp. 256–7.

the authorities in Russia, Austria and Venice and the journeys undertaken by Danilo, Vasilije and Sava and others acting on their behalf testify poignantly to the Montenegrins' attempts to develop links with the powers which they believed could protect them and engender a degree of prosperity. Also, the considerable number of émigrés, especially to Russia, offered them an additional though somewhat opaque window on the outside world.

Yet the end of the eighteenth century saw a weakening of the link with Russia, which had been one of the most important developments of this period. That a shared Orthodoxy lay at the root of this connection was ironic given the notorious vagueness of the Montenegrins, who had originally been so much admired in Russia as resolute defenders of Orthodoxy against Islam, on the doctrinal basis of their religion. An Austrian report of the time noted 'Except that they keep the fast, they have no religion.' Religious practice was heavily influenced by traditional beliefs and local superstitions. Priests were often poorly educated, more at ease bearing arms than discussing matters of doctrine. As Petar himself was to show, fame as a fearless leader of men in battle was still, as in Joan of Arc's France, compatible with sainthood. Yet despite the loosening of bonds with Russia, the newly-consecrated Petar Petrović set off there in 1784 on yet another supplicant journey. His pre-eminent position in Montenegrin history (assured by an astonishing victory against the feared Kara Mahmud) was still far in the future.

5. Montenegro in the time of Petar I (1774–1830)

At the time of Petar's ordination the western Balkans were in a state of upheaval, prey to constant fighting as a result of the Porte's inability to control local upstarts whose rivalries and territorial ambitions directly threatened Montenegro. The country's position was perilous since neither its traditional ally Russia nor its neighbours Venice and Austria showed any interest in offering protection. At this time too Montenegro was a society economically stretched to the limit. It still had no access to the sea, and famine remained a threat, leading to a consistently high rate of emigration.

The new Vladika, like his predecessors, lacked the authority to face down such challenges. He did not control the election of tribal chiefs; he was unable to levy taxes; with no army or forces at his disposal apart from the members of his own clan he could not contain the inter-tribal conflict or prevent the habitual cross-border raiding which invited Muslim retaliation. What authority he possessed was moral rather than temporal. It enabled him to mediate in disputes, plead causes, call down curses or utter threats of excommunication, but not to impose his decisions or enforce order. The Vladika's effectiveness thus depended largely on force of personality, a tall order in a society where every man was a warrior with strong local loyalties and where travel on foot or, rarely, by horse and mule was the only effective means of communication.

But if character was what counted, Petar I had it in abundance; his presence impressed not only his fellow-countrymen but, even more important and for the first time, the outside world. As one of the few educated Montenegrins—the others tended to be monks or from abroad—Petar was necessarily the principal contact with representatives of foreign governments and influential individuals. In this respect, the times would soon be more propitious as the military campaigns of the Napoleonic wars drew fighting men from many countries to Kotor and the surrounding coastal region. Petar understood that outside involvement offered opportunities for Montenegrin aggrandisement, both territorially and in terms of his small country's international prestige, and although his vastly exaggerated hopes inevitably led to disappointments, he was right to see the wars as contributing to it. The attention Montenegro attracted through exposure to the outside world was far greater than its size and military contribution warranted, and contemporary accounts stressed Petar's personal part in this. Simply put, Petar I put Montenegro on the map, and in this way opened a new chapter in his country's history.

The Ottoman renegade, Kara Mahmud

Yet Petar I's years as Vladika could hardly have begun less auspiciously. In 1785, at the beginning of his time in office, he was still in Russia where he had arrived some months earlier with the aim of restoring close relations with the court, which had been badly damaged over the years by the political intriguing of Montenegrin malcontents.[1] Petar, as head of the Montenegrin Church, attached great importance to reviving the Orthodox connection with Russia, but his immediate concern was to enlist Russian protection against the powerful Muslim renegade, Kara Mahmud Bušatlija, whose ambitions represented the gravest threat to Montenegro. Although Montenegro was isolated and its position appeared desperate, Petar's mission was ill-timed: in June 1785 Kara Mahmud chose to launch a long-planned attack, while the Russians, far from welcoming his overtures, simply expelled him from the country.[2]

Mahmud Pasha Bušatlija was the son of the former Ottoman governor of Skadar, whom he succeeded in 1779. Modelling himself on the great Albanian hero Skanderbeg,[3] Kara Mahmud (Black

---

[1] See Živković, *Istorija Crnogorskog Naroda*, vol. 2, pp. 260–1.
[2] Živković, *Istorija Crnogorskog Naroda*, p. 262.
[3] Skanderbeg, after the name taken by Gjergj Castriot, the Albanian nobleman who led a revolt against the Porte in 1443–68, and not to be confused with the Islamicised son of Ivan Crnojević who later took the same name.

Mahmud), as the young Bušatlija was known in the West, soon led a revolt against the Porte during which he laid claim to part of Albania as well as Montenegro. Taking advantage of Petar's absence and the tribes' disunity, Kara Mahmud was able to detach the chiefs of some of the *nahije* closest to the Ottoman border and thus facilitate his entry into the Katuni *nahija*, the principal locus of Montenegrin resistance to his expansionist plans. Petar, disillusioned by his experience in Russia, returned home the following February to find large parts of the country pillaged and on the verge of starvation. Cetinje had been sacked and the monastery destroyed once more.

In this grim situation it was at least a consolation to find the Katuni *nahija* no longer occupied. Pressed by lack of supplies, Kara Mahmud had remained in Cetinje, which had only one well, for just six days before withdrawing via the coastal territory of the Paštrovići, an Orthodox tribe which from the time of the Treaty of Passarowitz had been under Venetian jurisdiction.[4] Next Kara Mahmud summoned the Paštrovići leaders to a meeting where he demanded that they swear allegiance to him. When they refused he had them executed, and pillaged and burnt their territory. Venice protested to the Porte which, wishing to avoid piling on further troubles at a time when Venice had refused all help to the Montenegrins, redoubled its efforts against the renegade, but to no avail. Not only did Kara Mahmud manage to defeat the first force the sultan sent against him, but in 1787 he succeeded in burning the Turkish fleet at anchor in the Bojana river.[5]

Kara Mahmud's successes against the Porte had aroused the interest of Russia and Austria, which jointly had designs on the Ottoman Empire. When conflict between these Christian powers and the Ottomans broke out in 1787, Montenegro too began to attract the attention of Russia and Austria as they sought support from Balkan Christians against the Porte. In a welcome new development both Catherine II of Russia and the Habsburg Emperor Joseph II now wooed Montenegro, offering financial support, military advisers and volunteers to further the war effort. At the same time Joseph II sent his representatives to Kara Mahmud to seek his

[4] See Chapter 3.
[5] See Lenormant, *Turcs et Monténégrins*, pp. 216–19.

participation on the Austro-Russian side, but Mahmud, believing that the Porte would eventually win, slaughtered the envoys and sent their heads to the sultan to confirm his change of heart.

In 1791 the Austrians signed the Treaty of Sistova, with the Ottoman government, broadly guaranteeing a return to the *status quo* before the war. The following year at Jassy (Iaşi in modern Romania), the Russians signed a separate peace whereby they acquired further territory in what is now Ukraine, giving them a border with the Ottoman Empire. The Montenegrins, who in their customary manner had entertained excessive hopes of the war, were awarded no gains; on the contrary the Treaty of Sistova, to which Britain was a signatory, specifically designated Montenegro as a province of Turkey.[6] Nonetheless the Montenegrins continued their defiant stance towards Kara Mahmud with Petar supporting the Brda tribes in their refusal to pay the tribute demanded by Mahmud despite the risks involved. The Montenegrins' position was indeed perilous though Petar, a wily diplomatist, attempted as best he could to maintain good relations with both Venice and Vienna and thus a lifeline to the outside world. But his efforts were often vitiated by the depredations wrought by his fellow Montenegrins. In 1795 one such affray in the market-place at Kotor left thirty dead, leading the Venetians to bar the Montenegrins from access to the market.[7]

In 1796 Kara Mahmud decided to impose his control once and for all on the rebel Piperi and Bjelopavlići tribes, both of which not only refused to pay tribute but were constantly blockading and attacking Turkish caravans seeking to pass from Podgorica to Nikšić through their tribal territory. Despite Mahmud's warnings Petar, as head of the Montenegrin chiefs, was determined to come to their aid. Battle was joined at Martinići near Spuž in the territory of the Bjelopavlići on 11 July. The Montenegrins were divided in their customary fashion into two forces under Vladika Petar and the civil governor Jovan Radonjić who, having accepted Petar's pre-eminence, had been permitted to retain his office. Before the battle Petar

[6] Lord Loftus to the Earl of Malmesbury, 19 April 1858, Document no. 47 published in *Montenegro: Political and Ethnic Boundaries 1840–1920*, vol. I, edited by Beitullah Destani, Chippenham (Wilts): Archive edition, 2001, pp. 72–3.
[7] Živković, *Istorija Crnogorskog Naroda*, vol. 2, p. 285.

delivered the following philippic much quoted by Montenegrin historians:

Gentle Knights [*Vitezovi*] and dear Brothers—
Our mortal enemy did not accede to my appeal to refrain from further bloodshed and leave our unfortunate brothers the Highlanders alone, but I trust in Almighty God that you will this day drive this cruel Satan in shame from our borders. He recruited an unnumbered army, but it is weak and miserable and above all God will help us. We came here, dear knights and heroes, to shed our blood against our foes. We came to show them [the value of] our faith, our name and our beloved freedom, that we are Montenegrins, that we are a people willing to fight for freedom to the last drop of blood and sacrifice our lives on the frontiers [defended by] our immortal ancestors, but we will not allow the enemy to enter alive into our free and beloved mountains, which our great-grandfathers, grandfathers and fathers and we ourselves have defended with our blood.[8]

Whether or not they were inspired by Petar's words, the Montenegrins succeeded against all odds in overcoming Kara Mahmud's much larger force. Mahmud himself was wounded, but he survived and, deeply humiliated by the defeat, plotted revenge. In September the same year he led a large army into the Lješnjani *nahija*. This time his aim was to crush Montenegro completely, and to ensure success he had even enlisted a number of French officers from Bonaparte's revolutionary forces together with his mainly Albanian army. The second battle took place at Krusi (near Podgorica) on 4 October 1796. Some accounts describe Mahmud's troops as caught in a narrow defile between the two sections of the Montenegrin army so that many of them were cut to pieces. Others refer to the Albanians retreating in confusion across the plain to the Morača river, where many drowned.[9] Mahmud himself was captured and beheaded, and his head was carried back in triumph to be placed on display in Cetinje.

The victory at Krusi was to be one of the most celebrated in Montenegrin history. It not only conclusively removed the threat posed by Kara Mahmud and secured a period of peace with the

[8] Quoted by Živković, *ibid.*, pp. 291–3 (the present author's translation).
[9] See John Gardner Wilkinson, *Dalmatia and Montenegro*, London: John Murray, 1848, vol. I, part 2, pp. 489–90, and Stevenson, *History of Montenegro*, p. 165.

Ottoman Empire, but gave Montenegro a significant increase in territory by allowing the annexation of the Brda region inhabited by the Piperi and Bjelopavlići tribes. Reports of the Montenegrins' victories over the notorious Kara Mahmud spread far beyond Montenegro's borders, not only among the Slavs of Serbia and Bosnia, but as far as Russia and France. The *British and Foreign Quarterly Review* (of July 1840) described the battle of Krusi as 'the most glorious and decisive of all that ever took place between the Montenegrins and the Turks'.[10] The triumph of Montenegro seemed briefly complete when in 1799 a Turkish *firman* recognised that it had never been a vassal of Turkey.[11] But while the Montenegrins were to claim it as an important precedent, amounting to formal recognition of what was by now *de facto* independence, the concession was soon retracted.

First steps on the road to unity

One of the effects of this period of constant warfare was to stimulate the process of internal unity the better to resist the pressure of external enemies. Even before the critical battle at Krusi the assembly of tribal chiefs meeting at Cetinje had adopted an act known as the *Stega* (fastening), which proclaimed the unification of the Montenegrin heartland with the Brda. Two years later, in 1798, the tribal leaders met at the Stanjevići monastery to form the first organ of central government above the chief's assembly, the *praviteljstvo suda*[12] (court) whose fifty members, presided over by the Vladika, were supposed to fulfil a combination of administrative and judicial functions. At the same time the tribal leaders agreed to adopt a law code (*zakonik*) for Montenegro and the Brda, based on tribal custom, to which a further body of law was added in 1803. In principle these steps were intended to signal a real increase in the central power of the Vladika, but in practice the change was often more apparent than real. Many disputes continued to be dealt with locally by tribal

---

[10] *Ibid.*, p. 489.

[11] *Foreign Office Handbook on Montenegro*, November 1918, p. 13.

[12] The *praviteljstvo suda* soon became known as the *kuluk* (*kuluk* = unpaid work), in recognition of the fact that its members received no payment. (See Andrijašević and Rastoder, *History of Montenegro*, p. 81.)

leaders according to traditional practices. Although the Vladika himself would at times attempt to arbitrate, tribes at any distance from Cetinje were largely free to continue their traditional raiding and feuding in defiance of the new laws.

Contending with empires

Externally Montenegro was soon caught up in the wave of further European wars which followed the convulsion provoked by the French Revolution. In 1797 Napoleon launched his Mediterranean campaign, which inflicted defeats on both Venice and Austria. When the fighting spread to the Dalmatian coast the Montenegrins were able to seize a stretch of coastal territory from the Venetians, but the gains proved ephemeral. In the Treaty of Campo Formio signed in that year France and Austria divided the Venetian lands in the Mediterranean between them. Cetinje was forced to look on in dismay when the Habsburg Empire displaced Venice as the controlling power on the Adriatic coast with jurisdiction over Kotor and surrounding territory.

Unable either to capitalise on these events or even to protect his people from their impact, Petar I continued to seek support from Russia where the less imperialistically ambitious Paul had succeeded his mother, Catherine II, in 1796. Abandoning her anti-Ottoman policies, Paul sought instead to improve relations with the Porte, and in 1799 joined an alliance—directed against France—with Britain, Austria and the Ottoman Empire. Paul's formal relationship with the Porte and with Austria can hardly have commended itself to Petar I since it precluded Russia supporting either of Montenegro's principal foreign policy goals, namely to win international recognition, which was naturally resisted by Turkey, and to acquire an Adriatic port, to which Austria was strongly opposed. But the Vladika was not about to put any disappointment he felt at these developments above the need to attract Russian backing both as a defence against possible aggression by predatory neighbours and as a source of much-needed material aid. Petar's blueprint for future relations envisaged a fresh start after the difficulties of the preceding twenty years: in return for financial and military protection Montenegro would place itself under the formal patronage of the Emperor of Russia, a proposal recalling the dreams of Vladika Vasilije.[13] Paul responded with an immediate gift of 3,000 roubles for the Cetinje monastery and promised to send a Russian fleet to protect the Orthodox population of the area and to restore the regular subsidy.[14]

As in the past, however, the relationship did not proceed smoothly. Petar's plans went awry when, following Paul's assassination in 1801, he dispatched an envoy, Stevan Vukotić, to convey his greetings to the new tsar, Alexander I. Instead of securing a continuation of the subsidy as instructed, Vukotić chose instead to denounce Petar for contacts with French agents in Dalmatia. Despite his renewed hopes of Russia, Petar had judged it prudent to maintain contact with the French, but his clever diplomacy was now about to backfire. A Russian envoy of Serbian origin, Colonel Marko Ivelić, was sent to Montenegro as part of a plot to overthrow Petar and replace him with a member of the Vukotić clan. Not surprisingly Russian-Montenegrin relations plummeted, but Petar, though briefly threatened, was not to be dislodged. Successfully securing the backing of the majority of the chiefs, he was able to outmanoeuvre Ivelić and in time effect a reconciliation with St Petersburg. As relations improved, the Russians first established a consulate in Kotor and then increased their representation by appointing a prominent diplomat, the Tsar's personal envoy Stevan Andrejevich Sankowsky, to intensify contact with Montenegro. For the Montenegrins such tangible proof of renewed Russian interest was welcome, and as would soon become apparent, it prepared the ground for closer military co-operation.[15]

By 1805 Russia, Austria and Britain had resumed their war against Napoleon with both a French fleet and a Russian one under Vice-Admiral Senyavin competing for influence in the Adriatic. At the end of that year Austria suffered defeat by France at Austerlitz and under the Treaty of Pressburg was forced to surrender its Dalmatian territories, including the Gulf of Kotor, to the French. This dramatic turn of events greatly alarmed the people of the coast. The

---

[13] Živković, *Istorija Crnogorskog Naroda*, vol. 2, p. 381.
[14] See Jelavich, *History of the Balkans*, vol. 1, p. 120.
[15] See Živković, *Istorija Crnogorskog Naroda*, vol. 2, pp. 322–3.

Orthodox tribes to the south of Kotor declared themselves ready to throw off the French occupiers and join the Montenegrins while the Catholic population stood aside, as reluctant to be ruled by the French as they were to join Montenegro and wishing only to be allowed to continue as subjects of the Emperor of Austria. But after centuries confined to the mountains the Montenegrins were not about to let slip an opportunity to gain possession of a stretch of Adriatic coastline—any more than were the commanders of the Russian fleet still hovering offshore.

Despite the risks involved, Petar I lost no time in summoning the assembly of tribesmen which on 27 February 1806 voted to demand the surrender by Austria of all its fortresses on the coast to the newly-formed alliance of Montenegrins, Russians and *Bocchesi* (as the coastal population of the Gulf of Kotor region or *Boka* were known), or expect an attempt to take them by force. Faced with such an ultimatum and lacking the time to consult his superiors, the Austrian commandant chose simply to retreat and to leave the coast, including the vital Spanish fort (Forte Mare) of Herceg Novi (Castelnuovo), in the hands of the Montenegrins and a number of Russian detachments which Senyavin, acting without authorisation and at his own risk, had sent ashore to provide further support. Kotor too was swiftly taken over by the Russians and Montenegrins. Intense diplomatic efforts to put an end to the crisis involving all three powers—Russia, Austria and France—failed to resolve it and left the Russians and Montenegrins in occupation. As Russian and French naval forces clashed off the Dalmatian coast, some 3,000 Montenegrins joined the *Bocchesi* in attacking the French, their efforts adding significantly to the number of casualties.[16]

However, in May 1806, despite those efforts, the French General Lauriston succeeded in taking Dubrovnik (Ragusa), which was then besieged by Russian and Montenegrin forces. Although Dubrovnik withstood the siege, the combined Slav forces were able to hold the town of Cavtat just to the south and the surrounding territory. For the next few weeks the French in Dubrovnik had to endure constant harrying by bands of Montenegrins, and the besieged city was only

[16] Živković, *Istorija Crnogorskog Naroda*, pp. 324.

relieved by the arrival of a substantial contingent of French troops at the end of June. Forced to abandon the city and its immediate environs, the Russians and Montenegrins managed to maintain their control of the shores of the Gulf of Kotor over the next few months. It was only in September with the arrival of Napoleon's commander General Marmont (later Marshal and Duke of Ragusa) that the French were able to enforce their claim to all the surrounding coastal territory. Marmont's fellow-countryman Colonel Vialla de Sommières, subsequently commandant of Castelnuovo (Herceg Novi) and for six years governor of the French-ruled province of Cattaro (Kotor), left the following account of the Montenegrins' offensive tactics and eventual defeat:

When the French force approached Castel Nuovo, it was suddenly attacked by 10,000 Montenegrines, united to the Russian troops, who had landed on the banks of the Saturina [Sutorina]. Our army was thus thrown into disorder, and was obliged to retreat by Ragusa, which the Montenegrines entered in the confusion of the pursuit. They immediately took possession of the town, levied contributions, laid waste Old Ragusa, and burnt Santa Croce, better known by the name of Gravosa, or the Port of Ragusa. In a second engagement they were, however, completely defeated and dispersed, being unable to sustain the regular attack of our battalions. The Russians, who had placed great reliance on the Montenegrines, were, in consequence, obliged to re-embark precipitately; renouncing, on the one hand, the advantages of an excellent position, and on the other, the aid of a numerous squadron, which, while it intercepted the entrance to the mouths of the Cattaro, would have dealt destruction along the plain of the Salterns, Sutorina, which we occupied. Forty-eight hours sufficed for the retreat of the enemy's force. The Vladika, who, two days before, had been animating the courage of his hordes, and leading them on with extraordinary courage and skill, now hastily retired to the convent of Savina, which was covered by the line of Castel Nuovo and the Spanish fort. There he rallied his forces, and, on the third day commenced his march towards Montenegro.[17]

Meanwhile, from the other side a Russian naval officer serving under Admiral Senyavin, Vladimir Broniewski, had also been recording his impressions of the methods of warfare employed by

---

[17] L. C. Vialla de Sommières, *Travels in Montenegro*, London: Philips & Co., 1820, p. 2.

Russia's Montenegrin allies, including those that risked leading to possibly fateful misunderstandings:

> A Montenegrin never craves for mercy; and whenever one of them is severely wounded, and it is impossible to save him from the enemy, his own comrades cut off his head. When at the attack of Clobuk [Klobuk] a little detachment of our troops was obliged to retreat, an officer of stout-make, and no longer young, fell on the ground from exhaustion. A Montenegrin perceiving it ran immediately to him, and, having drawn his yatagan, said, '*You are very brave, and must wish that I should cut off your head: say a prayer, and make the sign of the cross.*' The officer, horrified at the proposition, made an effort to rise, and rejoined his comrades with the assistance of the friendly Montenegrin. They consider all those taken by the enemy as killed. They carry out of the battle their wounded comrades on their shoulders; and let it be said to their honour, they acted in the same manner by our officers and soldiers.[18]

Broniewski's account goes on to describe in detail the Montenegrins' exceptional skill as marksmen as well as their predilection for the guerrilla tactics of harassment and surprise, but his conclusions highlight both their strengths and weaknesses as a fighting force:

> Their extraordinary boldness frequently triumphed over the skill of the experienced bands of the French. Attacking the columns of the enemy in front and flank, and acting separately, without any other system than the inspirations of personal courage, they were not afraid of the terrible battalion fire of the French infantry...
>
> [They] cannot withstand regular troops beyond their mountains; because destroying everything with fire and sword, they cannot long keep the field; and the advantage of their courage in assisting our troops, and the fruits of victory, were lost by their want of order. During the siege of Ragusa, it was never possible to know how many of them were actually under arms, because they were constantly going to their homes with spoil, whilst others joined the army in their places, and after a few days of indefatigable exertion, returned to the mountains, to carry away some insignificant trifle.[19]

Short-lived though they were, the joint operations with the Russians had been enough to arouse the Montenegrins' expansionist

---

[18] Quoted in Wilkinson, *Dalmatia and Montenegro*, vol. 1, part 2, p. 434.
[19] *Ibid.*, p. 437.

dreams, which as always took little account of St Petersburg's hard-headed attitude to collaboration with the small Balkan countries. With an enthusiasm worthy of his predecessor Vladika Vasilije, Petar sent a letter to Tsar Alexander I proposing the creation of a large Slav state, to include modern Hercegovina, Dalmatia, Dubrovnik and part of Albania. Although Dubrovnik would be the capital, Montenegro would be at its heart and Vladika Petar the prince, his position secured by Russian patronage.[20] How badly misplaced Petar's hopes in Russia had been soon became evident when the Russians, having settled their differences with the French under the Treaty of Tilsit in 1807, readily sacrificed Montenegrin interests in pursuit of broader European goals. As part of the package agreed at Tilsit the Russians accepted that the Kotor region should be ceded to France. With the fortresses of the Gulf of Kotor in French hands, the Montenegrins were again confined to their mountains. Petar I is said to have lamented during a meeting with Vialla de Sommières: 'When shall I behold the seas, or rather the commerce of the world set at liberty?'[21]

After their victory on the coast the French had plans to advance further into 'Illyria', as they called their Dalmatian territories. At the time Napoleon himself expressed an interest in Montenegro and was reported to have written to General Marmont: 'How is it that you never speak to me of the Montenegrins? It doesn't do to have an inflexible character. Send agents among them and try to win over this country's agitators.'[22] So, attempting to conciliate the natives of the interior, Marmont held a meeting with Vladika Petar in August 1807. The encounter was lively, and the Vladika was prepared, as ever, to argue Montenegro's case. When the General remonstrated with him over the Montenegrins' practice of cutting off the heads of their enemies (they were alleged to have used the head of the unfortunate French General Delgorges for a football after the siege of Herceg Novi), Petar is said to have remarked that the French had themselves publicly cut off the heads of their own King and Queen

---

[20] Banac, *The National Question*, p. 274 and Jelavich, *History of the Balkans*, vol. 1, p. 121.

[21] Vialla de Sommières, *Travels in Montenegro*, p. 80.

[22] Extract from the French journal *Moniteur* of 20 June 1858 and quoted in *Montenegro Political and Ethnic Boundaries*, vol. 1, p. 226.

in a square in Paris.[23] Seemingly the exchange was not harsh enough to prevent Marmont from recording a generally favourable impression: 'This Vladika is a splendid man, of about fifty-five years of age, with a strong spirit. He conducts himself with nobility and dignity. His positive and legal authority is unrecognised in his country, but his personal influence is unlimited.'[24]

Despite the attempted thaw, relations with the Montenegrins soon began to deteriorate when the French came to believe that the tribesmen and the Vladika in particular were behind their problems with the population of the coastal region. To try to force the Montenegrins into line they attempted to establish a consulate in Cetinje, a move that Petar I steadfastly opposed. Armed incidents continued and markets on the coast were again closed to Montenegrins. In the hinterland too clashes continued between French and Ottoman detachments and Montenegrin tribesmen. In 1811 the French planned a major attack on Montenegro, only to abandon it when they met with strong resistance from the Piperi. Subsequent attacks, launched from both Hercegovina and Skadar, were also pushed back—in one such encounter Petar himself was wounded.[25] Hostility—magnified on the Montenegrins' part by their view of the French as allies of the hated Turk—reached such a point of intensity that Napoleon threatened to make of Montenegro a Monte Rosso.[26] But before he could make good his threat, the fear of French reprisals against Montenegro was removed by a rapid turn-about in world events. In 1812 Napoleon began his fateful invasion of Russia, leading to the catastrophic defeat of his army and eventually to his own fall from power. A British naval contingent stationed in the Adriatic established its main naval base on the nearby island of Vis, from where in 1813 they began the reconquest of Dalmatia. Hoping to succeed where their earlier efforts had failed, the Montenegrins began to pursue contacts with the British contingent, commanded by Captain William Hoste whose journal recording his campaigns in the Adriatic was published in London in 1833. His journal entry for 13 October 1813

---

[23] See Vialla de Sommières, *Travels in Montenegro*, p. 24.
[24] Živković, *Istorija Crnogorskog Naroda*, vol. 2, p. 329.
[25] See Houston, *Nikola and Milena*, p. 37.
[26] *Foreign Office Handbook on Montenegro*, November 1918, p. 13.

describes his arrival in the Gulf of Kotor and includes his first reflections on the Montenegrins:

[The Gulf] is twenty miles in length and three or four in width, with sufficient water for men-of-war, forming together the completest port in the world. Extremely high mountains are on both banks. The lower regions are inhabited by a people called Bocchesi, the upper parts by a race of men almost savages. One of these mountains is called the Monte Negro, whence the natives are denominated Montenegrins. The Austrians are the rightful sovereigns of the country, but it was ceded to the French at the last peace with Austria. Since that time the Montenegrins have carried on hostilities with the French and give them no quarter, but they are such a ferocious set that no-one likes to have anything to do with them. The chief person among them is their archbishop, who is of a very different nature from his adherents. He is a man of education, has been some time in Russia, and is very much respected by everybody. His influence is almost unbounded with the Montenegrins, except in the article of plunder. He has made several overtures to our Government for assistance, which have not been listened to till now.[27]

Almost immediately, however, the persistence of the Montenegrins paid off and a mere three days later (on 16 October) Hoste's journal records a joint British-Montenegrin assault on Herceg Novi and the Spanish fort at the end of the Gulf of Kotor, which resulted in the capture of the town. This success was swiftly followed by an attempt on Kotor, with the Montenegrins attacking by land and the British by sea. Although the Austrians had pledged support for the attempt, their troops were held up in Zadar (Zara) on the Croatian coast, forcing Hoste to look for help from the abundantly willing Montenegrins. By this stage Hoste's initially favourable impression of Petar—'a commanding figure; and of a mild but majestic aspect'[28]—had undergone some revision as he noted the 'deep game' the Vladika was playing:

His evident aim in paying court to us is to procure powder and ammunition, of which he is in great want, but I am mistaken if a hundredth part of it will be expended against the French. Unless some power sends a large regular force, he and his hordes will overrun Cattaro and its neigh-

---

[27] Richard Bentley (ed.), *Memoirs and Letters of Captain Sir William Hoste*, London, 1833, vol. 2, p. 187.
[28] *Ibid.*, p. 191.

bourhood, which, barren as it is, is, I am told, a paradise compared to the Monte Negro.²⁹

In January 1814 Hoste and his sailors finally secured the surrender of Kotor, after dragging cannons up the precipitous mountainside and firing down upon the town. The operation was an exhausting undertaking in which Hoste's men were helped, not by the Austrians who were nowhere to be seen, but by the Montenegrins who acted throughout under a Russian flag. Montenegrin zeal was, however, to place Hoste in an invidious position when the Austrians finally arrived at Herceg Novi. By this time Petar had set up a 'Central Commission', composed half of members from Montenegro and half of *Bocchesi*, which, with the apparent acquiescence of the population of the *Boka*, was to oversee a union of both territories. Naturally Petar himself was to head the Commission, and Kotor was to be the new capital.³⁰

However, a hitch appeared, when shortly afterwards the Austrian general, Milutinović, made his belated appearance at Herceg Novi and requested Hoste's assistance in conveying his troops to Kotor in order to avoid clashing with the Montenegrins, who now held the intervening territory and were threatening to provoke 'civil war'. Confessing himself to be in 'a most awkward position', Hoste declined to assist the Austrians and departed for Dubrovnik after simply handing over the keys of the city to the civil magistrate and thus to the *'Bocchesi* themselves'. Although he wished, as he put it, neither to offend the Russian flag nor to give Austria cause for complaint by allowing the Vladika to enter Kotor, his decision earned him a rebuke from the British Ambassador in Vienna, the Earl of Aberdeen, who regretted Hoste's enlistment of barbarians to achieve his objective.³¹ Fortunately for Hoste, his actions in the Gulf of Kotor, soon to be followed by similar success at Ragusa, did not ultimately blight his career. Overlooking any slight to his own commander, Milutinović, Francis I of Austria awarded Hoste the Order of Maria Theresa. At home, Hoste's courage and endurance in the course of a campaign that inflicted lasting damage on his health took considerably longer

---

²⁹ *Ibid.*, p. 209.
³⁰ *Ibid.*, pp. 231–2.
³¹ Letter from the Earl of Aberdeen to Captain Hoste of 23 February, 181, *ibid.*, pp. 234–5.

to achieve acknowledgement; however, the British government eventually awarded him a knighthood.

Fate proved to be less kind to the Montenegrins, since the Russians, Austria's allies, intervened on their account with the Vladika in order to secure the Montenegrins' withdrawal from all the lands around the Gulf of Kotor. Shortly afterwards at the Congress of Vienna in 1815, the Concert of Europe confirmed the Habsburg Empire's possession of the Kotor region which, together with the whole of Dalmatia, remained a separate administrative unit under the control of the House of Habsburg until its fall in 1918. Ruled by an appointee of the Austrian Crown and denied political representation, the local population were, however, able to enjoy a degree of religious liberty thanks to laws enacted by Napoleon's revolutionary regime. Such a concession—frustrating the pressure for conversion exerted by the Catholic Church—would have important consequences for the Orthodox majority in the *Boka* region allowing them to retain a sense of separate identity even while benefiting from the social and economic development that was to take place under the Austrians.[32] This dispensation, had they even been aware of it, could have afforded little consolation to the Montenegrins, who had as ever hoped for more from Russia. As it was, they faced a wasteland, partly of their own making, in which—in the absence of outside aid—some 2,000 Montenegrins starved to death.[33]

The devastation and bloodshed which accompanied the tribesmen's embroilment in the Napoleonic wars in the Adriatic put Montenegro on the map as far as the wider world was concerned, but did so in a way that lastingly affected outsiders' perceptions of Montenegrins.[34] In the aftermath of the campaign, officers' accounts of Montenegrin exploits were swiftly followed by those of ethnographers and other interested travellers from many parts of Europe. Almost all, irrespective of their country of origin or gender, depicted

---

[32] Ćirković, *The Serbs*, p. 188.
[33] Milovan Djilas wrote: 'A wasteland remained wherever the Montenegrins had passed: partly they and partly the colonials [the Austrians], as well as the Russians and the French, razed and looted everything within reach' (*Njegoš*, p. 51)
[34] See Cathy Carmichael and Božidar Jezernik, 'Gender and the Construction of Montenegrin National Identity before 1918', in Wojciech Burszta, Tomasz Kamusella and Sebastian Wojciechowski (eds), *Nationalism across the globe: An overview of the nationalisms of state-endowed and stateless nations*, Poznan: Wyzsza Szkola Nauk Humanistyeznych i Dziennikarstwa, 2005.

the Montenegrins as 'born warriors'.[35] As to whether or not their savagery was of the 'noble' variety opinion was by no means so unanimous, although for the most part English-speakers and, more surprisingly given the circumstances, the Montenegrins' French adversaries tended to take a broadly positive view.[36]

Relations with Serbia

Intense preoccupation with events in the Gulf of Kotor had meanwhile prevented the Montenegrins from becoming closely involved in the anti-Ottoman campaign that was being simultaneously waged in Serbia. From 1804 the Serbs, under the *hajduk*-cum-revolutionary leader Djordje Petrović[37] or Karadjordje (Black George), had been engaged in their own struggles, first against rebel janissaries who had attacked and slaughtered many local Serbian leaders, and later, as the original uprising took on more nationalist colouring, against the janissaries' nominal masters, the Ottoman Turks. Despite this, St Petersburg had not responded in the two years immediately following the Serbian uprising to Karadjordje's quest for allies in pursuit of his wider rebellion against the Ottoman Empire principally because Russian foreign policy interests at the time required that out of fear of his ally Napoleon the sultan should not be antagonised. Wishing to remain on side with Russia, the Montenegrins tended to follow St Petersburg's lead despite their sympathy for the Serbian cause. In January 1804 Petar I had sent a letter to the abbot of the Dečani monastery in South Serbia indicating Montenegro's readiness to support the Serbian uprising, but by the following year his letters to the illiterate Karadjordje were urging restraint.[38] However, Russian pressure may not have been the only factor: there are indications that the Vladika himself had doubts about supporting an uprising at a time when he was cautioning the Rovčani and Mora-

---

[35] See Vesna Goldsworthy, *Inventing Ruritania: The Imperialism of the Imagination*, New Haven and London: Yale University Press, 1998, p. 218n.

[36] See, for example, Stevenson, *History of Montenegro*, p. 172n, and Alis Nolte, *Essai sur le Monténégro* (Calmann-Lévy, 1907), republished by the National Library 'Radosav Ljumović', Podgorica, 1996, p. 34.

[37] The clan came originally from Hercegovina and was related to the Petrović clan of Njeguši.

[38] Michael Boro Petrovich, *A History of Modern Serbia 1804–1918*, New York: Harcourt Brace Jovanovich, 1976, vol. 1, p. 26.

čani tribes, on the fringes of Montenegro, to remain quiescent in order to avoid provoking Ottoman reprisals.[39] Needless-to-say, the tribesmen did not always heed the Vladika's advice, with the result that both parties continued to launch attacks across the ill-defined border with Hercegovina.

From 1806, when the Russian attitude towards the Serbian uprising became more openly positive after the outbreak of war with the sultan, Petar's policy followed suit. In 1807 the withdrawal of Montenegro's forces from the coast under the provisions of the Treaty of Tilsit freed sufficient troops for co-operation with Serbia, but in 1809 the Montenegrins joined with Serbs from Serbia and Hercegovina in an attack on the Ottoman fortress towns of Nikšić and Klobuk in Hercegovina, only to suffer defeat. The experience appears to have reinforced Petar's cautious attitude since he continued to urge the tribesmen to wait for the opportune moment rather than risk destruction at the hands of the Turks. When Karadjordje appealed in a letter to Petar 'to show your love for Christianity by attacking the enemy and advancing to us', Montenegrin support was not forthcoming.[40]

Like the Montenegrins, the Serbs had allowed themselves to become dependent on Russian support for their stand against the Turks, for which they received backing for as long as Russia continued to wage war against Ottoman Turkey during the Napoleonic wars. But, as in Montenegro, Russia was never tempted to put the interest of fellow-Slavs in Serbia above its own foreign policy interests, and in consequence its support for the Serbian uprising fluctuated in accordance with its oscillating attitudes to France and the Ottoman Empire. Thus when Napoleon's Russian campaign compelled St Petersburg to withdraw forces from the Balkans in 1812 in order to defend the homeland, Karadjordje was left in a highly vulnerable position. In 1813 the Ottomans counter-attacked and overwhelmed the Serbs, who were further weakened by divisions among themselves. Karadjordje fled for his life to Austrian territory.

In 1815, however, Vladika Petar was in touch with Karadjordje's rival and successor as rebel leader, the Serbian warlord-cum-livestock farmer, Miloš Obrenović, through the abbot of Oštrog mon-

---

[39] Živković, *Istorija Crnogorskog Naroda*, vol. 2, p. 358.
[40] See 'Dreams of the Montenegrin Man', www.njegos.org/mnhisotyr/hist2.htm. p.1 accessed 10/10/02.

astery. Miloš, like Karadjordje, was illiterate, but politically he proved far more astute: instead of seeking out-and-out military confrontation with the Ottoman Empire he sought to reach a political agreement which made him the pre-eminent leader of the Serbian *pashalik* of Belgrade under the suzerainty of the sultan himself. But after 1817, when news reached Montenegro of Karadjordje's return to Serbia and his betrayal and execution at the hands of Miloš, Montenegrin indignation at the manner of the revolutionary leader's death—Miloš sent his rival's head to the sultan as a token of his loyalty—led to a period of estrangement.[41]

Relations had thawed somewhat by the time of the Greek national uprising of 1821, but while Petar always professed to sympathise with Serbia's struggle, his relations with Miloš showed that for him Montenegro's interests continued to take precedence over his readiness to help the Serbs. Thus in June 1821, in reply to Miloš's request for support in the face of a prospective attack against Serbia by the Bosnian rebel leader Husein Pasha, Petar replied in a reprise of his reaction to a similar event in 1807 that he was unable to help because his own forces were fully occupied resisting the Turks, both on the borders of Hercegovina and at Skadar.[42] Petar's attitude can be explained by a highly significant battle which had been fought the previous year at the river Morača in which Montenegrin forces had been in action in support of the Rovci and Moračani tribes, who were attempting to break away from Ottoman control and join 'free' Montenegro: the resulting stand-off required a high state of vigilance.[43]

Miloš was a skilled and ruthless tactician, but Petar too possessed a calculating side. Whatever his reservations about Miloš and his unwillingness to jeopardise Montenegrin interests in the Serbian cause, the Vladika ensured that his relations with Miloš would remain good enough to allow him to relieve the acute pressure on his country's scarce resources by arranging for a number of its people to settle permanently in Serbia.[44] Although most Montenegrin emigrants at this time went to Serbia, desperate over-population im-

---

[41] Živković, *Istorija Crnogorskog Naroda*, vol. 2, p. 365.
[42] *Ibid.*, p. 366.
[43] Banac, *The National Question*, p. 275.
[44] *Ibid.*, p. 367.

pelled others to find work in Istanbul where many were employed as guards and janitors. A third group sought employment in Russia.[45]

Relations with Austria

Conscious of the tribesmen's reputation as doughty fighters, the Habsburgs continued to look to Montenegro as a source of recruits to help to protect their frontier against the Ottomans. However, Petar I and indeed the assembly of chiefs were opposed to wide-scale recruitment, at first because of the threat posed by Kara Mahmud and later because of Montenegrin engagement in the Gulf of Kotor and many lesser military entanglements. The Montenegrins' differences with the Habsburgs were aggravated when first the Treaty of Sistova in 1791 and then the Treaty of Vienna in 1815 failed to address its interests or even accord the country a specific mention.

Despite such impediments in the relationship, Petar I was enough of a realist to understand that he had no alternative but to maintain good relations with a powerful neighbour whose occupation of the principal Adriatic ports gave it an effective stranglehold over Montenegro's ability to import munitions and, in times of threatened starvation, wheat. Yet Petar was not always able to keep his fellow-clansmen under control, a situation which continuing lack of clarity over borders exacerbated. Even when, in November 1820, a protocol attempting to settle the frontier dividing Montenegrin from Austrian territory was signed and a joint court introduced, the Montenegrins' tradition of roaming in search of pasture or plunder led to sporadic conflict often resulting in the Montenegrins' temporary exclusion from coastal markets.

Difficulties arose too from time to time through the intriguing of the Radonjić clan, who traditionally provided Montenegro's civil governors but tended to be pro-Austrian in political orientation. In 1802 Jovan Radonjić's attempts to embroil Austrians and, at other times, Russians, in internal Montenegrin politics were ended by his death, but his son Vuko continued the family's efforts to supplant the Petrovići as Montenegro's premier clan by intriguing with Russia while simultaneously joining forces with Petar's opponents at home. Matters came to head in 1818 when the assembly voted to dismiss

[45] Živković, *Istorija Crnogorskog Naroda*, p. 528.

Vuko Radonjić following flagrant attempts to involve outside powers in Petar's overthrow. Two years later Vuko sought and was granted a pardon for the offence, and was thereafter permitted to return to his old position as governor, with the power struggle between the governor and the Vladika conclusively resolved in the latter's favour.[46] Writing in 1820 of his earlier travels in Montenegro, Vialla de Sommières remarked: 'The governor is now only a secondary agent, without influence, power or any other prerogatives other than mere external honours. Every thing is executed by the order of the vladika, and nothing without him... He uses his authority with all the moderation that can be expected, and the people revere, love and obey him.'[47]

Petar I's place in Montenegrin history

The esteem in which the Vladika was so widely held proved to be lasting: no figure in Montenegro history—not even St Vasilije, the miracle-worker of Ostrog—has been more venerated by his countrymen. And, although he was canonised by his successor principally to consolidate the hold of the Petrović clan on power, Petar I's appearance, demeanour and conduct as described and sketched by contemporaries together bear out the picture of a man of impressive, if not wholly unimpeachable, moral qualities, and an undeniable charisma. That Petar cultivated his venerable image is scarcely open to doubt. A contemporary sketch by Vialla de Sommières shows a majestic, white-bearded figure, arrayed in his metropolitans's robes and with staff and prayerbook in hand, his gaze at once mild and far-seeing. Hoste's journal records that Petar received him wearing 'a purple silk robe and cassock with a red ribbon, like that of the Order of the Bath, and a star upon his breast', adding that 'when he goes into battle, he is covered with orders and stars.'[48] But while Petar shared his fellow-Montenegrins' fondness for personal adornment—possibly influenced, in his case, by a familiarity with the Russian court and the Orthodox hierarchy—he seemingly attached little

---

[46] But after the death of Petar I, Radonjić again fell foul of the Petrovići and in 1830 found himself once more in exile. See below.

[47] Vialla de Sommières, *Travels in Montenegro*, p. 65.

[48] *Memoirs and Letters of Sir William Hoste*, journal entry of 16 October 1813, p. 191.

importance to other aspects of physical comfort. Hoste later records
an uncomfortable meeting at his house on the coast, 'a wretched
hovel [which] contained but two chairs, is about ten feet square, and
was crowded with Montenegrins; [where] it rained in torrents, and
we were, moreover, wet to the skin.'[49]

Admittedly such saintliness and forbearance is hard to reconcile
with Broniewski's description of the Vladika leading his Montenegrins in person against the enemy 'like wolves on a white flock'.[50]
Naturally courage and ruthlessness in battle only heightened Petar
I's standing among his countrymen and even to a certain extent
among foreign contemporaries, although, we may suspect some
exaggeration by Broniewski since Petar was already approaching
sixty at this stage and was thus hardly in his fighting prime. But even
if Petar's reputation has been inflated both by sympathetic contemporary observers such as Vialla de Sommières and posthumously by
his compatriots, his qualities clearly eclipsed those not only of his
Montenegrin predecessors but also his Serbian counterparts. Where
the latter were illiterate, Petar spoke several languages, among them
Italian, Russian, some German and a little French, and his political
sagacity seems preferable to Karadjordje's brutality and Miloš's
treachery.[51]

When Petar I died in October 1830 he was well into his eighties
and much enfeebled, and had withdrawn from public life. But for
almost the entirety of the forty-six years that he remained at the head
of his people Petar worked to improve their lot in ways that were as
much practical as theological. The Montenegrin diet, restricted as it
was, benefited greatly from the introduction of the potato which
Petar brought back from his visit to Russia in 1786.[52] And although

---

[49] *Ibid.*, journal entry of 29 October, 1813, p. 205.
[50] See Živkovic, *Istorija Crnogorskog Naroda*, p. 259, and Carmichael and Jezernik,
'Montenegrin National Identity before 1918', p. 4.
[51] Vialla de Sommières, *Travels in Montenegro*, p. 62. This is not to deny that both
Karadjordje and Miloš were courageous and able military leaders, or to belittle
Miloš's undoubted qualities as a political operator. And although Petar too could
be ruthless and indeed in some instances ordered the execution of rebels, his par-
doning of the civil governor Vuk Radonjić was in marked contrast to both
Karadjordje's and Miloš's brutal methods of disposing of their political rivals.
[52] See Wilkinson, *Dalmatia and Montenegro*, vol. 1, part 2, p. 413. Later however the
Montenegrins' dependence on the potato brought its own problems, see below.

Montenegro had neither doctors or hospitals, the Vladika took a keen interest in improving public health, imposing controls designed to curb the spread of plague, discussing vaccination with foreign visitors and persuading Russian and Austrian doctors to come to Cetinje in order to learn from them more effective treatment for a range of illnesses. In his role as metropolitan Petar was similarly active, ordering the monasteries to provide bread for the poor, mediating in disputes, and issuing numerous pastoral letters whereby he attempted to curb inter-tribal bloodshed and discourage raiding.[53] But, as Hoste observed, the means available to Petar were mainly confined to letters of exhortation and liberal use of the threat of excommunication. Some twenty years after the battle of Krusi had secured their incorporation among the Montenegrin tribes, Petar wrote to the Bjelopavlići: 'How long is it that I have been teaching, begging and imploring you to live in peace and in concord with one another, to labour for the sake of your own welfare and good name, to love your freedom and to fortify it, that you might never forget the cruel lot which your fathers and forefathers endured under Turkish tyranny and oppression?'[54]

Petar's inability to suppress Montenegrin lawlessness was thus hardly surprising. Nor, given the international factors ranged against him, could he reasonably have been expected to achieve his other major aim of gaining an outlet to the Adriatic, although for a tantalising moment he glimpsed its possibility. Set against these failures, his period as Vladika saw the area under Montenegro's control become significantly enlarged by the addition of the Brda region, although Montenegrin territory at this stage remained divided northwest and south-east by the Zeta and Bjelopavlići valleys, and was therefore vulnerable to being cut in two by Ottoman attacks. For his own part Petar in his old age spared neither himself nor the Montenegrins; on the contrary he professed himself to be both dissatisfied with his achievements and sickened by the violence of Cetinje: 'Had I done this for any other people on earth, they would have been grateful and I would have lived among them in happiness and joy, and my name would have been held by them in eternal love, but

[53] Živković, *Istorija Crnogorskog Naroda*, pp. 527 and 537.
[54] Quoted by Djilas, *Njegoš*, p. 60.

among you my heart has shrivelled from misdeeds and my old age has become embittered so that I take joy in nothing.'

Yet in laying claim to the role of martyr was Petar not being over-dramatic or even disingenuous? Certainly he was, as we have seen, far from pacifist in outlook, and was at times undeniably harsh. But for all that, and despite his failure to weld his flock into a unified people, Petar I's reign had been marked by significant advances in building a sense of common identity. Partly this was because the constant external danger was at the same time a powerful stimulus towards unity. Divided, the Montenegrin tribes stood little chance of resisting predatory outsiders, whereas together, as we have seen, they could in certain circumstances prove a most formidable fighting force—although, as in former times, Montenegro needed outside support if only to secure the money for the arms and ammunition on which its survival depended.

Here once again the character of the Vladika counted: Petar I succeeded, not least through his personal charisma and commitment, in drawing the world's attention to his country's struggle. His consequent contribution to Montenegro's prestige was a significant marker on its path to statehood.

6. Crucible of Resistance: Montenegro under Njegoš (1830–51)

However exemplary the role of Petar I may have been in the eyes of many of his compatriots, his ranking in the wider Serbian pantheon was overtaken by his nephew and immediate successor Petar Petrović II, a man who, paradoxically, had little of Petar's supposed saintliness and whose life-span was less than half of his. At his birth in 1813 Petar Petrović II was given the name Rade Tomov after his father Tomo Petrović, Petar I's younger brother. On ordination he took his uncle's name, Petar, but in South Slav history he is known as Njegoš after his birthplace, the hamlet of Njeguši in the Katuni *nahija* of Montenegro.

Like his uncle, Njegoš was a religious ruler and would-be centraliser, but his impact on his people's history was due less to his spiritual and political activities than to his poetry. However, his fame as a poet did not come immediately. As Milovan Djilas points out, some thirty years elapsed before scholars began to draw attention to the importance of his work.[1] Once established, however, his reputation was assured, at least until dissenting voices were raised in the present age. In particular, his great epic poem *The Mountain Wreath*, crystallised for Serbs and Montenegrins everywhere the nationalistic spirit of the age.[2] As we have already seen, the poem's setting is early eighteenth-century Montenegro and it takes as its immediate subject the alleged massacre of Muslim converts in the time of Vladika Danilo. However, its broader message—that of the need for Serbian Orthodox Christians to rise up against their Ottoman

[1] Djilas, *Njegoš*, p. 464.
[2] See Chapter 4.

Muslim oppressors—emerges powerfully from the poem's dramatic choruses and monologues, recounting the Kosovo disaster and glorifying the fourteenth century Serbian hero Miloš Obilić, assassin of the Ottoman Sultan Murad. Not only is tyrannicide celebrated, but the poem insists that a murderous struggle between Christians and Muslims is the price to be paid for future liberty:

> *As Wolf does on the Sheep impose his might,*
> *So tyrant lords it over feebler fellow;*
> *But foot to place upon the Tyrant's neck*
> *To bring him to the consciousness of Right—*
> *This of all human duties is most sacred!*
> *If thou canst calmly bloody sword embrace,*
> *If thou canst swim through blackest night,*
> *Such sacred strife shall sanctify thy dust.*
> *Europe's cleric from his Christian altar*
> *Doth scoff and gibe at Asia's Minaret:*
> *With thunderous strokes the Asiatic club*
> *Shatters those fanes where Crucifix is reared,*
> *Blood innocent is shed within our shrines,*
> *And relics scatter'd to the winds in dust.*
> *Above a world of travail God keeps silent:*
> *The Crescent and the Cross, great Symbols twain,*
> *Do no advantage gain save in a world of slain.*[3]

For most of the modern period *The Mountain Wreath* popularised Montenegro as the crucible of resistance to foreign oppression and did so at a time when struggling against foreign oppressors, particularly those of an alien faith, was seen as particularly noble. That the country was small, poor and mountainous added to the piquancy of its plight and the heroism of its struggle.

By 1913 *The Mountain Wreath* had been translated into at least ten languages, an indication of its unprecedented literary popularity.[4] But its real significance, for the historian at least, was political: it tapped into the prevailing social and political unrest with an ideology which, as Vladimir Dedijer has pointed out, 'added to the element of divine determinism … the principle of voluntarism', implying in

---

[3] *The Mountain Wreath of P. P. Nyegosh, Prince Bishop of Montenegro*, transl. James W. Wiles, pp. 104–5, lines 616–32.
[4] *Ibid.*, p. 11.

other words, 'that the outcome of a struggle depends also on the positive action of people themselves.'[5] *The Mountain Wreath*'s celebration of religiously sanctioned violence as the catalyst for political liberation struck a powerful chord among radical Serbophile youth well after Njegoš's time. Historians have often commented on the fact that the young Gavrilo Princip, whose assassination of the Archduke Franz Ferdinand in Sarajevo in 1914 sparked off the First World War, knew the whole of *The Mountain Wreath* by heart.[6] Even in Tito's time schoolchildren continued to recite it, and it was extolled both as a model of literary achievement and for its patriotic contribution to Slav (by this time, Yugoslav) liberation.[7]

But it was not simply posthumously that Njegoš dominated the Montenegrin scene. Most of what was written about the Montenegro of his time was the work of foreigners—officials, scholars or simply curious travellers—for whom Njegoš, like his uncle Petar before him, was the natural point of contact. Six feet seven inches tall, handsome, agreeable in manner and dressed in national costume, he was the epitome of the romantic Balkan hero, at once poet and chieftain.[8] Impressed by his physical presence and Romantic aura and by his ability to speak foreign languages, outsiders were quick to acknowledge his impact on all aspects of Montenegrin social and political life.

As we saw in an earlier chapter, it is only recently that the reputation of Njegoš and his poetry has come under attack as critics have linked the anti-Muslim rhetoric of *The Mountain Wreath* to the ethnic cleansing and fratricidal murder perpetrated by Serbian extremists in the most recent Balkan wars.[9] The question of the way in which a glorified and uncritical recycling of the past has shaped national consciousness throughout the Balkans is indeed a vital one as later generations try to absorb the lessons of a decade of war, but it

[5] Vladimir Dedijer, *The Road to Sarajevo*, New York: Simon and Schuster, 1966, p. 254.

[6] *Ibid.*, pp. 259–60.

[7] *Ibid.*

[8] See Pavlowitch, *Serbia: The History behind the Name*, p. 40 and David A. Norris: *In the Wake of the Balkan Myth: Questions of Identity and Modernity*, London: Macmillan, 1999, p. 26.

[9] See Judah, *The Serbs*, p. 77, and Chapter 4 above.

takes us far beyond nineteenth-century Montenegro and cannot be fully answered here. Instead we are concerned with Njegoš as an historical figure, set within the context of his times and country.

Montenegro in the 1830s

As the previous chapter showed, Montenegro had changed in some key respects over the forty-six years of Petar I's rule. Important victories over Kara Mahmud had underscored Montenegrin autonomy and resulted in territorial enlargement. The consequent increase in population was felt to be important although the total number of people living in fully liberated territory remained tiny.[10] Montenegro had been drawn into the campaigns generated by Napoleon's short-lived conquest of Dalmatia, and as a result at least some Montenegrins were aware of the nationalist and liberationist ideologies given currency by the French Revolution. Moreover, the impact of this nationalist ideology had been magnified by events in Serbia where first Karadjordje and then Miloš Obrenović had led national Serbian uprisings with partial success against the Ottoman Empire. In 1830 a Turkish *firman* recognised Serbia as an autonomous state and Miloš as hereditary prince. Although Montenegro had long proclaimed its independence from Ottoman rule, and would never countenance a parallel offer, such developments in Serbia were not without impact. By 1830 Montenegro was at last much better known abroad, and even had a handful of travelled and educated citizens.

[10] A study by the Scottish economist Michael Palairet puts the population at somewhere between 47,000 and 58,000 for the year 1838. This figure represents a marked reduction in comparison with the estimates traditionally given for mid-nineteenth century Montenegro. For example Wilkinson in 1848 estimated Montenegro's population as between 80,000 to 107,000. (*Dalmatia and Montenegro*, vol. 1, part 2, p. 405.) However, Palairet's research shows that most figures given for Montenegro's population in the eighteenth and nineteenth centuries were exaggerated for political and military reasons and offers a more reliable estimate based on average family size and projecting back from tax registers, which are first available from archival sources for the year 1868. (See Michael Palairet, 'The Culture of Economic Stagnation in Montenegro', *Maryland Historian*, XVII, 1986, pp. 17–42.)

These then were significant changes, but much remained the same. The Sublime Porte continued to claim Montenegro as part of the Ottoman Empire, although the empire's internal weakness meant that they could neither levy taxes nor subdue the country militarily.[11] Seen from the Ottoman point of view, the Montenegrins were a group of rebellious infidels, addicted to plunder, whose leaders were prepared to engage in any stratagem or join any alliance to further their campaign against the empire. For their part the Montenegrins continued to see themselves as irrevocably committed to the struggle for freedom, a stance which demanded that the empire's problems—in particular the threat posed by renegade Muslim warlords—be turned wherever possible to Montenegro's advantage. However, Montenegro still lacked internationally recognised borders. Thus its fate remained at the mercy of international political developments and of foreign governments whose political and financial support had constantly to be solicited in order to ensure Montenegro's survival.

If much remained uncertain in Montenegro's relations with the Great Powers, life closer to home was equally precarious. Economic activity lagged well behind other Balkan regions. The vast majority of the population continued to live a spartan, even brutalising existence; their world view remained traditional, focusing almost exclusively on the struggle with the Turks. Here the causes for hostility were not only political and personal—the need for vengeance against an enemy—but also social and economic. As Michael Palairet has explained, economic stagnation—itself the result of persisting with traditional 'transhumance' grazing practices despite having only limited pasturage around which to move their livestock—

---

[11] From the end of the Napoleonic wars it was apparent that the Ottoman Empire was beset by structural weaknesses and divisions that threatened its survival. After attempting to curb the power of the janissaries and provincial potentates in the 1820s, the Sublime Porte embarked in the 1830s on a massive programme of reform known as the *Tanzimat* or 'reordering'. But changes to the vast conservative bureaucracy and to the structure of the empire were hard to implement, due partly to obstruction by the religious authorities and governing class at the centre, but also, especially on the empire's borderlands, to the resistance of powerful Muslim landowners whose own powers were directly threatened by the reforms.

together with a cultural reluctance to undertake other forms of legitimate work caused male Montenegrins to see banditry as 'an attractive solution to their need for ready cash'.[12] Banditry had consistently fuelled conflict with the country's neighbours, and would continue to do so throughout Njegoš's time.[13] Emigration—generally but not always accurately seen as an alternative to banditry—continued for some to be the only response to the great difficulty of Montenegro's economic situation.[14]

The harsh conditions of life astonished foreign travellers, as is clear from the memoirs of such men as Vialla de Sommières and John Gardner Wilkinson. In his account published in 1848, Wilkinson describes some houses or shacks in the more remote parts of the interior as 'inferior even to the cabins of Ireland, made of rough stones piled the one on the other, or of mere wicker work, and covered with the rudest thatch, the whole building being merely a few feet high'. And in the year when famine in Ireland reached its point of greatest devastation, he detects further similarities: 'The poverty of this [Montenegrin] people, their pig, and their potatoes, are also points of resemblance with the Irish: and I regret to find that, since I visited the country, they have in like manner been suffering from the failure of the potato crop, upon which they depend so much for their subsistence.'[15]

The primitive nature of Montenegrin life was not a question only of material poverty. Taking heads was still a practice that conferred honour on the taker particularly if the victim was a Turk, while internally the blood feud continued to play a prominent part in enforcing an unforgiving moral code.[16] Prowess and courage in

---

[12] Palairet, 'The Culture of Economic Stagnation in Montenegro', pp. 28–9.

[13] Palairet suggests that rulers such as Njegoš, who made a show of suppressing banditry, only did so in order to attract support for Montenegrin statehood and international recognition, rather than through any conviction that it was socially or morally reprehensible. (See *ibid.*, p. 29.)

[14] Palairet notes that many Montenegrin emigrants—particularly those who went to farming areas—showed little enthusiasm for the activities of ploughing and tilling the soil and instead returned to banditry. (*Ibid.*, pp. 32–3.)

[15] Wilkinson, *Dalmatia and Montenegro*, vol. 1, part 2, p. 418.

[16] For a more detailed description of Montenegrin tribal life see Christopher Boehme, *Blood Revenge: The Anthropology of Feuding in Montenegro and other Tribal Societies*, University of Kansas Press, 1984.

battle and raiding were not simply widely esteemed; they were the only virtues a real man could take pride in. Merchants were seen as money-grubbing, effete and above all foreign; artisans' skills were neither widely acquired nor admired, and therefore had to be imported. Almost all physical labour was done by women, again a fact that shocked contemporary foreign observers. Wilkinson commented: 'In Turkey, and in Montenegro, man is equally "a despot, and woman a slave"; but the difference in the two countries is that in one she is an object of caprice, and part of the establishment, as a horse is a member of its master's stud; in the other, she is the working beast of burthen, and his substitute in all laborious tasks.'[17] Not surprisingly women aged early and relationships between the sexes were unsentimental in the extreme. Children were given an early introduction to the harsh realities of life.[18] Entertainment consisted largely of sporting contests exhibiting feats of strength, and evenings spent listening to tales of heroic exploits chanted to the accompaniment of the traditional Montenegrin instrument, the one-stringed *gusle*.[19] Religion, closely linked with traditional beliefs in demons, spirits and curses, evoked a God who inspired fear and imposed judgement, rather than one embodying qualities of mercy and love.[20]

This then was the political, social and moral climate into which Njegoš was born and which nurtured his literary talent, which was honed by extensive reading and familiarity with both the classics and the Romantic nationalist ideology of his times. Although this blend of influences was later to develop into a form of pan-Serbian nationalism which, transformed and transmitted through Njegoš's poetry, influenced generations of Greater Serbians, Njegoš's early life was

[17] Wilkinson, *Dalmatia and Montenegro*, vol. 1, part 2, p. 421.

[18] As late as the 1920s Milovan Djilas's memoir of his early years, *Land without Justice* (New York, 1958), describes a life remarkable for the austerity which characterised not only ordinary living conditions but even relationships within the family. A still more detailed picture of the extreme poverty characteristic of the Dinaric regions is given in Rudolf Bićanić, *How the People Live: Life in the Passive Regions (Peasant Life in Southwestern Croatia, Bosnia, and Hercegovina; Yugoslavia in 1935)*; Research Report no. 21, Department of Anthropology, University of Massachusetts, September 1981.

[19] Wilkinson, *Dalmatia and Montenegro*, vol. 1, part 2, pp. 440–1 and 447.

[20] Boehme, *Blood Revenge*, pp. 66–9.

unremarkable and he was by no means his uncle's first choice when it came to appointing Montenegro's next Vladika.

Petar Petrović Njegoš: early years

Petar I's unhappy final years had been further blighted by his failure to find a successor—a Petrović who was both literate and a monk—capable of carrying on his role. His first choice, his nephew Mitar Stijepov, died while studying in Russia; his second, another nephew Djordje Savov, wrote from St Petersburg to inform his uncle that he wished to enrol in an officers' school in St Petersburg rather than become a bishop. Literate monks being in short supply in the Petrović clan, Petar I still had not formally appointed a successor at the time of his death on 19 October 1830.[21] Rather it was the Petrović clan, determined as ever to keep out potential rivals from among the Radonjići and supported by Petar's former secretary Simo Milutinović Sarajlija, who moved quickly to ensure that the new Vladika should be one of their own.

Their most credible candidate was the seventeen-year-old Rade Tomov, whose 'pleasant physiognomy and …good nature' had been remarked on by his uncle following the lack of success with his other nephews. However, Rade was not a monk. His early life had not suggested any sense of vocation, and his education consisted of eighteen months' tuition under a priest, Josif Tropović, at Topla on the Gulf of Kotor and a short period in Cetinje, where he studied for a time under Simo Sarajlija. But these deficiencies were of little importance when weighed against the Petrović interest in keeping the metropolitanate within the clan. Wasting no time, the Petrovići dressed Rade in his uncle's cassock and proceeded to have him ordained as an archimandrite before any further theological objections could be raised. At the same time the Petrovići's traditional opponents the Radonjići, believing that Rade's youth and the rushed manner of his ordination might indeed attract opposition, began to campaign against

[21] The testament read the day after Petar's I death in which Rade Tomov was designated as his successor is thought by some to have been forged by Petar's secretary, Simo Milutinović Sarajlija, who had been Rade's tutor in Cetinje. This view is supported by the fact that Rade had not been ordained which was established practice for a prospective Vladika. (See Djilas, *Njegoš*, pp. 64–5.)

him in a manner reminiscent of the power struggle which had followed the death of Vladika Vasilije.[22]

The Petrovići struck back violently: first the civil governor of Montenegro, Vuko Radonjić, who had been exiled in 1818 and then permitted to return, was accused of intriguing with Austria. There is no firm evidence either way to support or refute these accusations.[23] However, he was put on trial and sentenced to death, although the sentence was commuted by Njegoš, first to imprisonment and then exile, in a well-timed display of clemency. Vuko's educated and well-travelled brother Djuzo Radonjić was murdered by one of the Petrovići on his own saint's day. Other members of the Radonjići came to a violent end, either murdered in raids or driven out with their families after their houses had been set on fire. Vuko died in 1832, shortly after his expulsion to Kotor. By 1831 Sarajlija had also fled to Kotor after falling out with Njegoš, although he was permitted to return shortly afterwards on the understanding that the new relationship was to be on the young man's terms.[24] Although subsequently foreign visitors to Montenegro always remarked on Njegoš's civilised demeanour and unfailing courtesy, these early encounters with potential rivals and critics suggest from the outset an intransigent and ruthless side to his nature.

Challenges to Njegoš's youthful authority were never likely to stop with the downfall of the Radonjići. Montenegro was far too fractious and divided a society for that. The first serious revolts against central authority broke out in the 1830s shortly after Njegoš became Vladika; a decade later in 1846–7 Njegoš was still having to resort to force to maintain his hold over tribesmen who had been wooed away by the ambitious Pasha of Skadar.

---

[22] Živković, *Istorija Crnogorskog Naroda*, p. 510.

[23] Djilas, for example, contests these allegations (*Njegoš*, pp. 81–3) while Živković insists upon their validity (*Istorija Crnogorskog Naroda*, pp. 510–11).

[24] Whatever the immediate cause of this short-term disagreement—Djilas suggests it was because Sarajlija had 'taken liberties' by trying to impose his own decisions—in a broader sense Sarajlija had a strong influence on the young Rade during the time spent under his instruction. A much-travelled Serb from Sarajevo—hence the name Sarajlija—he helped to to awaken the young Rade's interest in both metaphysical and nationalistic ie pan-Serbian themes. (See Djilas, *Njegoš*, pp. 85–6 and 271.)

Montenegro's evolving institutions

Traditionally the Cetinje monastery and the institution of Vladika had survived as a result of Russian support, but in Petar I's final years the relationship with Russia had cooled. In 1831, with the generally pro-Austrian governorship in abeyance, the connection with Russia was reactivated with important consequences for Montenegro. Encouraging steps in this direction had been taken somewhat earlier when two Montenegrins, Ivan Ivanović Vukotić and his nephew Matija Vučićević, originally from the Ottoman-ruled plain of Zeta but both long resident in Russia, returned to Montenegro. Vukotić, who had served for a time as a non-commissioned officer in the Russian army, brought with him substantial funds acquired as a result of a Russian legacy.[25] In turn Vukotić recruited the lame Dimitrije Milaković, originally from Mostar but educated in Novi Sad and Vienna, who was to become Njegoš's secretary in place of Sarajlija. Over the years Milaković used his knowledge of foreign languages and literary skills to assist the Vladika, remaining unobtrusively at his side until Njegoš's death in 1851.[26]

Meanwhile Vukotić styled himself a general although he was no such thing, conscious no doubt of the Montenegrins' willingness to suspend disbelief where anything touching on Russian grandeur was concerned. Yet Vukotić was not all empty pretensions. In 1831 he set about transforming Petar I's court or *kuluk* into a more effective body, the senate, which was composed of the most powerful chiefs of Montenegro and the Brda. This new institution aimed to co-opt the headmen to the centre and in so doing to limit their capacity for disruption and factionalism. Initially Vukotić was its president, and his nephew acted as his deputy.[27] At the same time the senate's effectiveness was to be enhanced by an additional body, the *gvardija*—part regional police force, part court—which was to have representatives in the tribal territories and its headquarters in Rijeka Crnojevića. Central authority was to be further strengthened by increasing the size of the Vladika's personal guard, known as the *perjanik* after the feather (or *pero*) worn in the guardsmen's caps.[28]

[25] See Houston, *Nikola and Milena*, p. 42.
[26] Djilas, *Njegoš*, p. 108.
[27] *Ibid.*, pp. 8–91.
[28] While the *gvardija* was responsible for dealing with minor offences on the spot,

Forwards and backwards on the road to state-building

The following year, 1832, the nineteen-year-old Njegoš took his first steps as a military leader, launching an attack against the Muslims of Podgorica who at the time were engaged in helping the Sublime Porte to subdue rebellious local potentates in both Bosnia and Albania. As in earlier times when the Vladika and the civil governor jointly led their men into battle, Njegoš, still at this stage an archimandrite, shared the command of the army with Ivan Vukotić, who had encouraged Njegoš in planning the attack. To bolster their hopes of success, the Montenegrins secured a promise of additional help from the disenchanted Albanian Hoti clan. Nonetheless, for Njegoš to expose himself to the risk of launching an assault on the Ottoman centre of Podgorica was foolhardy. Not only did such an attack risk jeopardising his hopes of being consecrated as metropolitan (or Vladika) in Russia, which was at this time an ally of the Porte, but it also discounted the fact that the Montenegrins' guerrilla style of mountain warfare was ill-suited to taking Podgorica, a walled city on the plain. With the scales thus loaded against them, two further factors—the tribesmen's lack of proper planning and the Ottomans' use of cavalry—ensured the failure of the Montenegrin campaign. Both Vukotić's and Njegoš's forces were compelled to withdraw, taking with them many wounded. For Njegoš, who would never again lead Montenegrins into battle against the Turks, the defeat was a lasting source of regret. For Montenegro generally the failed attack on Podgorica spelt disaster: the Ottoman vizier, Reshid Pasha, seized on it as a convenient provocation and proceeded to raze Montenegrin territory, impaling and hanging many of the unfortunate Montenegrins he was able to capture.[29]

Pressure from Russia discouraged the Montenegrins from seeking revenge. Nevertheless, relations with their Muslim neighbours were maintained; mostly they were bad, but occasionally were more amicable or at least utilitarian when the Montenegrins attempted to form tactical alliances with 'Turkish' renegades in order to enlist their assistance against the central authority of the Sublime Porte.

more serious matters were brought before the senate. (See Živković, *Istorija Crnogorskog Naroda*, p. 513 and Houston, *Nikola and Milena*, p. 44.)

[29] See Djilas, *Njegoš*, pp. 95–7, for a full account of the debacle.

But such practices involved risk, and, as we shall see, the long-term gains did not always justify the short-term benefits. In particular tactical alliances against the Sublime Porte risked Russian displeasure, a danger that Njegoš sought to neutralise by cultivating close ties with Jeremija Gagić, an ethnic Serb who served as the Russian consul in Dubrovnik.[30] This gambit proved rather more fortunate. Although Gagić carried out his reporting duties conscientiously, and at times severely criticised Montenegrin conduct, his instincts were on the whole pro-Montenegrin, and his advice, in a world where educated opinion was so often lacking, both well-judged and necessary.

However, it was Vukotić rather than Gagić who in 1833 instigated one of the most important but contentious policy changes introduced under Njegoš—the levying and collection of taxes. Without taxes there could be no certain foundation on which to build a state, no standing army, and no capacity for the state to take independent action which did not depend either on plunder or on the charity of others. But this innovation was anything but acceptable to the Montenegrins. With their long history of resistance to Ottoman tax collectors they were only with the greatest difficulty to be persuaded to part with scarce resources, and attempts to force compliance led to conflict on a number of occasions.

Montenegro's attempts at state-building were not simply a question of strengthening the territory's internal organisation; they also required outside recognition of Montenegrin institutions and above all of the Vladika's authority. Accordingly in 1833 Njegoš decided to make the journey to Russia, where he hoped to be consecrated as metropolitan and received by Tsar Nicholas I, a step which marked a significant departure from traditional practice whereby Montenegrin metropolitans had been consecrated by the patriarch of Peć, either in Peć itself or later in Sremski Karlovci. Journeying via Trieste and forced to bide his time in Vienna, Njegoš made the acquaintance of the famous Serbian language reformer, Vuk Stefanović Karadžić, whose Greater Serbian views were to have a considerable influence on Njegoš's poetry and indeed on his political thinking in the years to come.[31] But if Njegoš was impressed by his encounter

---

[30] *Ibid.*, pp. 108–9.

[31] Vuk Karadžić was born Vuk Stefanović in a western Serbian village but later adopted the Montenegrin clan name Karadžić in recognition of the fact that his

with the older Karadžić, the linguist was similarly struck by Montenegro's young ruler. As he commented in a letter to his friend, the Serbian poet and archimandrite Lukian Mušicki, 'Petar Petrović is not yet twenty years old, but bigger and more handsome than any grenadier in Vienna! Not only does he know Serbian very well to read and write, but he also composes fine verses … He thinks that there is no finer language in the world than our popular tongue (and he's right to think so, even if it were not true).'[32]

Coming from the desolate wilderness of Montenegro, the young archimandrite was sufficiently moved by his first sight of St Petersburg to send a breathless account of his impressions to Vuk Karadžic, in which he took care to strike the right lofty poetic tone.

I barely remembered this morning that I promised to write [to] you from St Petersburg. The vastness of the city, the symmetry of its streets, the majesty of its buildings, and thousands of similar sights which are new to me are the cause of this tardiness of mine. Is it any wonder that I am tardy and find it hard to sit down and write when I hardly know if I am on earth, for I think that I have been lifted by the wing of Daedalus to observe from the air, as in a dream, the capital of a truly great tsar who is one with us in religion and race …[33]

Fortunately for the Montenegrins, the visit to Russia fulfilled expectations: Njegoš returned with gifts of money, books and icons

---

forebears had originally come to Serbia from the lands of the Karadžići clan around Drobnjak in Montenegro. Karadžić's fame derives from his development of a standardised and simplified orthography for the Serbian language which made written Serbian accessible to ordinary people to an extent that had not been possible previously when all literary and liturgical works had been printed in an archaic form of Church Slavonic. But Karadžić's linguistic research led him to formulate views about the identity of the South Slavs which made him lastingly unpopular with much of the peninsula's non-Orthodox population and fuelled the development of Greater Serbian nationalism. His view was that all those who spoke the *štovakian* dialect—characteristic of western Hercegovina but also of Montenegro, Bosnia and Dalmatia and much of Croatia—were Serbs, irrespective or their religious affiliation. Along with his sympathy for Karadžić's Greater Serbian ideology, Njegoš supported his language reforms and later had all his works published in Cetinje printed in Karadžić's orthography.

[32] Quoted in Duncan Wilson, *The Life and Times of Vuk Stefanović Karadžić*, Oxford: Clarendon Press, 1970, p. 274.
[33] Quoted by Djilas, *Njegoš*, p. 114.

and with the first printing press Montenegro had possessed since the time of the Crnojević. The setting up of the printing press was no easy matter since everything—machines, type and paper—had to be transported from St Petersburg up the mountain tracks to Cetinje. Nor were there more than a handful of literate Montenegrins able to read the books. Despite the unpromising circumstances Njegoš was to print a number of his own poems; also works by Sarajlija and a collection of Montenegrin proverbs assembled by Vuk Karadžić who, after his encounter with Njegoš in Vienna, had spent some months in the autumn of 1834 and the following summer pursuing his linguistic studies in Montenegro. Persisting with his attempt to bring education to his fellow-Montenegrins, Njegoš established the first elementary schools for boys—one in Cetinje and one in Dobrsko Selo—and in 1836 began the printing of Montenegro's first periodical to which he gave a somewhat uncharacteristic name for Montenegro: *Grlica* (Turtledove).[34]

While Njegoš had been away in Vienna and Russia, the ambitious Vukotić had used the Vladika's absence to take more power into his own hands. But Njegoš himself was sufficiently strengthened by the visit to Russia and by his consecration to push Vukotić aside and install his own brother Pero as leader of the senate and his cousin Djordje as Pero's deputy.[35] Exiled together with his nephew, Vukotić attempted to blacken Njegoš's reputation in Russia. While their intriguing threatened to undermine him abroad, the Vladika still faced challenges to his authority at home from rebellious tribesmen whose many causes for discontent now included the abomination of taxes. Perhaps it was the Russian experience which led him to respond with a particularly adroit move—the canonisation of his uncle Petar I on the fourth anniversary of his death in October 1834. With a saint in the family Njegoš could reinforce the temporal power derived from the new institutions with the threat of spiritual sanctions.[36]

[34] Neither the periodical not the printing press was destined to survive long. While *Grlica* endured till 1839, the printing press lasted into the time of Njegoš's successor, Prince Danilo, when the type was melted down for use as shot in the continuing warfare against the Turks. See Ćirković, *The Serbs*, p. 190, and Djilas, *Njegoš*, p. 132.
[35] Jelavich, *History of the Balkans*, vol. 1, p. 250.
[36] Djilas, *Njegoš*, p. 139.

The local Orthodox population responded to the creation of the new saint with enthusiasm, flocking to Petar's tomb in Cetinje, but in the adjacent Ottoman and Austrian territories the authorities viewed the development with unease. In reality the Vladika's hold on power was not yet entirely firm. Criticism of him, supported on this occasion by Gagić, now included the charge of channelling Russian funds into the hands of his clansmen, the Petrovići.[37] In the course of 1836 discontent with the autocratic and centralising tendencies of Njegoš's rule, exacerbated by food shortages and demands for taxes, gave rise to rebellions in the Crmnica and Rijeka *nahije* which were suppressed by two prominent Petrovići, Njegoš's cousins Djordje and Stanko Stijepov.

At the same time a more complex situation was developing along Montenegro's northern borders with Hercegovina where the Orthodox tribesmen around Grahovo—still feudatories of the Muslim ruler of Hercegovina—were refusing to pay the *harač*. Recognising the need for outside assistance, the rebels proclaimed themselves subjects of the Vladika and invoked Montenegro's support. Determined to crush the rebels, Ali Pasha Rizvanbegović, vizier of Mostar in Hercegovina, attacked Grahovo at the beginning of August 1836 with an army of many thousands, seizing captives and burning the town to the ground. As honour demanded, the Montenegrins prepared a counter-attack to rescue the captives, gathering together a few hundred men under the leadership of Njegoš's younger brother Joko Petrović and eight close kinsmen.[38] At first they were successful in liberating the local clan leader and his followers, but disaster followed when the Montenegrins confronting the combined forces of Ali Pasha Rizvanbegović and Resulbegović of Trebinje were surprised by a fresh contingent of cavalry, led by the feared Ottoman commander Smaïl Aga Čengić. In the ensuing melée Joko, still in his teens, and Stanko Stijepov's son Stevo were among forty Montenegrins hacked to death. Smaïl Aga had Joko's severed head placed on display; the inhabitants of Grahovo fled but after being refused sanctuary in neighbouring Austrian territory were eventually forced to swear an oath of loyalty to the Ottoman vizier and beg to be allowed to return home. The real affront to Njegoš's authority came when

[37] Djilas, *Njegoš*, p. 141.
[38] See Živković, *Istorija Crnogorskog Naroda*, p. 413.

the Grahovići, fearing further retaliation, refused to avenge the deaths of the Petrovići, including that of the Vladika's own brother.[39] News of the defeat soon filtered abroad. When the reports reached Russia they added to earlier criticisms of Njegoš's profligacy with Russian money a further charge of reckless and provocative conduct in his relations with the Turks. Njegoš needed to put the record straight, even more so at a time when Montenegro urgently needed further aid. He therefore sought permission to make a second trip to Russia, in the course of which he intended to refute the charges against him. At first the Russians proved unresponsive and the Vladika was obliged to remain for some time in Vienna before receiving permission to proceed to St Petersburg. The enforced delay in the Habsburg capital gave him a further opportunity to meet men outside his milieu and, most important, to spend time with Vuk Karadžić who, following his recent research in Montenegro, was working on a detailed ethnographical study in German entitled *Montenegro und die Montenegriner*.[40] Reports of Njegoš's meetings with Karadžić and other kindred spirits in Vienna brought him to the attention of the Austrian Chancellor Metternich who, having ignored him on his previous visit, now noted: '[He has] spiritually and physically developed; has little respect for the principles of religion and monarchy and is not firm in them, given to liberal, revolutionary ideas; to be placed under surveillance.'[41] The Chancellor's suspicions of Njegoš were increased by the young man's request for a visa to visit France. Metternich determined to keep a check on any revolutionary tendencies and ordered Austrian agents to maintain surveillance of the Montenegrin's activities both abroad and at home.

[39] Djilas, *Njegoš*, pp. 141–3.

[40] Based on this research Karadžić had already published in 1834 'A View of Montenegro', an article that was was intended to present a favourable view of Njegoš to the world and to challenge the widespread image of Montenegro as little more than a nest of bandits. By contrast, *Montenegro und die Montenegriner, ein Beitrag sur Kenntniss der europäischen Türkei und des serbischen Volkes (Montenegro and the Montenegrins: A Contribution to the Knowledge of European Turkey and the Serbian People)*, published in 1837, presented an unvarnished picture of the primitive state of Montenegrin society at the time with an accuracy that Njegoš found embarrassing. See Wilson, *Vuk Stefanović Karadžić, 1787–1864*, pp. 294–5 and 401–2.

[41] Djilas, *Njegoš*, pp. 144–5.

In 1837 Njegoš finally gained permission to visit Russia, and this time was considerably less overawed. For their part the Russians took a more critical look at the young metropolitan, noting some instances of 'unmonkish' behaviour, in particular his fondness for the company of women.[42] Despite this, Russia not only continued the annual subsidy paid to Montenegro but even increased it, and from 1837 for a time provided wheat to tide the population over a particularly severe famine. But the Russian connection, though it offered at times the only source of desperately-needed funding, was geopolitically something of a liability. Fear of Russia gaining control of a seaport on the Adriatic ensured that Austria remained determinedly opposed to this long-standing Montenegrin goal.[43] Later all the Powers, including Italy, came to share the belief that Montenegrin access to the Adriatic risked Russian penetration into the Mediterranean, thus ensuring that when Montenegro finally gained Great Power approval in 1878 for access to the sea it was only under Austrian supervision.

The visit to Russia encouraged Njegoš to undertake further measures to strengthen his own authority within Montenegro: the number of *perjaniks* and the size of the *gvardija* were both significantly increased after he returned home, and those who disturbed the peace by feuding and raiding across the frontiers were more harshly punished.[44] The effect was observed by the Russian envoy Ozeretskovsky, sent back with Njegoš to report to St Petersburg on the state of the country. He wrote approvingly: 'Senators, captains, the *gvardija* and *perjaniks*—all only await his [Njegoš's] nod, and I don't believe that another country in the world exists where the orders of the ruler are carried out so precisely and quickly from the lowest to the greatest.'[45]

As Njegoš's personal authority increased, so too did the attraction for him of the trappings of power. From 1838 the Vladika abandoned his priestly robes in favour of the colourful costume of a mountain chief, which was now construed as Montenegrin national

---

[42] Djilas, *Njegoš*, p. 152.
[43] Jelavich, *History of the Balkans*, vol. 1, p. 250.
[44] Živković, *Istorija Crnogorskog Naroda*, pp. 51–7. Njegoš was in fact responsible for setting up Montenegro's first prison.
[45] *Ibid.*, p. 518 (my translation).

dress.[46] A form of national decoration for heroism, the Obilić medal (after the great Serbian hero of the battle of Kosovo) was introduced, and Njegoš himself now began to favour the use of princely rather than ecclesiastical titles.[47] He embarked on the construction of a new residence which, though scarcely a palace, was far better appointed than the monastery where shortly before he had been forced to move from room to room in order to accommodate the Saxon King Friedrich Augustus. The king was an enthusiastic naturalist who had come to Montenegro to study the country's exceptional flora. Njegoš was said to be at once bemused by the king's passion for 'grasses' and infuriated by German press reports highlighting the primitive character of Montenegro.[48]

Determined to live down such insults, Njegoš involved himself closely in the planning and supervision of the twenty-five-room residence, soon to be dubbed the Biljarda after the billiard table, which he had transported from the coast on the backs of a team of strong men. But if the Biljarda, with its introduction to gentlemanly pursuits, was intended to dispel the charge of primitivism, it was perversely ill-sited: the windows of Njegoš's apartment overlooked an unfinished round tower festooned with stakes on each of which was impaled a decapitated Turkish head. For European visitors the spectacle held a grisly fascination. John Gardner Wilkinson's description of the tower as it appeared during his visit to Cetinje in 1844 is but one of many:

On a rock, immediately above the convent [Cetinje monastery], is a round tower, pierced with embrasures, but without cannon; on which I counted the heads of twenty Turks, fixed upon stakes, round the parapet, the trophies of Montenegrin victory; and below, scattered upon the rock, were the fragments of other skulls, which had fallen to pieces by [sic] time; a strange spectacle in a Christian country, in Europe, and in the immediate vicinity of a convent and a bishop's palace. It would be in vain to expect that, in such a condition, the features could be well-preserved, or to look for the Turkish physiognomy, in these heads, many of which have been exposed for years in this position, but the face of one young man was remarkable; and the contraction of the upper lip, exposing a row of white teeth, conveyed an

---

[46] Djilas, *Njegoš*, p. 154.
[47] *Ibid.*, p. 158.
[48] *Ibid.*, p. 155.

expression of horror, which seemed to show that he had suffered much, either from fright or pain, at the moment of death.[49]

Wilkinson elsewhere recounts his attempt to persuade the Vladika to have the Montenegrins abandon the practice of cutting off and displaying the heads of their enemies. Njegoš immediately agreed in principle, only to come up with a serious objection: the Turks would never agree to do the same thing, and in these circumstances any first move to discontinue head-taking by the Montenegrins would be construed as weakness and serve simply to invite attack. Agreeing with Njegoš, Wilkinson determined to act as honest broker and duly tackled Ali Pasha Rizvanbegović on a subsequent visit to the Hercegovinian capital, Mostar.[50] But the vizier's reaction mirrored that of the Vladika: he was, of course, willing to abandon the practice but doubted the good faith of the Montenegrins, who were known for their wanton cruelty. At Wilkinson's instigation letters were exchanged between the vizier and Njegoš, but, since the custom continued well into the twentieth century the initiative clearly foundered.[51]

If lack of trust prevented the Vladika and the vizier from reaching an understanding on the practice of head-taking, it did not prevent them from co-operating on other occasions when this seemed mutually advantageous. At first, as we have seen, this was far from being the case; Ali Pasha's brutal campaign of 1836 had left the tribal lands around Grahovo scarred but far from quiescent and, despite attempts by Russia and Turkey to rein in the belligerents, clashes between the Christian *raia* (subject peasantry) and their Ottoman overlords were continually breaking out. In 1838, however, Russian pressure on Njegoš—increased during his second visit to St Petersburg—induced him to sign a peace treaty with Ali Pasha who was being similarly pressured by representatives of the Sublime Porte.[52]

---

[49] Wilkinson, *Dalmatia and Montenegro*, vol. 1, part 2, pp. 511–12.

[50] *Ibid.*, vol. 1, part 2, pp. 475–6, and vol. 2, pp. 74–88.

[51] Djilas describes the practice of head-taking as continuing into Prince Nikola's reign when the prince himself issued an interdiction in 1876. Not wishing to disobey their prince, the Montenegrins instead took to taking ears and noses as battle trophies, a practice that continued on occasion even during the First World War. (See Djilas, *Njegoš*, p. 245.)

[52] Although this treaty, signed in 1838, was to keep the peace for less than a year, the Montenegrins saw it as deeply significant. Njegoš wrote immediately to the Russian consul, Gagić, pointing out that the Ottoman side's willingness to sign

But the treaty brought about only the briefest of pauses before the clashes and beheadings continued. All this was no doubt to be expected, but the same could not be said of the development of a relationship which was to see Njegoš and Ali Pasha rejoicing together, if not overtly at least complicitly, at the downfall of a man who had become their shared enemy—Smaïl Aga Čengić, Ottoman hero of the battle of Grahovo.[53]

Encounters with adversaries—Smaïl Aga Čengić

Indeed such was Smaïl Aga's contribution to the victory that the Sublime Porte had granted him the fiefdom of Gacko and Tališa (modern Kolašin and Pljevlja) in Hercegovina, which at that time covered an area larger than the whole of Montenegro. From his position as a great landowner, the ambitious Smaïl Aga was soon seen as threatening his fellow *beys*, among them his erstwhile ally Ali Pasha Rizvanbegović. The next step in the drama seems to have been caused by a mix-up of correspondence when, inadvertently or not, Prince Miloš of Serbia informed Ali Pasha that the *aga* was attempting have the Porte move against him.[54] In a bid to save himself Ali Pasha turned to Njegoš, whom he knew to be seeking revenge for the death of his brother Joko at Grahovo. Njegoš needed little urging but for a time had difficulty in persuading the chiefs of the local tribe, the Drobnjaci, to agree to the assassination of Smaïl Aga, not through any reluctance to see the reviled *aga* despatched but rather because they feared the Porte's retaliation. It was therefore not till 1840, four years after Joko's death, that a leader of the Drobnjaci, Novica Cerović, managed to ambush Smaïl Aga near the little village of Mijetičak north of Nikšić. When Smaïl and his retinue attempted to flee they discovered that a spy, who had infiltrated their camp posing as a *gusle* player, had hobbled the horses. The *aga* was shot and his head brought to Njegoš who, according to one account, 'threw it in the air like an apple, and as he caught it

---

amounted to effective recognition of Montenegro as an independent state. See Živković, *Istorija Crnogorskog Naroda*, pp. 465–6.

[53] See Djilas, *Njegoš, pp.* 180–1.

[54] *Ibid.*

...cried, "So you too have come my way, poor Smaïl!'" As further proof of his pleasure Njegoš made Cerović a senator.

The death of Smaïl Aga set in train a series of attacks and counter-attacks in which both Montenegrins and Turks died. Anxious to conceal his part in the plot, Ali Pasha ordered an attack on the Drobnjaci, in which some seventy clan members died.[55] Seeking at the same time to shore up his own position he attempted to reach agreement with Njegoš over the disputed borderlands, since to do so would remove a pretext for intervention by the Porte. Njegoš's position was difficult; however lamentable he found the deaths of the Drobnjaci, he could not ignore the fact that the renegade Ali Pasha was not only his enemy's enemy but a man who might play a useful part in helping Montenegro secure its wider aims—a viable expanse of territory and recognition by the Great Powers, which wanted peace and an end to the continuing skirmishing in the borderlands around Montenegro. After a series of false starts a second pact to replace the earlier one of 1838 was signed in Dubrovnik in 1842 by both men in the presence of Austrian and Russian representatives. Eye-witness accounts tell of the two rulers striving to outdo each other in the finery of themselves and their retinues. At first it seemed that Njegoš, being so much younger, taller and more handsome than the vizier, was certain to eclipse his rival, but Ali Pasha proved to be the more cunning: emerging suddenly from the building in which the talks were being held he began to scatter coins with liberal abundance. As the local populace rushed forward to gather them up the Montenegrin chiefs could be seen to be among them. Having convincingly demonstrated Montenegro's poverty to all and sundry, the vizier was deemed to have triumphed.[56] Bested though he was, Njegoš seems not to have borne a grudge since, wishing no doubt to facilitate the negotiations, he even accepted the drunken Ali Pasha's bizarre invitation to become his blood brother.[57]

Osman Pasha Skopljak

If the details seemed picaresque, the reality was more sobering. The Sublime Porte had appointed as governor of Skadar Osman Pasha

[55] Djilas, *Njegoš.*
[56] *Ibid.*, p. 187.
[57] *Ibid.*

Skopljak, who was both an exceptional general and son-in-law of the late Smaïl Aga. That Osman Pasha was of Serbian stock did nothing to diminish his enmity towards Montenegro, or indeed towards Njegoš personally. His father Suleiman Pasha had been instrumental in crushing the Serbian uprising of 1813,[58] and Osman Pasha was prepared to follow in his footsteps. In 1843 he invaded Montenegro from Lake Skadar, seizing the islands of Vranjina and Lesendro. With the conquest of these two small but strategically positioned islands, Osman Pasha had gained a stranglehold over Montenegro, cutting off trading access to Podgorica as well as the use of the lake itself for essential excursions to Skadar on the opposite shore. Advised of the position, the Porte now attempted to turn this situation to its political advantage. Njegoš was offered a status equivalent to that of Prince Miloš of Serbia: recognition as ruler of Montenegro provided that he in turn accepted the overall sovereignty of the Sublime Porte. The Vladika rejected the offer with derision on the grounds that he was already ruler of a free country, whose independence had been assured not by the whim of the sultan but the readiness of the Montenegrin people to die in defence of their land.[59] For all his braggadocio Njegoš must have realised that the position was hopeless. With little artillery at their disposal, the Montenegrins' attempt to break the blockade could be no more than symbolic. The only real avenue open to them was to secure foreign intervention. Njegoš therefore set about trying to enlist outside support. No opportunity, it seemed, could be passed up to involve foreigners. On one such occasion, an English traveller Charles Lamb, who was visiting Montenegro with his wife in the autumn of 1843, was taken by boat to join the Vladika for lunch at a military emplacement overlooking the lake. As Lamb recalled,

The place where we sat was a most picturesque situation. The Turkish balls kept whizzing past, forming, as his Highness remarked, beautiful music. Indeed, it seemed to me we were very nearly in the line a well-directed shot ought to have taken; but, of course, it was not my place to speak.[60]

[58] *Ibid.*, p. 102.
[59] *Ibid.*, p. 195.
[60] Charles Lamb, 'A Ramble in Montenegro', *Blackwood's Edinburgh Magazine*, no. 57, January 1845, p. 44.

If such contrived displays of nonchalance could do little more than burnish his romantic reputation among a susceptible public, Njegoš genuinely hoped for more from his appeals to the Great Powers. But Russia did nothing; France, though sympathetic, failed to intervene; and Britain in those pre-Gladstonian days sided with the Ottoman Empire. When Njegoš attempted to arrange for the construction of ships to re-take the islands, Austria intervened to prevent it, and refused to supply the Montenegrins with the munitions they needed for a counterattack. Njegoš was powerless, a humiliation he found difficult to accept. Over the following years he and Osman Pasha continued their bitter stand-off as the vizier of Skadar, retaining his loyalty to the Sublime Porte, sought further ways to inflict a final, fatal blow on the Montenegrin ruler.

In 1847 severe drought followed by famine offered Osman Pasha the opportunity of enticing the chiefs of the Crmnica to revolt against Cetinje's authority in exchange for much-needed wheat.[61] Njegoš, at the time in Vienna overseeing arrangements for the publication of *The Mountain Wreath*, was caught off-guard. The situation was inherently more threatening in that the rebels included important tribal chiefs, among them Markiša Plamenac, a leader of one of the most lastingly famous of all the Montenegrin clans, and as such a potential threat to the Petrovići. But some members of the tribe remained loyal, and the rebellion was on the point of failing when Osman Pasha sent troops to reinforce the rebels. Njegoš returned to find a Turkish army already on the ground in the Crmnica *nahija*. Wisely he did not lead the resistance himself but sent his battle-hardened cousin Djordje at the head of a large body of Katuni tribesmen to put down the rebellion. Plamenac fled to seek refuge with the vizier, going so far as to persuade him to fortify yet another rocky islet, Grmožur, on Lake Skadar. Njegoš countered by building a defensive tower on the opposite shore overlooking the lakeside port of Virpazar through which he hoped to safeguard river traffic entering the lake. Predictably things did not go well for Markiša Plamenac. One Montenegrin version of the story recounts that he was overcome by remorse and offered to betray Osman Pasha by calling on his own clansmen to help him take back Grmožur for

---

[61] Djilas, *Njegoš*, p. 221.

Montenegro.[62] But if this were so it was not enough to save him. Plamenac was shot and his kinsmen were refused leave to bury him in Montenegro.

Undeterred by his lack of success, Osman Pasha was soon involved in fomenting a second rebellion, this time among the Piperi on the eastern fringes of what was then Montenegro. Again Njegoš was able to suppress the rebellion and had its instigators shot. While Njegoš had succeeded in circumventing Osman Pasha's attempts to undermine Montenegro's fragile unity, his hatred for the pasha unsurprisingly grew. Each man conspired to have the other murdered even while letters, in which each expounded his own uncompromising ideology, continued to pass between them. For one reason or another, all these attempts were fated to end in failure. An assassin sent by Njegoš, having reached Skadar, suffered a very un-Montenegrin loss of nerve while for his part Njegoš survived attempts to poison him and blow up his headquarters.[63] Possibly the ensuing stalemate had its benefits since in the wake of these dramatic incidents, tension between the two sides eased and the situation along Montenegro's southern borders became for the time being more stable.

Relations with the Great Powers

Throughout the period that Montenegro had battled continually with the Turks its relations with other Powers had not stood still. Contact with Austria had, as we have seen, been marked by suspicion on both sides, exacerbated by Montenegrin pillaging and the lack of clarity over borders. The old line of definition with the Venetian dominions was an obvious starting point for negotiations, but matters had been continually complicated by the way in which a clan's territory often overlapped on to the other side of this former frontier, and by the tribesmen's tradition of seeking pasturage for their cattle and sheep with no regard for formal borders. However, in 1841 an agreement defining the frontier between Montenegro and Austria was signed as part of Njegoš's attempt to secure his country's recognition as a state. How far this served Montenegro's interests is debatable since the agreement was not seen by any outside power as

[62] *Ibid.*, p. 226.
[63] Houston, *Nikola and Milena*, p. 49.

confirming its international identity and was only secured after Njegoš had agreed to its complete withdrawal from the coast. This latter move had several damaging aspects. First, the withdrawal necessitated the sale of two monasteries, both admittedly dilapidated: Majine, situated in Austrian territory on the plain of Budva and once a favourite residence of Vladika Danilo, and Stanjevići near Budva, where both Vladika Sava and Petar I had spent much of their time. Second, this agreement over borders resulted in the forfeiture by Montenegro of any claim to provide the spiritual leader for the Orthodox population on the coast. However, Russia, having close relations with Austria at the time, was strongly in favour of such a settlement, and pressure was put on Njegoš to sign the agreement. He did so believing that a resolution of the relationship with Austria might assist his attempt to gain recognition of Montenegro's status from Turkey. In return he was paid a considerable sum for the monasteries, money that was still held in a Russian bank at the time of his death.[64] The only tangible benefit Montenegro had to show for the loss of its lands and monasteries was an improvement in trading relations between the two sides.[65]

If commerce flourished, relations between Austria and Montenegro were soon complicated by the latter's support for the burgeoning Slav nationalist movement, which, by the mid-1840s, had gained significant support among South Slavs in the Habsburg Empire. The emergence of what came to be called the Illyrian movement, a forerunner of 'Yugoslavism', was first stimulated by Napoleon's short-lived conquest of Dalmatia and the consequent influence of the liberationist and nationalist ideologies that flowed from the French Revolution. In common with the Revolution's other romantic nationalist offshoots, the Illyrian movement saw a common cultural and linguistic heritage as evidence of a people's right to form a single political unit. As might be imagined, Njegoš's natural interest in cultural and linguistic matters and his visits to Vienna and Italy exposed him to these ideas, which were further nurtured through contacts with Slav intellectuals in territories ruled by the Habsburgs, as well as in Serbia itself. Naturally these contacts were not to the

[64] Djilas, *Njegoš*, pp. 165–6.
[65] Živković, *Istorija Crnogorskog Naroda*, p. 536.

liking of the Austrian authorities. Indeed such was their concern that a decade after Metternich's suspicions of Njegoš led him to place the young man under observation and prevent him from gaining a visa to travel to France, they increased their surveillance of Njegoš, employing a number of informers and intercepting all his correspondence. This proved an over-reaction: as events were to show, Njegoš played little more than a walk-on role in the tumultuous events of 1848 despite his undoubted sympathy with the nationalist movements.

In 1847, the year in which Njegoš published *The Mountain Wreath*, Croats in the Habsburg-ruled territories, resenting the attempted imposition of Hungarian as the official language of government throughout the Hungarian half of the empire, declared Croatian to be their official language. In 1848 when the city of Vienna fell under the control of the revolutionaries, the Slav population in the Hungarian territories sided with the House of Habsburg, while seeking at the same time to promote their own pan-Slavist national agenda.[66] Their movement in Croatia was led by a Croatian colonel, Josip Jelačić, to whom the Croatian *sabor* (assembly) gave the title of *Ban*. At the same time the pan-Slavist aims of Jelačić and his Illyrianists found support among Orthodox Serbs living within the Habsburg Empire, largely in the area of Vojvodina or along the old Military Frontier (*Vojna Krajina*) between the Habsburg and Ottoman Empires.[67] At first Njegoš also supported Jelačić but he became disillusioned with the Illyrianists when he saw that their support of the old Habsburg authorities against the Hungarians would not lead to any real freedom for the Slav peoples within the Habsburg Empire and was indeed likely to retard any future hope of a larger pan-Slavist union to include the Serbs.

In fact Njegoš's pan-Slav views had, as might be expected of a churchman, a strongly Orthodox slant and were thus more focused

[66] See Jelavich, *History of the Balkans*, vol. 1, pp. 315–21.
[67] The origin of the Military Frontier goes back to the end of the fifteenth century when the Ottomans, having taken Bosnia and much of Croatia and Dalmatia, settled Serbs and Vlachs into the newly conquered lands. In the course of the next two centuries many of these people, together with other Serbian refugees from Ottoman rule, crossed over into what had by then become Habsburg territory. There the Habsburgs allowed them to settle and retain their Orthodox faith in return for defending the frontiers of the empire.

on contemporary Serbia, on Bosnia and Hercegovina (which at the time had a majority Orthodox population) and on the sacred Serbian heartland of Kosovo than on anything happening in Habsburg lands. By 1848 Serbia was no longer under Prince Miloš but had returned to the previous dynasty in the person of Aleksandar Karadjordjević, son of Karadjordje. Njegoš was in contact with Aleksandar by letter but he corresponded more extensively with Ilija Garašanin, his most important minister and the leading figure on the Serbian national scene. Garašanin, who had also been politically active under Prince Miloš, is famous in Serbian history for his document *Načertanije*, a draft outline of Serbia's foreign policy objectives which in effect amounted to a plan for a Greater Serbia, inspired by belief in the need to re-create Tsar Dušan's medieval Serbian empire.[68] At the time Garašanin kept his document secret, but he discussed his political ideas with sympathisers, and since he was obsessed with Serbia's need to gain access to the sea, Montenegro was of particular interest to him. He and Njegoš never met, but their correspondence reveals Njegoš's admiration for the Serbian statesman's political ideals and his own identification with the cause of Serbdom:

Thanks be to the Illustrious Prince and Sovereign and to you, his councillors, for whatever thought you may from time to time lend this bloody Serbian crag. This will win you the honour of posterity when our people are raised up in spirit...... My dear and esteemed Mr Garašanin, as backward as our Serbian state of affairs is in our century, it is no wonder that I have been exhausted by this bloody cathedra to which I ascended these twenty years ago. Everyone is mortal and must die. I would be sorry for nothing now save for not seeing some progress among our whole people and for not being able in some way to establish the internal government of Montenegro on a firm foundation, and thus I fear that after me there will come back to Montenegro all those woes which existed before me, and that this small folk of ours, uneducated but militant and strong in spirit, will remain in perpetual misery. There is not a Serb whom Serbdom loves more sincerely and respects more than you, and there is not a Serb who loves and respects you more than I.[69]

In April 1848 a Serbian emissary, Matija Ban, paid a secret visit to Cetinje in order to discuss with Njegoš plans for an uprising in Old

[68] Tim Judah, *The Serbs*, pp. 56–7.
[69] Taken from a letter written by Njegoš to Garašanin in July 1850, and quoted by Djilas, *Njegoš*, p. 408.

Serbia (as Macedonia was then called), Bosnia and Hercegovina, which would be timed to exploit the opportunities offered by wider revolutionary events in Europe. He also brought funds with which to assist Montenegro.[70] Both Njegoš and Garašanin saw their homelands as playing a part in instigating rebellion against Turkey in Ottoman-ruled territories, but crucially they differed over priorities. Where Garašanin focused principally on southern Serbia, and Kosovo, Njegoš was for obvious reasons more immediately concerned with the situation in Bosnia and Hercegovina. But despite these differences of emphasis, there was an overall concurrence of aims in which Njegoš accepted Aleksandar Karadjordjević as having the prime claim to be the dynastic ruler of a united Serb people, while he himself would be content with the religious office of patriarch.[71]

This neatly dovetailing prospect was not to be realised. The escalation of tension within the Habsburg territories and the change of priorities to securing the liberation of Slavs in those territories distracted attention from attempts to stimulate an uprising in the Turkish-ruled territories, a course of events which Njegoš would bitterly regret. Ill as he already was by this time with the tuberculosis that would soon kill him, there was little he could do to influence major events beyond Montenegro's borders. Not only did the Great Powers, in particular France and Britain, favour the preservation of the European balance of power and hence the Ottoman Empire, but the Porte itself, having embarked on a programme of military reform with a consequent increase in efficiency, had finally succeeded in re-establishing its authority over Bosnia. The chief agent of this success was the formidable newly-appointed vizier of Bosnia, Omer Pasha Latas, originally a Serb from the Lika district of Croatia.

As Njegoš's hopes for national expansion and liberation collapsed so too did his health. Hoping to avoid the uncertainty which preceded his own accession to office, Njegoš nominated as his successor Danilo, son of Stanko Stijepov, and his own great-nephew. With Montenegro still in 1850 without a single trained doctor, Njegoš, in the hope of postponing the end, spent much of this year in the warmer climate of Italy. Here he was disturbed by reports of Omer

---

[70] Živković, *Istorija Crnogorskog Naroda*, p. 531.
[71] Djilas, *Njegoš*, p. 409–10.

Pasha's plans to invade Montenegro and attempted to gain permission to make one final trip to St Petersburg to enlist Russian support and assistance against attack. Nicholas I refused Njegoš's request and with his health deteriorating rapidly, he returned to Cetinje where he died on 19 October 1851, shortly before his thirty-eighth birthday. Garašanin wrote: 'Montenegro has lost its Sovereign and Serbdom a worthy pillar.'[72] And he was right: great Montenegrin though he was, Njegoš undoubtedly saw himself as a Serb. Michael Boro Petrovich, historian of Serbia, describes him as a great Serbian patriot: he simply saw no conflict in this position.[73] That would only come later when a common border made two dynasties redundant.

Legacy

Given the enormous prestige Njegoš enjoyed both in his lifetime and since, how durable was his impact on his country's fortunes? Politically he had been an ambitious and able ruler, although given the scope of his ambition he was inevitably disappointed. While as a military leader he had experienced failure, socially and politically the balance-sheet showed much to his credit. He founded the first schools in Montenegro, established the senate and a police force, and through the force of his personality and the efficacy of his actions helped to build the underlying unity required by any new state. But he was certainly not above employing spies and resorting to brutality to crush opposition.

Njegoš was Montenegro's last theocratic ruler. Stevan Pavlowitch describes him as the last theocratic ruler in Europe, although the Pope might be thought to have a claim to that title.[74] His successor Danilo was to insist on becoming a secular ruler, thereby indicating that he would no longer accept the limitations on his authority that could be associated with the possession of purely ecclesiastical powers. For Montenegro this move away from episcopal ruler to prince was vital in terms of securing eventual recognition because, as Ivo Banac points out, it undercut the Porte's argument that Montenegro was merely another Ottoman province, enjoying, in typical Ottoman

---

[72] Djilas, *Njegoš*, p. 463.
[73] Michael Boro Petrovich, *History of Serbia*, vol. 1, p. 234.
[74] Pavlowitch, *Serbia: The History behind the Name*, p. 40.

fashion, religious freedom under an ecclesiastical leader.[75] Danilo could never have taken such a politically significant step had Njegoš not prepared the ground, both by the centralising changes he introduced and by the prestige he imparted to the office during his twenty-one years as Vladika.

But we also need to look beyond his reign to his influence on both Montenegrins and Serbs a century and a half later. Here was a ruler who, while fiercely ambitious for his own state of Montenegro, saw no contradiction between that ambition and being a Greater Serb. His willingness to accept a subordinate position to Aleksandar Karadjordjević was evidence of that, and this was because he encapsulated the duality of the Montenegrin/Serb conundrum. As his exchanges with Garašanin demonstrated, all Orthodox Montenegrins were in Njegoš's eyes Serbs. They occupied a different space but they were as much Serbs as their Orthodox brethren in Belgrade. It is this which caused him to be revered by the Greater Serb nationalists of the 1990s, who were often seen carrying his portrait at demonstrations in support of nationalist leaders. And, despite its uncompromising and intolerant message, when the national theatre in Podgorica reopened in 1997 it was a dramatic version of *The Mountain Wreath* which was chosen for the inaugural performance, attended somewhat incongruously by the Grand Mufti.

[75] Banac, *The National Question*, p. 275.

7. Montenegro and the anti-Ottoman Wars: the Road to Independence (1850–80)

European writers and travellers of the 1840s had found in the Montenegro of Njegoš a beguiling reflection of their own Romantic sensibilities. However, as the century advanced officials and diplomats were to take a less rosy view of Montenegro: 'this small but very unquiet state'[1] became a diminutive but significant factor in the dangerous diplomatic and political rivalries encompassed by the Eastern Question. Under successive rulers, Montenegro's involvement in the anti-Ottoman wars of the period twice threatened to provoke a wider conflict which, given the European Powers' competing interests in the volatile Balkan region, risked spilling over on to the wider European stage. Despite misgivings the Powers repeatedly intervened in defence of Montenegrin interests—in 1853, in 1858 and again in the period 1875–80. And it was finally thanks to this series of interventions that by 1880 Montenegro could be said to have largely achieved the goals to which its rulers had so long aspired—significant territorial enlargement, internationally recognised independence within legally constituted borders, and an outlet to the Adriatic.

Getting there had not been easy; sacrifices had been made and allegiances placed under strain. The wars of the 1850s and even more the uprising in Hercegovina in 1875 and its aftermath resulted, as we shall see, in the loss of many lives and civilians being driven

---

[1] Sir George Hamilton Seymour, British Ambassador at Vienna, in a memorandum to the Foreign Secretary, the Earl of Malmesbury, of 6 March 1858. Published in Beitullah Destani (ed.), *Montenegro Political and Ethnic Boundaries 1840–1920*, London: Archive Editions, 2001, vol. 1, document no. 6, 'Correspondence relative to Montenegro January 1857 to January 1859', memorandum, no. 12, p. 45.

from their homes. On the political and diplomatic level long-standing friends and supporters of Montenegro had at times stood aside only to be replaced by new ones, as first the French Emperor Napoleon III and later the British Prime Minister W. E. Gladstone evinced strong support for the Black Mountain. But while monarchs and statesmen rallied to Montenegro's defence and poets (Tennyson) and war correspondents (Arthur Evans, W. J. Stillman, G. A. Henty and W. T. Stead), penned passionate pieces on the Montenegrins' behalf, official despatches revealed the strain of trying to keep Montenegrin ambitions in check in a climate embittered by old enmities and inflamed by rising nationalist aspirations. Public opinion, especially in Russia, France and Britain, may have been firmly on the side of Christian Montenegro but in foreign ministries and chancelleries the policy for the region—driven by competing views of national self-interest—was more often characterised by mistrust and exasperation.

Danilo succeeds Njegoš and becomes Montenegro's first secular ruler

In Montenegro itself the death of Njegoš in 1851 unleashed the by now familiar rivalries associated with the succession as his kinsmen vied with one another to dominate the political scene. Njegoš's will named his nephew Danilo, then aged twenty-five, as his heir, but the dead ruler's brother, Pero Tomov, president of the senate and a significant figure in his own right, was determined to limit the power of the young Vladika designate to ecclesiastical affairs while ensuring that political and military control remained in his own hands. Initially Pero's position seemed unassailable. At the time of his uncle's death Danilo was in Vienna on his way to a seminary in St Petersburg. Pero, supported by those chiefs who favoured a more aggressive policy against the Turks, announced that he had assumed the late Vladika's powers, taking pains to inform the Russian consul in Dubrovnik, the Austrian representative in Kotor and the authorities in Belgrade that he had done so with the senate's blessing.

Danilo met the challenge head-on. Abandoning his plans for further study, he returned immediately to Cetinje where he summoned the chiefs and demanded that they honour his uncle's will. In a society where a man's physical appearance was important Danilo's physical presence did little to recommend him to his fellow Montenegrins. His small stature and green bulging eyes earned him the nickname of 'Little Rabbit'[2] but there was nothing soft or timid about his character. His decisiveness and forceful personality, together with the support he had secured from St Petersburg, were enough to secure the chiefs' backing of him as Njegoš's designated heir. Not content with being simply an ecclesiastical ruler, he next demanded that the chieftains prepare a memorandum petitioning the tsar to agree to his becoming a hereditary prince. Danilo wished to marry and to pass on his position to any son he might have, instead of the traditional Montenegrin pattern of succession from uncle to nephew. Again Danilo got his way, and having secured the chiefs' supposedly spontaneous demand, set off in 1852 for St Petersburg where he sought recognition as the ruler of a principality, rather than consecration as metropolitan. Unsurprisingly the Orthodox hierarchy of St Petersburg opposed the secularisation of office Danilo's move implied and tried to prevent it by insisting on accommodating him in the Alexander Nevski monastery where his predecessor Vladika Vasilije had been buried. Preparations were also begun for Danilo's consecration. But he did not co-operate, refusing to fast, pray or don priestly apparel. Eventually his uncompromising approach paid off. In April 1852 the tsar finally received him, saluting him as Prince of Montenegro.[3] Backed by Russia, and having assured himself that Austria too was prepared to tolerate his change of designation, Prince Danilo returned to Cetinje to impose his authority and crush his opponents. Pero and Njegoš's cousin Djordje, another potentially threatening rebel, were forced to flee the country.

This early demonstration of Danilo's energy and willpower foreshadowed his later full-blown authoritarianism. Emboldened by his new status, he tightened his grip on Montenegro's institutions, nominating another member of his clan to the position of metropolitan and insisting on choosing the senators himself rather than, according

---

[2] Or '*Zeko*'. Later however the harsh measures Danilo instigated against would-be rebels earned him the nickname of 'Thunderbolt'. (See Djilas, *Njegoš*, p. 252 and Houston, *Nikola and Milena*, p. 67.)

[3] Milan Jovićević, *The Montenegrin Royal Marriages*, The Museums of Cetinje, 1988, pp. 24–5.

to past practice, allowing the *zbor* to do so. Danilo was equally unyielding in the choice of his future wife, rejecting in turn the daughters of the Serbian prince Aleksandar Karadjordjević and of a wealthy Viennese banker Baron Sina in favour of a beautiful fifteen-year-old whose father Marko Kvekić was a merchant in Trieste. Darinka Kvekić's family lacked wealth and nobility but, since they originated from the coastal town of Herceg Novi, they had what many assumed to be the compensating advantage of close ties with Montenegro.

The celebration of the marriage was fixed for early 1855. As a sign of Austrian assent Field-Marshal Marmula agreed to act as chief witness at the wedding. The bride set sail from Trieste for Kotor on a Lloyds steamer on 21 January, and the following day rode up through the snow to Cetinje on a white horse, escorted by six fine-looking young men and a growing crowd of curious Montenegrins. Various contemporary accounts describe the arrival of the half-frozen princess in Cetinje where her future husband, waiting to greet her, was said to have counselled his young bride to be 'stout-hearted [since] it is not easy to be a princess among these wolves'.[4] But Darinka, like Danilo, was strong-willed and ambitious and far from faint-hearted. She was also extravagant, something Montenegro could ill afford. Soon she had transformed the austere Biljarda into something resembling a rich Central European merchant's mansion, introducing fine furniture, improving the food and wine, and even managing to have her way in her preference for using the French language.[5] Visitors were impressed, but Montenegrins, who required only modesty and industry of their women, were less dazzled by the display than dismayed by her lavish spending.

Danilo defends Montenegrin unity

By 1855 the realisation of Danilo's personal ambitions had been matched by similar success politically, although this ultimately called for foreign intervention and was not achieved without casualties. Even before his marriage, and shortly after his return from Moscow,

[4] *Ibid.*, pp. 26–7.
[5] *Ibid.*

Danilo had faced a threat from the Croatian Serb turned Ottoman general Omer Pasha Latas, the redoubtable vizier of Bosnia. Having subjugated the renegade *beys* of Bosnia, Omer Pasha's ambition was to impose imperial control on the wider region. Montenegro's decision to declare itself a secular principality thus came as an affront to the Porte, which had never accepted any formal loss of sovereignty over it. In 1853, as a first step, Omer Pasha attempted to detach the Piperi tribal region from Montenegro, promising the tribesmen immunity from certain taxes and grants of much-needed land.[6] A group of Montenegrins chose this moment to respond, seizing the old Crnojević capital of Žabljak on the foreshores of Lake Skadar. If, as has been suggested, Danilo was complicit in the attack, he had misjudged Omer Pasha's response. At the last moment, sensing the danger, Danilo ordered the Montenegrin forces to withdraw but he was too late to prevent the pasha from seizing on this provocation as an excuse to launch a full-scale invasion of Montenegro.

Determined to inflict a crushing defeat on Montenegro, the Turks struck the principality with four separate forces advancing at once.[7] With Montenegro facing disaster—even the lead type from Njegoš's former printing works had been melted down for shot[8]— Danilo appealed for help to both Russia and Austria. Austria, concerned at the impact an Ottoman invasion might have on its own South Slavs, responded forcefully, sending an envoy, Count Leiningen, to warn the sultan that failure to prevent the attack would lead to an Austrian intervention.[9] Subsequently the Austrian government was to use this as an illustration of its even-handedness, demonstrating the Habsburg Empire's readiness to act on behalf of populations under attack irrespective of whether they were Christian or Muslim. But the British, at least, suspected a less altruistic reason for Austria's action. A confidential memorandum from the consul in Istanbul to the Earl of Malmesbury, the Foreign Secretary, claimed that the Habsburg authorities had received secret intelligence of

---

[6] See Jelavich, *History of the Balkans*, vol. 1, p. 252.
[7] *Foreign Office Handbook on Montenegro*, November 1918, p. 17.
[8] See Chapter 6.
[9] Russia also exerted pressure on the Ottoman Empire through the Foreign Minister Count Nesselrode. (See Stevenson, *A History of Montenegro*, p. 184.)

Russia's intention to 'take advantage of the religious connection between the Eastern and Western Churches in order to invade Turkey', something the Austrians were determined not to allow.[10] Montenegro may therefore have been of no more than incidental importance; nonetheless Austria's interest in keeping Russia out of the Balkans as trouble brewed in the Crimea may in part have been responsible for its change of attitude towards its troublesome neighbour. Whatever the motive, Count Leiningen's intervention with the sultan almost certainly saved the principality from disaster. On 3 March 1853 peace was agreed on the basis of the territorial *status quo*. Most satisfactorily for the Montenegrins, the Austrians accepted that the wording of this treaty referred back to the Ottoman *firman* of 1799 in which the Sublime Porte recognised that Montenegro was no longer under Ottoman suzerainty. Danilo sent a message of thanks to Emperor Franz Joseph.

Danilo's authority had been challenged on a second occasion before his wedding and the successful consolidation of his position in 1855. The threat this time came from rebellious tribesmen rather than from external aggressors and involved the most recently incorporated Brda tribes—the Piperi, the Kuči and the Bjelopavlići. The outbreak of the Crimean War (1853–6) had encouraged the war party in Cetinje to urge an attack on Turkey at a time when it was engaged in hostilities against Montenegro's traditional protector, Russia, but the Austrians strongly opposed such a move and Danilo, much indebted to them, felt obliged to maintain a neutral stance in the war despite the active opposition of his uncle Djordje Petrović. This deviation from the traditional pro-Russian/anti-Turkish posture inevitably provoked a strong reaction to the point where some of the tribesmen, aggrieved as much by Danilo's determination to enforce taxation as by his neutrality, rose in revolt. The Piperi, Kuči and Bjelopavlići went so far as to declare themselves an independent state,[11] but Danilo immediately suppressed the revolt, forcing many of the rebellious tribesmen to flee to neighbouring territories to escape crushing indemnities or even execution.

---

[10] See Destani (ed.), *Montenegro: Political and Ethnic Boundaries*, vol. 1, document no. 38, pp. 62–3.
[11] *Foreign Office Handbook on Montenegro*, November 1918, p. 18.

Danilo marked the success of his campaign by promulgating a new law code, drafted with the help of a Russian adviser, and a draconian tax regime, which he was able to enforce with the army led by his brother Mirko. Mirko Petrović, a figure notorious in Montenegrin history for his bellicosity, was later considered even by his fellow-countrymen, who honoured and feared him in almost equal measure, as too warlike to succeed his brother in governing the country. He was not about to show compassion to the rebels. Those who had refused to pay Danilo's taxes or attempted to avoid payment by going over to the Ottomans were punished ruthlessly: men, women and children were massacred, villages burned and whole families driven into exile. On one occasion the heads of men, women and children were placed on stakes in a priest's apiary—'it was a reign of terror such as not even Montenegro had known.'[12] Certainly clan resistance, for so long a major problem in Montenegro, was effectively broken, but Danilo had alienated a number of the tribes and made many enemies, one of whom was probably his future assassin.

Manoeuvring between the Powers

It was at this time, with Russia in a weak position during the Crimean War, that Danilo set about consolidating relations with France.[13] His approach paid off since Napoleon III proved a sympathetic ally, providing Danilo with his most influential adviser Monsieur Delarue and taking a consistently pro-Montenegrin line throughout the protracted diplomatic wrangling which followed the settlement of the Crimean War. Ready to explore any avenue which might result in the enlargement of Montenegro's territory, and in particular the accession of a port on the Adriatic, Danilo toyed briefly with accepting a nominal form of Turkish suzerainty, an approach which provoked outrage among traditional Montenegrins and was soon abandoned.[14] In 1856 the victory of the Western Powers—France, Britain and Piedmont, fighting in defence of

[12] Djilas, *Njegoš*, p. 253.
[13] Alone among the Powers, France had its representative on the spot: M. Hecquard, a well-known writer on Albania, was sent as consul to Cetinje in 1855.
[14] Houston, *Nikola and Milena*, p. 63.

Turkey—had led to the Treaty of Paris under which the victors took on the role of protecting the Ottomans' Christian subjects, a right previously claimed on behalf of the Orthodox by the defeated power, Russia.[15] The 14th Protocol of the treaty[16] specifically denied Russia the right of protection over Montenegro, stipulating that any special relationship would henceforth be based solely on the bond of 'mutual sympathy'. Meanwhile the Turkish representative at the Peace Conference in Paris, the grand vizier Mehmed Emin Ali Pasha, repudiating the earlier *firman*, maintained that in the view of the Sublime Porte Montenegro remained an integral part of the Ottoman Empire; however, he accepted that his government had no intention of altering the *status quo*. Ali Pasha's statement was immediately rejected by the Montenegrins. On 31 May 1856 Prince Danilo addressed a note to the Powers setting out Montenegro's demands: recognition of its independence, the extension of its frontiers to the north and south, the establishment of a legally recognised frontier with the Ottoman Empire, and the annexation of the port of Bar.[17]

Over the next two and a half years the Powers, including Austria and Prussia as co-signatories of the Treaty of Paris, devoted an inordinate amount of time attempting to resolve the problem posed by the status and frontiers of Montenegro. As exasperated ministers and diplomats were forced to recognise, a question which, in the words of the Austrian Foreign Minister Count Buol, 'ought to be as insignificant as Montenegro'[18] was made deeply complex by its bearing on the wider issue of preserving the integrity of the Ottoman Empire. At the time the Western Powers and the British and Austrian governments in particular saw the survival of the Ottoman Empire as vital in order to limit Russian expansionism in the region, and were considerably irked to have their broader policy aims frustrated by the manoeuvrings of Prince Danilo and his advisers at the head of fewer than 100,000 Montenegrins.

---

[15] Russia's longstanding claim to have gained the right to intervene with the Sublime Porte over the fate of Orthodox Christians within the Ottoman Empire was based on a number of treaties and subsequent guarantees going back in the first instance to the 1774 Treaty of Kuchuk Kainarji.

[16] Henceforth referred to as the Treaty of Paris.

[17] Stevenson, *History of Montenegro*, pp. 185–7.

[18] Destani (ed.), *Montenegro: Political and Ethnic Boundaries*, vol. 1, document no. 13, p. 47.

Such manoeuvrings were of course only possible because remaining post-war differences in the Powers' perceptions of their own interests continued to be played out in the acutely sensitive borderlands of the great empires. Naturally the Powers in closest proximity, believing their interests to be most directly affected, took the strongest stand. Thus Austria, fearing the effect of nearby liberationist movements on its own Slav population, insisted on Montenegro recognising the sultan's authority and justified its position by reference to the 1791 Treaty of Sistova, to which Britain had been a signatory.[19] Equally wary of allowing Russian influence to enter the Adriatic, the Austrian government was also adamantly opposed to any suggestion of Montenegro gaining access to the sea. British Tory ministers, whose interests were less directly involved, took a more nuanced view, preferring to describe Montenegro's status as 'obscure' while nevertheless inclining towards the Ottoman position. By contrast France, with its recent revolutionary history, tended to be more sympathetic to the Montenegrin position. Lastly, while in Russia public opinion remained consistently pro-Montenegrin, officials attached far more importance to Russia's own political goals and were accordingly unwilling to risk further humiliating defeat on behalf of their co-religionists.

With Austria and Britain taking a lead, the Powers at first attempted to regulate the Porte's relations with Montenegro by putting together a settlement under which it would be offered more arable land in return for accepting, at least in principle, the status of a vassal state of the Ottoman Empire. Danilo rejected this and used a visit to Paris in 1857 to argue Montenegro's case. The highly favourable impression he made on the emperor considerably strengthened France's support for the Montenegrin cause and led Napoleon III to push the other Powers to recognise Montenegro's claim to independence.

At this juncture the growing division between the Powers over Montenegro's formal status suggested that the best way forward lay in bypassing the sovereignty issue in favour of securing a recognised

---

[19] In so doing Austria chose to overlook the treaty involving the exchange of lands concluded separately with Montenegro in 1842 and in which there had been no reference to the Ottoman Empire's sovereignty over Montenegro, nor to the need for the sultan to approve arrangements made by his vassal. See Destani (ed.), *Montenegro: Political and Ethnic Boundaries*, vol. 1, inclosure 1 in no. 297, p. 219.

border between Ottoman-ruled territory and Montenegrin lands. Under such an arrangement the Montenegrins were still to be offered an increase in cultivable land in order to remove any justification for the territorial incursions that in the past had often spilled over into wider warfare.[20] But even with the sovereignty question officially placed on one side, the delineation of the frontier proved far from straightforward as disputes continued over the territory which such an arrangement would entail. In particular the Porte was adamantly opposed to any expansion in the direction of Serbia since this might lead the two principalities to unite and declare independence, thereby cutting off Ottoman access to Bosnia.[21] Meanwhile, as negotiations continued over which countries should be represented on the commission intended to delimit the borders, skirmishing between Montenegrins and their Ottoman-ruled neighbours broke out, both in the south along the shores of Lake Skadar and in the north where Montenegrins had become involved in an uprising launched by Christian subjects of the Porte in Hercegovina.

As the risk of wider conflict grew, Austria's denunciations of the prince's policies became ever more emphatic. An article on Montenegro published on 2 March 1858 in *Ost Deutsche Post* was considered sufficiently representative of the official government view to warrant its inclusion in a despatch sent to the Foreign Office by the British ambassador in Vienna, Sir Hamilton Seymour. The anonymous correspondent began by sounding a note of alarm:

The existence of a so-called state like Montenegro is a comical curiosity in the system of European states; but it assumes the character of a dangerous anomaly when one considers the conduct of that so-called State for a series of years, particularly since the self-accomplished secularisation of the Vladika dignity, but, most of all, by the breach of the peace committed by it at this time.

A little later the tone of the article becomes increasingly strident:

What is Montenegro? A barren rocky district of rather more than eighty square miles (German), with not more than 120,000 inhabitants, hardly

[20] In 1855 the average holding of a Montenegrin peasant amounted to no more than a quarter of a hectare of arable and meadow land. See Jozo Tomasevich, *Peasants, Politics and Economic Change in Yugoslavia*, Stanford University Press, 1955, p. 128.
[21] Destani (ed.), *Montenegro: Political and Ethnic Boundaries*, vol. 1, document no. 107, p. 102.

tinged by the lowest degree of civilization. The whole population possesses only two or three schools, and priests who can neither read nor write are as common as workmen are uncommon. Manufacturers, engineers, physicians etc., are quite unknown. In the whole country there is not a single road; out of 300 villages the chief town of Cettinge [*sic*] alone has more than 1,000 inhabitants. The lowest degree of production, such as is due to Nature itself with the least help of man, and by the side of this the constant trade of arms, such as it is, carried on by brigands; this is the sum total of Montenegrin activity. And the despot of such a tribe challenges the Sovereign of a great empire, his own suzerain Lord, nay he dares to throw down the gauntlet to the whole of Europe. He dreams of the erection of a great national empire, the centre of which shall be Montenegro, and the head of which he shall be himself. Is not such an ambition open madness? Shall a lunatic with impunity strike a spark which might set the whole world in flames?[22]

The battle of Grahovo

Rage as it might, *Ost Deutsche Post* could do little to curb the actions of the Montenegrins. In May 1858 a combined Montenegrin-Hercegovinian force, under the prince's brother, Mirko Petrović, captured the important town of Grahovo some 50 km. east of Dubrovnik. While the scale of the Montenegrin victory could hardly be doubted—several thousand Turkish soldiers were killed in the battle[23]—there were suspicions of Montenegrin treachery in which Monsieur Delarue, the French secretary to the prince, was thought to be involved.

Two accounts of what happened at Grahovo exist. Both refer to two separate engagements—one on 11 May in which the Montenegrins came off worse, and a second two days later when the mountaineers attacked a convoy of some 300 *bashi-bazouks* (irregulars) bringing supplies to the Ottoman forces. The resulting carnage was frightful: many of the feared irregulars were cut to pieces, some having their lips and noses hacked off according to contemporary Montenegrin practice. When, the next day, a relieving Ottoman force saw what had happened to their comrades, they panicked and fled back to Trebinje.

[22] Quoted in Destani (ed.), *Montenegro: Political and Ethnic Boundaries*, vol. 1, inclosure no. 11, pp. 44–5.
[23] Some reports put overall Turkish casualties as high as 6,000 out of a total force of 8,000 (Houston, *Nikola and Milena*, p. 66).

So far Turkish and Montenegrin accounts agree, but they differ over what happened next. M. Delarue himself relates that when he tried to advise the commandant of the remaining and by now encircled Ottoman forces, Hussein Pasha, not to attempt to accompany him to Trebinje for a meeting with Kemal Effendi—the commissioner sent by the Porte to negotiate with Montenegro—the commandant insisted on leaving and was cut down despite the secretary's attempts to save him. The Turkish account claims that Delarue, after promising Hussein Pasha safe conduct, broke his word and allowed the Montenegrins and Hercegovinian tribesmen to attack him.[24]

Unable finally to determine whether or not Delarue's conduct had been treacherous on this occasion, British official reports of the time reflect increasing distrust of Danilo. A despatch of 14 June 1858 from Horace Rumbold, who had been sent to Dubrovnik by the Foreign Office to investigate the Grahovo affair, reports a conversation the officer had with Milorad Medaković, former secretary to Danilo—and earlier to Njegoš—on board a Dalmatian steamer travelling to Dubrovnik According to Medaković:

Prince Danilo is much what he is represented to be by the Austrians: he is ignorant, though not wanting in considerable quickness of apprehension; uncertain of purpose in all but his unbounded ambition and unrelenting cruelty; perfidious in the highest degree, and at times unfathomable even to those most familiar with him.[25]

Scrupulously Rumbold cautioned against accepting Medaković's account uncritically; the former secretary, he noted, had his own reasons for opposing Danilo and strongly supported Danilo's replacement by Djordje Petrović, head of a group of exiles living under Austrian protection at Zadar. Nevertheless Rumbold, who in

---

[24] Papers contained in Foreign Office files show British representatives of the time as disagreeing over whether Delarue and the Montenegrins did behave treacherously. Mr Rumbold claims, on the personal authority of Hussein Pasha, that Delarue did indeed issue a safe-conduct, which was not then honoured by the Montenegrins. However, Mr Rumbold goes on to acknowledge Delarue's honourable conduct in attempting to defend the life of Hussein Pasha, noting that the latter accepted that the secretary had tried to defend his life, only to become separated from him after twice having his horse shot from under him. (See Destani (ed.), *Montenegro: Political and Ethnic Boundaries*, vol. 1, pp. 215–21.)

[25] *Ibid.*, p. 216.

this report described Montenegro's independence as 'a real fact',[26] made no secret of his own views of Danilo, whom he excoriated as the 'chief author and promoter' of all local pan-Slav movements, particularly since the 'bloody deed of Grahovo'.[27]

However, worse was to follow as Montenegrin forces continued to clash with their Muslim neighbours in neighbouring Ottoman-ruled territory. In one particularly grave incident near Kolašin in July 1858 the Montenegrins were reported to have burnt houses, massacred the men and carried off into Montenegro perhaps as many as 200 women and children.[28] Danilo disowned the perpetrators and promised to punish them severely, but the atrocities committed did little to improve the standing of the prince and his Montenegrins in most European chancelleries. The French government proved an exception since Napoleon III attempted to ensure that France replaced Russia in exerting paramount influence on Montenegrin affairs. On 15 May, just days after the Montenegrin victory at Grahovo, the French had shown their support for Montenegro by despatching two ships of the line to the Adriatic, a measure doubtless intended to discourage Austria from going to the assistance of the Turks.[29] Despite arousing apprehension, the ships docked quietly in Dubrovnik and, when the Austrians made no forceful response, soon sailed away. French support for Montenegro proved more enduring since they were reported soon afterwards to be offering the Montenegrin government a sum roughly equivalent to the subsidy the principality had received from Russia.[30]

However, a solution to the frontier problem needed to be found if further and even more serious incidents were to be avoided. Ever the pragmatists, the British attempted to mediate between the French and Austrian positions, and towards the end of 1858 their efforts finally met with success. Following further tortuous negotiations, the five Powers—Britain, France, Russia, Austria and Turkey—reached agreement together with a Montenegrin delegate on a new border with Turkey based on the *status quo* in 1856, a time when

[26] Destani (ed.), *Montenegro: Political and Ethnic Boundaries*, vol. 1, p. 218.
[27] *Ibid.*
[28] *Ibid.*, pp. 275–87.
[29] *Ibid.*, vol. 1, inclosure 1, no. 200, p. 150.
[30] *Ibid.*, p. 253. The sum in question was 4,600 ducats.

Montenegrin forces were occupying Grahovo. When the agreement was finally implemented the following spring Montenegro gained not only the town itself but additional territory around it. However, it failed—principally as a result of British and Austrian opposition to a French- and Russian-sponsored proposal—to obtain an outlet to the Adriatic. Nor, despite its clear *de facto* independence, was Montenegro granted *de jure* international recognition since this was deemed to be injurious to Turkey. Finally Danilo was forcefully warned that any further incursion into Ottoman territory of the kind committed by his countrymen at Kolašin would result in the Powers abandoning Montenegro to its fate.

Danilo's assassination; the impact of his rule on Montenegro

Danilo's nemesis was not to be at the hands of the Great Powers. In August 1860 he was shot dead by one of his own countrymen in a village near Kotor where he was accompanying his wife Darinka, whom her doctors had ordered to undertake a regime of sea-bathing. The assassin, Todor Kadić, was a member of the aggrieved Bjelopavlići tribe. Danilo did not die immediately but was carried wounded back to the house of his agent in Kotor. By the next morning a large crowd had assembled in the open space in front of the bazaar of Kotor, threatening to burn the town if their prince was not handed over to them. Only when Darinka sent a message saying that Danilo was not yet able to travel to Cetinje because of the pain he was suffering but would be handed over to them as soon as he could travel did the tribesmen agree to disperse peacefully. The prince died that evening and his body was later borne through the streets by Austrian soldiers who fired a volley of cannon shots in a salute.

For all Austria's honouring of Danilo after his death there remained suspicions that the Austrian authorities had in some way been complicit in his assassination. Certainly the Austrian government had long wished to see him overthrown and replaced by one of the band of Montenegrin exiles under their protection at Zadar over whom they assumed that they would have more control. Nevertheless whether the assassin acted for political reasons or out of a desire for personal vengeance has never been conclusively established. As two Scottish women who visited Montenegro the Christmas after Danilo's death noted in their memoir, there were plenty of reasons to suppose that he had been vulnerable on both counts.[31] Yet despite his ruthlessness, his deceptions and his dangerous political brinkmanship, Danilo was in many ways an able ruler whose reforms, if they can be so called, benefited his country. Although his death caused an ambitious plan to found a new capital, Danilovgrad, by the river in the fertile Bjelopavlići plain to be dropped, there was no doubting his prodigious energy. He not only overcame the divisive influence of the Montenegrin clan chiefs but his reorganisation of the army did much to make the national forces more disciplined and effective. In 1855 he organised the country's first census, which, correctly or not, put the population at 80,000. He also arranged for a small number of prominent Montenegrins to be sent abroad to receive an education. It could even be argued that through his marriage he introduced Montenegrins for the first time to some of the more humanising aspects of Western civilisation. Darinka is credited with securing the removal of the heads previously displayed on the tower in Cetinje.[32]

Shortly after Danilo's death Darinka left Cetinje accompanied by her year-old daughter Olga. A mere two years later she returned with Olga to live in Cetinje but her attempts to exert her influence over Danilo's successor, and involve herself in political life in Cetinje increased her unpopularity. She eventually departed again in 1867 having in the intervening time been a considerable drain on the finances of Montenegro.[33] In 1892 Darinka died of pneumonia in Venice, as did her daughter only four years later; both were buried in the Cetinje monastery.[34]

[31] According to Mackenzie and Irby the assassin was swiftly apprehended and later executed in Kotor. The women note that before he died, the assassin confessed to having been instigated in his act by Austria but they also record hearing of 'a hundred versions [for his murder] based on a private quarrel'. (G. Muir Mackenzie and A. P. Irby, *Travels in the Slavonic Provinces of Turkey-in-Europe* (second edition in two volumes), London: Daldy, Isbister and Co., 1877, p. 215.)

[32] M. G. Lejean, 'Voyage en Albanie et au Montenegro' (1858), *Le Tour du monde. Nouveau journal des voyages*, Paris: Librairie Hachette, 1er semester de 1860, p. 85.

[33] Darinka returned to Cetinje in 1862 in the immediate aftermath of Montenegro's defeat at the hands of the Ottoman general, Omer Pasha Latas, and attempted to involve herself in the peace negotiations which were at that time taking place through the mediation of the Powers. See Jovićević, *Montenegrin Royal Marriages*, p. 41.

[34] *Ibid.*, p. 27.

Nikola Petrović: the new prince

Danilo had no male heirs and his brother Mirko, now known as the 'Sword of Montenegro',[35] was considered too bellicose and uneducated to succeed him. In itself such a consensus of opinion against Mirko might be seen as evidence of the progress made towards more civilised values in Danilo's time. That Danilo himself shared the general view of his brother is confirmed by the fact that in 1857, shortly before leaving for Paris, he designated his young nephew—Mirko's son Nikola Petrović—as his successor.[36] Nikola's preparation for this role had begun as early as 1852 when he was sent for schooling to Trieste and then in 1856 to Paris where, under the patronage of Napoleon III, he was enrolled in the famous Lycée Louis-le-Grand. However, at the time of his uncle's death in 1860 Nikola was already back in Cetinje after apparently suffering some health problems in Paris.[37]

Nikola was born in 1841, and thus only nineteen at the time he inherited the title of prince. He came under pressure almost immediately to marry the girl to whom he had been betrothed since childhood, the thirteen-year-old Milena Vukotić. Milena had been carefully chosen with an eye to avoiding the defects which the Montenegrins perceived in her predecessor. Still virtually a child and having received no more than basic education, she embodied the qualities of modesty and dutifulness which the Montenegrins thought befitted a woman. Family connections were equally in her favour: her father Petar Vukotić, a senator from the nearby village of Čevo, was admired as a soldier, and after Mirko's death from cholera in 1867 he emerged as Montenegro's foremost military commander.

Omer Pasha Latas

The prince had hardly settled into his new role when he was faced with the challenge of restraining his subjects who were clamouring to support an uprising against the redoubtable Omer Pasha Latas launched by their co-religionists in the frontier districts of Hercegovina.

[35] *Foreign Office Handbook on Montenegro,* November 1918, p. 21.
[36] Jovićević, *Montenegrin Royal Marriages,* p. 37.
[37] *Ibid.*

The Powers' experience of trying to reach a settlement after the battle of Grahovo had left them determined to impress on Nikola the importance of avoiding further military adventures. Nikola co-operated after a fashion, allowing the Turks to re-provision their fortress at Nikšić by transiting Montenegrin territory but doing little to prevent Montenegrin tribesmen from crossing the frontier to fight alongside their kinsmen in Hercegovina. Meanwhile the old pattern of economic raiding across the borders increased, largely because of the temporary weakening of Ottoman control in Hercegovina in the wake of the Montenegrin victory at Grahovo.[38]

The Ottomans were bound to respond as soon as circumstances permitted. Omer Pasha laid his plans accordingly, first putting down the revolt in Hercegovina and then taking advantage of the long winter months to impose a blockade on Montenegro, thereby cutting supplies of essential arms and ammunition.[39] By the spring of 1862 Omer Pasha had finalised preparations for an invasion. Dividing his army, he struck Montenegro at its weakest point at both ends of the so-called 'funnel of Montenegro', a narrow tongue of Montenegrin land only twelve miles long, which separated the Porte's Albanian-inhabited territory from Ottoman-ruled Hercegovina.[40] Pressed from north and south of the funnel, Montenegrin forces came under simultaneous attack from a third force to the east as Omer Pasha used the far more numerous troops at his disposal to drive home his advantage. Serbia, appealed to for help by the Montenegrins, agreed to co-operate but then failed to act in time. For two months the Montenegrin commanders Mirko Petrović and Petar Vukotić were able to hold out before the Turks succeeded in driving them from the funnel, cutting the country in two. Still the Montenegrins did not give up: Mirko, having made a largely successful withdrawal, was able to launch a resistance campaign defeating the enemy in two separate engagements despite what was by then a serious lack of armaments. The imbalance in forces and supplies meant that the Montenegrins could not hope to hold out for long and, worse still, their major ally France was too deeply involved in Napoleon III's

---

[38] Palairet, 'The Culture of Economic Stagnation in Montenegro', p. 29.
[39] *Foreign Office Handbook on Montenegro*, November 1918, p. 22.
[40] *Ibid.*

Mexican adventure to give support. In Britain Palmerston took the side of the sultan, although Montenegro's plight attracted some support from fellow Christian sympathisers and a subscription fund was launched in Athens. It was not enough: when Omer Pasha struck again the Montenegrins suffered a decisive defeat near Rijeka Crnojevića on Lake Skadar.

The scale of the defeat convinced Nikola that further resistance was futile. Briefly it seemed that Cetinje again faced destruction;[41] under terms dictated by the Ottoman commander, the Ottomans were to erect fortifications along a substantial part of the border between Spuž and Nikšić, and Mirko Petrović was to be expelled from Montenegro. At this late hour Montenegro's friends abroad—Russia and France—became active in the matter, insisting that the Convention of Scutari (Skadar) should nullify these provisions and instead include certain concessions to Montenegro. Hence the principality was allowed to retain its 1859 frontiers, rent further arable lands from the Ottomans, and even use the port of Bar provided the provisioning involved did not include munitions or arms. To restore the balance to some degree in the Porte's favour, the Montenegrins were required to give up raiding, abandon their support for rebels in Ottoman-ruled lands and to desist from the practice of building fortresses on the frontier.

Both sides had suffered heavy losses. In Montenegro up to 6,000 men had been killed or wounded, and the country was ravaged by the war and now desperately in need of a period of peace to allow the population to recover and rebuild their lives.[42] The ensuing

---

[41] W. J. Stillman, sent as war correspondent of *The Times* to cover the uprising in Hercegovina a few years later, casts doubt on the real nature of the threat to Cetinje. 'Omar [*sic*] himself', Stillman writes, 'said at Constantinople to a friend of mine, that if the Prince had sent 5,000 fresh men against his army when it reached Rijeka he could not have offered an effectual resistance, and would have been forced to abandon his conquest.' (W. J. Stillman, *Herzegovina and the Late Uprising: the causes of the latter and its remedies*, London, 1877, fn. p. 5.) This, of course, begs the question whether the Montenegrins, having suffered so many casualties, could at this stage have put 5,000 fresh men into the field.

[42] While this figure may be on the high side, there is no doubt that the war had greatly increased the level of hardship faced by the population. Visiting Cetinje in the winter of 1861, Mackenzie and Irby record, 'It was melancholy to note the increase of begging; we could scarcely walk a step without being pursued by

thirteen years from 1862 to 1875, when Montenegro would once again become involved in insurrection in Hercegovina, saw the principality formally at peace although the lack of a real economic base dimishished the benefits such a respite might have brought.

Moving forward: progress at home, frustration abroad

Over these years Prince Nikola's youthful experience of a world beyond his country's confines led him to introduce a number of changes, intended to move the country in the direction of the modern world. Many schools offering elementary education were opened in different parts of the principality including, in Cetinje, the first school for girls, established with Russian help in 1869. Communications were improving. In 1869 Montenegro was for the first time connected to the outside world by telegraph, and two years later the first post office was established. In 1874 construction began on a proper road linking Cetinje and Kotor, funded by Austria-Hungary. But the prince's broad education, knowledge of languages, and experience of 'civilised' Europe were not shared by the mass of his subjects, over whom he ruled with the autocratic powers, if not in the despotic manner, of his predecessor Prince Danilo. The evident contradiction implicit in such an approach was later at least partly the cause of Nikola's undoing, but at the time widespread acceptance of his style as one of paternalistic benevolence helped to earn him the respect of his people and the admiration of an increasing number of foreign visitors.

However, Nikola's early successes did not extend to realising his people's dearest wish—the acquisition of an Adriatic port. In 1861 the Scottish women travellers Mackenzie and Irby had noted sympathetically the words of an old 'highlander' they encountered near Cetinje: 'Tell your great English Queen that we Montenegrines [*sic*] can no longer live without a bit of sea.'[43] Perversely Nikola's

---

little children praying for alms.' Both France and Russia, they observe, had sent grain to Cetinje to provide relief for Montenegro in a situation made worse by the recent drought. (*Travels in the Slavonic Provinces of Turkey-in-Europe*, pp. 225 and 243.)

[43] *Ibid.*, p. 271.

failure to achieve this aim in 1866 owed much to the opposition of the British government which, together with France, opposed the sultan's offer to cede Montenegro a coastal strip near Spič fearing, as Austria did before them, that control of the port might fall into the hands of Russia.[44] Typical of this attitude was that of Disraeli:

As for Montenegro, it has got about that Russia is intriguing for a port under the pretence of increasing the territory of Montenegro. No such thing: we renounce the idea. Montenegro need have no port. Only a little garden to grow cabbages and potatoes.[45]

Shut off from the sea, Nikola turned his thoughts in other directions. Although Serbia had failed to come to the aid of Montenegro in time to save it from Omer Pasha's devastating attack of 1862, the strongly nationalistic and anti-Ottoman programme pursued by Serbia's ruler, Prince Mihailo Obrenović, commended itself to his Montenegrin counterpart. In 1860, the year of Nikola's accession, Mihailo had returned to rule Serbia for the second time after sixteen years' exile in Europe and, once in power, had entrenched his control through a combination of legalistic and despotic measures before turning his attention to ensuring that Serbia became the leading nation in a pan-Balkan alliance intended to free the Christian population from Ottoman rule. Mihailo's time in exile had convinced him that if Balkan Christians were to achieve this goal they would have to do it themselves. In the view of Mihailo, as of revolutionaries elsewhere, Serbia with its more educated population and by far the largest army in the Balkans was the natural leader of any liberation movement.[46]

The initiative was launched shortly after Mihailo came to the throne but soon ran into problems with Greece over the future division of Ottoman lands in Macedonia. Meanwhile there was further uncertainty over whether a future South Slav state would include Slav peoples currently ruled by the Habsburgs. The immediate focus thus fell on the unification of historic Serbian lands, which were widely accepted as including Montenegro, as well as

---

[44] *Foreign Office Handbook*, November 1918, p. 24.

[45] Quoted by Vladimir Dedijer, *The Road to Sarajevo*, New York: Simon and Schuster, 1966, p. 45.

[46] Petrovich, *A History of Modern Serbia*, vol. 1, p. 314.

Bosnia, Hercegovina, Kosovo and part of Macedonia.[47] At this stage co-operation between Mihailo and Nikola was already well advanced; in November 1860 Mihailo had taken the initial step of sending the Serbian intellectual Vuk Karadžić on a mission to Montenegro. Ostensibly this was in order to convey formal notification of Mihailo's succession to the Montenegrin prince, but the more important part of Karadžić's mission was to win Nikola's approval for Belgrade's pan-Balkan alliance system. Both for romantic nationalistic and for more selfish dynastic reasons, Cetinje was prepared to support this project.

Nonetheless progress towards the alliance remained incremental. Mihailo had become godfather to two of Nikola's daughters, and this was intended to move the relationship between the two dynasties along.[48] But it was only in 1866 when Austria, always deeply opposed to Serbian expansion, had been defeated by Prussia and was temporarily incapacitated that the signing of the Serbian-Montenegrin agreement finally took place. After a grandiose preamble stating that the two princes 'having in view, on the one hand, their sacred duty, and, on the other, the sorry state of the Serbian people in Turkey, and inspired by the same patriotic desire to work in sincere concord for the liberation and unification of their people', the agreement committed the signatories to instigate an uprising against Turkey which it was hoped would prepare the way for the liberation of all Serb people and their unification in a single state.[49] The detail of the agreement further contained the key points that in the event of victory Serbia and Montenegro would unite under the Serbian prince; that Nikola and his family would retain their titles and privileges; that Montenegrin officials would keep their positions and salaries while enjoying equal rights with Serbians; and that neither Montenegro or Serbia would declare war on or negotiate with Turkey without the other.[50]

For all the high-flown sentiment of the preamble, each of the princes approached the agreement with his own agenda and signed it with reservations. Mihailo was childless and was thought likely to

---

[47] Jelavich, *History of Serbia*, vol. 1, pp. 333–4.
[48] Houston, *Nikola and Milena*, London, 2003, p. 97.
[49] Petrovich, *A History of Modern Serbia*, vol. 1, pp. 323–4.
[50] *Ibid.*

remain so. Nikola had therefore hoped the agreement would contain written confirmation of his understanding that he or his son would in due course succeed to the throne of the joint state and was duly disappointed when it failed to do so. For his part Mihailo found reason to doubt Nikola's commitment to the agreement when negotiations between Montenegro and the Porte over outstanding border questions, which had been ongoing since 1862, concluded with the Porte acceding to Montenegro's demands, rounded off by the presentation to Nikola of a small yacht.[51] He was not mistaken. Only four years after the agreement was signed Nikola was expressing doubts in the senate over Serbia's reliability as a military partner. But by this time Mihailo was dead, assassinated in Belgrade's Košutnjak park in 1868 in a conspiracy which has never been fully elucidated. The network of Balkan alliances he had painstakingly put together with Montenegro, Greece and Romania died with him.

Strengthening ties with Russia and the growth of nationalist sentiment

Even with Mihailo still alive Nikola had been looking for additional support both to pay his bills and to bolster Montenegro's position in the world. In 1868 and again in 1869 he travelled to Russia, where his efforts met with considerable success. But perhaps the most gratifying and in the long run most consequential result of the visits was the close relationship Nikola forged with the imperial family itself. Graciously received by Tsar Alexander II and presented by him with the sabre of the Serbian King Milutin Nemanjić, the Montenegrin prince was able to arrange for four of his daughters to be educated at Russian expense in the famous Smolny Institute designed to offer education to women.[52] While one of the princesses died young in St Petersburg, two—Stana and Milicia—later married grand dukes and, through their position in the imperial family, exercised a baleful influence on the tsarina herself.[53]

---

[51] Petrovich, *History of Modern Serbia*, vol. 1, p. 324.
[52] Nikola and Milena had nine daughters in all, although at this stage only the four eldest were old enough to be sent to St Petersburg for schooling.
[53] Jovićević, *Montenegrin Royal Marriages*, p. 43. On the influence exercised by the Montenegrin princesses see Chapter 8.

Nikola had succeeded in placing Montenegro's relations with Russia on a satisfactory, even enviable footing, but he had no wish to damage his standing with the other Powers. He therefore took care to ensure that Montenegro observed a formal neutrality while at the same time covertly continuing to permit his subjects to involve themselves in nationalistically-inspired military engagements beyond the country's borders. Thus in 1870, while maintaining an official neutrality, Montenegrins actively assisted their kinsmen in the *Boka* who had rebelled against Austrian rule and rejoiced when they defeated the Austrians and forced them to conclude a disadvantageous peace.

Nationalist sentiments similarly inspired the founding in 1871 of the country's first newspaper, the *Crnogorac* (the Montenegrin), which was soon banned in neighbouring countries because of its vociferously anti-Ottoman and anti-Austrian tone. In 1873 it was replaced, at Nikola's instigation, by the less strident *Glas Crnogorca* (Voice of Montenegro), a change undertaken in order to keep in step with Russia which by then had joined Austria and Germany in the Three Emperors' League.[54] But while Nikola gave the appearance of acting in such as way as to mollify Montenegro's outside backers, he was in reality far from accepting the existing state of affairs and was instead seeking to change both the status and the borders of Montenegro. A better indication of his intentions is provided by the attention he devoted to the reorganisation of the army. The defeat suffered by the Montenegrins in 1862 had revealed grave weakness in their forces, in particular their reliance on outmoded weaponry—mainly long Turkish daggers or *yataghans* and obsolete Albanian-made muskets, often beautifully ornamented with silver and mother of pearl but unwieldy and inaccurate if used on the move. Changes introduced by Nikola in 1870 replaced the old tribal basis of military organisation with an army divided along more conventional lines into battalions and with two significant innovations—a cavalry corps and a mountain artillery unit equipped with a battery of cannon and appropriate ammunition. With Russia and Serbia providing financial help, the Montenegrins began to acquire more up-to-date rifles and Serbian officers assisted with

---

[54] John D. Treadway, *The Falcon and the Eagle: Montenegro and Austria-Hungary, 1908–1914*, West Lafayette: Purdue University Press, 1998, p. 13.

training. Given that every Montenegrin between the ages of fifteen and sixty was liable to be called up to fight in case of need, it is hard to produce figures for the number of men under arms. Numbers given by different sources range between 17,000 and 35,000, the lower figure being the more realistic estimate.[55] The use to which this new army might be put became still more apparent after an incident in October 1874 when up to twenty-two Montenegrins were murdered at Podgorica in reprisal for a Turk found dead in Montenegro.[56] Tensions soared and Nikola protested to the Powers, who were eventually able to defuse the situation and prevent it from escalating into full-scale conflict. However, the following year, 1875, marked the onset of a crisis which was to convulse Europe for the rest of the decade, signalling a new and critical phase in the century-long Eastern Question.

The Hercegovinian uprising

Although the grievances that sparked the uprising in Hercegovina in 1875 were of local origin, widespread misrule across the vast Ottoman Empire provided the background for rapidly spiralling revolt. Throughout the 1870s the Porte's economic ills and internal convulsions advertised only too clearly the progressive erosion of Ottoman power. A succession of sultans had displayed remarkable incompetence while spending unimaginable amounts on the upkeep of their own courts. One writer on the empire described the then reigning Sultan Abdul Aziz (1861–76) as having 5,500 courtiers and servants, 600 horses, 200 carriages and a harem of 1,000 to 1,500 women.[57] Partly as a result of such extravagance and partly through sheer fiscal incompetence and an inability to tackle

---

[55] See Stevenson, *A History of Montenegro* p. 192. *A Handbook of the Montenegrin Army* prepared by the General Staff and published in 1909 (His Majesty's Stationery Office, London, p. 7) put the total strength of the army on a war footing at 50,000 (which was probably an overestimate), but noted that such a high number of recruits would not be immediately available in the event of a war since many were at the time living in America and elsewhere as immigrant workers.

[56] *Foreign Office Handbook on Montenegro*, November 1918, p. 24. Stevenson (*ibid.*, p. 193) puts the number at twenty-two; other sources at seventeen.

[57] Philip Mansel (in *Sultans in Splendour*) quoted by A. N. Wilson, *The Victorians*, London: Hutchinson, 2002, p. 393.

the incurable imbalance in trade, the empire's financial system was in ruins and in 1875 the Ottoman government was forced to declare bankruptcy.[58] Shortly afterwards Abdul Aziz was overthrown in a military coup (he subsequently committed suicide) and replaced by Sultan Murad V.

It was against such a background of administrative incompetence and increasing economic and political turmoil that in mid-1875 simmering discontent in Hercegovina boiled over into open insurrection after Ottoman officials launched a renewed campaign to force payment of taxes at a time when the province was suffering from severe drought. Success at Grahovo in Danilo's time had re-awakened longstanding Montenegrin dreams of further territorial gains in Hercegovina, while Serbia had ambitions in neighbouring Bosnia. Nevertheless, the timing of the insurrection suited neither the Serbs nor the Montenegrins, both of whom were under strong pressure from both Russia and Austria-Hungary to keep the peace.[59] Because of its close kinship ties with Hercegovina, Montenegro was already sheltering many Hercegovinian refugees, and public opinion was clamouring for outright intervention. Moreover, the sense of impending Montenegrin involvement was heightened when a number of refugees, who were returning from Montenegro to their home district of Nevesenje in Hercegovina, were arrested by an Ottoman patrol, violating the guarantee of safe-passage home which Nikola had earlier secured from the Porte. Refusing to recognise the Ottoman right of arrest, the returning refugees chose to resist and in the ensuing fight several of them were killed. The remnants of the band fled back into Montenegro, fanning indignation and prompting the remainder of their kinsmen still sheltering in the principality to return home and join in the anti-taxation rebellion now spreading through Hercegovina and into Bosnia.[60]

The Ottoman governor of Hercegovina, Dervish Pasha, attempted to put down the revolt, but his brutal methods of repression only

[58] Mansel, *Sultans in Splendour,* pp. 393–4.
[59] Petrovich, *A History of Modern Serbia,* vol. 2, p. 381. In 1867 Austria became Austria-Hungary after Hungarian nationalists had succeeded in raising Hungary's status to that of a separate state equal to Austria but under a common Emperor, Franz Joseph.
[60] Stillman, *Herzegovina and the Late Uprising,* pp. 10–11.

The battle of Vucji Do: a key Montenegrin victory
in the 1876–7 war.

Lessons in Cetinje. Montenegrin high school
opened in 1869 with Russian support, among the
first schools for girls in the Balkans.

Above medallion of Montenegrin rulers, arranged around Vladika Saint Petar of Cetinje. *Right* Prince Danilo (1826–60), nicknamed 'the little rabbit' because of his short stature and bulging green eyes (painting by Johann Boss, 1853).

Village scene from the Brda: early 20th-century photograph by the British historian of Montenegro, Alexander Devine.

King Victor Emmanuel III and Queen Elena of Italy. Official photos of the couple were designed to minimise the difference in height between them.

King Nikola, *c.* 1910 (photograph *Peoples of All Nations*, ed. J.A. Hammerton, vol. 5, London, 1922).

Queen Milena, *c.* 1910 (photograph *ibid.*).

Royal family portrait commemorating proclamation of the kingdom of Montenegro, August 1910.

Back row from left Grand Duke Peter Nikolayevich, Prince Franz Joseph of Battenberg, Princess Vjera, Princess Ksenija, Crown Prince Danilo, Prince Mirko, Prince Petar.

Seated from left Crown Princess Milica–Yutta, Princess Ana of Battenberg, Queen Elena of Italy, Queen Milena, King Nikola I, Grand Duchess Milica Nikolayevna, King Victor Emmanuel III of Italy, Princess Natalia.

Seated front, from left Princess Jelena Karadjordjevic, Princess Marina Romanov, Crown Prince Alexsandar Karadjordjevic of Serbia.

incited further insurrection in the province, uniting Orthodox and Roman Catholics in a common anti-Ottoman cause. By this time Nikola, already issuing medals for bravery to those of his subjects who were fighting unofficially on the side of the rebels, had come out openly in favour of a war of liberation. In a similar vein the exiled contender for the Serbian throne and grandson of Karadjordje, Petar Karadjordjević, who would later enlist as a volunteer in the campaign, declared himself for war.[61] But Prince Milan of Serbia, successor to the murdered Mihailo, though coming under increasing pressure from domestic public opinion, prevaricated, and chose instead what to many seemed an inopportune moment to marry his Romanian bride.[62]

Montenegrin military commanders were already in the field, ostensibly to pacify the insurgents; it was a simple step to reverse what had never been more than a token opposition into active support for the rebels. Soon Nikola's father-in-law Petar Vukotić and the 'old Turk-fighter'[63] Peko Pavlović—men from the same Čevo district of the Katuni *nahija*—were openly fighting alongside the native Hercegovinian leader Mico Ljubobratić and his band of rebels. Meanwhile, what had started as a local insurrection rapidly assumed the dimensions of an international crisis: in December 1875 Austria-Hungary issued an ultimatum to the Ottoman Empire demanding the suppression of tax farming and a guarantee of religious liberty in Bosnia-Hercegovina, while Prussia under Bismarck went further, proposing that Austria itself should annex the two provinces. Britain under Disraeli at first retained a pro-Ottoman stance, but the isolationist position became untenable after 1876 when the revolt spread to Christians in Ottoman-ruled Bulgaria, bringing down the full force of Ottoman repression and provoking indignation across Europe. Outraged by Disraeli's refusal to spring to the defence of the oppressed Christian population, Gladstone, already sixty-six and in retirement, re-entered the political fray. His

---

[61] Petrovich, *A History of Modern Serbia*, vol. 2, p. 382. Petar, who formed his own fighting unit, fought under the *nom de guerre* Petar Mrkonjić. (See Dušan Bataković, *The Serbs of Bosnia and Herzegovina*, Paris: Dialogue, 1996, p. 57.)

[62] *Ibid.* p. 383. I am indebted to Petrovich for much of the above account.

[63] Stillman, *Herzegovina and the Late Uprising*, p. 18.

opening sally in what was to become the over-riding political issue
of the day had been an impassioned denunciation of the atrocities
committed by the *bashi-bazouks*, published in September 1875 in a
pamphlet entitled *Bulgarian Horrors and the Question of the East*. Capturing the public mood, this became an instant bestseller with
40,000 copies sold within the first four days and 200,000 by the end
of the month.[64] A Russian translation followed and soon the pamphlet enjoyed popularity in St Petersburg.[65] In Britain, political
divisions over the Eastern Question threatened to 'balkanise' national
politics;[66] in Russia, the government was coming under increasing
pressure from pan-Slavists to take action on behalf of their co-religionists. Still official Russia, constrained by its adherence, together
with Germany and Austria-Hungary, to the principles of the Three
Emperors' Alliance, hung back although a retired Russian general,
Mihail Cherniaev, renowned for his Central Asian campaign, was
already in Serbia and offering to lead the Serbs into war. Not to be
outdone, Nikola seized on the occasion of Sultan Murad's succession
to the hapless Abdul Aziz to proclaim that 'the time had come to
restore the Serbian empire, which had fallen with the first Murad
and should revive with the fifth'.[67]

With Cherniaev on the spot and Nikola already encouraging
military action, Prince Milan could no longer delay. On 16 June
1876 he agreed to the signing of a treaty of alliance with Montenegro and on 2 July the forces of both armies launched simultaneous
but separate advances into Ottoman territory.[68] At the end of June
Nikola had received a delegation of Hercegovinian rebels begging
him to accept the title of Prince of Hercegovina, a request with
which, the Great Powers willing, he was only too ready to comply.

[64] Richard Shannon, *Gladstone, Heroic Minister, 1865–1898*, London: Allen Lane,
    1999, p. 172.

[65] Goldsworthy, *Inventing Ruritania*, p. 29.

[66] *Ibid.*

[67] *Foreign Office Handbook on Montenegro*, November 1918, p. 25. In fact Murad was
    only slightly more fortunate than his predecessor: a few months after his ac-
    cession he suffered a breakdown under pressure of events and abdicated in fav-
    our of Abdul Hamid II, who by contrast displayed exceptional staying power,
    remaining in office till 1909.

[68] Petrovich, *A History of Modern Serbia*, vol. 2, p. 386.

The Montenegrin strategy entailed not only the capture of Nikšić and surrounding lands north-east of Grahovo in Hercegovina, but also Podgorica on the plain north-east of Lake Skadar.

In Hercegovina, as we have seen, fighting had in fact been taking place between Montenegrin irregulars and Ottoman forces long before any formal joint declaration of war. However, the initial advance of the Montenegrin army proper into Hercegovina was soon checked as the Montenegrins, not wanting to risk an encounter at this stage with a stronger Ottoman force and facing protests from Austria-Hungary, decided to pull back to positions near the border of their own territory. Nevertheless it was here, in the vicinity of Vučji Do, that in July 1876 the Montenegrins won one of the most crucial battles of the entire war when they defeated a far larger body of the Ottoman army under Ahmed Mukhtar Pasha, governor of Mostar and commander of the main Ottoman force in Hercegovina.[69] Other victories followed, at Fundina, Trijebač and Krstac and, most important, in the Bjelopavlići valley along the Zeta river, which opened the way to Podgorica.

Such was the interest sparked by the crisis abroad, particularly in Britain, that several foreign correspondents—pioneers in the field—were by this time already travelling in the province and filing reports. One such, W. J. Stillman of *The Times*, met leaders of the insurgents and while making no secret of his sympathy for the rebel cause, attempted to convey to them the importance of moderating their demands 'if they wished England to interest herself in a favourable settlement of the affair'.[70] As an eye-witness to a number of battles, Stillman gave his reactions to the brutality of combat:

The whole thing [an encounter in 1876 near Duži, close to the Austrian frontier] excited in me a disgust and a horror which I never before in my life experienced, though it was neither my first experience under fire nor of this kind of fighting. The most vividly conscious feeling in this melange was pity for the brave men of the hill [the Turks besieged in the fortress]... The wounded were coming in faster.... Almost every man had an amputated

[69] Numerous trophies from the battle, including an especially fine collection of Ottoman banners, remain in the Cetinje museum. The victory is also celebrated in a striking picture by the Montenegrin painter, Petar Lubarda.
[70] W. J. Stillman, *Herzegovina and the Late Uprising*, p. 47.

nose to show, and they all said there were many killed and wounded, and more of the former than the latter.[71]

Seeking to explain the Montenegrin victories over generally much larger Ottoman forces, Stillman observed: 'The generalship on both sides [is] bad, but on that of the Turks atrocious.'[72]

Meanwhile the Serbs had experienced nothing but disaster. The bleak picture was completed by the revolt's failure to generate a Balkans-wide uprising among the subject Slav peasantry. Serbia's fighting forces were divided into four separate armies. Cherniaev, still without official Russia's backing, commanded the largest of these, while the other forces were led by inexperienced local officers.[73] Burdened with obsolete equipment and poorly organised—a situation not helped by the presence of thousands of poorly disciplined and often drunken Russian volunteers—all four armies suffered major defeats. To the south the situation was particularly perilous with the Ottomans poised to march north through the now open Morava valley and thence on to Belgrade.

As disputes broke out between the Serbian leadership and Cherniaev—denounced by one exasperated Serbian officer to the Premier, Ristić, as that 'Russian madman'[74]—Prince Milan appealed to Tsar Alexander II to intervene to save Serbia from disaster. Now, as Serbia's fortunes reached their lowest ebb, official Russia, having been reluctant to intervene earlier, reacted strongly.[75] Faced with a Russian ultimatum, the Porte agreed to an armistice in November 1876 and Russia undertook responsibility for conducting negotiations on behalf of Serbia and Montenegro at a peace conference to be held in Istanbul.

But even while this conference was in progress, the Russian and Austrian Foreign Ministers, Gorchakov and Andrássy, as representatives of the Three Emperors' Alliance, were conducting their own negotiations with a view to defining their respective roles in the

[71] Stillman, *Herzegovina and the Late Uprising*, p. 108.
[72] *Ibid.*, p. 121.
[73] On Serbia's part in the war, see Petrovich, *A History of Modern Serbia*, vol. 2, pp. 386–95.
[74] *Ibid.*, p. 388.
[75] *Ibid.*, p. 389.

Balkans. In return for accepting Russian military intervention in
the crisis, Austria-Hungary acquired the right to occupy Bosnia-
Hercegovina, while Russia was forced to agree not to interfere
directly in Serbia or Montenegro, while being permitted to co-
operate militarily with them only beyond their own borders. Meanwhile the delegates at the conference in Istanbul failed to agree a
solution that satisfied the European Powers, since the Porte claimed
to have introduced measures guaranteeing the full equality of all
citizens within the Ottoman Empire and thereby removing the need
for any further intervention by the Powers.[76] Nor was the conference any more successful in satisfying the demands made by
Montenegro. Nikola had asked for an increase in territory to include
both Nikšić and the little port of Spič, north of Bar, but the sultan
refused to yield Nikšić and both Austria and Italy maintained their
opposition to a Montenegrin outlet to the sea. Other changes to
Montenegro's borders, put to the Porte by Lord Salisbury at the conference, also proved unattainable. With Serbia, however, matters proceeded differently since the Serbian government, with approval
from Russia and Austria, agreed to settle under terms that were no
more advantageous. Nikola, angry and disappointed and still formally at war with the Porte, declared a formal end to the alliance with
Serbia.[77]

Thus, disillusioned with Serbia, the Montenegrins were over-
joyed when on 24 April 1877 the Russians, finally goaded into
action by pan-Slavists at home after the failure of the Constantinople
(Istanbul) peace conference, officially declared war on the Porte. The
Russians had been anxious to avoid war partly through fear of
encouraging any form of closer Anglo-Austrian co-operation in
opposition to such a move against the Ottoman Empire, and partly
because they had reason to doubt their own military capabilities.[78]
Nor were they any more confident of the military capacities of their
potential Balkan allies. These, in turn, had their own reasons for
hanging back—exhaustion in the case of Serbia, fear of creating
conditions for a new Russian protectorate in Romania, and anti-war

[76] Jelavich, *History of the Balkans,* vol. 1, p. 356.
[77] Petrovich, *A History of Modern Serbia,* vol. 2, pp. 390–2.
[78] Jelavich, *History of the Balkans,* vol. 1, p. 356.

pressure on Greece from its British allies, combined with concerns over backing for a Greater Slav state in the region.[79]

Unconstrained by these considerations Montenegro returned to the fray, fighting as before on two fronts—in Hercegovina to the north and along the present-day Albanian border in the south. Here the Montenegrins succeeded in defeating renewed Ottoman attempts to advance into the principality through the Duga pass, leaving them free to devote the bulk of their forces to the capture of Nikšić. As a major Ottoman town commanding the route through Hercegovina to the provincial capital of Mostar, Nikšić had long been a principal goal for Montenegrin military strategy and been blockaded almost since the beginning of the uprising in Hercegovina.[80] Dragging on through the bitter winter of 1876, the siege had brought the inhabitants to the brink of starvation, and Nikola, wishing to gain favour with the Powers, offered more than once to permit its re-supply by a route traversing Montenegrin territory. But his assurances counted for little since the relieving Ottoman soldiers were attacked in a battle which left many dead and allowed the Montenegrins to capture a substantial quantity of arms and much-needed ammunition.

In September 1877 the town finally fell to Montenegrin forces. The jubilation in response to its surrender was witnessed in Cetinje by the eminent archaeologist Sir Arthur Evans, who had been acting as correspondent for the *Manchester Guardian* during the war. Already displaying literary pretensions, Nikola had sent a telegram announcing Nikšić's surrender in the form of a poem addressed to Princess Milena, which he instructed her to read to the inhabitants of Cetinje. But in the excitement generated by the news, as Evans noted, the young princess had difficulty performing her role.

The Princess now stepped forth onto the balcony and informed the crowd, amidst a breathless silence, that Nikšić was taken. She had intended to read her husband's poetic telegram, but was cut short by a tremendous 'Živio!' (Evviva!) and a simultaneous volley from the guns and pistols of her loyal subjects, and retired kissing her hand.

[79] Jelavich, *History of the Balkans*, pp. 357–8.
[80] *Foreign Office Handbook on Montenegro*, November 1918, p. 26.

Cetinje's inhabitants filled the streets as the celebrations got underway.

Ancient veterans, grim, rugged mountain giants, fall about each other's necks and kiss each other for very joy. The wounded themselves are helped forth from the hospitals, and hobble along on crutches to take part in the rejoicings; men, in the ambulances, dying of their wounds, lit up, I was told, when they heard these tidings, and seemed to gain a new respite of life. Crowds are continually bursting into national songs, and hymns, broken at intervals with a wild Živio! Živio! And ringing hurrahs which Czerno-gortzi [*sic*], as well as Englishmen, know how to utter. The big, ancient bells of the monastery, and the watch-tower on the rocks above, peal forth. The bronze cannon—a gift from the sister Principality—is dragged out, and salvoes of artillery tell every upland village that Nikšić has fallen.[81]

The outpouring of national feeling which accompanied the capture of Nikšić could be explained not simply by the access it afforded to a large and relatively fertile plain but, more important, by the thought that it presaged the realisation of their long-held hopes for the incorporation of Hercegovina. But here they were to be disappointed: Austria–Hungary, fearing the possible consequences for its own Slav population, categorically ruled out any Montenegrin attempt to advance to Trebinje and thence to the provincial capital of Mostar. Blocked in Hercegovina, the Montenegrins turned again to the southern front, focusing their attack on the seaport they had so long desired. A string of military successes allowed them to occupy Spič, Bar and Ulcinj, and their subsequent advance on the main Ottoman centre of Skadar was only checked by news of the armistice of 31 January 1878 that Russia, after defeating the Ottomans at Adrianople (Edirne), had been forced to call after heavy pressure from the European Powers.[82]

The impact of the anti-Ottoman wars

The anti-Ottoman wars of 1876–78 saw the Montenegrins' fame at its height, and nowhere more than in Britain, where in May 1877 their heroic struggle was eulogised by both Gladstone in the House of Commons and by Tennyson, the Poet Laureate, in his famous

[81] Arthur John Evans, *Illyrian Letters*, London: Longmans, Green, 1878, pp. 186–7.
[82] Petrovich, *A History of Modern Serbia*, vol. 2, p. 395.

sonnet 'Montenegro'. Gladstone's speech was later described by one
witness as a 'feat of parliamentary courage, parliamentary skill, parliamentary endurance and parliamentary eloquence [which would]
always be unequalled',[83] while another claimed: 'I have heard many
listeners of cool temperament declare the passage about the Montenegrins and onwards to have been the most thrilling deliverance that
could ever be conceived.'[84] Gladstone said:

> A portion of those unhappy people are still as yet making an effort to
> retrieve what they have lost so long, but have not yet ceased to love and to
> desire. I speak of those in Bosnia and Herzegovina. Another portion—a
> band of heroes such as the world has rarely seen—stand on the rocks of
> Montenegro, and are ready now, as they have ever been during the 400
> years of their exile from their fertile plains, to sweep down from their fast-
> nesses and meet the Turks at any odds for the re-establishment of justice
> and of peace in those countries.[85]

Tennyson's sonnet, which appeared on the front page of *The Nineteenth Century* in the same month as this speech, was composed at the
Grand Old Man's request to accompany an article he himself had
written on Montenegro.[86] It was the only poem Tennyson ever devoted exclusively to the Balkans, and in the eyes of the British public
did for the Montenegrins what 'The Charge of the Light Brigade'
had done for British soldiers fighting in the Crimean War. Moreover, Tennyson's son, Hallam, maintained that it was the poem his
father always 'put first among his sonnets', and it enjoyed enormous
popularity throughout the rest of the nineteenth century.[87]

> *They rose to where their sovran eagle sails,*
> *They kept their faith, their freedom, on the height,*
> *Chaste, frugal, savage, arm'd by day and night*
> *Against the Turk; whose inroad nowhere scales*
> *Their headlong passes, but his footstep fails,*
> *And red with blood the Crescent reels from fight*

[83] A. J. Balfour quoted by Shannon in *Gladstone, Heroic Minister,* p. 201.
[84] John Morley, *The Life of William Ewart Gladstone,* London: Macmillan, 1903,
vol. 2, pp. 566–7.
[85] *Ibid.,* p. 567.
[86] William Ewart Gladstone, 'Montenegro: A Sketch', *The Nineteenth Century,*
no. 3, May 1877, pp. 360–79.
[87] Quoted by Goldsworthy, *Inventing Ruritania,* p. 33.

Before their dauntless hundreds, in prone flight
By thousands down the crags and thro' the vales.
O smallest among peoples! rough rock-throne
Of Freedom! Warriors beating back the swarm
Of Turkish Islam for five hundred years,
Great Tsernogora! Never since thine own
Black ridges drew the cloud and brake the storm
Has breathed a race of mightier mountaineers.[88]

Needless to say it did not take long for translations to appear in the Balkans. In the same month as it was published in England the first Serbian version, a collaborative effort by W. J. Stillman and the Serbian poet Ljubomir Nenadović, came out in Novi Sad, at that time across the border in Habsburg-ruled Vojvodina but already a centre of Serbian cultural and intellectual life.[89] From then on the sonnet appeared regularly in translation and was learned by heart by generations of Serbian and Montenegrin children, helping to anchor yet more firmly in the popular mind the prevailing myths of Montenegrin life.

Gladstone's article that accompanied Tennyson's sonnet began, like his speech in the House of Commons, by describing the glories of Montenegrin history, but is perhaps most interesting when it turns to the principality's future in which he was himself to play a by no means inconsiderable part:

Montenegro, which has carried down through four centuries, in the midst of a constant surge of perils, a charmed life, we may say with confidence will not die. No Russian, no Austrian eagle will build its nest in the Black Mountain. The men of Tsernagora, who have never allowed the very shadow of a Turkish title to grow up by silent prescription, will claim their portion of an air and soil genial to man, and of free passage to and fro over the land and sea which God has given us. It is another question whether their brethren of the Serbian lands will amalgamate with them politically on an extended scale, and revive, either by a federal or an incorporating union, the substance, if not the form, of the old Serbian State. Such an arrangement would probably be good for Europe, and would go some way

---

[88] Alfred Lord Tennyson, 'Montenegro', *The Nineteenth Century*, p. 359; and in any edition of his collected works.
[89] Goldsworthy, *ibid.*, p. 34. Goldsworthy points out that the translation of the sonnet was included in a despatch from a Montenegrin battlefield.

to guarantee freedom and self-government to the other European provinces of Turkey, whether under Ottoman suzerainty or otherwise.[90]

Gladstone's moment to influence Montenegro's future would come
not with the armistice of January 1878 nor with the ensuing Treaties
of San Stefano and Berlin when he was still opposition, but in 1880
by which time, aged seventy-one, he was again Prime Minister.

The Treaty of San Stefano

At first Montenegro appeared to have little need of help: the Treaty
of San Stefano, signed on 3 March 1878, awarded the principality a
vast increase in territory, effectively tripling its size.[91] Serbia was by
no means so fortunate, receiving only a 240-square-km. swathe of
land to the south. The other major beneficiary of San Stefano was
Bulgaria, transformed by the treaty into a new state whose vast
increase in territory aroused fears of Russian strategic control of the
region through its dominance of the new Bulgarian proto-state.
Meanwhile Romania, which had entered the war on the side of
Russia, was required to give up southern Bessarabia while Greece
and, most important, Austria-Hungary made no gains. Fears of
Russia's preponderance were such that Britain sent a fleet to the
Dardanelles, while Austria-Hungary too saw the altered balance of
power as deeply threatening to its own interests. Matters could not
be left as they were if war was to be avoided between Russia on one
side and Britain and Austria-Hungary on the other, and with the
strong possibility of France and Germany being drawn in.

The Congress of Berlin

As tension mounted Russia drew back, accepting the need for the
issue to be addressed by a new congress, which would meet in Berlin

---

[90] Gladstone, 'Montenegro: A Sketch', p. 378.
[91] The territory originally awarded to Montenegro stretched as far as the junction
of the rivers Drina and Lim to the north; to the east it was nearly contiguous
with Serbia; to the south it included Ulcinj and Bar and the territory as far as the
Bojana river, and Lake Skadar, but not the town itself which was left to Turkey;
to the south-east it included the lands of the Hoti and Tuzi tribes as well as
Gusinje and Plav, the latter all predominately Albanian-inhabited districts. See
Destani (ed.), *Montenegro: Political and Ethnic Boundaries*, vol. 2, p. 369.

under the chairmanship of the German Chancellor Otto von Bismarck, who reluctantly agreed to assume the role of 'honest broker'.[92] A practitioner of *Realpolitik* and dismissive in equal measure of small nations and the collapsing Ottoman Empire, Bismarck was determined to ensure that any new treaty reflected the interests of the Great Powers, establishing a balance of power which would prevent further conflict over the Balkans.[93]

The ensuing Treaty of Berlin was a watershed in nineteenth-century history, but while the Powers that mattered had to be won over and their interests propitiated, the smaller countries of southeast Europe were treated as so many passive witnesses to their fate. Some argue that these small aggrieved nations attempted to ape Great Power methods by going on the offensive whenever they felt strong enough to enlarge their own national territories at their neighbours' expense. But the reality was that, for a time at least, major wars were avoided.[94] Nonetheless, despite periods of considerable instability notably in 1903 and 1908, it was not until the small states found themselves able to act together in the First Balkan War of 1912 (having learned that they could do nothing on their own) that they became major actors themselves.

This is not to minimise the widespread dissatisfaction at the Great Powers' outright imposition of national borders, fostering revanchism with effects in the region that are felt to this day. But in 1878 the concern of the Congress of Berlin was to guarantee peace for the immediate future by rectifying the destabilising position created by the Treaty of San Stefano. Thus Russia received southern Bessarabia at the expense of Romania to make up for its loss of 'Big Bulgaria' awarded under that treaty, while Austria-Hungary was granted the right to occupy and administer Bosnia and Hercegovina to balance Russia's territorial gains. Romania, Serbia and Montenegro were recognised as independent states and awarded, to varying degrees, increases of territory.[95] Yet all three were left unsatisfied: Romania

---

[92] Jelavich, *History of the Balkans*, vol. 1, pp. 359–60.
[93] On the Congress of Berlin and its consequences see W. N. Medlicott, *The Congress of Berlin and After*, London: Methuen, 1938 and Misha Glenny, *The Balkans, 1804–1999: Nationalism, War and the Great Powers*, London: Granta, 1999, pp. 136–50.
[94] A notable exception was the Graeco-Turkish war of 1898.
[95] Greece too, formally independent since 1830, was left unsatisfied since its claim to more land was left dependent upon the outcome of Graeco-Turkish negoti-

received only the northern and not the southern part of Dobrudja, which instead went to Bulgaria; Serbia, despite gaining the southern towns of Niš and Pirot, found its designs on Bosnia dashed; and although Montenegro saw the territory under its control doubled from its pre-San Stefano size, it nevertheless resented the Berlin Treaty's cut-back on the huge territorial gains awarded under the Treaty of San Stefano. Nor were the non-Slav peoples any happier. Greece, independent since 1830, was awarded territorial gains on paper, but since these were dependent on what proved to be long-drawn-out Graeco-Turkish negotiations, it saw no immediate benefit (some territorial gains eventuated three years later). The Albanians got nothing.

Just as Serbia had sought to acquire Bosnia, Montenegro had hoped to take over the whole of Hercegovina, territory it had long seen as its natural hinterland. But although the Treaty of Berlin maintained the fiction of Ottoman sovereignty over Bosnia and Hercegovina, it was clear to both Serbia and Montenegro that Austria-Hungary, having once secured the right to administer the two provinces, was never going to permit their return to Ottoman control.[96] Nor would the Dual Monarchy willingly countenance any further expansion by the new Slav states into the territories it controlled, which included, in addition to Bosnia and most of Hercegovina, the strip of land separating Montenegro from Serbia, known as the Sandžak of Novi Pazar.

For all the dissatisfaction engendered by the Congress of Berlin, Montenegro appeared to have emerged from it in a far better position than Serbia. To the north, in what had been Hercegovina, it kept Nikšić, a town which would soon lose both its Muslim population and distinctive Turkish houses and markets as incoming Montenegrins and its local Orthodox Hercegovinians set about eliminating all traces of the 'oriental'.[97] Arthur Evans was once again

---

ations which eventually, three years later, resulted in some territorial gains. (See Glenny, *The Balkans*, p. 149.)

[96] *Ibid.*, p. 147.

[97] In fact the Treaty of Berlin was strikingly modern in some of its provisions since it stipulated equality under the law irrespective of religious affiliation. This was evidently not enough to reassure the Muslim inhabitants of Nikšić, most of whom decamped at the earliest opportunity rather than test the liberal pro-

an eyewitness and his account, though generally favourable to the Montenegrin side, was not without sympathy for the departing Muslims.

> It has been a striking sight to watch the long cavalcades of Turkish fugitives, sometimes as many as sixty at a time, streaming out of town. Now and then one of the little ones would look disconsolate enough, but the women were muffled in long white sheets, so that you could hardly see so much as a nose, and the men were too proud to betray any symptom of regret, and were even dressed out in their brightest holiday costume. How dull look the Montenegrins who escort them beside these brilliant Orientals! How strange and characteristic is this transformation of which I am at this moment a witness![98]

With Nikšić came access to its well-watered and fertile plain, a considerable boon for the Montenegrins. Moreover the town's capture was followed by the opening of a telegraph station, a step which led to a significant improvement in communications within the country. Nikšić was not the only gain Montenegro was to acquire in what had formerly been Hercegovina: further to the north and west they were also granted the Banjani, Drobnjaci and Piva districts and, to the south of Nikšić, the strategically vital Duga pass.

But with Austria-Hungary now firmly entrenched in the north, the main thrust of Montenegro's expansion was henceforth to be almost exclusively southwards into areas that contained ever greater concentrations of Albanians. Land-hungry as they were and convinced moreover of their historic right to these lands, the Montenegrins were not inclined to let questions of ethnic or religious allegiance stand in their way. But the progressive incorporation of so many reluctant citizens was subsequently to prove deeply problematic.[99] Among the most important of such centres acquired in 1878 was the former Ottoman fortress of Podgorica, then still largely a Muslim town which, once transferred into Montenegrin hands, became the biggest concentration of population in the

---

visions of the treaty. (See Article 27 of the Treaty of Berlin, quoted in Medlicott, *The Congess of Berlin*, Appendix 2, p. 414.)

[98] Arthur Evans, *Through Bosnia and Herzegovina on Foot during the Insurrection, August and September 1875*, New York: Arno Press and New York Times, 1971, pp. 195–6.

[99] Banac, *The National Question*, p. 275.

country. Other centres similarly assigned to Montenegro under the Treaty of Berlin were considerably less populous, but still had particular resonance: Spuž, formerly an important centre of oppressive Ottoman control and Žabljak, the old medieval capital. Turning to the east, the treaty confirmed the principality's possession of the districts of Gusinje and Plav, where the populations included large concentrations of recusant Slav Muslims and unconsenting Albanians. Finally, the treaty granted Montenegro what might have been expected to be its most treasured gain—an outlet to the Adriatic at Bar, but Bar was to prove a disappointment since it was only gained at the cost of handing over the nearby promontory of Spič to the Austrians and returning Ulcinj—captured by the Montenegrins in January 1878—to the Ottomans. Montenegro's strip of coastline was thus extremely small. Moreover its effective control of the port of Bar was severely restricted by Article 29 of the treaty which stated that Montenegrin waters should remain closed to warships of all nations, and further stipulated that all Montenegrin ships using the port should fly the Austrian flag.[100] These provisions were, of course, directed principally against Russia but they were seen as humiliating and were resented all the more because the Austrians' capacity to control the entrance to the bay of Bar from the promontory of Spič ensured Montenegrin compliance. All in all, the Congress of Berlin left Prince Nikola and the Montenegrins deeply disappointed and for a simple reason: although the Ottoman Empire had been forced into retreat, Montenegro now found itself effectively ringfenced by Austria-Hungary.[101]

Worse however was to follow since the provisions pertaining to Plav and Gusinje proved unenforceable. Their Albanian inhabitants had no wish to exchange their largely unfettered existence for Prince Nikola's rule and were prepared to fight to resist it. Envoys sent by the sultan to persuade them to comply met a hostile response, culminating in the death of one of the Porte's most valued diplomats, Mehmed Ali Pasha, who was killed as he tried to flee from a burning house in Djakovica together with his unfortunate host.[102] In 1879

---

[100] See Medlicott, *The Congress of Berlin*, Appendix 2, p. 414.

[101] See *Foreign Office Handbook on Montenegro*, November 1918, p. 27. Mehmed Ali Pasha, originally from Brandenburg, had been a member of the Ottoman delegation at the Congress of Berlin.

[102] *Ibid.*, p. 28.

fighting broke out between Montenegrins and Albanians whose nationalism had been fanned by the activities of the Prizren League. This broadly representative body, reflecting for the first time Albanian nationalist aspirations, was formed in response to the Treaty of San Stefano's proposed, but never fully implemented, transfer of Albanian-inhabited regions to Slav control. At first members of the Prizren League sought purely to protect Albanian interests from Slav expansionist policies, and therefore accepted Ottoman sovereignty as an additional bulwark. Later however it became a potent force in the drive to replace Ottoman rule with full Albanian sovereignty.

Fearing a reopening of the Eastern Question over a matter of as slight concern as Montenegro's southern frontier, the Great Powers swung back into action. As always, outsiders acted in accordance with their own interests, and thus Italy, united since 1860 and now emerging as a Power in its own right, sought to check the increasing predominance of Austria-Hungary in the western Balkans. Accordingly Count Corti, the Italian Ambassador to the Sublime Porte, suggested a compromise whereby Montenegro should renounce its claim to the towns of Gusinje and Plav in exchange for only a part of the Gusinje district and additional territory between Podgorica and Lake Skadar. The proposal was accepted by Montenegro in April 1880 but once again ran into strong resistance from the local Albanians.[103] Few doubted that the Porte had a hand in strengthening their opposition, although officially it endeavoured to appear cooperative while maintaining the right to protect the interests of its co-religionists.[104] A second conference held in Berlin suggested giving Montenegro Ulcinj and an accompanying strip of coastline as far south as the Bojana river in place of Count Corti's rejected proposals. This too was rejected by the Porte on the grounds that it would prove unacceptable to the predominantly Albanian population.

---

[103] *Foreign Office Handbook on Montenegro*, November 1918, p. 28.

[104] A despatch of 2 October 1880 from the Foreign Secretary, Earl Granville, to the British ambassador to the Sublime Porte observes: 'It has been apparent throughout all these transactions that the Turkish authorities, while professing to be unable to overcome the resistance of the Albanians, have been stimulating it, and making use of the loyalty of the Albanians to the Sultan as a means of delaying the settlement, not only of this frontier question, but of the other questions pending with the Porte which the Sultan and his advisers are doing their utmost to evade.' (Destani [ed.], *Montenegro: Political and Ethnic Boundaries*, vol. 2, p. 374.)

Two years after the Berlin Congress attempts to delineate Montenegro's southern border had reached an embarrassing impasse. It was at this point that Britain, where Gladstone had returned to power in April 1880, intervened to end the stalemate. Determined to resolve the issue in the Montenegrins' favour, Gladstone persuaded the other Treaty Powers to assemble a fleet, which in September sailed into the Adriatic port of Dubrovnik. The fleet's presence was intended as a naval demonstration since the Powers were reluctant to order the bombardment of Ulcinj and cautioned the Montenegrins against attacking by land. On the side of the Ottomans the commander-in-chief of their forces based at Skadar, Riza Pasha, alternated continuing prevarication with more menacing utterances stating that 'force will be repulsed by force'.[105] Ignoring Riza Pasha's threats, Gladstone's response was neatly targeted to strike at the empire's vital commercial interests: failure to hand-over Ulcinj to the Montenegrins would result in the British seizure of the important Ottoman custom-house at Smyrna (modern Izmir) on the Anatolian coast. After months of prevarication this threat finally proved effective: on 25 November the local Ottoman commandant Dervish Pasha marched against the town at the head of a contingent of troops who opened fire on the Albanians, crushing any further resistance. Twenty-four hours later Prince Nikola's cousin, Božo Petrović, accompanied by 4–5,000 Montenegrins, entered the town where they were, according to one Foreign Office report, 'received ...by the Mahommedan inhabitants in a by no means unfriendly manner'.[106]

Britain's—and indeed Gladstone's—role in securing Ulcinj for Montenegro was recognised fulsomely. Even before the Montenegrins had entered the town Mr Kirby Green, the British consul general at Scutari, was called in by Prince Nikola to receive his expression of gratitude, an experience he later recalled in his report to Earl Granville:

Later in the evening [of 29 November] the Prince asked me, in the presence of his Ministers, to declare to Her Majesty's Government, in his name and that of his country, that England had acquired the right to require of Montenegro, at any and at all times, to be guided by her advice. His

---

[105] Destani (ed.), *Montenegro: Political and Ethnic Boundaries*, vol. 2, p. 374.
[106] Despatch no. 420, Captain Sale to Earl Granville, 30 Nov. 1880. (*Ibid.*, p. 662.)

Highness said he did not wish to diminish the value of the ties which exist between Montenegro and Russia, nor of the obligation of the Principality towards the Austrian Empire; but, nevertheless, he solemnly declared that neither of these would ever be found to outweigh the counsels of Her Majesty's Government.

Expressing his own opinion, Mr Kirby Green added:

The satisfaction shown to me by the Prince and Princess, and all other Montenegrins, at the settlement of their frontier has been so genuine, and their determination to attribute it nearly entirely to the disinterested action of the English has been so evident, that I have no hesitation in expressing the belief that, on all important occasions when the foreign relations of the Principality are concerned, the wishes of the British Government will undoubtedly meet with the attention which has now been spontaneously promised.[107]

These were heady days for Montenegro. With the long struggle for sufficient land, a seaport and full international recognition of its independence apparently over, Nikola could be excused his encomium, whether or not he had any intention of honouring its sentiments. However, Mr Kirby Green, seemingly swept away by his sense of involvement, might be seen to have seriously misjudged British enthusiasm for involvement in Montenegrin affairs, although this remained undimmed for as long as Gladstone was alive. As the author of the Foreign Office's own *Handbook on Montenegro* observed in 1918: 'Gladstone's successors cared nothing about the "smallest among peoples", and relations soon cooled as British diplomacy lost interest in the Black Mountain.'[108]

Little by little Russia too reduced its political support for Montenegro, although close ties were maintained at the dynastic level as Nikola's daughters made advantageous matches with Russian grand dukes. From now until the closing years of Nikola's reign, relations with Montenegro's neighbours—Austria-Hungary and Serbia— would come into sharper focus as, with the Balkans now more or less at peace, the more distant Powers finally felt free to turn their attention elsewhere.

[107] Despatch no. 425, Kirby Green to Earl Granville, 30 Nov. 1880. (*Ibid*, p. 668.)
[108] *Foreign Office Handbook*, November 1918, p. 30.

8. Montenegro on the International Stage

The Merry Widow, Franz Lehar's famous comic opera, opened in Vienna on 30 December 1905, just eleven days after Nikola had granted Montenegro its first constitution. The operetta's action takes place in the Paris legation of Pontevedro, a mythical little Balkan country, where a celebration to mark the reigning prince's sixty-fourth birthday is about to take place. As at least some of the audience would have known, Nikola Petrović, born in 1841, had turned sixty-four only two months earlier. For others any lingering doubts concerning the identity of the little Balkan country would have been quickly dispelled by the amusing discovery that the principality is not only seriously strapped for cash, but is represented at its legation in Paris by a cast of characters which includes the Pontevedrian envoy Baron Mirko Zeta, Count Danilo Danilowitch, sometime secretary to the legation, and, best of all, the legation's clerk Njegus.

The personal mission of the envoy Baron Zeta is to ensure that Pontevedro retains the fortune of one of its few wealthy citizens, who just happens to have been at one time the object of Count Danilo's affections—the eponymous Merry Widow.[1] How this is achieved is easily imagined. On the operetta's opening night, however, the evident enjoyment of the Viennese audience was doubtless heightened by the unexpected jokes at their small but troublesome neighbour's expense.[2] Official Montenegro was predictably less amused, and Montenegrin students in Vienna held demonstrations to protest at the slight upon the national dignity.[3] But if Nikola and

---

[1] See Andrew Lamb, 'Lehar's Immortal Merry Widow: Libretto' (London: EMI Classics, 1994), pp. 7–12.

[2] Karl-Dietrich Gräwe, 'Pontevedro in Paris', Hamburg: Deutsche Grammophon, 1994, pp. 18–20.

[3] See Goldsworthy, *Inventing Ruritania*, pp. 47 and 219.

the court were inclined to take heart at such signs of support from the country's more privileged youth, they were soon proved wrong. Viewed with hindsight, the opera's timing, subject matter and, most of all, the students' response to it had their fair share of irony. In the English version of the operetta, staged in London in 1907, Njegus sings 'I was born by cruel fate in a little Balkan state.'[4] Within just over a decade, the 'cruel fate' lamented by the Pontevedrian clerk would prove to be an epitaph for the Petrović dynasty, and in the forefront of those who welcomed its downfall were the Montenegrin students themselves.

The 1905 constitution—Montenegro's first—was in itself an attempt to dampen growing dissatisfaction over the autocratic nature of Prince Nikola's rule. But the experiment, which Nikola never really meant to succeed, was soon exposed as a sham as many of those who disagreed with the prince were dismissed from office. After accusations of a bomb plot, they were put on trial, found guilty and punished. From 1907 the dynasty was being compared unfavourably with a by now more liberal Serbia under Nikola's son-in-law Petar Karadjordjević. Increasingly Nikola was forced to counter his loss of popularity with harsh actions against his political opponents and, from 1910–11 onwards, with attempts at territorial aggrandisement. Apparently bolstered by enormous territorial gains during the two Balkan Wars, the regime suffered considerable damage when Skadar (or Scutari as it was consistently known to the Powers at this time), won with much loss of life, was wrested from them and incorporated in the new state of Albania created under the settlement imposed following the Conference of Ambassadors in 1913. Worse was to come as suspicions over Nikola's dealings with Austria, and the military incompetence of his sons, further undermined the standing of the Petrović dynasty and the country generally, in particular vis-à-vis Serbia.

1880–1900: fin-de-siècle Montenegro

Perhaps none of this was foreseeable in 1880, when Nikola could look with satisfaction at his achievements where international recognition and access to the sea were concerned. In marked contrast

---

[4] The additional libretto was written by Basil Hood and Adrian Ross.

with the turbulent pre-recognition period and what was to follow, the last two decades of the nineteenth century were a time of relatively peaceful internal development, while on the external front Nikola's policies—in particular the remarkably successful marriages of his daughters—appeared set to boost Montenegro's standing among European states, despite its diminutive size.

The peace spurred attempts to open the country up to the world. With Austrian help new roads and bridges were built, including the important network linking Nikšić, Podgorica and Cetinje with Kotor on the coast. In 1879, when the project was still less than half complete, two English travellers making the journey up from the coast came across labourers blasting rocks, 'a ...picturesque gang of navvies ... clad in their shaggy sheep-skin jackets and white woollen pantaloons', and noted approvingly how 'Prince Nikita—surnamed by his people "the road-maker"—was pushing the work vigorously forward.'[5] Despite the enthusiasm, a combination of interruptions, the sheer scale of the task and fear of facilitating access to putative foreign aggressors delayed completion of this crucial link in the road network till the turn of the century.[6] Though similarly delayed, the first Italian-built rail line from Bar to Virpazar on Lake Skadar was completed in 1908. Italian interest in Montenegro, stimulated by an ambition to resume Venice's place in the Adriatic at the expense of Austria, was boosted by the marriage of Nikola's daughter, Jelena, to Crown Prince Victor Emmanuel of Italy in 1896. Italian companies established shipping routes and handled an increasing trade in food, oil and tobacco. Italy's proximity also led to the installation of international telegraph lines from 1880 and, in 1904, the radio-telegraph—the first in the Balkans—which connected Bar in Montenegro with Bari in Italy.[7]

Outside interest in the Montenegrin economy went hand in hand with progress in foreign relations. International recognition in 1878 had been followed by the establishment of several diplomatic missions in Cetinje, first Russia and France and then, in 1879, Britain, Austria-Hungary, Italy and the Ottoman Empire. Subse-

---

[5] Anonymous, 'Montenegro as we saw it', *Scribner's Monthly,* December 1880, p. 28.
[6] Treadway, *The Falcon and the Eagle*, pp. 10–11.
[7] *Ibid.*, p. 15.

quently Greece, Serbia, Bulgaria, Germany and the United States also established diplomatic relations though not all of them sent envoys to Cetinje. What the staff of these various missions made of life in Cetinje, which, apart from the few official buildings, still had no more than a hundred single-storey stone houses, is easily imagined. A few days in Cetinje in 1879 were enough to convince the anonymous correspondent of Scribner's Monthly that 'life in the Montenegrin capital was not... a continual delirium of excitement', an impression borne out by his exchange with the doleful secretary to the Austrian Legation who confided that he found Cetinje like 'being shut up in a sarcophagus'.[8]

Royal marriages

When it came to winning friends Montenegro's greatest asset turned out—rather surprisingly in such a male-dominated society—to be Nikola's nine statuesque and attractive daughters, five of whom made highly favourable marriages connecting the Petrovići with some of the greatest royal houses of Europe. Conscious of Cetinje's inability to provide fitting education for his daughters, the prince was more than happy to accept an offer from Tsar Alexander II to enrol the eldest ones in the prestigious Smolny Institute in St Petersburg. At first only the two eldest, Zorka and Milica, were sent but they were soon joined by their younger sisters Anastazija (Stane), Marija, Jelena and Ana. Although the girls were afforded the same treatment as might be shown to Russian royal children, it was not enough to prevent Marija from contracting tuberculosis from which she died in St Petersburg at the age of sixteen. Of the three remaining daughters one, Sofija, died in infancy while the two youngest, Ksenija (Xenia) and Vjera, were kept in Cetinje, possibly as a result of an incident in St Petersburg involving their elder sister Jelena.[9] Ksenija, an intelligent girl with a forceful personality, later became her father's confidante and adviser, a role to which—as subsequently

[8] Anon., 'Montenegro as we saw it', p. 289.
[9] Jelena was unwittingly the cause of a duel in which a young man, Carl Gustaf von Mannerheim, the future field-marshal and President of Finland, was seriously wounded. The incident, which received wide coverage in the European press, led to Jelena's departure from St Petersburg before she had completed her education.

became apparent—she was not well suited and which cannot be said to have benefited her father's cause.[10]

So many daughters—he also had three sons—presented Nikola with the problem of securing their marriages, for failure to do so would place a heavy burden on an already poverty-stricken state. After an education befitting Russian princesses, they were unlikely to find suitable husbands in Montenegro, and in desperation the prince planned to build a convent on the little island of Vranjina in Lake Skadar where his daughters would live out their lives as nuns.[11] However, the princesses were saved from this fate when Zorka, following a visit to Vichy in 1882 with her mother and sisters, received a proposal from Petar Karadjordjević, exiled pretender to the Serbian throne and grandson of the famed Karadjordje. For Nikola the decision whether to accept the offer was a difficult one, since for all its evident attractions the proposal introduced a number of dynastic complications. It was true that this suitor appeared to have few prospects of regaining the throne of Serbia where his rival Prince Milan Obrenović had just proclaimed himself king. Still, the fact that Petar's reputation as a brave fighter in Hercegovina during the war had earned him a certain following in Serbia would undoubtedly prejudice Milan against the match and undermine any remaining hope of a Petrović succession to the Serbian throne. On the other hand it would clearly be impolitic for Nikola to turn down a grandson of Karadjordje and in so doing lose a prospective husband for at least one of his daughters.[12] He decided to press ahead, attempting to placate Milan by asking him to act as witness (*kum*) to the marriage. Far from mollifying Milan the offer further enraged him,[13] and Nikola turned to Tsar Alexander III who agreed to assume the role in his stead.

After the wedding Petar and Zorka took up residence in Cetinje where they soon attracted a number of Karadjordjević supporters

[10] See below.

[11] Jovićević, *Montenegrin Royal Marriages*, pp. 95–6.

[12] *Ibid.*, p. 98.

[13] On hearing the news he was said to have exclaimed: 'Could not that naked beggar from that hungry gorge spare me? Instead he dared to catch me in his perfidious, base trap, and asked me to be godfather to the murderers of Prince Mihailo.' Vojvoda Gavro Vuković, *Memoari*, quoted by Houston in *Nikola and Milena*, p. 184.

and family members, so forming a sort of Serbian opposition in exile. Milan's apprehensions about the marriage proved well-founded as the Karadjordjevići, with Zorka fully involved, began plotting to march on Belgrade with 5,000 men, hoping in this way to put pressure on the Serbs to overthrow Milan and proclaim Petar king in his place.[14] Nikola, cautioned by Vienna, intervened at the last moment to bring a halt to the uprising—an act that incurred Petar's lasting hostility and led after Zorka's death to the family eventually departing from Cetinje.[15]

In 1889, six years after Zorka's marriage to Petar, Milica, Nikola and Milena's second daughter, received a proposal in the course of a visit by her father to Russia. Milica's husband-to-be was the Grand Duke Pyotr Nikolayevich, a first cousin of Tsar Alexander III and grandson of Nicholas I. In St Petersburg news of the engagement was welcomed in pro-Slav circles around the tsar as much as it was in Cetinje. Presiding over an official dinner to mark the occasion, Alexander proposed a toast to the health of Nikola, 'the only sincere and faithful friend of Russia'.[16] The marriage took place a few months later—a grand event in the Peterhof attended by representatives of many of the royal houses of Europe. On the day before the wedding the engagement of yet another daughter was announced. Stane, a year younger than Milica, was to marry Prince Georgi Maximianovich, Duke of Leichtenberg; two children were born of the marriage, but it ended in divorce in 1906. A year later, at the age of forty, Stane married Grand Duke Nikolai Nikolayevich, brother of Pytor Nikolayevich.

Known in Russia as the black princesses, the two sisters were to exercise a baleful influence on the Russian royal family through the closeness of their relationship with the unhappy Tsarina Alix. As a foreigner she had received a somewhat cold reception at the hands of Russian noblewomen and was looking for solace as she struggled to

---

[14] *Ibid.*, pp. 186–7.

[15] The Karadjordjevići's position in Montenegro became still more difficult after the abdication of King Milan in 1889 in favour of his son, the thirteen-year-old Aleksandar Obrenović. Milan's abdication led to an improvement in Serbian-Montenegrin relations which Nikola supported, a stance that led him to try to rein back on Karadjordjević plotting from Montenegro.

[16] *Ibid.*, p. 285.

overcome her fears for the health of the haemophiliac tsarevich, her only son. Her superstitious nature soon found a sympathetic counterpart in Milica and Stane. Of the two sisters Milica possessed the stronger character, and is widely thought to have introduced the tsarina to Grigory Rasputin, who came to exercise such a disastrous influence over the Russian royal family.[17] But the sisters' good relationship with Rasputin did not last, nor did they remain so close to the tsarina. Milica grew jealous of the relationship between the tsarina and her 'holy man', but her attempts to come between them backfired when the sisters found themselves the ones excluded from the royal circle.[18] For as long as the sisters retained their influence they were able to ensure a favourable hearing for Nikola in St Petersburg; their subsequent loss of influence was felt in Montenegro when, under pressure from the tsarina and Rasputin, the tsar refused Nikola's request to go to war with Austria-Hungary following its annexation of Bosnia-Hercegovina in 1908.[19]

If Nikola had been fortunate to marry his three eldest daughters so successfully, the marriage of his fifth daughter was without doubt the most dazzling of his matrimonial coups. The Italian House of Savoy had been attempting for some time to find a bride for Crown Prince Victor Emmanuel, a far from easy task since the prince was at once physically unprepossessing—he was so small that Kaiser Wilhelm II nicknamed him 'the dwarf'—and notoriously difficult to please.[20] However, his mother Queen Margherita, undeterred, had singled out the tall and athletic Jelena, a match she described as 'for the good of the dynasty'.[21] There was also in Italian eyes the attraction of expanded influence in the Adriatic through the Montenegrin connection.

For the marriage to take place there was one important obstacle to be overcome—Jelena's conversion from Orthodoxy to Catholicism,

---

[17] Edward Radzinsky, *Rasputin: The Last Word*, London: Weidenfeld & Nicolson, 2000, pp. 69–70.

[18] *Ibid.*, pp. 85–6.

[19] *Ibid.*, pp. 133–4.

[20] R.J.B. Bosworth, *Italy, the Least of the Great Powers: Italian foreign policy before the First World War*, Cambridge University Press, 1979, p. 260. As Bosworth points out, the Kaiser was scarcely more flattering about Jelena, whom he described as 'the daughter of a Black Mountain cattle thief'.

[21] *Ibid.*, p. 13.

a step that the traditionally pro-Russian Montenegrins found difficult to accept. Eventually an ingenious solution was found by arranging for Jelena's conversion to take place on board a ship while she and some of her family were making the crossing from Bar to Bari. This avoided the obvious embarrassment of a Montenegrin princess renouncing Orthodoxy on Montenegrin soil, and further eased the Italian monarchy's position by allowing the future queen to step ashore in Italy as a Catholic.[22] Queen Elena, as she was known in Italy, fulfilled her role admirably. Loved for her beauty, sweet nature and good works and for being a devoted mother to her five children, she is still regarded as Italy's most popular queen.

Of Nikola's three remaining daughters only one was to marry: the sixth, Princess Ana. In 1897, a year after her sister Jelena, Ana was married to Franz Joseph of Battenberg. The marriage, though politically of less consequence than those of her elder sisters, brought with it interesting dynastic connections. Franz Joseph's eldest brother Alexander was for a time Prince of Bulgaria, while two other brothers, Princes Henry[23] and Louis, were married respectively to Queen Victoria's daughter Beatrice and to her granddaughter Victoria of Hesse. The connection gave Nikola a basis for arranging two meetings with Queen Victoria, the second in the course of a state visit in 1898, when he stayed at Windsor Castle.[24] Nikola seems from the Queen's diary to have made a favourable impression, appealing no doubt to her proclivity for the exotic: 'He was wearing his beautiful, picturesque national dress ...I found the Prince most kind and pleasant and pleased with everything.'[25]

Nikola had developed a taste for foreign visits from which he hoped to derive some political and financial benefit either for his family or for the country.[26] He nonetheless experienced some

---

[22] Houston, *Nikola and Milena*, p. 206.

[23] This much-loved son-in-law of Queen Victoria died a year before Ana's marriage to Franz Joseph during a campaign against King Prempeh of Ashanti. See Houston, *ibid.*, p. 226. Prince Louis became an admiral in the British navy, and his son, also Louis, was Lord Mountbatten of Burma.

[24] R. J. Kennedy, *Cettinje to Windsor: being an account of the visit of the Prince of Montenegro to Her Majesty the Queen*: May 1898.

[25] Quoted by Houston, *ibid.*, p. 178.

[26] *Ibid.* p. 170.

qualms when in 1883, in response to an invitation from Sultan Abdul Hamid II, he embarked on a first visit to Istanbul, seat of Montenegro's age-old enemy the Sublime Porte. Although Nikola found the Ottoman capital squalid, he was gratified by the fulsome reception accorded to him by Abdul Hamid and noted with satisfaction the sultan's tacit recognition of Montenegro's territorial gains made at Ottoman expense. A second visit in 1899, with a larger party that included Princess Milena and Prince Mirko, met with an equally flattering reception, no doubt partly because Abdul Hamid, by this time reviled by the Powers as responsible for the Armenian massacres of 1895–6, was predisposed to welcome any friends from abroad. Nikola too was determined to preserve the friendship even to the extent of pressing a reluctant Milena to agree to an offered visit to the sultan's harem, which in spite of herself she enjoyed.[27]

This same year Crown Prince Danilo became engaged to Augusta Charlotte, princess of the German duchy of Mecklenburg-Strelitz, who on her conversion to Orthodox Christianity took the name Milica Yutta. The dynasty's anxiety for the crown prince to produce an heir was evident in the marriage being celebrated almost immediately after the young princess's arrival in Montenegro and her conversion. Although the new princess was made welcome by the Montenegrins and by her parents-in-law in particular, Danilo, who had shown no enthusiasm for marriage, was clearly not greatly enamoured of his new wife. Their union produced no children. Despite his handsome appearance, the crown prince was in many ways a disappointment and—unforgivable in his countrymen's eyes— preferred German culture to Russian ways and showed little natural sympathy for the ordinary Montenegrin. Haughty and distant in his manner, he nonetheless saw the need for constitutional reform and was instrumental in pushing his father to accept the country's first constitution in 1905.[28] His subsequent failure to impress as a military leader in the Balkan Wars, together with his reluctance to embrace the Petrović-Njegoš cause after 1916, suggest that if he had ever succeeded his father he would have been unlikely to secure the continuation of a Montenegrin monarchy.

[27] *Ibid.*, p. 175.
[28] *Ibid.*, pp. 236–8.

Nikola's second son Mirko was ultimately to prove just as great a disappointment and, what was worse, he complicated Montenegro's crucial relations with Serbia. Unlike Danilo, Mirko was far from lacking ambition; he was intent on securing a Balkan throne for himself and was at different times mentioned as a candidate for the thrones of Bulgaria and Serbia as well as for the position of governor in Ottoman-ruled Macedonia and Albania.[29] But his character, at once wayward and self-indulgent, hardly marked him out for such a role, and he was unsuccessful in every one of these endeavours.[30] Nor were his prospects advanced by his decision to marry Natalija Konstantinović, daughter of a member of an exiled branch of the Obrenović family. The marriage led to difficulties with King Aleksandar Obrenović, who suspected Mirko, probably correctly, of harbouring designs on the Serbian throne.[31] The marriage was almost equally displeasing to Mirko's brother-in-law Petar Karadjordjević who, since he himself nurtured hopes of ousting King Aleksandar, resented any formal link between the Petrovići and the Obrenovići even where they were, as he was, exiled opponents of the Serbian king.

Relations with Serbia

Relations between the Petrovići and the Obrenovići had in fact suffered complications earlier when attempts to negotiate a Balkan alliance to expel the Turks from the whole Balkan peninsula broke down. Nikola and Aleksandar disagreed over the projected division of future liberated territories, in particular over who should acquire the historically and religiously significant town of Prizren.[32] The set-

[29] *Ibid.*, p. 241.

[30] Joyce Cary's description of the three princes is illustrative: 'Danilo a stolid-looking fellow, Mirko with a flash air and Peter .... the most popular'. (*Memoir of the Bobotes*, London:Readers' Union Michael Joseph, 1965 [prev. publ. University of Texas Press, 1960], p. 108.)

[31] See Slobodan Markovitch, *British Perceptions of Serbia and the Balkans, 1908–1906*, Paris, 2000, p. 94.

[32] Nikola had composed a poem dreaming of the day he would lead his people to recapture Prizren which, set to music, became immensely popular at this time. 'There, over there, beyond those hills,/ Ruined lies, they say/ My Emperor's Palace; there they say,/ Once heroes had gathered/ There, over there ... I see

back to relations came as something of a shock after the success of Nikola's first-ever visit to Belgrade on St Vitus's Day in 1896, which had been marked by scenes of pan-Serbian celebration.[33] The return visit of King Aleksandar to Cetinje in April 1897, when he angrily rejected the Montenegrin territorial proposals, marked the beginning of a deterioration in relations which gained pace after Aleksandar's father, ex-king Milan, returned to Serbia towards the end of that year. The Montenegrins, taking their lead from the Russians, viewed Milan as dangerously close to Austria-Hungary, while Milan for his part was convinced, not without reason, that Cetinje was the centre of an anti-Obrenović campaign aimed at securing a Karadjordjević restoration. The fact that Montenegro granted asylum to the Serbian Radical leader Ranko Tajsić after his attempt to assassinate Milan in 1899 could only lend credence to these accusations.[34] In such a climate of poisoned relations earlier speculation over a possible marriage between King Aleksandar Obrenović and Nikola's second-youngest daughter Ksenija was destined to come to nothing.[35] It was a fate that Ksenija was fortunate to escape since Aleksandar and his wife, the widely detested Draga Mašin, were murdered in Belgrade by officers of the palace guard in June 1903. Within four days Petar Karadjordjević was proclaimed king in the palace where his predecessor had died.

The demise of the Obrenović dynasty did not however end Nikola's trouble with Belgrade. Although ordinary people had played no part in the officers' coup, Petar Karadjordjević himself was popular principally as a result of his participation in the 1875–8 war in Bosnia-Hercegovina. Moreover, Petar's education at the French military academy of Saint-Cyr and his long years of exile in Paris and Geneva had converted him into something of a liberal—he had even translated John Stuart Mill's essay *On Liberty* into Serbian.[36]

By contrast Nikola had experienced no such evolution. His political instincts were highly conservative, not to say autocratic.

Prizren!/ It is all mine—home I shall come! Beloved antiquity calls me there/ Armed I must come there one day.' Quoted by Houston, p. 123.

[33] Petrovich, *A History of Modern Serbia*, vol. 2, p. 499.
[34] *Ibid.*, p. 501.
[35] Houston, *Nikola and Milena*, pp. 213–19.
[36] Banac, *The National Question*, pp. 142–3.

Changes to the system of government introduced in 1879 had replaced the old senate with a council of ministers, a high court and a privy council with a legislative role. But since Nikola himself had the last word over who was appointed to every institution, the effect was to increase rather than diminish his personal control. Local government too had been reformed at this time with the division of the country into captaincies, but this centralising reform simply weakened the old tribal system, which had not been without its democratic aspects. A new law code introduced in 1888 did little to diminish Nikola's power since he continued to select the judges.

Montenegro thus entered the twentieth century with the traditional system of government virtually intact. The ruler as an institution was connected with all the decisive events in public life, and Nikola treated the state as if it were his family domain. Foreigners often commented on the Ruritanian aspect of Cetinje—the miniature capital had its own theatre and reading room which, already in 1879, was stocked with newspapers from all parts of Europe, among them the *Illustrated London News* and, somewhat surprisingly in view of the country's poverty, a pamphlet entitled *Die Private Spekulation an der Börse [sic]*.[37] There were no regular budgets till 1907. Russian subsidies supplemented by Austrian loans provided the bulk of the country's financial resources, which were insufficient to cover the basic requirements of the population. Grain and textiles had to be imported, although Nikola attempted to improve agriculture by creating an experimental farm at Danilovgrad and ordering every Montenegrin to plant a vine.[38]

Everything from court procedure down to details of his subjects' national dress was determined by the prince. At the beginning of the twentieth century Montenegrin men still wore caps with a scarlet top encircled by a black band in mourning for defeat at the field of Kosovo as part of a picturesque costume which rarely failed to elicit favourable comment from foreign visitors. Less romantic observers might have construed Nikola's whimsical attempt to harness support for the dynasty by invoking a mythical past as indicative of his ap-

[37] 'Montenegro as we saw it', Anon., p. 290. Perhaps the explanation lay in Nikola's personal fondness for speculating on the Stock Exchange, as discussed below.
[38] *Foreign Office Handbook on Montenegro*, November 1918, p. 30.

proach to his subjects—that of an increasingly outdated type of nineteenth-century ruler—and perhaps even of an eloquent absence of ideas for the future. For while Nikola focused on such small things, he often misread the larger picture—one of the reasons why Montenegro's success in the wars of 1875–8 failed to resolve the problem of land hunger or significantly increase the general level of prosperity. Montenegro's territorial acquisitions had been accompanied by an initial increase of population of some 116,000 inhabitants, which included some 50,000 non-Orthodox, split more or less evenly between Albanian Catholics and Muslims.[39] Yet within a relatively short time most of these had fled their lands as a result of strong-arm tactics employed by the Montenegrins.

Nearly all the land in the Kolašin region had been taken from the Moslems, whom the Montenegrins massacred or drove away after conquering them. Even their graveyards had been levelled or ploughed over beyond recognition. The blood enmity between the two faiths had been so great that the Moslems themselves moved away, abandoning their houses and farms. It was not only the agas and begs who fled, but also the Moslem peasants who owned most of the land. The seizure of Moslem lands was regarded as a reward for the horrors and carnage and heroism of war.[40]

Bar, Nikšić and Ulcinj lost up to half of their pre-war population and Podgorica up to two-thirds.[41] The loss of so many non-Orthodox craftsmen and merchants who might have helped to develop Montenegro was particularly damaging given Montenegrins' lack of experience of commerce and manufacturing. As the anonymous correspondent of *Scribner's Monthly* observed at the time: 'The Montenegrin is a fighting man or he is nothing, never having been taught any peaceable pursuits and reared as he has been from childhood only to use of arms.'[42]

Far from benefiting the population as a whole, lands abandoned by departing Muslims were frequently given to Nikola's supporters, leading to widespread resentment. For many ordinary Montenegrins the outlook was as bleak as ever. With little to fall back on, emigration was often the only available solution.

[39] Pavlowitch, *Serbia: The History behind the Name*, p. 73.
[40] Djilas, *Land without Justice*, p. 24.
[41] Houston, *Nikola and Milena*, p. 140.
[42] Anon., 'Montenegro as we saw it', p. 284.

The exodus in turn created further problems because many of the emigrants did not remain abroad permanently but returned home to Montenegro after years of living under a less autocratic regime. In this regard Petar Karadjordjević's Serbia represented a particular problem since it allowed Montenegrin emigrants to experience a freer and more prosperous but nonetheless Orthodox Slav society under a relatively enlightened ruler, a comparison clearly to Nikola's disadvantage. It was from Serbia that much of the trouble of the next few years was to come.

Nascent opposition

By 1905 growing discontent with Montenegro's sclerotic political system had forced Nikola to seek a solution. In a political climate influenced by reforms in Russia and Serbia, as well as by the need to attract foreign loans, he agreed to the drawing-up of a first constitution. Like Tsar Nicholas II, however, Nikola did not envisage these changes as genuinely diminishing his control and insisted on a document which preserved the paramount position of the country's hereditary ruler. Specifically it guaranteed him the right to name ministers, initiate laws and, most important, declare war and peace and represent the state in all its contacts with foreign governments.[43] Further constitutional provisions proclaimed the Montenegrin Church autocephalous, and with no apparent sense of irony guaranteed religious freedom for all. At the same time the prince allowed an element of press freedom and introduced free and compulsory education up to the end of elementary school. Despite unprecedented levels of debt Montenegro inaugurated its own currency, based on a silver unit, the *perper*, and its own national bank.

The constitution established an assembly, to be partly nominated by Nikola and partly elected. Yet such was the growing opposition that despite its partly nominated character, the assembly elected in 1906 contained a majority of members who based their programme on that of the Radical Party in Belgrade. Renaming the assembly 'the Serb Skupština in Montenegro',[44] they saw their role as being

---

[43] Jelavich, *History of the Balkans: Twentieth Century*, vol. 2, CUP, 1983, pp. 35–6. See also *Foreign Office Handbook on Montenegro*, November 1918, pp. 38–9.

[44] Report from Des Graz to Viscount Grey of 7 March 1907. PRO, FO 371/279/ 8439.

to check the authority of the prince. This opposition group, the People's Party, known as *klubaši* (the clubmen), took advantage of the new press freedom to found its own newspaper, the *Narodna misao* (National Idea) which began for the first time to circulate opinion critical of the ruling circles and of the prince.[45] In a parallel move Montenegrin students in Belgrade issued a pamphlet entitled *The Voice of Montenegrin University Youth on the Circumstances in Montenegro*, which took an intensely pro-Serbia line, accusing Nikola of seeking only to preserve his dynastic interests by means which included conspiring with Austria-Hungary.[46]

Having released the liberal genie from the bottle, Nikola was at a loss how to react. First he set about prosecuting the students, but this guaranteed them a wave of sympathy—some of it from as far away as Moscow and St Petersburg—which forced him to back down. The prince then attempted to co-opt his opponents, and after staging a public reconciliation with the student leaders, proceeded to enlist a representative of the *klubaši*, Marko Radulović, to form an administration. The attempt at co-existence was short-lived: Radulović resigned after Nikola intervened to circumvent his attempts to release political prisoners and introduce some degree of financial accountability. His successor Andrija Radović, a sometime supporter of Nikola, was similarly obstructed in his attempted reforms and soon tendered his resignation. Abandoning any attempt at conciliation, Nikola unleashed a vitriolic campaign against the *klubaši*, closing down their papers, issuing denunciations and even encouraging punishment squads to administer beatings, effectively driving much of the opposition underground. Predictably such tactics failed to achieve their goal, tending instead to play into the opposition's hands by highlighting the repressive nature of the regime and driving even the prince's long-time supporters into the opposing camp; Andrija Radović and Gavro Vuković, respectively Nikola's former prime minister and former foreign minister, were among the latter.[47] In an attempt to drum up support for his own position the prince promoted a dynastic party, the True People's Party or *pravaši*, and installed

---

[45] Houston, *Nikola and Milena*, p. 274.
[46] Banac, *The National Question*, p. 278.
[47] Houston, *Nikola and Milena*, p. 276.

a new premier, Lazar Tomanović, to head an administration widely
seen as composed of Nikola's placemen.

The constitutional experiment was leading to disaster, a view
which seemed confirmed when on 5 November 1907 several bombs,
manufactured in Kragujevac in Serbia, were discovered in Cetinje,[48]
where pro-dynastic circles not unreasonably saw the fact that certain
Belgrade papers had published reports of Nikola's assassination
the day before the bombs' discovery as proof of the Serbian government's implication.[49] Contemporary reports from the British
Legation in Belgrade sought to exonerate the Serbian authorities,
suggesting that Austria, in an attempt to discredit the Serbian government, might have been behind the plot.[50] Nikola, however, continued to insist on Serbian involvement. The alleged perpetrators—
over 150 of them—were arrested and put on trial, and the sentences
handed down were harsh: several 'conspirators' received death sentences although these were eventually commuted. Even some of
those once close to Nikola did not escape suspicion and punishment.
The former Prime Minister Andrija Radović was sentenced to
fifteen years' imprisonment although, according to Britain's representative in Cetinje at the time, 'his connection with the conspiracy
could only have been of the most indirect kind.'[51]

Austria's annexation of Bosnia-Hercegovina

The impact of these events was such that diplomatic relations
between Serbia and Montenegro were formally broken off. That a
deeper rift did not open up was due not to mollifying action by
either side but to Austria-Hungary's sudden annexation on 6 October 1908 of the provinces of Bosnia and Hercegovina; these, though
still nominally under Ottoman sovereignty, had been administered
by the Dual Monarchy since the Congress of Berlin. Austria's action
had been prompted by the Young Turk revolution of July 1908 and
was designed to thwart any attempt by the new regime in Istanbul

[48] Treadway, *The Falcon and the Eagle*, p. 19.
[49] Des Graz to Viscount Grey, 18 November 1907, PRO, FO 371/279/33877.
[50] Whitehead to Grey, 15 June 1908, PRO, FO 371/480/20496.
[51] Beaumont to Grey, 5 July 1910, PRO, FO 371/929/24721.

to reactivate Turkey's formal claim to sovereignty over the two provinces. In particular Vienna was embarrassed by the Young Turks' plan to allow Bosnia and Hercegovina to elect representatives to the new Ottoman parliament, which was to meet in Istanbul—a concession contrasting with the Habsburgs' refusal to allow the provinces representation.

Austria's pre-emptive move provoked consternation in much of Europe and great hostility in Serbia and Montenegro. The annexation dealt a major blow to the Serbian and Montenegrin governments, both of which nurtured hopes of eventually obtaining recognition of their long-held claims to, respectively, Bosnia and Hercegovina. Nikola's first reaction to the crisis was to attempt to make the most of it by demanding compensation in the form of territory in Hercegovina. Austria immediately rejected this proposal, offering instead to modify Article 29 of the Treaty of Berlin, which guaranteed Austrian control over the Montenegrin coast, in return for Montenegro's acquiescence in the annexation. Disappointed, Nikola changed his approach, issuing a public declaration in which he both denounced the annexation and declared that, in view of Austria's actions, he no longer considered his country bound to observe Article 29 and now demanded the right to assume total control over Montenegro's coast. Meanwhile the Montenegrin populace had been making their outrage felt by staging violent anti-Austrian demonstrations in Podgorica, Bar, Nikšić and elsewhere. In Cetinje Nikola's two youngest daughters, Ksenija and Vjera, took to the streets at the head of a procession of women carrying anti-Austrian placards and singing national songs.[52] Montenegro began a boycott of Austro-Hungarian products which, by initiating a trade war, proved unsurprisingly to be far more damaging to Montenegro.

The crisis caused by the annexation led to a temporary thaw in relations between Belgrade and Cetinje, prompting Nikola and his estranged son-in-law Petar Karadjordjević to reach agreement on an offensive-defensive alliance against Austria-Hungary, which they signed on 24 October 1908 as a prelude to a broader military pact to include Turkey. There was even an initiative, launched by the Serbian Prime Minister Nikola Pašić, to demand compensation from

[52] Treadway, *The Falcon and the Eagle*, p. 26.

Austria-Hungary in the form of a corridor through Bosnia to connect Serbia and Montenegro.[53] For a time the situation appeared to hover on the brink of war, but the decision by the Young Turks to accept the Austro-Hungarian action as a *fait accompli* rather than join with Serbia and Montenegro against the Dual Monarchy, and most important, Germany's commitment to fight in any future war alongside Austria, ensured that plans for a local war eventually faded. Although Serbia and Montenegro were both forced to fall into line with the rest of Europe, the climb-down created deep resentment. As the Austrian ambassador in Belgrade minuted at the time, 'Here all think of revenge, which is only to be carried out with the help of Russia.'[54]

The brief détente in Serbian-Montenegrin relations did not survive the end of 1909. In the autumn of that year Montenegrin authorities put down an attempted uprising which they claimed was supported, like the 1907 bomb plot, by elements in Serbia dedicated to the overthrow of the Petrović dynasty. The conspirators—a group of disaffected liberals with links to the *klubaši*—were swiftly arrested and brought before a military tribunal in Kolašin, where they received heavy sentences;[55] several were put to death.[56] Nikola used the occasion as an excuse to crack down more widely on his political opponents, but the severity of the response provoked widespread reaction, especially in Belgrade where crowds demonstrated and newspapers fulminated against Nikola's autocratic regime.[57] As Serbian-Montenegrin relations hit a new low-point, the Petrovići readjusted their relations with Austria-Hungary, prompted partly by rumours of a further plot to assassinate Nikola. The prince's second son Mirko suggested just how far they were prepared to go in

[53] Petrovich, *History of Modern Serbia*, vol. 2, p. 558.
[54] Duncan Townson, *Dictionary of Modern History, 1789–1945*, London: Penguin Books, 1994, p. 96.
[55] Banac, *The National Question*, p. 279. Banac records that one of the conspirators, sentenced to death *in absentia*, was Puniša Račić, who in 1928 assassinated the Croatian deputy Stjepan Radić and four of his colleagues in the chamber of the Yugoslav Parliament. See Chapter 10.
[56] Despatch from Henry Beaumont to Viscount Grey of 7 December 1909. PRO, FO 371/44523.
[57] Treadway, *The Falcon and the Eagle*, p. 53.

achieving this rapprochement when he told the Austrian representative in Cetinje: 'Montenegrins are not Serbians, neither cowards
nor traitors, nor regicides. [...] We do not want to have anything to
do with Serbia.'[58]

From prince to king

It was in this essentially unpromising climate that Nikola chose to
unveil a scheme of his own devising—that of elevating Montenegro
from a principality to a kingdom. Timed to coincide with the prince's
fiftieth jubilee, the proposal evoked a mixed response from the
Powers which, despite their reservations and some uncertainty over
the issue of representation, ended by accepting it. Henry Beaumont,
the British chargé d'affaires at Cetinje, noted at the time:

The decision, ... though unlikely to raise opposition, may be open to
criticism. The Prince, by his campaigns in 1876–78 against the Turks, by the
matrimonial alliances of his daughters, by his literary and histrionic talents
is an interesting personality and occupies a picturesque and unique position
among the Sovereigns of Europe, but with a Civil List of £6,000 a year,
with a capital still in the very earliest stage of civilisation and as the ruler of
some 200,000 poverty-stricken barbarous peasants, an increase in rank
rather than adding to his dignity seems to show a want of the sense of proportion and may expose him to the reproach of vanity, or of jealousy of the
status of his son-in-law King Peter, which I believe to be the real explanation of his alleged ambitions.[59]

Others tended to be more indulgent. The British Embassy in
St Petersburg observed:

The general impression produced here by the announcement that the ruler
of Montenegro was about to assume the Royal dignity was, I should say,
one of good-humoured astonishment. I am informed that the Emperor
looked at the event chiefly from the humorous point of view.[60]

The Serbian reaction, however, was predictably hostile. The Belgrade daily *Politika* wrote:

The whole tendency of the Cetinje celebrations is towards supremacy
among the entire Serbian people.[...] Serbia alone is called upon to be the

[58] Treadway, *ibid.*, p. 57.
[59] Beaumont to Grey, April 1910. PRO, FO 371/929/12960.
[60] O'Beirne to Grey, 6 September 1910, PRO, FO 371/929/32992.

plenipotentiary representative and leader of all the other branches of the Serb people.[61]

Meanwhile life in Cetinje was immediately given over to the impending celebrations, as attested by a flurry of diplomatic correspondence between Cetinje and European capitals. Much of it contained speculation as to whether King Petar would consent to attend. The recent vilification of Petar and his Prime Minister Nikola Pašić in the Montenegrin press and political circles meant that Petar's presence, while in protocol terms desirable, was likely to raise hackles in both Serbia and Montenegro. In the event Petar declined the invitation on grounds of health, sending in his stead Crown Prince Aleksandar but not the prime minister. However, if Nikola felt slighted by his Belgrade son-in-law, he had reason to be gratified by the presence of his Italian counterpart (and son-in-law) King Victor Emmanuel, as well as King Ferdinand of Bulgaria, Crown Prince Constantine of Greece and his two Russian sons-in-law, Grand Dukes Nikolai Nikolayevich and Pyotr Nikolayevich, who represented the tsar. Apart from the family element, the strong Slav character of the representation was noteworthy: the tsar, notwithstanding his amusement at the occasion, honoured Nikola by making him a field-marshal in the Russian army, and showered further decorations and promotions on his sons.[62] Other European powers—Britain, France, Germany and Austria-Hungary—as well as the United States,[63] sent formal congratulations, but made do with the participation of their local representatives. In a well-orchestrated display of popular devotion the assembly and clergy expressed their joy at Nikola's elevation. Nikola responded graciously: he not only pardoned some of those convicted for the 1907 bomb plot, but did not fail to point out that his coronation signified the restoration of the old Serbian line of kings who once ruled in Zeta, making him by implication the embodiment of a more ancient dynasty than the king presently reigning in Belgrade.[64]

[61] Petrovich, *A History of Modern Serbia*, vol. 2, p. 596.
[62] Treadway, *The Falcon and the Eagle*, p. 63.
[63] The United States was content to send its representative in Athens to Cetinje with a letter of congratulations from President Taft. (Beaumont to Grey, 12 September 1910, PRO, FO 371/929/33887.)
[64] *Ibid*.

The presence of so many dignitaries and the staging of such a spectacle could not be achieved cheaply. Observing the beautification of Cetinje, Beaumont reflected that the cost—some 150,000 crowns—was roughly equal to the entire amount spent in a year on education in Montenegro.[65] Privately even Victor Emmanuel was said to have thought the whole affair ridiculously extravagant.[66] Looking to rebuild his finances in the aftermath of the celebrations, Nikola was able to point to a Russian decision to grant Montenegro an annual subsidy of 600,000 roubles to help train and equip its army.[67] In return Nikola had to undertake not to conclude alliances without Russia's consent, as well as accepting that the country would place 'all of the armed forces of the Kingdom at the disposal of His Imperial Majesty at his first call'.[68] Serbia, which had recently concluded its own alliance with Bulgaria, was not included.[69] For Russia the signing of the convention was a clear attempt to reassert Russian influence in the face of Montenegro's rapprochement with Austria-Hungary.

The Balkan Wars

Nikola did not intend his quest for allies and financial support, still less his royal status,[70] to constrain his ambitions, which now included extending his kingdom to Northern Albania, involving in particular the capture of Scutari (Skadar). In 1910 the Catholic Malissori tribe in the Northern Albanian Highlands had risen in revolt against Turkish rule, provoked by the Young Turks' programme of Ottomanisation, and this presented Nikola with an opportunity to pose as the Malissoris' champion, offering them his protection as ruler in place of the sultan. Soon a number of tribes—the Hoti, Shali, Grudi and Kastrati—had crossed the border into Montenegro to avoid

---

[65] Beaumont to Grey, 15 August 1910, PRO, FO 371/929/63.
[66] *Ibid.*
[67] Beaumont to Grey, 16 November 1909, PRO, FO 371/694/41000.
[68] Quoted by Petrovich, *A History of Modern Serbia*, vol. 2, p. 597.
[69] *Ibid.*
[70] As Edith Durham observed: 'A king must have a kingdom. The Powers would not otherwise have allowed him to be king. Soon there will be war.' (*The Struggle for Scutari*, p. 17, quoted by Treadway, *The Falcon and the Eagle*, p. 66.)

taxes and escape Ottoman reprisals. This scenario pleased neither Russia nor Austria-Hungary. Russia, still recovering from its defeat in the 1905 Russo-Japanese war and from the attempted revolution the same year, had no wish to see the Balkan *status quo* disturbed, while Austria-Hungary saw its tutelage of the Malissori and of Albania in general as fundamental to its policy of containment of Slav and Italian influence in the region.

Conscious of the need to placate the powers, Nikola first played the diplomatist, persuading the Albanian rebels to seek accommodation with the Porte in exchange for increased autonomy.[71] But when a second Malissori revolt broke out in 1911, Montenegro again lent covert assistance to the rebels and offered shelter to refugees. At the same time, despite the generally poor state of Montenegrin-Serbian relations, Nikola proposed taking joint action against Turkey in Macedonia, a proposal that Serbia, under strong pressure from Russia, turned down. Russia then increased its pressure on Montenegro, threatening to halt the military subsidy if Nikola continued his backing of the Malissori. With the Powers working together to urge restraint, Turkey and the Malissori signed a peace agreement in August 1911, apparently putting an end to the crisis.

One prime consequence of the Malissori crisis was a weakening of the Montenegrin-Russian relationship; the Montenegrins, resenting Russia's interference, struggled to diversify their sources of financial support. Austria-Hungary was, as always, the obvious alternative, but Nikola cast his net widely, attempting to attract loans from Britain, France and Italy, while keeping a watchful eye open for developments which might offer him the possibility of expanding southwards in an anti-Turkish war.

In the event it was Italy that provided the pretext through its attack on Ottoman-ruled Tripoli in September 1911, shortly after the signing of the Turkish-Malissori peace agreement. Nikola's immediate reaction was to suggest an Italian-Montenegrin alliance to invade Albania. The Italians turned down the offer, but neither their rejection nor Austro-Hungarian warnings had any real impact on the prince's objective of gaining Scutari and even of establishing

[71] Treadway, *The Falcon and the Eagle*, p. 74.

himself as ruler of a greatly enlarged Balkan state with its capital in Prizren.

For the other Balkan states Italy's attack on Turkish-held Tripoli was similarly a call to action. They too sought territorial expansion into the lands still ruled by the Ottomans and claimed justification from the continued oppression in these lands of their co-religionists, as well as the right of occupation supposedly conferred by historical memory.[72] If one of the Powers could break the peace in this way, the Balkan states could by the same token hope to get away with an attack on Turkey's European possessions, particularly since Italy's action had left the Ottoman Empire in disarray thereby maximizing their chances of success. Moreover to delay further was dangerous since there was always the risk that Austria might take pre-emptive action in the Sandžak, just as it had done in 1908 in Bosnia-Hercegovina, or even annex Macedonia.

Even as Nikola plotted his intervention he continued to assure the Austrians of his commitment to peace, an undertaking that the Austrians were disinclined to believe. Nevertheless they drew some comfort from the apparent continuing poor state of Serbian-Montenegrin relations, which were further aggravated at the beginning of 1912 by the decision of the Ecumenical Patriarch in Constantinople to appoint a Montenegrin candidate, Archimandrite Gavrilo Dožić, as Metropolitan of Prizren in place of a Serbian candidate, and by resentment over Montenegro's acceptance of a significant loan from Austria-Hungary.[73]

In March 1912 secret negotiations between Serbia and Bulgaria, which had been going on since the beginning of Italy's Tripolitan war, culminated in a nominally defensive treaty which in reality was intended to lay the foundations of a future offensive alliance directed by the Balkan states against Turkey. Given the parlous state of Serbian-Montenegrin relations, Serbia ensured that Montenegro knew little of these negotiations. By contrast the relationship between Nikola and King Ferdinand of Bulgaria was close, and when

---

[72] Pavlowitch, *Serbia: The History behind the Name*, p. 83.
[73] In December 1911 Montenegro was granted a loan of 1.3 million crowns by the Boden-Credit-Anstalt of Vienna, in an attempt to encourage Nikola to continue to keep the peace. (Treadway, *The Falcon and the Eagle*, p. 91, and Houston, *Nikola and Milena*, p. 297.)

Ferdinand attended the ceremonies to mark Nikola's self-designation as king, the two new kings—Ferdinand had been raised from reigning prince to king by a compliant Grand National Assembly in 1908[74]—were reported to have agreed that, if Turkey were to give up the Sandžak, whether voluntarily or compelled to do so by force of arms, Montenegro should receive the western third.[75] It was therefore not surprising that in May 1912 the Bulgarians should propose extending the Serbian-Bulgarian treaty to include Montenegro, but the Russian Foreign Minister Sazonov argued against it both on the grounds of continuing hostility between Serbia and Montenegro, and because of the risk that, with Montenegro involved, the alliance would soon become known to Austria-Hungary.[76] However, Bulgaria did not abandon the idea of bringing in Montenegro, and after concluding a bilateral agreement with Greece in May embarked upon secret negotiations with Nikola and his prime minister, which were conducted largely in Vienna 'right under the noses'[77] of the Austrian Emperor Franz Josef, his ministers and officials.

With the last piece of this Balkan jigsaw now in place, the Serbian-Montenegrin agreement called for a joint declaration of war on the Ottoman Empire by 14 October at the latest,[78] but Nikola was determined to steal a march on Serbia and declared war alone on 8 October.[79] Although he had promised the Powers never to fire the first shot in any Balkan conflict, he was determined to miss

---

[74] Crampton, *A Concise History of Bulgaria*, p. 134.
[75] Ernst Christian Helmreich, *The Diplomacy of the Balkan Wars, 1912–1913*, London and Cambridge, MA, 1938, p. 83.
[76] *Ibid.*, p. 85.
[77] Thaden, *Russia and the Balkan Alliance*, quoted by Treadway, *The Falcon and the Eagle*, p. 106.
[78] Treadway, *ibid.*, p. 107.
[79] Rumour had it that Nikola's precipitate declaration of war was timed to allow him to make a killing on the stock exchange. The charge—repeated at the time of the evacuation of Scutari in May 1913—remains unproven. However, as Helmreich points out, Montenegro's intentions were hardly a secret. Both the Russian and French foreign ministries were informed of the timing of the declaration on October 6 two days before it was made. Montenegro had many other reasons for wanting to get in first, the most prominent of which was likely to be that advanced by Count de Salis, British representative in Cetinje at the time—outdoing Serbia. (See Helmreich, *The Diplomacy of the Balkan Wars*, pp. 140–5.)

nothing of the symbolism of the occasion as his tiny country launched its attack on the mighty Ottoman Empire. Choosing uncharacteristically to forgo a moment of personal glory, he allowed his
youngest son to make the first move. The veteran Balkan traveller
Edith Durham was invited to witness the scene:

We started for the little hill from which Podgorica takes its name. The rain
ceased; the sun came out and sparkled on the coarse grass. About three
quarters of the way up we halted by the perianiks [*sic*] and saw the King in
full Montenegrin costume, standing brilliantly white against the sky, on the
summit, with Prince Mirko and a small suite. The air was crystal clear. An
endless quarter of an hour dragged by. So peaceful was the scene it was hard
to realise that the long-talked-of status quo was about to be shattered and
the map of Europe changed. In the strain of excitement all possible and
impossible results of the approaching fall of the Turk whirled through my
mind. Boom! The big gun roared from Gradina, on the height to our left,
fired by Prince Petar. ... I looked at my watch; it was 8 a.m. And we were at
war.[80]

In fact all the Balkan states had begun to mobilize even before the
signing of the final agreements. Montenegrin forces were naturally
much the smallest and least well equipped of all the Balkan armies.
Despite the reforms of 1895, the army remained essentially a militia,
composed of all able-bodied male Montenegrins between the ages
of eighteen and sixty-two. On the eve of the First Balkan War, Montenegro was able to put into the field some 35,600 men, 126 field-
guns, and one small cavalry unit consisting of thirty men and an
officer. By contrast Serbia had 230,000 infantry and 3,000 cavalry,
Bulgaria 350,000 infantry and 5,000 cavalry, and Greece 110,000
infantry and 1,000 cavalry. Greece also had a navy with over 11,000
men, Bulgaria too had some naval as well as air capacity, and Serbia
had a fledgling air force of some ten aeroplanes.[81]

Compared with its allies, Montenegro not only had pitifully small
forces, but very limited artillery, almost no motorised transport and
no field hospitals. Some of these deficiencies—notably the transport
of munitions and supplies—were made good by women, who traditionally fulfilled the role of porter. Moreover the Montenegrins,

[80] Durham, *The Struggle for Scutari*, p. 187.
[81] Richard C. Hall, *The Balkan Wars, 1912–1913: Prelude to the First World War*,
London and New York: Routledge, 2000, p. 18.

accustomed to an almost constant state of conflict along their border with Albania, were hardened to warfare. But although this gave them some advantage over their less seasoned allies, this border skirmishing, while making for brave individuals, had done little to weld the Montenegrins into an effective and well-trained army.[82]

The allied Balkan force of four different national armies faced an enemy which, as a great empire, was essentially multi-national. If the Ottomans were not to depend on troops from European Turkey, many of whom were of the same nationality as their adversaries and hence potentially unreliable, they would have to transport soldiers from Anatolia. The process was inevitably cumbersome and liable to be disrupted by the Greek navy. The Ottomans faced other problems too, in particular the failure to achieve standardisation of weaponry and a high level of illiteracy, both of which made the use of modern weaponry problematical. Finally they had to conclude their war with Italy in North Africa before they could turn their full attention to the Balkan theatre. This last problem was quickly overcome with the signing of a peace agreement on 15 October, but the Ottoman army still faced delays in transporting men and officers from the North African front to the Balkan peninsula where, given the existing logistical and manpower difficulties, they could have been expected to play a useful part in preventing an Ottoman defeat in the First Balkan War.[83]

The Siege of Scutari

The major battles of this war were fought, not in the western Balkans but in the eastern theatre of Thrace, gateway to the ultimate prize of Istanbul, the city still referred to by the Powers as Constantinople. Here the Ottoman armies at first suffered terrible defeats, losing Thrace and Macedonia before rallying sufficiently to retain three small pieces of territory in eastern Thrace including—significantly for the future—Gallipoli. By contrast, Montenegro's aspirations focused on the western Balkans where, in the case of Kosovo

---

[82] *Ibid.*

[83] Under the agreement, signed at Ouchy in Switzerland, the Turks ceded Tripoli and Cyrenaica while Italy undertook to vacate the Dodecanese islands and Rhodes, a commitment that remained unfulfilled until after the Second World War. (See Hall, *The Balkan Wars*, p. 20.)

and the Sandžak of Novi Pazar, they clashed with those of its ally Serbia. In the first place Nikola had fixed his sights on Prizren, an Albanian-inhabited town revered by Serbs as the burial-place of the great fourteenth century ruler Tsar Dušan. His second objective was the important city of Scutari, a prize that promised both economic and political rewards. Once part of Tsar Dušan's great Serbian empire and subsequently capital of Zeta under the Balšas, the city possessed a symbolic significance which Nikola hoped to exploit in his attempt to lay claim to the leadership of the Serb people.[84] And, given the initial support he had received from the Catholic Albanian Malissori, he was far from averse to expanding his claims to take in a sizeable portion of Albania. Scutari was also an important commercial city, the economic and administrative capital of northern Albania, offering access both to the lowland area around Lake Skadar and beyond it to territory stretching as far as the River Drin. It could thus offer Montenegro what it had lacked for so long, namely hope of a viable economic future.[85]

Montenegro's strategy involved attacking on several fronts at once. While the Eastern Division of the army under General Janko Vukotić, Queen Milena's cousin, struck out immediately for the Sandžak, the remaining forces were themselves divided in order to launch a two-pronged attack on Scutari as they advanced from the north and south of Lake Skadar. General Martinović led the attack from the north, while General Bošković, sharing the command with Prince Danilo, approached along the southern shore of the lake, intending to squeeze the city in a pincer movement and so force its surrender. Hopes rose when the Montenegrins took Tuzi, a significant milestone on the way to Scutari, and captured a large number of prisoners.

Meanwhile, the Sandžak force had met with rapid success, taking Bijelo Polje and Berane by 16 October, and Plav and Gusinje a few days later. Pressing on, Vukotić's forces 'liberated' the thirteenth-century Serbian monastery at Dečani and captured the Serb holy city of Peć but failed to reach Prizren, which was taken instead by the Serbs. By contrast, after their early successes the Scutari detachments

---

[84] *Handbook on the Balkan States*, Part 1, issued by the Historical Section of the Foreign Office, Peace Handbooks Series, London, 1920, p. 60.

[85] Hall, *The Balkan Wars*, p. 55.

soon ran into difficulties. The unexplained death of General Boško-vić—possibly by suicide, but giving rise to rumours that implicated one of the princes—was an early sign of the problems of morale which were to dog the Montenegrin campaign and tarnish the reputation of the dynasty. At the time the episode was hushed up and Danilo assumed sole command of the Zeta detachment,[86] but more troubles were to follow. The first indication of this was the halting of the advance on Scutari by General Martinović's forces from the southern side of Lake Skadar, probably to ensure that the city would fall to Danilo, who had taken the longer northern route around the lake.[87] The delay allowed Scutari's defenders, under Hussein Risa Bey, to bring in reinforcements. These included a number of Albanian irregulars and, more significantly, the 8,000-strong *redif* (militia) force under an ambitious local Albanian commander, Essad Pasha Toptani, whose scheming led ultimately to the city's fall.

Most observers of the war had expected Scutari to fall quickly to the Montenegrins, although even a cursory glance at the local topography should have cautioned against such an assessment. To the west, south and east were three large hills, respectively Taraboš, Brdica and Bardanjolt, on which the Ottomans installed artillery and machine-gun emplacements. At the same time they fortified the flat plain of Stoj just to the north of Scutari with trenches and barbed wire.[88] If the city were not to surrender, its capture would require an assault force prepared to grapple with barbed-wire entanglements under a hail of artillery fire. In fact this was exactly what happened as the Montenegrin besiegers were ultimately too few to cut the city off completely, a situation which allowed the defenders to hold out by continuing to bring in supplies and reinforcements from the south. As the siege lengthened, the Montenegrins' shortage of firepower prompted them to launch ever more reckless attempts to breach the city's defences; conducted under enemy fire, these led inevitably to heavy loss of life. Such tactics revealed the fundamental weakness of the Montenegrin army—the lack of training and strategic planning which, accompanied by heroic self-sacrifice, alternatively impressed and horrified observers. For Edith Durham,

---

[86] Houston, *Nikola and Milena*, p. 298.
[87] Treadway, *The Falcon and the Eagle*, p. 112.
[88] Hall, *The Balkan Wars*, pp. 55–6.

a one-time friend of Montenegro who had turned into a bitter critic, the spectacle of the charging Montenegrins was singularly appalling: 'They rushed like a pack of wolves, howling war cries, and had no notion of how to take cover or spread.'[89] But the twenty-one-year-old Irishman and future novelist Joyce Cary, then in search of adventure and enlisted as a stretcher-bearer on the Montenegrin side, was struck by the selfless heroism and pathos of a line of elderly bomb-throwers whose task was to clear a pathway for younger fighters across the wire.

There were forty of them, all old men and special volunteers. They offered themselves because as they said it would not matter if they got killed. Several of them were wearing the long white frock, blue breeches and white stockings of civil dress, and their coats blew out ludicrously behind them as they hurried on their rheumatic old legs over the stones. .... Several of the old men went down, but two thirds of them got their bombs into position and lighted. They came trotting back with short steps and long jumps as men do over rough ground, falling one by one all the time. When they passed immediately above the wall and the soldiers waiting there, they threw up their caps to shew them that the wire was broken. ......the Turks were firing point blank at them from fifty yards. Some of those who threw their caps too high waited gravely for them to come down again, as if it was a game of cup and ball.[90]

The situation for the attackers was made even worse by heavy rain which soon turned the foreshores of Lake Skadar into quagmires of mud through which struggled soldiers and wounded men, and mules bearing ammunition and stores.[91] Inside the besieged city the Baghdad-born General Riza imposed an iron grip on the inhabitants, ordering all food, fuel and other supplies to be handed over to his supervision in order to ensure rationing and prolong the siege. The Ottoman general had pledged himself never to surrender and threatened to execute anyone who dared to suggest treating with the enemy.[92] As the stakes were raised, Montenegrins began the deliberate targeting of civilians, but still Scutari and the fortress on Mount Taraboš held out.

---

[89] Durham, *The Siege of Scutari*, quoted by Houston, *Nikola and Milena*, p. 298.
[90] Cary, *Memoir of the Bobotes*, p. 115.
[91] Houston, *ibid.*, p. 299.
[92] *Ibid.*

What he failed to achieve by military means Nikola now attempted to gain by diplomatic measures. Initially Austria-Hungary appeared willing to condone Montenegro's capture of Scutari, but only in return for possession of the heights of Mount Lovćen which over-looked the Austro-Hungarian port of Kotor. For Nikola this was a step too far, not to be contemplated even when it came with the added sweetener of a promised customs union with the Dual Monarchy. He knew his people well enough to understand that if Lovćen, Montenegro's original Black Mountain, were to be surrendered, he would lose their support and quite possibly his throne.[93] Thus the negotiations came to nothing. Montenegrins returned to pursuing the siege, while the furious Austrians determined that, even if the Montenegrins took Scutari, they would never be allowed to retain it.[94]

In November the besieging Montenegrin forces were boosted by the arrival of most of General Vukotić's division which, after capturing much of the Sandžak and the western portion of Kosovo, had marched back across the snowy passes of the Dinaric ranges to join the force encamped around Scutari. By this time too the victorious Serbian Third Army had consolidated its occupation of western Kosovo and pressed on to the Adriatic where it had taken a portion of the coast including the great citadel of Alessio (Alb. Lezha), burial-place of the great Albanian hero Skanderbeg. From there it made contact with the Montenegrin forces outside Scutari. However, Nikola was loath to allow the Serbs a role in the city's capture. As one foreign observer and war-correspondent Lev Bronstein, better known to history as Leon Trotsky, put it,

During the war, friction between Serbia and Montenegro did not cease… the Serbs have a modern army, whereas the Montenegrins have a primitive militia quite unsuitable for complicated strategical operations. The Montenegrins are brave, good at impetuous onslaughts, and merciless, in which qualities they resemble the Albanians. Like the latter, however, the Montenegrins are absolutely incapable of planned operations, lack endurance, and easily lose their heads when things go wrong. This is very clearly apparent in their utter helplessness before Scutari, where they have not even managed to cut the garrison off from Alessio. However, Prince [*sic*] Nikola

---

[93] Treadway, *The Falcon and the Eagle*, p. 126.
[94] *Ibid.*

is not willing on any account to let the Serbs have the 'glory' of taking Scutari. The Serbian forces have played no part in the battle for this fortress, although the 1st Army was free to do so.[95]

For Trotsky, Nikola was the epitome of the petty reactionary, and his regime was 'comparable [to one] maintained in some out-of-the-way rural district in Russia by His Honour the Superintendent of Police'. Writing in 1912 he observed the mounting frustration caused by Montenegro's lack of military success and speculated about its likely effect on the fate of the Petrović dynasty:

> In Montenegro itself there is much dissatisfaction with the doubtful successes won by the country's forces, which have suffered heavy losses. [...] It may be expected that this war will lead, in Montenegro, as in Turkey, to internal reforms, which will put an end to the tyranny and the financial indecencies now reigning on the Black Mountain. Whether Nikola Njegoš will be able to hold out is difficult to forecast. But anyone has the right to consider the need for a distinct Montenegrin dynasty not proven.[96]

While Nikola kept the Serbs at arm's length the situation in front of Scutari remained at a stalemate, but the Balkan allies' rapid successes in Thrace and Macedonia were threatening meanwhile to upset the delicate balance of power within Europe. The early twentieth-century diplomatic alignments of the Great Powers into two hostile camps—Austria-Hungary, Germany and Italy in the Triple Alliance and France and Russia, later to be joined by Britain, in the Triple Entente—made the prospect of any alteration to the *status quo* particularly perilous. For Austria-Hungary the Serbian army's arrival on the shores of the Adriatic was already a step too far; any prospect of the Slav states being granted a permanent Adriatic port, which might become a Russian port, was a red line that could only be crossed at the risk of a conflagration. On 12 November Austria-Hungary and Italy demanded Serbia's withdrawal from Albania, Montenegro's abandonment of the siege of Scutari, and the creation of a viable state of Albania, and emphasised the point by ordering an initial mobilisation of forces. Russia, which had earlier mobilised in support of the Balkan states, now received assurances of backing from France, while Austria-Hungary was promised similar support by Germany. With Bulgaria poised outside Istanbul and threatening to upset the balance further, it seemed as if Europe was on the brink of war. As Russian belligerence waxed and waned it was even rumoured that the Montenegrin 'black princesses' had succeeded in influencing the tsar to take a stronger stand against Austria's pro-Albanian policy by bribing Rasputin.[97]

The London Conference of Ambassadors

News of an armistice, when it came on 3 December, was greeted with great relief. The Powers convened two separate but inter-connected peace conferences in London. The first, known as the St James Conference, was between the belligerents. Although Montenegro sent a delegation led by a former prime minister Lazar Mijušković, Nikola did not call off the offensive at Scutari. The second and ultimately more meaningful assembly was the Conference of Ambassadors, which sought to reach a position of adjust-ment and reconciliation between the Great Powers themselves. On 20 December the conference, presided over by the able and gen-erally impartial British Foreign Secretary, Sir Edward Grey, agreed to establish an independent Albanian state, although the task of deter-mining its actual borders was handed over to a commission which would report at a later date.[98] The Powers also guaranteed Serbia access to the Adriatic but only through a neutral free port in what was to be designated as Albanian rather than Serbian sovereign ter-ritory.[99]

If the ambassadors representing the Powers made some progress, the same could not be said for the belligerents. Although at first the Ottomans were ready to concede all territory west of Adrianople to the Balkan allies, which in effect meant Scutari along with Janina, their offer did not prove acceptable to the Greeks or the Bul-garians.[100] Fighting around Janina thus resumed, while in Scutari,

---

[97] Helmreich, *The Diplomacy of the Balkan Wars*, p. 217.

[98] An Albanian national assembly meeting in Vlorë had already proclaimed the independence of Albania on 28 November 1912. See Hall, *The Balkan Wars*, p. 72.

[99] Treadway, *The Falcon and the Eagle*, p. 130.

[100] In fact the belief that the Ottoman Grand Vizir Kamil Pasha was about to concede Adrianople to the Bulgarians was the prime reason for the Young Turks' coup of 23 January 1913, which overthrew the regime and proposed the

where it had never really stopped, the debilitating struggle continued. With so much at stake, Nikola was convinced that if Scutari were to fall before the signing of a final peace treaty, the Powers would not seek to overturn a *fait accompli*. It was therefore especially galling to the Montenegrins that the Turkish General Riza, despite prohibition on re-provisioning during the so-called armistice, managed to have supplies brought into Scutari, thereby threatening to prolong the siege. In the end, however, Riza's success in securing some re-provisioning was not enough to save him or the city. On the night of 30 January, on his way home after a dinner with his rival and second-in-command Essad Pasha, Riza was murdered by unknown assailants. Although it was never conclusively proved, Essad Pasha remained the prime suspect on the basis of *cui bono*.

The death of this capable general greatly encouraged the Montenegrins, who by this time had reluctantly accepted Serbian aid. Together the two Slav states attempted an all-out assault on Mount Taraboš, losing several thousand men without precipitating Scutari's fall. In London, Scutari was at the forefront of international attention. Grey feared it was 'a bomb which might set the whole of Europe on fire'.[101] With the peace of Europe hanging in the balance Russia, though not willing to join the other Powers, reluctantly agreed not to stand in their way, and a fleet tasked with imposing a naval blockade and consisting of ships representing the five remaining Powers set sail under the command of the British Vice-Admiral Sir Cecil Burney. It reached the Adriatic coast in early April by which time even Serbia, under heavy pressure from the Powers, was about to fall into line. Not so Nikola; as impervious to the Powers' threats as to their attempts to cajole him with bribes, he appeared determined to have his prize.[102] But while Montenegro continued to hold out alone against the Powers and the fleet blockaded the port of Bar, events on the ground took a dramatic turn. On 22 April, after several days of secretive negotiations, Essad Pasha surrendered the city.

---

partition of that city. The Balkan states refused this offer and fighting resumed at the beginning of February. See Hall, *The Balkan Wars*, pp. 78–9.

[101] Quoted in Treadway, *The Falcon and the Eagle*, p. 132.

[102] For a discussion of the various inducements offered to the Montenegrins see R. J. Crampton, *The Hollow Détente: Anglo-German Relations in the Balkans, 1911–1914*, London: George Prior Publishers, 1979, pp. 90–3.

In Cetinje Edith Durham was woken before it was light by big guns firing in celebration. The king and his daughters appeared on the palace balcony and a jubilant crowd sang Nikola's anthem, 'Let me see Prizren'.[103] Although the Montenegrins could not claim a military victory—indeed it was generally accepted that the scheming Essad Pasha had made a treacherous bargain with Nikola[104]— the prospect of Montenegrins re-entering the old capital of Zeta after more than 500 years was rapturously received. In Sofia and across Russia pro-Slav sentiment erupted. In Belgrade the crowds could not be prevented from showing their delight, although the authorities took pains to stress that the city had fallen to Montenegro without a fight.[105]

Scutari, when the Montenegrins entered on 24 April, was desperate in the extreme. Edith Durham, who entered the city on the same day in the company of a Mr Loch of *The Times* described the scene that awaited them: 'In the poorer houses [the occupants] lay on the ground in the last stages of misery. Tortoises, frogs, hedgehogs, dandelions had all been used as food. [...] I saw a man drop in the street, and I fed a skeleton child.'[106] Another eyewitness, Joyce Cary, was one of the first three over the bridge in Scutari after the surrender. Cary, who unlike Durham was sympathetic to the Montenegrins, nonetheless recalled: 'The crowds peered in silence from the dark caverns of the open stalls. Every man and woman of them expected massacre that nightfall, but their attitudes and looks expressed for the most part nothing but indifference made easy by famine.'[107]

The expected massacre by Montenegrin soldiers did not take place, a fact uncharitably ascribed by Nikola's detractors to his awareness

---

[103] Durham, *The Struggle for Scutari*, p. 275.
[104] See Crampton, *The Hollow Détente*, p. 90. While the details of any financial arrangement are unknown, the fact that Essad Pasha was able to march out of the city with over 20,000 men who left behind only their heavy guns aroused suspicion. Once Essad Pasha had reached the safety of Tirana he proclaimed his refusal to recognise the provisional government of Ismail Kemal, which had been set in place by the Powers, instead declaring himself to be the ruler of Albania.
[105] Treadway, *The Falcon and the Eagle*, pp. 142–3.
[106] Durham, *The Struggle for Scutari*, p. 279.
[107] Cary, *Memoir of the Bobotes*, p. 151.

that the eyes of the world were upon them. Elsewhere, in Peć, Djakovica and Gusinje, Montenegrin troops carried out a widespread policy of forced conversions, to which the alternative was generally death.[108] The Montenegrins were especially feared for their practice of facial mutilation. As a Montenegrin schoolteacher explained to Edith Durham on the eve of the war, 'It is our old national custom... how can a soldier prove his heroism if he does not bring in noses? Of course we shall cut noses; we always have.'[109]

But Montenegrins were far from alone in perpetrating a catalogue of barbarity during the Balkan Wars. Trotsky, who was not squeamish, filled his despatches with appalled eye-witness accounts of atrocities committed by Serbs and Bulgarians in Kosovo and Macedonia,[110] and there is no shortage of testimony implicating the other members of the Balkan alliance.[111] The authoritative and impartial Carnegie Report of 1914, which investigated the causes and conduct of both Balkan Wars, produced graphic evidence of atrocities committed by all sides including Ottoman soldiers, who even as they retreated sometimes avenged themselves upon the civilian populations whom they encountered.[112] Of course such practices were far from new. It was the scale of the action taken against civilian populations that distinguished the Balkan Wars from previous centuries of warfare. Already in 1914 the Carnegie Report expressed the view that much of the violence was attributable to new nationalist ideologies which conceived of terror inflicted on

---

[108] Malcolm, *Kosovo*, pp. 254–6.

[109] Durham, *The Struggle for Scutari*, p. 185.

[110] Trotsky's war correspondence contains an overwhelming number of such instances. To take but one: 'The horrors actually began as soon as we crossed the old frontier [with Old Serbia]. ... Burning was going on all around us. Entire Albanian villages had been turned into pillars of fire ... This was the first real, authentic instance I had seen in the theater of war, of ruthless mutual extermination between men. Dwellings, possessions accumulated by fathers, grandfathers, and great-grandfathers, were going up in flames. In all its fiery monotony this picture was repeated the whole way to Skoplje.' (Trotsky, *The Balkan Wars*, p. 267.)

[111] *Ibid.*

[112] Carnegie Endowment for International Peace, *Report of the International Commission to Inquire into the Causes and Conduct of the Balkan Wars*, Washington, 1914.

civilians as a means of removing populations from territory the conquerors intended to make solely and permanently theirs.[113]

In the case of Scutari it was the Albanian civilian population that had borne the brunt of the suffering throughout the siege, although casualties among the Montenegrin combatants were also appallingly high. General Martinović, who with General Vukotić led the first Montenegrin entry into Scutari on 24 April, attempted to win over the populace by arranging for supplies of bread to be distributed twice a day, and even set up the first street lamps in the hope of reconciling the world at large to Montenegrin possession of the town.[114] But neither he nor his successor, Scutari's short-lived civil governor Petar Plamenac, stood any real chance of making headway with the Albanian population who, whether Catholics or Muslims, were never going to be cajoled into throwing in their lot with Montenegro, and eight months under siege had served only to strengthen that determination. If any further incentive to resist Montenegrin blandishments had been needed, there was still the presence of the Powers' flotilla just offshore.

For the Austrians Montenegro's occupation of Scutari in defiance of the Powers was the final straw. Not only did it challenge their determination to see Scutari incorporated within an independent Albanian state; it also complicated relations within the Triple Alliance by bringing into the open the rivalry that existed between two of its members—themselves and Italy—over control of the Adriatic.[115] As the Austrians prepared to take action against the Montenegrins with or without the say-so of the other Powers, the outcome was felt to depend upon whether Russia was prepared to stand by and permit such a move. Grey himself was deeply pessimistic. The British ambassador in St Petersburg reported, 'the political outlook is blacker than at any other period of the crisis.'[116] Then at the eleventh hour on 4 May 1913 Nikola, correctly calculating that the odds were irrevocably stacked against him, backed down and agreed to evacuate Scutari in exchange for a substantial

[113] Hall, *The Balkan Wars*, pp. 136–8.
[114] Cary, *Memoir of the Bobotes*, p. 152.
[115] Bosworth, *Italy, the Least of the Great Powers*, pp. 224–32.
[116] See Crampton, *The Hollow Détente*, pp. 90–1, and Treadway, *The Falcon and the Eagle*, p. 148.

foreign loan.[117] Europe reacted with relief. As the Russian foreign minister was reported to have said, 'King Nikola was going to set the world on fire to cook his own little omelette.'[118] But now the extraordinary period throughout which Montenegro on its own had confronted the Powers and brought Europe to the brink of war was drawing to a close.[119]

Nikola's note of capitulation, drafted for him by the British minister at Cetinje, Count de Salis, endeavoured to extract the best from the situation: 'This position [of my government] conforms to the established principles of justice. I affirm once more, with my people, our right consecrated by history and by conquest. My dignity, as well as that of my people not allowing me to submit to an isolated summons, I entrust the fate of the city to the hands of the Powers.'[120] And despite Nikola's games of brinkmanship, and suspicions that he had sought to make large gains on the stock market by engineering the crisis over Scutari,[121] the Powers took a generally sympathetic attitude to Montenegro hoping in this way to ensure the small state's future stability. Among those advocating leniency was King George V, who personally suggested awarding Montenegro some increase of territory.[122] Serbia too seemed disposed to be generous when it came to agreeing the new and, for the first time, directly contiguous Serbian-Montenegrin border in the Sandžak, although in the light of the increasing unpopularity of Nikola's regime Belgrade's generosity would be seen to contain a high level of self-interest.

---

[117] Grey wrote: '... the various methods to be employed to induce Montenegro to evacuate Scutari gave rise to tedious problems. At one extreme was the suggestion to land troops and compel the evacuation; at the other was a proposal to give Montenegro money—in other words, to bribe the ruling authority to leave the place. We ourselves would not co-operate in the use of troops, but were ready to join in a naval demonstration. Eventually a blend of the threat of coercion and the offer of money compensation settled the matter to the satisfaction of Austria, perhaps also to the satisfaction of the King of Montenegro, and this danger to European peace was laid to rest.' (*Twenty-five Years, 1892–1916*, vol. 1, London: Hodder & Stoughton, 1925, pp. 270–1.)

[118] Radzinsky, *Rasputin*, p. 189.

[119] See Crampton: 'The Scutari crisis had been the most dramatic and dangerous of the problems created by the Balkan wars.' (*The Hollow Détente*, p. 93.)

[120] Helmreich, *The Diplomacy of the Balkan Wars*, p. 324.

[121] Treadway, *The Falcon and the Eagle*, p. 276.

[122] *Ibid.*, 154–5.

Nikola was certainly in need of help. While Montenegrins initially reacted calmly to the news of their country's surrender of
Scutari, a sense of failure, accompanied by resentment, soon emerged for which Nikola and the Petrović dynasty were widely held
responsible. The bitterness provoked by Montenegro's forced surrender found its expression in one final act of vengeance. Just before
the international fleet under Vice-Admiral Burney was due to take
over control from the departing Montenegrins, a fire, starting myste-
riously in the bazaar, razed Scutari's entire commercial quarter to
the ground.

In political terms, the failure of Montenegro's war aims dealt a
disastrous blow to Nikola's hopes of challenging Serbia's position of
pre-eminence in the Serb world. For outsiders the dream had always
appeared far-fetched but any hope that it would continue to play a
useful purpose in terms of domestic politics receded as Montenegrins not only digested the extent of Serbia's territorial gains, but
also weighed up the respective military leaderships, noting in particular the lamentable performance of Prince Danilo when compared
to that of the Serbian Prince Aleksandar. Edith Durham observed:

All Europe knew that the Servian army was superior to the Montenegrin.
The Montenegrins were intensely embittered, and spoke openly and
angrily against the King and especially against the royal princes. The anti-
dynasty party said freely that the Petrovitches were the bane of the land.
Much anger was expressed against Princess Xenia [Ksenija], who was said
to have undue influence with the King...[123]

The Peace of London marking the end of hostilities was signed on
30 May 1913, but although it put an end to the Balkan nations' joint
campaign against Turkey, it marked no more than an interlude
between two periods of war. In the summer of that year the Second
Balkan War broke out when the former members of the Balkan
pact—Serbia and Greece fell out with their former ally Bulgaria as
they sought to obtain a greater share in the carve-up of conquered
territory. On the night of 29–30 June Bulgaria seized the initiative
by launching a surprise attack on Serbian positions. Given Montenegro's indebtedness to Serbia over the Scutari campaign and the
strength of pro-Serb feeling in Cetinje, Nikola had had little choice

[123] Durham, *The Struggle for Scutari*, p. 272.

but to support his former Serbian ally, although in reality he had no wish to see Serbia make further gains. Soon the defeated Ottoman Empire had also joined the fight against Bulgaria, exploiting the opportunity to take back the city of Adrianople which had been lost to Bulgaria following an appalling five-month siege in the First Balkan War.

This time the Powers kept their distance and the peace of Europe was not threatened to anything like the extent it had been by the First Balkan War.[124] Yet the loss of life was greater. Though exhausted by the previous war, Montenegro sent troops to fight alongside the Serbs, more than 12,000 men from the Montenegrin division joining the Serbian 3rd Army fighting near Veles in central Macedonia. Many Montenegrins took part in the bloody battle of Bregalnica south-east of Skopje (16,000 Serbian and Montenegrin casualties as against 20,000 on the Bulgarian side), which ended in victory for the Serbs. Further Bulgarian defeats followed, most notably the rout of the 2nd Bulgarian Army by the Greeks at Salonika, which forced the Bulgarians to retreat. Although the Bulgarians briefly showed some signs of rallying, their position became wholly untenable when Romania entered the war on 10 July 1913.[125] On 31 July, after thirty-three days of fighting, both sides agreed to an armistice followed by peace negotiations scheduled to take place in Bucharest. Montenegro sent its representative—the new Prime Minister, General Janko Vukotić—to sit at the victors' table alongside the Serbs, Greeks and Romanians. But since it had no direct territorial claims to make on Bulgaria its participation amounted to no more than an expression of solidarity aimed at securing a favourable division of the Sandžak in forthcoming bilateral negotiations with Serbia.

The terms of the Treaty of Bucharest of August 1913 saw Bulgaria divested of most of the territory for which it had fought in the First Balkan War. Serbia and Greece were the principal victors, dividing the greater part of Macedonia between them. There was to be a new independent state of Albania under a constitutional monarchy whose neutrality would be guaranteed by the Powers. Serbia and Montenegro were to have a common border after settling the divi-

---

[124] However, a potential flashpoint existed over Russia's desire to evict Turkey from Adrianople. See Crampton, *The Hollow Détente*, pp. 102–7.
[125] Hall, *The Balkan Wars*, pp. 120–1.

The Tribes of Old Montenegro and the Brda, 1913

sion of the Sandžak. The Porte kept Adrianople and Romania acquired southern Dobrudja, both at Bulgaria's expense. Together with Bulgaria, the Ottoman Empire was the other great loser: at the end of the Balkan Wars the former imperial power retained no more than the city of Istanbul and a strip of Thracian hinterland in Europe. For all its attempts at judicious redistribution, the Treaty of Bucharest left none of the small Balkan nations states satisfied, while the Great Powers were apprehensive over the likely effect of the settlement on the peace and stability of Europe. Turkey and Bulgaria remained aggrieved, ready to make common cause against Serbia when an opportunity presented itself. As Sir Edward Grey wrote, 'The settlement after the Second Balkan War was not one of justice but of force. It stored up inevitable trouble for the time to come.'[126]

Effect of the Balkan Wars on Montenegro

For the present Serbia was in the ascendant, having greatly enhanced its prestige and that of the monarchy while doubling the size of the territory under its control. Thus when frontier negotiations began between Serbia and Montenegro in November 1913, Serbia went out of her way to accommodate its small neighbour, conceding to it the possession of Pljevlja, Bijelo Polje, Berane, Mojkovac, Peć and Djakovica. But with the momentum towards Serbian-Montenegrin unification gathering pace in Cetinje and Belgrade, it was difficult to avoid detecting an opportunist angle to the Serbia agenda. Djakovica, an Albanian-inhabited town, was itself twice the size of Montenegro's largest city, Podgorica. Certainly the impact of Montenegro's expansion was dramatic; the little country now stretched for over 14,443 square kilometres and had some 450,000 inhabitants. But since much of the new land was relatively infertile and the added population lacked any sense of shared religious or ethnic identity, the net effect was to be a drag on Montenegro's financial and administrative capacities rather than a panacea for its economic and political woes.[127]

Predictably, the apparent closeness with Belgrade aroused anxiety in Austria-Hungary, concerned now by the threat that an enlarged Serb-inhabited state with an outlet to the Adriatic would present to the subject Slavs within the Austro-Hungarian Empire. Should this

[126] Grey, *Twenty-five Years*, vol. 1, p. 263.
[127] Treadway, *The Falcon and the Eagle*, p. 161.

happen Austria-Hungary made clear its intention of occupying the Adriatic coast south of Kotor as far as the Albanian border. Nor was it possible, on this occasion, for the Montenegrin regime to balance its present difficulties with Austria-Hungary by following the traditional pattern of moving closer to Russia. Official Russia's exasperation with Montenegrin obduracy over Scutari had not diminished and was still in marked contrast to popular feeling as reflected in the Russian press during the siege. The tsar therefore suspended the vital military subsidy paid to Montenegro while simultaneously refusing to help with war costs.[128] In a fit of pique, Nikola wrote to the Dowager Empress Marie of Russia to request the closure of the Russian-financed school for girls, which had been founded in 1869 by her order. If sweeping aside one of the few avenues for improvement open to girls in Montenegrin society seemed unimportant at the time, offering Russia a pretext for abandoning its support of an independent Montenegro in favour of the far more expedient political union with Serbia could hardly have been more damaging.

As the dynasty's popularity declined, the other institutions of government strengthened. Montenegro's financial problems demanded a more balanced and consistent approach to potential allies and benefactors, and in this context the new Montenegrin foreign minister, the Western-educated Petar Plamenac, was able to demand Nikola's signature on a foreign policy document which underlined the government's commitment to friendly relations with Russia, France and Britain and provided indirectly the basis for a Franco-Italian loan of 6 million francs, although this was barely enough to meet the most urgent needs. Meanwhile the Great Powers debated the modalities of the loan of 30 million francs, subsequently increased to 40 million, which had been promised to Montenegro in exchange for its withdrawal from Scutari. However, the payment was never made since before the details could be finalised Montenegro, together with the rest of Europe, was once again at war.[129]

In the meantime Montenegro's financial situation was growing ever more desperate. The cost of the war, estimated by one source at 100,000,000 francs,[130] had left the country ruined. Arriving in Montenegro just before the outbreak of war, Joyce Cary had noted

---

[128] Treadway, *The Falcon and the Eagle*, p. 161.
[129] *Ibid.*, p. 166.
[130] Hall, *The Balkan Wars*, pp. 138.

Cetinje's similarity to 'a small Irish country town... The Government buildings are exactly like a convent, the Royal Palace like a Court House, the Embassies like a row of small Doctors' and Lawyers', and the Crown Palace like the local Squire's. But it is cleaner than any town one ever sees in Ireland ..., and it is lighted by electricity.'[131] Used to the poverty of early twentieth-century Ireland, Cary may have taken an over-sanguine view. Certainly the post-war situation, with the country still struggling to deal with the consequences of many dead and wounded, was so bad as to verge on the desperate. Although perhaps one-third of the adult male population of working age were abroad and sending home their remittances, Montenegro simply lacked the money to pay wages, including those of the army, and was facing protest demonstrations.[132]

The political climate was not improved by the conduct of the younger members of the dynasty. The reputation of the still childless Prince Danilo had been badly damaged by his conduct during the Balkan Wars and his fondness for spending time abroad. Now Nikola's second son Mirko announced his separation from Princess Natalija to whom he had been married for eleven years. Nikola's own conduct was erratic—not only did he still allow the army to provoke frontier incidents with both Albania and Austria-Hungary, but there were questions regarding his misappropriation of a fund intended by its Russian provider to furnish poor Montenegrin girls with dowries.

As the pressure for union with Serbia grew stronger, elections in March 1914 brought the People's Party (the old *klubaši*) to power. For the new government and its supporters the solution to Montenegro's financial difficulties and political backwardness was a union between the two Serb states, which since the end of the Balkan Wars had shared a 200-kilometre-long frontier. Nikola had little choice but to pretend to go along with them, describing himself as committed to 'the hope of an approaching union', but with the proviso that it allowed for the continuation of both royal houses.[133] From Belgrade his son-in-law King Petar reacted sensitively, expressing his

[131] Cary, *Memoir of the Bobotes*, p. 14.
[132] Pavlowitch, *Serbia: The History behind the Name*, p. 86. Also Treadway, *The Falcon and the Eagle*, p. 173.
[133] Treadway, *The Falcon and the Eagle*, p. 175

preference for some form of Serbian–Montenegrin commonwealth and suggesting imperial Germany as a possible model.[134] The new government accordingly opened negotiations with Belgrade for a military, diplomatic and financial union. The Serbian Prime Minister, Nikola Pašić, himself put forward a programme for the merger of the two armies as well as the amalgamation of the ministries of justice, finance and communication. So far at least there had been no mention of a single dynasty, but Russia's foreign minister Sazonov commented that Nikola was being allowed to 'die by inches'.[135]

[134] *Ibid.*

[135] Jannine Leadbetter, 'The End of Montenegro, 1914–1920', *South Slav Journal*, vol. 14, no. 3–4, London, 1991, p. 49.

9. From the First World War to Loss of Statehood

Appalling as the horrors of the Balkans Wars appeared to outsiders, they were no more than a pale foreshadowing of the Great War that was to follow. Nor did the year between the signing of the Treaty of Bucharest and the assassination of Archduke Franz Ferdinand in Sarajevo by the young Bosnian Serb Gavrilo Princip amount to a true peace.[1] In Montenegro the end of the siege of Scutari had been followed by a succession of border incidents as the Montenegrins attempted to encroach on Albanian lands to the south in anticipation of the findings of the international border commission, while to the north and in the Sandžak there were disputes between Montenegro and Austria-Hungary over various scraps of territory. Meanwhile Serbia continued to crush any sign of Albanian resistance in Kosovo and in Macedonia,[2] where Greece too subjected its newly-conquered population, especially Albanian Muslims, to an ongoing campaign of repression.[3] More generally, Serbia's success in the Balkan Wars strengthened support for Yugoslavism among the South Slav population of the Habsburg Monarchy and nourished nationalist secret societies in Serbia and elsewhere dedicated to the liberation of brother-Slavs still under Austro-Hungarian rule. In response Austria-Hungary, fearful for the future of the empire and already harbouring resentment over Serbia's actions in the Balkan wars, came increasingly to view Serbia as the Piedmont[4] of the Balkans

---

[1] Princip's family, members of the Jovičević clan, were originally from the rocky region of Grahovo in Montenegro, migrating to the Hercegovinan side of the border at the beginning of the eighteenth century. (See Dedijer, *The Road to Sarajevo*, p. 29.)

[2] Malcolm, *Kosovo*, pp. 256–8.

[3] Hugh Poulton, *Who are the Macedonians?* London: Hurst, 1995, pp. 74–5.

[4] *Pijemont* was in fact the name of the publication produced by the secret terrorist society, the 'Black Hand', dominated by Colonel Dimitrijević, '*Apis*', who played

and Serbian nationalism as a lethal force which had to be crushed if it could not be contained.

In such a political climate the assassination in Sarajevo on 28 June 1914 of Archduke Franz Ferdinand, heir to the Habsburg Empire, provided the pretext and spark for Austria-Hungary's declaration of war against Serbia. More than three weeks were to pass before Austria-Hungary delivered an ultimatum to Serbia, but the delay was due to the Austrian authorities' need to assure themselves of the support they required both from Germany and from the Hungarian part of the empire, as well as to allow time to get in the harvest before the peasants were mobilised for war. Serbia's compliance with all but one of the ten demands of the ultimatum—that of allowing Austrian officials to conduct their own investigation of the murder on Serbian soil—was never going to be enough for the hawks within the Habsburg administration who from the beginning were determined to take military action. On 28 July, a month after the Archduke's assassination, they had their way. One week later all the European powers were at war.

If war between Austria-Hungary and Serbia could be seen as the predictable consequence of the Archduke's assassination, the chain of events set in motion by Princip's action could hardly have been foreseen. The cataclysm of the Great War led, beyond the millions of deaths, to the collapse of the autocratic empires of Russia, Turkey and Austria-Hungary and swept away four great reigning dynasties—the Ottoman sultanate, the Habsburgs, the Hohenzollerns and the Romanovs. With them went the Petrović dynasty in circumstances which left Nikola and his sons almost wholly discredited and which rebounded—many would argue unjustly—on the future of the country. When in 1918 an assembly in Podgorica, composed only of those with impeccably pro-Serbian views, voted to depose Nikola and unite with Serbia, few outside voices were raised against them. Although a series of missions was despatched by the Great Powers to look into the consequent unrest and rebellion, the Allies

---

an important part in the plot to murder Franz Ferdinand as well as being a leading participant in the murder of King Aleksandar Obrenović and his wife Draga Mašin. See David Mackenzie, *Apis: the Congenial Conspirator: The Life of Colonel Dragutin T. Dimitrijević*, Boulder, CO: East European Monographs, 1989, especially pp. 123–37.

lacked the political will to challenge what was by then a Serbian *fait accompli*. The following year the fate of Montenegro was sealed at the Paris Peace Conference, where its demise as an independent state was graphically symbolised by an empty chair.

Preparations for war

After Franz Ferdinand's assassination Montenegro, exhausted by the savage fighting of 1912–13, was not eager at first for another war.[5] In particular Nikola, despite his conviction that Princip's action would unleash war between Austria-Hungary and Serbia, sought to avoid being dragged into Serbia's quarrel;[6] indeed his first reaction was to damp down support for Serbia among pro-Serbia nationalists within Montenegro while attempting to negotiate the country's possible neutrality in return for Austria's agreement to permit its expansion into Albania, and perhaps even a return to Scutari.[7] But Austria's ability to deliver was always in doubt, while Nikola was finding increasing difficulty in ignoring the growing pro-Serb sentiments among his own population. Hence his telegram of support to Aleksandar Karadjordjević, assuring his grandson: 'My Montenegrins are on the frontier prepared to fall in the defence of our independence.'[8] These fine words on closer examination amounted to a statement which—as the cynical British representative in Cetinje, Count de Salis, pointed out—'pledged him to no more than resistance to an attack which at that time was not threatened'.[9]

Nevertheless on 29 July, the day after the Austro-Hungarian Empire declared war on Serbia, Nikola, recognising the growing strength

[5] Treadway, *The Falcon and the Eagle*, pp. 184–5.
[6] Nikola's Foreign Minister, Petar Plamenac, was widely thought to have been involved in secret negotiations with the Austro-Hungarian government, which were injurious to the Allies before the outbreak of war. Indeed, as early as 1912 Plamenac is reported to have invited the Austrians to enter the Sandžak in order to provide a barrier between the two Serb states so preventing Serbia's becoming a danger to Montenegrin independence. See G. P. Gooch and Harold Temperley (eds), *British Documents on the Origins of the War, 1898–1914*, vol. XI, HM Stationery Office, 1926, p. 336.
[7] *Ibid.*
[8] *Ibid.*, p. 167.
[9] De Salis to Grey, 24 March 1916, PRO, FO 371/2711, p. 1.

of popular opinion, ordered the general mobilisation of the Montenegrin army. On 1 August the Montenegrin *Skupština* (assembly), ·galvanised into action by the news of Russia's general mobilisation the previous day, passed a resolution calling for Montenegro to fight alongside Serbia. On 5 August diplomatic relations with Austria-Hungary were broken off, and two days later Montenegro was officially at war. With a combination of trite aphorism and prescience, Nikola told the departing Austro-Hungarian military attaché: 'God is my witness that I never willed the war, for I know what is at stake. Destiny fulfils itself; it is stronger than the human will.'[10]

Despite the drain on its resources of manpower and munitions during the Balkan Wars, Montenegro managed to mobilise some 47,000 soldiers whose numbers were increased to 50,000 by the return of some citizens from abroad.[11] Although Nikola remained titular commander-in-chief, a Serbian general Božidar Janković was appointed chief of the general staff with his headquarters in Cetinje and other Serbian officers were placed in key positions. Nikola could not openly oppose this decision since it had the backing of Russia as well as considerable popular support, but he was unhappy with a move he saw as limiting his forces' capacity to act independently as well as his own ability to make territorial claims in the event of an overall victory by the Allied forces.

Serbia and Montenegro at war

Realistically, however, the general picture was hardly encouraging. The odds stacked against the two Slav states in the war against Austria-Hungary could hardly have been higher: together the populations of Serbia and Montenegro amounted to no more than 4.75 million, while they faced an adversary with a population of some 52 million. At the outbreak of war the Russian military mission, which had been withdrawn in displeasure at Montenegro's conduct in initiating the First Balkan War without prior Russian approval, had still not returned to Cetinje. Instead the Russians backed the despatch of a Serbian military mission under General Janković.

[10] Treadway, *The Falcon and the Eagle*, p. 199.
[11] Rastoder, 'A Short Review of the History of Montenegro', p. 126.

With a Serbian general now in command, Montenegro's army was deployed in a way that afforded maximum support to Serbia. It was divided into four divisions with the greatest concentration of forces along the frontier with Hercegovina, while a smaller number of battalions were stationed around Pljevlja in the Sandžak, and along the frontier with Albania. Early on Montenegrin forces occupied the coastal land around Budva, but were forced to yield Pljevlja to the Austro-Hungarian army. By mid-August 1914, however, the impressive victory of the Serbian army at Cer in north-western Serbia—the Entente's first victory—had reversed the situation, forcing the Austrians to pull back across the Sava and Drina rivers, abandoning not just north-western Serbia but also the Sandžak, including Pljevlja.

Instructed by their Russian allies to relieve the pressure they were experiencing on the Galician front, Serbian forces then pushed on into Bosnia, while the Montenegrins advanced in support as far as Pale and Jahorina, within sight of the Bosnian capital, Sarajevo.[12] Serbian and Austro-Hungarian forces clashed again at Mačkov Karmen in early September with both sides suffering heavy casualties. But while the Austrian General Potiorek was able to call up massive reinforcements, the Serbian army could at this stage do nothing to compensate for casualties suffered at Cer,[13] a situation made still more acute by the overall lack of supplies and ammunition. In the crisis Belgrade had to be abandoned. Threatened with total collapse, Serbia's position was only saved by the arrival of fresh troops and ammunition via the port of Salonika. Recognising that the enemy forces were spread too thinly, the Serbian commander General Mišić counter-attacked across the Kolubara river in central Serbia to win his country's second great victory of the war. Belgrade was re-taken, leaving Serbia to experience a period of respite before the tables were again turned as Bulgaria, enticed by promises from the Central Powers to restore land lost to Serbia after the Treaty of Bucharest,

---

[12] See Vladimir Dedijer, Ivan Božić, Sima Ćirković and Milorad Ekmečić (eds), *History of Yugoslavia*, New York: McGraw-Hill, 1974, p. 476 (trans. by Kordija Kveder from the Serbo-Croatian, *Istorija Jugoslavije*, 1972).

[13] Austrian losses of some 6,000–10,000 killed and 30,000 wounded exceeded Serbian deaths estimated at between 3,000–5,000 dead and over 15,000 wounded. (Glenny, *The Balkans*, p. 316.)

followed the example set earlier by Turkey and, in the autumn of 1915, entered the war.

Meanwhile the Montenegrin forces that had entered Bosnia in support of the Serbian offensive had had much less success. In late October 1914 they were defeated at Glasinac in Hercegovina and thereupon withdrew to the right bank of the Drina. Although Montenegrins subsequently participated in the Serbian offensive to drive the Austrians back across the Drina, diplomatic reports of the time question the degree of support shown by them to their Serbian allies in the ensuing battles in Bosnia and Hercegovina.[14] In reality Nikola appreciated the threat posed to his kingdom and dynasty by a Serbian victory, and saw the European powers' involvement in the wider war as offering him a chance to improve his own and Montenegro's chance of survival through territorial expansion into Albania. He therefore ignored a number of warnings from Britain and Russia[15] not to attack Albania at a time when the conflict demanded an all-out campaign against Austria–Hungary, and his government concocted a series of grievances against Albania designed to open the way for their recapture of Scutari. Nikola, backed by a chorus of ministers, continued to offer assurances to the Allies, as Montenegrin troops took up position around Scutari, prompting the surrender of the frightened inhabitants.[16] On 27 June 1915 they entered the town, coolly informing the Allies that they had done so at the inhabitants' request 'to restore order'.[17]

As Nikola had surmised, the Allies in response were not in a position to do more than issue a collective note stating their refusal to recognise Montenegro's occupation of Scutari. The Serbian General Janković, who had strongly opposed the Montenegrin action,

[14] De Salis to Grey, March 24, 1916, PRO, FO 371/2711, p. 9.

[15] France's attitude was more ambiguous. Intent on gaining concessions for projects which included road-building and other public works in Scutari and Montenegro, the French representative in Cetinje did not join the chorus warning Nikola against attempting to recapture the city. (See De Salis to Grey, 24 March 1916, PRO, FO 371/2711, p. 18.)

[16] Colonel Philips, commanding the British detachment to Scutari and Alessio, had withdrawn in response to orders at the end of July 1914 immediately after the Austro-Hungarian declaration of war on Serbia. (*British Documents on the Origins of the War*, vol. XI: *The Outbreak of War*, p. 196.)

[17] *Ibid.*, p. 197.

resigned his command and returned to Serbia on the orders of the Serbian Prime Minister, Pašić. He was succeeded by another Serb, Colonel Petar Pešić, who, arriving in Montenegro having been made aware of the population's support for the capture of Scutari, argued against confronting Nikola over this issue. He added in a revealing coda: 'Should our [Serbian] interests demand that Montenegro be brought into a hopeless situation, it would be better to use another pretext and not the issue of Skadar [Scutari].'[18] Despite an undertaking to its allies, Montenegro continued the campaign in northern Albania throughout June and into July with a view to defeating the local Malissori tribesmen and consolidating possession of all the land as far south as the River Drin. However, by late summer the offensive had stalled and a truce was concluded, leaving the Montenegrins in uneasy occupation of Scutari and the surrounding valleys but unable to dislodge the Malissori from their strongholds in the high mountains.

Meanwhile the balance of forces in the wider war had been changed dramatically, first by Italy's engagement on the side of the Entente in May 1915, secured by the promise of territory which included South Tyrol, Trentino and Trieste and a substantial part of the Adriatic coast, and subsequently by Bulgaria's decision in October 1915 to enter the war on the side of the Central Powers. That this had taken so long was partly due to a division in public opinion. The opposition, wooed by the Allies and sensitive to the country's war-weary state, were at least initially opposed to Bulgaria's engagement, but finally King Ferdinand and the Prime Minister Vasil Radoslavov yielded to the blandishments of the Central Powers, who promised to restore the territory in Macedonia lost in the Second Balkan War, as well as granting additional territory in Thrace. Clearly the Allies' support for Serbia ruled out their offering Bulgaria the same inducement of Serb-held territory in Macedonia, and this, added to the fact that the Central Powers appeared to be winning at this stage, clinched Bulgaria's decision in their favour and, through it, Serbia's fate in the war.[19]

[18] Quoted by Banac, *The National Question*, p. 282.
[19] See R.J. Crampton, *History of Bulgaria*, pp. 140–3. By this stage the Italian offensive had stalled and the Allies had failed in their attempt to capture the Dardanelles and link up with Russia. Germany had taken Poland and Lithuania and part of Belorussia.

At a stroke Bulgaria's action tightened the noose around Serbia, which had previously faced the Austro-Hungarians to the north but now, cut off from re-supply by sea to the south, was in a parlous situation. On top of this Serbia was also suffering the ravages of a typhus epidemic which broke out in late 1914 and by the summer of 1915 had infected over half a million people.[20] With events conspiring so much in their favour, the Central Powers had no intention of experiencing the humiliation of further reverses at the hands of the small Slav states. Germany, some of whose own soldiers now formed part of an expanded joint force, insisted that command be entrusted to the highly capable Field-Marshal von Mackensen, who almost immediately set about bombarding Belgrade.

Serbs and Montenegrins in retreat

The Serbian capital fell within less than three days and the Serbian army began to pull back to the south in the direction of the cities of Kragujevac and Niš. Within a week the Bulgarian army was advancing across Macedonia and into southern Serbia to attack the Serbian army from the rear, and a few days later on 22 October Austro-Hungarian troops launched an offensive from Dalmatia against Montenegro. In spite of facing encirclement and annihilation, the Serbian government and high command decided against surrender and chose instead to lead the army and much of the civilian population on an epic journey of retreat into the Sandžak and thence through Montenegro or Kosovo to the Albanian coast.

Accompanied by the seventy-six-year-old King Petar and the severely asthmatic Field-Marshal Putnik, who had to be carried in a litter because of his inability to mount a horse, part of the retreating Serbian army took the direct route from Prizren across the Shala mountains to Scutari. Meanwhile other remnants of the army were retreating by way of the perilous Čakor pass across the Accursed (*Prokletije*) mountains through Andrijevica and Kolašin in Montenegro to the coast. With them went the relics of the thirteenth-century Serbian King Stefan (the First-Crowned) to be placed for safe-keeping in Ostrog monastery, and a vast straggling multitude of civilians over cart and sheep tracks which soon degenerated into a

[20] Dedijer *et al.*, *History of Yugoslavia*, p. 484.

sea of mud.[21] Milovan Djilas, then a small child, recalled some of the Serbian soldiers passing through the wooded hills near his family home 'four hours downstream' from Kolašin:

> The news had spread of their dying along the roadside of hunger and fatigue, each dead man with a coin placed in his mouth… There was little bread, and some who had gave none, nor could it be bought at any price. It seems as though our people pitied the Serbians more than they helped them. They did not even help as much as they were able. The Serbians passed through Montenegro as through a foreign land, savage and soulless.[22]

The battle of Mojkovac

Perhaps local peasants could have done more to help, but for the most part, and often in defiance of orders emanating from Nikola and the government in Cetinje, Montenegrin forces valiantly defended the line of Serbian retreat, fighting along the Drina and Lim rivers where they saved many Serbians at the cost of Montenegrin lives.[23] Here, on the eastern front at Mojkovac above the Tara river in January 1916, Montenegrin soldiers fought the most costly battle of the war as they struggled to protect the retreating Serbs from all-out assault by the 47th division of the Third Austro-Hungarian army. From the outset the imbalance of forces appeared to make an Austro-Hungarian victory a near-certainty: the Montenegrins, under General Vukotić, had a force of 6,500 men; the vastly better-equipped Austro-Hungarian force, commanded by the Austrian General Wilhelm von Rendel, some 14,000. With the odds stacked against them and in sub-zero blizzard conditions the Montenegrins struggled to defend positions that were vital to their line of defence. Slowly the combination of mountainous and heavily forested terrain and appalling weather turned the battle in the Montenegrins' favour since the soldiers, unable to fire their weapons, were forced to engage in ferocious close combat.[24] But when the Montenegrins eventually prevailed they were astonished to receive

---

[21] G. Gordon-Smith, *Through the Serbian Campaign: The Great Retreat of the Serbian Army*, London, 1916, p. 157.

[22] Djilas, *Land without Justice*, pp. 44–5.

[23] De Salis to Grey, 24 March 1916, PRO, FO 371/2711, p. 9.

[24] Šćekić, *Travelling through Montenegro*, p. 203.

orders not to pursue the enemy in order to consolidate the victory. Thrown into confusion, a few Montenegrin soldiers set off in the wake of the retreating Serbian army but most simply returned to their villages or took to the hills from where they would later take part in the resistance against the Austrian occupation.

Devastating as it was, the Serbs' long march across the mountains of Albania and into exile on Corfu allowed the Serbian leadership to avoid surrender and ultimately made it possible for Serbs, marching from Salonika with Allied support, to play an active part in their country's liberation.[25] By contrast Montenegro's situation at the beginning of 1916 was one of great confusion in which events, though tragic, permitted neither the myth-making nor the eventual triumphant return that partly compensated the Serbs for their suffering. In this respect the battle of Mojkovac, though frequently portrayed as exemplifying Montenegrin selflessness in the Serb cause, did not in fact play as important a part in saving Serbian lives as earlier encounters with the Austro-Hungarian forces had done. Indeed, by the time the battle was fought, most Serbian soldiers had already crossed into northern Albania and were battling their way down the coast between Scutari and Durazzo, the city now known as Durrës.[26] Nor did it have any influence on the overall course of affairs since, as the bitterly disappointed Montenegrin combatants discovered, the battle was being fought at the very time that Nikola and his government were in the throes of negotiating surrender.

The loss of Mount Lovćen

What had happened is difficult to piece together since the chain of events is far from clear, leading to differing views on how blame should be apportioned. Obviously Montenegro could not resist long on its own once Serbia had fallen, and thus from October 1915, when the Austro-Hungarian army launched its offensive in Bosnia, Montenegrin troops, concentrated on the eastern frontier as ordered by the Serbian high command, had begun to pull back in tandem with Serbian forces. But while Cetinje supported and indeed

---

[25] Of the 350,000–400,000 who set out, more than 240,000 died or were captured during the retreat. See Pavlowitch, *Serbia: The History behind the Name*, p. 97.

[26] Djilas, *Land without Justice*, p. 162.

ordered the withdrawal, some local commanders continued, as we have seen, to provide strong support to the retreating Serbian forces.

In the middle of November the Allies obtained reports suggesting that the Austrians were preparing to attack from the coast, presumably with the object of capturing Mount Lovćen. Despite this Colonel Pešić, the Serbian chief of staff, did not consider that it was necessary to bring in reinforcements to strengthen the defences of either the mountain or the coast road from Kotor to the town of Budva, which the Montenegrins still held. Instead the main part of the Montenegrin army remained in the north between the mouth of the Piva river and Čakor,[27] while Serbian troops, which still at this stage could have been made available to reinforce the defences of Lovćen and the coastal region, were not deployed.[28]

On 7 January the Austrians began firing on the Montenegrin defenders on Lovćen from their forts in Kotor. On the night of the 9th they occupied the summits of Kuk and Krstac, which had previously been evacuated by Prince Petar and the Montenegrins. Budva too was speedily evacuated. In both cases the Montenegrins surrendered almost immediately, having taken no more than a few casualties.[29]

Montenegro sues for peace

The surrender of Lovćen opened the way to Cetinje. In the early hours of 11 January the king left his capital soon followed by members of the diplomatic corps. On 13 January Nikola himself sent a telegram offering a truce to the Emperor Franz Joseph, while two government ministers conveyed in person the same offer to the Austro-Hungarian general, Weber von Webenau. Discussions continued over a few days with Nikola refusing to sign the formal surrender demanded by the Austrians so long as this included an undertaking to hand over those Serbian soldiers who remained on Montenegrin territory. While Nikola stalled, the Austrians continued their advance towards the Bojana river, threatening—in conjunction with the Bulgarians, who were continuing their march

[27] Rastoder, 'A Short Review of the History of Montenegro', p. 127.
[28] De Salis to Grey, March 24, 1916, PRO, FO 371/2711, p. 9.
[29] *Ibid.*, p. 11.

northwards up the Albanian coast from Puka—to cut off the Montenegrins' escape route from the Albanian port on the gulf of San
Giovanni di Medua (Shëngjin) south of Scutari. Pressed from north
and south, Nikola and a small retinue finally left Montenegro on
19 January for Scutari and thence for Italy, without signing a formal
surrender. What remained of the Montenegrin army was assigned to
the control of General Vukotić, who despite being Queen Milena's
cousin favoured union with Serbia. Petar Pešić and the remaining
Serbian forces had left the country the day before. A week later, with
the Montenegrin government and army mired in confusion, General
Vukotić finally signed an instrument of capitulation[30] and the government of the country was taken over by the commander of the
Austro-Hungarian Third Army, Herman von Kövess, who was succeeded on 26 February by General Weber himself.

How fully were Nikola and his close circle to blame for Montenegro's surrender? Later his political opponents attributed both
the surrender and the events leading up to it to the Petrović's pre-
arranged treachery, claiming that both princes, Petar and Danilo, in
the belief that the Central Powers would emerge as victors from the
war, had for some time been involved in secret negotiations with
their representatives.[31] Evidence available at the time suggests that
these accusations were well-founded.[32] Danilo's pro-Austrian incli-
nations had long been known and, in the course of 1915 a number of
legations had become aware of frequent communications between
Prince Petar and the Austrian military commander in Budva, a Major
Lompar.[33] The lack of concern shown by the king and his close circle in the face of the Austrian advance across the Danube was equally
suggestive of some form of prior collusion.[34] Subsequently both
Nikola and his prime minister, Lazar Mijušković, attempted to justify the decision to yield Lovćen without a struggle by suggesting
that the Montenegrin defenders were starving and by exaggerating

---

[30] Rastoder, 'A Short Review of the History of Montenegro', p. 127.
[31] See for example the document entitled 'The Question of Montenegro', prepared and presented by Andrije Radović, Radovan Bosković and Janko Vukotić,
Paris, 1919, p. 9.
[32] De Salis to Grey, 24 March 1916, PRO, FO 371/2711, pp. 8–11.
[33] *Ibid*.
[34] Palairet, 'The Culture of Economic Stagnation in Montenegro', pp. 17–42.

the number of their casualties. But their statements in no way accorded with the accounts given by French officers stationed nearby at Njeguši, who instead described the Montenegrins as simply abandoning their posts when they received news that peace had been agreed.[35]

But if Nikola and his close family acted dishonourably, the Serbian high command appears also to have been playing a double game. How else can one explain the fact that, given the strategic importance of Mount Lovćen and foreknowledge of Austrian intentions, the Serbian commander Colonel Pešić took so sanguine a view of its defences?[36] As the historian Ivo Banac has pointed out, the Serbian authorities needed to ensure Montenegro's surrender on less than honourable terms in order to prevent the Petrović dynasty from benefiting from Serbia's own defeat. Such an interpretation is supported by Pešić's comments in which the Serbian general takes credit for his own part in securing King Nikola's disgrace:

Did [my critics] stop to think of the situation that our whole people would have had to face had not King Nikola sent that *dépêche*[37] to Franz Joseph, and that in addition to the Serbian supreme command we also had the Montenegrin supreme staff at the Salonika front, and that upon the breach of that front and entrance to the Fatherland—besides King Petar there was also King Nikola?[38]

Djilas, whose own father was strongly opposed to the policies of King Nikola, was later convinced of the spoiling role played by the Serbian authorities:

There was another reason for the shameful unmilitary fall of the Montenegrin army. This was the sinister and moot role of the Serbian gov-

---

[35] *Ibid.*

[36] De Salis wrote: 'Colonel Peshitch, the Serbian chief of staff of the Montenegrin army continued to think that for various reasons, and especially on account of the relatively small number of troops at the disposal of the enemy, Montenegro was not for the moment threatened, while he considered the arrangements he had made were quite sufficient to secure both the Lovtchen positions and the coast-road from Cattaro to the town of Budua in possession of the Montenegrins. Colonel Peshitch insisted more than once that adequate steps had been taken, though he did not carry out a plan of placing a division of Serbian troops behind the Montenegrin lines at Budua.' (*Ibid.*, p. 9.)

[37] That is, the telegram asking for peace. See below.

[38] Banac, *The National Question*, p. 282.

ernment. This government, and its representative in the Montenegrin high command, Colonel Petar Pešić, not only did nothing to overcome the pusillanimity of the Montenegrin leaders, whose whole policy, in both war and peace, had already boiled down to the bare preservation of power, but they encouraged it. It was the Serbian government that saw to it that the Montenegrin army did not retreat with the Serbian [army], to make sure that at the end of the war there would not be two armies and two dynasties, which would have complicated, and perhaps made impossible, the estab- lishment of a united state. Resentment against the Serbians, [our] brethren, remained long after, bitter and deep.[39]

As both Pešić and Djilas make plain, Nikola was censured for not ensuring that the Montenegrin army retreated with the Serbians. His failure to join his son-in-law Petar Karadjordjević and grandson Aleksandar in Corfu was likewise a cause for criticism. But his decision not to do so was understandable in the light of the very poor relations that existed between him and the Serbian prime minister-in-exile in Corfu, Nikola Pašić. In 1916 Pašić, already seventy-two years old, remained a force to be reckoned with. From the beginning of the war he had made clear his post-war goal of a unitary state, comprising in the first instance Serbia, Montenegro and Bosnia–Hercegovina, although he was also prepared to accept a Yugoslavia which included Slovenes and Croats provided it was on his terms—in reality an extension of the kingdom of Serbia.[40] Nikola, on the basis of past experience, was already only too well aware of the Serbian prime minister's expansionist ambitions. On the small island of Corfu he would have come under extraordinary pressure to accept Pašić's policies, a step he not unreasonably wished to resist. Instead Nikola's objective for the remainder of the war was to try to keep the Allies to their pre-war promise of restoring the independence of small states—Serbia, Belgium and Montenegro (the last-named, of course, under the Petrović dynasty).

Nikola's government-in-exile

With this goal in mind Nikola set about forming a government-in- exile, first in Bordeaux where he had gone shortly after reaching

[39] Djilas, *Land Without Justice*, pp. 163–4.
[40] Glenny, *The Balkans*, p. 369.

France at the end of January, and later in Neuilly-sur-Seine outside Paris. Although there were successes—recognition of his government-in-exile by the governments of France, Russia, Britain, Italy and Serbia and the negotiation of a subvention from the Allies—disagreements among the exiles undermined what was already a weak position, playing into the hands of Nikola's political opponents. In particular St Petersburg, although it had recognised Nikola's government, had not convincingly reaffirmed the old ties of friendship between Russia and Montenegro. Dismayed by the king's conduct during the war, the Russian authorities instead determined to keep their distance and hardened their support for the idea of a single state under the Kardjordjević dynasty. Accordingly the Russian subsidy was withdrawn in 1916 when St Petersburg also refused Nikola's request to take refuge in Russia[41]—one decision which, in view of future events, worked in Nikola's favour.

Immediately on arrival in France Nikola reappointed Lazar Mijušković as his prime minister, but jealousies and political disagreements with many of those around the king, in which Mijušković became embroiled, soon led to the latter falling from favour. He was replaced by the more politically adroit Andrije Radović who, despite having been imprisoned by Nikola at the time of the bomb plot, agreed to take on the role of prime minister. Unsurprisingly, however, Radović's agenda differed substantially from Nikola's and he lost no time in advocating his own solution to the dynastic question. As a long-time member of the pro-Serbia camp he had in fact co-ordinated his moves with Pašić, and his proposal was aimed at facilitating the unification of Serbia and Montenegro.[42] In August 1916 Radović proposed that the single throne would be occupied alternately by a Karadjordjević then a Petrović: first Nikola would abdicate in favour of the Prince Regent Aleksandar, who would in turn be succeeded by Nikola's heir Danilo, and so on.[43] Crown Prince Danilo, who had earlier left Montenegro ostensibly on grounds of health, was in favour of the proposal, but his influential sister Ksenija argued strongly against it. Nikola, though at one time

---

[41] Rastoder, 'A Short Review of the History of Montenegro', p. 128.

[42] Banac, *The National Question*, p. 283.

[43] Petrovich, *A History of Modern Serbia*, vol. 2, p. 640.

appearing not to be opposed to the idea, finally, with encouragement from Italy, came out against it. His decision was at best a tactical mistake: Radović resigned and went over openly to the Pašić camp, accepting financial support from the Serbian government-in-exile on Corfu for what was henceforth to become an anti-Petrović campaign.

Backed by Pašić, Radović became the head of the Montenegrin Committee for National Unification, a body founded in Geneva in 1917. As a result Pašic effectively withdrew his recognition of Nikola's government, choosing to treat the entirely biddable Montenegrin Committee as the competent legal authority. With Serbian support the Committee launched a newspaper *Ujedinjenje* (Unification), which from its first issue in April 1917 became a strident voice in favour of Serbian-Montenegrin union.[44] In August the Montenegrin Committee declared itself in favour of the Corfu Declaration of July 1917, which set out the principles governing the creation of a future common state for the South Slavs.[45] In so doing they accepted the Declaration's overall aim of creating a unitary state based on a constitutional monarchy under the Karadjordjević dynasty, thereby assenting to the disappearance of a separate Montenegrin dynasty and to Montenegro's future union with Serbia.[46] Nikola and his supporters had not been consulted.[47]

Radović's *volte face* left Nikola exposed and forced to cast around for another reliable figure to head his government. His first choice, the former minister and old friend Simo Popović, excused himself on the grounds of old age; his second, Simo's namesake Evgenije Popović, another loyal but none-too-enthusiastic recipient of the honour, accepted. But there was no disguising the fact that Nikola, by now seventy-five years old, was becoming increasingly marginalised and isolated even among his own supporters.

[44] Petrovich, *A History of Modern Serbia*, vol. 2, p. 640.
[45] The Declaration stated that the Croats, Serbs and Slovenes were one people; there was no mention of the other Yugoslav peoples—the Macedonians, Albanians, Bosnian Muslims or the Montenegrins. (See Jelavich, *History of the Balkans*, vol. 2, p. 146.)
[46] See the *Report of the Central Europe Department of the Foreign Office*, 18 April 1923, p. 3.
[47] Houston, *Nikola and Milena*, p. 333.

Austrian occupation and resistance

Meanwhile the situation in Montenegro under Austro-Hungarian occupation was rapidly becoming desperate. At first the occupiers did not treat the population with excessive harshness, although they displayed a 'severity accompanied by ... orderliness' that kept people wary and wholly unreconciled to their presence.[48] But as pockets of resistance began to manifest themselves the Austrians increasingly resorted to stronger measures and at times treated the civilian population with considerable brutality.[49]

Ironically the unofficial leader of the resistance was Brigadier-General Radomir Vešović, the man who had been charged with disbanding the Montenegrin army and negotiating terms with the occupying Austro-Hungarian forces after the departure of King Nikola and the internment of Prince Mirko. The prince, who had been left by his father in nominal charge of the country, was already suffering from the tuberculosis which had carried off his two young sons some ten years earlier and was to kill him two years later in Vienna.[50] Even if he had been temperamentally so inclined, he was thus hardly in a position to organise a resistance movement. By contrast Vešović, having failed to reach any satisfactory agreement with the occupiers, was soon involved in what can best be described as a spontaneous resistance movement. Since the army had traditionally been organised on a militia basis, some of the disbanded soldiers chose to take to the hills with their weapons and form *komiti* (guerrilla) bands rather than return in peace to their villages.[51] When an Austrian patrol was sent out to bring in Vešović, the general refused to go quietly, and killed the man sent to arrest him. His action and subsequent escape sparked an upsurge of sympathetic resistance, especially among his Vasojevići kinsmen, and a harsh campaign of reprisals by the Austrians.[52]

[48] Djilas, *Land without Justice*, p. 60.
[49] *Ibid.*
[50] Petrovich, *A History of Modern Serbia*, vol. 2, p. 625. Mirko and Natalija's two eldest children, Stevan and Stanislav, died from tuberculosis in 1908 and 1907 respectively.
[51] See Rastoder, 'A Short Review of the History of Montenegro', p. 127, and www.geocities.com/veldes 1/weber.html, accessed on 4 January 2004.
[52] Djilas, *Land Without Justice*, p. 61. Djilas, however, explains that Vešović later had a change of heart, returned from the woods, and called on others to surrender.

The father of Milovan Djilas was one of the many thousands of those taken prisoner and held in camps by the Austrians, while others who attacked the Austrians directly or committed acts of sabotage were hanged on public gibbets erected in the countryside.[53] To the fear occasioned by the reprisals were added the constant depredations of indigenous guerrillas, some of whom behaved more as bandits, stealing from the local population rather than helping them. As early as 1916 the German press was reporting: 'In Montenegro there is no more bread, no flour, no tobacco, no salt and no oil.'[54] By 1917 famine, never far removed from the lives of ordinary Montenegrins, was becoming an everyday reality.

Defeat of the Central Powers and arrival of the Serbian army

Coming almost on top of the two Balkan Wars, the First World War and occupation by the Central Powers inflicted terrible hardship from which Montenegro would struggle to recover in the neglectful environment of the first Yugoslavia.[55] But in the autumn of 1918 the deadlock which had kept the Allied lines at Salonika almost unchanged from 1916 was finally broken following the victories of the Allies on the Western Front. In September the Allies—duly reinforced and including Greek, Serbian and some Montenegrin troops—launched a successful offensive in Macedonia, and the resulting collapse of Bulgaria brought about the rapid retreat northwards of German and Habsburg troops. As the Central Powers retreated, the Serbian First Army marched north, defeating the

---

[53] Rastoder claims that by 1918 the Austrians had interned some 9,500 'intellectuals and officers'. See 'A Short Review of the History of Montenegro', p. 127.

[54] Houston (quoting Alexander Devine), *Nikola and Milena*, p. 334.

[55] In fact the post-war situation in Montenegro was even worse than in Serbia. According to Rastoder Montenegrin military losses amounted to some 20,000 men. (See Andrijašević and Rastoder, *History of Montenegro*, p. 153.) At the same time many civilians lost their lives through deliberate reprisals, banditry, famine and disease. In 1955 the economic historian Jozo Tomasevich estimated Montenegro's combined loss of population due to the First World War as 51,400, which seems an enormous number in a country whose population at the time was well under 400,000. (*Peasants, Politics and Economic Change in Yugoslavia*, Oxford University Press, 1955, p. 225.)

German divisions at Niš and finally liberating Belgrade on 1 November. On 6 November Austrian troops, prompted both by an upsurge of internal guerrilla activity and the imminent arrival of the Allies, marched out of Cetinje.

In Montenegro the withdrawal of the Austrian forces was followed rapidly by the advance of bands of Serbian irregulars moving north from Macedonia and, shortly afterwards, units of the advancing Serbian army. To these were added French, British and Italian troops who, in line with the decision taken by the Inter-Allied Commission at Versailles, were under the overall command of the French general formerly leading the Allied offensive on the Salonika front, Franchet d'Esperey. The arrangements put in place by the French commander on the spot, General Venel, gave Serbian troops—rapidly reconstituted as 'Yugoslavs'—complete control of the interior of the country, while other Allied forces were largely disposed along the coast.[56] At the same time the French government turned down all of Nikola's requests to return, claiming that the situation in the country was too insecure to allow him to do so safely.[57] The Allies' *de facto* policy was thus in contrast to the formal position by which they continued, though with little enthusiasm, to recognise Nikola and his government as officially in charge of the country. In this their official position remained in line with the principles elaborated in President Wilson's famous 'Fourteen Points' of January 1918, Point 11 of which read:

Romania, Serbia and Montenegro should be evacuated; occupied territories restored; Serbia accorded free and secure access to the sea; and the relations of the several Balkan states to one another determined by friendly counsel along historically established lines of allegiance and nationality; and international guarantees of the political and economic independence and territorial integrity of the several Balkan States should be entered upon.[58]

---

[56] *Ibid.*

[57] Petrovich, *A History of Modern Serbia*, vol. 2, p. 663. Petrovich further points out that Pašić had already made arrangements with the Serbian high command to ensure that Serbian forces would enter Montenegro before the return of King Nikola. (*Ibid.*, p. 640.)

[58] Quoted in Petrovich, *ibid.*, p. 653. In fact, as Petrovich indicates, the British prime minister David Lloyd George had similarly affirmed Britain's commit-

The Podgorica Assembly

The political vacuum left in Montenegro by the Austrians' departure was filled by the appointment of a National Council[59] whose membership and organisation owed much to Lieut.-Colonel Dušan Simović, a representative of the Serbian High Command and leading advocate of Pašić's centralised Serb-dominated state.[60] As soon as it was appointed the Council announced its intention of uniting Montenegro and Serbia. Meanwhile members of a second body, the Provisional Central Executive Committee, in fact an arm of Radović's Montenegrin Committee, moved into action overseeing both the setting up of local centres of government and the organisation of elections for a Grand National Assembly, intended to pronounce definitively upon the future of Montenegro. Significantly the Assembly was to take place in Podgorica, away from Cetinje and the tribes of Old Montenegro with their long history of support for Montenegrin independence. Ballot papers were distributed: green for those supporting the continuation of an independent Montenegro and white for those in favour of unification with Serbia.

Elections for the delegates to the Podgorica Assembly took place over two weeks in mid-November with the opposing parties taking their names from the colour of their ballots—the Greens or *zelenaši*, corresponding roughly to the old *pravaši*, and the Whites or *bjelaši*, approximately equivalent to the former *klubaši*.[61] With the Serbian army in control of the countryside and Radović's Montenegrin Committee actively engaged on the ground, the result—victory for the Whites, whose candidates gained almost the totality of the votes—was never in doubt. Nor, given the composition of the Assembly, could there be any uncertainty about the outcome of the

---

ment to the restoration of both Serbia and Montenegro in a speech he made three days earlier to the trade unions outlining the country's war aims. (*Ibid.*, p. 652.)

[59] The three members of this committee were Svetozar Tomić, an official from the Ministry of Public Instruction in Belgrade, Pierre Kosović, a high school teacher, and Janko Spassojević, of whom only the last was a Montenegrin. (See 'Report by the Count de Salis on Montenegro', 21 August 1919, PRO, FO 608/46.)

[60] Petrovich, *A History of Modern Serbia*, vol. 2, pp. 672–4 and 678.

[61] However both sides contained a range of political opinion. See below.

322   *From the First World War to Loss of Statehood*

deliberations of its 168 members[62] when they were summoned to meet on 24 November. Within two days the Assembly had proclaimed the deposition of King Nikola and the unification of Serbia and Montenegro under the Kardjordjević dynasty. The accompanying resolutions passed by 163 representatives—five, pleading illness, did not participate—endorsed the establishment of an Executive Committee to administer Montenegro until the arrangements for the union could be brought to a conclusion. A twelve-member delegation was sent to Belgrade under the leadership of Archbishop Gabriel Dožić of the Montenegrin Orthodox Church,[63] and there the Montenegrins were joined by delegates from the National Council representing Croats, Slovenes and Serbs from Slav lands formerly ruled by Austria-Hungary. Driven by growing anxiety over Italian military advances in Istria, coupled with the need to secure a recognised 'Yugoslav' seat at the Peace Conference, the National Council yielded to Belgrade's demand for a speedy conclusion to the process of creating the new state. On 1 December 1918 Prince-Regent Aleksandar proclaimed the new Kingdom of Serbs, Croats and Slovenes (*Kraljevstvo Srba, Hrvata i Slovenaca* or SHS). Montenegrins received no mention. Instead their National Executive handed over authority to the new state, declaring: 'Montenegro enters into its new fatherland not only as a pure Serbian land, but purified of all dark and criminal elements.'[64] The reference to Nikola and his court could not be misunderstood.[65]

Nearly nine decades later, the Podgorica Assembly remained a subject of contention for supporters and opponents of an independent Montenegro. For supporters it was an illegal assembly not approved by the 1905 Montenegrin Constitution or by the regular *Skupština*.[66] By contrast, opponents discounted the 1905 Consti-

[62] The original number of members—168—was subsequently increased to 176. (See 'Report' by Count de Salis on Montenegro, of 21 August 1919, PRO, FO 608/46, p. 5.)
[63] Petrovich, *A History of Modern Serbia*, vol. 2, p. 679.
[64] Quoted by Leadbetter, 'The End of Montenegro', p. 61.
[65] *Ibid.*
[66] As these supporters of Montenegrin independence point out, Article 36 of the 1905 Constitution specifically prohibited the division or secession of all or any part of Montenegro without the agreement of the ruler and the People's

tution which they saw as having been imposed by an autocratic ruler, and argued that the exceptional situation caused by war and occupation more than justified the different procedures undertaken by the Assembly.[67] Yet even leaving aside the question of the Assembly's legality, there are solid grounds for believing it to be an unrepresentative body whose role was to affix its imprimatur to the decision on unification which, since it was demanded by the Serbian authorities and indeed by a part of Montenegro's population, was to be imposed on all without further consultation or delay.[68]

To begin with, the elections were organised with such speed that some of the more inaccessible communities were unaware that they were taking place until they were over. An American intelligence officer, formerly an adviser to President Wilson, spoke of them as being 'railroaded through'.[69] At the same time a number of would-be voters—mainly officers returning from internment in Hungary—were prevented from voting until it was too late. Added to this was the proximity of Serbian troops and, more threateningly, of armed bands under the control of Kosta Pećanac, a man already

---

Assembly. See Srdja Pavlović, 'The Podgorica Assembly in 1918: Notes on the Yugoslav Historiography (1919–1979) about the Unification of Montenegro and Serbia', *Canadian Slavonic Papers*, vol. XLI, no. 2 (June 1999), p. 173.

[67] *Ibid.*

[68] See, for example, Ivo Lederer who writes: 'There is of course no question that Serbian agents did indeed enter Montenegro in October and November 1918 to spread unionist propaganda and that Serbian influence was exerted in the Podgorica Assembly.' However, he goes on to stress that pro-Serbian Montenegrins played a still larger role in promoting the unionist cause. (*Yugoslavia at the Paris Peace Conference: A Study in Frontiermaking*, New Haven, 1963, p. 114.) A number of recently published documents also back up claims that considerable sums of Serbian money were devoted to bribing candidates. (See Pavlović, 'The Podgorica Assembly in 1918', p. 161.)

[69] Comments by Major Furlong quoted by de Salis ('Memorandum respecting the Incorporation of Montenegro in the Jugoslav Kingdom', 18 April 1923, PRO, FO 371/8903.)

On Major Furlong's mission, see Wayne Vucinich, 'An American View of Conditions in Montenegro 1918–1919', *Balkania (Annuaire de l'Institut Balkanique)*, Belgrade (1982–3), vols XIII–XIV. A second report, by a Captain Brodie, sent out in connection with a special mission to Albania in January 1919, reported that his informants had described the Podgorica Assembly as 'a farce' (PRO, FO 371/8903).

known in Macedonia as a forceful propagandist in the Serbian cause.[70] When it came to the Assembly itself, there were further questions over the conduct of proceedings. One account, purporting to be by an eye-witness, read as follows:

They smoked, talked, shouted as in a café. There was no voting; the resolutions were declared to be carried by unanimity. Anyone who attempted to object was howled down. Objections were raised that members, even those from Cetinje itself, were not the persons elected. But no hearing could be obtained. Some Albanians were sent forcibly to represent the country of Ipek [Peć], but they protested in vain that they had no wish to take part in the proceedings. All this was under the shadow of the bayonet.[71]

The Christmas rising

One of the Assembly's first acts was to order the confiscation of Petrović property, while at the same time forbidding members of the family to return to Montenegro. The move was designed to cut off both financial and moral support to political opponents. Despite this, a growing resistance movement soon emerged whose supporters included, besides a dwindling band of Petrović loyalists, a body of Montenegrins opposed to what they saw as an act of outright annexation. Preparations for an uprising against the new authorities began almost immediately and came to a head with a rising on the eve of the Orthodox Christmas in 1918.

The date, recalling the 'Montenegrin vespers' of 1702, had been chosen for its symbolic significance, since the organisers, aware that they could not realistically expect a military victory, hoped nonetheless to dramatise Montenegro's situation and thus bring it to the attention of the Allies who were already gathering in Paris for the Peace Conference. The chief instigator of the rebellion was Jovan Plamenac, an ambitious but somewhat erratic character who was later to serve as the last prime minister of Nikola's government-in-exile. With a rebel force composed mainly of tribesmen from Old Montenegro, the Greens launched a determined assault to oust the

---

[70] Pećanac became a Chetnik leader during the Second World War when he collaborated with the Germans. He was subsequently caught and shot by rival Chetniks under the command of Draža Mihailović.

[71] 'Report' by Count de Salis on Montenegro of 21 August 1919, PRO, FO 608/46.

White defenders from the capital.[72] The Whites, though fewer in number, had the advantage of better weaponry and the assurance of further support on the way from more distant tribes in favour of union with Serbia. As the risk of wider conflict escalated, General Venel, still in overall command of Montenegro, travelled to Cetinje to impose a separation of forces. By this stage those killed on both sides numbered 20–30 with many more wounded, but the attempt by the Greens to break into the town had failed. Seeking to pacify the situation, Venel allowed those insurgents prepared to lay down their arms to return to their homes. Some took advantage of the offer but others fled to the hills or placed themselves under Italian protection either at San Giovanni di Medua (Shëngjin) in Albania or, like Plamenac, in Italy itself.[73]

Despite the exodus sporadic guerrilla action continued, prompting the reinforcement of the Serbian troops,[74] who proceeded to carry out harsh reprisals—the French military authorities took no restraining action. Although both sides perpetrated outrages—plundering, burning and raping—the superior fire-power and strength of the Whites inevitably meant that the Greens and their alleged supporters bore the brunt of the suffering. Worse still, while the majority of Whites lived in the towns and of Greens in the small villages and the countryside, the conflict divided tribe from tribe, at times cutting through clan and family loyalties and opening divisions that would outlive the new Yugoslav state itself. Djilas's memoirs convey something of the confusion and the turmoil of the times when his own father, no royalist but opposed to unification on

[72] Earlier the Greens had briefly occupied Rijeka Crnojevica and Virpazar and attempted to besiege Nikšić as well as attacking Cetinje. (See Rastoder, 'A Short Review of the History of Montenegro', pp. 130–1, and Banac, *The National Question*, p. 286.)

[73] Rastoder, 'A Short Review of the History of Montenegro', p. 131. The Italians had occupied Bar since capturing it in October 1915, a fact that enabled many of the Greens to make their escape from Montenegro on board Italian vessels.

[74] See the 'Memorandum respecting the Incorporation of Montenegro in the Jugoslav Kingdom' 18 April 1923. PRO, FO 371/8009. Pro-unification forces operating inside Montenegro were termed 'Yugoslav' following Prince Regent Aleksandar Karadjordjević's proclamation of the Kingdom of the Serbs, Croats and Slovenes on 1 December 1918. However, as de Salis noted in early 1919, the fact that all the soldiers occupying Cetinje during his visit attended Orthodox church services made it 'seem evident that all of them are Serbs of one country or another'. (See de Salis's 'Report' of 21 August 1919, p. 4.)

terms which he saw as humiliating to Montenegro, found himself obliged by circumstances to enlist on the side of the authorities.[75] Djilas describes his father's involvement in the suppression of a rebellion by the Rovči who refused to recognise the new Serbian authorities, preferring instead to be governed by their own traditions and rules. When a patrol of gendarmes sent into Rovci territory was attacked and some killed, the army was sent in with devastating consequences:

Their houses were burned down; they were pillaged and beaten. The women had cats sewn in their skirts and the cats were beaten with rods. The soldiers mounted astride the backs of old men and forced them to carry them across the stream. They attacked the girls. Property and honour and the past—all this was trampled upon.[76]

At a gathering held near Nikšić in mid-1919 the rebels, meeting to discuss tactics, decided to continue the military campaign.[77] The number of insurgents was probably at this stage no more than 1,000, fewer certainly than in earlier days since a proportion of those who had fled after the failure of the 'Christmas rising' had reassembled, with Italian backing, in Gaeta on the coast between Rome and Naples and at camps in different parts of the Italian mainland, from where they launched several small unsuccessful incursions into Montenegro. What is more difficult to determine is what proportion of the broader population opposed Montenegro's incorporation in Serbia, whether they did so for doctrinal reasons—loyalty to the monarchy or because they wished to preserve Montenegro's identity or autonomy, perhaps within a larger Yugoslavia—or simply because they resented the hasty and coercive manner in which the union with Serbia had been enacted. Djilas, for example, claims that at first a majority of the population, though for very disparate reasons, were opposed to the new regime.[78] Ivo Banac too sees the Greens at that time as having the passive support of the larger part of the population. Their failure to mobilise more active support stemmed from organisational weakness and the lack of an underlying unity of purpose. As a result they succeeding only in provoking reprisals,

[75] Djilas, *Land Without Justice*, p. 89.
[76] *Ibid.*, p. 97.
[77] Banac, *The National Question*, p. 287.
[78] Djilas, *Land Without Justice*, p. 93.

'which grew into wholesale political terror'.[79] In support Banac quotes the observation of one official report on the attitude of the population around Cetinje of January 1920: 'Today, in this district, the overwhelming majority of people, from children to old men, except for a third of the townspeople, are opposed to the [established] order.'[80] But Cetinje was a notorious stronghold of loyalism and support for Montenegrin independence; elsewhere in the country the situation was notably different.

Although the insurgents had failed to hold any of the main towns, the unrest did have the effect of drawing outside attention to the situation in Montenegro. From France Nikola, who was held at least partly responsible for the uprising and was thus under pressure, sent a letter to the rebels urging them to return home and keep the peace. In return he was able to secure an undertaking from the Allies promising that the Montenegrin people should be given the opportunity to make a free and independent choice regarding the future status of their country. But Nikola's message, calling for the rebels to lay down their arms in return for the promise of future elections, did not get through to the people in its intended form after he had entrusted it to his cousin Božo Petrović. Božo was himself associated with the rebels, giving General Venel the excuse simply to throw the message away and arrest the messenger.[81] The king's call for the rebels to cease their campaign was then widely broadcast without any reference to his demand for elections, leaving many in Montenegro with the impression that he was seeking nothing but their surrender.[82]

The international context

Where the Allies were concerned, however, Nikola did not lose any opportunity of reminding them of letters from both US President

---

[79] Banac, *The National Question*, p. 286.
[80] *Ibid.*, p. 287.
[81] Nebojša Čagorović, 'The Empty Chair: Montenegro at the Peace Conference', unpubl. MA thesis, King's College London, August 1995. General Venel was subsequently relieved of his duties following a complaint made by Nikola and his government-in-exile about his active interference in the conflict in favour of the authorities in Belgrade. See Srdja Pavlović, 'Myth and Reality among the South Slavs: Montenegro and Serbia in the Creation of the Kingdom of the Serbs, Croats and Slovenes', Ph.D. thesis, Dept of History and Classics, University of Alberta, Edmonton, Canada, 2003.
[82] Houston, *Nikola and Milena*, pp. 341–2.

Woodrow Wilson and the French prime minister Georges Clemenceau promising to respect Montenegro's independence. Clearly such a stance implied Montenegro's participation in the Paris Peace Conference. Yet in the weeks leading up to the opening of the Conference on 18 January 1919, the Allies, divided among themselves and uncertain of the situation on the ground in Montenegro, continued to prevaricate. Notwithstanding the drift of their policy towards full acceptance of the *status quo* in Montenegro, the Allies continued to despatch a series of missions, both military and civilian, over a period which extended from the beginning of 1919 up to the elections for the Constituent Assembly of the Kingdom of the Serbs, Croats and Slovenes (SHS), held in November 1920. The first of these missions, the Inter-Allied Commission, had visited Montenegro in January 1919 and consisted of British, Italian and American representatives, led by the French commander-in-chief, General d'Esperey. The ensuing report recommended unification while advocating the continued deployment of Allied forces in the region, but this latter course was over-ruled when the Allied troops were withdrawn in mid-1919, leaving Montenegro under the control of a Serbian—later renamed Yugoslav—occupation force. By contrast, other missions that followed largely concluded that whatever the economic necessity of Montenegro's union with the new Yugoslavia, its real wishes had not been reflected in the Podgorica Assembly or in the country's forced incorporation into the Kingdom of the Serbs, Croats and Slovenes.[83]

With missions coming and going, the strongest support for a separate seat for Montenegro at the Conference came from Italy, where both family loyalty and Italian self-interest argued in favour of

[83] Such missions included that of Woodrow Wilson's one-time special military advisor, Major Charles Furlong, and of Count de Salis, whose report, written in August 1919, was never published. Although Lord Curzon, Foreign Secretary at the time, told the House of Lords that this was to protect de Salis's informants, it is not hard, given the report's strong criticism of Serbian methods and implied criticism of Allied policy, to discern a less charitable motive. (See de Salis's report of 21 August 1919, PRO, FO 608/46.) Instead the British government sent yet another mission led by the historian and army officer Harold Temperley, which sent a report more to their liking. Temperley found that support for Nikola had substantially diminished, while 'all the intelligentsia in Montenegro, except for those who are on trial for high treason or in the entourage of King Nicholas, are practically unanimous in Serb favour'. (Temperley to Curzon, 12 October 1920, PRO, FO 371/6193.)

continuing Montenegrin independence.[84] At the other extreme was France which, despite continuing to provide shelter for Nikola and his government-in-exile, had both financial and political reasons for taking a strongly pro-Serbian line.[85] In between were the other Entente governments—the United States and Britain; Russia of course was now under Bolshevik rule. But whereas President Wilson, in contrast to his more hard-headed ministers and officials, appeared personally sympathetic,[86] the British prime minister Lloyd George, despite disquieting reports from his officials on Serbian actions in Montenegro, had concluded in private that an independent Montenegro would 'serve no useful purpose'.[87] The result was a fudged decision that in attempting to exculpate the Allies of any blame that could arise over their treatment of Montenegro played squarely into the hands of Pašić and his pro-unification supporters inside the country. Montenegro, the Conference decided, was 'in principle' to be granted one delegate at the Conference, but the rules of designation would 'not be established until such a time when the political situation of that country will be clarified'.[88] In practice this meant leaving the field clear for the three delegates of the proto-Kingdom

---

[84] After the war Italy sought to increase its own territorial gains in Dalmatia as part of a broader ambition to make itself mistress of the Adriatic. As a small state an independent Montenegro would be weaker and more susceptible to Italian influence, thus giving Italy a potential foothold in this strategically important part of the Adriatic while weakening the position of a Serbian or Yugoslav state.

[85] France had close economic and political relations with Serbia in the pre-war period, owning one of the most powerful of the Serbian banks. In addition, the French were keen to see a powerful South Slav state which could act as a check to the expansionist ambitions of both Germany and Italy.

[86] Wilson expressed considerable understanding for the pro-independence view in Montenegro, once remarking: 'The sympathies of the people of the United States are as much with Montenegro as with Serbia.' At the same time the US government was aware of the activities of a particularly strong American-based pressure group, the Montenegrin Committee for National Unity (the MCNU), which took a virulently anti-Petrović and pro-union line. Finding the picture impossibly confused and concerned to make progress on the bigger questions before the Conference, Wilson ultimately failed to follow up his initial sympathy for the advocates of Montenegrin independence with concrete support. (See Ivo J. Lederer, *Yugoslavia at the Peace Conference*, Yale University Press, 1963, pp. 115 ff; Čagorović, 'The Empty Chair'; and Leadbetter, 'The End of Montenegro', p. 56.)

[87] Quoted by Lederer, *ibid.*, pp. 114–15.

[88] *Ibid.*, p. 116.

of the Serbs, Croats and Slovenes who, since the kingdom had not been officially recognised by the time the Peace Conference opened on 18 January 1919, were admitted in the name of Serbia alone.[89] While the Allies prevaricated, Montenegro was represented by an empty gilt chair.[90]

In March reports that Italy was working with Plamenac to facilitate the training of Montenegrin cadres to lead a new insurrection caused alarm at the Peace Conference.[91] Nikola took advantage of the general uncertainty to repeat his request for permission to address the Conference, and in March he was allowed to have his statement read to the Council. But any hope of receiving a serious hearing was vitiated by outrageous claims made on his behalf for lands extending into both northern Albania and Hercegovina and amounting to an effective doubling of the national territory.[92] In May Nikola's government-in-exile appealed personally to Woodrow Wilson, but by then the Conference had devised a new form of words—'Yugoslavia including Montenegro'—implying that the issue of separate Montenegrin representation was already considered closed.[93] As if this were not enough, the Allies finally conceded official recognition to the Kingdom of the Serbs, Croats and Slovenes—the United States did so in February, and Britain and France in June.[94] Almost concurrently a change in government in Italy re-

[89] *Ibid.*, p. 113.

[90] Harold Nicolson, *Peacemaking, 1919*, London, 1943, p. 123.

[91] Lederer, *Yugoslavia at the Paris Peace Conference*, p. 166. Although the Montenegrin army-in-exile was formally under Montenegrin command, Italy controlled the purse strings and was thus able to ensure, particularly after the formation of the Nitti government in June 1920, that the incursions launched in its name were no more than minor and, from Italy's point of view, opportunistically-designed, irritants. (See Rastoder, 'A Short Review of the History of Montenegro', pp. 132–3.)

[92] The statement was read on Nikola's behalf by General Ante Gvozdenović and included, besides demands for separate representation at the Peace Conference and for further territory, a request for the Allies to oversee genuinely free elections. (See Lederer, *Yugoslavia at the Paris Peace Conference*, p. 116; Houston, *Nikola and Milena*, p. 343; and Čagorović, 'Montenegro at the Paris Peace Conference'.)

[93] Lederer, *Yugoslavia at the Peace Conference*, p. 116.

[94] *Ibid.*, p. 205. Lederer points out that Italian recognition, though not formally enunciated, 'may be considered to date in effect from the signing of the Treaty of Versailles on June 28, 1919'.

sulted in a tailing off of Italy's hitherto strong support for an independent Montenegro. The new Nitti government swiftly tabled a proposal whereby Italy would offer to give up all claims to the Dalmatian and Quaterno islands in exchange for full sovereignty over Mount Lovćen and the Gulf of Kotor, with a view to establishing a naval base that would take advantage of the Gulf's incomparable position. The proposal was rejected at once: Italian domination of two such strategically vital positions was unthinkable, a point on which all members of the SHS delegation immediately agreed, and with the American delegate supporting them, the proposal fell away.[95]

The Paris Peace Conference formally ended in January 1920, and unfinished business was handed over to the Conference of Ambassadors. By this time the 'Montenegrin Question' was no longer on the agenda. The separatists' hopes suffered a series of further blows in the course of 1920, first in January when the Italian troops were suddenly withdrawn from Montenegro, and again with the signing on 12 November of the Treaty of Rapallo, which awarded Italy concessions in Dalmatia and the islands in exchange for its recognition of the Kingdom of Serbs, Croats and Slovenes. Italy's rationale for supporting an independent Montenegro was thereby removed. France, which had long been looking for a pretext, used it as an excuse to sever its remaining formal links with the Petrovići.

In Montenegro as elsewhere in the new Kingdom of the Serbs, Croats and Slovenes, the signing of the Treaty of Rapallo was followed on 28 November by elections for representatives for a new Constituent Assembly to replace the *Privremena Skupština* (Provisional Parliament) in which Montenegro had been granted twelve out of a total of 296 delegates, half the number awarded to Vojvodina but on a par with the region of Dalmatia.[96] With no party opposed to the union with Serbia standing in the election, and a number of captured Greens facing political trials, electoral absenteeism in Montenegro was, to quote Banac, 'exceptionally high'.[97] Andrija

[95] Lederer, *Yugoslavia at the Paris Peace Conference*, p. 232. This is not to say that the Nitti government immediately ceased to exploit the Montenegrin question; rather their government continued to do so wherever they thought it might serve Italy's broader interests and to this end maintained Italian troops in Montenegro until June 1920.
[96] *Ibid.*, pp. 170–1.
[97] Banac, *The National Question*, p. 287. Banac puts absenteeism among the Cetinje

Radović, Nikola's former prime minister turned uncompromising political opponent, barely held his seat. Such clear signs of dissatisfaction suggested less nostalgia for Nikola and his circle than hostility to rule from Belgrade, as can be seen from the fact that the Communist Party (KPJ) in Montenegro won an impressive 38% of the vote, by far the largest share of the vote and a percentage equalled only in Macedonia.[98]

Death of King Nikola

On 1 March 1921 in Cap d'Antibes near Cannes, Nikola died at the age of seventy-nine, clutching a small handful of stony earth he had taken with him when he fled Montenegro.[99] He was buried not in France but at San Remo in Italy, where his son-in-law and daughter, the Italian king and queen, oversaw the funeral arrangements.

After his father's death Danilo, who had no belief in an independent Montenegro, abdicated in favour of his nephew Mihailo. Milena was briefly regent but the Royalist movement, increasingly divided, did not endure for long after Nikola's death.[100] The Italians

---

tribe (the highest) at 50.38%, but absenteeism in other tribal areas of Old Montenegro was only slightly lower at between 48 and 45%. By contrast, a British delegation sent out at the time to observe the elections put the overall level of abstention at 32.69% [of those inscribed on the voters' lists] and considered that, in view of the factors militating against electoral participation in Montenegro—voter illiteracy, distance to the polls, the holding of the election on a Sunday—'the number of persons who refrained from exercising their voting rights on political grounds can be regarded as so small as to be negligible'. (See Bryce to Lord Curzon, 16 December 1920, PRO, FO 371/8903, pp. 23–8.) It was a conclusion that the British government, following earlier reports to the contrary, were more than happy to accept.

[98] John R. Lampe, *Yugoslavia as History: Twice there was a Country*, Cambridge University Press, 1996, p. 122. See also Aleksa Djilas, *The Contested Country: Yugoslav Unity and the Communist Revolution, 1919–1953*, Harvard University Press, 1991, p. 63.

[99] Djilas, *Land without Justice*, p. 196.

[100] Houston, *Nikola and Milena*, p. 253. A Foreign Office despatch reporting from Belgrade at the time noted that Nikola's death was being 'handled respectfully by the Press in view of his Late Majesty being the grandfather of the Prince Regent of Serbia. There was [the report added] some sarcastic comment at the

ordered the closure of the remaining military camp at Gaeta—the remnant of Nikola's Montenegrin army. Barred from returning home, most of this dwindling band of loyalists went into permanent exile, scattering as far afield as Turkey and Argentina.

Nikola's loss of his small kingdom and the disappearance of the Petrović dynasty[101] were hardly events such as to cause surprise at a time when so many of the great European royal houses were being swept away. Realistically it represented the culmination of a long process of disenchantment with autocratic rule which began at least as early as 1905 when Nikola's attempt to stem rising discontent by enacting Montenegro's first constitution had fallen on unreceptive ground. The last twenty years of his rule were less than edifying: the king emerges as vain and duplicitous, still at times politically nimble but often failing to take in the full strategic picture in pursuit of tactical advantage. Yet he does not appear as the entirely discreditable character portrayed by his fiercest critics[102] and if he had not reigned till well into the twentieth century, when demands for political and social change multiplied, he would no doubt have been remembered more kindly.

It does not seem likely that, even without Nikola, independent Montenegro would have survived for long. Serbia's position at the end of the war as the only South Slav state with an army, coupled with the single-minded determination of its Prime Minister Nikola Pašić and his supporters, was enough to ensure Serbia's predominance *vis-à-vis* all the South Slav nations—though not, for Croats and Slovenes at least, with the total loss of national identity implied by Montenegro's unification with Serbia. Furthermore, Monte-

---

news of the renunciation by Prince Danilo in favour of the young Prince Mihailo,' [with] reports from Belgrade's *Tribuna*, styling Milena 'the Merry Widow'. (PRO, FO 371/6193.)

[101] The nominal head of the House of Petrović at the time of writing—Nikola, son of Mihailo and King Nikola's great-grandson—is an architect living in Paris.

[102] Criticism of Nikola was naturally strongest among his own countrymen and in Serbia. The debate was eagerly taken up by foreigners, among whom Nikola had both passionate admirers and ferocious critics. In Britain the best known of the former included Alexander Devine (*Montenegro in History, Politics and War*, London: T. Fisher Unwin, 1918) while two British women, Edith Durham and Rebecca West, were among the most vituperative.

negrin Whites tended both to be better educated and to live more often in the small towns than in far-flung villages, and they had strong support among the educated youth. In time their views were always likely to prevail, and perhaps they would have done so sooner if the Serbs' methods had been less coercive.

In the 1920s the insurgency abated, although support for the cause did not entirely vanish from the political scene. In 1925 an amnesty was granted to the pro-Petrović émigrés, which allowed Jovan Plamenac, among others, to return home.[103] Other Greens formed the Montenegrin Party, which soon abandoned the armed struggle in favour of federalist goals.[104] But the divisions within Montenegrin society did not disappear, and remained as permanent fault-lines, liable to re-open when outside events created new stresses.[105]

For the outside world the 'Montenegrin Question' had simply ceased to exist. Russia, Montenegro's old protector, remained caught up in the aftermath of the Revolution. France had long looked to its interests in Serbia, and Italy, having signed the Treaty of Rapallo, had largely lost its focus on Montenegro. In Britain too the voices in support of an independent Montenegro gradually fell silent. Some vestiges of unease remained. Harold Nicolson, who as a young British diplomat attended the Paris Peace Conference, wrote fourteen years after the close of the Conference:

I disliked and distrusted King Nikita, yet I felt he was almost in the right. I had a passion for the Jugoslav State, and yet I felt they had behaved badly about all those bayonets and that Podgoritza Assembly. I knew it would be better in the long run, for economic and political reasons, were Montenegro to be absorbed by Serbia, or, as we then preferred to phrase it, 'admitted into close union with the Serb, Croat and Slovene State'. Yet I felt extremely uncertain whether such a solution was in fact desired by the Montenegrin people themselves. Here was a case in which dynastic interests on the one hand were balanced against the union of a fine and liberated people. It was awkward to reflect that the balance of right inclined towards the dynasty, and the balance of wrong towards the Serbian liberators. It was in connection with this problem of Montenegro that my early faith in Self-

---

[103] Banac, *The National Question*, p. 290. Banac notes that Plamenac at this time became a member of Pašić's National Radical Party.
[104] *Ibid.*
[105] *Ibid.*

Determination as the remedy for all human ills became clouded with doubts and reservations.[106]

However, by 1920, its fate sealed, Montenegro became the only nation that had entered the Great War on the side of the victorious Allies and finished it without its independence restored.

---

[106] Harold Nicolson, *Peacemaking: 1919*, London, 1934, p. 124.

10. The Interwar Years and the Second World War

In the summer of 1941, while Serbia remained sullenly acquiescent under the German-controlled government of General Milan Nedić and Croatia and much of former Bosnia-Hercegovina were yoked together in the quisling independent state (Nezavisna Država Hrvatska—NDH) of the Croatian fascist Ante Pavelić, rebellion broke out in Montenegro. On 13 July lightly armed villagers headed for the towns and succeeded in seizing back the principal garrisons of the Italian occupying forces. The Italians had been taken by surprise, although the trigger had been provided by the previous day's proclamation of the 'independent' state of Montenegro by a group of Montenegrin Greens who were willing to accept the status of a puppet state under an Italian king provided it meant breaking free of Serbia.

The rebellion, spontaneous and poorly organised, was soon put down by the Italians, reinforced with troops who were largely Albanians and Sandžak Muslims. However, its significance was to prove long-lasting. For the Communists—even though they had yet to take over organisation of the resistance in Montenegro—the territory's suitability as the fulcrum of popular revolution appeared confirmed. It was not only that Montenegrins with their heritage of martial spirit, poverty and alienation were by temperament and tradition likely to prove naturally zealous revolutionaries, but their country's mountains, gorges, caves and forests offered ideal terrain for the guerrilla fighting which the Communists, opposed by much stronger conventionally armed forces, were compelled to employ.

Four years of bitter fighting during the Second World War did nothing to alter that perception as Tito's Partisans zigzagged in and out of Montenegro (and Bosnia-Hercegovina) in their attempts to avoid encirclement and annihilation at the hands of both foreign and domestic enemies. The cost to Montenegro and Montenegrins was enormous—the countryside ravaged, towns destroyed, and a death-rate that saw a greater percentage of Montenegrins killed than any other national group apart from Jews and Roma.[1]

The interwar years

Following the turmoil and carnage of the war years, the interwar period in Montenegro, far from offering a new start, was characterised by neglect, stagnation and widespread disillusionment. Although the repressive political climate discouraged open dissent beneath the surface discontent was accumulating and not simply among traditional Greens. Even the former Whites, who had naturally invested much hope in the new union, were forced to recognise that the regime was failing to address the economic and social ills which had placed Montenegrins near the bottom of the heap in the new Yugoslav state. Officially Montenegrins were considered Serbs, and while many of them at the time found this designation acceptable, others resented the sweeping away of state traditions and symbols and the way their people had been pushed aside and overruled on all issues of self-governance by influential Serbs from Serbia proper. It was not merely that Montenegrin officers were expected to join a national army which, despite incorporation of officers from the former Montenegrin and Habsburg armies, retained its old Serbian command structure. More wounding, given its long association with Montenegrin self-rule, was the blow dealt to the autocephalous Metropolitanate of the Montenegrin Orthodox Church, which in September 1920 was formally subsumed into the union of Yugoslav Orthodox churches—an institution placed under the authority of the Serbian Patriarch with his see in Belgrade.[2]

[1] Christopher Bennett, *Yugoslavia's Bloody Collapse: Causes, Course and Consequences*, London: Hurst, 1995, p. 45.
[2] Banac, *The National Question*, p. 221. In reality, as Lampe points out, the different branches of the Orthodox Church continued to observe their own practices and traditions until 1931, when under King Aleksandar's dictatorship complete unification took place. (See John R. Lampe, *Yugoslavia as History: Twice there was a country*, Cambridge University Press, 1996, pp. 165–6.)

As with the church, so with civil administration: reorganisation spelt increasing centralisation. In 1922 a decree was promulgated dividing the new state into thirty-three different French-style prefectures (*oblasti*) for administrative purposes. The region around Cetinje was designated the Zeta *oblast* while the northern area including Bijelo Polje and Pljevlja became part of a prefecture centred on the Bosnian town of Užice. The reorganisation of government did contain provisions that envisaged some measure of local autonomy, but with the Interior Minister retaining the power to suspend certain acts of the local assemblies and the prefects charged with maintaining order in the different *oblasti* appointed from Belgrade, there was no mistaking where real power was located. The situation was little different in the courts. Although the legal code from Nikola's time remained in force, by 1925 the Ministry of Justice could overrule decisions taken by local courts and dismiss judges.[3]

Parliamentary elections were held in the Kingdom in 1920, 1923, 1925 and 1927. Electoral boundaries were redrawn so that Montenegro—treated as a single constituency and entitled to return eight members—was again confined to its pre-Balkan Wars borders. This effectively halted any process of political integration between the populations in the recently acquired territories and the pre-war territory, a fact that was to be significant in the future.[4] Already in the 1920 parliamentary elections, Montenegrin resentment of its treatment by Belgrade had found expression in the high level of support given to the Communist Party. In 1921, the year in which an attempt was made on the life of the Prince-Regent Aleksandar Karadjordjević, the Communist Party (KPJ) was banned after a young Bosnian Muslim Party member assassinated the Interior Minister who had been responsible for introducing certain anti-Communist regulations. Though forced underground, the Party continued—as later events would confirm—to gather adherents, especially in Montenegro. In a sense this appeared paradoxical given its officially centralist outlook, but in a political landscape dominated by pro-Serbian parties, and lacking other channels through which to voice their dissent, many Montenegrins saw support for the Communists or

---

[3] Lampe, *Yugoslavia as History*, pp. 137–8.
[4] Andrijašević and Rastoder, *History of Montenegro*, p. 200.

their various front organisations as the most effective means of expressing their opposition to Serbian nationalism and hegemony.

Elsewhere in the territories formerly controlled by the Habsburgs or the Ottomans the new government had at least gained credit among the peasantry for its extensive land reform programme. But Montenegro, like Serbia proper, was already a land of smallholders, and with plots averaging no more than a couple of hectares per family[5] there was clearly no scope for land redistribution within its borders. Emigration—the traditional solution—was also declining, partly in response to more restrictive US legislation introduced in the 1920s. In its place the government organised the resettling of many thousands of Montenegrins from the barren karst regions on land expropriated from estate-owners in Kosovo and Macedonia or in formerly Habsburg-ruled Vojvodina. The small plots, the different farming methods required to cultivate the marshy lowlands of Macedonia or flat plains of Kosovo, and the lack of equipment needed to farm the new land meant that these emigrants often had a struggle to succeed. Finding themselves in competition with the local minorities, particularly in Kosovo, the new settlers were easily enlisted as rank-and-file members of nationalist and anti-Albanian campaigns.[6] Some however became Communists and within a short time their membership outnumbered that of Albanians in the Party.

If the land resettlement programme was storing up problems for the future, it appeared at the time to be the new Yugoslavia's single noteworthy achievement. Certainly there were a host of problems to be tackled in managing the pre-war debt burden, the intermittent poor harvests and ongoing border disputes with neighbouring countries, yet among the many difficulties facing the young state the one which most gravely and consistently threatened its stability was the so-called national question, and in particular relations between the two largest groups—the Serbs and the Croats.

Throughout the early 1920s cabinets led by the aged Nikola Pašić succeeded one another as his Radical Party proved unable to form lasting coalitions or enact a comprehensive legislation programme. As a wholly Serb party it could not command support from other

[5] Jozo Tomasevich estimates land ownership in Montenegro in 1912 as a little over one third of a hectare of arable and meadow land *per capita*. (*Peasants, Politics and Economic Change*, p. 128.)

[6] See Lampe, *Yugoslavia as History*, p. 147.

ethnic groups like the Croats or Macedonians, both of whom found increasing cause for discontent with what they saw as Serbian predominance. Other ethnically-based parties were unable to secure sufficient votes while those few parties—principally the Democrats—that attempted to attract support across the country's ethnic divisions ultimately failed to prosper. Reformers like the Slovene Anton Korošec, who argued for a confederal solution to the country's problems, met with no success. Most Serbs and in particular Pašić's conservative Radicals remained wedded to their concept of a unitary state, which in effect meant rule by Serbia. But if the Slovenes and Macedonians, like the Montenegrins, lacked the numbers to challenge the system, this was not the case with the Croats whose volatile leader Stjepan Radić, at the head of the immensely influential Croatian Peasant Party (HPSS), pursued a zigzag course between supporting and boycotting the Parliament, seeking to gain a better deal for Croats while stopping short of precipitating the state's collapse. Serb leaders performed similar political gymnastics in an atmosphere poisoned by Serbian authoritarianism and widespread corruption. Political dialogue was going nowhere; parliament was paralysed and tensions mounted.

The crisis, when it came, was triggered by a Radical deputy Puniša Račić, who, though Montenegrin-born, considered himself a Serb and was a militant Greater Serbia nationalist. In 1909 he had been sentenced *in absentia* for his part in the Kolašin plot.[7] On 19 June 1928 Račić, incensed by Stjepan Radić's criticism of Radical Party deputies, drew a gun in the chamber and fired a number of shots, killing two Croatian deputies and wounding three others including Radić. When Radić died of his wounds some two months later, 100,000 Croats took to the streets of Zagreb. A government of national unity under the Slovene Korošec failed to reassure Radić's successor, who used the crisis to demand that the Kingdom of the Serbs, Croats and Slovenes be re-cast as a federal structure. In December riots broke out in Croatia on the tenth anniversary of the proclamation of the new state.[8] On 6 January 1929, the Orthodox Christmas, King Aleksandar dismissed Parliament and suspended the Constitution.

---

[7] Banac, *The National Question*, p. 279.
[8] See Lampe, *Yugoslavia as History*, pp. 158–9.

Aleksandar lost no time in tightening control, signalling his determination to break with the past and unify the country by changing its name to Yugoslavia. What remained of local autonomy was swept away; political parties and civil liberties were abolished. Not satisfied with the state's division into administrative prefectures, Aleksandar introduced a system of nine provinces (*banovine*), drawn up in such a way as to cut across the old borders. At the same time the historic names such as Croatia and Montenegro were abolished and replaced with the names of rivers and other natural features. In a deliberate piece of gerrymandering Croatian-inhabited areas sometimes found themselves on opposite sides of the new provincial borders while in former Bosnia-Hercegovina the lines were drawn in such a way as to prevent any one province having a Muslim majority.[9] Montenegro—now part of a new Zeta province—was rather better off since, rather than being split into two, it gained territory that would include part of the previously Serbian Sandžak and some of Kosovo and Hercegovina as well as the historic city of Dubrovnik. The loss of so splendid a part of what they saw as their patrimony shocked many Croats, whose mortification was only further increased when the provincial capital of Zeta province was declared to be Cetinje.[10] A flurry of new legislation focused on increasing standardisation throughout the kingdom. Nikola's old legal code disappeared, being merged into a single legal system; the Orthodox Church completed the unification process begun ten years earlier by implementing a single set of regulations to ensure uniform practice through Yugoslavia. Police surveillance increased and the regime's political opponents including some 100 Montenegrin Communists were locked up, or fled abroad mostly to the Soviet Union.

In 1931, partly in response to diplomatic pressure, Aleksandar slackened his hold on power and promulgated a new constitution,

---

[9] *Ibid.*, p. 164.

[10] The pre-war borders of Zeta province provided the basis for Tito's post-war borders of the new Republic of Montenegro, which incorporated the Gulf of Kotor within Montenegrin territory. It is somewhat ironic that Montenegro, having failed before the First World War to gain the outlet to the Adriatic via Scutari to which it had long aspired and for which it was prepared to risk almost everything, gained instead in the immediate post-Second World War period the splendid Adriatic 'fjord' of Kotor, which it had not seriously expected would form part of any prospective plan for its territorial enlargement.

but in reality the restoration of political liberties was something of a sham. A largely appointed senate was a check on a national assembly whose democratic credentials were already heavily compromised by an extremely complicated electoral system. Country-wide lists were drawn up on the basis of very strictly defined provisions for the selection of candidates, and the winning list—which was naturally intended to be the government's—was then awarded an automatic two-thirds of the seats.[11] Under this system elections in 1931 to a new reduced 306-seat national parliament gave 219 seats to Serbs and 55 to Croats but only 2 each to members of parliament from the formally unrecognised provinces of Montenegro and Macedonia.[12] It was hardly a recipe for assuaging discontent, and in December 1934, while on a visit to France intended to strengthen Yugoslavia's connections with the principal anti-fascist powers—France and Britain—Aleksandar was assassinated in Marseilles together with the French Foreign Minister Louis Barthou. The assassin, a Macedonian, had links with a Croatian extremist organisation—the Ustasha (Uprising) Party of Ante Pavelić, who in 1929 had fled to Italy where he received help from Mussolini's Fascist regime. Because Aleksandar's heir Prince Petar was still a minor, a regency was declared under his cousin Prince Paul (Pavle).[13] The English-educated Paul retained his predecessor's 1931 Constitution, while allowing some relaxation of police surveillance and the very stringent political laws.

With most political attention still focused on Serb-Croat relations, Montenegro had become more and more a backwater, both politically and economically. For example, the longest-lasting inter-war government—that of Milan Stojadinović (June 1935–February 1939)—contained no Montenegrin (or Croatian) ministers, and there were only four in the entire inter-war period (1918–41), years that saw no fewer than thirty-nine governments with 819 ministerial mandates. Electoral support for the regime-sponsored coalition declined progressively as the population, largely on dwarf farms, were at the mercy of local middlemen. The unreasonable profit

[11] Lampe, *Yugoslavia as History*, pp. 166–7.

[12] *Ibid.*, pp. 166–7.

[13] He is here referred to as Prince Paul, the name by which he was internationally known. Strictly Paul was the senior regent; there were two others who hardly counted.

margins left them struggling to cope with unfavourable price differentials between what they received for the small amount of grain they could sell when the harvest had just come in, and the price they had to pay as the crop year advanced and their own supplies were exhausted.[14] Despite the continuing poverty (in 1938 national income in Montenegro was only 31 per cent of the Yugoslav average)[15], almost no funds were allocated to economic development, nor was there any serious attempt to tackle the absence of any major infrastructure, apart from the development of military facilities in the Gulf of Kotor.

The inter-war years had been characterised by three principal concerns—disputes over the organisation of the state, ethnic tensions and socio-economic problems—but by the late 1930s, although none of these had been satisfactorily resolved, strategic matters featured ever more prominently in the public mind as the *Anschluss* of 1938 gave Germany a common frontier with Yugoslavia, and Italy's readiness to involve itself in Croatian affairs was becoming ever more ominous. The deteriorating international situation finally proved a catalyst for disputatious Serbian and Croatian politicians. In August 1939 Stojadinović's successor as prime minister, Dragiša Cvetković, signed an agreement (*sporazum*) with the leader of the Croatian Peasant Party, Vladko Maček, whereby the Serbs agreed to an autonomous Croatia within significantly enlarged borders. The agreement was supported by Montenegrin federalists who chose to see it as a first step on the path to a fully federal system with Montenegro having equal status, but rejected by Montenegrin unionists.

In any event agreement had come too late. The outbreak of war only two weeks later placed immense strains on the Yugoslav state whose leaders now devoted most of their energy to trying to keep out of the war. In the course of 1940–1 Prince Paul came under increasing pressure to adhere to the Tripartite Pact between Germany, Italy and Japan. Mussolini's bungled attack on Greece forced Hitler to go to his ally's rescue. Britain's support for Greece increased German apprehensious over Yugoslavia as an Allied foothold in the Balkans. The Bulgarian government's adherence to the Tripartite Pact in March 1941 was the last straw. On 25 March the government

---

[14] Tomasevich, *Peasants, Politics and Economic Change*, p. 610.
[15] Andrijašević and Rastoder, *History of Montenegro*, p. 183.

of Yugoslavia formally put its signature to the pact only to be overthrown two days later, together with the regent, in a popular revolt led by military officers and aided by British agents in Belgrade. Prince Paul was replaced by the seventeen-year-old Petar whose majority was advanced to allow him to be proclaimed king. General Dušan Simović, one of the principal plotters and the military officer in charge of Serbian forces at the time of the Podgorica Assembly (November 1918), became prime minister.

The Axis attacks

Hitler did not wait long before responding to the provocation of the Belgrade coup. On 6 April 1941 450 bombers pounded Belgrade as part of 'Operation Punishment'.[16] Podgorica too was hit as airfields all over Yugoslavia were put out of action. Land forces entered Yugoslavia simultaneously from Austria, Hungary, Romania and Bulgaria. Italy followed Germany, bombing Dalmatia and despatching troops—the Messina, Centauro, and Marche divisions—into Montenegro, which they entered on 17 April. On 22 April an attempt to rescue British diplomats and dependents who had been evacuated from Belgrade to the Gulf of Kotor by road ended in farce. A British submarine, the *Regent*, entered the Gulf but after being discovered and fired on from two German planes, crash-dived taking with it Italian officers who had gone aboard to negotiate the safe conduct of the diplomatic staff and leaving behind the Royal Navy officer who had gone ashore to arrange the departure.[17]

In the absence of resolute leadership, surrounded and facing twenty-four German, twenty-three Italian and five Hungarian divisions and some 2,200 enemy aircraft Yugoslavia had little hope of holding out.[18] Zagreb fell on 10 April and Belgrade two days later. King Petar flew from Nikšić in Montenegro to Greece on 15 April.[19]

[16] Less than half the number of planes used over Serbia and Montenegro by NATO nearly sixty years later.

[17] Giacomo Scotti and Luciano Viazzi, *Le Aquile delle Montagne Nere: Storia dell'occupazione italiana e della guerra in Montenegro (1941–1943)*, Milan: Mursia, 1987, pp. 57–8.

[18] Jozo Tomasevich, *The Chetniks: War and Revolution in Yugoslavia, 1941–1945*, Stanford University Press, 1975, p. 65.

[19] When young King Petar and his entourage fled to Nikšić en route to Cairo, they left behind them orders for the despatch of the Royal Treasury, which was to

On 17 April while in Belgrade Generals Cincar-Marković and Janković were putting their signatures to the act of capitulation, the Italian Messina division, which had come up the coast from Scutari to the Gulf of Kotor, had captured almost the entire Yugoslav navy and despatched a column of troops to occupy Cetinje. Following Yugoslavia's surrender, over 200,000 prisoners, 12,000 of them officers, were transported to provide forced labour in Germany and Italy.[20] Meanwhile the country's dismemberment began immediately, leaving a complex chequerboard of different jurisdictions. Germany and Italy divided Slovenia between them; Serbia was placed under direct German rule. Italy and Germany shared responsibility for occupying most of former Croatia, which was nonetheless proclaimed the Independent State of Croatia (NDH). Bulgaria took most of Macedonia, apart from the western third which went

---

follow by road convoy to Montenegro. Among other things the treasury contained large quantities of banknotes, some 60 tons of gold in ingots, precious jewellery, two relics alleged to be the hand of St John the Baptist and a splinter of the True Cross, and a famous Byzantine icon, the 'Virgin of Philerme'. The icon of the Virgin, popularly attributed to St Luke, had been the property of the Knights of St John of Jerusalem when they settled in Rhodes in 1307. After Rhodes fell to the Ottomans in the early sixteenth century, the icon accompanied the knights to Malta. After Napoleon conquered the island in 1798 the icon ended up, together with the other relics, in the possession of Tsar Paul of Russia. At the time of the Russian Revolution it was given to Empress Maria Feodorovna and after her death eventually presented to King Aleksandar of Yugoslavia. On arriving in Montenegro in April 1941 the icon was hidden in Ostrog monastery and then disappeared for more than fifty years before its discovery by scholars in the reserve collection of Cetinje National Museum in 1998. The banknotes meanwhile had been hidden in a cave outside Nikšić whose whereabouts were discovered when the Italians came across local people, who had managed to find a way through the partly dynamited entrance to the cave, attempting to exchange sacks of notes for silver coinage. The ingots too were eventually discovered—some of them in a Nikšić pharmacy and the rest at the bottom of a well in the house of a priest in Herceg Novi from where they were eventually retrieved and transported back to Italy. (See www.stjohndc.org/ stjohndc/English/Serbia/Pilgrimage/Plgrm6.htm accessed on 22/09/2004 and Scotti and Viazzi, *Le Aquile delle Montagne Nere*, p. 47 and pp. 56–7.)

[20] Stevan K. Pavlowitch, *A History of the Balkans, 1804–1945*, London and New York: Longman, 1999, p. 311. Jozo Tomasevich (*The Chetniks*, pp. 73–4) gives a more detailed breakdown of figures and points out that the vast majority of prisoners were Serbs. The Germans subsequently allowed most of the non-Serb prisoners of war to return home.

to Italian-ruled Albania. The Italians directly annexed a portion of the Adriatic coast from Zadar to Split, thereby obtaining another desirable foothold on the Adriatic.

Italy's ambitions to extend its influence to the other side of the Adriatic made Montenegro a natural focus of attention. The fact that Queen Elena, wife of the Italian King Victor Emmanuel III, was King Nikola's daughter suggested to the Italians that they might realise their goal of achieving an Italian protectorate there by promising to restore the monarchy. Naturally the Italian government did not envisage Montenegro as having any real independence; rather Elena herself would assume a tutelary role over whoever was to become the future ruler of the new kingdom. A number of Montenegrin federalists, the former Greens,[21] seemed likely to cooperate.

Misreading the level of support for 'independence', the Italians took a relatively relaxed approach to the occupation of Montenegro. In April Mussolini appointed Count Serafino Mazzolini, a diplomat and prominent fascist to the post of civil governor, while the number of troops deployed there was reduced to some 10,000, divided among approximately twenty garrisons.[22] Mazzolini's first step was to announce the creation of an advisory council, naming a prominent separatist, Sekula Drljević, as prime minister. However, Drljević, though committed to Montenegrin independence, was not a supporter of the Petrović dynasty, nor was there widespread support for a monarchy within the country even among those who favoured separation from Serbia. Nonetheless, the Italians remained convinced that exploiting the royal connection would bring the vast majority of Montenegrins around to accepting what effectively amounted to a vassal state.

The question of which royal personage should be approached was controversial. As the Italian foreign minister, Count Galeazzo Ciano, wrote in his diary on 21 May:

It seems that the idea of Prince Michael [Nikola's grandson Mihailo] for the position is not popular in Montenegro. They do not know him; he has married a Frenchwoman and until now has lived on the pay of Belgrade.

---

[21] As explained in the preceding chapter, by 1925 the majority of Greens had come round to supporting the Montenegrin Party, which now stood for Montenegrin autonomy within a federal Yugoslavia. See also Banac, *The National Question in Yugoslavia*, pp. 289–91.

[22] Scotti and Viazzi, *Le Aquile delle Montagne Nere*, pp. 61–2.

On the other hand, the consensus of opinion is unanimous in favour of the Queen. She is the one who ought to wear the crown of the Petrovichs. Such a solution would also be very pleasing to me, because it would tend to place the country solidly in our hands. For the time being the King [Victor Emmanuel] is recalcitrant. Now we have sent Mazzolini to explain to him how matters stand we hope that he will give his consent. As for the frontiers, the King would like to restore Montenegro to its 1914 borders. This is impossible. Albania would start an uprising, and we know from experience how invincible is the bitterness provoked by deceit on the part of allies. Versailles teaches us this lesson.[23]

However, Victor Emmanuel continued to object to Queen Elena taking the crown. Ciano in turn objected to the king's favourite Nikolai Romanov—a distant Petrović, who Ciano feared might resemble his father Prince Roman, 'prototype of a blockhead'.[24] When the young man rejected the 'honour' there was little choice but to return to Prince Mihailo, but he too refused on the grounds that the Allies would eventually win the war. Ciano's frustration was palpable: 'I never dreamed we should waste so much brainpower on a country like Montenegro.'[25]

Undeterred, the Italian king visited Cetinje in May. Although it was billed as a private visit, the queen did not accompany him. The Italian authorities had been active handing out cloth for Italian flags and dragooning civil servants, students and schoolchildren out onto the streets where they were instructed to welcome the king with cries of '*Evviva!*' and fascist salutes. But despite Cetinje's reputation as the centre for opposition to Belgrade, there were few flags to be seen while the only gestures of support came from a handful of separatists and nostalgic royalists. The Montenegrins were not to be won over.[26]

The 13 July uprising

Within a few weeks Montenegrin recalcitrance became transformed into open revolt. The immediate trigger for the uprising was

---

[23] Hugh Gibson (ed.), *The Ciano Diaries, 1939–1943*, New York: Doubleday, 1946, p. 355 (entry of 21 May 1941).

[24] *Ibid.*, p. 356 (entry of 22 May 1941). Prince Roman Petrovich Romanov (as he styled himself) was the son of Princess Milica and the Russian Grand Duke Pyotr Nikolayevich. The throne was offered to Roman's elder son Nikolai.

[25] *Ibid.*, p. 357 (entry of 26 May 1941).

[26] Scotti and Viazzi, *Le Aquile delle Montagne Nere*, p. 67.

the convening of an assembly in Cetinje on 12 July, St Petar's Day, at which a group of Italian-backed separatists proclaimed Montenegro's independence, reading out a declaration that had been prepared in Rome. Far from welcoming the idea of a protectorate, most Montenegrins were outraged at the affront to their independence. To compound their sense of injury the so-called state had already been divested by the Italians of significant chunks of its territory. Not only had they reassigned to a Greater Albania lands surrounding Peć and Dečani that Montenegro had gained after the First Balkan War and territory around Ulcinje and Tuzi that had been part of Montenegro since 1878;[27] they had also detached a strip of land running from the Gulf of Kotor to Budva for direct annexation to Italy as part of the separate *Governatorato* (military district) of Dalmatia.[28] The Montenegrins' anger at the Italians' action was reinforced by their traditional belief in Mother Russia: the peasants were eager for a war that they believed would soon end in a decisive victory for the Red Army.[29]

The first assaults on Italian garrisons took place in Old Montenegro. The country was well-stocked with arms left behind by the defeated Royal Yugoslav army. Within days almost the entire population from former Royal Army officers and local Communist Party agitators to ordinary villagers, and even some Serbs fleeing Hercegovina to escape Ustasha massacres, had turned upon the occupiers. The Italians were wholly taken aback by the rapid spread of the uprising. On 17 July Ciano noted in his diary:

The Montenegrin insurrection continues; in fact, it is assuming greater proportions. If it did not have a deep and bitter significance, it would be

---

[27] Victor Emmanuel, no doubt on Queen Elena's prompting, opposed the handing over of former Montenegrin territory to a Greater Albania, but Mussolini overruled him.

[28] Andrijašević and Rastoder, *History of Montenegro*, p. 210.

[29] Vladimir Dedijer, *The War Diaries of Vladimir Dedijer*, 3 vols, Ann Arbor: University of Michigan Press, 1990, vol. 1, p. 151. Like Milovan Djilas' memoir *Wartime*, Dedijer's diary is an invaluable record of the war, one that has the particular advantage of being written contemporaneously. A journalist before the war, Dedijer became the Partisans' official diarist and later Tito's biographer. He served in Tito's post-war government as minister for information before falling out with his master after publicly supporting Djilas in 1954. He was later put on trial, was dismissed from the KPJ, and after further harassment moved abroad. In 1970 he returned to Yugoslavia.

grotesque that war exists between Italy and Montenegro. We hope that our military men will settle it without having to call for German intervention.[30]

It was not only the Italians who were caught unawares. The Communists too were unprepared for an outbreak of spontaneous violence on such a scale. At the beginning of July the Communist Party chief Josip Broz Tito[31] had despatched one of his chief lieutenants, Milovan Djilas, to his native Montenegro with instructions to organise a campaign of guerrilla attacks. 'Be careful not to incite a general uprising,' Tito told him. 'The Italians are still organised and strong, and they will break you. You should begin with minor operations.'[32] However, Tito knew little of the reality on the ground where the Communists, though well represented in Montenegro, were far from enjoying the support of the general population. Nor were the members of the Party in Montenegro—till only a short time before among the most hardline opponents of engagement in what they saw as an 'imperialist war'—even united among themselves over what stand to take in the battle against the occupier.[33]

Some divisions arose from internal doctrinal disputes, but others were attributable to personality clashes. In particular the two Party members closest to Tito—Milovan Djilas and the Jewish intellectual and veteran Communist, Moša Pijade—were almost always on opposing sides irrespective of the issue. When Pijade, who had been forced to flee for his life from Nazi-occupied Belgrade, found himself the subject of rumours about a planned escape by boat to join the British, he blamed Djilas for circulating them. Djilas strenuously denied this, but his treatment of Pijade was often less than tactful: typically he excluded Pijade from the meeting of the Montenegrin Provincial Committee of the KPJ on 8 July 1941 at which the Communists debated what position they should take on the armed uprising. This was an error of judgement for which Djilas was to pay dearly since it allowed Pijade to avoid any responsibility for dis-

[30] Gibson (ed.), *The Ciano Diaries*, p. 378.
[31] In his early days as leader of the underground Communist Party Josip Broz was known by a number of assumed names. Later his Communist Party colleagues settled on Tito, a name that caused much confusion to Axis and Allied powers alike during the War.
[32] Djilas, *Wartime*, pp. 8 and 25.
[33] As late as May 1940 the Montenegrin Communist Party had been criticised by the central leadership of the KPJ for advocating the demobilisation of soldiers,

obeying Tito's orders over the uprising, and to lay the blame on Djilas.

In reality, as the debate of the KPJ Provincial Committee showed, the Party in Montenegro was simply overwhelmed by the scale and violence of the popular uprising. Despite the initial confusion the Communists felt they had little choice but to back the uprising, exploiting the opportunities it afforded for extending their political influence locally while making the most of their own unblemished reputation compared to the tarnished image of the Royal Army. Hoping to win more converts to the cause, the Party leadership came out in favour of a broad military command structure, including former Royal Army officers. As the foremost exponent of this approach, Djilas went so far as to offer the command to a well-known former Royal Army officer, Colonel Bajo Stanišić of the Bjelopavlići clan. The Colonel's reputation rested on his regiment's success on the Scutari front in the first half of 1941, the only successful operation by the Royal Army during the war. However, Stanišić turned the offer down, maintaining that the uprising was premature.[34] Although not obviously hostile to the Communists at this stage, he subsequently became one of the principal Chetnik[35] commanders, collaborating with the Italians in attacks on the Partisans before being killed by them after the capture of Ostrog monastery by Partisan forces in 1943.

On 18 July, the day after Stanišić's rejection of the KPJ's offer and with the uprising in full swing, the Communists established the pon-

---

the refusal of military discipline, and even desertion in order to prevent proletarian lives being wasted in an imperialist war. See Tomasevich, *The Chetniks*, p. 83 and Djilas, *Wartime*, p. 18.

[34] The uprising was premature in the sense that it could not have led to a lasting victory. But it was a major event by the standards of engagements in occupied Europe and tied down substantial Axis forces which would have been deployed elsewhere.

[35] The term Chetnik (*Četnik* in Serbian) comes from the Serbian term *četa* or armed band and was adopted during the Second World War by the Orthodox followers of the royalist military commander and nationalist leader, Draža Mihailović. Although the term was subsequently used to describe both Serbs and Montenegrins, at the time of the uprising the non-Communist resistance forces in Montenegro cannot strictly be described as Chetniks. The term 'nationalist' is therefore used here to describe them up till the time of their establishing formal links with Mihailović.

derously-named 'Provisional Supreme Command of National Liberation Troops of Montenegro, the Gulf of Kotor and Sandžak', and set about allocating titles and responsibilities. As Tito's chief delegate in Montenegro, Djilas occupied the top-ranking political position. Blažo Jovanović, one of the most prominent Montenegrin Communists and a member of the influential Piperi tribe,[36] was named as political commissar. His kinsman Arso Jovanović, though not yet a Communist, was appointed military chief.[37]

Unlike the Communists, the Montenegrin nationalists in 1941 had no separate, organised command structure, nor in any meaningful sense did they come under the control of the leader of the Serbian nationalist resistance force, the former Royal Yugoslav Army colonel turned Chetnik commander, Draža Mihailović, who was himself in touch with the royal government-in-exile from his headquarters at Ravna Gora in southwest Serbia. At a time when they sought the widest possible support for their struggle against the occupier, the Montenegrin Communists were unable to agree on cooperation through a single individual or organisation, but instead combined forces with a number of other nationalists and former Royal Army officers, among them the future Chetnik leaders Major Djordje Lašić and Captain Pavle Djurišić.

At first events moved rapidly in favour of the insurgents. The first day of the revolt—13 July—was particularly bloody as peasants armed with everything from rifles and pistols to scythes and pitchforks overran several garrisons in Old Montenegro and on the coast, setting fire to barracks and killing and wounding many Italians. Where possible, the Italians replied in kind, led by the 'blackshirts' whom the insurgents had determined to execute wherever possible.[38] Meanwhile the insurgents had cut down telephone and tele-

---

[36] The Piperi were particularly strongly represented in the Communist leadership having, in addition to Blažo Jovanović, three other clan members in the original provincial leadership. Shortly afterwards another prominent member of the clan and effectively the military chief at the time of the uprising, Arso Jovanović, joined the Party. Subsequently Jovanović became Tito's commander-in-chief before siding with Stalin in 1948 at the time of his split with Tito. See Djilas, *Wartime*, pp. 16 and 452, and Chapter 11 below.

[37] Djilas, *Wartime*, pp. 28–9.

[38] Scotti and Viazzi, *Le Aquile delle Montagne Nere*, pp. 100–1.

graph lines and blocked the roads, severing communications with inland Montenegro. With no news getting through, the Italians at first believed that apart from Cetinje the rebellion was confined to the Virpazar-Budva-Rijeka Crnojevića triangle, causing them to delay sending for reinforcements and allowing the insurgents to capture almost all the garrisons and liberate the main towns apart from Podgorica, Nikšić, Cetinje and Pljevlja. Within a few weeks most of upland Montenegro had been liberated, the Italian garrison at Cetinje cut off, and many thousands of Italian soldiers killed or taken prisoner.[39] As the rest fled to the coast or barricaded themselves in the main towns, Mazzolini left hurriedly for 'consultations' in Italy.[40]

But surprise and enthusiasm could only carry the Montenegrins so far. On 15 July the Italian supreme command ordered General Alessandro Pirzio Biroli, a veteran of Italy's inglorious Abyssinian campaign and the commander of all Italian forces in Albania, to assume command of the overall campaign to take back the country. Operational command was awarded to General Luigi Mentasti who was given *carte blanche* in Montenegro as Italian reinforcements began arriving in their thousands. While the insurgents continued their successful progress through eastern Montenegro, the Italians unleashed a campaign of reprisals in the Montenegrin heartlands, shooting civilians from villages where Italian forces had been ambushed. With only days to go in his position as civil commissioner, Mazzolini protested at the brutal treatment of civilians he found on his return to Cetinje, but his protests evoked no response. On the contrary the ill-treatment of the population was becoming ever more widespread. On 24 July Mussolini stripped Mazzolini of his post and abolished the civil command. Arriving from Tirana to assume overall charge of both civil and military affairs, General Pirzio Biroli commented: 'This is a people ready for anything and sustained by a mystical fanaticism... Those who are captured with

[39] As always there are conflicting figures given by different sources. Dedijer, quoting the Partisan military chief, Arso Jovanović, gives no figures for Italians killed but refers to 4–5000 being taken prisoner. (Dedijer, *War Diaries*, vol. 1, p. 460.) Djilas puts the number of prisoners at 3,000 (*Wartime*, p. 26).
[40] Thomas Fleming, *Montenegro: The Divided Land*, Rockford, Illinois: Chronicles Press, 2002, p. 133.

arms and therefore shot don't bat an eyelid in front of the firing squad.'[41]

Lacking the heavy weaponry and recognising their inability to withstand the advance of a fully equipped army backed by a campaign of aerial attacks, the Communist leadership sought refuge in a deserted settlement on the rocky slopes of Mount Kamenik. While the leaders hesitated over whether to continue with a large-scale insurgency or confine themselves to guerrilla warfare, ordinary villagers, reduced to panic at seeing their hamlets burnt and livestock decimated, began to return home. Many had joined the insurrection in the mistaken belief that Soviet intervention, ensuring no more than a few weeks' fighting, was imminent, and were demoralised by the prospect of a long war.

By late August the Italians were back in greater numbers. With reinforcements from no fewer than six divisions, including many Albanian and Slav Muslim irregulars, they had soon managed to take back most of the towns. Villages were bombed from the air, and motorised columns continued the mopping-up on the ground. In the process the restraint that had characterised the initial phase of the Italian occupation was completely abandoned; many of the Albanians and some local Muslims, most notably those in the ethnically divided town of Berane, were happy to settle old scores.[42] In September Sekula Drljević, the leading Montenegrin Green at the time of the declaration of independence, was dismissed from office and transferred to Italy.[43] At the same time many thousands of

[41] Scotti and Viazzi, *Le Aquile delle Montagne Nere*, p. 195.

[42] The atmosphere around Berane was already tense due to the fact that the town had seen particularly violent fighting in the course of the uprising. The anger of the town's Orthodox population had been sparked off by the Carabinieri's execution of a number of prominent townsmen whom they falsely accused of being Communists. Anger at the executions swelled the ranks of the insurgents attacking the town's Italian garrison. The Carabinieri put up fierce resistance which was only broken when the Montenegrin rebels, urged on by the former Royal Army officer turned nationalist leader, Pavle Djurišić, burned the garrison to the ground. See Djilas, *Wartime*, pp. 28–9 and 40, and Scotti and Viazzi, *Le Aquile delle Montagne Nere*, pp. 150–5.

[43] He later escaped, possibly with Italian connivance, and made his way to Croatia where, abetted by the German and Ustasha authorities, he set up a Montenegrin State Council with the aim of creating a fascist-sponsored 'independent' Montenegrin state. See Tomasevich, *The Chetniks*, p. 209, and below.

Montenegrin prisoners, including women, children and the elderly, were interned locally or sent to camps in Albania and Italy.[44] The XIV Army Corps of the Italian Ninth Army, together with additional forces roughly equivalent to six divisions, were stationed permanently in what from the beginning of October 1941 was redesignated as the *Governatorato* of Montenegro.[45] The presence of so many Axis soldiers in such a small territory was extraordinary and in itself justified the uprising in terms of tying up such a large force: one source describes it as involving 23 per cent of the entire occupation force in Yugoslavia to control approximately 3 per cent of the country's population.[46] Yet in one respect at least the Montenegrins could consider themselves fortunate: harsh as the Italian occupation was at particular times, it never approached the level of severity and cruelty which the German and the Ustasha regimes inflicted on Montenegro's neighbours.

First divisions between Communists and nationalists

The nationalists had played an undeniable part in the uprising, but in the wake of the harsh Italian reprisals some of their leaders were already scaling down their earlier commitment to resistance in the hope of retaining the support of the local population. Quick to sense a widening of the gap between the Communists and nationalists, General Pirzio Biroli sought to initiate secret contacts with certain nationalist leaders. Some responded by concluding local truces with the Italians, but at this stage these were largely in the regions to the south and east where the local nationalist bands, engaged in

---

[44] Again precise figures are difficult to establish, both for those killed and for numbers taken prisoner. The British historian Stephen Clissold calculated that in a little over a month about 5,000 Montenegrins were killed and some 7,000 wounded as a result of the Italians' campaign to subdue the country (see Scotti and Viazzi, *Le Aquile delle Montagne Nere*, pp. 242–3). On the Italian side well over 1,000 died and more were wounded. The number of prisoners taken from Montenegro to Italy or Albania was about 10,000, but many more were interned in Montenegro itself. In Kotor the population was subjected to equally harsh measures. Kotor's Jewish population was rounded up and sent by ship to concentration camps in Durazzo (Durrës).

[45] Scotti and Viazzi, *Le Aquile delle Montagne Nere*, p. 362.

[46] Franco Boiardi (ed.), *Italia e Montenegro*, Bari: Laterza, 1997, p. 104.

hostilities against Sandžak and Albanian Muslims, saw the Italian occupiers as the lesser evil.[47]

Back in overall control, the Italians were content to remain largely in the towns, leaving the countryside subdued if not wholly pacified. The Communist leadership, who had been hard-pressed by the lack of food in the mountains, took the decision to descend from their refuge to the village of Radovče, north of Podgorica. This was Piperi territory, long distinguished by its strong support of the Communists. Nonetheless the leadership's decision was not altogether a wise choice. Not only did it reinforce the notion that the Montenegrin Partisans were too closely bound up with the Piperi but, more important, it was too close to the large Italian garrison in Podgorica, whose presence would soon compel the leadership to take to the hills again. However, in one sense, the Communist leadership's choice of Radovče was serendipitous. The village was not too far from the coast, and when on 20 September a mission from the Royal Yugoslav government-in-exile was landed from a British submarine at the little seaside town of Petrovac, south of Budva, a group of Communist scouts watching from the mountains above were able to guide the mission's members up along local tracks to the leadership's headquarters before either the Italians or the nationalists, with whom the mission had hoped to make initial contact, were even aware of their arrival.[48]

[47] Milazzo, *The Chetnik Movement*, p. 45.
[48] A second mission led by a Slovene and Royal Yugoslav naval officer, Lieutenant Rapotec, landed on the Dalmatian island of Mljet on 27 January 1942 but then disappeared for many months before turning up in Istanbul in July 1942 where Rapotec was interrogated by British agents. A third British mission consisting of Major Terence Atherton, his radio operator Patrick O'Donovan, and a Royal Yugoslav officer landed near Petrovac in Montenegro in February 1942 and was escorted by Montenegrin Partisans to Tito's then headquarters at Foča. Tito had grave suspicions about Atherton's intentions, particularly because he believed that the British were somehow behind the resurgence of support for the Chetniks in Montenegro. These suspicions seemed confirmed when on the night of 15 April Atherton and his radio operator disappeared from Foča in the company of several Chetniks. They were believed to be intending to make their way to Mihailović's headquarters, at that time still in Serbia. But neither Atherton nor Donovan ever arrived. Their bodies were never found but both were presumed to have been murdered, probably for the large number of gold sovereigns that Atherton carried in his money-belt. Subsequently Chetniks and Partisans accused each other of responsibility for the murders. Mihailović informed the Allies

The mission sent by the British consisted of three Montene-grins—Majors Ostojić and Lalatović and a radio operator[49]—and one British officer, a former mining engineer and fluent Serbo-Croat speaker, Captain D.T. 'Bill' Hudson. Though a member of the joint mission, Hudson was unaware of the instructions given to his colleagues by the Royal Yugoslav government-in-exile which, on the basis of reports emanating from Yugoslav intelligence sources in Cairo, was anxious to make contact with a certain Colonel Mihai-lović who was reported to be leading guerrilla bands loyal to King Petar from a base in southwestern Serbia. Meanwhile Hudson had been sent with somewhat vague instructions from the Special Oper-ations Executive based in Cairo requiring that he report on all the resistance groups operating in Yugoslavia.[50] It was only after his arrival in Montenegro that he received a message from Cairo inform-ing him of Mihailović's presence in Serbia and ordering him to proceed urgently to the Colonel's headquarters at Ravna Gora with a cipher which would enable him to transmit coded messages to the British.[51]

The Montenegrin Communist leadership received the Hudson mission warily and were not reassured when the two Yugoslav offi-cers revealed their determination to make contact with nationalist bands in Serbia. However, Hudson claimed that the British gov-ernment was ready to help all resistance movements engaged in

---

that Atherton's murder had caused him to 'declare open warfare on all Partisans'. However, what little circumstantial evidence there is suggests that the murder was carried out by Spasoje Dakić, the leader of a small renegade band of nation-alists. See Walter R. Roberts, *Tito, Mihailović and the Allies, 1941–1945*, New Brunswick, NJ: Rutgers University Press, 1973, pp. 54–5, and F. W. D. Deakin, *The Embattled Mountain*, Oxford University Press, 1971, pp. 173–6.

[49] Ostojić later became one of Mihailović's closest collaborators, playing a pro-minent part in organising Chetnik forces during Operation Weiss (see below). The radio operator Veljko Dragičević was from the beginning sympathetic to the Partisans. He married a Montenegrin and later joined the Partisans, serving as a radio operator until he and his wife were killed at Drvar in May 1943. See Djilas, *Wartime*, p. 71.

[50] The Balkan arm of the SOE was composed mainly of experts on Yugoslavia, some of whom had been involved in the 27 March coup against Prince Paul. In order to increase their scanty knowledge of what was happening inside Yugo-slavia they had set up listening posts in Cairo and Malta.

[51] Deakin, *The Embattled Mountain*, p. 130.

fighting the Axis Powers. Although his attempt at reassurance had little effect on his hosts,[52] Hudson was soon sending ciphers to Malta, in which he painted a positive picture of the Communists' strength and organisation within Montenegro, and suggesting that they were more deserving of British support than the local nationalists.

Mistrust of the mission may well have prompted the Montenegrin leadership's decision to accompany Hudson's party as, following instructions, it set off on about 13 October for Mihailović's headquarters at Ravna Gora in Serbia. There was even a proposal that the mission should be ambushed and its members killed, a suggestion that Djilas refused to take seriously. Communists and nationalists were still, in theory at least, committed to a common struggle against the occupation but the relationship was daily becoming more strained.

On the nationalist side Hudson's arrival in Ravna Gora coincided with the British government's decision to recognise Mihailović as the only legitimate commander of all the resistance forces in Yugoslavia—a vital development for the Chetniks since it made them the exclusive beneficiaries for the time being of both Allied propaganda and of material support.[53] External backing of this sort enabled the Chetniks to attract followers more easily among the population who, given the ferocity of German reprisals in Serbia, were also increasingly inclined to favour the Chetniks' more cautious approach of avoiding outright attacks on the occupiers in order to conserve their forces in preparation for an eventual Allied landing in Yugoslavia.[54]

In direct contrast to the Chetnik position, the Communists remained committed to attacking the enemy wherever possible, even welcoming reprisals in the belief that they could convert a passive population into recruits to the Partisan cause. Not surprisingly given these differences, the earlier limited cooperation between Partisans

---

[52] Djilas, *Wartime*, p. 72.

[53] Mihailović's recognition by the Allies was accompanied by a series of quick promotions. In December 1941 he was promoted brigadier-general, in January 1942 he was appointed the government-in-exile's Minister of the Army, Navy and Airforce, and in June the same year he was made chief of staff. (Tomasevich, *The Chetniks*, p. 144.)

[54] On 16 September the Germans announced a policy of killing 100 Serbs for each German killed and fifty for each German wounded. (Tomasevich, *The Chetniks*, p. 146.)

and Chetniks was giving way to increasing mistrust as the reality of their two very different approaches to occupation became clear. The situation appeared slightly improved after a meeting between Tito and Mihailović on 27 October in the village of Brajići when Tito offered Mihailović the supreme command, though with the understanding that had the offer been accepted he, Tito, would have refused to serve under him.[55] Almost immediately, however, the agreement collapsed as clashes broke out between Communists and Chetniks culminating in an unsuccessful attempt by the Chetniks to capture Užice, but success against the Chetniks on this occasion was not enough to guarantee the future security of Tito's forces at Užice. With the base coming under increasing attack from German forces, Tito was forced to make his way south across the mountains into the Sandžak and ultimately into eastern Bosnia, where he established new headquarters at the town of Foča.

Montenegrin Communists renew the offensive

Meanwhile in Montenegro Djilas and his close collaborators, convinced that only a spectacular strike against the enemy could halt the slide in their support, were determined to launch a renewed assault against the occupiers, irrespective of the consequences. Using only tried and tested young men, they succeeded in ambushing a column of enemy trucks laden with food, money and armaments at an isolated spot known as Jelin Dub above the gorge of the Mala river near the village of Bioče, north of Podgorica. Fifteen Italians were killed and seventy captured for the loss of only one attacker dead and one wounded.[56]

The Italians struck back, executing peasants from a neighbouring village who had signed up as members of the pro-Italian guard. In turn the Communist leadership decided to retaliate by killing some of their Italian prisoners. Somehow the prisoners themselves learned of this plan and pleaded with their Montenegrin captors to intervene. Moved by the entreaties of ordinary soldiers with whom they had shared food and heavy loads over the previous days, Djilas's men

---

[55] Roberts, *Tito, Mihailović and the Allies*, p. 34. Tito had held one previous meeting with Mihailović on 16 September near Valjevo in western Serbia.

[56] Djilas, *Wartime*, pp. 73–4.

urged their leaders to spare the prisoners' lives. Djilas and the other leaders hesitated but then relented, freeing the ordinary soldiers and offering to spare the officers in exchange for some of their own prisoners. The Italians agreed and an exchange of prisoners followed.

The apparent turnabout in the Communists' fortunes led some left-leaning separatists, among them Petar Plamenac and Novica Radović, to try to involve them in further talks with the Italians aimed at achieving a halt to the killing.[57] When the Communist leadership somewhat surprisingly agreed to the offer of talks, the Italians proposed an amnesty (except for those who had killed Italian soldiers) in exchange for the cessation of hostilities and the surrender of weapons. The Communists countered by demanding a complete Italian withdrawal. Both demands were almost equally unrealistic and the talks ended having achieved nothing beyond demonstrating that the Italians had given up all hope of making headway with the separatists and were now prepared to seek compromises even with Communists.[58]

The improvement in Communist morale did not last long. At the end of October Tito had ordered a leading Montenegrin Communist and Politburo member, Ivan Milutinović, at that stage still in Užice, to return to Montenegro to set up a new local military and political command from which Djilas was to be specifically excluded. Other prominent members included Blažo Jovanović, appointed chief of staff, as well Arso Jovanović, by now a member of the Communist Party, and Peko Dapčević, a veteran of the Spanish Civil War and later one of the Partisans' most prominent generals.[59] Besides re-ordering the local hierarchy, Milutinović on Tito's orders promulgated a number of rules intended to improve cohesion and boost recruitment, among which was the instruction to refer to Tito's resistance forces as 'Partisans' instead of the previously used term 'guerrillas'. But the most important of the tasks Tito entrusted to Milutinović at this time involved the despatch of 2,500–3000 Montenegrin Partisans across the Sandžak into Serbia where they

[57] *Ibid.*, p. 76.
[58] *Ibid.*, pp. 76–7.
[59] Other leading members were Bajo Sekulić, who was given the title of 'Vice Commandant', and Budimir Tomović who was appointed head of the Montenegrin branch of the Communist Youth Organisation or SKOJ.

were to assist their Serbian comrades in the struggle to secure their country's future liberation.

For Djilas dismissal from the official command was just the first in a series of blows. On 2 November his brother Aleksa was killed by Montenegrin militia fighting on the side of Italian forces in the hunt for Partisan saboteurs. Subsequently the Partisan leadership abandoned Radovče for the greater safety of Gostilje on the slopes of Mount Zlatibor, just across the border in Serbia. Scarcely had the leadership moved into their new headquarters when a further letter from Tito singled out Djilas as principally to blame for the failure of the uprising[60] and ordered him to make his way to supreme command headquarters, still at this stage at Užice.

In later years the Communist leadership were determined to draw some positive conclusions from the uprising despite its failure to achieve its ambitious goals. In this they were at least partly right: the uprising had transformed the Montenegrin Communists from an underground organisation into a core part of the Partisan resistance movement which, despite suffering the most serious reverses, would survive to fight repeated engagements and emerge eventually as victors. Post-war Yugoslav historiography, throughout the Tito era and beyond, continued to depict the insurrection as a highly significant event—at once a genuine popular movement and the first and most unequivocal uprising of the entire war.

The period of 'Left Deviation'

If the Montenegrin Partisans had shown flexibility in their dealing with both the Italian prisoners and the left separatists, it was scarcely characteristic of their general approach.[61] The momentary truce

---

[60] In his letter to Djilas, quoted on p. 79 of *Wartime*, Tito says that the uprising had been the right decision but not sufficiently prepared, and that from the beginning Partisan tactics should have been adopted. At the Fifth Party Congress in 1948, Tito partly apologized to Djilas in private. (Conversation with Milovan Djilas's son, Aleksa.)

[61] The Partisan leadership, however, formally forbade its forces to carry out atrocities and ethnic cleansing of the Muslim minorities in Montenegro. On 25 July 1941, after nationalist forces led by Pavle Djurišić and Nikola Trifunović proposed driving out the Muslim population in the area between Berane and Rožaje, the Berane Committee of the Montenegrin Communist Party issued a directive

with the Italians soon broke down as the Partisans launched a series of attacks on telegraph lines and bridges, culminating in a particularly violent encounter on 9 November in which a considerable number of Italians died.[62] Moreover, as the Partisans began to retake some of the terrain lost after the crushing of the uprising, their return was accompanied by a spate of executions of their fellow Montenegrins. Many of those executed were denounced as spies or collaborators but others were in reality simply prominent citizens judged to be 'class enemies', a category that included former members of parliament, judges and larger landowners. Caught between the Partisans' excesses and fear of Italian reprisals, many villagers turned instead to the nationalist bands as offering some degree of protection. So counterproductive was this upsurge of extremism that the Communists themselves later denounced it as an example of 'left deviation', a fundamental error for which Djilas was blamed. But it was in his absence from Montenegro, from November till the following March, that some of the worst atrocities were perpetrated including the macabre events that took place outside Kolašin over Orthodox Christmas of 1941–2. Here fanatical young Partisans carried out a particularly gruesome series of executions of prominent townspeople in a field where the bodies were then dumped together with that of a tortured dog at a site they dubbed the 'Dogs' Graveyard'.[63]

If Djilas cannot be held accountable for the carnage at Kolašin or atrocities that occurred over the winter of 1941–2, he was by his own admission involved in the executions of some civilians and prisoners. His account of the period, *Wartime*, published in the United States and Britain in 1977 at a time when publication was impossible in Yugoslavia, is a work that must stand as one of the great memoirs of warfare of modern times.[64] In it Djilas admits to ordering or

---

which threatened to punish with death by firing squad the pillaging and burning of Muslim houses and possessions or any other excesses directed against Muslims. See Scotti and Viazzi, *Le Aquile delle Montagne Nere*, pp. 207–8.
[62] *Ibid.*, pp. 343–4.
[63] Fleming, *Montenegro: The Divided Land*, pp. 136–7.
[64] *Wartime* was of course written over thirty years after the events it describes, yet the sense of immediacy it conveys, the author's readiness to admit his own errors of judgement, its focus on events in Montenegro through the eyes of a Montenegrin, combine to make it not only a primary source of indisputable value but

acquiescing in both the burning of villages[65] and the execution of individuals who were in no way collaborators but were deemed by virtue of their occupation or social position to be 'reactionaries' and class enemies:

It became increasingly clear to me that our imprudent, hasty executions, along with hunger and war weariness, were helping to strengthen the Chetniks.[66] Even more horrible and inconceivable was the killing of kinsmen and hurling of their bodies into ravines—less for convenience than to avoid the funeral processions and the inconsolable and fearless mourners. In Hercegovina it was still more horrible and ugly: Communist sons confirmed their devotion by killing their own fathers, and there was dancing and singing around the bodies. How many were executed in Montenegro and Sandžak at that time? I don't know but several hundred doesn't seem exaggerated.[67] All too lightly the Communists destroyed the inherited, primeval customs—as if they had new and immutable ones to replace them with. By retrieving the bodies from the ravines and giving them solemn burial, the Chetniks made impressive gains while pinning on the Communists the horrible nickname of 'pitmen'.[68]

---

one that has the compelling ring of truth. Yet precisely for this reason there is a need to be wary of accepting all of Djilas's assertions at face value, when clearly both the passage of time and the need to explain and justify certain actions which the later Djilas was bound to find reprehensible is likely to have coloured his presentation of some of the events described. On this point see Scotti and Viazzi, *L'Inutile Vittoria: La tragica esperienza delle truppe italiane in Montenegro*, Milan: Mursia, 1989, especially. pp. 243–51. Regrettably Djilas's memoir has no counterpart on the Chetnik side.

[65] In fact after a number of villages including Ozrinići near Nikšić and Donji Zagarač in Old Montenegro, had been razed, Djilas and Milutinović together came to the conclusion that the burning of villages was counterproductive and called a halt to the practice. See *Wartime*, p. 155.

[66] The nationalists in Montenegro were by this stage becoming better known by the name already used in Serbia—Chetniks.

[67] It should be remembered that executions carried out by the Partisans during this period were certainly matched by those carried out by Montenegrin Chetniks, which included other prominent citizens of Kolašin who were executed at around that time for sympathising with the Partisans (see below). The Chetniks also carried out large-scale massacres against Muslim civilians during this period. One such massacre in the Pljevlja district in February 1942 is described in a Chetnik report to headquarters at Zaostro near Berane as resulting in the deaths of 'about 1,200 armed men and around 8,000 civilians, women, old people and children' (see Scotti and Viazzi, *L'Inutile Vittoria*, p. 140).

[68] Djilas, *Wartime*, p. 149.

Partisan excesses were not the only reason why the winter of 1941
saw ordinary villagers deserting the Partisans and turning for support to local nationalists. In early December the Partisans' prestige
had been deeply damaged by a failed attack on the Italian garrison at
Pljevlja which left them with over 300 dead and two to three times
that number wounded. Milutinović believed that in order to send
the Montenegrin Partisans into Serbia in compliance with Tito's
orders he had first to drive the Italian forces out of Pljevlja, a key
point in their battle to control the Sandžak. As he was to discover, his
plan to reduce the garrison and capture the town was over-ambi-
tious. Pljevlja was heavily fortified and defended by the highly capable Alpine Pusteria Division.[69] Tito, who had been initially consulted
by Milutinović, had already expressed grave doubts over the viability
of the plan, but was forced by the German assault on Užice, which
was taking place at the time, to focus on securing the safe passage of
his forces out of Serbia to the exclusion of all other matters.

Hoping for both glory and booty, Milutinović went ahead with
catastrophic consequences. Although some Partisan units fought
bravely, others had melted away even before battle was engaged,
thereby providing the nationalists with a demonstration of Partisan
military ineptitude, if not actual cowardice, which they were quick
to exploit. On hearing the news Tito blamed both Arso Jovanović,
the commander, and Milutinović for the defeat, although it was not
until Arso Jovanović broke with Tito over the split with Stalin in
1948 that his role in the debacle at Pljevlja resurfaced to set the seal
on his disgrace.[70]

The beginning of Chetnik collaboration

The carnage at the Dogs' Graveyard near Kolašin had revealed just
how far relations between Chetniks and Partisans had deteriorated

[69] One of the liaison officers appointed by the Germans to be stationed alongside
the Pusteria Division in Pljevlja was Lieutenant Kurt Waldheim, the future Sec-
retary-General of the United Nations. Italian documents and private diaries
mention both his fondness for political argument, something not encouraged by
Italian authorities, and his friendly and informal behaviour. See Scotti and
Viazzi, *Le Aquile delle Montagne Nere*, pp. 318–19.
[70] *Ibid.*

in Montenegro since the days of the July uprising. In Serbia too relations between the two military formations were breaking down. Earlier agreements on a limited degree of cooperation reached after Tito and Mihailović had met on two occasions—in September and October 1941—near Ravna Gora had failed to prevent continuing clashes between Partisans and Chetniks.[71]

As news of the rift between them filtered through to Montenegro it played into the hands of those nationalist leaders who were already contemplating a policy of collaboration.[72] Thus far the different Chetnik bands in Montenegro had tended to act in isolation with little overall co-ordination, a state of affairs which continued well into 1942 (and even beyond) despite a serious attempt by Mihailović in December 1941 to assert his control over the Montenegrin Chetniks by formally appointing Pavle Djurišić, who had fought alongside the Partisans at Berane during the July uprising, and Djordjie Lašić, respectively as commanders for the Sandžak and Old Montenegro. Possibly Mihailović's strategy for Montenegro was 'premature',[73] but more probably his appointees were by nature closer to the Montenegrin tradition of warlords—men who attracted a following of guerrilla fighters motivated by personal loyalty and prepared to switch allegiances and countenance all manner of betrayals in the interest of their own survival and those of their immediate families.

In February 1942, having built up his guerrilla army, Djurišić returned to continue the cycle of revenge after the bloodbath of nationalist supporters at Kolašin, defeating the Partisans and killing two leading members—Budo Tomović, secretary of the Montenegrin Communist Youth, and Bajo Sekulić, a member of the central staff and close colleague of Djilas. For Djurišić as for other Chetnik commanders in Montenegro at this time the Partisans had become the real enemy.

To hasten their defeat and improve their own situation a number of what might loosely be called Chetnik leaders, all former Royal Army officers, reached agreements with the occupying forces. The

[71] Roberts, *Tito, Mihailović and the Allies*, pp. 31–7.
[72] Tomasevich, *The Chetniks*, p. 209.
[73] Milazzo, *The Chetnik Movement*, p. 47.

first commander to do so was Colonel Bajo Stanišić—he to whom Djilas had originally offered the command of the July uprising. In early February Stanišić suddenly withdrew his units from the combined resistance forces surrounding Danilovgrad, thereby allowing the Italians to break out and defeat the Partisans.[74] Almost immediately after this he sent a representative to establish a link with the Italian commander of the Tauro Division and within a short time was receiving supplies from the Italians.[75] Stanišić was at this time still the leader of a quasi-autonomous group, which he styled the National Liberation Army of Montenegro and Hercegovina.[76] Djurišić was, by contrast, one of the Montenegrin leaders with official links to Mihailović, but soon he too was negotiating with Italians, concluding his own agreement with Pirzio Biroli and thereby obtaining a free hand for his Chetniks against the Partisans in areas under the control of the Venezia Division.[77]

On 9 March a number of Chetnik leaders met at Cetinje[78] and, in a move possibly encouraged by Mihailović,[79] they formed a Montenegrin National Committee and elected General Blažo Djukanović as commander of all so-called nationalist forces in Montenegro. Stanišić then became the intermediary through which this body sought and achieved a satisfactory understanding with the Italians. By this stage it had become apparent that Stanišić, for all his protestations of independence, was nonetheless in contact both with the Italians, from whom he was receiving supplies, and Mihailović, with whom he maintained a direct correspondence.[80]

The Partisans' situation deteriorates

As the Chetnik commanders drew closer to the Italians, the situation for the Partisans in Montenegro was worsening. An assembly held at

---

[74] Milazzo, *The Chetnik Movement*, pp. 81–2.
[75] *Ibid.*
[76] Scotti and Viazzi, *L'Inutile Vittoria*, p. 148.
[77] Tomasevich, *The Chetniks*, p. 210.
[78] *Ibid.*, p. 210. Milazzo (*The Chetnik Movement*, p. 82) wrongly claims that this meeting took place at Podgorica.
[79] Tomasevich, *The Chetniks*, p. 210.
[80] Milazzo, *The Chetnik Movement*, p. 82 and Scotti and Viazzi, *L'Inutile Vittoria*, pp. 183–4.

Ostrog monastery on 8 and 9 February 1942 failed in its attempt to harness popular support by setting up a National Liberation Council intended to lay the foundations for a future Government of Montenegro.[81] Meanwhile increasing hunger among the population was encouraging yet more defections among the Partisans' peasant supporters, while drops of arms, food and medicine long expected from the Soviet allies failed to arrive. So concerned was Tito at the prospect of losing Montenegro that in March 1942 he ordered Djilas to return to Montenegro to replace the now out of favour Milutinović. Not only was Montenegro a traditional bastion of Communist support, but its loss would rule out the prospect of the Partisans in Serbia receiving help by sea, as well as forfeiting large tracts of country best suited to guerrilla warfare. Tito therefore authorized Djilas to do whatever was necessary, including the burning of whole villages to discourage their inhabitants from going over to the Chetniks.[82]

By the end of March 1942 Montenegro was ravaged, the people were cowed and concerned only with the struggle for survival. The Partisans' brutal policy of reprisals and executions was alienating not only the local population but also their own supporters as Djilas discovered when he returned after a four-month absence. 'Don't such death sentences cause fear and dread not only among the population, but within the party itself? How else', Djilas asked in a report dated 27 March and sent to headquarters in Užice, 'is one to explain that on territory liberated by the Partisans, the Chetniks have been successful in inciting such panic that the Partisans don't encounter a single soul?'[83] In response the Central Committee ordered a halt to unjustified executions. The killings became fewer, perhaps, but they did not stop, and nor did burning of villages and settlements. Just five days after Djilas's report to headquarters over thirty members of the Karadžići clan were deemed guilty of conspiracy and executed in Šavnik. Many of them, as Djilas himself observes, were condemned

---

[81] See Scotti and Viazzi, *L'Inutile Vittoria*, pp. 179–82. Scotti and Viazzi claim to have found no trace in Yugoslav documents of an Assembly resolution declaring the liberated territory of Montenegro to be an integral part of the Soviet Union, as claimed by the diplomat turned historian Walter Roberts. (*Tito, Mihailović and the Allies*, p. 55.)

[82] Djilas, *Wartime*, p. 146.

[83] *Ibid.*, p. 156.

solely on the basis of clan affiliation, although the Partisans themselves would have argued that while such a penalty was extreme, it was a reaction to the clan's known nationalistic and anti-Communist fanaticism.[84]

The Third Offensive

In an attempt to stem the haemorrhaging of support the Partisans set about reorganising their forces, reforming the chain of command by creating highly mobile units of younger fighters, many of them Party members.[85] The reorganisation was the more urgent since the Partisans were about to come under renewed attack, which for the first time would involve a co-ordinated offensive by the Axis powers and Ustasha forces operating together with Chetnik units[86] and conducted over an area stretching from Bosnia and Hercegovina through the Sandžak and into Montenegro. The combined attack—the Third Enemy Offensive in Partisan terminology—was launched on 11 March with Tito's headquarters at Foča coming under German aerial bombardment, while in Montenegro the Italian forces were assisted by some 12,000 'collaborationists' under the overall command of Major Ostojić.[87] These forces included the formations commanded by Djurišić and Stanišić and the brigade of former Greens led by the old Montenegrin *vojvoda* General Krsto Popović, as well as a number of Muslim detachments and semi-detached Chetnik bands.[88]

---

[84] The infamous Radovan Karadžić, leader of the Bosnian Serbs in the 1992–5 Bosnian war, is a member of the Karadžići clan. Born in 1945 in Šavnik in Montenegro, he is too young to have seen and remembered the killings, but in a society where such events remain firmly embedded in oral history it is not difficult to imagine the part which accounts of the Partisans' actions may have played in Karadžić's own psychological make-up.

[85] Djilas, *Wartime*, p. 151.

[86] An extreme example of Chetnik collaboration with anyone who could help them crush the Partisans.

[87] Scotti and Viazzi, *L'Inutile Vittoria*, p. 293. Ostojić, having made his way to Mihailović's headquarters in October 1941, had been appointed by the latter as commander of the Chetnik forces in the border regions of Sandžak and Montenegro.

[88] *Ibid.* Although originally a Green, Popović had belonged to the faction that had previously come to terms with the reality of the First Yugoslavia to the extent of calling themselves 'federalists' and redefining their platform as that of demanding

The Partisans, now divided into their smaller and more flexible units, were under-equipped and vastly outnumbered by their adversaries. Recognising that the circumstances left them extremely exposed at their base in Piperi territory close to Podgorica, the leadership moved to Gornje Polje near Nikšić, the headquarters of the veteran Communist and legendary Montenegrin fighter, Sava Kovačević.

For a time the renewed energy injected into the Partisans by reorganised fighting formations allowed them to claim some minor victories and slow the pace of the enemy advance. Believing against all odds that an offensive might yet reverse the tide against them, they launched a major attack on Kolašin in the middle of May authorised by Djilas, only to suffer a devastating defeat. To make matters worse, the Partisans on this occasion outnumbered the Chetniks by three or four to one, although the Chetniks were more than compensated by the abundant supply of munitions they received from the Italians. The Partisans had not wished to fight for a town they knew would soon be abandoned. There was no disguising the fact that the Chetniks were advancing relentlessly on all sides. Besides lacking ammunition, the Partisans, now concentrated mainly in the barren and snow-covered uplands of Sinjajevina, were desperate for food.

Tito arrives in Montenegro

At this hopelessly inopportune moment Tito arrived in Montenegro after abandoning Foča on 10 May, just in time to escape the combined onslaught of German and Ustasha forces, leaving behind only a scattering of committed Communists. Ironically the situation in Montenegro was beginning to resemble that in Foča. On 21 May Vladimir Dedijer, the dedicated Communist and journalist chosen

---

equal status for Montenegro within a federal Yugoslavia. After the Axis invasion, he had cooperated in support of the Italian attempt to create a puppet state believing that it would allow Montenegro to break free of its subordinate relationship with Serbia. Subsequently the number of Montenegrins prepared to rally to the separatist cause and to serve under Popović's command allowed him to form a separate brigade, which was then formally incorporated within the Italian army.

by Tito to keep an official record of the Partisan struggle, made the following entry in his diary:

We will, perhaps, have to evacuate Montenegro. The Četniks are hitting us with automatic weapons. They have obtained cannons and mortars from the Italians. At Mojkovac they struck us with heavy machine-guns, while on our side the Aleksa Djilas Battalion had to bury their automatic rifles for want of ammunition. There is hunger. For the last twelve days our battalions on the Kolašin front have had only a third of a pound of bread per soldier per day, along with the same amount of stringy mutton. For days the only food to be had for some units was grass. And the Četniks eat Italian rations.[89]

With no choice but to retreat, Tito took the bold decision to strike out to the northwest where the enemy had not succeeded in completely closing the gap. If this were successful, he planned to push on into new territory in western Bosnia where he was hopeful of securing both fresh supplies and new recruits to the cause. Tito's 'Long March'—the name by which this epic journey was to be known—was executed in stages, with the Partisans first calling a halt in the isolated valley of the Sutjeska between the Maglić and Zelenagora mountain ranges, just across the border from Montenegro. Here the two Montenegrin brigades—the Fourth and Fifth—that were to play so important a part in subsequent fighting were formed. But the barren country of Hercegovina could not support so many Partisans. Leaving behind the Fifth Montenegrin brigade (commanded by Sava Kovačević), together with a brigade from the Sandžak, to maintain a Partisan presence in eastern Hercegovina, Tito and the rest of the Partisan units struck out for Bosnia, once again on the offensive, this time against the Ustasha forces of the Croatian fascist puppet ruler Ante Pavelić and his German overlords.

The Partisans' departure from Montenegro was naturally the best possible news for the Chetniks. Indeed so favourable were the circumstances for them there and so rapid was the growth of their support that in May 1942 Mihailović decided to save his forces from the German onslaught taking place in Serbia by heading for Montenegro, where he established his headquarters on the slopes of Sinjajevina not far from Mount Durmitor. Meanwhile the Italians in Montenegro, freed from the constant threat of Partisan attacks, were

[89] Dedijer, *War Diaries*, vol. 1, entry for 21 May 1942.

keen to use the Chetniks to carry much of the burden of the occupation for them, principally the policing of the countryside and the suppression of any sign of pro-Partisan activity. As early as November–December 1941 General Pirzio Biroli, in recognition of the cooperation shown by 'loyal nationalists' in Montenegro, had instituted a civil administration with Montenegrin placemen named as the heads of various departments of government. But the fact that each Montenegrin was shadowed by an Italian official ensured that the administration was a sham from the start.[90]

On 24 July 1942 Pirzio Biroli took the policy of co-opting Chetniks a step further when he signed a formal agreement with General Blažo Djukanović of the Chetnik officers' Montenegrin National Committee. The Italian general thereby approved the formation of three 'flying detachments', each of about 1,500 men and commanded by a Montenegrin leader. These were the pro-Mihailović Chetnik Pavle Djurišić, the nominally independent nationalist Bajo Stanišić,[91] and the federalist Krsto Popović. In order to attract men of completely opposing political tendencies—in other words, both Whites and Greens—the Italians convinced them all of the need to defeat the Partisans as a first priority, and then promised Djurišić and Stanišić assistance in their aim of forming a Greater Serbia while assuring Popović that the destruction of the Partisans would only be a prelude to eradicating the Chetniks whose eventual defeat would make possible the restoration of an independent Montenegro.[92]

In this way the Italians succeeded in achieving an arrangement that appeared to serve the interests of all sides. They themselves had gained what effectively amounted to an auxiliary force able to ensure the pacification of the more remote areas of Montenegro, thereby obviating the need for additional Italian troops, which were now required to deal with increasing disorder in Albania. The Chetniks were granted considerable freedom of manoeuvre in rural areas plus guaranteed pay, rations and arms for the men directly involved and

---

[90] Scotti and Viazzi, *Le Aquile delle Montagne Nere*, pp. 375–6.

[91] Stanišić's 'Army of National Liberation' was nominally autonomous but he had already cooperated with Major Ostojić in the course of the Third Offensive and was himself directly in touch with Mihailović whose aims for a Greater Serbia he largely shared. See Scotti and Viazzi, *ibid.*, pp. 184–6.

[92] Scotti and Viazzi, *L'Inutile Vittoria*, p. 148.

sufficient food for their families.[93] Finally the federalists, who already had troops officially serving as auxiliaries in the Italian army,[94] hoped to benefit from an arrangement that saw them treated on an equal footing with the much more numerous Chetniks.

With Mihailović now in Montenegro the question arises as to how far he himself approved of the official relationship with the Italian occupiers. The subject remains controversial with historians falling broadly into two camps: on the one hand are those who argue that the presence of Mihailović in Montenegro and his contacts with Hercegovinian and Montenegrin Chetnik leaders demonstrate that he must have known and approved of their collaboration with the Italians, and on the other those who maintain that his failure to denounce General Djukanović and other Chetnik collaborators in western Yugoslavia was based on the Chetnik leader's unwillingness to admit to his lack of control.[95] The balance of evidence suggests that his acceptance of the need to collaborate was based on his view that this was a necessary evil if he were to achieve his ultimate goal of a Serb-dominated and monarchical post-war Yugoslavia or, if there were no alternative, a Greater Serbia. As the Italian historians Scotti and Viazzi comment in *L'Inutile Vittoria*, Mihailović's relationship with the Italians constituted perhaps 'a unique instance in history of an army minister and commander of the same army deploying it not against the enemy (the occupying troops) but alongside the enemy against a national liberation army'.[96]

---

[93] In the case of the Chetniks, the 3,000 men incorporated in the Italians' auxiliary force represented only a small proportion of their fighting men. Tomasevich quotes an internal memorandum of the Italian Foreign Ministry as putting the overall number of Chetnik forces at 31,500 with the caveat that 'the figure is totally unrealistic, except possibly as an estimate of the number who could be mobilized in areas under Chetnik control'. (*The Chetniks*, p. 212.)

[94] Scotti and Viazzi, *L'Inutile Vittoria*, pp. 184–5.

[95] Among the first group are the historians Jozo Tomasevich (*The Chetniks*, p. 211) and Matteo Milazzo (*The Chetnik Movement*, pp. 93–5), while the second group includes the British-Yugoslav historian Stevan Pavlowitch (talk with Pavlowitch on 19 April 2004) and the French academic Antoine Sidoti (*Partisans et Tchetniks en Yougoslavie durant la Seconde Guerre Mondiale: Idéologie et mythogenèse*, CNRS Editions, Paris, 2004). Needless to say, the subject arouses still stronger feelings among historians from within the different parts of the former Yugoslavia.

[96] Scotti and Viazzi, *L'Inutile Vittoria*, p. 190.

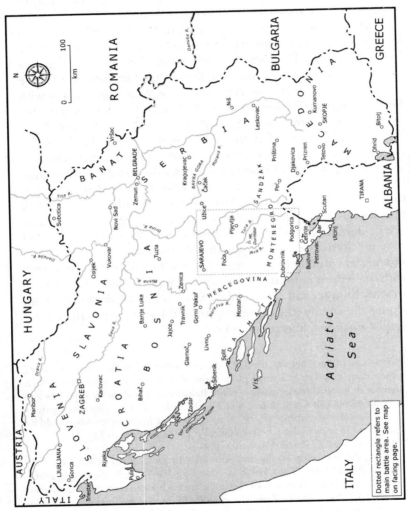

Yugoslavia during the Second World War

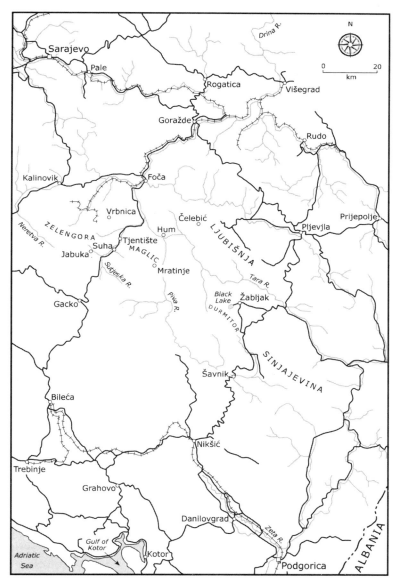

The Main Battle Area during the Fourth and Fifth Offensives

The Yugoslav context: the 'Long March'

The *modus vivendi* reached between the Italians and the Chetniks meant that by the middle of 1942 the focal point of the resistance had moved out of Montenegro (and Serbia) to Bosnia, where the larger part of Tito's Partisans was following a north-westerly route lying largely between the Italian and German zones of occupation.[97] The initial stages of the march were particularly harrowing as men and women, many still in their teens and at times in a state of near-starvation, had to fight their way through countryside dominated by Ustasha units.

By August 1942, however, the Partisans had captured the small town of Livno in central Bosnia from where they were able to extend their control over further swathes of territory to the north and west. On 5 November they captured the important town of Bihać, significant subsequently politically as it saw the creation at the end of November of what came to be called the Anti-Fascist National Liberation Council of Yugoslavia or AVNOJ.[98] This was to be the political arm of the liberation struggle ostensibly representing all the political parties engaged in the fight to free Yugoslavia from fascist oppression. AVNOJ adopted a restrained programme intended to seduce doubters both inside and outside Yugoslavia into believing that the Partisans were not bent on creating a Communist Yugoslavia after the war.[99]

The 'Long March' was a great achievement for the Partisans. Fighting over four months and covering a distance of some 300 kilometres, they transformed themselves from a force threatened with annihilation in both Serbia and Montenegro into a highly disciplined army whose numbers were being constantly replenished by new recruits to the cause. Success had been achieved through ruthless methods—Chetnik and Muslim villages had been burnt and hundreds of Chetniks executed, many at the hands of Montenegrin Partisans who were ready to take revenge for their own losses and no less ready when it came to booty.[100] Yet within the NDH the Par-

---

[97] Fitzroy Maclean, *Disputed Barricade: The Life and Times of Josip Broz Tito*, London: Jonathan Cape, 1957, p. 186.

[98] Antifaštistićko Veće Narodnog Oslobodjenja Jugoslavije.

[99] Roberts, *Tito, Mihailović and the Allies*, p. 78.

[100] Djilas, *Wartime*, p. 191.

tisans' ruthlessness did not begin to approach that of the Ustasha, whose actions at times left even the German occupiers appalled.

Operation Weiss; the Fourth Offensive

In the midst of war waged against both occupiers and domestic enemies, the Partisans' success at Bihać could be no more than a respite. In December 1942 Hitler announced his intention to crush resistance in the Balkans which was not only tying up too many German divisions but also posed a particular risk in the event of a possible Allied invasion of Yugoslavia. In January 1943 the German commander in the Balkans General Löhr, the Italian chief of staff General Ugo Cavallero, the commander of the Italian Second Army General Mario Roatta, a representative of the Ustasha, and the maverick Chetnik leader for Dalmatia and Hercegovina, Dobroslav Jevdjević, met in Rome to plan a campaign that would be known by the Germans as Operation Weiss and by the Partisans as the Fourth Offensive.[101] The first stage of the plan was to involve the use of German, Italian and Ustasha troops to encircle the Partisans in the barren uplands of Bosnia before proceeding to destroy them;[102] the second stage was to disarm and neutralise the Chetniks. The Italians, however, had reservations about proceeding against the Chetniks with whom they had cooperated closely in Montenegro, Dalmatia and Hercegovina, and although they reluctantly assented to German demands for their disarmament, they continued clandestinely to arm them and to rely on them as auxiliary forces.

In fact the Chetniks were more ready than ever to act against the Partisans, whom they now regarded as the principal threat to their plans for a Serb-dominated, monarchist Yugoslavia. By January the volunteer units of both Djurišić and Stanišić were preparing to march north. From the village of Donje Lipovo on the slopes of Sinjajevina Mihailović gave his approval to Chetnik participation in Operation Weiss, as his communications with the Hercegovinan leader Jevdjević make clear.[103] On 19 January, the day before it was launched, a delegate from General Djukanović's staff at Cetinje was

[101] Roberts, *Tito, Mihailovic and the Allies,* pp. 103–4.
[102] Fitzroy Maclean, *Tito: A Pictorial Biography,* London: Macmillan, 1980, p. 67.
[103] Milazzo, *The Chetnik Movement,* pp. 114–16.

flown to Split in an Italian plane with instructions to coordinate Montenegrin Chetniks' movements with overall Italian strategy.[104]

At the end of January four German and three Italian divisions and several Ustasha brigades equipped with tanks and artillery and with air support attacked the Partisans from the north. But the immediate plan to encircle the Partisans did not work because Tito, having already decided on a spring breakthrough back into Montenegro,[105] had already moved the best of his fighting forces, including the First and Second Proletarian Divisions, to the south and out of the range of immediate enemy encirclement. These forces now continued to fight their way though Bosnia in the direction of the River Neretva, taking with them some 4,000 sick and wounded Partisans. Tito's ultimate aim was to reunite his forces, including those left behind in the north to hold off any German attack, and break through into the wild mountainous country of eastern Bosnia and Montenegro where he could resume the offensive. But the immediate situation was desperate. Food supplies were short, temperatures had fallen, typhus had broken out, and the number of sick—both Partisans and civilians— was growing by the day. A desperate plea to the Soviets for aid was turned down 'on account of insurmountable technical difficulties'.[106]

On 6 March Tito decided to take the only course of action open to him by forcing a passage across the Neretva river. It was a daunting enterprise: the Partisans faced overwhelming enemy numbers on all sides—the Germans to the north and east, the Italians to the west and the Chetniks in a commanding position in the mountains beyond the river.[107] The fording of the river was led by the Second Proletarian Division, commanded by the Montenegrin General Peko Dapčević who successfully stormed the Chetnik positions on Mount Prenj, clearing a way for the main Partisan force to follow.[108]

---

[104] *Ibid.*, p. 116.

[105] As Walter Roberts explains, Tito needed to return to Montenegro in order to be closer to Serbia, which he believed he needed to control in order to dominate Yugoslavia. (*Tito, Mihailovic and the Allies*, p. 100.) In addition, the move back into Montenegro would enable his forces to establish contact with Albanian Partisans.

[106] Quoted by Maclean in *Disputed Barricade*, p. 206.

[107] *Ibid*, p. 212.

[108] *Ibid*.

With 4,000 wounded to transport under intense enemy aerial bombardment, the whole perilous operation took over a week to complete, but its success left the way open for the return to Montenegro.

The day after the first crossing of the Neretva Tito sent a message to the German headquarters in Zagreb via their communications centre in western Bosnia, stating that the Partisans were prepared to carry out an exchange of prisoners. When the Germans agreed, the Partisans sent three negotiators—the commander of the First Proletarian Division Koča Popović, the Serb lawyer from Croatia Vladimir Velebit, and Milovan Djilas (the latter two under false names)—to the Bosnian town of Gorni Vakuf, and later to Zagreb, for talks with the enemy. Unexpectedly the Partisans' written proposals included not only the exchange of prisoners but an offer to call a ceasefire. Furthermore the third point of their proposals included the statement that they considered the Chetniks to be their main enemy, noteworthy as an indication that the Partisans, in this instance at least, were prepared to do what they had always attacked the Chetniks for doing—tactically collaborating with the enemy in order to gain the upper hand against their domestic foes, even if they never contemplated fighting under Axis command. The Communists later defended the tactic as an attempt to buy time while the Partisans were under maximum pressure,[109] and indeed, as Tomasevich argues, the Partisans' long record of hostilities against the occupiers, both before and after, would seem to bear this out.[110] In the end, however, although the exchange of prisoners, which included Tito's former wife Herta, was agreed, the ceasefire got nowhere. Ribbentrop himself intervened to impose a veto, a move subsequently strongly endorsed by Hitler who was said to have remarked: 'One does not negotiate with rebels—rebels must be shot.'[111]

[109] Djilas, *Wartime*, p. 244.

[110] Tomasevich, *The Chetniks*, p. 246. See also Milazzo, *The Chetnik Movement*, pp. 134–5. However, the post-war Tito regime was determined to prevent knowledge of these proposals getting out and damaging the integrity of the Partisan myth of relentless struggle against the enemy, brotherhood and unity, etc. All mention of the negotiations was thus suppressed until revealed by Roberts (*Tito, Mihailović and the Allies*) in 1973 and subsequently admitted by Djilas in *Wartime* in 1977.

[111] Roberts, *Tito, Mihailović and the Allies*, p. 110.

'Operation Schwarz'; the Fifth Offensive

By late April 1943 the majority of the Partisans, having defeated a combined Chetnik and Italian force at the confluence of the Drina and Piva rivers, had successfully crossed once again into Montenegro where they were advancing rapidly, driving the fleeing Chetniks before them. So great was the Chetnik disarray that in May Mihailović, having again failed to hold the line against the Partisans, this time between Nikšić and Bijelo Polje, and receiving a warning that the Germans too were preparing to pursue him into Montenegro, decided to return with about 2,000 of his followers to Serbia.[112]

The Germans, though originally determined to annihilate all the resistance forces in Yugoslavia, were now resolved to crush the Partisans at all costs and at the earliest possible opportunity while continuing to proceed more slowly against the Chetniks.[113] Nevertheless in the spring, against Italian wishes, they succeeded in disarming many of the Chetniks, including Colonel Djurišić whom they sent to an internment camp in Ukraine. At the same time they began planning a new anti-Partisan offensive to take place at the end of May. Determined this time to leave nothing to chance, the Axis commanders assembled a force of some 117,000 men under General Rudolf Lüters, including the crack Prince Eugen Division and part of the SS Brandenburg Division, as well as Italian and Bulgarian forces, to crush a mere 20,000 Partisans.[114]

Operation Schwarz began on 15 May 1943. The Partisans were in great peril. Mountain wildernesses, which for centuries had offered refuge to the Montenegrins, could be turned against them by an enemy possessing great technological superiority and with trained and highly mobile alpine units.[115] Captain William Deakin, a British officer who had previously been an Oxford don and a literary assistant to Winston Churchill, dropped by parachute on Mount Durmitor just in time to share the experience of the Fifth Offensive. He gave a graphic account of the terrain and its military significance.[116]

[112] Tomasevich, *The Chetniks*, pp. 249–50.
[113] There was in fact some informal and spontaneous collaboration between German and Chetnik forces in an area west of Kolašin during Operation *Schwarz*. See Tomasevich, *The Chetniks*, p. 253.
[114] *Ibid.*, pp. 251–2.
[115] Maclean, *Disputed Barricade*, pp. 218–19.
[116] In May SOE in Cairo had picked up a message from Tito requesting them to

Mount Durmitor rises at its highest summit of Bobotov Kuk to over seven thousand feet. Precipitous cliffs in scattered clusters dominate the highland plateau, which towers above the sheer plunge of the river canyons of the Tara to the east and the Piva to the west, protecting on either flank this mountain fastness. There are no tracks leading across the higher slopes, and eternal snows crown the uplands. Save for rare stone sheepfolds and the wood cabins of shepherds on the bare pastures there are no signs of human settlement...

This region was now designed [*sic*] by the enemy as a field of destruction of the Yugoslav National Liberation Movement, whose main forces were pressed into the rugged barren triangle marked by the gorges of the Tara and Piva rivers and the mountain ranges. The battle in progress was a race for the heights, and for the river crossings.[117]

In this race the Partisans were hampered most of all by the need to transport the sick and wounded, a practice which, despite its evident costs, had become a defining tenet of the Partisan approach to war. They were short of food and lacked any form of defence against air attacks, but most of all they needed a viable plan of escape. Blocked to the south and east by a heavy concentration of German troops around Nikšić and Pljevlja, Tito had originally decided to move north towards Foča, but by the time his advance forces had cleared a way, the Germans had moved troops there blocking the route.

One alternative remained—to move the main body of forces north-westwards across the Piva gorge and then, having traversed the pitted, rock-strewn surface of Maglić massif, to cross the Sutjeska river before disappearing into the mountains of Bosnia, where the Fifth Bosnian Division under the command of Arso Jovanović

---

send a British liaison officer to join the Partisans in order to report back on their effectiveness in fighting the Axis forces. By this time the British already knew from Enigma intercepts of Chetnik collaboration with the enemy. They therefore agreed to Tito's request, and Captain Deakin, accompanied by Captain William Stuart and a team of four, were dropped by parachute on to a small plateau on Mount Durmitor where they were awaited by the Partisans. Later there were accusations that the delay had been responsible for the very heavy casualties suffered by the Partisans. Tito denied this but there is no gainsaying the fact that the Partisans' escape from encirclement on Durmitor was a very close-run thing and that Tito had taken a major risk in order to ensure the presence of a British witness to the Partisans' battle against the Axis powers.

[117] Deakin, *The Embattled Mountain*, p. 10.

awaited them.[118] This choice of route required a division of forces since there was no hope of so many Partisans weighed down by the burden of the wounded making the river crossings as a single formation. But a division of forces would assist their escape by preventing the Germans concentrating their attack in one place.[119] Moreover this move was favoured because Tito had at least partly secured the route a week earlier when he sent a small advance force to take up a position on Mount Vučevo which dominated the Maglić massif and was thus fundamental to securing the crossing of the Sutjeska valley. Now he followed up, reinforcing the troops on Vučevo and despatching a second small force to secure a crossing of the Sutjeska at Suha where a bridge across the river stood alongside an old Austrian fort. By this stage the Germans had realised what was afoot and a race for Mount Vučevo ensued, with the Partisans beating their adversaries to the summit by fifteen minutes.[120]

With Axis forces closing in on all sides the main body of Partisans began the crossing of the Piva gorge. Conditions were appalling. The Partisans struggled 1,000 metres down a single muddy track and across a rope bridge to the other side of the gorge before facing an equally steep scramble up the other side, all under the pounding of German bombers. Remarkably most of the Partisans managed the crossing and to shelter for the night in caves on the mountainside below the ruined village of Mratinje. There, just before leaving Montenegro, Tito took the decision to divide his main force again, ordering the First and Second Divisions to continue on the chosen route across the Sutjeska, while the Third and Seventh Divisions, transporting the central hospital with the sick and wounded, were to make a perilous retreat back along the way they had come before turning east and fighting their way across the gorge of the Tara river and into the Sandžak. Tito and most of the leadership, as well as the British mission, accompanied the first group while Djilas, accompanied by the Executive Committee of AVNOJ, was placed in charge of the second group responsible for the wounded.

By 6 June Tito's forces had crossed the terrain separating the Piva gorge to a point overlooking the Sutjeska, having stopped on the

---

[118] Maclean, *Disputed Barricade*, p. 223.
[119] Djilas, *Wartime*, p. 260.
[120] Maclean, *Disputed Barricade*, p. 224.

way to bury the Communist Party archives together with all their heavy weapons. But in the meantime the Germans had brought up reinforcements, which they had positioned along the far bank of the Sutjeska, leaving no more than a five kilometre gap between the villages of Tjentište and Suha, still in Partisan hands. Here the Partisans staged a precarious crossing of the river at the spot where the Sutjeska emerges from a 1,000-metre deep canyon.[121] The Germans believed the ring to be closed and issued an order stating that 'no able-bodied man was to leave the ring alive'.[122] Against all odds and with suicidal recklessness, men of the First and Second Proletarian Brigades spearheaded a breach through the ring to get through to the main Foča-Kalinovik road.[123] Once again the enemy tried to close the circle but too late. On 13 June the main force of Partisans crossed the road, continuing across the Sarajevo-Višegrad railway and on into the forests of Bosnia.

Meanwhile, although it seemed barely possible, the Third and Seventh Divisions had fared even worse than their comrades with Tito. Having returned to the Tara to find the Germans already occupying the far bank and all possible crossing points lost, Djilas decided to send the Seventh Division, too stricken by typhus and hunger to fight its way out, in the wake of Tito and the supreme staff and to entrust to them the walking wounded. He and Milutinović remained with the Third Division commanded by Sava Kovačević while the supreme staff agonised over what to do with the seriously wounded. Contrary to all previous Partisan practice, Tito agreed to Djilas's suggestion that the wounded be left behind, hidden in caves along the Piva together with medical staff who volunteered to stay with them. The best they could hope for was discovery by friendly peasants or to remain hidden until the Partisans were able to return for them; but the chances of rescue were slim and a number of the wounded committed suicide rather than be discovered by the enemy.

It was now too late for the Third Division to catch up with the Seventh Division which was trailing after Tito and the supreme staff. An attempt by members of the First Dalmatian Brigade to occupy

[121] Dedijer, *War Diaries*, vol. 2 (entry for 6 June 1943), p. 288.
[122] Maclean, *Disputed Barricade*, p. 226.
[123] Deakin, *The Embattled Mountain*, p. 20.

the hills on the left bank of the Sutjeska and secure the crossing failed. The Germans were entrenched both above the river and on the other bank but there was no alternative but to cross. In fact, instead of falling on them immediately, the Germans allowed the Partisans to cross the river and begin the ascent before opening fire with machine-guns from concealed bunkers on the other side. Calling on his men to follow, Sava Kovačević led the charge up the mountain, dying in the attempt. Others followed only to be cut down alongside him. In the chaos that followed the remnants of the Third Division broke into small groups, each struggling on its own to break the German line. Of the 1,200 members of the division who had attempted to make the crossing about half eventually got through to rejoin their comrades. Left behind along the Piva, the wounded were not so fortunate. Almost all were discovered by Axis forces using tracker dogs. They were then slaughtered, together with some 230 doctors and nurses—half the trained staff of the central hospital—who had remained with them.[124]

On 16 June the Germans called a halt to Operation Schwarz. In the course of its duration some 6,000 Partisans had lost their lives, as had some thousands of civilians in the districts of Durmitor and Piva. Determined to prevent all possibility of the Partisans' returning in the future to reclaim territory they had formerly liberated and then abandoned as they had done in Croatia, the Germans employed ruthless reprisals designed to cow the local population into lasting submission. Partisan sympathisers of both sexes and all ages were hunted out and murdered, villages burnt, livestock killed; whole clans were exterminated. Afterwards Deakin, an eye-witness to many of these events, wrote of Durmitor: 'The mountain was wreathed in flames and ashes of villages and settlements. The scattered dead lay, spilt in heaps, as if by a giant hand, across this landscape of the moon.'[125]

Italy capitulates

Although the war was far from over, the centre of action now moved well outside Montenegro with Tito, Ranković and Djilas moving on to Croatia while Peko Dapčević and his Second Proletarian

---

[124] Dedijer et al., *History of Yugoslavia*, p. 648.
[125] Deakin, *The Embattled Mountain*, p. 32.

Division returned to Montenegro both to prevent any Chetnik resurgence and to prepare a base from which to stage a future return to Serbia.[126]

On 24 July 1943 Mussolini fell from power. When this was followed by the capitulation of Italy on 8 September, the Venezia Division in Montenegro went over to the Partisans. Formed into special 'Garibaldi' brigades, these men went into combat with the Partisans against the Germans, fighting with particular success in the area around Pljevlja.

Without their Italian protectors, and indeed without Djurišić, one of their most able commanders, the Chetniks were extremely vulnerable. Krsto Popović's separatists, who had already distanced themselves from the Chetniks in order to avoid being disarmed by the Germans, were pinning their hopes on the emergence of an autonomous Montenegro under Axis patronage, now increasingly unlikely.[127] The Partisans, who had profited from the Italian withdrawal by seizing a substantial quantity of arms, lost no time in attacking the centres of Chetnik support in Berane and Kolašin. Striving to deal with the mounting chaos in Chetnik ranks, the remaining Chetnik leaders—Djukanović, Stanišić and Lašić—attempted to reorganise their forces, many of whom were now joining the Partisans or simply disappearing into the forests. Although Mihailović had ordered the Montenegrin Chetniks to resist the German occupation forces as they arrived in Montenegro to take over from the Italians, there is evidence that Stanišić at least ignored this order and tried to reach an understanding with the Germans based on their common enmity towards the Partisans.[128]

But whether or not an understanding between the Chetniks and the Germans was indeed reached, it was never acted upon since in October 1943 Partisan forces surprised Djukanović and Stanišić at Ostrog monastery. Djukanović and a number of his followers were tricked into surrendering by Blažo Jovanović, who promised that they would be put on trial after the war, but the Partisans executed them on the spot. When Stanišić, who had not surrendered, appeared at a window of the monastery, he was killed by a sniper.[129]

[126] Djilas, *Wartime*, p. 302.
[127] See Milazzo, *The Chetnik Movement*, p. 146 and below.
[128] Tomasevich, *The Chetniks*, p. 348.
[129] Djilas, *Wartime*, p. 351.

Lašić was now the only surviving Chetnik commander in Montenegro of any importance and his followers numbered no more than hundreds.[130]

The German occupation

Meanwhile on 26 September 1943 the Germans had set up a military government, Area Command no. 1040, in Montenegro under General Wilhelm Keiper, who presided over a Montenegrin Administrative Council composed of quisling representatives of both the Greens and the Whites. At the same time, the German area command reached agreements with the so-called 'national forces', effectively Chetniks, under the command of a Major Jovo Djukanović, and attempted to use these forces together with German troops in actions against the Partisans in Montenegro in December 1943 and again in April the following year but with little success.[131]

In an attempt to remedy the lack of leadership and rebuild Chetnik ranks in Montenegro, the Germans released Djurišić, together with some of his captured followers, back into Montenegro. Believing that Djurišić's strong support among Montenegrin Chetniks and his known Greater Serbia sympathies would boost a fighting force with cross-border support in Serbia and Montenegro, the Germans helped Djurišić establish the quisling Montenegrin Volunteer Corps;[132] he was even awarded the Iron Cross, supposedly the only non-German ever to receive it.[133] The German operations in Montenegro and the Sandžak were principally aimed at preventing a Partisan breakthrough into Serbia which, as all sides now recognised, would be the crucible in the battle for Yugoslavia. In the spring of 1944 the Germans sent members of a parallel Serbian Volunteer Corps, followers of the Serbian fascist Dimitrije Ljotić, to assist Djurišić in operations against the Partisans in the Sandžak.

In the middle of July the Germans launched Operation *Draufgänger* (in Partisan terminology Operation Andrijevica) in the hope

---

[130] Milazzo, *The Chetnik Movement*, p. 164. He was later killed in an Allied bombing raid over Podgorica. (Tomasevich, *The Chetniks*, p. 351.)
[131] Tomasevich, *The Chetniks*, p. 349.
[132] *Ibid.*
[133] http://ww.google.com/search?sourceid+navclient&ie+UTF-8&rls= GGLC,GGLS:1970-. Accessed on 30/01/2005.

of preventing the Partisans entering Serbia from Montenegro. To this end they despatched additional troops, specialists in mountain warfare from Greece, who were ordered to encircle and destroy those Partisans still in the region between the Piva and Tara rivers as part of a largely concurrent Operation *Rübezahl* (Operation Durmitor). These actions managed to delay the Partisans' entry into Serbia but could not prevent it.

Meanwhile Djurišić's close cooperation with the Germans continued in Montenegro until December 1944. Although the military results were insignificant in changing the balance in the Germans' favour, they did afford Djurišić and his force of roughly 7–8,000 men food supplies at a time when these were in increasingly short supply within the province and much of the population was going hungry.[134]

The Partisans' role in the final victory

As Germany's position in the Balkans weakened, the Partisans' strength increased, giving rise to further political developments. In November 1943 the Partisan leadership convened a second meeting of AVNOJ in Jajce in Bosnia to declare it the legitimate government of Yugoslavia in opposition to King Petar's government-in-exile. Tito was given the title of Marshal and his control over the armed forces was reaffirmed. Significantly for Montenegro, the elected Assembly of AVNOJ reaffirmed the federal character of post-war Yugoslavia, guaranteeing Montenegro equal status with the other constituent units—Serbia, Croatia, Slovenia, Bosnia-Hercegovina and Macedonia.

To add to their sense of progress, the Partisans' advance at the internal level was beginning to be matched by attention and assistance from abroad; by now they were receiving help from the British in the form of air support and arms on a large scale. A British military mission headed by the former diplomat and friend of Churchill, Fitzroy Maclean, was dropped into Bosnia in January and was shortly

---

[134] Tomasevich points out that the Italians had imported almost three times more food into Montenegro than the Germans ever did, accounting for the increasing occurrence of hunger and, in some cases, starvation. (*The Chetniks*, p. 351.)

afterwards followed by a Russian mission bringing with it experts in Partisan warfare.[135]

In the spring of 1944 the Germans launched a final unsuccessful assault—Operation Rösselsprung (meaning a knight's move in chess)—against Tito. He narrowly escaped death in a daring raid by paratroopers on his headquarters at Drvar in Bosnia, but was evacuated by a Soviet plane to Bari in Italy and from there was taken by a British ship to the rocky Adriatic island of Vis, where from his headquarters in a cave on the slopes of Mount Hum he continued to direct the resistance under British protection.

In the summer of 1944 pressure on the government-in-exile in London forced King Petar to dismiss his intensely anti-Partisan prime minister-in-exile, Mr Purić, and send his replacement, the Croat Dr Ivan Šubašić, to negotiate with Tito on Vis. In contrast to his predecessor, Dr Šubašić was prepared to play the role, as he saw it, of mediator between the royal government and the Partisans. In fact Tito's dominance on the ground in Yugoslavia meant that there was no question of Šubašić's entering the negotiations as an equal although he did have one card to play—Tito's need for international recognition. The imbalance nonetheless led to an agreement—that King Petar's government would recognise AVNOJ as the single political authority within Yugoslavia, and the Partisans as the official army; settling the question of a monarchy would be left till after the war. As Mihailović was stripped of his official position, Tito and the KPJ were beginning to see the future government of a liberated Yugoslavia as within their grasp. Nevertheless, they still did not entirely trust the British whom they feared might insist on a division of Yugoslavia to allow the return of a royal government to Serbia. Nor did Tito wish to allow the Soviets a completely free hand in the liberation of Serbia. The most effective means of forestalling this was to ensure that Partisan troops played a prominent part there.

Accordingly in August many of Peko Dapčević's troops, still based in Montenegro, were ordered to enter Serbia where they were to be joined by additional Partisan units from eastern Bosnia, some nine divisions in all. As a result, those units left behind were exposed to a combined offensive by German and Albanian troops resulting in the loss of some of the Montenegrin territory the Partisans had con-

---

[135] Maclean, *Disputed Barricade*, pp. 250–1.

trolled.[136] The sacrifice nevertheless seemed worth making for an army that now had victory in its sights. A second senior Partisan general, Koča Popović, was sent into Serbia where Communist recruits were re-appearing after years spent underground. In Macedonia too the Partisans under the Montenegrin Svetozar Vukmanović-Tempo were growing in strength. By the middle of September the Bulgarians had switched sides, transferring to Partisan control the areas they had occupied in Serbia and Macedonia.

As Partisan divisions continued to pour into Serbia, King Petar issued an appeal on 12 September to all Yugoslavs to join with Tito to defeat the Axis forces, further undermining Chetnik morale. At the beginning of October with Partisan agreement, the Red Army forces crossed the Danube into Serbia, presaging the arrival of a massive Soviet force with tanks and artillery on Yugoslav soil. Inevitably, given their numbers and heavy weaponry, the Red Army forces did most of the fighting against the occupiers, but Tito remained determined that the Partisans should feature prominently in the liberation of Belgrade.[137]

On 14 October Peko Dapčević and his units arrived on the outskirts of the capital. With Soviet support his forces managed to break through the German lines of defence south of the city. On 20 October the First Proletarian Division seized Kalemegdan, the old Ottoman fortress in the centre. Tito, determined to make the most of the Partisans' role in this costly victory,[138] had arranged with the Soviet commander Marshal Tolbukhin that a Partisan general should lead the column of victorious troops into the capital. Given the significant contribution of Montenegrin Partisans to the war effort, it was appropriate that this role should fall to one of the Montenegrins, Peko Dapčević, who duly entered the city on a white horse.

[136] Djilas, *Wartime*, p. 398, and Tomasevich, *The Chetniks*, pp. 409–10.

[137] The conduct of the Red Army, in particular the widespread rape of local women, shocked the Partisans whose own strict moral code had largely curbed atrocities directed specifically against women and children. Nor were the Chetniks normally guilty of such atrocities against Partisan women, a restraint not shown to Muslims.

[138] As Tomasevich points out the figures for the casualties incurred by the participants in the capture of Belgrade—Partisan losses at 2,953 as against those of the Russians at about 1000—tend to belie the claim made by some historians that the Partisans played an insignificant part in the liberation of Belgrade. (See Tomasevich, *The Chetniks*, p. 418.)

The beginnings of Tito's Yugoslavia

Meanwhile on other fronts since the summer of 1944 the Germans had experienced defeat after defeat. Progress in Western Europe and in Italy meant that the Allies were advancing towards the Balkans whence the Germans were attempting to make an orderly withdrawal. In this context there was an urgent need for the Allies to consider the political future of Yugoslavia. In October Stalin and Churchill met in Moscow to agree on a post-war division of influence throughout Eastern Europe and the Balkans and in particular to find a solution over the frontiers of Poland. On the basis of a few figures jotted down by Churchill on a half-sheet of paper with the aim of creating an atmosphere conducive to reaching a settlement on Poland, they determined that the division of interest in post-war Yugoslavia should be on a fifty–fifty basis.

In November 1944 Tito and Šubašić met again to sign a draft agreement on the setting up of a joint government that would in due course hold elections to decide on the political future of the country. In the absence of King Petar, who was not to return to Yugoslavia until the people had been given a chance to vote on the future of the monarchy, there was to be a regency council. For Tito the agreement provided the cover he needed to secure international recognition. On 7 March 1945 a new government was formed with twenty ministers from Tito's National Liberation Committee and just six from the former royal government-in-exile. Tito assumed the positions of prime minister and defence minister while Šubašić became foreign minister, a role in which he was to have no real influence. At the Yalta conference, where the victorious Allies met to decide on the post-war settlement, Tito had gained the international recognition he required. From now on he and his close collaborators in the KPJ would rule the country according to their own precepts with little regard for agreements reached at Yalta.

Against this background of political development, the fighting in Yugoslavia continued from late autumn through till May with the German army trying to save as many of its forces as possible by battling its way out to the north. As German units withdrew they were joined by troops pulling out of Greece across Albania and into Montenegro. The German 21st Corps from Greece and their 91st Corps from Kosovo converged in Montenegro as, running out of fuel and food and under attack from Allied planes, they traversed the Lim valley heading north towards the Drina river.[139] With them went Djurišić's Chetniks, hastening out of Montenegro where they found themselves both increasingly threatened by Partisan attack and unable to secure supplies from the ravaged countryside. In Montenegro, the Sandžak and Serbia the Chetniks could do little more than try to survive in the hope that the Allies, once the fighting in the Balkans was finally over, would reconsider their support for the Partisans and offer the Chetniks and Mihailović a secure position in the future government of the country.[140]

It was with these considerations in mind that, as the winter of 1944 approached, Mihailović moved his own troops from the Sandžak into northeastern Bosnia where food supplies were more easily obtainable. Similarly imperilled, Djurišić decided to jettison his own plan for escape through Albania to Greece and accept Mihailović's order to move his troops to Bosnia. In February 1945 Djurišić joined Mihailović near Majevica mountain north of Tuzla where they remained, still partly under the shelter of the Germans, but at ever-increasing risk from Partisan attack and with ebbing hopes of Allied intervention in their favour. Despite the harsh conditions they had experienced in Montenegro and the Sandžak, Djurišić's troops were in better condition than those of Mihailović; they were also better trained and personally loyal to their leader rather than to Mihailović.[141] Mihailović did not inspire confidence; he could not decide on a fixed plan of action, and still less could he continue to remain in a position of increasing vulnerability. Finally, against the wishes of the majority of his followers, he decided to head for Serbia.[142]

By the spring Djurišić had had enough of Mihailović's indecision and decided to escape by breaking with him and leading his men

---

[139] Djilas, *Wartime*, p. 446.

[140] Tomasevich, *The Chetniks*, pp. 429–30.

[141] *Ibid.*, p. 440.

[142] In fact Mihailović had fallen victim to a Partisan plan whereby the Partisans sent false coded messages intended to lure him back into Serbia by emphasising the strength of Chetnik support that he could count on there. After a number of failed attempts, the Partisans finally succeeded in capturing Mihailović in January 1946 after he was betrayed by a former follower. He was subsequently put on trial, found guilty and executed. See Tomasevich, *The Chetniks*, pp. 458–61.

north to Slovenia where he hoped to be rescued by the Allies.[143] To assist in this plan Djurišić made contact through emissaries with Sekula Drljević, the former Montenegrin quisling prime minister who, having 'escaped' from Italian custody, had set up residence in Zagreb, where he had established a *modus vivendi* with Pavelić's Ustasha government. In Zagreb he had set up a Montenegrin State Council as a prelude, he believed, to establishing an autonomous Montenegro, in effect a puppet German-Ustasha state. Drljević now promised to help Djurišić and the two apparently agreed that Djurišić's forces would co-operate in the setting up of a Montenegrin National Army. In the event Djurišić sent only his sick and wounded to join Drljević and attempted to head off on his own towards Slovenia. Drljević and his Ustasha allies then succeeded in entrapping Djurišić and many of his followers. Perhaps he had always intended to do so since, as a fervent believer in Montenegro's independence, he could never have found a lasting common cause with a Greater Serbia Chetnik like Djurišić. Djurišić's followers had by this time suffered serious losses after fighting their way through Bosnia. Regardless of any suspicion he might have had, Djurišić was thus forced to agree to negotiations with Drljević's representatives and their Ustasha allies. However, on his way to the meeting Djurišić was attacked and killed together with some other leading Chetniks and a number of Orthodox priests.[144] Some of his followers escaped and managed to reach Slovenia where they were intercepted by the Partisans and killed. In all only about a quarter of Djurišić's entire force survived. But justice finally also caught up with Drljević and his wife: both were killed in a revenge attack by supporters of Djurišić after they had managed to escape into Austria in the closing days of the war.[145]

The deaths of Djurišić and Drljević spelt the end of any hope for the revival of anti-Communist forces within Montenegro. In reality there had been no prospect of any other ending to the war in the Balkans since October 1944 when the dramatic downturn in German fortunes and likewise those of the remaining Chetniks made

[143] *Ibid.*, pp. 446–9.
[144] According to one unsubstantiated report, he was taken to Jasenovac concentration camp where he was boiled alive. (Conversation with Aleksa Djilas.)
[145] See Tomasevich, *The Chetniks*, pp. 351 and 446–9.

recovery wellnigh impossible. Fighting therefore only to save their lives, the anti-Partisan forces struggled on in Montenegro till the beginning of 1945 and elsewhere in Yugoslavia up to and beyond the date of Germany's surrender on 7 May 1945.

On 15 May, the date the war officially ended in Yugoslavia, the new representative for Montenegro in the central government of 'Democratic Yugoslavia', Djilas, had returned to a Montenegro where the foundations were being laid for a Republican government which would ensure Montenegro's autonomy on an equal basis with that of its larger neighbours—Serbia, Croatia, Bosnia-Hercegovina and Macedonia. It was to be a fresh beginning, launched amid formal celebrations, but the recollections of its new official representative depict Montenegro as still for the time being a land devastated by war:

It seemed to me [Djilas wrote] as if all of Yugoslavia was synthesized in Montenegro, in the boundless confidence of the victors and the silence and shame of the vanquished. There were scorched walls along torn-up, demolished roads; rivers without bridges; railroad tracks with splintered, ripped-out ties. In the forests, outlaws—four to five hundred in Montenegro... Titograd [Podgorica] was so devastated by Allied bombings—they say there were over twenty—that it resembled an archaeological excavation through which only one path had been cleared. The people of Podgorica had scattered to the villages or to the caves around the Morača river. From these caves there still came smoke and the cry of children.[146]

[146] Djilas, *Wartime*, p. 445.

11. Montenegro in the Second Yugoslavia

The Tito years at a glance

In many accounts of the Tito period Montenegro is lost from view, swallowed up in the mass of statistics given for the new Yugoslavia. Nor would many Montenegrins of the time have found this state of affairs unacceptable. In their enthusiasm for the new state they were unmatched by any of their fellow-Yugoslavs, not even by the generally pro-Yugoslav Muslims of Bosnia-Hercegovina.[1] Throughout the forty-six-year life of the second Yugoslavia such enthusiasm would be carefully nurtured since the federation's new rulers recognised that the ballast provided by the smaller nations played a vital part in balancing traditional Serb-Croat rivalries and thus in helping to keep the Yugoslav ship afloat.

The end of the Second World War left Montenegrins once more divided. Added to the divisions between winners and losers were those which cut across clans and families. Public exultation over the glorious victory achieved by the Partisans (36% of whose generals were Montenegrins) was accompanied by private grief at the cost of a civil war which scarcely left any family untouched. Certainly Montenegro's sacrifice had not been unnoticed—its change of status[2] constituted an acknowledgement of the outstanding part

[1] Whereas Montenegrins generally saw Yugoslavism as positive, something they embraced and had been prepared to fight for, for all but some Muslims Yugoslavia's association with Slavdom made it an ideology that they accepted, as it were, by default.

[2] The term 'Republic' did not come into use immediately. Instead the ruling body—in effect a single representative, legislative and executive institution—was known from July 1944 as the Montenegrin Anti-fascist Assembly of People's Liberation (CASNO). However, agreement on the federal organisation of post-war Yugoslavia had been agreed at the second meeting of AVNOJ in November

Montenegrins had played in the liberation struggle. Aid was beginning to come in, and the young especially were full of belief in the future and in the better world they would help to build. But with up to 50,000 Montenegrins dead,[3] with towns flattened (Podgorica had suffered some seventy Allied bombardments), roads and bridges destroyed, settlements and livestock burnt and part of the displaced population reduced to scavenging and living in caves, the task of reconstruction might well have appeared sisyphean to even the most optimistic. Instead the new leadership set about the undertaking with revolutionary zeal, imposing a rigidly orthodox system whose political underpinning owed much to Stalin's 1936 constitution with its entirely fictitious federation of 'nations'.[4] It was an orthodoxy for which the russophile Montenegrins were to pay a particularly heavy price when, three years after the Partisans' total victory, the country was again convulsed by ideological conflict following Tito's split with Stalin.

By the mid-1950s, however, Montenegro was the focus of intense efforts to tackle centuries of under-development. Millions of dinars were invested in mining, hydroelectric projects and industrial plants.[5] In the new Yugoslavia Montenegrins were everywhere—in the senior levels of public administration, in politics, in the security and the diplomatic services, and in the army. Not surprisingly the Tito

---

1943 (see Chapter 10). The creation of CASNO represented an intermediate stage before the term 'Republic' was officially confirmed following the promulgation of the constitution of the new Federal People's Republic of Yugoslavia (FNRJ) in January, 1946. In 1963 the state's name was changed to the Socialist Federative Republic of Yugoslavia (SFRJ). See Chapter 12.

[3] Bennett, *Yugoslavia's Bloody Collapse*, p. 45. As always, figures on the number of dead are controversial. This figure, though possibly on the high side, is, as Bennett points out, given additional credence by the fact that it reflects a rare degree of Serb-Croat consensus on this subject. Rastoder suggests a lower figure of 37,000 deaths (Andrijašević and Rastoder, *History of Montenegro*, p. 226).

[4] See Aleksa Djilas, *The Contested Country: Yugoslav Unity and Communist Revolution, 1919–1953*, Harvard University Press, 1999, pp. 166–7. The nature of post-war Yugoslav federalism is further considered below.

[5] For the years 1947–56 Shoup lists the average annual expenditure *per capita* in thousands of dinars as follows: Serbia 4.56; Croatia 6.18; Slovenia 7.94; Bosnia-Hercegovina 4.59; Macedonia 5.53; and Montenegro 8.69. See Paul Shoup, *Communism and the Yugoslav National Question* (hereafter referred to as *The Yugoslav National Question*), New York: Columbia University Press, 1968, p. 231.

years were for many the best years in Montenegro's entire history. The Federal People's Republic of Yugoslavia (FNRJ)[6] seemed to offer Montenegrins both a balm for wounded political pride and a vision of Yugoslavism that they took somewhat ingenuously to heart. Unfortunately, however, the high level of heavily capital-intensive investment did little to resolve Montenegro's deep-rooted economic and social problems. Instead the last years of the Tito era saw the Montenegrin economy failing to perform and unemployment and social discontent rising—so much so that by the late 1980s, as Yugoslavia was poised to fall apart, the credit Montenegro had earned through its wartime achievements had largely been spent and it remained among the poorest and least developed of the Republics.

The immediate post-war years (1945–7)

The revolutionary spirit that characterised the immediate post-war years had both positive and negative consequences. On the positive side the Communist Party sought immediately to consolidate the myth it had begun to cultivate during the war—that of the equal contribution made by all the nations of Yugoslavia in the struggle to defeat fascism and liberate the Yugoslav people.[7] Fundamental to the success of this struggle was the spirit defined by the Partisan slogan 'bratstvo i jedinstvo'—brotherhood and unity. In Montenegro this meant in particular attempting to rebuild relations with Muslims and Albanians who had actively or passively supported the Axis side during the war, a goal more successfully realised with the former than with the latter.[8] But if the new regime's policy of ethnic and

---

[6] Federativna Narodna Republika Jugoslavija.

[7] Aleksa Djilas, *The Contested Country*, p. 162. Aleksa Djilas points out that this equality was not, however, considered as applying equally to all the *peoples* of Yugoslavia: not only the Germans and Italians (most of whom had by this time either been expelled or had left out of fear) but also Hungarians and Albanians were largely excluded.

[8] Many Albanians had joined the notorious Skenderbeg SS Division, which was responsible for atrocities perpetrated against Serbs and Montenegrins during the occupation, while even Albanian Communists in Kosovo actively preferred union with Albania to incorporation within Yugoslavia. Tito did not support this and instead proposed a form of Balkan federation, which was also to include Bulgaria. Nothing came of this proposal and in December 1944 Albanians in Kosovo launched a revolt against Serbian rule which lasted till mid-1945. See Lampe, *Yugoslavia as History*, p. 223 and Shoup, *The Yugoslav National Question*, pp. 104–11.

religious tolerance was widely enforced and, at least on the surface, accepted, its capacity to motivate the masses represented a still more striking achievement. Rural youth especially responded with great enthusiasm to the call to participate in the country's reconstruction, even if in Montenegro the rebuilding came up at times against the problem of traditional attitudes to physical labour, which was seen as humiliating for males in a warrior nation. As Milovan Djilas recalled, 'When UNRRA [United Nations Relief and Rehabilitation Agency] sent pickaxes and shovels, the Montenegrins allegedly returned them: "That must be for some other fraternal republic— not for us!"'[9] But despite such obstacles and at times in the face of protests from their own supporters, the Communist leadership made no attempt to hinder UNRRA's distribution of aid on both sides of the Chetnik-Partisan divide. Nor did the Communist Party in Montenegro bow to Partisan expectations by expropriating the property of former Chetnik fighters in order to compensate the needy on their own side.[10]

Unsurprisingly given the conditions that had spawned it, the new regime was soon showing signs of the excesses characteristic of its absolutist nature, alongside more positive features. Like their counterparts in the Central Committee of the Communist Party of Yugoslavia (KPJ), the Montenegrin leadership showed no hesitation in distributing the spoils of victory among their own, an egregious example being Blažo Jovanović, president of the government and secretary of the Party, established in the villa of the former British legation to the Montenegrin court, and with other party members similarly rewarded according to rank.[11]

Nor was Montenegro exempt from the horrendous practice of revenge killings although remarkably, given the bloodletting of the war years, the level of atrocity was low in comparison to many other regions of Yugoslavia. For the first two years after the war some former Chetniks managed to hold out in the forests making the roads unsafe for official travellers, but by 1947 with most of the 'ren-

---

[9] Milovan Djilas, *Wartime*, p. 445.

[10] Banac writes: 'In an attempt to heal the wounds of war the KPJ [Communist Party of Yugoslavia] was lenient to Chetnik families, at least by the stern standards of Montenegro'. (*With Stalin against Tito*, Ithaca NY: Cornell University Press, 1988, p. 171.)

[11] Djilas, *Wartime*, p. 445.

egades', as the new regime called them, killed or having surrendered, Montenegro was largely pacified.[12] Nevertheless executions did occur, for example some non-political academics and students in Cetinje in November 1944 where the only motive appears to have been social class or educational attainment. Montenegrins were also well represented in the new post-war security service, the State Security Administration (UDBa) which in 1946 replaced its war-time equivalent, the Department for the Protection of the People (OZNa). UDBa was headed by a Serb, Aleksandar Ranković, whose agents operated 'in every block of flats, in every street, in every village and in every barrack room'[13] to report any evidence of anti-state behaviour. When it was suggested to Tito that OZNa might no longer be necessary after the war, he replied: 'If OZNa puts fear in the heart of those who do not like our kind of Yugoslavia, all the better for the Yugoslav people. We shall never listen to such advice.'[14]

But while those categorised as enemies of the state were harshly treated—arrested, imprisoned and sometimes executed—others, deemed worthy by their actions or social class, were duly rewarded. Poor Montenegrins without sufficient land to live on, for instance, benefited significantly from the expulsion of minorities—in particular the German population of Vojvodina—when they were resettled on the expropriated land.[15]

On past form the Montenegrins could be counted on to be territorially acquisitive, and the new leadership soon showed themselves just as ready as the country's traditional rulers to press the case for more land. As early as January 1944 Montenegro was asserting the right to add the Sandžak—hitherto treated by the Communists as a separate unit—to the embryonic Montenegrin federal unit, a move denounced and described as 'premature' by the Central Committee of the KPJ.[16] But by the following March its robust[17] attitude to the acquisition of territory had been successful in ensuring the return to

[12] Milovan Djilas, *Rise and Fall*, London: Macmillan, 1983, p. 6.
[13] Quoted by Lampe, *Yugoslavia as History*, p. 234.
[14] Quoted by Maclean, *Disputed Barricade*, p. 312.
[15] Aleksa Djilas, *The Contested Country*, p. 171.
[16] Banac, *With Stalin against Tito*, p. 101.
[17] *Ibid.*, p. 104: Banac describes Montenegro's approach to territorial issues as 'especially aggressive'.

Montenegro of that part of the Sandžak—Pljevlja and Bijelo Polje—which it had originally acquired after the First Balkan War.[18] In addition Montenegro had secured possession of the invaluable Gulf of Kotor, together with the adjacent Sutorina peninsula (the latter also claimed by Bosnia-Hercegovina), an area it had long coveted and one where Orthodox Serbs outnumbered Catholics by almost two to one.[19] Favourable as they were, these adjustments by no means exhausted the territorial ambitions of the Montenegrin leadership, who continued to press for the Dalmatian city of Dubrovnik, as well as Hercegovina and Metohija (the western half of Kosovo). All these claims were turned down when the borders of the Republics were fixed by the 1946 constitution.

The 1946 constitution

At the end of 1945 federal elections took place in a political climate that intimidated and silenced the regime's critics and prevented any opposition party from standing. Such overkill was unnecessary since it was likely at that time, even in essentially free and fair conditions, that elections would have produced a Communist-dominated Constituent Assembly.[20] Unsurprisingly the Assembly's first act in November 1945 was to abolish the monarchy and proclaim the Federal People's Republic of Yugoslavia.[21] Shortly afterwards the Assembly voted unanimously to adopt the new state's constitution. The Republics swiftly followed suit: in Montenegro a Constituent Assembly voted to adopt a new Montenegrin constitution on 31 December 1946.

Drafted principally by Tito's chief Communist theorist and Politburo member, the Slovene Edvard Kardelj, Yugoslavia's 1946 constitution gave formal recognition to Montenegro's position as

[18] The decision to divide the Sandžak between Serbia and Montenegro was not well received by local Communists who had been led to expect autonomous status after the war. When this was refused, Moša Pijade was sent with a special commission to explain the decision to them, after which they agreed, though with the President dissenting, and voted to dissolve the Assembly. (See Shoup, *The Yugoslav National Question*, p. 118.)

[19] Banac, *The National Question*, p. 104.

[20] Aleksa Djilas, *The Contested Country*, p. 159.

[21] *Ibid.*

Tito's Yugoslavia

one of six federal Republics within Yugoslavia and to Montenegrins as one of the state's five constituent nations.[22] As innumerable commentators have pointed out, this constitution—the first of four drafted by Kardelj—was modelled extensively on the Soviet constitution of 1936, and differed from it significantly only in its failure to grant to its different nations the right to an independent foreign

---

[22] The new federal Yugoslavia contained six Republics as well as Vojvodina, an autonomous province (*pokrajina*), and Kosovo-Metohija (or Kosmet, as Kosovo was then known), an autonomous region (*oblast*), but only five constituent nations since Bosnian Muslims were not at this time considered a 'nation' or *narod* in themselves. The 'nations'—Serbs, Croats, Slovenes, Macedonians and Montenegrins—corresponded to those Slav peoples who, as the Communists explained it, had no home elsewhere. Albanians, Hungarians, Germans and others who had 'mother' states outside Yugoslavia were considered national minorities—*narodnosti*. In 1971 Bosnian Muslims were also declared to be a *narod*.

policy and independent armed forces.[23] However, like its Soviet counterpart the 1946 constitution did grant Yugoslavia's nations (*narodi*) the right to self-determination, which included the right to secede from the federation.[24] Interestingly Tito at first opposed the granting of both these rights but was subsequently persuaded to concede them, in reality a meaningless gesture since there was never any chance of their being exercised. Formally supreme legislative and executive power was invested in the bicameral National Assembly, which consisted of a Federal Council elected on a population basis—one deputy for every 50,000 people—and a Council of Nationalities with thirty members from each Republic, twenty for Vojvodina and fifteen for Kosovo.[25] But despite the presence of a handful of opposition members, both chambers were no more than 'rubber-stamp parliaments';[26] instead real authority rested with the Communist Party and, beyond that, with the ultimate arbiter, Marshal Tito himself.

For all the simplicity at the top, federal Yugoslavia was a complicated creation with a plethora of ministries and administrative structures. In addition to six federal ministries—foreign affairs, defence, transport, the navy, the postal services and foreign trade—there were republican ministries, as well as nine hybrid federal-republican ministries which covered such areas as interior, finance, justice, industry, agriculture, mines, forestry, labour and construction.[27] Overlapping responsibilities restricted the degree of sovereignty exercised by the Republics, as did the federal government's right to appoint its own representative to sit in the republican government. Moreover the diminution of sovereignty was potentially greater in the cases of Bosnia–Hercegovina, Macedonia and Montenegro where the republican constitution did not contain a clause requiring that the governments of the Republics approve of the particular candidate selected. The other three Republics—Serbia, Croatia and Slovenia—had promulgated their own constitutions a

---

[23] Aleksa Djilas, *The Contested Country*, p. 167.

[24] This theoretical right extended to the *narodi*—those who had their own homeland Republic; it did not include the Albanians of Kosovo since they were only a national minority or *narodnost*.

[25] Lampe, *Yugoslavia as History*, p. 230.

[26] The term is used by Lampe, *ibid*. p. 232.

[27] Aleksa Djilas, *The Contested Country*, p. 160.

month later, and these included a provision that any such representative of the central government could only be chosen with the approval of the republican government.[28] Despite such limitations and the inherent centralism of the Communist system, the Republics did not altogether lack a voice at the centre. As Aleksa Djilas points out, 'the party leaders of the republics were ....people with their own revolutionary, wartime and political biographies, with roots in the party of their region and nation, and with reputations and personal authority.'[29] As such their views were likely to carry a certain weight at the political centre.

Montenegrin national identity

Concurrently with the debate over borders, Montenegro's new republican status had provoked a degree of dissension—some even within the KPJ—over the issue of separate Montenegrin nationality. Among the dissenting voices was that of the Serbian Politburo member and close wartime associate of Tito, Sreten Žujović, who argued strongly in favour of Montenegro's unification with Serbia.[30] So too did the leader of the (Serbian) Democratic Party, Milan Grol,[31] who, though shortly to withdraw his party from the 1945 election campaign as a result of Communist Party threats, had not yet been completely silenced. Describing the separation of Montenegrins from Serbs as an expression of 'imagined nationality', Grol dismissed the idea that the case for a separate Montenegrin Republic could be based on either national or economic arguments.[32]

Irrespective of the provenance of such views, Tito was unlikely to be swayed by them since Greater Serbianism—seen as the defining characteristic of Karadjordjević Yugoslavia—was something the

[28] See Shoup, *The Yugoslav National Question*, p. 114.

[29] *Ibid.*, p. 174.

[30] In 1948 Žujović, known as *Crni* (Swarthy), was to side with the Cominformists against Tito. See below.

[31] Together with Dr Šubašić, who became foreign minister, Milan Grol had received a position (that of vice-premier) in the Provisional Government of Yugoslavia of 7 March 1945 in order to comply with the Yalta Agreement's provision that AVNOJ be expanded to include members of the pre-war parliament. But Tito never intended the appointments to be more than a cover to ensure recognition of his regime, and both opposition figures were effectively neutralised within months of their being appointed.

[32] Grol also believed that Macedonia should be part of Serbia.

Communists were determined to suppress. In its place would come Yugoslavism, of which the eventual triumph would be assured by the march of history. In the meantime, however, allowing national characteristics to exist alongside a growing sense of Yugoslavism was seen as necessary, at least during an initial period, in order to promote reassurance particularly over the delicate issue of national equality—an equality which to the Communists meant not only a levelling of individuals but also ensuring that no one nation would prove able, as in the past, to dominate another.

It was here that Montenegro had a complex role to play on the larger Yugoslav stage: as a separate Republic it could act as a balancing element, counteracting rather than enhancing Serbian predominance. At the same time a sense of internal balance needed to be found to try to bridge the divisions within Montenegro between what Banac has called 'Serbophiles and nativists',[33] or broadly between the old Whites and Greens. Djilas, Montenegro's representative in the central government and in charge of propaganda or 'Agitprop', appeared to be seeking consensus when he wrote in 1947: 'Montenegrins belong to the Serb branch of the South Slavic tribes.'[34] This view of Montenegrins as Serbs with special characteristics chimed in well enough with the majority view within the Politburo, and—more important—found favour with Tito, who had seen at first hand what tenacious Partisans Montenegrins made, and believed they could also be good Yugoslavs. Already in 1946 the Montenegrin Communist leadership were displaying strong Yugoslavist instincts, arguing in favour of a common school curriculum in such critical areas as history and literature in the run-up to agreement on the constitution.[35] That the Montenegrins were unsuccessful on this occasion did not seem to diminish Tito's regard for them.[36] He en-

---

[33] Banac, *With Stalin against Tito*, p. 105.

[34] *Ibid.*

[35] In voting for a uniform curriculum for the critical subjects of history and literature, the Montenegrins were joined by the Macedonians and the Bosnians, but the Serbs, Croats and Slovenes, who voted against, won the day. (See Lampe, *Yugoslavia as History*, p. 233.) In 2004 the character of school texts again became a political issue in Montenegro with the pro-independence camp insisting on translating school texts into what they termed the 'Montenegrin' language.

[36] In *Tito: The Story from Inside* (first trans. by Vasilije Kojić and Richard Hayes, New York: Harcourt Brace Jovanovich, 1980; London: Weidenfeld and Nicolson, 1981, p. 19). Djilas observes that, according to Tito's family account, his

gaged a Montenegrin driver Prlja, a former Partisan from Podgorica, who was soon lording it over everyone.[37] Tito's liking for Montenegrins even extended rather bizarrely to King Nikola. As Djilas, who had elsewhere remarked on a fondness for medals which Tito shared with Nikola, recalled: 'When I commented on the despotic and melodramatic character of the later reign of the Montenegrin King Nikola, Tito objected: "Oh, no, we young people thought him charming, brave, patriotic, a true Yugoslav."'[38] In the summer of 1946 Tito made a brief tour of Montenegro. On 13 July 1946, the fifth anniversary of the Montenegrin uprising against the Axis invasion, Podgorica was renamed Titograd—allegedly at Djilas's suggestion.[39] Two years later Titograd became the Republic's administrative capital.

The 1948 split with Stalin

In this broadly promising climate few outside Montenegro anticipated that the Republic's relationship with the centre would soon be disturbed in a way that raised the most serious conflicts of loyalty. The source of the trauma was the dramatic rift between the Communist Parties of Yugoslavia and the Soviet Union, evidence of which began to appear in 1947. Up till that time, despite the wartime and early post-war frustrations which the Yugoslav Communists had experienced with the Soviet Union,[40] Tito and the KPJ had been admirers of Stalin and were determined both to remain loyal allies of the Soviet Union and to keep Yugoslavia in step with

---

branch of the Brozes came to Zagorje (Tito's birthplace in Croatia) from the border region between Bosnia and Dalmatia probably in the sixteenth century but before that they could trace their origins to the Montenegrin Kuči tribe.

[37] Djilas, *Tito: The Story from Inside*, p. 101. Prlja's particular story did not end well: he was caught stealing tyres and spare parts, and committed suicide rather than face the disgrace.

[38] *Ibid.*, pp. 101 and 111.

[39] Fleming, *Montenegro: The Divided Land*, p. 157.

[40] In addition to Moscow's failure to deliver any help to the Partisans until the last year of the war, and the depredations carried out by Soviet soldiers following the Red Army's entry into Yugoslavia, there were more recent causes for concern: Stalin had failed to support Tito's post-war government over Trieste, and had criticised the Yugoslavs' attempt to intervene in Greece on the side of the Communists.

other 'progressive nations' by maintaining membership of the Soviet-dominated organisation of Communist parties or Cominform.[41] However, in contrast to the situation in other Eastern Bloc countries where post-war 'liberation' leading to Communist regimes had come through military intervention by the Soviet Union, the Yugoslavs themselves were largely responsible for achieving their liberation after years of battling the Axis powers. In the view of Yugoslavia's new leaders at least, their wartime experience had moulded them into independent-minded patriots who resented Soviet attempts to infiltrate the Party and state structures and were determined to defend Yugoslav sovereignty. Given Stalin's radically different agenda, this view was bound to lead to conflict.

The first signs of trouble were not long in emerging. As it became apparent that the Kremlin's vision of the future envisaged keeping Yugoslavia as a source of the raw materials required for Soviet needs rather than allowing it to industrialise, the Yugoslavs' refusal to fall in with Stalin's plans marked the initial signs in the deterioration of the relationship between Tito and Stalin. Nor was Stalin any happier about the high-profile visits that Tito had begun to make to other Eastern Bloc countries after the war. The situation came to a head as a result of the meeting between Tito and his Bulgarian counterpart Georgi Dimitrov at Bled in August 1947 to sign an agreement on a future customs union without first obtaining Moscow's approval. The final breach came in January 1948 with the publication in *Pravda* of a federation plan, announced by Dimitrov, which was to include not only Yugoslavia and Bulgaria but also Hungary, Romania, Czechoslovakia, Poland, Albania and Greece.[42]

Stalin had not been consulted. In early 1948 he summoned both Tito and Dimitrov to Moscow. The Bulgarian complied but Tito sent Kardelj to join Djilas, who had already been in Moscow for a month waiting to follow up a previous meeting with Stalin when the Soviet leader—to Djilas's astonishment—had invited Yugoslavia to 'swallow Albania' rather than merge with it.[43] Deeply angered by

---

[41] The Cominform had replaced an earlier organisation, the Comintern, in October 1947.

[42] R. J. Crampton, *The Balkans since the Second World War*, London: Longman, 2002, p. 30.

[43] Milovan Djilas, *Conversations with Stalin* (trans. from the Serbo-Croatian by Michael B. Petrovich), New York: Harcourt, Brace & World, 1962, p. 143.

Tito's non-compliance, Stalin perversely demanded that both leaders immediately agree to form a Yugoslav-Bulgarian Federation before proceeding to incorporate Albania.[44] Before leaving Moscow Kardelj reluctantly signed a document agreeing that Yugoslavia would consult the Soviet Union on foreign policy; with it came the realisation that Stalin would accept nothing less than Yugoslav subservience in a system of entrenched Soviet hegemony.

Yugoslavia's challenge to Stalin could not go unpunished. In an escalating campaign of retaliation the Soviet Union first cancelled negotiations on a trade agreement before recalling all Soviet advisers from Belgrade and finally inviting the Yugoslavs themselves to depose the country's leaders.[45] Other satellite states were enjoined to back the Soviet operation to beat the Yugoslavs into submission. In June 1948, after Yugoslavia had refused to attend a Cominform meeting in Bucharest, they collectively agreed to expel Yugoslavia from the Cominform and issued a declaration describing Yugoslavia as a 'Turkish terrorist regime'.[46] But Tito and his close colleagues refused to be intimidated. Of the leading Party members around Tito only Streten Žujović and the previously disgraced Croatian Party leader and Politburo member Andrija Hebrang sided with the Soviets. Žujović had already been stripped of Party membership and joined Hebrang in prison in May that year.[47] As the hostilities continued into 1949, Yugoslavia's predicament grew desperate. With other Eastern Bloc countries cowed into upholding the Soviet position, the Yugoslav leadership faced a real risk of annihilation as a result of either military action from outside or rebellion within. In response they instigated a ruthless crackdown on anyone suspected of having links with Moscow or supporting the Cominform position.

Outside Tito's immediate circle the split with Moscow soon began to take its toll on the Party itself where, although it caused confusion at all levels, the main impact fell on local elites, nowhere

---

[44] *Ibid.*, p. 177.

[45] Jelavich, *History of the Balkans*, vol. 2, pp. 325–6.

[46] *Ibid.*

[47] Later Žujović recanted and was set free in 1952, but the real circumstances surrounding Hebrang's death—he is alleged to have committed suicide in prison in 1952—remain puzzling. The Tito regime propagated one version of what happened, which is still disputed both by former Chetnik supporters and by Croatian nationalists, each of whom has his own, different explanation. See Jasper Ridley, *Tito: A Biography*, London: Constable, 1994, pp. 312–14.

more so than in Montenegro. A variety of factors—historic, political and cultural—combined there to ensure that a significant proportion of the membership would find supporting the KPJ's now aggressive anti-Soviet campaign impossible. First, for Montenegrin Communists, the centuries-old devotion to Russia had been heightened by their new-found admiration for the Soviet people as the instigators of the October Revolution,[48] for Stalin himself as leader of the international Communist movement, and finally, as proclaimed by official propaganda, for the Soviet Union's glorious role in the Second World War. Added to this was the fact that in Montenegro traditional mores—a lethal combination of dogmatism and idealism—had given rise to a more rigid and in that respect more Stalinist view of Communism, as the period of 'left deviation' had already established.[49] Thirdly, as Banac points out, despite the favourable treatment accorded to Montenegrin Partisans after the war, there were simply too many of them for everyone to receive due recognition and remuneration.[50] Coming on top of the discontent generated by Montenegro's complete subordination to Serbia in the First Yugoslavia—a situation that had earlier resulted in particularly high levels of support for the Communist Party—continued postwar resentment of Belgrade's determination to maintain hegemony over Montenegro engendered a naïve and uncritical attitude towards the Soviet Union. As one Montenegrin Communist observed of the growing dissension around him, 'I do not know what all this is about, but I know that Russia is great and Stalin is mighty.'[51]

The split with Stalin thus threw the Montenegrin Communist Party into confusion, with many of the leading figures, such as Blažo Jovanović, secretary of the KPJ's regional committee for Montenegro, and Veljko Vlahović, the Yugoslav deputy foreign minister and director of the Party newspaper *Borba*, torn over which way

---

[48] Banac, *With Stalin against Tito*, pp. 164–5.
[49] Even before the Second World War, as well as in the immediate post-war period, a number of factional groups had broken away from the Montenegrin Communist Party, the best known of which was the group around Berane headed by Petko Miletić. Miletić's faction, like most of the factionalists, advocated a particularly rigid and puritanical interpretation of Communist ideology. See Shoup, *The Yugoslav National Question*, p. 51, and Banac, *With Stalin against Tito*, p. 165, for more on the development and significance of factionalism.
[50] Banac, *With Stalin against Tito*, p. 171.
[51] Quoted by Banac, *ibid.*

to go.[52] Both Jovanović and Vlahović finally joined in the condemnation of those who had sided with Stalin, and subsequently tried to conceal the high proportion of prominent Montenegrin Communists who rejected the Yugoslav leadership's position. But not all the defections could be hushed up. After four Montenegrin Republican ministers were suddenly removed from office in August 1948, followed shortly afterwards by another unexplained top-level 'resignation', the reality was that the majority of the local Montenegrin leadership had come down on the Soviet side.[53]

Along with high-ranking politicians arrested and detained were other prominent Montenegrins, two of them—Stefan Mitrović and Radovan Zogović—former friends and colleagues of Djilas who, as students of literature and revolutionary poets, were active with him in Agitprop.[54] Zogović, very popular with Party members, was eventually spared the worst and subjected only to a brief period of detention, but Mitrović's particularly harrowing case is indicative of the level of tragedy afflicting some Montenegrin families at the time. Mitrović himself was sent to the prison camp the authorities established on the island of Goli Otok,[55] where he went mad; two of his sisters and a brother had already been executed during the war; another brother was expelled from the Party and went mad in prison; a fourth brother became a traitor, and yet another brother who had vanished during the war was never seen again.[56]

The defections of so many high-level Montenegrins shook the Republic to its core. Despite the cost, the survivors within the Party justified the crackdown by reminding themselves of what was at stake—the risk of Soviet intervention to link up with centres of internal opposition within the Party and conceivably, given its high ratio of Cominformists, within Montenegro itself.

In Montenegro, as elsewhere in Yugoslavia, the fundamental belief that 'Cominformism had to be torn up by the roots'[57] gave rise

---

[52] Banac, *ibid.*, pp. 165–6, and Milovan Djilas, *Rise and Fall*, p. 210.
[53] Banac, *ibid.* Banac names the individuals concerned as Božo Ljumović, former secretary of the KPJ regional committee for Montenegro and Yugoslavia's ambassador to Poland, Vuko Tmušić, Niko Pavić, Blažo Borovinić and Radivoje Vukićević.
[54] *Ibid.*, p. 167.
[55] For Goli Otok, see below.
[56] See Djilas, *Rise and Fall*, p. 224.
[57] *Ibid.*, p. 240.

to an extremist culture in which sons were encouraged to denounce parents, wives to divorce husbands, and siblings to approve each other's execution. As the level of political and social paranoia grew, people were arrested simply for failure to report suspect conversations, and for reading or listening to material that was deemed to have pro-Soviet content.[58] Overall about a third of the total Communist Party membership in Montenegro, some 5,000 people, are thought to have aligned themselves with the pro-Soviet tendency, a level of support far beyond that existing anywhere else in Yugoslavia.[59] So grave was the threat to overall Yugoslav security that in the summer and autumn of 1948 a full division of the security service (UDBa) was seconded to Montenegro to engage the growing number of rebels who had taken to the hills and to close the borders with Albania.[60]

Like their predecessors, OZNa, the UDBa did not hesitate to take the most drastic measures when events in Montenegro briefly threatened to get out of hand. In the summer and autumn of 1948 there were outbreaks of violence in the Zeta valley where many Party members fought alongside the rebels, some of whom had entered Montenegro from Bosnia-Hercegovina.[61] When rebellion also broke out in the Montenegrin part of the Sandžak in 1949 it looked briefly as if Montenegro might form a launching-pad for a wider uprising against the central government. But UDBa struck back, reducing the rebel strongholds and killing or capturing those involved. Elsewhere potential leaders who stepped out of line were

[58] *Ibid.*, p. 240.

[59] In the past the figures were covered up by the Communist authorities, leading to considerable confusion as to the real number of those who sided with the Soviet Union. Banac cites the first detailed breakdown of figures on the Cominformists produced by Professor Radovan Radonjić of the University of Titograd (now Podgorica) in 1983, which puts the number of Montenegrin Cominform supporters at just over 5,000 and those arrested and convicted at 3,439 or 21% of all arrested or convicted Cominformists in Yugoslavia. (See Banac, *With Stalin against Tito*, p. 150.) Pavlowitch agrees, putting the percentage of those imprisoned for 'Cominformism' in Montenegro at roughly 20% of the Yugoslav total at a time when, as he notes, the Republic represented approximately 2.6% of Yugoslavia's population. (Pavlowitch, *Serbia: The History behind the Name*, p. 166.)

[60] *Ibid.* p. 167. The military wing of UDBa was called KNOJ (*Korpus narodnog oslobodjenja Jugoslavije*).

[61] Banac, *With Stalin against Tito*, pp. 234–5.

liquidated to guard against further insurgency. One such incident took place at that time near Bijelo Polje, where eleven or twelve prominent local officials, led by the local secretary of the regional committee, Ilija Bulatović, took to the woods. They were pursued by UDBa agents, failed to attract local supporters and eventually surrendered one by one. None of those who did so returned alive to Bijelo Polje.[62]

Despite such bloody incidents, most of those arrested in Montenegro were not killed. Instead they joined their compatriots from the other Republics in prison camps established, on Tito's orders, on one of two uninhabited islands off the Adriatic coast of Dalmatia—Sveti Grgur (Saint Gregory) and Goli Otok (Naked Island), the latter a former marble quarry, waterless, utterly barren and exposed both to the summer heat and Adriatic gales. Most Montenegrins ended up on Goli Otok, having been sentenced for periods ranging from two to sixteen years. Occasionally a prisoner would receive the death sentence, but this was normally commuted in recognition of Tito's reminder to Party loyalists: 'Our revolution does not eat its children.'[63]

Although the prisoners escaped death, they were spared little else since the prevailing belief was that the renegades needed to be entirely broken before beginning their re-education as good Titoists.[64] They were thus subjected to repeated humiliations and purposeless, backbreaking toil with the object of eradicating any vestige of resistance. Spying and denunciation were encouraged to create a climate of fear. Worse still, the decision was taken to encourage the prisoners themselves to direct the brutalities, which even extended to the occasional lynching. Knowledge of the atrocious conditions on the island was hushed up, allowing the authorities to stick to their official version—that the camps were merely centres for social and political rehabilitation. Even years later people were afraid to speak out.

Despite the reign of terror on Goli Otok and the prospect of still worse punishment, revolts did break out. One attempted revolt was organised by a Montenegrin, Colonel Vladimir Dapčević, brother of the famous Peko. The plotters were discovered and their pun-

[62] Djilas, *Tito: The Story from Inside*, p. 80.
[63] Quoted by Banac, *With Stalin against Tito*, p. 247.
[64] *Ibid.*

ishments increased.⁶⁵ A member of the army's political directorate, Vladimir Dapčević, had been caught and arrested in autumn 1948 on the border with Hungary. As a senior military figure he was only one of a number of his army colleagues to side with Stalin against Tito. His crime had been to become involved in what for Titoists was the most shocking example of treachery when he joined his fellow-Montenegrin Arso Jovanović, Tito's wartime chief of the general staff, in plotting a military coup. Before the war Jovanović had been an officer in the royal army, only joining the Communist Party in August 1941.⁶⁶ Later he had spent more than a year at the top Soviet military school at Voroshilov and returned to Yugoslavia as the crisis was escalating in the spring of 1948, still imbued with belief in the Soviet Union.⁶⁷ When their plan to overturn the regime failed, Jovanović and his fellow-plotters decided to escape across the border to Romania. By ill-luck they happened to run into border guards on the lookout for cross-border smugglers and, challenged by the guards, Jovanović fired a shot and in return received a fatal head wound. Dapčević fled into the forest while a third major figure in the attempted escape, Major-General Branko Petričević-Kadja, made his way back to Belgrade, hoping to convince the Party leadership that the whole affair was the result of a hunting accident.⁶⁸ Meanwhile, Dapčević after hiding in the forest attempted to make his way across the Hungarian border where he was arrested three months later. Both men were sentenced to twenty years in prison but released in 1955.⁶⁹

⁶⁵ *Ibid.*, pp. 130 and 250.
⁶⁶ In *Rise and Fall*, p. 229, Djilas mentions the fact that many former royal army officers subsequently sided with Stalin against Tito. In Jovanović's case the time he had spent in the Soviet Union just before the split may provide an explanation but, as a more general phenomenon, the correlation is surprising.
⁶⁷ Banac, *With Stalin against Tito*, pp. 129–30.
⁶⁸ Djilas, *Rise and Fall*, pp. 213–15. Djilas notes that at the time there was considerable scepticism about the official version of events surrounding Jovanović's death, giving rise to the conviction that he was killed in Belgrade and his body transported to the Romanian border. It must be said that, given his position, it was surprising that Jovanović did not organise a more ambitious means of escape such as commandeering a plane.
⁶⁹ Following his release from prison in 1955 and, after attempting to set up a new pro-Communist party, Dapčević fled once again, this time to Albania and thence in 1960 to the Soviet Union. In 1968 he moved to Brussels where he began to write articles critical of Tito. According to Jasper Ridley's account, the Yugoslavs

Meanwhile investigations into the failed coup revealed a link with the Soviet military attaché in Belgrade.[70] The Soviet Union struck back, accusing the Yugoslav secret police of cold-bloodedly murdering Jovanović. As the tension between the two sides rose, so too did the risk of Soviet attack.[71] In August 1949 Tito announced in Skopje that Yugoslavia would defend itself if attacked, a stance which gained credence the following month by the Acheson-McNeil declaration stating that the United States and Britain would defend Yugoslavia against a Soviet attack.[72] Stalin drew back but the Soviet Union continued to operate an economic freeze, excluding Yugoslavia from COMECON, the Communist Bloc's equivalent of the Marshall Plan, and putting pressure on previously friendly countries to cancel trade agreements with Yugoslavia.[73]

The beginnings of Yugoslavism

Yugoslavia's survival demanded dramatic readjustment at every level—ideological, military, political and economic. At the economic level the Soviet and Eastern Bloc blockade did not take long to bite particularly because the 1948 harvest had been poor. This made fulfilment of Yugoslavia's Five Year Plan, highly dependent on Soviet aid, difficult to implement.[74] Nonetheless the Yugoslav lead-

---

plotted with the Romanians to lure Dapčević to Romania from where he would be surrendered to the Yugoslav security services. This duly took place and Dapčević was put on trial in Belgrade and charged with entering Yugoslavia illegally in order to organise subversive activities. He was defended by a well-known Montenegrin defence lawyer, Jovan Barović, who revealed the truth about Dapčević's capture in Romania thereby saving him from the death penalty although he was still sentenced to twenty years' imprisonment. Barović continued to appear for the defence in celebrated cases involving those charged with offences by the regime. He was killed in February 1969 when a lorry ran into his car outside Belgrade. (See Ridley, *Tito: A Biography*, pp. 404–5.)

[70] Banac, *With Stalin against Tito*, pp. 129–30.

[71] Ridley observes that the Czechoslovak leader Klement Gottwald suggested to Stalin during a meeting in the Crimea in September 1948 that the Red Army should enter Yugoslavia and overthrow Tito, advice rejected by Stalin at the time. (*Tito: A Biography*, p. 294.)

[72] Djilas, *Rise and Fall*, pp. 253 and 259.

[73] Jelavich, *History of the Balkans*, vol. 2, p. 327.

[74] Dennison Rusinow, *The Yugoslav Experiment, 1948–1974*, London: Hurst, 1977, p. 35.

ership, still concerned to prove themselves the real inheritors of Marxism–Leninism and reluctant to abandon the economic orthodoxy established by the Soviet Union, continued to establish plans for heavy industry, such as iron and steel production and vast thermo-electric schemes in the underdeveloped regions—Macedonia, Bosnia-Hercegovina and Montenegro. The aim was to equalise economic conditions within Yugoslavia while providing 'jobs for the boys from the backwoods who had contributed so much manpower to the Partisan army and the new regime'.[75] Cynical as this may sound, the Communists, many of whom were themselves from these 'backward regions', had come to power believing strongly in the need to right the injustices from which their peoples had suffered.

In 1949, recognising that the crisis threatened by declining food stocks could no longer be ignored, Yugoslavia's economic planners turned their attention to agriculture. Here too they aimed to enforce orthodox Communist methods by eradicating 'backwardness' and accelerating the collectivisation of agriculture. Ironically the measures they employed—the expulsion of the German population, the confiscation of land, the large-scale resettlement and the pressures, penalties and threats applied—were tantamount to classic Stalinism. Unsurprisingly they provoked widespread resistance in many parts of Yugoslavia, including Serbia, where peasant smallholders responded by slaughtering livestock and cutting production. However, in Montenegro, where peasants on tiny uneconomic plots had little to lose, 'the collectives spread like wildfire.'[76] The enthusiasm was not matched by results: by 1951 Montenegro had had 44.7% of its land collectivised, but with little apparent economic benefit.[77] It was still a food-importing economy.

In 1950 a major drought combined with the harsh consequences of the country's isolation forced the Yugoslav leadership to turn to the United States for aid that Truman was prepared to supply to ensure that Yugoslavia maintained its distance from the Soviet Union and the Eastern Bloc. The effect of this economic lifeline was to allow the leadership to strike out on a new 'Yugoslav road to socialism',[78]

[75] *Ibid.*, p. 21.
[76] Djilas, *Rise and Fall*, p. 251.
[77] Banac, *With Stalin against Tito*, p. 135.
[78] See Rusinow, *The Yugoslav Experiment*, p. 50.

accompanied by an ideological campaign which attacked Soviet imperialism while vaunting the 'originality' of Yugoslavia's solution.[79]

In the search for ways to survive alone while differentiating itself from Soviet practice, the KPJ developed the idea of 'socialist self-management', a concept which was to become the hallmark of the Titoist regime and, over the next twenty years, the subject of scores of scholarly works of exegesis.[80] In essence 'self-management' envisaged replacing centralised state control with the decentralising of the economy, of the Party and of local communes, all of which were to be placed in the hands of the workers. In this way genuine democracy would provide a safeguard against the excessive bureaucracy and the abuse of power and privilege which the Yugoslavs saw as deforming the Soviet system, and would lead eventually to the 'withering away of the state', as required by Marx, and to the disappearance of the ethnic problems engendered by Yugoslavia's various nations.

Put into practice, the new ideology led within a short time to the virtual abandonment of forced collectivisation of agriculture and, at the political level, to a degree of decentralisation involving the transfer to the Republics of some of the previously federal economic ministries, including mining, agriculture and forestry.[81] But however fundamental these changes appeared to be and despite constant tinkering with the system, it was soon apparent that the devolution of power to people's committees and workers' councils and even to the Republics themselves, was not a recipe for curing Yugoslavia's economic and political ills. Far from increasing efficiency and accountability, the people's committees made appointments on the basis of political soundness rather than technical competence, while the workers' councils tended to award wage increases at the expense of investment. And the Republics naturally enough put their own interests before the broader interests of Yugoslavia as a whole. Despite the contradictions inherent in the self-management system, the Yugoslav leadership pressed ahead with further changes. In November 1952, at the Sixth Party Congress, the Communist Party

[79] Aleksa Djilas, *The Contested Country*, p. 175.
[80] According to Milovan Djilas's own account, he first hit upon the idea after re-reading *Das Kapital* and encountering Marx's concept of the 'free association of producers'. See Rusinow, *The Yugoslav Experiment*, pp. 50–1.
[81] Rusinow, *The Yugoslav Experiment*, p. 57.

acknowledged its readiness to abandon the Soviet model of a hierarchal and monolithic party, imposing its control from above in favour of a more democratic movement in touch with the grass roots by changing the Party's name to the League of Yugoslav Communists (SKJ).[82]

By 1953 the move away from Stalinist practice was thought to require significant amendments to the Yugoslav constitution. Rather than envisaging a withering away of the federal state that Marx foresaw, the new constitutional law of 1953 seemed, as Lampe puts it, 'directed towards a withering away of the republics'[83] which, built round the 'nations', were destined to become redundant once true democracy and devolution of power to the people had succeeded in eradicating nationalism in favour of Yugoslavism.[84] With the constitutional changes introduced in 1953 the Republics lost not only the theoretical right to sovereignty and secession granted under the 1946 constitution, but also saw the curtailing of their previous powers to administer justice.[85] At the same time additional changes in federal government further undermined the authority of the Republics. The previous Federal Council of Nationalities, where all the Republics had equal representation, was replaced by an expanded Federal Council where representation was directly related to the number of voters, a reform that obviously disadvantaged a small republic like Montenegro. However, a further significant change—the creation of a new Federal Executive Council (SIV),[86] which imposed a dual system of authority at the federal level of government (in addition to the SKJ itself)—could be seen in retrospect to have worked in the opposite direction, enhancing the strength of some national groups at the expense of others. Crucially there was no requirement that the Republics be represented proportionately to their population, an oversight that allowed Serbs and Montenegrins to be considerably over-represented while Croats in particular were under-represented. For example, in 1958 Montenegro with roughly 3 per cent of the population had four representatives on the

---

[82] In Serbo-Croat '*Savez Komunista Jugoslavije*', but in English often referred to as the LCY. This change of name was also proposed by Djilas.
[83] Lampe, *Yugoslavia as History*, p. 257.
[84] Aleksa Djilas, *The Contested Country*, pp. 176–9.
[85] Lampe, *Yugoslavia as History*, p. 257.
[86] *Savezno Izvršno Veče*.

SIV while Croatia with 22 per cent of the population had only five.[87] Despite such glaring inconsistencies the enthusiastic framers of the 1953 constitution shared the heady belief that the national question had already been solved.[88]

The Djilas affair

But even as the changes were ushered in, another crisis was brewing which was to have a profound impact within Yugoslavia while ensuring that its instigator, the native Montenegrin Milovan Djilas, would become a historic figure as postwar Communism's first, and arguably most important, dissident.[89] Ever since the mass imprisonments on Goli Otok Djilas had been preoccupied with the revolution's failure to produce the genuinely democratic society for which he had fought during the years of Partisan struggle. Believing that changes in the early 1950s—most notably the development of the socialist self-management project and the re-branding of the Communist Party as the League of Communists—heralded the liberalising movement he wished to see, Djilas chose the anniversary of the Russian Revolution[90] to make an impassioned speech attacking the Soviet leadership's betrayal of the goals of the revolution and promising that Yugoslavia would remain steadfast in their defence. The speech was greeted with rapturous applause. To many of the audience Djilas's role as Tito's heir seemed confirmed, but his mother, who had only heard the speech over the radio, was nearer the mark when she remarked to her daughter-in-law: 'It is not good for Djido when they clap more for him than Tito.'[91]

    Although he took no part in framing the 1953 constitution, Djilas found further encouragement in its provisions, so much so that he

---

[87] Shoup, *The Yugoslav National Question*, table on p. 274.
[88] Aleksa Djilas, *The Contested Country*, p. 180.
[89] See Borka Božović, 'Osvajanje sloboda nikada nije završen proces', *Danas*, 5–6 February 2005.
[90] In fact the anniversary of the October revolution took place during the Sixth Congress of the KPJ, that is on 7 November according to the Gregorian (New Style) calendar, which replaced the Julian (Old Style) calendar on 31 January 1918. In *Rise and Fall* Djilas writes that he suddenly remembered the significance of the date and suggested to Tito that they mark it at the beginning of the afternoon session. Djilas's speech was the result. (See *Rise and Fall*, p. 296.)
[91] *Ibid.*

was soon using the Party paper *Borba* to publish articles intended to speed up the transition to a more democratic and humane form of socialism.[92] At first Tito seemed to approve when Djilas showed him the articles, but when Djilas moved on from criticising Stalinist thinking within the Party to calling for a further downgrading of the role of the Party and launching specific attacks on the abuse of privilege within its higher echelons, Tito's consent changed to anger.[93] Djilas pressed on, interrupting his writing on one occasion to take the leading left-wing British politician Aneurin Bevan and his wife Jennie Lee, with whom he had forged a close friendship during a visit to Britain, on a short tour of Montenegro (and Bosnia) where they could fulfil Bevan's desire to see 'backward areas and the real people'.[94] Shortly afterwards he returned to Montenegro to participate in the 1953 election campaign, where in a one-horse race he was duly nominated in Titograd as the Party's official candidate.[95]

Back in Belgrade, Djilas's articles were eliciting an enormous response, strengthening his resolve to press ahead with his criticism of the Party. At the beginning of 1954 he published 'Anatomy of a Moral', an article that focused on the experience of another famous Montenegrin Peko Dapčević, the Partisan general and war hero. Dapčević had recently married a beautiful young actress who was shunned by the wives of the Partisan elite, ostensibly on the grounds that she had not shared the Partisans' wartime experience. Djilas went to her defence in an excoriating article that attacked the hypocrisy and degeneracy of the Partisan *nouveau riche*. Although he did not name names, the people involved—mostly wives of senior Party members—were all readily identifiable. Worse still, the case was clearly recognised as a paradigm for the moral fall from grace of the top echelons, whom Djilas castigated as a caste corrupted by their abuse of power.[96]

---

[92] Woodford D. McClellan, 'Postwar Political Evolution' in Wayne S. Vucinich, (ed.), *Contemporary Yugoslavia: Twenty Years of Socialist Experiment*, Berkeley: University of California Press, 1969, p. 138.

[93] Rusinow, *The Yugoslav Experiment*, p. 84.

[94] Djilas, *Rise and Fall*, p. 327. Bevan was to die shortly afterwards. Djilas dedicated his famous book, *Conversations with Stalin*, to the memory of Aneurin Bevan, but the book's publication in 1962 earned him another prison sentence.

[95] *Ibid.*, p. 337.

[96] Rusinow, *The Yugoslav Experiment*, p. 84.

Djilas was summoned to appear before the Central Committee at its third plenum where Tito and Kardelj rebuked him at a meeting which, contrary to normal practice, was broadcast live to the country.[97] Privately Tito told him that 'his "case" was having the greatest world repercussion since [the] confrontation with the Soviet Union.'[98] At the plenum most of his fellow Montenegrins— Blažo Jovanović, Veljko Vlahović, Svetozar Vukmanović-Tempo and even Peko Dapčević—joined in the attack against him. Apart from his family, his only support came from two Serbs—his former wife Mitra Mitrović and Dedijer who, although he avoided a prison sentence, was ostracised by the Party and subsequently went into voluntary exile.[99] Escaping with a warning on this occasion,[100] Djilas continued to write, and completed a first draft of *Land without Justice*, an autobiographical account of his early life in Montenegro, in 1954, the same year as he resigned from the Party.[101] In Montenegro his fall from grace might have been expected to provoke strong reactions, but there were no public protests. Although the trauma of 1948 may partly explain this, the traditional Montenegrin inclination towards the most doctrinaire form of Communism was also likely to have been a contributing factor. In a display of just such orthodox self-righteousness the Nikšić Communists insisted on returning money Djilas had donated to the local library rather than accept help from a 'contaminated' source. Now divested of his previous positions in the Party and government and rather hard-up, Djilas used the money to buy a typewriter.[102]

In 1956 Djilas was put on trial after publishing a statement condemning the Russian invasion of Hungary. At his trial before the

---

[97] *Ibid.*, p. 85. Exceptionally, too, the conflict with Stalin in 1948 had also been broadcast live.

[98] Djilas, *Rise and Fall*, p. 355.

[99] Rusinow, *The Yugoslav Experiment*, p. 86.

[100] Not wishing to be classed as a Stalinist abroad, Tito chose not to expel him from the Party, though Djilas tendered his own resignation in March 1954. (See Djilas, *Rise and Fall*, pp. 363 and 369.) At the beginning of 1955 he was put on trial and given a suspended sentence after being interviewed by the *New York Times*.

[101] The title was taken from Njegoš's *Mountain Wreath*. See Djilas, *Rise and Fall*, p. 366.

[102] *Ibid.*

Belgrade district court the chief judge described him as a Montenegrin, provoking Djilas to make his only comment: 'I object. The statement should show that I am a Yugoslav.' Hitherto he had made much of his Montenegrin background—*Land without Justice* had finally been published in the United States that same year—so that at first sight the interjection seems puzzling. Of course, as his American editor and fellow Montenegrin William Jovanovich pointed out in his introduction to *Land without Justice*, Djilas may have been concerned that the authorities would use the heretical and warlike reputation of Montenegrins against him, but he was determined to demonstrate that it was not he but the Yugoslav leadership who had abandoned revolutionary principles, and no doubt wanted to record his continued adherence to the Communists' belief in the withering away of nations and eventual triumph of Yugoslavism.

Whatever the motive, Djilas's scruples did him no good and he was duly sentenced to three years' imprisonment. The following year he was again before the courts after *The New Class*, a particularly hard-hitting attack on the bureaucratisation of the revolution and the corruption of its ideals, was smuggled abroad and published in the United States. Perhaps his most influential and certainly his most subversive book, *The New Class*, written in just three months, earned Djilas a seven-year sentence on top of the one he was already serving, amounting to ten years in all. Allowed out of prison in 1961, he was sentenced again in 1962 after publication of *Conversations with Stalin*. This work not only broke all the rules with its frankness in revealing the thoughts and manipulations of the top Yugoslav leadership in their dealings with Stalin immediately after the war, but also offended the Soviet leader Leonid Brezhnev with whom Tito was by this time attempting to establish better relations.[103]

Djilas was finally released in December 1966, having spent nine years in Sremska Mitrovica prison outside Belgrade, of which twenty-two months were in solitary confinement. During this time he continued to write; often, when he was denied writing materials, on prison toilet paper which was regularly confiscated by the guards. All three books written in prison were set largely if not exclusively in Montenegro—a biographical study of Njegoš, a volume of short stories entitled *The Leper and Other Tales*, and a third book—part

[103] Rusinow, *The Yugoslav Experiment*, p. 121.

fiction, part history and reflection—called simply *Montenegro*, evidence perhaps of Djilas's tendency to associate his native land with suffering and victimhood.[104] Out of prison but not free of surveillance and harassment, Djilas continued to produce books and articles. In the late 1960s, with Yugoslavia's desire to build better relations with the West, he was permitted to travel to the United States and Britain where his status as Communism's foremost dissident ensured him a wide audience for his lectures and journalism. However, in the 1970s, as Tito sought to rein back the liberal changes affecting the country, his passport was withdrawn and his books and articles were banned in Yugoslavia. Even after Tito's death in 1980 the ban remained in force until 1989, when following the fall of Communism permission was finally given for him to travel abroad and publish his work at home. He died in Belgrade in 1995 and was buried in his birthplace, the village of Podbišće in Montenegro.

As the foremost Montenegrin of his time and a prolific writer on Montenegro, Djilas has occupied a prominent role in this narrative, one that may nonetheless seem to require further explanation. After all, apart from his youth and the admittedly highly important war years, most of his eventful life was lived beyond Montenegro's borders, while his dissident status and steadfast support of democratic values did not gain him a significant following among Montenegrin Communists. On the contrary, when in the mid-1960s liberal movements began to attract supporters in Serbia, Croatia, Slovenia and even to some extent Macedonia, Montenegrins showed a conspicuous lack of enthusiasm, matched only in Bosnia-Hercegovina. Yet, paradoxical as it may seem, Djilas's convictions and his determination to stand by them regardless of the cost owed much to his early experience in Montenegro. The clue to his motivation, as David Pryce Jones has pointed out,[105] is provided by the autobiographical *Land without Justice*, a work in which the typically Montenegrin

[104] The thought is prompted by Djilas's description of his state of mind following his ousting from the inner circle of the Communist Party at the third pleneum: 'I was in the throes of a moral and intellectual crisis, the heir to the legacy of suffering of my family and my native Montenegro. ...' (*Tito: The Story from Inside*, p. 164.)

[105] David Pryce-Jones, 'Remembering Milovan Djilas', *The New Criterion* (on line), http://www.newcriterion.com/archive/18/oct99/djilas.htm, accessed 24 Nov. 2004.

cycle of violence, suffering and rebellion leads the young Djilas to an inevitable conclusion: 'Were not the first impulses towards Communism those arising out of a desire to put an end to the world of force and injustice and to realise a different world, one of justice, brotherhood and love among men?'[106] Romantic, idealistic yet prepared to go to extremes to realise his ideals, Djilas was strongly influenced in his outlook on life by his Montenegrin background and boyhood. Later, natural intelligence and strength of purpose brought him close to the pinnacle of power—he was generally considered to be Tito's chosen successor—but once there, a sense of justice and an asceticism, both surely derived from his early life in Montenegro, not only prevented him from tolerating the abuses of privilege and power by his closest colleagues and former wartime comrades but drove him to denounce it and suffer the consequences with a tenacity many rightly saw as heroic.

The economic impact

By 1966, when Djilas emerged from prison, Yugoslavia itself was changing. Economic reforms enacted in 1965 introduced a degree of liberalisation including some exposure to market forces, access to European markets and permission for Yugoslavs to work in the West. In 1966 Tito's feared Minister of the Interior, Aleksandar Ranković, was swept aside, ushering in a period of increased cultural and intellectual freedom and with it further improvements in education. Montenegrins benefited from the latter—literacy levels, formerly low, continued to rise.[107] Many Montenegrins embraced education as offering a way out of poverty, preferring something they saw as conferring high status to less befitting mercantile pursuits. However, moves towards economic liberalisation were a different matter since they threatened to erode the privileged situation which Montenegro had enjoyed since the end of the war.

---

[106] Milovan Djilas, *Land without Justice*, p. 305.
[107] Before 1941 the level of illiteracy in Montenegro was approximately 56 per cent, reduced to just under 6 per cent by 1991. (See Šerbo Rastoder, 'A Short History of Montenegro', p. 137.) Taking a shorter period, Lampe gives the following, not necessarily incompatible, figures for illiteracy: 26.4% in 1953 as against 9.4% in 1988. (*Yugoslavia as History*, p. 332.)

Given its evident backwardness, Montenegro, as we have seen, had been a notable beneficiary of a principal plank of Communist economic policy intended to equalise development between the developed and less developed Republics. Under this policy it had not only obtained a highly disproportionate share of funds earmarked for the establishment of heavy industry in the initial Five Year Plan of 1947, but had continued to receive a particularly generous allocation from the Belgrade-based General Investment Fund from the time of its establishment in 1953.[108] At the same time Montenegro had gained considerably from a second method of redistribution—the practice of offering grants-in-aid to the Republics intended to equalise the provision of social services—in education, the payment of pensions, access to medical facilities and so on. So lamentable had been the state of social provision within pre-war Montenegro that during the 1950s half of the Republic's total revenue came from this source.[109] Naturally both policies, greatly valued by Montenegrins, helped to account for their marked enthusiasm for Yugoslavia and Yugoslavism, and were bound to be defended by the Montenegrin Communist Party when they were perceived as coming under threat. It was equally evident that such policies were open to abuse—Montenegro was often seen as wasting funds[110] and, given the General Investment Fund's adherence to the typical Soviet practice of promoting the rapid development of heavy industry,[111] led to the

---

[108] Shoup observes that in terms of overall economic assistance, Montenegro did much better than the comparably poor republic of Macedonia. (*The Yugoslav National Question*, p. 180.) Lampe notes that over the period 1952–60 Montenegro received 230 dinars for every 100 invested in Yugoslavia (*Yugoslavia as History*, p. 276).

[109] Shoup, *The Yugoslav National Question*, p. 230.

[110] Over this period Montenegro registered the highest *per capita* budgetary expenses of any Republic, almost twice as high as those of Serbia or Bosnia-Hercegovina. (See Shoup, *The Yugoslav National Question*, p. 231.) In addition to budgetary expenses, Montenegro received the second highest (after Slovenia) investment *per capita*, a fact which failed to alter its unenviable status as the least developed of the Republics. (*Ibid.*, p. 234.) Shoup's interpretation of such discrepancies is one shared by many non-Montenegrin Yugoslavs at the time: 'the use of political influence within the Party to obtain federal aid'. (*Ibid.*, p. 231.)

[111] Rastoder points out that the share of the industrial sector in the economy rose from 6 to 35 per cent between 1945 and 1990. ('A Short Review of the History of Montenegro', p. 37.)

Milovan Djilas, 1942

Visits to Cetinje by Tito, 1959 and late 1960s

The Presidents of the six Yugoslav Republics in Cetinje, 1991. *From left* Momir Bulatovic (Montenegro); Milan Kucan (Slovenia; Bosnia-Hercegovina); Slobodan Milosevic (Serbia).

Milo Djukanovic and business leaders, 1990. The photo was taken shortly before Djukanovic became, at the age of twenty-nine, Europe's youngest prime minister.

Monument to King Nikola unveiled in Cetinje by
Prime Minister Djukanovic, December 2005.

Pro-independence supporters celebrate at a rally in
Podgorica, three days before the referendum in
May 2006.

establishment of new industries in wholly unsuitable places where
they lacked access to the necessary raw materials and to markets.
A notorious refrigerator plant was built at Cetinje[112] while the steel
mill at Nikšić, built in 1953, had no rail connection to the Adriatic
until 1961 and no paved road to connect it with anywhere till 1963.
But such was the enthusiasm of the Montenegrins for the benefits of
Yugoslavism that the Nikšić steelworks were named after the
Slovenian Boris Kidrič, Yugoslavia's economic chief until his death
in 1953, rather than after a native Montenegrin. A still more ambitious project was the Bar to Belgrade railway, an undertaking
begun in 1954 but by the mid-1960s still unfinished[113] and already,
perhaps unfairly, attracting criticism from the other Republics as
both needlessly extravagant and indicative of a Serb-Montenegrin
bias in the distributions made by the General Investment Fund.
Although tourism, beginning in the late 1950s and increasingly
attracting not only fellow-Yugoslavs but also Russians and others
from the Eastern Bloc countries as well as West Europeans, proved a
more enduring success than the dinosaurs of heavy industry, it too
encountered infrastructural problems, for example insufficient water
and poor quality construction, while the Montenegrins themselves
were often said, at least by other Yugoslavs, to be temperamentally
ill-suited to operating service industries.

However ill-advised the investment, the mushrooming industries
had the obvious effect of drawing much of the previously scattered
rural population into the larger towns. For example, the population
of Nikšić, after it had suffered heavy bombing at the end of the war,
grew from only 4,000 at that period to 50,000 by the 1980s, while
over almost the same period the pre-war population of Podgorica
had multiplied five times as workers flocked to fill jobs at the huge,
environmentally disastrous aluminium plant on the edge of the
city.[114] Naturally such large population shifts changed the social
structure of Montenegro with villages and hamlets being abandoned

---

[112] Shoup, *The Yugoslav National Question*, p. 244.

[113] Subject to many interruptions and the cause of frequent inter-Republic disputes, the construction of the narrow-gauge railway, which involved no fewer
than 254 tunnels and some 214 bridges over its 476 km. length, was not completed until 1976.

[114] Set up in 1969, Kombinat Aluminijuma Podgorica (KAP) subsequently became
Montenegro's largest company. See Chapter 12.

as their inhabitants, especially the young, moved to the main towns.[115]
While access to education and health facilities improved, the environmental impact of such a rapid shift in population was largely
negative, not only because of the proliferation of drab concrete
blocks built to house the incoming population, but also because of
the tendency to build on any available flat land, thereby eliminating
much of the traditional small-scale agriculture which, better managed, could have proved of greater benefit to Montenegro. These
major changes in patterns of settlement did not, however, undermine the clan system. Instead, in a way often commented on by the
Republic's critics, the clan structure proved highly adaptable to
the Communist system, lending itself to clientism as well as the
strengthening of Party loyalties.

But while in the mid-1960s most Montenegrins were generally
content with their situation in the new Yugoslavia, others were
markedly less so. By this time, despite the efforts of a succession of
economic planners, it was apparent that the policy of establishing
large capital-intensive enterprises in the least developed regions in
order to equalise regional differences, far from achieving the desired
results, was producing a situation in which the poorer regions were,
in relative terms, falling progressively further behind. Meanwhile the
richer Republics—Slovenia, Croatia and parts of Serbia (including
Vojvodina)—were increasingly resentful at the burdens imposed on
their own economies by the subventions designated for the poorer
regions, a process which they claimed was holding back the country
as a whole.

For those with eyes to see it was already clear that economic differences were driving the Yugoslav Republics apart. More specifically Montenegrins, adept at exploiting both their Partisan past and
the resources of the clan system, were resented in the other Republics for the way they were seen as 'colonising the [federal] bureaucracy' in order to occupy positions of power.[116] Naturally this led to

---

[115] According to Rastoder, the proportion of town-dwellers in Montenegro grew
from 14.2 per cent in 1953 to 58.2 per cent in 1991. ('A Short Review of the
History of Montenegro', p. 137.)

[116] This applied equally to Montenegrins from Montenegro and to those who,
having moved to Serbia, considered themselves as Serbs. Marko Nikezić, Yugoslav foreign minister in 1965 (previously Yugoslavia's ambassador to the United
States), had a Montenegrin father and a French mother. Nikezić had spent part
of his childhood abroad and was a well-known liberal. In 1970 he became

snide jokes at Montenegrin expense, one of which spoke of Cetinje descending on Dedinje, a reference to the number of Montenegrins who had taken up residence in Belgrade's most exclusive suburb, while another claimed that when two Montenegrins met in the street they would greet each other not with the usual 'What are you doing?' (*Šta radiš?*) but with 'Where are you managing?' (*Gdje rukovodiš?*)[117]

Economic self-interest helps to explain why Montenegro, along with Bosnia-Hercegovina, remained throughout the Tito period both the most pro-Yugoslav of all the Republics, relatively untouched by currents of liberalism and nationalism that emerged elsewhere in the 1960s. But equally Montenegro's past—the love of Russia, the pre-war strength of the Communist Party and wartime support for the Partisans, even the often alluded-to 'rigid Manichean mores'[118]— all played their part in ensuring that it remained an outpost of Titoist orthodoxy. In 1963 Montenegro had a significantly higher ratio of Party membership per head of population (6.7%) than Serbia (5.3%), where Party Membership was in turn higher than in any of the other Republics.[119] Montenegrins were also heavily represented on the Executive Committee of the Yugoslav League of Communists, which in 1963 had four Montenegrins as compared with five Serbs, five Croats but only three Slovenes and three Macedonians.[120] Three years later in 1966 only Montenegro (apart from his native Serbia) offered any support to Ranković, the secret police chief and principal opponent of reform, at the time of his disgrace.[121]

Undermining the federation: the 1974 constitution

Unsurprisingly, therefore, the liberalising movement which, starting in Croatia over language issues in 1967 and later followed by broadly

---

president of the Central Committee of the Serbian Communist Party, from which position Tito removed him as part of his purge of liberal elements in the Communist Party in October 1972. See Lampe, *Yugoslavia as History*, pp. 303–4.
[117] Fleming, *Montenegro: The Divided Land*, p. 156.
[118] Banac, *The National Question in Yugoslavia*, p. 274.
[119] See Appendix B, National Composition of the Yugoslav Communist Party, in Shoup, *The Yugoslav National Question*, p. 269.
[120] *Ibid.*, p. 275.
[121] Lampe, *Yugoslavia as History*, p. 285.

parallel movements in Serbia, Slovenia and even to some extent Macedonia, had little impact in Montenegro. Montenegrins—like the Bosnian Muslims though for different reasons[122] were resistant to change, with the local Party acquiring a reputation as die-hards. Nonetheless Titoism, with its deliberate fostering of the 'smaller nations', was largely responsible for the strengthening of a sense of Montenegrin identity, especially at the expense of those who had previously defined themselves as Serbs, the old Whites. The 1961 census showed the percentage of the population defining themselves as Montenegrins as 81.3 per cent, as against only 3 per cent who saw themselves as Serbs.[123]

Montenegrins did not dissent when, in 1972, Tito suddenly cracked down harshly on the liberal reformists active in Croatia, Serbia, Slovenia and Macedonia, whom he saw as threatening the rule of Communist bureaucracy and even his own authority.[124] However, his next move, effectively a delayed response to this crisis, was to authorise the drafting of yet another constitution, a step which, had they recognised its ultimately destructive implications for the future of the federation, would have shocked them profoundly. But they did not. Nor did Tito or Kardelj, who was once again responsible for the drafting. Rather the intention was to provide for the governing of the state after Tito's death (he was now eighty-two years old) by strengthening the role of the Communist Party and ensuring through an elaborate system of checks and balances that no one man could enjoy the power that Tito had exercised during his lifetime.

---

[122] The hard-line approach of Communist Party officials in Bosnia-Hercegovina was due both to their awareness of the need to keep a lid on the ethnic problem of the Republic, as well as to the fact that the bulk of the country's military facilities were located in that Republic.

[123] Susan L. Woodward, *Balkan Tragedy: Chaos and Dissolution after the Cold War*, Brookings Institution Press, Washington, DC, 1995, p. 33.

[124] One indication of the strong level of resistance in Montenegro to the prospect of creating a Yugoslav-wide reform movement was the breaking up of a clandestine congress that took place in April 1974 at Bar on the coast of Montenegro. Documents seized at the time and produced at the trial in September 1974 of those arrested revealed the existence of a group of die-hard supporters of Soviet-style Communism, some of whom were found to be in touch with former Cominformists living in the Soviet Union. See Banac, *With Stalin against Tito*, pp. 263–6, and Rusinow, *The Yugoslav Experiment*, p. 334.

The 1974 constitution, an enormously complicated creation with 406 articles and 100,000 words was beyond the comprehension of most Yugoslavs. Among its most significant provisions was the setting up of a collective state Presidency, consisting of one representative for each Republic or province, plus Tito—with the provision that after Tito's death the Presidency would rotate on an annual basis among its members.[125] While the Presidency staff was selected on a republican basis, a second pillar of federal government, the Federal Executive Council (SIV), was exempted from the usual Titoist requirement of equal representation for all the nations—the so-called 'ethnic key'. This omission soon allowed its domination by Serbs and Montenegrins. The third and final pillar at the federal level was, of course, the League of Communists of Yugoslavia (SKJ).

As a guarantee for the continuation of Yugoslavia, the new constitution contained a number of serious weaknesses. Foremost among these, it allowed Republics to have an effective veto over legislation affecting all the other Republics, a recipe for creating paralysis at the federal level. When this was subsequently extended to Communist Party decisions as well, the future of the federation was clearly under threat.[126] At the same time the constitution permitted the devolution of further significant powers to the Republics (and the provinces) which, in addition to their own presidents and prime ministers, now had the right to initiate legislation and maintain their own missions abroad. Finally they retained the right to secede from the federation, although it was still not envisaged that they should exercise it. The effect, as Lampe has noted, was to create 'a confederation of single-party regimes'.[127]

From 1974 until his death in 1980 Yugoslavia held together largely through the force of Tito's personality as his widespread popularity enabled him to discipline the Party and continued borrowing helped to keep the state afloat and even to sustain an unearned rise in living standards. Meanwhile, however, politicians at the republican level were largely free to pursue their own frequently incompatible policies, strengthening their own power bases with little regard to

---

[125] Lampe, *Yugoslavia as History*, p. 305. Tito had already agreed to the setting-up of a collective Presidency, originally with twenty-three members, in 1971.
[126] *Ibid.*, p. 305.
[127] *Ibid.*, p. 299.

the country's wider interests. It was a state of affairs that fostered rivalry and led to wasteful duplication of facilities and resources. For example, Montenegro enlarged the port facilities at Bar even though Rijeka in Croatia already had adequate facilities for all Yugoslavia's maritime trade.[128] There was duplication too at the cultural level as each Republic allocated funds for prestigious local institutes and institutions. By 1974 Podgorica had a university with six faculties. This was followed two years later with the establishment of a Montenegrin Academy of Arts and Sciences. A national theatre and separate Montenegrin television channels and radio stations were soon established, together with the first daily newspaper with the nostalgically Communist title *Pobjeda*—Victory.[129]

Through all this Montenegrins retained their affection for Yugoslavia. In 1974 the Njegoš chapel on Mount Lovćen was replaced by a huge stone mausoleum designed by the Croat sculptor Ivan Mestrović. In Montenegro's schools children continued to recite the poems of the Slovene poet France Prešeren as often as they recited those of Njegoš. In 1979 following a hugely destructive earthquake in the vicinity of Kotor, Tito appealed personally to all Yugoslavs to aid their fellow-citizens by digging deep in their pockets. Each Republic could select the way it chose to respond. Serbia introduced a tax on workers' salaries while other Republics also donated generously. Montenegrins were touched; but the peoples of the other Republics, who at first were responsive to Montenegro's plight, soon made jibes about the Montenegrins' laziness and claims to special treatment. In the years following Tito's death in May 1980 Montenegrins, unlike Serbs who generally resented what they saw as the downgrading of Serbia's position during the Second Yugoslavia, continued to revere the Old Man's memory and to cling to their hopes for the continuation of a system that they rightly believed had worked greatly to their advantage. Typical of this confused and wishful thinking, perhaps, was the name given to the Montenegrin football team—*Budućnost*, Serbo-Croatian for 'Future'—when what they really wanted was more of the same. The numbers formally calling themselves Yugoslavs continued to climb (from 2.1% in 1961

[128] Bennett, *Yugoslavia's Bloody Collapse*, p. 75.
[129] *Pobjeda* had existed as a weekly publication in Montenegro since the war.

to 5.4% in 1981), lower than in Croatia, where many of those who did so in 1981 were likely to have been Serbs, and in Bosnia-Hercegovina, where 'Yugoslav' was still a popular form of self-designation for Muslims, but higher than in Serbia, where increasingly Tito's equalising policies were seen as being at Serbia's expense.[130] Still good Yugoslavs in 1984, they backed the Montenegrin President of the collective Presidency, Veselin Djuranović, and felt pride when during an official visit to Britain he was received by the Queen at Buckingham Palace: apart from Tito, they observed, no other Yugoslav had received such a magnificent reception.

However, the Montenegrins' optimism was hardly well-founded. As the 1980s progressed they, like other Yugoslavs, were made increasingly aware of the economic crisis facing the country. Tito's Yugoslavia had borrowed recklessly and by the mid-1980s the international debt was spiralling out of control. Meanwhile, as the banks continued to issue credits, inflation escalated and living costs soared. The federal government imposed austerity measures, a move which hit hard in Montenegro where industry had long been propped up by federal government subventions. Factories were forced to lay off workers, raising unemployment in Montenegro to 24% by 1984.[131] To add to the problem, Montenegrins from Kosovo, alarmed by deteriorating relations with Albanians, were leaving the province and so adding to the unemployment figures at home.

None of these problems was unique to Montenegro, but the fact that so much of the Montenegrin economy was centred on capital-intensive basic industry caused particular problems. With their more Western-focused export markets and better links with the rest of Europe, Slovenia and Croatia were better placed to confront the crisis. Even among the poorer Republics, Montenegro's dependence on mining and metallurgy and its poor infrastructure was a major disadvantage. As ordinary people struggled to make ends meet, disillusionment was beginning to grow and with it a Yugoslav-wide tendency, particularly pronounced in Serbia, Croatia and Slovenia, to blame those in other Republics for the problems experienced 'at

---

[130] Woodward, *Balkan Tragedy*, p. 33.

[131] *Ibid.*, p. 53. Unemployment figures in Montenegro were subject to considerable seasonal variation, particularly on the coast, where they were significantly affected by tourism.

home'.[132] Montenegro, as a 'favoured' Republic despite its continuing relative poverty, was one of the objects of this resentment. It still clung to its Yugoslavism but was facing the bitter truth that others were planning their exit from Yugoslavia while one man was planning to take the country over. They were to be caught in the middle.

[132] Lampe, *Yugoslavia as History*, p. 326.

12. The Djukanović Years

The Third Yugoslavia

As the Communist era drew to a close, in Montenegro as in other parts of Yugoslavia, the underlying national tensions, hitherto suppressed, were making their way to the surface. Worse still, the country's economic crisis, coming as it did with the collapse of Communism in the Soviet Union and across the Eastern bloc, fatally undermined the ideological underpinning of Yugoslavia's one-party regime with its cornerstone of 'brotherhood and unity'. Without Tito to hold the country together, and with resentment growing between the different Republics, the way was open for opportunistic and unscrupulous politicians to bang the drum of nationalism. Not only did the overall decline in the national wealth fuel resentment between Yugoslavia's individual Republics, but within the Republics nationalism's emphasis on the primacy of the core 'nation' was threatening the hitherto protected position of the various minorities. In Montenegro, given its history, such developments did not bode well for the interests of the non-Orthodox minorities—Slav Muslim or Albanian—any more than it did elsewhere in Yugoslavia. However, for Montenegrins the recrudescence of nationalism would have a further specific dimension: in addition to the division between the Orthodox and the various minorities, the focus on the 'core' nation would inevitably run up against the Orthodox population's long-standing ambivalence over national identity. Here the vital question was: what constituted the core—Serb or Montenegrin? At the political level such tensions were bound to rekindle the old divisions between Greens and Whites, fuelling a debate over the restoration of a Montenegrin state. Associated and running in parallel with it was the emergence of conflict over the proposed restoration of an autocephalous Montenegrin Orthodox Church. As time went on, the economic aspirations of different constituencies and interest groups would add their weight to the divisions over national identity and statehood, considerably complicating the picture.

Montenegro's position was aggravated by a lack of consistency among its politicians. During the heady days of Milošević's rise to power, the strength of support for his brand of Serbian nationalism found the pro-Serbia forces in the ascendant. But as Yugoslavia's disintegration degenerated into ever more bitter fighting between and within the Republics, and as Montenegro was excoriated for its inglorious role in the shelling of Dubrovnik, enthusiasm for war faded, promoting a groundswell of support for Montenegrin independence, subsequently captured and built on by the country's new political master, Milo Djukanović. The debate over Montenegrin national identity was rekindled during the Kosovo war and took yet another turn after the fall of Milošević. In the process every development—both internal and external—was liable to become grist to the mill of the different camps: the Orthodox Church, The Hague Tribunal and the prospect of EU membership. Of these the most important was the last, where the argument centred on which path could deliver quicker and better access to the EU with little attention being given by either side to what might happen once the panacea of EU membership had been obtained. Much of the debate consisted of nationalistically-slanted campaigns, albeit along opposing lines. Djukanović's ruling party favoured post-modern[1] rhetoric—Montenegro as the world's first ecological state and suchlike—but in reality was ready to exploit its brand of Montenegrin nationalism as a means of achieving the goal of independence. Equally, Djukanović's adversaries were strong on Greater Serbian rhetoric, with a particularly vocal contribution emanating from the Montenegrin branch of the Serbian Orthodox Church, a stance echoed by a part of the Serbian establishment including Prime Minister Koštunica.

Milošević's rise to power

With the rise to power in Serbia of Slobodan Milošević and the consequent disintegration of Tito's Yugoslavia, the peculiarly intense

---

[1] See Robert Cooper, *The Breaking of Nations: Order and Chaos in the Twenty-First Century*, London: Atlantic Books, 2004, pp. 26–37.

relationship between Serbia and Montenegro came under the spotlight again. But just as the sense of separate Montenegrin national identity had been largely submerged under the Karadjordjević parliamentary regime and subsequent dictatorship, so Milošević ensured that in the crucial years of Yugoslavia's disintegration, he could always count on at least one ally, Montenegro, in pursuing his brand of nationalism. As the son of Montenegrin parents himself, he knew how to play his hand, and a campaign begun in Kosovo and directed against the Albanians—a sizeable minority within Montenegro's borders—and in defence theoretically of Yugoslavia was aimed to unite many Montenegrins[2] behind the traditional banner of the defence of Serbdom and to appeal to their strong support for the Yugoslav idea.

From the time Milošević came to exercise full control in Serbia, having metaphorically defenestrated his former friend and mentor Ivan Stambolić at the 8th Plenary Session of the Serbian League of Communists,[3] he plotted to extend his power throughout the SFRJ.[4] A secret admirer of Tito (although they never met), he saw himself as occupying a similar position within Yugoslavia. Unfortunately for him, what Tito had achieved through the Partisan struggle others inside Yugoslavia were not prepared to concede without battling to defend their own interests against Serbian hegemony. Milošević's response to this was twofold: while increasing his hold over the Yugoslav army (JNA), he would attempt to control the collective and rotating eight-man state (i.e. federal) Presidency which had ruled Yugoslavia since Tito's death in 1980. His aim was to

[2] Montenegrins and northern Albanians resemble one another in many respects—in their tribal social structure, their patriarchal values and their strict moral code with its emphasis on heroic values. This results in a high degree of mutual understanding. Nevertheless, differences of language and religion, amplified by the persistent recycling of 'historical memories' as part of Milošević's policy at that time, ensured that the mythic view of the other held by each as the enemy—a view far more prevalent in the case of Serbs and Albanians—possessed sufficient resonance.

[3] He was rumoured to be behind Stambolić's actual death in 2000. See Slavoljub Djukić, *Milošević and Marković: A Lust for Power* (trans. from the Serbian *On, Ona i Mi*, by Alex Dubinsky), London: Ithaca, 2001, pp. 145–6.

[4] The Socialist Federative Republic of Yugoslavia, also frequently referred to therefore as the SFRY.

ensure that a new constitution, which had been mooted for some time, would reflect Serbia's concern to reinforce its own position, remove the secessionist clauses enabling the other Republics to break away, and reduce the power of Serbia's autonomous regions (Kosovo and Vojvodina) to obstruct Serbian policy. Under the arrangement of Tito's 1974 constitution, intended to prevent Serbian dominance while satisfying the increasing demands of Slovenian, Croatian and Albanian nationalists, each of Yugoslavia's six Republics had one vote in the federal Presidency. So too did Serbia's two autonomous provinces,[5] both of which had used their votes against Serbia on a number of occasions.

The anti-bureaucratic revolution; Milošević's placemen

Milošević now set out to gain control of the federal Presidency. After sweeping to power in Serbia on a wave of anti-Kosovar-Albanian sentiment, he and his supporters moved to use these populist tactics against the leaders of Serbia's autonomous provinces: Kosovo itself, where the Assembly was intimidated by Serb tanks into surrendering its autonomy in March 1989, and Vojvodina, where mass rallies of protesters shouting nationalist slogans of support for their brothers in Kosovo were successful in ousting the local Communist leaders, who found themselves cast in the role of old-style bureaucratic oppressors.[6]

After Vojvodina, Montenegro's similarly lacklustre leadership looked vulnerable to the Milošević-organised travelling roadshow of agitators. The economic situation had been deteriorating for some time. As funds began to diminish under the tough financial requirements imposed by the International Monetary Fund and experts called in to deal with the Yugoslav financial crisis, the people in the poorer republics were the first to feel the pinch. Montenegro had declared bankruptcy in 1987, and huge lay-offs of workers in the Republic's major industrial plants were in prospect. But if the

---

[5] The status of Kosovo, originally an autonomous region, was upgraded to that of an autonomous province in 1963.

[6] These supposedly spontaneous protests were accordingly described by their supporters as forming part of an 'anti-bureaucratic revolution'.

background to the protests lay in economic decline, they quickly took on a political and nationalistic hue as protesters began to express their dissatisfaction with the local leadership and proclaim solidarity with Serb and Montenegrin brothers in Kosovo.

Sporadic demonstrations in support of Serbs and Montenegrins in Kosovo had first broken out in August 1988 in the Montenegrin capital Titograd organised by members of Milošević's band of agitators. In Nikšić, the day after the fall of the leadership in Vojvodina, workers from the town's iron and steel works were prevented by police from joining up with protesters in Titograd, and a number of demonstrators were injured in an action that was to lead to the undoing of the Republic's leadership. The most significant of the protests on 7 October culminated in a violent clash between police and demonstrating steel workers, the first use of force to suppress a public protest since police had put down an attempted uprising by Kosovo Albanians in 1981.[7] With the shock waves extending widely beyond Montenegro, Milošević was able to use injuries inflicted in the police baton charge to good effect to accuse the local leadership of oppression. He was echoed by a leading Serb nationalist intellectual writer Dobrica Ćosić, who appealed to local leaders to 'prevent violence against citizens who are not satisfied with the existing state of society'. After the clash on 7 October the Montenegrin government led by Premier Vuko Vukadinović called for and received an immediate vote of confidence. But the same session of Parliament then voted separately against the Minister of the Interior and three other ministers, whereupon Vukadinović and the whole government resigned, the first government in Yugoslavia to do so since 1945. Although the Party leadership won a vote of confidence that month, and there was no immediate sense that the old power structure had collapsed, the writing was on the wall.

Far from quelling the protests, the police action seemed to encourage them, and over the next weeks the numbers of demonstrators grew. The fact that many of the Slav settlers in Kosovo were of Montenegrin origin ensured a favourable climate for the anti-Albanian brand of nationalism fostered by Milošević's placemen. Milošević was well aware that playing the anti-Albanian card would,

[7] Veseljko Koprivica and Branko Vojičić, *Prevrat '89*, Podgorica: Liberalni Savez Crne Gore, 1994, p. 200.

at least in the short term, unite Montenegrins of different traditions. How successful he was in this could be seen from the curious mixture of placards carried by the protestors. Together with those portraying Milošević were many of Tito and some of Njegoš, whose panegyric to Serbdom, *The Mountain Wreath*, has—as we have seen—been associated with strong anti-Muslim sentiment.[8] Within Montenegro itself different traditions honoured different aspects of Njegoš: Prince-Bishop of Montenegro and poet of a peculiarly Montenegrin heroic tradition, or alternatively the glorifier of the historic victories of the great Serb nation. However, other protesters had a different agenda.

Besides the economic grievances on which Milošević supporters were able to capitalise, a further current of opinion found its inspiration in the youth movements of Slovenia that were pushing for a clear break with Yugoslavia's Communist path and were seen as very much in the vanguard of East European reform.[9] Thus in contrast to the situation in Vojvodina and Kosovo, the protests in Montenegro brought together three different but in some cases overlapping constituencies: those concerned at the fate of Serbian and Montenegrin brothers in Kosovo; those brought low by economic hardship; and the educated but weakest strand, those who wanted true political and economic reform, a group further divided over the merits of socialist pluralism or multi-party pluralism.

Whatever the different agendas of the demonstrators may have been, their combined force led in January 1989 to the resignation of the party leadership, to be replaced by a group of young Communists, specially groomed for power by Milošević, known as the '*lijepi, mladi, inteligentni*', or 'bright young things'. Unlike the situation in other East European 'revolutions', this was a palace coup. Led by Momir Bulatović and Milo Djukanović, who had risen to the top of the League of Communists at that time, they took over the 'anti-bureaucratic revolution' in Montenegro.

While Bulatović appeared ostensibly affable and easy-going, Milo Djukanović (nicknamed 'the Razor', *Britva*, for his sharp tongue[10]),

---

[8] See Chapters 4 and 6.

[9] Author's conversation with Srdjan Darmanović, at the time a supporter of the pro-Slovenian element in the protests and currently director of CEDEM (Centre for Democracy and Human Rights) and professor of politics at Podgorica University.

[10] Veseljko Koprivica, 'From Enthusiasm to Wealth', AIM Podgorica, 28 October

the man who was to become Europe's youngest Prime Minister at the age of twenty-nine in 1991, is remembered by many of those who knew him at that time as inflexible and doctrinaire. Beginning his political career at a precocious age—he was the youngest member of the Central Committee of the Communist Youth Alliance of Yugoslavia[11]—Djukanović later emerged as a highly pragmatic figure able to portray himself, as to some extent he was, as an advocate of social reform and ethnic tolerance. However, in 1989 his rigidly Communist outlook soon led to disagreements with would-be democrats who had taken their inspiration from the Slovenian youth movement and aspired to the multi-party ideals that were beginning to find their mark elsewhere in Eastern Europe. The wrangling eventually led to the ousting of the young intellectuals like Srdjan Darmanović, Ljubiša Stanković and Miodrag Vlahović.[12] Milošević now had the Montenegrin vote under his belt and Bulatović, his protégé, at the age of thirty-four was the local party chief. His role in subsequent months was largely to be his master's voice in the tempestuous clashes of the federal Presidency.

Later that year, in a colourful interlude, King Nikola's remains were returned from Italy to the homeland he had fled seventy-three years earlier. Amid emotional scenes in Cetinje in October 1989, he was reburied with his wife and three of his daughters in the course of a three-hour-long Orthodox ceremony attended by over a quarter of Montenegro's population. 'All the former legations sported their old coats-of-arms and fresh coats of paint,'[13] and the heir apparent, the Parisian architect Prince Nikola, and his fashion designer wife Frans, were mobbed.

But monarchical sentiment was not going to be converted into political support. In the 1990 multi-party elections held throughout

---

1997, available at http://www.aimpress.ch/dyn/trae/archive/data/199710/71029-027-trae-pod.htm, accessed on 21 August 2005.

[11] Government of Montenegro website: http://www.gom.cg.yu/print.php?id=17&jezik=0, accessed on 12 Dec. 2004.

[12] Miodrag Vlahović was a founder member of the Association for a Yugoslav Democratic Initiative, one of the earliest opposition parties in Yugoslavia in 1989, before becoming in 1991 a leading member of the anti-war movement opposed to Montenegro's role in the invasion of Croatia. In 2004 he was appointed Montenegro's foreign minister.

[13] *The Times*, 2 October 1989.

Yugoslavia, though without any great enthusiasm in Montenegro and Serbia, the Montenegrin League of Communists—alone in Yugoslavia in not renaming itself—won an overwhelming victory in taking eighty-three of the 125 seats available. The results reflected both the popularity of the relatively new party leadership and the fact that Communism enjoyed more support in Montenegro than elsewhere. Bulatović won a decisive victory (76.1 per cent) in the simultaneous presidential elections.

Finally after the election, the Montenegrin League of Communists renamed itself the Democratic Party of Socialists (DPS), and while working hand in glove with Milošević's party, the Socialist Party of Serbia (SPS), resisted blandishments to unite with it. The nearest party to the DPS in terms of support was the Yugoslav-wide United Reform Party of the Yugoslav Prime Minister Ante Marković. As a liberal, democratic alternative to the nationalist parties and the League of Communists of Yugoslavia (SKJ) Marković's party was popular with the outside world but failed to achieve a breakthrough in any of the republican elections where it stood.[14] It never ran again in Montenegro. Marković's reformists narrowly out-performed the Narodna Stranka or People's Party (NS), a party which was strongly Serb nationalist and unitary: a Union of Serbia and Montenegro with Serb areas of Croatia and Bosnia thrown in for good measure. A party formed from two ethnic minority parties, of Albanians and Slav Muslims, took 10 per cent of the vote and subsequently broke up to run separately.[15]

Demise of the League of Communists of Yugoslavia and the descent to war

While the majority of Montenegrins saw themselves as remodelling rather than repudiating their Communist past, at the federal

---

[14] If the West had pressed for the federal elections to be held first, Marković's party might have been the strongest.

[15] At a time of escalating anti-Muslim and anti-Albanian tension the two minority parties were driven through a shared sense of vulnerability to run together on a single ticket. Subsequently, as the intensive anti-minority campaign in Montenegro abated under the leadership of Milo Djukanović (see below), the Muslim-Bosniak and Albanian parties felt sufficiently secure to run alone.

level the League of Communists of Yugoslavia had already imploded.[16] In January 1990 it fell to Bulatović to play a historic and dramatic role in the break-up of the federation at the fateful and final 14th Extraordinary Party Congress of the League of Communists of Yugoslavia. On 23 January, as first the Slovenes and then the Croats walked out of the Congress humiliated at the rejection of all their proposals to reform the Communist Party, Momir Bulatović was in the chair. With no representation of two of the six Republics left, Bulatović was in a quandary. He exercised his chairman's right to call a break for fifteen minutes, which, as he subsequently commented, 'lasted throughout history'.[17]

For eighteen months Yugoslavia teetered on the edge: Slovenia, with great efficiency, and Croatia, lagging behind, prepared their exit, arming their own territorial units. In Croatia the significant Serb minority was armed in turn by Milošević. Despite frantic international activity and dire warnings by the international community of the importance of maintaining the Federal Republic in place, the descent into war accelerated. Both Slovenia and Croatia declared independence on 25 June 1991, which led immediately to the JNA's forcible intervention in Slovenia. Ironically Milošević had not intended to go to war over Slovenia since he already understood—particularly following the demise of the SKJ—that it was no longer possible to dominate the whole of Yugoslavia and had decided to redefine his goal as controlling all Serbs in one state.[18] In the autumn of 1990, with this end in view, he had reached a private agreement with the Slovenian President Milan Kučan that Slovenia, a Republic that significantly lacked a Serbian minority, would be allowed to opt for independence, believing that as a *quid pro quo* it would not object to the dismemberment of Croatia.[19]

That the proposed exit by Slovenia did not go smoothly was due, not to any qualms on Kučan's part and still less on the part of Milošević, but to a decision by nostalgic Titoists on the general staff of the

[16] On the demise of the League of Communists see Louis Sell, *Slobodan Milošević and the Destruction of Yugoslavia*, Durham, NC: Duke University Press, 2002, pp. 60–1 and 104–5.

[17] Laura Silber and Alan Little, *The Death of Yugoslavia*, Penguin Books Worldwide, rev. edn, 1996, p. 81.

[18] See Sell, *Milošević and the Destruction of Yugoslavia*, p. 108.

[19] *Ibid.*, pp. 115 and 128.

JNA to make a stand in favour of Yugoslavia.[20] However, their intervention was futile: within ten days the JNA had been made to look
impotent and been forced to withdraw. It was a different story in
Croatia. The JNA needed to restore its military credentials after its
humiliation in the phoney ten-day war against Slovenia. When the
war with Croatia formally broke out in August 1991, the JNA, with
General Ratko Mladić playing a key role, enjoyed the full support of
the federal Presidency, a presidency now shorn of Slovenes and
Croats and hence a tool in Milošević's hands. A Montenegrin representative on the Presidency, Branko Kostić, was acting head of state
and commander-in-chief of the Yugoslav Army, but Milošević was
pulling all the strings.

At first the war focused on those parts of Croatia with Serb populations, a theatre at a good distance from Montenegro. But as the
battle for Vukovar[21] raged, the Yugoslav army attacked Dubrovnik
from Montenegro. JNA soldiers, supported by Montenegrin irregulars, earned a name for lawlessness and rapacity, which prompted a
torrent of international outrage and disapproval. Dubrovnik had no
military strategic value and was barely defended by the Croats. Nor
were there more than a few Serbs living there. Rather the attack
seemed to stem from pure vindictiveness or, according to some, from
the Montenegrins' traditional appetite for plunder,[22] and led to
headlines in the Western press likening the Yugoslav army to barbarian hordes. Although Montenegro was officially detached from
the war in Croatia and withdrew its reservists there in October 1991,
Montenegrin soldiers from their positions in the hills above Dubrovnik destroyed hotels, yachts and other signs of sophistication or civilisation with a wantonness that caused more damage to Milošević's
interests and game plan than he could possibly have anticipated.[23]

[20] Sell, *Milošević and the Destruction of Yugoslavia*, p. 145.
[21] Over the autumn of 1991 the town of Vukovar on Serbia's border with Croatia
in eastern Slavonia was besieged and bombarded by the JNA backed by Serb
paramilitaries. Hundreds of civilians died during the siege while more died,
presumed executed, when in November 1991 the town finally fell to JNA forces.
[22] On Montenegro's traditional banditry see Palairet, 'The Culture of Economic
Stagnation in Montenegro', pp. 28–9.
[23] In the year 2000 President Djukanović made an official apology to Croatia for
Montenegro's part in the 1991 attack on the coastal area around Dubrovnik.
Since then two prominent Montenegrins have been sentenced by The Hague
Tribunal for their part in the shelling of Dubrovnik—Admiral Miodrag Jokić,

Only days before the attack on Dubrovnik, with no apparent sense of irony, the Parliament of Montenegro had declared the country to be an ecological state. Its rhetorical ballast rings particularly hollow in the light of events only days away: 'We are fully aware that dignity and blessedness of a human being are intrinsically connected with blessedness and purity of nature … being committed to the struggle for the dignity of man, we are also called upon to struggle for the dignity of nature.'[24] The mindless sacking and looting around Dubrovnik for no rational purpose stood in contrast to a strategic bone of contention, which took more than a decade to resolve. The Prevlaka peninsula on the Croatian side of the border with Montenegro controlled access to the Gulf of Kotor, where the JNA's only remaining naval base was located. This led to the JNA's occupation of the peninsula in the first days of the war from which it finally withdrew a year later after an agreement reached between the then Yugoslav President Dobrica Ćosić and the Croatian President Franjo Tudjman for them to be replaced by a UN force to maintain its demilitarised status.[25]

The political and institutional landscape

As Croatia and Slovenia's departure from the SFRJ was followed by Bosnia and Macedonia, the bloody disintegration of Yugoslavia rekindled the identity question in Montenegro. The arguments of the Greens and the Whites were effectively re-run with those on the side of Serb nationalism enjoying the support of the hard-line Montenegrin Archbishop of the Serbian Orthodox Church, Amfilohije. Novak Kilibarda's People's Party was in the van of the campaign of the Whites and was seen as close to Radovan Karadžić's Serbian Democratic Party (SDS) in Bosnia and later to Koštunica's Democratic Party of Serbia (DSS). As a genuinely nationalist party, it sought to differentiate itself from Bulatović's DPS and its Serbian sister party, Milošević's SPS.

who was sentenced to seven years' imprisonment in March 2004, and Lieutenant General Pavle Strugar, who was sentenced to eight years in January 2005.
[24] Declaration of the Parliament of Montenegro, Žabljak, 20 September 1991.
[25] The agreement was brokered by Lord Owen and Cyrus Vance, the co-chairmen of the International Conference on the Former Yugoslavia (ICFY). See David Owen, *Balkan Odyssey*, London: Gollancz, 1995, p. 51.

On the other side of the equation stood the Liberal Alliance of Montenegro (LSCG). Founded in 1990 by a colourful and quixotic ex-public prosecutor Slavko Perović, the party saw itself as inheriting the historic mantle of the Greens. Pro-independence but paradoxically anti-nationalist (as understood in the Balkans) because the war was 'a Serbian war', the LSCG neither 'advocated the use of force, nor did it express hostility towards minorities'.[26] This placed it firmly at odds with Serbian nationalism and the Serbian Orthodox Church. Instead in 1993 the party put on record its support for the re-establishment of the Montenegrin Orthodox Church as a step towards its ultimate goal of achieving Montenegrin independence.[27] In a very real sense the tensions between the two churches reflected the wider political conflict in microcosm.

Support for an autocephalous Montenegrin Orthodox Church was not at this stage part of DPS policy, and it was not till Easter 2000 when President Djukanović sent official greetings to the Montenegrin Orthodox Church that the DPS really came off the fence over this issue. Rather the DPS was, if not equidistant, somewhere between the Whites and Greens, close to its Serbian sister party but distinct from it. It generally took a tolerant line towards minorities and indeed the period was characterised by some of the best interethnic relations in the former Yugoslavia.

Montenegro at The Hague Conference

While the fighting was escalating dramatically in Croatia, diplomatic activity was also intensifying. As early as September 1991 the European Community had set up a peace conference on Yugoslavia under the chairmanship of the former Secretary General of NATO (and before that British Foreign Secretary), Lord Carrington, who within a month had produced a detailed proposal to bring the

---

[26] Florian Bieber, 'Montenegrin politics since the disintegration of Yugoslavia', (hereafter referred to as 'Montenegrin politics since the disintegration') in Florian Bieber (ed.), *Montenegro in Transition: Problems of Identity and Statehood*, Baden-Baden: Nomos, 2003, p. 20.

[27] As George Schöpflin writes, 'Autocephaly has universally been seen as a mark of independent nationhood in the Orthodox world...' (*Nations Identity Power*, p. 359.)

Yugoslav crisis to an end: 'Arrangements for a general settlement'. The Carrington plan envisaged a loose association of sovereign or independent republics with adequate arrangements for the protection of minorities and possibly special status for certain areas. It also precluded unilateral changes of borders. But the elements in the plan that were attractive to Croatian Serbs applied equally to Kosovo Albanians and thus struck at the very heart of Milošević's rise to power. Milošević was therefore opposed to the Carrington plan, and in this expected full support from Montenegro.

Instead, on 18 October at a meeting of the peace conference in The Hague, Momir Bulatović, whose arrival was delayed because of a late-night sitting of the Montenegrin Parliament meeting to discuss the Carrington proposals, shocked the conference by announcing that he accepted them. He had been given authority by the Montenegrin Parliament to take a decision himself. He subsequently explained:

We thought the plan was quite enough. It made it possible for us to realise our own interests and to have the interests of the others also taken into account. It was an excellent means to put an end to the war, a war which affected us also in Montenegro, because 10 per cent of our population was mobilised for that war. I had been under enormous pressure. During a visit to the United States, they had treated me there as a savage—who is this person whose citizens are attacking and destroying Dubrovnik? We never needed Dubrovnik and, really, we could no longer allow ourselves to have our people die in vain, to have Montenegro acquire an unfavourable international reputation.[28]

This rational and principled explanation of his decision was contradicted by another participant at the conference, the then Italian Foreign Minister Gianni de Michelis. De Michelis maintained that he had been advised by the then Croatian representative on the federal Presidency, Stipe Mesić, that Montenegrin loyalty could be bought, and cheaply. Before the crucial meeting where Bulatović dissented publicly from the Milošević line, de Michelis claimed to have met Bulatović and to have pressed him to adopt an independent position. He recalled:

[Bulatović] told me… that Montenegro was interested in peace … and on the other hand he was very interested in the economic-development rela-

---

[28] Quoted by Silber and Little, *Death of Yugoslavia*, pp. 194–5.

tions with the European Community. He considered Italy Montenegro's natural channel to Europe.

At that time there were negotiations for the programme of cooperation between Italy and Montenegro. An important programme, about 30 or 40 billion lira in various projects, for Montenegro, a country of some 600,000 inhabitants.[29]

However promising Bulatović's rebellion was for the prospects of The Hague conference, not many were convinced that he would both hold his line and survive in his position. According to Henri Wejnaendts, a Dutch diplomat who was Carrington's aide, Milošević had dismissed Bulatović's rebellion with the words 'Bulatović will not stay president of Montenegro for long.'[30]

Indeed the heavens predictably fell in on Bulatović. As the tame Belgrade press cried traitor, Milošević's political agitators brought the crowds out on the streets again in Montenegro to demonstrate against Bulatović's line. He was ordered to Belgrade where, according to Bulatović himself,

There was a series of unpleasant meetings …the entire press in Belgrade labelled me a traitor. And some [of Milošević's men] would directly ask me whether I was a spy, whether I had received money from a foreign country. The next days were very explosive. The media would say I stabbed Milošević in the back.[31]

With his political future at stake, Bulatović yielded and eventually got himself out of the hole he had dug by agreeing to hold a referendum on the issue. On 30 October Serbia and Montenegro proposed an amendment to the Carrington plan, insisting that a clause be inserted declaring that the Federal Republic of Yugoslavia continued to exist for those who did not wish to secede. This was quickly rejected by Carrington and by all other participants. The conference was eventually irretrievably damaged when, with television images of the destruction of Vukovar and the wanton attack on Dubrovnik still fresh in minds, Hans-Dietrich Genscher, the German Foreign Minister, was able to reverse previous EU policy on keeping Yugoslavia together and force through the premature rec-

[29] Silber and Little, *Death of Yugoslavia*, p. 195.
[30] *Ibid.*
[31] *Ibid.*, p. 196.

ognition of Croatia and Slovenia, thereby in Carrington's words completely 'torpedoing' the peace conference.[32]

The fluctuating state of Serbian-Montenegrin relations

As the institutional kaleidoscope in the former Yugoslavia was shaken that winter by the recognition of Croatia and Slovenia and by the impending war in Bosnia, the leaders of Serbia and Montenegro contemplated their options. It was important for them to claim state continuity, in other words to maintain that they were the continuing state of Yugoslavia from which others had decided to secede. On the other hand, Bulatović, displaying a last flicker of independent political thought, attempted to chart a course for Montenegro which would steer between independence and Serbian domination. 'There is a minimum', he declared, 'below which Montenegro cannot go.' But Milošević's pro-Serbian support was too well marshalled, and Bulatović's platform met with little success.

On 1 March 1992 some 95.4 per cent of those voting in a referendum in Montenegro supported the maintenance of the union with Serbia, answering a question heavily skewed in favour of a 'yes' vote: 'Do you wish a sovereign Montenegro to remain in association with other Yugoslav republics that wish the same?' The turnout at 66.04 per cent was low by the standards of other Republics' referendums on their constitutional future, and diminished by the boycott called by both the Albanian and Muslim communities and by some of the opposition.[33] Nevertheless, the leadership in both Republics pressed on to the creation of the Federal Republic of Yugoslavia (FRY) on 27 April 1992 with only Serb and Montenegrin federal deputies—all of whose mandates had expired a year earlier—participating in the vote to adopt the constitution of the new two-member federation. The rush to claim state continuity, in other words to maintain that the FRY was really the prolongation of the SFRJ, allowed scant time for consideration of the constitution itself. As a result the April 1992 constitution adopted many of the provisions of the old SFRJ constitution, including most significantly its

---

[32] *Ibid.*, p. 199.
[33] Bieber, 'Montenegrin politics since the disintegration', p. 21.

insistence on equality of representation in federal institutions and on decision-making through consensus on federal issues, including crucial decisions on the armed forces.[34] The ill-considered outcome was, to say the least, anomalous: Montenegro, with approximately 6 per cent of the population, had an equal voice in federal decision-making. Indeed an increasing number of decisions were taken at the republican level, while at the international level Milošević took the decisions unilaterally.

Dissatisfaction with the new federation led to the opposition parties in Serbia and Montenegro boycotting the first elections to the federal Parliament called for May 1992.[35] Although the DPS together with two smaller Serbian-based parties—the Radicals (SRS) and a neo-communist party close to Milošević's wife Mirjana Marković (the JUL)—did run and were duly awarded seats, the authorities were not satisfied with the outcome while the opposition staged protests. New elections were scheduled for December 1992 to coincide with early presidential and parliamentary republican elections to be held simultaneously in both Republics. The Serb Socialist Party (SPS), irritated by Bulatović's initial support for the Carrington plan and by his now only lukewarm support for the war in Bosnia, promoted the candidacy of Branko Kostić, the last Montenegrin member of the rotating Yugoslav Presidency. Kostić, an unswerving Milošević supporter and a man once described as '*plus serbe que les Serbes*',[36] left no room for doubt on his pro-war stance when he described himself as the candidate for the 'Association of Fighters from the 1991–2 war'.[37]

As Kostić's challenge to Bulatović showed, there were already divisions between the governments of Serbia and Montenegro over Serbian support for the Bosnian war. In October the Montenegrin government took this a step further by promulgating a new consti-

[34] See 'Politics, Interests and the Future of Yugoslavia: an Agenda for Dialogue', in European Stability Initiative Discussion Paper, Berlin, Brussels, Sarajevo, 26 November 2001, p. 2.
[35] See Bieber, 'Montenegrin politics since the disintegration', to which I am indebted for this account of the political situation.
[36] Henry Wynaendts, *L'Engrenage. Chroniques yougoslaves, juillet 1991–août 1992*, Paris: Denoël, 1993, p. 51.
[37] *Udruženja ratnika, 1991–92*, mentioned by Bieber in 'Montenegrin politics since the disintegration', p. 22.

tution shorn of earlier nationalist references and recognising the existence of certain minority rights, a move which took cognizance of the growing sentiment within Montenegro against the war. How far did this reflect a real change of heart over the war by the government? Certainly the Montenegrin opposition parties—the LSCG and the small Social Democratic Party (SDP)—denounced them as insincere, believing that the DPS was stealing their clothes. However, it seems more probable that the government was responding both to the impact of UN imposed sanctions against the FRY (mainly in April 1992), which hit the smaller, tourist and maritime trade-dependent Montenegrin economy harder than it did the Serbian, and to the pressures imposed by an influx of Bosnian refugees.[38]

In the event Bulatović and Kostić both ran as presidential candidates for the DPS in the December elections, attracting in the first round 43.83 per cent and 23.74 per cent respectively. The liberal leader Perović garnered 18.33 per cent of the vote and Kilibarda of the People's Party 9.03 per cent. In the second round the Liberals and the small Social Democratic Party felt impelled to support Bulatović against the more vehemently nationalist Kostić, helping the former to win 63.29 per cent of the vote.

In the parliamentary elections the DPS maintained its grip on power, winning an overall majority of seats (forty-six of the eighty-five), if not of the popular vote, in the Montenegrin Parliament. It was nonetheless a significant achievement; in no other post-Communist country and not even in Serbia had the successor to the Communist Party managed to hold its grip on power so strongly.[39] As an indicator of the strain in relations between the DPS and the SPS, however, the DPS opened the government to a coalition with the Liberals, the People's Party and the Social Democrats. This was necessary for the DPS given the fissures in the country caused by the unpopular consequences of the Bosnian war.

The coalition allies soon fell out, however, as the Liberals and Social Democrats perceived that the DPS had no real intention of liberal reform or power-sharing. This period was nevertheless one of relative calm in relations between Serbia and Montenegro as the

---

[38] *Ibid.*, pp. 22–4.

[39] V. Goati, *Izbori u SRJ od 1990 do 1998: volja gradjana ili izborna manipulacija*, Belgrade: CESID, 1999, p. 179, quoted by Bieber, *ibid.*

two sister parties were both committed—largely as a result of the impact of sanctions—to bringing the war to an end and willing to co-operate with the international community. Djukanović and his allies occasionally took swipes at Serbia's autocratic rule and over-weening position in the FRY, but criticism was usually within acceptable bounds.

As prime minister Milo Djukanović was largely left in charge of running the economy and in mitigating the worst effects of sanctions. Inevitably, given the lack of alternatives, Montenegro, like Serbia, was soon prey to a number of sanctions-busting operations—everything from ill-fated pyramid schemes to large-scale cigarette smuggling—which in turn resulted in the emergence of a new class of shady profiteers with close links to the ruling party and, it was often claimed, to Djukanović himself.[40] Some commentators detect the first cracks in the Bulatović-Djukanović leadership as having appeared in this period when Djukanović began to argue in favour of Montenegro as an offshore investment tax haven with an economic system separate from Serbia's.[41] Bulatović meanwhile continued to be the only real liaison with Milošević on institutional affairs and constitutional matters. This division of labour was comfortable for a short period, and to the extent that anything could be said to be working effectively in Yugoslavia, Montenegro had succeeded in establishing a particular position for itself and retaining a certain freedom of movement, which was absent in Serbia. For instance, while Serbia abolished its own foreign ministry and subsumed it into the Federal Foreign Ministry after the break-up, Montenegro insisted on retaining its own separate republican foreign ministry, a relic of Tito's 1974 constitution.

The Montenegrin Foreign Minister in these early years (1992–5) was Miodrag Lekić, a non-party figure, former director of the cultural centre of Bar and SFRJ ambassador to Mozambique, whose views were far closer to Western chanceries than those of almost any other political figure in the FRY.[42] This led to his becoming

[40] See Bieber, *ibid.*, p. 25 and Nicholas Forster and Sead Husić, 'Probe into Montenegro's role in illegal cigarette trade', FT.com site accessed 9 August 2001.
[41] Branko Vojičić, 'The Worm that Turned', *Transitions*, July 1998, p. 58.
[42] In particular he advocated closer ties between Montenegro and Italy, a defusing of the tension along the border with Croatia, and the stationing of international

something of a favourite of Western diplomats and indeed a relatively popular figure in Western foreign ministries. Unfortunately the West failed to understand that Lekić needed to be supported by a liberal dose of carrots, rather than continuing to labour under sanctions applied to Montenegro and Serbia indifferently. If Montenegro's pro-Western orientation was to be deepened and maintained, the Republic had somehow to be differentiated and rewarded. This proved too difficult a concept for the West, and Lekić was therefore left dangling, encouraged only by regular pats on the back from Western embassies in Belgrade and the odd lunch and meeting with foreign ministers when overseas.

At the same time Milošević became increasingly irritated by Lekić's boldness and critical edge and insisted that Bulatović should remove him. In the event he was moved sideways, being appointed Yugoslav chargé d'affaires, later ambassador, to Italy at the beginning of 1995 but kept very much in a golden cage and isolated from any sensitive information. Instead it was the Yugoslav ambassador to the Holy See, Dojčilo Maslovarić, a personal friend of the Milošević family, who became the conduit for Milošević's serious interaction not just with the Vatican but also with the Italian state.

Lekić's successor as foreign minister, Janko Jeknić, a rally driver who enjoyed women and song, took a low profile politically and concentrated on encouraging cultural and academic links with the outside world. Bulatović meanwhile continued to handle delicate matters such as the territorial dispute with Croatia over Prevlaka and was in contact with Milošević as the latter, under pressure from international negotiators, began actively to play the role of peacemaker. It was, as one observer at the time put it, as though having been the pyromaniac, he volunteered to be the fireman.[43] When the Bosnian Serbs continued to oppose peace plans that Milošević accepted, Bulatović invariably supported Milošević. Bulatović accompanied Milošević to the vote at the Bosnian Serbs' Assembly in Pale in May 1993 to urge acceptance of the Vance-Owen peace plan for

---

monitors on the border with Bosnia-Hercegovina to enforce sanctions against Bosnian Serbs. See Stan Markotich, 'The Challenge of Balkan Peace: Tensions rise over Montenegro's Independence Moves', *Transition*, 26 July 1996, p. 59.

[43] Slavoljub Djukić, *On, Onai Mi*, Radio B92, Belgrade, 1997.

ending the war in Bosnia. Angered by the recalcitrance of his erstwhile protégés, Milošević increasingly but unavailingly tried to discipline them. When the Assembly, despite appeals from him and from Bulatović and the Yugoslav President Čosić, rejected the peace plan, this marked a watershed in the relations of Milošević and thus Bulatović with the Bosnian Serb leadership.

While Milošević continued to press the Bosnian Serbs to fall into line, Bulatović strongly supported him, most notably when in the summer of 1994 Milošević accepted the Owen/Stoltenberg—the latter Vance's successor as UN envoy—plan to place an embargo on the Bosnian Serbs to bring them to accept the international nego-tiators' map for the territorial division of Bosnia-Hercegovina while keeping it as one state. Montenegro had a key role to play, since it was required to police the embargo along the Bosnia/Montenegro border under international supervision. Although the borders re-mained porous,[44] the international community was satisfied that enough was being done and authorised the suspension of some minor sanctions on Serbia and Montenegro.

After a blockade lasting nearly a year on the River Drina between Serbia and Bosnia failed to resolve the stalemate with Bosnian Serb leadership, Milošević lost patience. As the summer of 1995 saw a succession of dramas and tragedies, including the Srebrenica massa-cre, the expulsion of the Krajina Serbs from Croatia and the capture of hundreds of UN peacekeepers as hostages by the Bosnian Serbs, Milošević summoned the Bosnian Serb leadership to Belgrade to be faced down by the full panoply of Serb/Montenegrin[45]/Yugoslav institutional life at state and church level: federal and republican Presidents, the chief of staff of the Yugoslav army and the Serbian patriarch.

The Dayton Accords and Djukanović's change of direction

The 'Patriarch gathering'—it was given this name although Patri-arch Pavle's role at the meeting was symbolic rather than active—

[44] Sell, *ibid.*, pp. 218–19.
[45] Montenegrin here implies Bulatović, rather than Djukanović, who was largely occupied with running the Montenegrin economy.

agreed to a joint negotiating team to engage with international negotiators and crucially to give the deciding voice in any dispute within the team to Milošević. Once the Bosnian Serbs, weakened by the subsequent NATO bombing and by a resurgent Croatian army trained by ex-US Army generals, had given up many of their 1992 gains thus facilitating the negotiation of the final map at the US-organised conference that autumn at Dayton, Ohio, Bulatović accompanied Milošević to Dayton along with the Bosnian Serbs Momčilo Krajišnik and Nikola Koljević. But Milošević took all key decisions personally in negotiation with the US team led by Richard Holbrooke. Bulatović was a loyal and unquestioning ally on whose vote Milošević could on this occasion absolutely depend, and whom he often 'brought to meetings to demonstrate that the Federal Republic of Yugoslavia consisted of more than just Serbia'.[46]

With the signing of the Dayton peace accords in November 1995 and the lifting of sanctions, Djukanović, aware of popular discontent with living standards, was ready to seize the opportunity to draw closer to Western countries while slackening the federal ties with Serbia.[47] He set out on an active mission in 1996 to bring foreign investment and trade to Montenegro, proposing again the creation of a tax haven. Critics suggested that this was simply a way of providing a front for the smuggling that had persisted throughout the sanctions period, particularly via Albania. One of the most profitable of these smuggling schemes involved importing petrol and other oil derivatives into Montenegro across Lake Skadar from Albania. Around 1,000 small motor launches were specially adapted for this purpose and the shores of the lake were dotted with small jetties.[48] There was even said to be an oil pipeline running under the lake itself. The Albanian government benefited through the receipts of a special tax while Montenegrin authorities took a large share of the profits.[49]

While sanctions lasted, the population, who depended upon revenues arising from smuggling for the payment of pensions and other benefits, had considered the government's involvement in

---

[46] Richard Holbrooke, *To End A War*, New York: Random House, 1998, p. 243.
[47] See Bieber, 'Montenegrin politics since the disintegration', pp. 27–8.
[48] See Draško Djuranović, 'Surviving the Sanctions', *Transitions*, July 1998, p. 60.
[49] *Ibid.*

sanctions-busting schemes as a necessary stratagem. Equally important, they were ready to accept the government's explanation for deteriorating living standards as being the direct result of the international blockade. Post-Dayton, however, the situation began to change. The removal of sanctions raised strong expectations of an improvement in living standards as shops in Podgorica and on the coast began to fill with designer goods. But with the United States still insisting on the operation of a so-called 'outer wall' of sanctions, tourists could not be attracted back in large numbers to Montenegro's dilapidated resorts since the inward investment needed to regenerate tourism (and to develop other industries) simply failed to appear. Almost the only tourists visiting Montenegro at this time were either from Serbia, where the economy was similarly affected, or groups from Israel or Russia, neither of which was large enough to make a significant impact on the economy. As Milošević began falling out of favour again with the West over Kosovo, Djukanović could see clear advantages in emphasising the difference between Montenegro and Serbia.

Against this background the ruling party of Bulatović and Djukanović managed to score a further success in federal and republican elections in Montenegro in October 1996, partly as a result of the government's ability to change the electoral rules in its own favour and partly through its ability to control the local media.[50] Montenegro's opposition parties complained with justification of the biased media coverage of the election campaign, but there was no serious attempt to suggest vote fraud on election day. By contrast, the opposition's victories in Serbia in municipal elections held at the same time in several major towns, including Belgrade, were annulled, unleashing a winter of discontent in the shape of three months of demonstrations.

Bulatović stood by Milošević at this critical time. As he later explained in his autobiography, 'Of course there are many things about which we had a difference of opinion and action. But not even with my brother do I agree on everything—yet it never occurs to me to deny that we are linked by destiny.'[51] Djukanović by contrast recognised in this moment an opportunity to re-cast himself as a

[50] Bieber, 'Montenegrin politics since the disintegration', pp. 28–9.
[51] Momir Bulatović, *Pravila Ćutanja*, Narodna Knjiga Alfa, 2004, p. 249.

political liberal and ally of the West, choosing to publicise his decision by sending a telegram of support to demonstrating students in Belgrade.

But Djukanović's dissatisfaction with Milošević's authoritarianism was not based merely, or even principally, on sympathy for the students. Rather it stemmed from the shrewd realisation that Montenegro needed to distance itself from Milošević's increasingly repressive policies if it was to gain access to the international financial resources needed to resuscitate its struggling economy. Prevented by Milošević from taking any political or economic initiatives to diversify external support for Montenegro,[52] Djukanović had become ever more frustrated as Milošević's new-found status as the Dayton peacemaker had hitherto robbed him of sufficient room for manoeuvre. But with Milošević's international respectability draining away, Djukanović was emboldened to voice increasingly sharp criticism of his behaviour and encourage other members of his entourage to do the same. Bulatović appeared unwilling or unable to hold him in check. As Milošević was increasingly angered by the criticism, relations between the two Republics became very cool. When the Montenegrin foreign minister, Janko Jeknić, died in a car accident in the mountains of Montenegro in the middle of one night, seriously injuring his companion, the funeral in January 1997 brought together all the leadership of Montenegro united by the shock of Jeknić's dramatic death. On Milošević's orders, Serbia sent no representation to the funeral, an insult that was compounded by the presence of a number of Western diplomats—the British, German, Italian and Canadian ambassadors and the British cultural attaché—who flew down from Belgrade especially for the event.

The rebuff was particularly hard to stomach since the two groups of leaders—Serbian and Montenegrin—were inextricably linked, belonging as they did to the successor parties to the old League of Communists in their own Republics. But in a gesture typical of Milošević, the Montenegrin leadership as a whole were being

---

[52] For instance, when Milo Djukanović and the then Montenegrin finance minister Predrag Goranović paid a working visit to the United States in April 1996 with a view to normalising relations, the FRY embassy in Washington, probably on Milošević's instructions, explicitly dissociated itself from the visit. Markotich, 'The Challenge of Balkan Peace', p. 58.

humiliated and punished for Djukanović's criticism of his autocratic behaviour. One of Djukanović's ministers, Goran Rakočević, whom Milošević subsequently forced Bulatović to demote to head of Montenegrin television and radio, told the British ambassador at the funeral that the insult to Montenegro was 'unforgivable'.[53] Djukanović decided to respond in kind. The next month in a magazine interview, Djukanović burnt his bridges with Milošević when he was quoted as saying: 'It would be completely wrong for Slobodan Milošević to remain in any place in the political life of Yugoslavia....Milošević is a man of obsolete political ideas, lacking the ability to form a strategic vision... surrounded by unsuitable individuals who are following the time-tested method of many authoritarian regimes.'[54] Djukanović's thinly veiled reference to Milošević's wife as 'unsuitable' was a particularly palpable hit.

The tensions between the two Republics now became mirrored by tensions within the leadership. Djukanović clearly felt that he had outgrown his junior partner status and wanted to take Montenegro in a different direction politically and economically. If Bulatović was not prepared to accommodate the change of tack he would have to be replaced as the helmsman. On the economic front Djukanović proposed the re-introduction of the *perper*, the old Montenegrin currency. But on the political front it was Bulatović who, on Milošević's instructions,[55] took the initiative. On 24 March Djukanović was forced to resign as deputy chairman of the DPS in a vote of the party executive by 65 votes to 7 with 20 abstentions.[56] Bulatović thus appeared to have the upper hand and sought to exploit it by

---

[53] Conversation with the author. Montenegrins take funerals particularly seriously, and often attend those of people they barely know as a gesture of respect.

[54] *Vreme*, 22 February 1997.

[55] Milošević had particular cause to seek the overthrow of Djukanović. Constitutionally debarred from standing for a third term as President of Serbia, he was endeavouring to preserve his hold on power by seeking to be directly elected as President of Yugoslavia (the FRY). Milošević knew that such a step, which would require a change in the constitution, needed the approval of the ruling elite in Montenegro and feared that Djukanović would not comply. In the event the DPS rejected the proposed change to the constitution, one which, given Montenegro's small population, would have been much to the Republic's detriment, but accepted Milošević's shift to the federal Presidency, an office which was thereupon endowed with 'executive' powers. See Robert Thomas, *Serbia under Milošević: Politics in the 1990s*, London: Hurst, 1999, pp. 336–9.

[56] *Ibid.*

demanding that Djukanović dismiss several members of his government including the deputy prime minister Slavko Drljević, a forceful advocate for a separate Montenegrin currency, and Vukašin Maras, head of state security, who was not only responsible for curbing the operation of Milošević's secret police in Montenegro but was also closely connected with 'transit' (in other words cigarette smuggling to Italy) and thus with the funds needed to keep Montenegro's economy afloat while the FRY was under sanctions.[57] Djukanović refused to comply. Although Bulatović was backed by pro-Milošević forces in Belgrade and by the tame Belgrade media, Djukanović received strong local support including that of the influential Speaker of the Montenegrin Parliament, Svetozar Marović.[58] Fighting for his political life, he was able to play both on the political conflict in Serbia, which was further blackening Milošević's name internationally, and on the pessimism many Montenegrins increasingly felt at the possibility of living standards ever returning to pre-Milošević levels, to seize control of the party.

In July 1997 Djukanović, having first gained support in Cetinje and his birthplace Nikšić, went on to secure the nomination of the DPS's main board as its candidate in the autumn's presidential elections. As the elections approached, the political gloves came off in Montenegro. Bulatović's campaign was the more traditional, based on familiar socialist principles, stressing Montenegro's links with Serbia and geared towards the lower-level DPS *nomenklatura*[59] and the majority Orthodox population. Naturally he had the support of Belgrade. Djukanović took an opposing line, rejecting Bulatović's pro-Serbian brand of nationalism and seeking to portray himself as a reformist and a 'moderniser',[60] whose outward-looking policies and Western contacts would help make Montenegrins part of mainstream Europe.

The election was very tightly contested. Bulatović had been slightly ahead in the first round, with Djukanović only winning in

---

[57] Two other resignations were also demanded—that of Goran Rakočević, still at the time Minister of Culture, and that of the head of the trade mission of Montenegro in Washington.

[58] Marović went on to become the only President of the Union of Serbia and Montenegro.

[59] Robert Thomas, *Serbia under Milošević*, p. 379.

[60] *Ibid.*

the second round with 50.8 per cent of the vote, largely due to the support of the non-Orthodox minorities, principally the Muslims/Bosniaks and Albanians who, for entirely understandable reasons, were opposed to backing Bulatović's pro-Serbian stance. Inter-ethnic relations in Montenegro, already considerably better than in most other republics, improved further after the 1997 elections when Djukanović's wooing of the minorities began to bear fruit. Meanwhile the narrowness of Djukanović's win led Bulatović first to claim electoral fraud—a charge rejected by international observers[61]—and then, clearly under Milošević's instructions, to organise demonstrations to prevent Djukanović from taking office. Unlike the Belgrade rallies, the protests threatened to turn violent, with some of Bulatović's supporters firing shots and carrying banners attacking 'Milo the Turk', a clear reference to Djukanović's pro-Muslim and Albanian policies.[62] Meanwhile pressure on the new government was increased by an ongoing, though undeclared, block-ade of Montenegro by Serbian customs officers and by a virulent anti-Djukanović campaign in the Milošević-controlled Belgrade media. The situation was for a while extremely tense as the possi-bility of a major violent confrontation led by Bulatović supporters and backed by Belgrade seemed to threaten Montenegro's stability.[63] But Bulatović had overestimated the extent of his support. In January 1998 a rally he had organised in Cetinje aimed at disrupting Djuka-nović's formal inauguration as President brought no more than 8,000 demonstrators on to the streets[64] and the Yugoslav army de-clined their support. Djukanović was sworn in at a ceremony atten-ded by fifty-seven ambassadors.[65]

In view of the bitter circumstances which had led to the split between the former close allies becoming formalised and irre-versible, it was no surprise when in March 1998, two months after Djukanović had taken office, Bulatović formed his own party, the

[61] See the OSCE/ODHIR: *Republic of Montenegro. Presidential Election 5 and 18 October, 1997, Final Report*, 1997, p. 5. Quoted by Bieber, 'Montenegrin politics since the disintegration', p. 31.

[62] Thomas, *Serbia under Milošević*, p. 382.

[63] *Ibid.*, p. 381.

[64] Šeki Radončić, 'Povratak na mjesto zločina', *Monitor*, 16 January 1998, cited by Thomas, *ibid.*, p. 385.

[65] *Ibid.*, p. 386.

Socialist People's Party (SNP), to contest republican elections scheduled for May. Djukanović's 'For a Better Life' coalition, as it was opportunistically named, included the Social Democrats (SDP) and the formerly nationalist People's Party (NS).[66] The Liberals, a party traditionally supporting Montenegrin independence but strongly critical of the DPS, declined to join the Djukanović coalition and lost out as a result. Similarly, minority parties ran but fared poorly as most Muslims and Albanians supported Djukanović's DPS to prevent Bulatović returning to a position of power. The former's coalition with a fraction less than half the votes (49.5 per cent) won forty-two of the seventy-eight seats while Bulatović could muster only twenty-nine. Bulatović's consolation came later that same month when Milošević, in flagrant violation of the spirit and letter of the federal constitution, named him Yugoslav prime minister. It was a move calculated to deepen divisions between Serbia and Montenegro.

NATO goes to war for Kosovo

And indeed with Djukanović now free to take Montenegro in a radically different direction, the policies of the two Republics increasingly diverged amid acrimonious exchanges. But while the war of words remained just that, relations between Serbia and Montenegro plumbed new depths in the spring of 1999 when Montenegro refused to side with Serbia during the NATO war over Kosovo. Djukanović went so far as to impose his veto in the Supreme Defence Council, a step that was in principle constitutionally binding, but which Milošević simply ignored. To compound the offence, Djukanović offered refuge to the opposition leader and future Serbian prime minister, Zoran Djindjić, who felt himself at risk in Serbia. Djukanović and Djindjić were personal friends and possibly business associates. Had Djindjić's assassination in 2003 not put an end to his political life, the two men might even, following Milošević's fall from power, have found a way to defuse the problem of Serbo-Montenegrin relations between them. At the time Djukanović's

---

[66] Novak Kilibarda explained his party's change of position by his own realisation of the errors committed by nationalists in both Serbia and Montenegro in the early Milošević period. (Interview with *Monitor*, 23 June 2000.)

anti-war stance carried with it real dangers to Montenegrin security, especially when NATO could not avoid striking Yugoslav armed forces' (VJ) sites in Montenegro itself and when 'collateral damage' included the killing of four children playing on a bridge over the river Lim near Murino in the north of Montenegro. Fortunately NATO, conscious of the delicacy of Montenegro's position, was successful in keeping Montenegrin casualties in single figures in contrast to the relatively large numbers killed in Serbia and Kosovo.

In spite of such restraint, tension in Montenegro continued to rise. The pressure was exacerbated by the presence in Montenegro of two armed forces: on the one hand, some 14,000 troops from the federal army under Belgrade's control, as well as the Seventh Military Police Battalion consisting of about 1,000 paramilitary personnel, and on the other hand the Montenegrin police who answered to Djukanović. The latter, numbering some 20,000 and well-armed with light infantry weapons through various dubious channels, reflected real fears that Montenegro could be Milošević's next target for destabilisation.

As if these strains were not enough, Montenegro had also to contend with the 80,000 Albanian refugees who had fled there to escape the Kosovo war. Representing more than 10 per cent of the population, they placed a huge economic burden on the tiny Republic. Most of the refugees returned to their homes in Kosovo but in a moment worthy of the (part-Montenegrin) film director Emir Kusturica, an Albanian group found itself crossing with groups of Serb refugees going in the other direction, fleeing from Kosovo and, as it were, taking their refugee places in Montenegro. Again it looked as though civil war could break out between those who felt that Montenegro was letting Serbia and Serbdom down and those of the Djukanović persuasion who were determined that Milošević should not drag Montenegro into another reckless, losing adventure. Ordinary people began mobilising on both sides mirroring the old divisions of Whites and Greens, often cutting through families. At this dramatic moment, the parties in Parliament concluded that civil war in Montenegro was to be avoided at all costs. While the verbal skirmishing continued, both sides instructed their supporters to draw back from the brink in a rare and perhaps unique instance of consensus on the national question. There were nonetheless real concerns that Milošević, as Yugoslav President and thus commander-in-chief, might seek to take control of the Montenegrin police, a step that would certainly have triggered conflict. But Belgrade's anticipated crackdown failed to materialise; Milošević made no move.[67] It had been a close-run thing, while from the West's viewpoint Montenegro had played a heroic role allowing Djukanović to relish his good standing with the international community. In contrast Serbia, with a weakened but by no means repentant Milošević still at the helm, was now an international pariah.

Djukanović was determined to turn the groundswell of international support to his government's advantage. A new 'platform' put forward in August 1999 to redefine the relationship with Serbia was ostensibly concerned with restoring the equality required under the 1992 constitution, but accompanying references to Montenegro's sovereignty and its people's right to self-determination allowed observers to glimpse an altered agenda, leading towards Montenegrin independence.

For the international community, preoccupied with the aftermath of the Kosovo conflict, this was a step too far. But Djukanović's ongoing opposition to Milošević and, in particular, his willingness to provide support for Serbia's opposition leaders ensured that he continued to receive strong international backing, both politically and in aid. One indication of the importance of the Montenegrin government's stance at this time is the fact that after Israel the country received more US aid *per capita* over the period 1999–2000 than any other, amounting to $55 million in 1999 and double that amount in 2000, in declared assistance.[68]

Meanwhile Milošević was hoping to capitalise in his own way on Serbian anger at NATO's bombing campaign by making the office of FRY President, which he had held since July 1999 after a sideways move from the Serbian Presidency, directly elected. Djukanović, over-confident perhaps following his new-found international popularity, was taken by surprise when in late June 2000 Milošević arbitrarily introduced the necessary changes to the FRY constitution to

[67] Srdjan Darmanović, 'Montenegro survives the War', *East European Constitutional Review*, vol. 8, no. 3, pp. 66–7.
[68] Dragan Djurić, 'The Economic Development of Montenegro' in Bieber (ed.), *Montenegro in Transition*, p. 155.

effect the direct election of both the Yugoslav President and the federal Parliament. Given Montenegro's tiny population, direct elections made its vote an irrelevance and were in contravention of Article 2 of the constitution, which guaranteed it an equal voice in the federation. On 8 July the Montenegrin Parliament passed a resolution rejecting the federal Parliament's amendments, a step facilitated by the opposition parties' decision not to oppose.[69]

When federal elections were scheduled for September 2000 Djukanović resisted intense international pressure to take part, arguing that the federation was now a sham and that participation would violate the Montenegrin Parliament's rejection of Milošević's constitutional amendments. Though understandable, Djukanović's decision was a miscalculation because, contrary to his expectations, the elections resulted in Milošević's defeat while leaving the Djukanović government unable to claim a role in his downfall on 5 October. It was from this time on that the international support Djukanović had previously enjoyed almost without qualification began to dwindle. The West now had a new best friend in the Balkans in the shape of the successful challenger to Milošević, Vojislav Koštunica, and thus Djukanović found himself relegated from his favoured position. Moreover, he was now expected to begin working with the newly-elected democratic government in Belgrade, especially after the Serbian republican elections three months later brought a democratic regime to power at the republican level to join the Koštunica regime at the federal level.[70] But for Djukanović and his allies too much had changed for them simply to agree to return to the old federation which they rightly claimed had never worked effectively since its inception following the earlier referendum in 1992.

---

[69] When federal elections were called in September 2000 the leader of the opposition SNP, Predrag Bulatović (a distant relation of Momir), issued a brave appeal to the Yugoslav army (VJ) to reject involvement in politics and remain in their barracks on election day. Fortunately the VJ agreed and the risk of conflict was averted.

[70] The message was stated explicitly by the US President's adviser on the Balkans, James O'Brian, who in the course of a visit to Podgorica on 14 October 2000 told Djukanović that following the fall of Milošević the United States did not support Montenegrin independence and urged the Montenegrin President to reach an agreement on the continuation of the federation through talks with the new leadership in Belgrade.

Moreover, from his assumption of the Presidency in 1998 Djukanović had *de facto* begun to pursue what has been described as a
policy of creeping independence. It was a policy that had been at
least tacitly accepted, if not encouraged, by the West at a time when
it had been particularly recognisant of Djukanović's forthright
opposition to Milošević.[71] In December 2000, believing that he was
still able to draw on the political capital he had accumulated with
Western countries, Djukanović reformulated his political 'platform'
of the previous year by calling for a union of independent states
guaranteeing both Serbia and Montenegro international recognition while preserving a number of common functions.[72] Far from
generating debate, the 'platform' met with a frosty response both
in Serbia, where it was seen as designed to benefit Montenegro at
Serbia's expense, and more generally when EU governments balked
at its proposal for separate seats for Serbia and Montenegro at the
United Nations. Yet the 'platform' had much to recommend it
when viewed against the less palatable alternatives available—an
unbalanced and unworkable federation or complete divorce.[73] By
2000 Montenegro was effectively a separate economic space from
Serbia. Montenegro had adopted the Deutschmark in 1999, which
the Montenegrin government saw as the right currency for the sort
of economic future—tourism, services etc.—that it sought to pursue. In 2002 it switched fairly painlessly to the Euro, a move adduced
by Djukanović's government as evidence of the success of its re-

[71] Western officials were careful never to give their formal blessing to Montenegro's independence project, instead promoting the concept of a genuinely democratic federation in a post-Milošević Yugoslavia. At the same time they
encouraged Djukanović in his opposition to Milošević, accepting and even
assisting his government's steps to distance Montenegro from Serbia in the
knowledge that this served their own interests.

[72] Shared functions included the areas of defence and foreign policy and the establishment of a common market. See 'Platform of the Government of Montenegro for Talks with the Government of Serbia on New Relations between
Two States', in *Europa South-East Monitor*, no. 19, January, 2001, published by the
Centre for European Policy Studies.

[73] Indeed the author took this view at the time, arguing in a paper delivered at
Chatham House that year that the proposal, which offered a possible way to
resolve the identity conundrum in Montenegro, was worth serious consideration. See also Peter Palmer, 'The EU and Montenegro: A Testing Ground for
the Common Foreign and Security Policy', *Reper* (Podgorica: CEDEM), no. 4,
October 2003, p. 23, for a relatively positive evaluation of this 'platform'.

formist and pro-European policies and apparently supported by a large majority of the population.[74] For similar reasons, and on the advice of EU and US missions despatched to offer advice on the economy, the Montenegrin government was reluctant to return to charging the higher customs rates which operated in Serbia. And, having set up its own national bank, it declared itself unwilling to return currency supply to Serbian control. It had tasted some of the fruits of *de facto* independence and enjoyed the experience. Djukanović had been fêted as an international statesman, being received by presidents and prime ministers, and had generally enjoyed red-carpet treatment. He calculated wrongly on the West's constancy in support and at first failed to appreciate the sensitivities aroused by the first rumours, particularly persistent in Italy, of his part in dubious financial and economic affairs.[75] And the more loudly Djukanović spoke about independence, the more unpopular he became with the EU, which responded by referring in Council of Ministers' statements to 'a democratic Montenegro in a democratic Yugoslavia'.[76]

With a chill setting in on the international front, Djukanović called early parliamentary elections in April 2001 in which he expected to win a strong endorsement for his by now openly pro-independence stance. In the event he experienced something of a reverse at the hands of an electorate disappointed by the failure of his 'For A Better Life' coalition to deliver a better deal to those outside his immediate circle. But despite the fall in his support, Djukanović was able to form a minority government, with additional parliamentary support from the Liberal Alliance of Montenegro whose overriding political goal remained the country's independence.

The EU becomes involved: the Belgrade Agreement

Meanwhile the international community, and in particular the European Union, had continued to harden its stance against such

---

[74] An opinion poll conducted in January 2002 showed that 80 per cent of those polled were reluctant to return to the dinar.

[75] The rumours persisted. As a result, when Djukanović travelled to Britain in 2002 the British Foreign Secretary, Jack Straw, declined to see him, pleading unconvincingly insufficient time because of an impending visit to India.

[76] EU Council of Ministers' conclusions 15 May 2001.

independence, a position it privately defended on grounds of *Realpolitik* since it could hardly challenge the Montenegrins' right to determine their own future on legal grounds. According to the 1991 Badinter Commission, set up to advise the then EC Conference on Yugoslavia, Montenegro, as a former full Republic of Tito's SFRJ, had the same entitlement to full independence and international recognition as those other former Republics—Slovenia, Croatia, Bosnia-Hercegovina and Macedonia—which attained their independence in 1991 and 1992. But the international community, basing its opposition on the roughly equal split within Montenegro over the issue of independence, made abundantly clear its reluctance to countenance any recognition of the result of a referendum to put the issue to the test.

In the eyes of Western governments, legal considerations in Montenegro's case were outweighed by geopolitical ones. According to this interpretation, independence for Montenegro, even if it were shown to be the wish of a majority of the population, could give the go-ahead to would-be independence seekers, first and most important in Kosovo but also in other potentially unstable areas—Macedonia and Bosnia-Hercegovina—within the broader region.[77] And since UN Security Council resolution 1244 establishing Kosovo's interim status in the wake of the 1999 war was specifically linked to the existence of the FRY, there was additional concern that Montenegrin independence and the break-up of the federation would leave Kosovo in limbo.[78]

Although fear of the domino effect was the main reason for the EU and, to a lesser extent, the US administration to oppose any move towards Montenegrin independence, it was by no means their only cause for concern. A second important reason for the EU offi-

---

[77] That concern about triggering moves for the independence of Kosovo was the principal reason for the EU's opposition to Montenegrin independence is beyond doubt. See for example the Report of the International Commission on the Balkans chaired by Giuliano Amato, *The Balkans in Europe's Future*, Sofia: Secretariat of the Centre for Liberal Strategies, 2005, p. 25.

[78] In fact this legal objection was subsequently addressed by the EU in the Belgrade Agreement of March 2002 in a clause which stated that Serbia would become the successor state to the FRY in the event of Montenegro's withdrawal from the state union. See Peter Palmer, 'The EU and Montenegro', p. 16.

cially to oppose the independence plans of the Montenegrin government was reluctance to countenance the growth of mini-states in
the region, which they saw as creating institutional problems for the
equilibrium of the EU.[79] From the European point of view, the
imbalance between small and large states within the Union is already
a delicate issue: a proliferation of small states among further would-
be applicants would only make steps towards achieving majority
voting on a wider range of issues more difficult.

Other antagonistic arguments concentrated on the deep divisions
within Montenegro over the issue of independence. Such divisions,
it was argued, could lead to internal destabilisation either by pro-
Yugoslav Montenegrins or by ethnic Albanians who might use
independence as an occasion to seek to secede from Montenegro
and join Albania. Finally, some international opposition to Montenegrin independence focused on the alleged lack of economic viability of prospective mini-states in the Balkans, arguing that these
would simply become centres for mafia-type crime and instability.
Italy, in particular, sought to highlight links between local mafia and
the Montenegrin government.[80] (The then Italian President Ciampi
in a visit to the region in January 2002 declined to meet Djukanović
and called for the maintenance of the union of Serbia and Montenegro.[81] Italian magistrates then issued preliminary indictments
against Djukanović in May 2002, alleging involvement in cigarette
smuggling and followed up with a request for his arrest in 2003, so
far not executed not least due to lack of jurisdiction.)

These, then, were the principal considerations weighing on Javier
Solana, the EU's High Representative, when, in November 2001, he
sought to 'deflect Montenegro's leaders from their independence

---

[79] The now stalled 'Giscard' European Constitution takes this EU view a step further by giving much less power to small states.

[80] A series of articles which appeared in the Croatian weekly, *Nacional*, in the
course of 2001, also made damaging allegations about the Montenegrin government's links to local and foreign mafias. At the time there were unsubstantiated
allegations that *Nacional* had received help from foreign intelligence agencies.
Whether or not this was so, the allegations damaged Djukanović personally.

[81] *I Discorsi del Presidente della Repubblica Italiana, Carlo Azeglio Ciampi*, published by
Ufficio per la Stampa e l'Informazione, Segretariato Generale della Repubblica,
Rome, 17 January 2002, pp. 1–2.

plans and to persuade them to renew their union with Serbia'.[82] Solana enjoyed strong support from the United States, and in particular from its veteran ambassador in Belgrade, in pressing Djukanović to retreat on independence. The US attitude carried weight with Djukanović precisely because he had hitherto considered the United States to be Montenegro's 'best friend' and believed that ultimately Washington would accept and even support Montenegrin independence.

Djukanović had little room for manoeuvre. Having consistently portrayed himself as pro-Western, he could hardly ignore the stated wishes of the EU and the broader international community, particularly when Montenegro's economic solvency depended heavily on the continuing inflow of Western (principally US) aid, and especially when he faced presidential elections later in the year. Seeking the best way out, Djukanović reluctantly accepted Solana's invitation to engage in fresh negotiations while insisting that he would not renounce Montenegro's economic reforms, which he claimed to be the real gains of his presidency.

At the Belgrade end Koštunica, the federal President, was under pressure either to act or to risk looking ineffectual, something he feared would weaken his position *vis-à-vis* his political rival, the Serbian prime minister Zoran Djindjić. But Djindjić himself was also aware of the need to remove the political uncertainty, which was proving a frustration to economic and political reform. Failure to resolve the Montenegrin issue was additionally delaying the restructuring of the over-large Yugoslav Army, which needed to be done if the state were to become a member of NATO's associate programme for aspirant members, Partnership for Peace (PfP). Such was the level of frustration that both the reformist wing of the Serbian ruling coalition, DOS, and a group of influential economists (G-17) were beginning publicly to float the notion that Serbia might be better off without Montenegro.

After some heavy diplomatic pressure Solana, in what was very much a personal initiative and without prior approval by the Council of Ministers, brought these Serbian-Montenegrin negotiations to a conclusion the following spring on 14 March 2002. The resulting

---

[82] Peter Palmer, 'The EU and Montenegro', p. 1.

Belgrade Agreement foresaw the creation of a new union on what might best be described as confederal lines. Not surprisingly the signatories to the agreement were all keen to present the prospective union in a different light according to their own preferred interpretations. For Solana the objective was to ensure that the union of Serbia and Montenegro—though in principle consisting of two separate entities—would remain, in a constitutional and legal sense, a single unit and thus, in international terms at least, little different from the old FRY. The EU therefore dismissed the Montenegrin side's demand for a separate UN seat, but in return conceded the demand for a referendum after three years of the Belgrade Agreement. By contrast Djukanović, in his presentation on the Belgrade Agreement, sought to emphasise the confederal element, stressing its preservation of Montenegro's separate economic system and its guarantee of Montenegro's right to revisit the question of a referendum three years on. After their initial shock, Djukanović's coalition partners the SDP—or most of them—came round to this view; in truth, they had little alternative. Conversely, the Montenegrin opposition parties making up the 'For Yugoslavia' coalition stressed the Agreement's federal elements, which they claimed as a victory for their own objectives under the new arrangement. Meanwhile the Liberals, arguing that the Agreement undermined the Montenegrin Constitution, sought unsuccessfully to challenge the Montenegrin leadership's right to sign it on these grounds. In Serbia the governor of the National Bank, Mljadan Dinkić, spoke of the Belgrade Agreement sarcastically as 'an original solution... unlikely to provide the basis for a lasting settlement'. In a similarly negative vein the then Serbian Finance Minister Božidar Djelić, while carefully describing the accord as 'a good solution in the political circumstances', went on to describe the state being proposed as an 'economic Frankenstein'.[83]

Exit the FRY; enter Serbia and Montenegro

The Agreement, besides being open to many interpretations, was sufficiently shorn of detail to leave the practical implementation still to be negotiated. Indeed it took a further year to adopt the Constitutional Charter of the new state, which was formally proclaimed on

[83] *Glas Javnosti*, 24 February 2002.

The Union of Serbia and Montenegro, February 2003

4 February 2003. This was a historic moment: the end of 'Yugo-slavia' and the beginning of 'Serbia and Montenegro' (SCG[84]) and with the latter the reappearance of the name of Montenegro in the international lexicon after its absence for more than eighty years; a name which had been cancelled by history joined the many other new state names in Eastern Europe which had reappeared after the fall of the Berlin Wall. Yet just as the demise of the old Yugoslavia passed almost without notice, so the new state's appearance was not accompanied by any celebrations: 'It was greeted more with relief that the wrangling was over than with fanfare or enthusiasm.'[85]

The difficulties surfaced almost immediately. First and foremost, both sides in the debate chose to interpret the timescale for a ref-erendum differently. Djukanović and his supporters attempted to argue that the clock had started ticking from the time of the sig-nature of the Agreement, a stance that would have led to a ref-erendum becoming due in the spring of 2005. For the Serbian side, as indeed for the EU, the timetable began with the three Parliaments (Serbian, Montenegrin and federal) adopting the Constitutional Charter foreseen under the Belgrade Agreement. This point of view prevailed, making the referendum on Montenegrin independence due in February 2006.

Harmonising the two very different economic systems as foreseen under the Agreement proved a nigh impossible task. To get round this Chris Patten, the then EU's external relations commissioner, put forward in July 2004 a twin-track proposal to allow the two entities to proceed towards relations with the EU in parallel without uni-fying their economic systems. In the circumstances this was a realistic measure, naturally well received by the Montenegrin gov-ernment, but also by the moderate wing of the Democratic Party in Belgrade together with leading members of the economic think-tank G-17, all of whom recognised the need to take account of two economies' systemic structural differences.[86] But while such prag-matism enabled negotiations to move forward, albeit slowly, the

[84] Srbija i Crna Gora, sometimes also referred to by the English acronym SAM.
[85] Peter Palmer, 'The EU and Montenegro', p. 22.
[86] For example, Montenegro was at the time considerably ahead of Serbia in the implementation of structural economic reform.

twin-track approach remained at odds with at least the spirit of the Belgrade Agreement, which spoke of the requirement to operate 'within a single economic space'.[87]

But it was not only at the economic level that the Belgrade Agreement was running into difficulties. Politically too the State Union spawned by the agreement was proving to be dysfunctional. Predictably the two parties were soon at odds over direct elections to the joint SCG Parliament, which were scheduled under the Constitutional Charter to take place in February 2005. But while the Serbian government passed the legislation needed to enable direct elections to go ahead, the Montenegrin government failed to do so, arguing disingenuously that with a referendum due in February 2006 the expenditure involved was unnecessary. With the impasse over the elections continuing into April 2005, the Serbian and Montenegrin governments, with the approval of Brussels, signed an amendment to the Constitutional Charter permitting the postponement of joint elections till the autumn of 2006. Djukanović had gained a victory, but at the cost of agreeing to abide by European standards in the organisation of any future referendum, a concession that some of his supporters—fearing EU interference—saw as a cause for regret. With the problem of direct elections solved for the moment, the European Council of Ministers at the end of April 2005 approved the Commission's positive feasibility study for Serbia and Montenegro, opening the way for the signing of a Stabilisation and Association Agreement (SAA), the first step on the path to EU integration. But if all sides welcomed the Council's decision as bringing them closer to the same final goal, they were far from agreeing on the immediate steps ahead. While EU officials and official Belgrade expressed the expectation that Serbia and Montenegro would proceed towards EU membership as one state, Djukanović insisted on Montenegro's right to hold a referendum on independence in the first months of 2006. No doubt he was gratified when the new US ambassador to the SCG entered the debate, stating that a referendum in Montenegro, provided it were properly conducted, would not endanger the stability of the region.[88]

---

[87] See Giuliano Amato *et al.*, *The Balkans in Europe's Future*, p. 26.
[88] See *VIP: Daily News Report*, no. 3066, 26 April 2005.

A crucial moment for Montenegro

In securing recognition of his right to call a referendum, Djukanović had moved the debate decisively forward. It was clear that despite the optimism evinced by its progenitors, 'Solania' (as the Union of Serbia and Montenegro was at first facetiously known in the region) deferred the solution to the problem of the relationship between Serbia and Montenegro rather than resolving it conclusively. And in domestic political terms Djukanović's coalition looked comfortably placed. Following parliamentary success in the October 2002 elections,[89] Djukanović moved to have himself appointed Prime Minister by the Parliament in January 2003, whereupon he stood down from the Presidency. His own candidate Filip Vujanović was successful in the May 2003 presidential election.[90] Furthermore, the DPS notched up more gains by taking control of local assemblies in the key municipalities of Nikšić, Tivat and Budva in a series of local elections in the spring of 2005, which added to Djukanovic's confidence that the referendum would be won. After sixteen months of boycotting Parliament, the opposition parties were in disarray, divided among themselves to such an extent that their ability to mount an effective challenge was severely diminished. Encouragingly for the pro-independence camp, Predrag Bulatović,[91] the leader of the strongest pro-Union party (the SNP), distanced himself from the smaller pro-Serbian nationalist parties, suggesting to outsiders that he was positioning himself to lead a credible opposition movement in the autumn 2006 parliamentary elections irrespective of future moves over independence. At the same time the old Liberal Alliance (LSCG) imploded: its former leader Živković formed a new Liberal Party which was still critical of Djukanović but returned to its tradi-

---

[89] Djukanović's 'Democratic List for a European Montenegro', won thirty-nine of the Parliament's seventy-five seats and could also count on two Liberal and two Albanian deputies for support on independence.

[90] At the third time of asking after two earlier elections were declared null and void owing to low turnout and obliging Parliament to remove the 50 per cent threshold for valid elections to take place. Vujanović won 63.3 per cent of the votes cast in a turnout of 48.5 per cent.

[91] Ironically, given Predrag Bulatović's position in the spectrum of Montenegrin politics, his grandfather and his great-uncle were the last Green rebel chiefs to be executed on 7 March 1929.

tional pro-independence stance. Against this political background Djukanović and his supporters' plans for a referendum, which they continued to insist must take place in the first part of 2006, took shape. In the summer of 2005 Djukanović stated that the referendum would take place in April 2006. This subsequently moved to May 2006, but with parliamentary elections due in the autumn of 2006, he was obliged to deliver on his referendum promise or risk a loss of credibility at home and abroad and even an early end to his political career.

In April 2005 two political groups—the 'Movement for an Independent European Montenegro' and the 'Movement for a European State Union'—were set up to lobby potential voters. Although not legally compelled to accept EU involvement, both sides had their own reasons for doing so. Djukanović needed to live up to his own proclaimed European credentials in order to garner the widest possible support, notably that of some minorities who, while more ambivalent about the independence project, were decidedly pro-European. For their part, the pro-Union parties sought the involvement of Brussels because they believed that the EU's past opposition to Montenegrin independence would lead to conditions being imposed that favoured the unionist position.[92]

The pro-Union bloc was particularly active in Serbia, where it was led by the academic Ljubomir Tadić, father of the Serbian President, and backed by figures who had long been prominent in Serbian nationalist circles including the well-known Montenegrin poet, Matija Bećković and, in the margins, Prime Minister Koštunica himself. Their prime concern was to secure voting rights for the approximately 260,000 Montenegrins living in Serbia. Their efforts failed when the Venice Commission[93] produced its recommendations for the conduct of the referendum in December 2005. Although this was a significant victory for the pro-independence side avoiding what would otherwise have been certain defeat, other recommen-

---

[92] See International Crisis Group's *Report on Montenegro's Referendum*, Europe Briefing No. 42, 30 May 2006.

[93] In May 2005 the Venice Commission had been invited by the Parliamentary Assembly of the Council of Europe to evaluate the referendum law passed by the Montenegrin government and to produce recommendations to ensure that the referendum was conducted according to international standards.

dations of the Venice Commission, subsequently adopted as EU policy, were considerably less favourable. The first requirement was that a valid vote for independence needed a majority turn-out. Given the weighty issue at stake this did not appear unreasonable but it opened the way for unionists in Montenegro to block a 'yes' vote by campaigning for a boycott. Aware of this, the EU introduced a further condition, insisting on a qualified majority of 55 per cent of voters in order, as Brussels claimed, to encourage pro-Union supporters to participate by providing them with a realistic chance of defeating their opponents. But if this proviso appealed to the opposition, it appeared unfair to the sovereigntists—as the pro-independence bloc now called themselves. Djukanovic and his DPS ultimately accepted this proviso under threat of non-recognition by the EU although the Social Democrats (SDP), his small coalition partner, and the Liberals refused to do so, and voted against the new referendum law necessitated by the EU's conditions.

The EU had raised the hurdle but they also simultaneously modified their earlier categorically pro-Union stance, assuming instead a more neutral position between the two blocs. No doubt this was facilitated by evolving attitudes to Kosovo where increasing acceptance of the inevitability of some form of independence meant that earlier fears of a Montenegrin break with Serbia producing an alleged 'domino' effect had markedly diminished. Furthermore, the Serbian government's repeated failure to honour its pledges to produce indicted war criminal General Ratko Mladić also probably contributed to a softening of the attitude of Brussels toward Podgorica. Having belatedly accepted that the Djukanović government could not be deflected from holding a referendum, Brussels began to engage constructively, appointing a former Slovak ambassador to Belgrade, Miroslav Lajcak, as Solana's special representative to mediate between the pro- and anti-independence camps. This was followed by the setting up of a Montenegrin Referendum Commission, consisting of an equal number of representatives from each side under the chairmanship of another experienced Slovak diplomat, Frantisek Lipka, who had the casting vote in the not unlikely event of disagreement. Such measures were important in helping to defuse tension surrounding the referendum issue. At least partly to blame for this tension was the conduct of the Serbian Orthodox Church (SOC) which increasingly promoted, from its metropolitanate in the old monastery of Cetinje, a highly radical form of Serbian nationalism. Metropolitan Amfilohije Radović, often spoken of as the next Patriarch of the Serbian Orthodox Church and closely connected to the ruling party in Serbia through his family relationship with Vojislav Koštunica's wife,[94] had consistently emphasised the divisions within Montenegrin society by his provocative statements and actions.[95] Thus it was surprising that in the last weeks before the referendum Amfilohije maintained a judicious silence, leaving the aged Serbian Patriarch Pavle to call from Belgrade for Orthodox Montenegrins to oppose Montenegro's secession from the 'motherland'.

While Amfilohije had adopted a quieter attitude, the unionist bloc ran an essentially negative campaign, highlighting the detrimental impact of Belgrade's assumed imposition of student fees and health care costs and raising concerns about the minorities' agenda in voting for an independent Montenegro. Koštunica's government in Belgrade also engaged on the side of the pro-Union bloc. Senior members of the Serbian government broadly hinted that Montenegrins would lose these privileges if their Republic left the Union. Furthermore, Koštunica's DSS provided campaign and policy advice, and reportedly even funds, to the pro-Union parties. By contrast, the Montenegrin government and its pro-independence supporters concentrated on projecting a positive message aimed at attracting young voters by linking a 'yes' vote with a bright, new European future.[96] In keeping with their determinedly positive approach, this

[94] Amfilohije is a cousin of Koštunica's wife, Zorica Radović.

[95] A notable example was the erection of a makeshift Serbian Orthodox Church on Mount Rumija near Bar (see Chapter 1), but the Archbishop also delivered a number of pronouncements calling down divine retribution on those who supported Montenegrin independence.

[96] It was therefore somewhat paradoxical that the Montenegrin government's campaign simultaneously made conspicuous use of symbols and motifs recalling the Petrović dynasty and Montenegro's traditional past. Thus the Crown Prince-in-exile Nikola Petrović was one of a number of speakers who addressed the sovereigntists' closing rally in Podgorica, the country's new flag, adopted on 12 July 2004, is based on King Nikola's personal red and gold standard incorporating the traditional emblem of the double-headed eagle, while the new national anthem, played constantly throughout the campaign and in its immediate aftermath, is the Montenegrin folksong, 'O Bright May Dawn', a version of which

bloc mostly avoided exploiting the potentially beneficial consequences of the EU's suspension of Stabilisation and Association
Agreement (SAA) negotiations with the SCG in early May 2006
(only days before the referendum) over Serbia's failure to hand over
the Bosnian Serb wartime leader General Ratko Mladić to the
Tribunal in The Hague. For a time, however, the government's
chances of success looked threatened by the decision of a third
political force in Montenegro—the Group for Changes (GZP), led
by Nebojša Medojević, a young electrical engineer with a flair for
economics—to throw its weight behind the 'no' campaign. Medojević, who in the past had identified himself as pro-independence,
explained his decision as motivated by his belief that the identity
issue was premature and divisive at a time when Montenegro faced
larger problems of poverty, unemployment and corruption. Certainly after seventeen unbroken years of Djukanović-controlled
government these problems persist: poverty continues to blight lives
not only in the rural areas in the north,[97] in Cetinje and even in much
more prosperous Podgorica while the challenge posed by crime and
corruption continues, most notably in the form of the still unsolved
killings of a number of prominent Montenegrins including one of
Djukanović's senior security advisers, the former editor-in-chief
of the opposition daily *Dan* and the deputy head of the Criminal
Police department; a still unresolved sex-trafficking scandal; and the
pervasive use of patronage appointments within the government.
Yet progress has been made especially in the early years of the new
millennium and the government's argument that Montenegro's prolonged period of constitutional uncertainty has hampered progress

---

(not the one adopted by the new state) was popularised by the Montenegrin
fascist Sekula Drljević during the Second World War.
[97] World Bank reports point out that poverty levels in northern Montenegro are
approximately twice as high as in the south and central parts of the country. And
despite the reforms and improvements put in place since 2000, GDP has still not
reached pre-transition levels. Overall growth of some 2.5 per cent is low for a
transitional economy, unemployment at 17 per cent remains troublingly high
and up to one third of the population is estimated by USAID to be economically vulnerable. Discontent with government policies, both economic and
political, clearly played a part when in the census returns of 2003 the number of
citizens describing themselves as 'Serbs' jumped from only 10 per cent in 1991
to 30 per cent.

carries some weight. In any case, Medojević, whose personal anti-
pathy for Djukanović is well known, failed to convince a sufficient
number of voters to come round to his view. He will therefore have
to work hard to transform his third force into a political party able to
challenge what has become the Djukanović juggernaut.

Montenegro decides

The referendum duly took place on 21 May 2006, with a turnout of
86.5 per cent. The way it was conducted was approved by international observers, including the respected and authoritative OSCE/
ODIHR mission. According to the referendum commission, 230,711
voters (55.5 per cent) voted in favour of independence and 184,954
(44.5 per cent) against. The opposition reneged on its agreement to
abide by the results claiming widespread irregularities even though
all pro-Union members of local polling boards signed off on the
results and no complaints were filed with the Montenegrin courts.
Given the international support, led by the EU, for the result and the
general very positive assessment of the referendum's conduct by the
observers, these complaints served little purpose beyond possibly
positioning the opposition parties for the forthcoming parliamentary elections. It was of course crucial that the 55 per cent barrier was
just cleared. Had a pro-independence vote fallen within the so-
called 'grey zone' of 50 to 55 per cent, the situation could have been
extremely difficult. There was a palpable sense of tension as the
results were awaited. A grey zone result could well have precipitated
rioting and anti-EU protests, nor would it have been the end of the
affair. The Montenegrin government pledged before the referendum that in the event of a grey zone result, Podgorica would remove
its officials from the Union government and call another referendum
in the near future. However, the result has secured independence.
Montenegro's Parliament duly declared independence on 3 June
(see Appendix) with widespread international support other than
the predictably mixed reactions from Belgrade. Thanks in part to the
EU and its mediators, the last few steps along the road have proved
less arduous and problematical than expected. Montenegro's admission to international organisations is also proving unproblematical. It
was admitted to the UN as its 192nd member state on 28 June 2006,

Montenegro in the critical year 2006

the anniversary of the battle of Kosovo in 1389. State succession issues with Serbia are however likely to drag on.

As the architect of independence, Djukanović will inevitably be seen as father of the nation, an impressive feat for someone still in his early forties. And it would indeed be wrong to under-rate the significance of his achievement. He did after all take on the EU's 'Foreign Minister', Javier Solana, and by extension the combined weight of the EU countries over an issue from which the United States had substantially disengaged. Djukanović's consciousness of his potentially historic role was already evident in December 2005 when he theatrically unveiled an imposing statue of King Nikola on horse-back in front of the Parliament building in Podgorica. Such concern for Montenegro's past will need to be paralleled by a similar sensi-tivity over its future if Montenegro is to prosper and to vindicate its claim to be an ecological state. There is a clear need to avoid the despoiling of the beautiful coast and to maintain a careful balance in establishing the proposed eco-tourism in the under-developed north of the country. Above all, the giant aluminium plant, KAP, outside Podgorica, an uneconomic concern and consumer of half the country's electricity, needs to be wound down and alternative employment created for its numerous workforce.[98]

Whether the Montenegrin state meets the environmental and economic challenges it faces is not a matter for a history but for the future. Yet one clear lesson to be drawn from the most recent events is the need to bridge the deep division at the heart of Montenegrin society. Roughly 50,000 more Montenegrins voted in favour of independence than against it, a substantial enough victory but one which still left some 45 per cent of the voting population on the losing side. Prosperity has a way of healing divisions and here the EU and international financial institutions can surely help.[99] Of course not all of those who voted against independence will in the future be reconciled to the new state: for a percentage of citizens, core beliefs about ethnicity are too deep for that. But many of those who voted against may well be won over by a more equitable distribution of wealth, particularly if it is coupled with a broad respect for minority rights which avoids thrusting 'Montenegriness' upon those who wish to celebrate the Serbian aspects of their culture and language.

Such a scenario will be easier to achieve if the divorce from Serbia is made as velvet as possible. This does not depend on Montenegro

[98] The Kombinat Aluminijuma Podgorica (KAP) was bought in 2005 by the Russian conglomerate Rusal. At the time of writing the plant's future is uncer-tain but there are concerns that Rusal may exploit Montenegro's bauxite mines at Nikšić before liquidating the company and leaving the country to deal with the environmental damage. Overall Russia's increasing stake in the Montenegrin economy has caused concern with a number of outsiders warning that the Mon-tenegrin government would be wise to avoid over-dependence on Russia par-ticularly given the dubious origins of some of the money invested.

[99] The obvious example is the Republic of Ireland, although the same cannot yet be said for less prosperous Northern Ireland.

alone: Serbia needs to come to terms with the new reality and to avoid the temptation to punish 'Montenegrin secessionists', something that a significant part of official Serbia clearly finds difficult to do. That both Serbia and Montenegro share the same goal of EU membership is helpful in so far as it facilitates continuing EU mediation, although there could be difficulties if Montenegro succeeds in stepping up its progress towards European integration while Serbia, unable to shake off its nationalist past, lags behind and becomes even more isolated internationally. Montenegro has already been successful in re-building good relations with the other countries to emerge from the former Yugoslavia and with Albania. The fact that Serbia and Montenegro are no longer 'two eyes in the one head' should be no bar to their becoming the closest of neighbours.

The closely interwoven relationship between Serbs and Montenegrins has been a recurring theme of this book and especially of its later chapters. To a large extent this has been unavoidable. The statehood issue was for Montenegro (though not for Serbia) a dominant preoccupation for much of the twentieth century and, since 1997, has eclipsed all other issues in Montenegro, deflecting attention from important economic problems and hindering the development of normal political life. Its resolution provides a fitting end point for this history and a new beginning for Montenegro.

Appendix: the Instrument of Independence

Proceeding from the centuries-long tradition of statehood and independence and the international recognition of the Principality of Montenegro at the Berlin Congress on July 13, 1878;

Based on the freely expressed will of citizens in the referendum on the state-legal status of the Republic of Montenegro held on May 21, 2006, conducted in conformity with international standards and in cooperation with the European Union;

Expressing its commitment to maintaining and promoting international peace and stability, reiterating its readiness to respect the principle of territorial integrity and sovereignty of all states, seeking to settle all international disputes by peaceful means, and promoting friendly relations and cooperation with all states on the basis of the principle of equality;

Based on the Decision on Proclamation of Independence of the Republic of Montenegro, and Article 81, paragraph 2 of the Constitution of the Republic of Montenegro

The Parliament of the Republic of Montenegro, at its session held on 3 June 2006 has adopted a

DECLARATION OF THE INDEPENDENT REPUBLIC OF MONTENEGRO

1.

The Republic of Montenegro, an independent state with full international legal personality, will continue to develop as a civic state, multiethnic, multicultural and multiconfessional society, founded on

477

the respect and protection of human freedoms and rights, minority rights, principles of parliamentary democracy, the rule of law and market economy, which will be further enhanced by promulgation of a new Constitution of the Republic of Montenegro.

2.

Proceeding from its restored independence, the Republic of Montenegro:

— accepting the principles laid down in documents of the United Nations, the Council of Europe, the Organisation for Security and Cooperation in Europe, and other international organisations, shall initiate the process for gaining a full-fledged membership of these organisations;

— shall accept and adhere to the rights and obligations that arise from existing arrangements with the European Union, the United Nations, the Council of Europe and the Organisation for Security and Cooperation in Europe, as well as other international organizations, that relate to Montenegro and are in conformity with its legal order, providing full support to the operation of their agencies and representations on its territory;

— confirms as its strategic priority an accelerated integration into the European Union, and is determined to continue to fulfil efficiently the conditions and requirements included in the Copenhagen criteria and the Stabilization and Association Process;

— is firmly determined to join European and Euro Atlantic (NATO) security structures and to continue to contribute to strengthening regional stability and security;

— committed to further progress in the process of accession to the World Trade Organization, stands ready to fulfil the obligations stemming from the membership of this organisation;

— shall continue and further the existing cooperation with the international financial institutions and commence the procedure to regulate its membership as an independent state;

— shall observe the principles of international law and the decisions of the International Court of Justice, and is determined to continue full cooperation with the International Criminal Tribunal for the former Yugoslavia in The Hague;

3.

The Republic of Montenegro shall establish and develop bilateral relations with the third states on the basis principles of the international law, accepting the rights and obligations stemming from existing arrangements and shall continue with active policy of good-neighbourly relations and regional cooperation.

4.

Reiterating its good faith, the Republic of Montenegro expresses particular interest and full readiness to address the existing mutual rights and obligations with the Republic of Serbia and develop good and friendly relations between the two states.

5.

The Declaration shall be published in the *Official Gazette of the Republic of Montenegro.*

Podgorica, 3 June 2006

PARLIAMENT OF THE REPUBLIC OF MONTENEGRO

THE SPEAKER

Ranko Krivokapić

Implementing the decision based on the free will of the citizens of Montenegro to restore the independence of the state of Montenegro and its full international and legal personality in the referendum held on May 21, 2006, organized in partnership with the European Union, and verified by the Report of Republic Commission for administering the referendum on state-legal status of the Republic of Montenegro, and exercising the right stipulated in the Article 2 of the Constitution of the Republic of Montenegro and Article 60 of the Constitutional Charter of the state union of Serbia and Montenegro, Parliament of Republic of Montenegro, at its session held on June 3rd, 2006, on the basis of the Article 81, paragraph 2 of the Constitution of the Republic of Montenegro, has adopted

THE DECISION ON THE PROCLAMATION OF INDEPENDENCE OF THE REPUBLIC OF MONTENEGRO

The Republic of Montenegro is an independent state with full international legal personality within its existing state frontiers.

The Republic of Montenegro, by restoring its independence, shall assume all matters that it had conferred on to the institutions of the state union by adoption of the Constitutional Charter of the state union of Serbia and Montenegro.

The Republic of Montenegro shall apply and adhere to international treaties and agreements that the state union of Serbia and Montenegro was party to and that relate to the Republic of Montenegro and are in conformity with its legal order.

Pending adoption of respective regulations of the Republic of Montenegro, regulations that were effective as regulations of the state union of Serbia and Montenegro on the day of entry into force of this Decision shall apply as the regulations of the Republic of Montenegro, provided that they are not in collision with the legal order and interests of the Republic of Montenegro.

The Republic of Montenegro shall determine the procedure of assuming the matters that have so far been administered by the institutions of the state union of Serbia and Montenegro, and by separate acts of the Parliament and the Government of the Republic of Montenegro it shall establish and make public the principles on which its internal and foreign policy shall be formulated and conducted.

This Decision enters into force from the date of its adoption and shall be published in the *Official Gazette of the Republic of Montenegro.*

Podgorica, 3 June 2006

RANKO KRIVOKAPIC (Speaker of the Parliament)

EXPLANATION

CONSTITUTIONAL AND LEGAL GROUNDS FOR ADOPTION

The Constitutional foundation for adoption of this Decision is defined in Article 81 paragraph 2 of the Constitution of the Republic of Montenegro that stipulates that the Parliament of the Republic of Montenegro shall enact laws, other regulations and general enactments as well as Article 11 of the Law on Referendum (*Official Gazette of the Republic of Montenegro* No. 9/01) that stipulates that the authority that called for the referendum ascertains the outcome of the referendum and passes the respective act, should the outcome of the referendum entail such an obligation

REASONS FOR ADOPTION

In the referendum on legal status of the Republic of Montenegro held on 21 May 2006, organised in partnership with the European Union, the citizens of Montenegro have decided that the Republic of Montenegro become an independent state with full international and legal personality. The decision of the citizens on independence of the Republic of Montenegro needs to be officially ascertained and proclaimed by the respective act of the Parliament, which is why adoption of this Decision has been proposed.

Simultaneously, the Decision on Proclamation of Independence, determined by the will of citizens, should regulate certain issues related to organisation and proceedings pending the adoption of new regulations, which has been accordingly proposed in specific provisions of this Decision.

GENEALOGIES
OF THE
MONTENEGRIN
AND SERBIAN
ROYAL HOUSES

House of Petrović-Njegoš

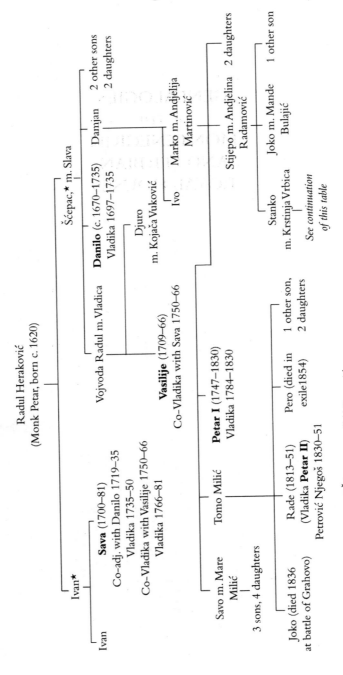

* All male descendants of Ivan and Šćepac are called Petrović.

House of Petrović-Njegoš *continued*

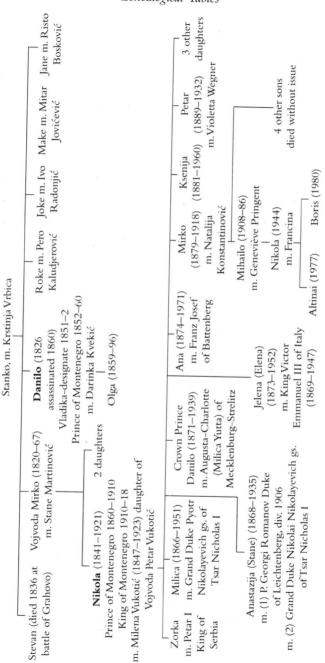

Stanko, m. Krstinja Vrbica

Stevan (died 1836 at battle of Grahovo)

Vojvoda Mirko (1820–67) m. Stane Martinović

Danilo (1826 assassinated 1860) Vladika-designate 1851–2 Prince of Montenegro 1852–60 m. Darinka Kvekić

Roke m. Pero Kaludjerović

Joke m. Ivo Radonjić

Make m. Mitar Jovićević

Jane m. Risto Bošković

Nikola (1841–1921) Prince of Montenegro 1860–1910 King of Montenegro 1910–18 m. Milena Vukotić (1847–1923) daughter of Vojvoda Petar Vukotić

2 daughters

Olga (1859–96)

Zorka m. Petar I King of Serbia

Milica (1866–1951) m. Grand Duke Pyotr Nikolayevich gs. of Tsar Nicholas I

Anastazija (Stane) (1868–1935) m. (1) P. Georgi Romanov Duke of Leichtenberg, div. 1906 m. (2) Grand Duke Nikolai Nikolayevich gs. of Tsar Nicholas I

Crown Prince Danilo (1871–1939) m. Augusta-Charlotte (Milica Yutta) of Mecklenburg-Strelitz

Jelena (Elena) (1873–1952) m. King Victor Emmanuel III of Italy (1869–1947)

Ana (1874–1971) m. Franz Josef of Battenberg

Mirko (1879–1918) m. Natalija Konstantinović

Ksenija (1881–1960)

Petar (1889–1932) m. Violetta Wegner

3 other daughters

Mihailo (1908–86) m. Geneviève Pringent

Nikola (1944) m. Francina

4 other sons died without issue

Altinai (1977)

Boris (1980)

House of Obrenović

Jevrem m. Maria Katardji of Moldavia

Miloš Obrenović
Prince of Serbia 1815–39
(interrupted 1858–60)

Mihailo
(1826–assassinated 1868)
Prince of Serbia 1840–2
(interrupted 1860–8)

Milan (c. 1819–39)
Prince of Serbia June–July 1839

Milan (1854–1901)
Prince of Serbia under a regency 1868–72
Prince of Serbia 1872–82
King of Serbia 1882–9 (abdicated)
m. Natalija Ketchko

Aleksandar (1876–1903)
Prince of Serbia under a regency 1889–93
King of Serbia 1893–1903
m. Draga Mašina, both assassinated 1903

House of Karadjordjević

Djordje Petrović (Karadjordje)
(c. 1768–1817)
1804–13
m. Jelena Jovanović

Aleksandar (1806–85)
Prince of Serbia 1842–58
m. Persida Nenadović

Petar I (1844–1921)
King of Serbia 1903–18
King of the Kingdom of Serbs, Croats
and Slovenes 1918–21
m. Lubica-Zorka Petrović Njegoš

Aleksandar (1888–assassinated 1934)
Prince Regent of Serbia 1914–18
Regent of Kingdom of Serbs,
Croats and Slovenes 1918–21
King of Kingdom of Serbs
Croats and Slovenes 1921–9
King of Yugoslavia 1929–34
m. Maria of Romania

Djordje (1887–1972)
Crown Prince of Serbia
(abdicated 1909)

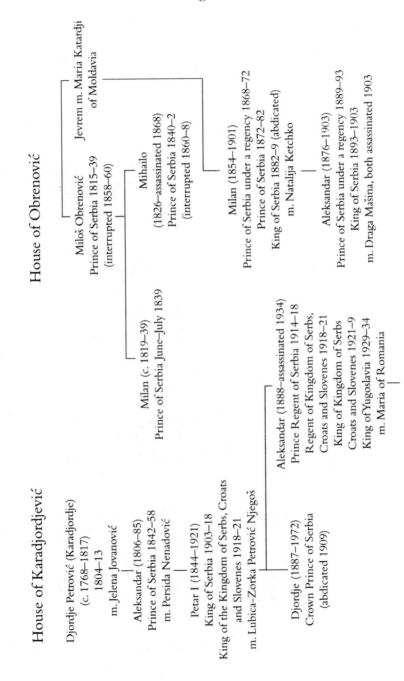

House of Karadjordjević *continued*

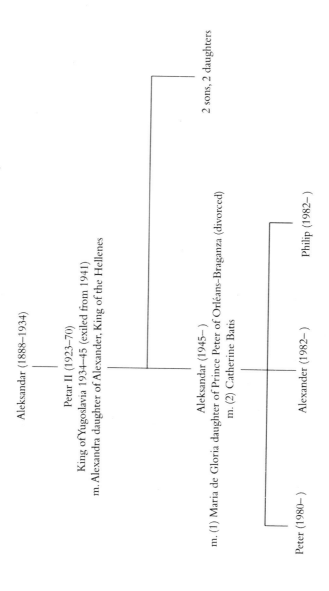

Aleksandar (1888–1934)

Petar II (1923–70)
King of Yugoslavia 1934–45 (exiled from 1941)
m. Alexandra daughter of Alexander, King of the Hellenes

Aleksandar (1945–)
m. (1) Maria de Gloria daughter of Prince Peter of Orléans-Braganza (divorced)
m. (2) Catherine Batis

2 sons, 2 daughters

Peter (1980–)

Alexander (1982–)

Philip (1982–)

Bibliography

Below are listed the works most frequently consulted by the author, including those referred to in the text. The listing does not claim to be exhaustive.

Books

Albertini, Luigi, *Origins of the War of 1914*, London, 1952–57.

Alexander, John, *Yugoslavia before Roman Conquest*, London: Thames and Hudson, 1972.

Allcock, John B., *Explaining Yugoslavia*, Hurst: London, 2000.

———, *and Antonia Young (eds) Black Lambs and Grey Falcons: Women Travellers in the Balkans*, New York, Oxford: Berghahn, 2000.

Anderson, Benedict, *Imagined Communities: Reflections on the Origins and Spread of Nationalism*, New York: Verso, 1991.

Andrijašević, Živko M., and Šerbo Rastoder, *The History of Montenegro from Ancient Times to 2003*, Podgorica: Montenegro Diaspora Centre, 2006.

Anzulović, Branimir, *Heavenly Serbia: From Myth to Genocide*, New York University Press and London: Hurst, 1999.

Baerlein, Henry, *The Birth of Yugoslavia*, 2 vols., London: Leonard Parsons, 1922.

Banac, Ivo, *The National Question in Yugoslavia: Origins, History, Politics*, Ithaca, NY: Cornell University Press, 1984.

———, *With Stalin against Tito: Cominformist Splits in Yugoslav Communism*, Ithaca, NY: Cornell University Press, 1988.

Bennett, Christopher, *Yugoslavia's Bloody Collapse: Causes, Course and Consequences*, London: Hurst, 1995.

Bićanić, Rudolf, *How the People Live: Life in the Passive Regions* (transl. and edited Joel M. Halpern and Elinor Murray Desplatović), Amherst: Dept of Anthropology, University of Massachusetts, 1981.

Bideleux, Robert and Ian Jeffries, *A History of Eastern Europe, Crisis and Change*, London: Routledge, 1998.

Bieber, Florian (ed.), *Montenegro in Transition: Problems of Identity and Statehood*, Baden–Baden: Nomos, 2003.

Boehm, Christopher, *Montenegrin Social Organisation and Values: A Political Ethnography of a Refuge Area Tribal Adaptation*, New York: AMS Press, 1983.

———, *Blood Revenge: The Anthropology of Feuding in Montenegro and other Tribal Societies*, University Press of Kansas, 1984.

Boiardi, Franco (ed.), *Italia e Montenegro*, Bari: Laterza, 1997.

Bonsal, Stephen, *Suitors and Suppliants: The Little Nations at Versailles*, New York, 1946.

Bosworth, R. J. B., *Italy, the Least of the Great Powers*, Cambridge University Press, 1979.

Brown, H. A., *A Winter in Albania*, Griffith, Faeran, London: Okeden and Welsh, 1888.

Burg, Steven L., and Paul S. Shoup, *The War in Bosnia-Herzegovina: Ethnic Conflict and International Intervention*, Armonk, NY: M.E. Sharpe, 1999.

Butler, Hubert, *Independent Spirit: Essays*, New York: Farrar, Straus and Giroux, 1996.

Carter, Frank W., *A Historical Geography of the Balkans*, London: Academic Press, 1977.

Cary, Joyce, *Memoir of the Bobotes*, London: Michael Joseph, 1965.

Ćirković, Sima M., *The Serbs* (transl. by Vuk Tošić), Oxford: Blackwell, 2004.

Clissold, Stephen, *A Short History of Yugoslavia*, Cambridge University Press, 1966.

Cohen, Lenard J., *The Socialist Pyramid: Elites and Power in Yugoslavia*, London: Tri-Service Press, 1989.

Cooper, Robert, *The Breaking of Nations: Order and Chaos in the Twenty-first Century*, London: Atlantic Books, 2003.

Crampton, R. J., *The Hollow Détente: Anglo-German relations in the Balkans 1911–1914*, Atlantic City, NJ: Humanities Press, 1979.

———, *A Concise History of Bulgaria*, Cambridge University Press, 1997.

———, *The Balkans since the Second World War*, London: Longman, 2002.

Cvijić, Jovan, *La Péninsule balkanique: Géographie humaine*, Paris: Armand Colin, 1918.

Dankoff, Robert and Robert Elsie (eds), *Evliya Çelebi in Albania and Adjacent Regions (Kosovo, Montenegro, Ohrid)*, Leiden: E. J. Brill, 2000.

Dapčević, Peko, *Kako Smo Vodili Rat*, Belgrade, 1946.

Deakin, F.W., *The Embattled Mountain*, Oxford University Press, 1971.

Dedijer, Vladimir, *Tito Speaks* (transl. from the Serbo-Croat *Josip Broz Tito*), London: Weidenfeld and Nicolson, 1953.

———, *The Road to Sarajevo*, New York: Simon and Schuster, 1966.

———, *The Battle Stalin Lost: Memoirs of Yugoslavia, 1948–1953*, New York: Viking Press, 1970.

————, *The War Diaries of Vladimir Dedijer,* (transl. from the fifth, unexpurgated edition of *Dnevnik* 1941–1944, Belgrade, 1945–1946), 3 vols, Ann Arbor: University of Michigan Press, 1990.

————, Ivan Božić, Sima Ćirković and Milorad Ekmečić, *History of Yugoslavia,* Serbian edn (transl. from *Istorija Jugoslavije,* Belgrade: Prosveta, 1972), New York: McGraw-Hill, 1974.

Denton William, *Montenegro: Its People and their History,* Daldy, Isbister & Co., 1877.

Destani, Beitullah (ed.), *Montenegro: Political and Ethnic Boundaries 1840–1920,* 2 vols, Chippenham, Wilts: Archive Editions, 2001.

Devine, Alexander, *Montenegro in History, Politics and War,* London: T. Fisher Unwin, 1918.

Djilas, Aleksa, *The Contested Country: Yugoslav Unity and the Communist Revolution, 1919–1953,* Harvard University Press, 1991.

Djilas, Milovan, *The New Class: An Analysis of the Communist System,* New York: Praeger, 1957.

————, *Land without Justice* (transl. by Michael B. Petrovich), New York: Harcourt Brace Jovanovich, 1958.

————, *Conversations with Stalin* (transl. by Michael B. Petrovich), New York: Harcourt Brace & World, 1962.

————, *Montenegro* (transl. by Kenneth Johnstone), London: Methuen, 1964.

————, *Njegoš: Poet, Prince, Bishop* (transl. by Michael B. Petrovich), New York: Harcourt, Brace and World, 1966.

————, *Wartime* (transl. by Michael B. Petrovich), New York: Harcourt Brace Jovanovich, 1977.

————, *Tito: The Story from Inside* (transl. by Vasilije Kojić and Richard Hayes), London: Weidenfeld and Nicolson, 1981.

————, *Rise and Fall* (transl. by John F. Loud), San Diego: Harcourt Brace Jovanovich, 1985.

Djukic, Slavoljub, *Milošević and Marković: A Lust for Power* (transl. by Alex Dubinsky from the Serbian *On, Ona i Mi*), Montreal: McGill-Queen's University Press: London: Ithaca, 2001.

Djurdjev, Branislav, *Turska vlasta u Crnoj Gori u XVI i XVII veku,* Sarajevo, 1953.

————, 'Karadagh' (Montenegro), *Encyclopaedia of Islam,* 2nd edn, 6 vols, Leiden: E. J. Brill, 1960.

Djurović, Milinko (ed.), *Istorija Crne Gore,* 3 vols, Titograd (Podgorica): Redakcije za Istoriju Crne Gore, 1967–75.

Doder, Duško and Louise Branson, *Milošević: Portrait of a Tyrant,* New York: The Free Press, 1999.

Durham, Edith M., *Through the Lands of the Serb*, London: Edward Arnold, 1904.

————, 'The Western Balkan Peninsula' in *Women of All Nations: A Record of Their Characteristics, Habits, Manners, Customs and Influence* (ed. T. Athol Joyce and N. W. Thomas), London: Cassell, 1909.

————, *The Struggle for Scutari*, London: Edward Arnold, 1914.

————, *Twenty Years of Balkan Tangle*, London: Geo. Allen & Unwin, 1920.

————, *Some Tribal Origins, Laws and Customs of the Balkans*, London: Geo. Allen & Unwin, 1928.

Durham, Thomas, *Serbia: The Rise and Fall of a Medieval Empire*, York: Ebor Press, 1989.

Edwards, Lovett Fielding, *A Wayfarer in Yugoslavia*, London: Methuen, 1939.

————, *The Yugoslav Coast*, London: B.T. Batsford, 1974.

Eraković, Aleksandar and Ljubiša Mitrović, *Sto dana koji su promijenili Crnu Goru*, Podgorica: Vijesti, 1997.

Evans, Sir Arthur John, *Illyrian Letters: A Revised Selection of Correspondence from the Illyrian Provinces of Bosnia, Herzegovina, Montenegro, Albania, Dalmatia, Croatia and Slavonia, Addressed to the Manchester Guardian during the Year 1877*, London: Longmans Green, 1878.

Fine, John V. A., *The Early Medieval Balkans: A Critical Survey from the Sixth to the late Twelfth Century*, Ann Arbor: University of Michigan Press, 1991.

————, *The Late Medieval Balkans: A Critical Survey from the late Twelfth Century to the Ottoman Conquest*, Ann Arbor: University of Michigan Press, 1994.

Friley, G. and Jovan Wlahovitj, *Le Monténégro contemporain*, Paris: Plon, 1876.

Gibson, Hugh (ed.), *The Ciano Diaries, 1939–1943: The Complete, Unabridged Diaries of Count Galeazzo Ciano, Italian Minister for Foreign Affairs, 1936–1943*, New York: Doubleday, 1946.

Glenny, Misha, *The Fall of Yugoslavia: The Third Balkan War*, London: Penguin Books, 1992.

————, *The Balkans, 1804–1999: Nationalism, War and the Great Powers*, London: Granta, 1999.

Goldstein, Ivo, *Croatia: A History* (transl. from the Croatian by Nikolina Jovanović), London: Hurst 1999.

Goldsworthy, Vesna, *Imagining Ruritania: The Imperialism of the Imagination*, New Haven and London: Yale University Press, 1998.

Gooch, G. P. and Harold Temperley (eds), *British Documents on the Origins of the War, 1898–1914*, vol. XI, London, 1926.

Gordon-Smith, G., *Through the Serbian Campaign: The Great Retreat of the Serbian Army*, London, 1916.

Grey, Viscount, of Fallodon, *Twenty-five Years, 1892–1916*, 2 vols, London: Hodder & Stoughton, 1925.

Hall, Richard C., *The Balkan Wars, 1912–1913: Prelude to the First World War*, London and New York: Routledge, 2000.

Helmreich, Ernst Christian, *The Diplomacy of the Balkan Wars 1912–1913*, Harvard University Press, 1938.

Holbrooke, Richard, *To End a War*, New York: Random House, 1998.

Hoste, William, *Memoirs and Letters*, vol. 2 (ed. Richard Bentley), London, 1833.

Houston, Marco, *Nikola and Milena: King and Queen of the Black Mountain*, London: Leppi, 2003.

Jelavich, Barbara, *History of the Balkans*, 2 vols, Cambridge University Press, 1983.

Jelavich, Charles and Barbara, *The Establishment of the Balkan National States, 1804–1920*, Washington University Press, 1977.

Jovićević, Milan, *The Montenegrin Royal Marriages*, Cetinje: Narodni Muzej Crne Gore, 1988.

Kaplan, Robert, D., *Balkan Ghosts: A Journey through History*, London: Macmillan (Papermac), 1994.

Kontler, Laszlo (ed.), *Pride and Prejudice: National Stereotypes in Nineteenth and Twentieth Century Europe East to West*, Budapest: Centre European University Press, 1995.

Koprivica, Veseljko and Branko Vojičić, *Prevrat, '89*, Podgorica: Liberalni Savez Crne Gore, Svjedočanstva Biblioteka, 1994.

Lampe, John R. and Marvin R. Jackson, *Balkan Economic History, 1550–1950: From Imperial Borderlands to Developing Nations*, Bloomington: Indiana University Press, 1982.

Lampe, John R., *Yugoslavia as History: Twice there was a Country*, Cambridge University Press, 1996.

Lederer, Ivo J., *Yugoslavia at the Paris Peace Conference*, Yale University Press, 1963.

Lenormant, François, *Turcs et Monténégrins*, Paris: Didier, 1866.

Mackenzie, G. Muir and Paulina A. Irby, *Travels in the Slavonic Provinces of Turkey-in-Europe*, 2nd edn in 2 vols, London, 1877.

Maclean, Fitzroy, *Disputed Barricade: The Life and Times of Josip Broz Tito, Marshal of Jugoslavia*, London: Cape, 1957.

———, *Tito: A Pictorial Biography* (first publ. Macmillan, London), New York: McGraw-Hill, 1980.

MacMillan, Margaret, *Peacemakers: The Paris Conference of 1919 and its Attempt to End War*, London: John Murray, 2001.

Malcolm, Noel, *Bosnia: A Short History* (2nd edn), London: Macmillan (Papermac), 1996.

———, *Kosovo: A Short History*, London: Macmillan, 1998.

Markovic, Čedomir and Rajko Vujičić, *The Cultural Monuments of Montenegro*, Novi Sad: Presmedij, 1996.

Mazower, Mark., *The Balkans*, London: Weidenfeld and Nicolson, 2000.

Milazzo, Matteo J., *The Chetnik Movement and the Yugoslav Resistance*, Baltimore, MD: Johns Hopkins University Press, 1975.

Milich, Zorka, *A Stranger's Supper: An Oral History of Centenarian Women in Montenegro*, New York: Twayne, 1995.

Mrvaljević, Jakov, *Kraj Crnogorskog Kraljevstva*, Cetinje: Narodni Muzej Crne Gore, 1989.

Nicolson, Harold, *Peacemaking 1919*, London, 1945.

Nolte, Alis, *Essai sur le Monténégro*, Paris: Calmann Lévy, 1907, republished by the National Library Radosav Ljumović, Podgorica, 1996.

Norris, David A., *In the Wake of the Balkan Myth: Questions of Identity and Modernity*, London: Macmillan, 1999.

Norwich, John Julius, *A History of Venice*, London: Penguin Books, 2003.

Obolensky, Dimitri, *The Byzantine Commonwealth: Eastern Europe 500–1453*, London: Phoenix Press, 1971.

Ostrogorsky, George, *History of the Byzantine State*, Oxford: Basil Blackwell, 1968.

Palairet, Michael, *The Balkan Economies c. 1800–1914*, Cambridge University Press, 1997.

Pavlowitch, Stevan K., *The Improbable Survivor: Yugoslavia and its Problems, 1918–1988*, London: Hurst, 1988.

———, *A History of the Balkans, 1804–1945*, Harlow: Longman, 1999.

———, *Serbia: The History behind the Name*, London: Hurst, 2002.

Petrović-Njegoš, Rade, *The Mountain Wreath of PP Nyegosh, Prince Bishop of Montenegro 1830–1851*, (transl. by James. W. Wiles), London: Geo. Allen Unwin, 1930.

Petrovich, Michael Boro, *History of Modern Serbia, 1804–1918*, 2 vols, New York: Harcourt Brace Jovanovich, 1976.

Poulton, Hugh, *Who are the Macedonians?*, London: Hurst, 1995.

Radzinsky, Edvard, *Rasputin: The Last Word* (transl. from the Russian by Judson Rosengrant), London: Weidenfeld and Nicolson, 2000.

Ramet, P. (ed.), *Nationalism and Federalism in Yugoslavia, 1963–1983*, Bloomington; Indiana University Press, 1984.

Rastoder, Šerbo, *Skrivana Strana Istorije: Crnogorska Buna I Odmetnički Pokret, 1918–1929, Dokumenti*, 4 vols, Cetinje-Podgorica, 2005.

Ridley, Jasper, *Tito: A Biography*, London: Constable, 1994.

Roberts, Walter R., *Tito, Mihailović and the Allies, 1941–1945*, New Brunswick, NJ: Rutgers University Press, 1973.

Rusinow, Dennison, *The Yugoslav Experiment, 1948–1974*, London: Hurst, 1977.

Scotti, Giacomo and Viazzi Luciano, *Le Aquile delle Montagne Nere. Storia dell'occupazione e della guerra italiana in Montenegro (1941–1943)*, Milan: Mursia, 1987.

————, *L'Inutile Vittoria. La tragica esperienza delle truppe italiane in Montenegro*, Milan: Mursia, 1989.

Sell, Louis, *Slobodan Milošević and the Destruction of Yugoslavia*, Durham, NC: Duke University Press, 2002.

Shoup, Paul, *Communism and the Yugoslav National Question*, Columbia University Press, 1968.

Sidoti, Antoine, *Partisans et Tchetniks en Yougoslavie durant la Seconde Guerre Mondiale. Idéologie et mythogenèse*, Paris: CNRS Éditions, 2004.

Silber, Laura and Alan Little, *The Death of Yugoslavia* (rev. edn), Penguin Books & BBC Books Worldwide, 1996.

Stevenson, Francis Seymour, *A History of Montenegro*, London: Jarrold, 1912.

Stoianovich, Traian, *Balkan Worlds: The First and Last Europe*, Armonk, NY: M.E. Sharpe, 1994.

Stillman, W. J., *Herzegovina and the Late Uprising: The Causes of the Latter and its Remedies*, London: Longman Green, 1877.

Strangford, Viscountess (Emily), *The Eastern Shores of the Adriatic in 1863 with a visit to Montenegro*, London: Richard Bentley, 1864.

Tanner, Marcus, *Croatia: A Nation Forged in War*, Yale University Press, 1997.

Temperley, Harold W. V., *History of Serbia*, London: G. Bell & Sons, 1919.

Thaden, Edward C., *Russia and the Balkan Alliance of 1912*, University Park: Pennsylvania State University Press, 1965.

Thomas, Robert, *Serbia under Milošević: Politics in the 1990s*, London: Hurst, 1998.

Thomson, Mark, *A Paper House: The Ending of Yugoslavia*, London: Hutchinson, 1992.

Todorova, Maria, *Imagining the Balkans*, Oxford University Press, 1997.

Treadway, J. A., *The Falcon and the Eagle: Montenegro and Austria-Hungary, 1908–1914*, West Lafayette, IN: Purdue University Press.

Trew, Simon, *Britain, Mihailović and the Chetniks, 1941–4*, London: Macmillan, 1998.

Tomasevich, Jozo, *Peasants, Politics and Economic Change in Yugoslavia*, Stanford University Press, 1955.

————, *The Chetniks: War and Revolution in Yugoslavia, 1941–1945*, Stanford University Press, 1975.

————, *War and Revolution in Yugoslavia, 1941–1945*, Stanford University Press, 2001.

Trotsky, Leon, *War Correspondence: The Balkan Wars, 1912–13*, ed. George Weissman and Duncan Williams, New York: Pathfinder, 1981.

Vialla de Sommières, L. C., *Travels in Montenegro*, London: Philips & Co., 1820.

Vucinich, Wayne S. (ed.), *Contemporary Yugoslavia: Twenty Years of Socialist Experiment*, Berkeley: University of California Press, 1969.

Vuković, Gavro, *Memoari*, Cetinje, 1996.

West, Rebecca, *Black Lamb and Grey Falcon: The Record of a Journey through Yugoslavia in 1937*, 2 vols, London: Macmillan, 1941.

West, Richard, *Tito and the Rise and Fall of Yugoslavia*, London: Sinclair-Stevenson, 1994.

Whitney, Warren, *Montenegro: The Crime of the Peace Conference*, New York: Brentanos, 1922; reprinted Podgorica, 2000.

Wilkes, John, *The Illyrians*, Oxford University Press, 1992.

Wilkinson, Sir J. Garner, *Dalmatia and Montenegro*, 2 vols, London: John Murray, 1848.

Wilson, Duncan, *The Life and Times of Vuk Stefanović Karadžić, 1787–1864*, Oxford: Clarendon Press, 1970.

Windt, Harry de, *Through Savage Europe: Being the Narrative of a Journey (Undertaken by a Special Correspondent of the Westminster Gazette) Throughout the Balkan States and Russia*, London: T. Fisher Unwin, 1907.

Woodward, Susan L., *Balkan Tragedy: Chaos and Dissolution after the Cold War*, Washington, DC: Brookings Institution Press, 1995.

Wynaendts, Henry, *L'Engrenage. Chroniques yougoslaves, juillet 1991–août 1992*, Paris: Denoël, 1993.

Wyon, R. and G. Prance, *The Land of the Black Mountain*, London: Methuen, 1905.

Živković, Dragoje, *Istorija Crnogorskog Naroda*, 2 vols, Cetinje, 1992.

Articles

Anonymous, 'Montenegro as we saw it', *Scribner's Monthly*, December 1880, pp. 276–93.

Carmichael, Cathy, and Božidar Jezernik, 'Gender and the Construction of Montenegrin National Identity before 1918' in Wojciech Burszta, Tomasz Kamusella and Sebastian Wojciechowski (eds), *Nationalisms Across the Globe: An overview of the nationalisms of state-endowed and stateless nations*, Poznan: Wyzsza Szkola Nauk Humanistycznych i Dziennikarstwa, 2005.

Darmanović, Srdjan, 'Montenegro: Destiny of a Satellite State', *Eastern European Reporter*, no. 27, March–April 1992, pp. 27–9.

Ford, Emmet B., 'Montenegro in the Eyes of the English Traveller, 1840–1914', *Südostforschungen* (Munich), no. 18, 1959, pp. 350–80.

Frazer, Rev. R. C. (published anonymously), 'Visit to the Vladika of Montenegro, Cetinje 1844', *Blackwood's Magazine*, no. 60, 1846, pp. 428–43.

Gladstone, W. E., 'Montenegro: A Sketch', *The Nineteenth Century*, no. 3, May 1877, pp. 360–79.

Goldsworthy, Vesna, 'Tennyson and Montenegro', *Tennyson Research Bulletin*, vol. 7, no. 1, November 1997.

Knežević, Saša, '"The Times" Coverage of the Montenegrin-Turkish War in 1862', *South Slav Journal*, vol. 21, no. 3–4 (81–82) autumn-winter 2000, pp. 60–9.

Lamb, Charles (published anonymously), 'A Ramble in Montenegro', *Blackwood's Edinburgh Magazine*, no. 57, January 1845, pp. 33–51.

Leadbetter, Jannine, 'The End of Montenegro', *South Slav Journal*, vol. 14, nos 3–4 (53–55), London, 1991, pp. 46–71.

Lejean, M. G., 'Voyage en Albanie et au Monténégro, en 1858', *Le Tour du monde, nouveau journal des voyages*, Paris: Hachette, 1er semestre de 1860, pp. 69–87.

Lopashich, Alexander, 'A Negro Community in Yugoslavia', *Man*, Nov. 1958, pp. 168–73.

Markotić, Stan, 'The Challenge of Balkan Peace: Tensions rise over Montenegro's Independence Moves', *Transitions*, 26 July 1996, pp. 58–61.

Palairet, Michael, 'The Culture of Economic Stagnation in Montenegro', *Maryland Historian*, no. 17, 1986, pp. 17–42.

Palmer, Peter, 'The EU and Montenegro: A Testing Ground for the Common Foreign and Security Policy', *Reper* (Podgorica: CEDEM), no. 4, October 2003, pp. 9–27.

Pavlović, Srdja, 'The Podgorica Assembly in 1918: Notes on the Yugoslav Historiography (1919–1970) about the Unification of Montenegro and Serbia', *Canadian Slavonic Papers*, vol. 41, no. 2, June 1999, pp. 157–76.

———, 'Who are the Montenegrins? Statehood, identity and civic society' in Florian Bieber (ed.), *Montenegro in Transition*, Baden-Baden: Nomos, 2003, pp. 83–106.

———, '*The Mountain Wreath*: Poetry or a Blueprint for the Final Solution?', available at http://www.univie.ac.at/spacesofidentity/Vol_4/_html/pavlovic.html

Pavlowitch, Stevan K., 'Unconventional Perceptions of Yugoslavia, 1940–1945', *East European Monographs*, 260(b), distrib. Columbia University Press, New York, 1985, pp. 67–105.

Rastoder, Šerbo, 'A Short Review of the History of Montenegro' in Florian Bieber (ed.), *Montenegro in Transition*, Baden-Baden: Nomos, 2003, pp. 107–37.

Seton-Watson, R.W., 'The Question of Montenegro', *The New Europe*, vol. 14, no. 181, 1 April 1920, pp. 265–73.

Thaden, Edward, 'Montenegro: Russia's Troublesome Ally, 1910–1912', *Journal of Central European Affairs*, vol. 18, July 1958, pp. 111–13.

Vucinich, Wayne S., 'An American View of Conditions in Montenegro, 1918–1919', *Balkania* (Annuaire de l'Institut Balkanique), Belgrade, 1982–3, vol. 13–14, pp. 271–9.

Other Material

Of the British archival material used in this study, the principal documents consulted were the Foreign Office's 'General Political Correspondence', series 371, housed in the Public Record Office.

Also consulted:

King's College London, Liddell Hart Centre for Military Archives, Papers relating to *The Death of Yugoslavia*, television documentary series (1941, 1985–96), Reference code: GB99 KCLMA The Death of Yugoslavia.

Handbooks on Montenegro, Serbia and the Balkan States

Prepared by the General Staff:

Handbooks of the Montenegrin Army, HMSO, 1909.

Prepared under the direction of the historical section of the Foreign Office:

Handbook on Montenegro, no. 20, HMSO, November, 1918.

Handbook on Serbia, no. 22, HMSO, December, 1918.

Handbook on the Balkan States (Peace Handbooks Series) vol. 3, HMSO, 1920.

Reports

Carnegie Endowment for International Peace, *Report of the International Commission to Inquire into the Causes and Conduct of the Balkans Wars*, Washington DC, 1914.

Report of the International Commission on the Balkans (chaired by Giuliano Amato), *The Balkans in Europe's Future*, Secretariat of the Centre for Liberal Strategies, Sofia, 2005.

Unpublished theses and papers

Čagorović, Nebojša, 'The Empty Chair: Montenegro at the Paris Peace Conference, 1919', unpubl. MA thesis for Dept of War Studies, King's College London, August 1995.

———, 'The War of the Churches: Montenegrin and Serbian Orthodox Churches, 1992–2003', delivered at a conference entitled 'After Yugoslavia: antagonism and identity revisited', held at the University of Kent, Canterbury, England, 29–31 March 2003.

News digest
VIP Daily News Report, published in Belgrade by Bratislav Grubačić from June 1993.

Index